SOURCES OF WESTERN CIVILIZATION

*VOLUME ONE · From the Ancient
World to the Reformation Era*

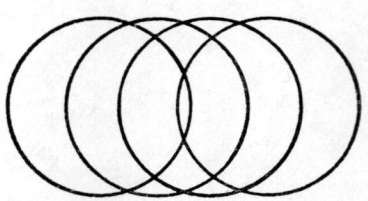

New York · Atlanta · Geneva, Ill. · Dallas · Palo Alto

SOURCES OF WESTERN CIVILIZATION

Edited by
Daniel D. McGarry · Clarence L. Hohl, Jr.
SAINT LOUIS UNIVERSITY

HOUGHTON MIFFLIN COMPANY · BOSTON

Copyright © 1962 BY DANIEL D. McGARRY AND CLARENCE L. HOHL, JR. ALL RIGHTS RESERVED, INCLUDING THE RIGHT TO REPRODUCE THIS BOOK OR PARTS THEREOF IN ANY FORM. *Printed in the U.S.A.*

PREFACE

THIS BOOK of readings is primarily designed for use in survey courses in European or Western civilization, though it should also prove usable in other types of courses (not necessarily in history) that focus on source documents. It originated in the twofold conviction (1) that students should be given an opportunity to see how subsequent historical accounts are based on earlier documentary sources, and (2) that direct contact, through such sources, with great minds and movements of history most effectively begets understanding and stimulates thought.

Most teachers find that a survey text is indispensable for providing continuity of narrative and a framework for ordering the place of men and movements, events and ideas, in relation to one another and to the whole picture. Some general knowledge of any historical time-slice is normally required before one can properly appreciate or fully understand its components. How, then, reconcile the need for a text with the desirability of some acquaintance with sources? Since it is unrealistic in these days of large enrollments to expect that the problem of supplementary reading can be wholly solved through the library, an obvious compromise is a selection of appropriate readings in inexpensive paperback form, designed to supplement and enrich the required textbook assignments.

This book is published in answer to this challenge. It provides an opportunity for reading in depth and for first-hand contact with events and ideas that have affected the direction and the character of Western civilization. Avoiding the common pattern of including a large number of fragmentary selections, we have limited the number of readings to fifteen in each of the two volumes, thus giving the student more than a cursory acquaintance with the sources. This plan permits the instructor, at his discretion, to assign the equivalent of one reading per week in each semester of the normal full-year survey course.

Given the restricted number of selections, it has not always been easy to choose among various possibilities. Thus, for ancient Greece, was it to be Herodotus, Thuycidides, Plato, Aristotle, or another? For modern Communism, was it to be Marx, Engels, Lenin, Stalin, or a representative Party voice rather than a personality? Almost every historical segment posed such a problem. The considerations underlying each specific choice are, we believe, made clear in the introductory notes to the various selections; but we have first of all set up the following guide lines: (1) Each reading should exemplify an important phase or aspect of human development; (2) it should be of intrinsic interest to the student-reader; (3) it should have a reasonable degree of unity and completeness — in fact, several works are given in actual or virtual entirety.

We hope, then, that this collection of source documents will acquaint the student with some of the great wellsprings of Western history; that it will enable him to experience, beyond the broad sweep and inevitable generalizations of the survey, the immediacy of human events, the realistic detail of life and action, the power of ideas, and the quality of mind of acute observers and original thinkers; and that, in doing these things, it will whet his appetite for history.

DANIEL D. MCGARRY
CLARENCE L. HOHL, JR.

CONTENTS

I. The Ancient Mediterranean World: Western Civilization Begins   1

1. The First Western Men Fight to Preserve Their Freedom   2
   HERODOTUS, from *History of the Persian Wars*

2. Transition from Republic to Empire Among the Practical Romans   31
   SUETONIUS, from *The Lives of the Caesars: Julius Caesar*

3. The Divine Salt and Leaven: Christ and His Church   63
   EUSEBIUS, from *Ecclesiastical History*

II. The Early Middle Ages: Western Civilization Gets a New Start   91

4. Uncivilized Indo-Europeans: The German Barbarians Before the Invasions   92
   TACITUS: *Germania*

5. The Frankish Empire: An Amalgam of Christian, Roman, and German Elements   116
   EINHARD, *Life of Charlemagne*

6. Benedictine Monasticism: A Corporate Attempt to Realize Christ's Counsels   141
   ST. BENEDICT OF NURSIA, from *The Rule of St. Benedict*

III. The High Middle Ages: The Blossoming of a Church-Centered Civilization   173

7. The Church Militant and Overseas Expansion in the Near East   175
   FULCHER OF CHARTRES, from *Chronicle of the First Crusade*

8. The Making of England: Norman Conquest and Consolidation   210
   WILLIAM OF MALMESBURY, from *Chronicle of the Kings of England*

9. The Scholastic Union of Faith and Reason   246
   ABELARD, *The Story of My Misfortunes*

IV. The Renaissance: Revision and Transition   281

10. The Birth of Renaissance Humanism in Italy   283
    FRANCESCO PETRARCH, *Selection from His Correspondence*

11. The Artistic Renaissance in Italy   315
    GIORGIO VASARI, from *Lives of the Most Eminent Painters, Sculptors, and Architects*

12. The New Politique   359
    NICCOLÒ MACHIAVELLI, *The Prince*

V. The Reformation: The Rending of Religious Unity   405

13. The Protest Begins   407
    MARTIN LUTHER, from *An Address to the Christian Nobility of the German Nation*

14. A Soldier Forges a Militant Spiritual Army   434
    IGNATIUS OF LOYOLA, *Autobiography*

15. Political and Religious Unrest in Reformation Europe   475
    VENETIAN DIPLOMATIC REPORTS, from *Papers Relating to English Affairs*

SECTION I

The Ancient Mediterranean World: Western Civilization Begins

WESTERN CIVILIZATION gradually emerged in Mediterranean Europe during classical antiquity. It derived principally from Greek, Roman, and Christian elements. The Greek contribution was paramount in intellectual and artistic fields; the Roman, in social organization and practical application; the Christian, in the spiritual and religious realms. Western civilization thus obtained, so to speak, a Greek mind, a Roman will, and a Christian heart. In the readings that follow in Section I, each of these three elements is presented at a turning point which was crucial for the future course of Western civilization. Herodotus, in his *History of the Persian Wars,* recounts the final victory of the Greeks in their long struggle against the menace of engulfment by the Persian colossus to the east. Suetonius, in his life of Julius Caesar, tells of the pivotal years when Rome evolved from republic to empire. And Eusebius of Caesarea, in his *Ecclesiastical History,* gives a vivid account of the Christian Church in its perilous passage through the last of the persecutions to full acceptance in the Roman Empire.

1

The First Western Men Fight To Preserve Their Freedom

HERODOTUS

The ancient Greeks enjoy the distinction of having been the originators of Western civilization, "the first Western men." The Hellenes, as they called themselves from a reputed common ancestor named Hellas, gave to Western civilization certain distinguishing characteristics. These include rationality, objectivity, appreciation of nature, broad humanism, love of freedom, democratic ideals, and a restless quest for truth and beauty. The Greeks were the founders of our philosophy and science, forms of literature and norms of aesthetics, democratic convictions and political theory.

Among the branches of learning originated by the Greeks was history; and Herodotus, the author of our first selection, is known as "the father of history." Herodotus was born about 484 B.C. at Halicarnassus, a Greek city in far southwestern Asia Minor. His native city-state was, at the time, under Persian domination; and his familiarity with the Persian Empire was later to serve him well in his account of the struggle between the Persians and the Greeks. The offspring of a prosperous, aristocratic Greek family, Herodotus apparently received a liberal education, strong in literature, as was customary among upper-class Hellenes. Although he became a citizen of Halicarnassus on reaching manhood, he was soon banished, probably for political reasons. This circumstance worked to his advantage, for it encouraged him to travel extensively, so that he visited most of the places he wrote about — Egypt and Lydia, Iraq and Iran, Scythia and the Danubian lands, the Aegean islands and Italy. Herodotus also changed his principal place of residence from time to time. Although he used Samos as his base of operations for a while, he spent most of his time at Athens, then at its height during its so-called Golden or Periclean Age. Apparently from a desire to regain citizenship, he concluded his life as one of the first colonists of the Greek settlement of Thurii (Thurium) in southern Italy. There he died about 425 B.C.

Although preceded by the quasi-historical poets such as Homer, and by the sixth-century Ionian logographoi (compilers, writers of sayings) such as Hecataeus, the work of Herodotus is our earliest surviving extensive, connected, organized prose treatise of a historical nature. The present division of the work into nine books, each named after a muse, was, however, a later innovation by an Alexandrian editor. The Greek word historia, which Herodotus applied to his work, means inquiry, investigation, researches. It subsequently came to be the accepted designation for historical accounts.

The main theme of Herodotus' history was for the Greeks their most glorious achievement and greatest pride: their repulse of the Persian colossus. At the outset Herodotus informs us that his purpose is "to prevent the great and wonderful actions of the Greeks and the Barbarians from losing their due meed of glory; and withal to put on record what were their grounds of feud" (I, Prol.). The "grounds," or background materials, in fact occupy over half the work: the first five books, representing over four-sevenths of the whole, contain accounts of the rise and history of Persia, Persian customs, institutions, and the like, together with similar information on other peoples such as the Egyptians, Scythians, Lydians, Indians, and Arabians, as well as the Greeks themselves. Attention may shift from marriage customs to methods of embalming mummies, from Scythian scalp-collecting to the Persian postal system, and from governmental intrigues at Susa to the cause of the annual flooding of the Nile. The fifth book, which is transitional to the main narrative, is chiefly concerned with the rebellion of the Ionian Greeks of western Asia Minor and nearby Aegean islands against Persian overlordship, a revolt aided by the Athenians. The remaining four books deal with the actual story of Persian attempts to conquer Greece, though these too digress into geography, anthropology, social and political institutions, biology, literature, mythology, and the numerous other topics into which the author's fertile curiosity led him.

In both manner and matter, the history of Herodotus presents the key characteristics which the Greeks transmitted to Western civilization. Greek rationality is exemplified by the organization and unifying theme of the narrative, by the intelligent manner in which the story is presented, and by the accounts of the reasoned processes whereby the Greeks arrived at decisions. Greek objectivity shines forth in the generally impartial presentation of the enemy Persians. Greek love of liberty and devotion to democracy illumine a narrative whose central theme is the victory of freedom over despotism. Yet diversity among the Greeks themselves is amply evidenced: Athenian inventiveness, enterprise, and intellectual amplitude, spiced with freedom; Spartan conservatism, deliberation, and moral rectitude, seasoned with a certain naïveté.

The title and general approach, the extent to which Herodotus "inquires" into backgrounds, and his numerous digressions illustrate the wide-ranging intellectual curiosity of the Greeks. Herodotus is a great storyteller largely because of his vivid interest in all things human. His literary humanism is shown by his intimate acquaintance with Greek poetic, rhetorical, and dramatic arts. Herodotus has been called a "son of Homer," not only because of his great admiration for and frequent quotation of Homer, but also because his account has the traits of an epic in prose. It is also replete with the teachings and devices of contemporary Greek rhetoricians, and has dramatic qualities which bear unmistakable traces of the Greek theatre of the day. Although occasionally skeptical, the History bears witness to Greek religious beliefs and practices, which often stand in contrast to other Greek characteristics. Though everything is grist for his mill, Herodotus is usually careful to make clear what he is relating as known fact, what as first-hand observation, and what as hearsay. He can describe a phoenix in credulous detail, but he is scrupulous in acknowledging that he himself has never seen one. He can recount gossip and anecdotes and tales of marvels, but he can also shrewdly analyze contrasting methods of fighting and show insight in recognizing the influence of sea power on history.

The History of Herodotus merits our special attention because it covers a critical period when emerging Western civilization beat off a threat of annihilation from the East. And it is interesting to note that the dominant theme, in broad outline, was the same in the fifth century before Christ as it is in the twentieth century after Christ: a struggle for the survival and ascendance of Western democracy against Eastern dictatorship, of individual freedom against regimentation, of unshackled objectivity against prejudiced fanaticism. The dauntless Greeks, who managed against overwhelming numerical odds to achieve success at Marathon, Thermopylae, and Salamis, contributed to the survival of that fragile yet priceless treasure known as Western civilization, which it is still our task to preserve and nourish.

The selections given here from the History of the Persian Wars comprise about five per cent of the whole work and are taken largely from the final four books, which relate the story of Persian attempts to subjugate Greece. This permits a reasonably connected and complete presentation of the high points of the main narrative, notably the critical battles of Marathon, Thermopylae, and Salamis.

HERODOTUS OF HALICARNASSUS

FROM *History of the Persian Wars* *

THESE are the researches[1] of Herodotus of Halicarnassus,[2] which he publishes, in the hope of thereby preserving from decay the remembrance of what men have done, and of preventing the great and wonderful actions of the Greeks and the Barbarians from losing their due meed of glory; and withal to put on record what were their grounds of feud. (I, Prol.)

. . . . .

Thus did the Athenians increase in strength.[3] And it is plain enough, not from this instance only, but from many everywhere, that freedom is an excellent thing; since even the Athenians who, while they continued under the rule of tyrants, were not a whit more valiant than any of their neighbours, no sooner shook off the yoke than they became decidedly the first of all. These things show that, while undergoing oppression, they let themselves be beaten, since then they worked for a master; but so soon as they got their freedom, each man was eager to do the best he could for himself. So fared it now with the Athenians. (V, 78) ...

While Onesilus was engaged in the siege of Amathus[4] King Darius[5] received tidings of the taking and burning of Sardis[6] by the Athenians and Ionians;[7] and at the same time he learnt that the author of the league, the man by whom the whole matter had been planned and contrived, was Aristagoras the Milesian.[8] It is said he no sooner understood what had happened, than, laying aside all thought concerning the Ionians, who would, he was sure, pay dear for their rebellion, he asked who the Athenians were and, being informed, called

---

* Translated by George Rawlinson (London: J. Murray, 1858–60).
[1] Inquiry, investigation, or history [*historia*].
[2] Halicarnassus: a Greek coastal city in southwestern Asia Minor, south of Miletus, for some time under Persian rule.
[3] Herodotus has just recounted the Athenians' overthrow of their tyrants and re-establishment of democracy, followed by their success against a formidable coalition of their enemies.
[4] Amathus, a city on the southern coast of Cyprus, refused to join other Cypriots in revolting against the Persians and was accordingly besieged by Prince Onesilus of Salamis, another city on the island.
[5] Darius I, King of the Persians, 522–486 B.C.
[6] Persian provincial capital of Lydia, in west-central Asia Minor.
[7] Term applied to Greek inhabitants of Western Asia Minor and neighboring Aegean islands.
[8] Greek coastal city in southwestern Asia Minor.

for his bow, and placing an arrow on the string, shot upward into the sky, saying, as he let fly the shaft, "Grant me, Zeus, to revenge myself on the Athenians!" After this speech, he bade one of his servants every day, when his dinner was spread, three times repeat these words to him, "Master, remember the Athenians." (V, 105) . . .

Meanwhile the Eretrians,[9] understanding that the Persian armament was coming against them,[10] besought the Athenians for assistance. Nor did the Athenians refuse their aid, but assigned to them as auxiliaries the 4,000 landholders to whom they had allotted the estates of the Chalcidean Hippobatae. At Eretria, however, things were in no healthy state; for though they had called in the aid of the Athenians, yet they were not agreed among themselves how they should act; some of them were minded to leave the city and to take refuge in the heights of Euboea, while others, who looked to receiving a reward from the Persians, were making ready to betray their country. So when these things came to the ears of Aeschines, the son of Nothon, one of the first men in Eretria, he made known the whole state of affairs to the Athenians who were already arrived, and besought them to return home to their own land, and not perish with his countrymen. And the Athenians hearkened to his counsel, and crossing over to Oropus, in this way escaped the danger.

The Persian fleet now drew near and anchored at Tamynae, Choereae, and Aegilia, three places in the territory of Eretria. Once masters of these posts, they proceeded forthwith to disembark their horses, and made ready to attack the enemy. But the Eretrians were not minded to sally forth and offer battle; their only care, after it had been resolved not to quit the city, was, if possible, to defend their walls. And now the fortress was assaulted in good earnest, and for six days there fell on both sides vast numbers, but on the seventh day Euphorbus, the son of Alcimachus, and Philagrus, the son of Cyneas, who were both citizens of good repute, betrayed the place to the Persians. These were no sooner entered within the walls than they plundered and burnt all the temples that there were in the town, in revenge for the burning of their own temples at Sardis; moreover, they did according to the orders of Darius, and carried away captive all the inhabitants.

The Persians, having thus brought Eretria into subjection, after waiting a few days, made sail for Attica, greatly straitening the Athenians as they approached, and thinking to deal with them as they had dealt with the people of Eretria. And because there was no place in all Attica so convenient for their horse as Marathon, and it

---

[9] Eretria was a principal city on the western coast of the large Greek island of Euboea, located opposite Attica.

[10] Darius sent a great expedition overseas against Greece, directed primarily against Eretria and Athens, in 490 B.C.

lay moreover quite close to Eretria, therefore Hippias, the son of Pisistratus, conducted them thither.[11]

When intelligence of this reached the Athenians, they likewise marched their troops to Marathon,[12] and there stood on the defensive, having at their head ten generals, of whom one was Miltiades. (VI, 100–103) . . .

And first, before they left the city, the generals sent off to Sparta a herald, one Pheidippides, who was by birth an Athenian, and by profession and practice a trained runner. This man, according to the account which he gave to the Athenians on his return, when he was near Mount Parthenium, above Tegea, fell in with the god Pan, who called him by his name, and bade him ask the Athenians, "wherefore they neglected him so entirely, when he was kindly disposed towards them, and had often helped them in times past, and would do so again in time to come?" The Athenians, entirely believing in the truth of this report, as soon as their affairs were once more in good order, set up a temple to Pan under the Acropolis, and, in return for the message which I have recorded, established in his honour yearly sacrifices and a torch-race.

On the occasion of which we speak, when Pheidippides was sent by the Athenian generals, and, according to his own account, saw Pan on his journey, he reached Sparta on the very next day after quitting the city of Athens. Upon his arrival he went before the rulers, and said to them: —

"Men of Lacedaemon,[13] the Athenians beseech you to hasten to their aid, and not allow that state, which is the most ancient in all Greece, to be enslaved by the barbarians. Eretria, look you, is already carried away captive, and Greece weakened by the loss of no mean city."

Thus did Pheidippides deliver the message committed to him. And the Spartans wished to help the Athenians, but were unable to give them any present succour, as they did not like to break their established law. It was then the ninth day of the first decade; and they could not march out of Sparta on the ninth, when the moon had not reached the full. So they waited for the full of the moon. (VI, 105–106) . . .

The Athenians were drawn up in order of battle in a sacred close belonging to Hercules, when they were joined by the Plataeans, who came in full force to their aid. Some time before[14] the Plataeans had

---

[11] Hippias, former Athenian tyrant, had been overthrown and exiled in 510 B.C.

[12] The plain of Marathon, site of the famous battle of that name (490 B.C.), was on the eastern coast of Attica, to the northeast of Athens.

[13] Spartans.

[14] Some time between 519 and 509 B.C., Plataea, a small city-state to the west of Attica, had submitted to the rule of Athens.

put themselves under the rule of the Athenians; and these last had already undertaken many labours on their behalf.... (VI, 108) ...

The Athenian generals were divided in their opinions; and some advised not to risk a battle, because they were too few to engage such a host as that of the Medes,[15] while others were for fighting at once; and among these last was Miltiades. He therefore, seeing that opinions were thus divided, and that the less worthy counsel appeared likely to prevail, resolved to go to the polemarch, and have a conference with him. For the man on whom the lot fell to be polemarch,[16] at Athens was entitled to give his vote with the ten generals, since anciently the Athenians allowed him an equal right of voting with them. The polemarch at this juncture was Callimachus of Aphidnae; to him therefore Miltiades went, and said: —

"With thee it rests, Callimachus, either to bring Athens to slavery, or, by securing her freedom, to leave behind thee to all future generations a memory beyond even Harmodius and Aristogeiton. For never since the time that the Athenians became a people were they in so great a danger as now. If they bow their necks beneath the yoke of the Medes, the woes which they will have to suffer when given into the power of Hippias are already determined on; if, on the other hand, they fight and overcome, Athens may rise to be the very first city in Greece. How it comes to pass that these things are likely to happen, and how the determining of them in some sort rests with thee, I will now proceed to make clear. We generals are ten in number, and our votes are divided; half of us wish to engage, half to avoid a combat. Now, if we do not fight, I look to see a great disturbance at Athens which will shake men's resolutions, and then I fear they will submit themselves; but if we fight the battle before any unsoundness show itself among our citizens, let the gods but give us fair play, and we are well able to overcome the enemy. On thee therefore we depend in this matter, which lies wholly in thine own power. Thou hast only to add thy vote to my side and thy country will be free, and not free only, but the first state in Greece. Or, if thou preferrest to give thy vote to them who would decline the combat, then the reverse will follow."

Miltiades by these words gained Callimachus; and the addition of the polemarch's vote caused the decision to be in favor of fighting. Hereupon all those generals who had been desirous of hazarding a battle, when their turn came to command the army, gave up their right to Miltiades. He however, though he accepted their offers, nevertheless waited, and would not fight, until his own day of command arrived in due course.

Then at length, when his own turn was come, the Athenian battle

[15] Medes: used synonymously with Persians. The Persian army is estimated to have been about five times the size of that of the Athenians and Plataeans.
[16] The polemarch in earlier times was in charge of military matters.

was set in array, and this was the order of it. Callimachus the polemarch led the right wing; for it was at that time a rule with the Athenians to give the right wing to the polemarch. After this followed the tribes, according as they were numbered, in an unbroken line; while last of all came the Plataeans, forming the left wing. And ever since that day it has been a custom with the Athenians, in the sacrifices and assemblies held each fifth year at Athens, for the Athenian herald to implore the blessing of the gods on the Plataeans conjointly with the Athenians. Now as they marshalled the host upon the field of Marathon, in order that the Athenian front might be of equal length with the Median, the ranks of the centre were diminished, and it became the weakest part of the line, while the wings were both made strong with a depth of many ranks.

So when the battle was set in array, and the victims showed themselves favourable, instantly the Athenians, so soon as they were let go, charged the barbarians at a run. Now the distance between the two armies was little short of a mile. The Persians, therefore, when they saw the Greeks coming on at speed, made ready to receive them, although it seemed to them that the Athenians were bereft of their senses, and bent upon their own destruction; for they saw a mere handful of men coming on at a run without either horsemen or archers.[17] Such was the opinion of the barbarians; but the Athenians in close array fell upon them, and fought in a manner worthy of being recorded. They were the first of the Greeks, so far as I know, who introduced the custom of charging the enemy at a run, and they were likewise the first who dared to look upon the Median garb, and to face men clad in that fashion. Until this time the very name of the Medes had been a terror to the Greeks to hear.

The two armies fought together on the plain of Marathon for a length of time; and in the mid battle, where the Persians themselves and the Sacae had their place, the barbarians were victorious, and broke and pursued the Greeks into the inner country; but on the two wings the Athenians and the Plataeans defeated the enemy. Having so done, they suffered the routed barbarians to fly at their ease, and joining the two wings in one, fell upon those who had broken their own centre, and fought and conquered them. These likewise fled, and now the Athenians hung upon the runaways and cut them down, chasing them all the way to the shore, on reaching which they laid hold of the ships and called aloud for fire.

It was in the struggle here that Callimachus the polemarch, after greatly distinguishing himself, lost his life; Stesilaus too, the son of Thrasilaus, one of the generals, was slain; and Cynaegirus, the son of Euphorion, having seized on a vessel of the enemy's by the ornament

---

[17] The Greeks probably made the charge on the run to compensate for their deficiency in archers and cavalry and to employ their heavier-armed, more athletic infantry at full advantage.

at the stern, had his hand cut off by the blow of an axe, and so perished; as likewise did many other Athenians of note and name.

Nevertheless the Athenians secured in this way seven of the vessels, while with the remainder the barbarians pushed off, and taking aboard their Eretrian prisoners from the island where they had left them, doubled Cape Sunium, hoping to reach Athens before the return of the Athenians. The Alcmaeonidae were accused by their countrymen of suggesting this course to them; they had, it was said, an understanding with the Persians, and made a signal to them, by raising a shield, after they were embarked in their ships.

The Persians accordingly sailed round Sunium. But the Athenians with all possible speed marched away to the defence of their city, and succeeded in reaching Athens before the appearance of the barbarians; and as their camp at Marathon had been pitched in a precinct of Hercules, so now they encamped in another precinct of the same god at Cynosarges. The barbarian fleet arrived, and lay to off Phalerum, which was at that time the haven of Athens; but after resting awhile upon their oars, they departed and sailed away to Asia.

There fell in this battle of Marathon, on the side of the barbarians, about 6,500 men; on that of the Athenians, 192. Such was the number of the slain on the one side and the other. . . . (VI, 109–117) . . .

After the full of the moon, 2,000 Lacedaemonians came to Athens. So eager had they been to arrive in time, that they took but three days to reach Attica from Sparta. They came, however, too late for the battle; yet, as they had a longing to behold the Medes, they continued their march to Marathon, and there viewed the slain. Then, after giving the Athenians all praise for their achievement, they departed and returned home. (VI, 120) . . .

Now when tidings of the battle that had been fought at Marathon reached the ears of King Darius, the son of Hystaspes, his anger against the Athenians, which had been already roused by their attack upon Sardis, waxed still fiercer, and he became more than ever eager to lead an army against Greece. Instantly he sent off messengers to make proclamation through the several states, that fresh levies were to be raised, and these at an increased rate; while ships, horses, provisions, and transports were likewise to be furnished. So the men published his commands; and now all Asia was in commotion for three years, while everywhere, as Greece was to be attacked, the best and bravest were enrolled for the service, and had to make their preparations accordingly.

After this, in the fourth year, the Egyptians whom Cambyses had enslaved[18] revolted from the Persians; whereupon Darius was more

[18] Cambyses (Persian monarch, 529–522 B.C.) had conquered the Egyptians in 526–525 B.C.

hot for war than ever, and earnestly desired to march an army against both adversaries. (VII, 1) . . .

After Egypt was subdued, Xerxes,[19] being about to take in hand the expedition against Athens, called together an assembly of the noblest Persians, to learn their opinions, and to lay before them his own designs.[1] So, when the men were met, the king spoke thus to them: —

"Persians, I shall not be the first to bring in among you a new custom — I shall but follow one which has come down to us from our forefathers. Never yet, as our old men assure me, has our race reposed itself, since the time when Cyrus overcame Astyages, and so we Persians wrested the sceptre from the Medes.[2] Now in all this God guides us, and we, obeying his guidance, prosper greatly. What need have I to tell you of the deeds of Cyrus and Cambyses, and my own father Darius, how many nations they conquered, and added to our dominions? You know right well what great things they achieved. But for myself, I will say that, from the day on which I mounted the throne, I have not ceased to consider by what means I may rival those who have preceded me in this post of honour, and increase the power of Persia as much as any of them. And truly I have pondered upon this, until at last I have found out a way whereby we may at once win glory, and likewise get possession of a land which is as large and as rich as our own — nay, which is even more varied in the fruits it bears — while at the same time we obtain satisfaction and revenge. For this cause I have now called you together, that I may make known to you what I design to do. My intent is throw a bridge over the Hellespont and march an army through Europe against Greece, that thereby I may obtain vengeance from the Athenians for the wrongs committed by them against the Persians and against my father. Your own eyes saw the preparation of Darius against these men; but death came upon him, and balked his hopes of revenge. In his behalf, therefore, and in behalf of all the Persians, I undertake the war, and pledge myself not to rest till I have taken and burnt Athens, which has dared, unprovoked, to injure me and my father. Long since they came to Asia with Aristagoras of Miletus, who was one of our slaves, and, entering Sardis, burnt its temples and its sacred groves; again, more lately, when we made a landing upon their coast under Datis and Artaphernes, how roughly they handled us you do not need to

---

[19] Xerxes (486–464 B.C.) meanwhile succeeded his father, Darius I (522–486 B.C.), as Persian monarch.

[1] Although these speeches may have no historical validity, they may be considered as embodying Persian as well as Greek views.

[2] The Medes and the Persians were related Indo-European peoples who, after occupying the Iranian highlands, proceeded to subjugate adjacent lands. At first the Medes were ascendant; but in 550–549 B.C. the Persians revolted and established a Persian dynasty on the throne. Medes as well as Persians continued to occupy governmental posts.

be told. For these reasons, therefore, I am bent upon this war; and I see likewise therewith united no few advantages. Once let us subdue this people, and those neighbours of theirs who hold the land of Pelops the Phrygian, and we shall extend the Persian territory as far as God's heaven reaches. The sun will then shine on no land beyond our borders; for I will pass through Europe from one end to the other, and with your aid make of all the lands which it contains one country. For thus, if what I hear be true, affairs stand: The nations whereof I have spoken, once swept away, there is no city, no country left in all the world, which will venture so much as to withstand us in arms. By this course then we shall bring all mankind under our yoke, alike those who are guilty and those who are innocent of doing us wrong. . . . (VII, 8) . . .

Now after Xerxes had sailed down the whole line and was gone ashore,[3] he sent for Demaratus[4] the son of Ariston, who had accompanied him in his march upon Greece, and bespake him thus: —

"Demaratus, it is my pleasure at this time to ask thee certain things which I wish to know. Thou art a Greek, and, as I hear from the other Greeks with whom I converse, no less than from thine own lips, thou art a native of a city which is not the meanest or the weakest in their land. Tell me, therefore, what thinkest thou? Will the Greeks lift a hand against us? Mine own judgment is that, even if all the Greeks and all the barbarians of the West were gathered together in one place, they would not be able to abide my onset, not being really of one mind. But I would fain know what thou thinkest hereon."

Thus Xerxes questioned; and the other replied in his turn, "O King! is it thy will that I give thee a true answer, or dost wish for a pleasant one?"

Then the king bade him speak the plain truth, and promised that he would not on that account hold him in less favour than heretofore.

So Demaratus, when he heard the promise, spoke as follows: —

"O King, since thou biddest me at all risks speak the truth, and not say what will one day prove to have lied to thee, thus I answer. Want has at all times been a fellow-dweller with us in our land, while Valour is an ally whom we have gained by dint of wisdom and strict laws. Her aid enables us to drive out want and escape thraldom. Brave are all the Greeks who dwell in any Dorian land;[5] but what I am about to say does not concern all, but only the Lacedaemonians.[6] First, then, come what may, they will never accept thy terms, which would reduce Greece to slavery; and further, they are sure to join

---

[3] The following conversation purportedly took place after Xerxes, having crossed the Hellespont and arrived in Thrace, reviewed his great army and fleet before proceeding with his attack on Greece, in 480 B.C.
[4] A former Spartan king who had gone over to the side of the Persians.
[5] The Peloponnesus; southern Greece.
[6] Spartans.

battle with thee, though all the rest of the Greeks should submit to thy will. As for their numbers, do not ask how many there are, that their resistance should be a possible thing; for if a thousand of them should take the field, they will meet thee in battle, and so will any number, be it less than this, or be it more.

When Xerxes heard this answer of Demaratus, he laughed and answered: —

"What wild words, Demaratus! A thousand men join battle with such an army as this![7] Come then, wilt thou — who wert one, as thou sayest, their king — engage to fight this very day with ten men? I trow not. And yet, if all thy fellow-citizens be indeed such as thou sayest they are, thou oughtest, as their king, by thine own country's usages, to be ready to fight with twice the number. If then each one of them be a match for ten of my soldiers, I may well call upon thee to be a match for twenty." . . .

Demaratus answered him, "I knew, O King, at the outset, that if I told the the truth, my speech would displease thine ears. But as thou didst require me to answer thee with all possible truthfulness, I informed thee what the Spartans will do. And in this I spake not from any love that I bear them — for none knows better than thou what my love towards them is likely to be at the present time, when they have robbed me of my rank and my ancestral honours, and made me a homeless exile, whom thy father did receive, bestowing on me both shelter and sustenance. What likelihood is there that a man of understanding should be unthankful for kindness shown him, and not cherish it in his heart? For mine own self, I pretend not to cope with ten men, nor with two, nay, had I the choice, I would rather not fight even with one. But, if need appeared, or if there were any great cause urging me on, I would contend with right good will against one of those persons who boast themselves a match for any three Greeks. So likewise the Lacedaemonians, when they fight singly, are as good men as any in the world, and when they fight in a body, are the bravest of all. For though they be freemen, they are not in all respects free; Law is the master whom they own; and this master they fear more than thy subjects fear thee. Whatever it commands they do; and its commandment is always the same: it forbids them to flee in battle, whatever the number of their foes, and requires them to stand firm, and either to conquer or die. . . ." (VII, 101–104) . . .

. . . At this time the heralds who had been sent into Greece to require earth for the king returned to the camp, some of them empty-handed, others with earth and water.[8]

---

[7] One authority estimates the Persian army as having numbered 180,000 men.
[8] Xerxes, like Darius before him, had sent out heralds to the various city-states of Greece, demanding earth and water as tokens of submission and recognition that he was the lord of land and sea.

Among the number of those from whom earth and water were brought, were the Thessalians, Dolopians, Enianians, Perrhaebians, Locrians, Magnetians, Malians, Achaeans of Phthiotis, Thebans, and Boeotions generally, except those of Plataea and Thespiae. These are the nations against whom the Greeks that had taken up arms to resist the barbarians swore the oath, which ran thus, "From all those of Greek blood who delivered themselves up to the Persians without necessity, when their affairs were in good condition, we will take a tithe of their goods, and give it to the god at Delphi." So ran the words of the Greek oath.

King Xerxes had sent no heralds either to Athens or Sparta to ask earth and water, for a reason which I will now relate. When Darius some time before sent messengers for the same purpose, they were thrown, at Athens, into the pit of punishment, at Sparta into a well, and bidden to take therefrom earth and water for themselves, and carry it to their king. On this account Xerxes did not send to ask them. . . . (VII, 131–133) . . .

To return, however, to my main subject, — the expedition of the Persian king, though it was in name directed against Athens, threatened really the whole of Greece. And this the Greeks were aware of some time before; but they did not all view the matter in the same light. Some of them had given the Persians earth and water, and were bold on this account, deeming themselves thereby secured against suffering hurt from the barbarian army; while others, who had refused compliance, were thrown into extreme alarm. For whereas they considered all the ships in Greece too few to engage the enemy, it was plain that the greater number of states would take no part in the war, but warmly favoured the Medes.

And here I feel constrained to deliver an opinion which most men, I know, will mislike, but which, as it seems to me to be true, I am determined not to withhold. Had the Athenians, from fear of the approaching danger, quitted their country, or had they without quitting it submitted to the power of Xerxes, there would certainly have been no attempt to resist the Persians by sea; in which case, the course of events by land would have been the following. Though the Peloponnesians might have carried ever so many breastworks across the Isthmus, yet their allies would have fallen off from the Lacedaemonians, not by voluntary desertion, but because town after town must have been taken by the fleet of the barbarians; and so the Lacedaemonians would at last have stood alone, and, standing alone, would have displayed prodigies of valour, and died nobly. Either they would have done thus, or else, before it came to that extremity, seeing one Greek state after another embrace the cause of the Medes, they would have come to terms with King Xerxes; and thus, either way Greece would have been brought under Persia. For I cannot understand of what possible use the walls across the Isthmus could have been, if the king had had the mastery of the sea. If then a man should now say that the Athenians were the saviours of Greece, he would not exceed the truth. For they truly held the scales; and whichever side they espoused must have carried the day. They too it was who, when they had determined to maintain the freedom of Greece, roused up that portion of the Greek nation which had not gone over to the Medes; and so, next to the Gods, *they* repulsed the invader. Even the terrible oracles which reached them from Delphi, and struck fear into their hearts, failed to persuade them to fly from Greece. They had the courage to remain faithful to their land, and await the coming of the foe. (VII, 138–139) . . .

King Xerxes pitched his camp in the region of Malis called Trachinia,[9] while on their side the Greeks occupied the straits. These straits the Greeks in general call Thermopylae (the Hot Gates); but the natives, and those who dwell in the neighbourhood, call them Pylae (the Gates).[10] Here then the two armies took their stand; the one master of all the region lying north of Trachis, the other of the country extending southward of that place to the verge of the continent.

The Greeks who at this spot awaited the coming of Xerxes were the following: From Sparta, 300 men-at-arms: from Arcadia, 1,000 Tegeans and Mantineans, 500 of each people; 120 Orchomenians, from the Arcadian Orchomenus; and 1,000 from other cities: from Corinth, 400 men: from Phlius, 200: and from Mycenae eighty. Such was the number from the Peloponnese. There were also present, from Boeotia, 700 Thespians and 400 Thebans.

Besides these troops, the Locrians of Opus and the Phocians had obeyed the call of their countrymen, and sent, the former all the force they had, the latter 1,000 men.[11] For envoys had gone from the Greeks at Thermopylae among the Locrians and Phocians, to call on them for assistance, and to say, "They were themselves but the vanguard of the host, sent to precede the main body, which might every day be expected to follow them. The sea was in good keeping, watched by the Athenians, the Eginetans, and the rest of the fleet. There was no cause why they should fear; for after all the invader was not a god but a man; and there never had been, and never would be, a man who was not liable to misfortunes from the very day of his birth, and those misfortunes greater in proportion to his own greatness. The assailant therefore, being only a mortal, must needs fall from his glory." Thus urged, the Locrians and the Phocians had come with their troops to Trachis.

The various nations had each captains of their own under whom

---

[9] To the north of the pass of Thermopylae, on the way to the heart of Greece.
[10] In the narrow pass of Thermopylae the Greeks fought their famous delaying action in 480 B.C.
[11] Several Greek city-states thus furnished contingents.

they served; but the one to whom all especially looked up, and who had the command of the entire force, was the Lacedaemonian, Leonidas.[12] . . . (VII, 201–204) . . .

. . . He had now come to Thermopylae, accompanied by the 300 men which the law assigned him, whom he had himself chosen from among the citizens, and who were all of them fathers with sons living. On his way he had taken the troops from Thebes, whose number I have already mentioned, and who were under the command of Leontiades the son of Eurymachus. The reason why he made a point of taking troops from Thebes and Thebes only was, that the Thebans were strongly suspected of being well inclined to the Medes. Leonidas therefore called on them to come with him to the war, wishing to see whether they would comply with his demand, or openly refuse, and disclaim the Greek alliance. They, however, though their wishes leant the other way, nevertheless sent the men.

The force with Leonidas was sent forward by the Spartans in advance of their main body, that the sight of them might encourage the allies to fight, and hinder them from going over to the Medes, as it was likely they might have done had they seen that Sparta was backward. They intended presently, when they had celebrated the Carneian festival, which was what now kept them at home, to leave a garrison in Sparta, and hasten in full force to join the army. The rest of the allies also intended to act similarly; for it happened that the Olympic festival fell exactly at this same period. None of them looked to see the contest at Thermopylae decided so speedily; wherefore they were content to send forward a mere advanced guard. Such accordingly were the intentions of the allies.

The Greek forces at Thermopylae, when the Persian army drew near to the entrance of the pass, were seized with fear; and a council was held to consider about a retreat. It was the wish of the Peloponnesians generally that the army should fall back upon the Peloponnese, and there guard the Isthmus. But Leonidas, who saw with what indignation the Phocians and Locrians heard of this plan, gave his voice for remaining where they were, while they sent envoys to the several cities to ask for help, since they were too few to make a stand against an army like that of the Medes.

While this debate was going on, Xerxes sent a mounted spy to observe the Greeks, and note how many they were, and what they were doing. He had heard, before he came out of Thessaly, that a few men were assembled at this place, and that at their head were certain Lacedaemonians, under Leonidas, a descendant of Hercules. The horseman rode up to the camp, and looked about him, but did not see the whole army; for such as were on the further side of the wall (which had been rebuilt and was now carefully guarded) it was not possible for him to behold; but he observed those on the outside,

[12] The Spartans were recognized as the best foot-soldiers in Greece.

who were encamped in front of the rampart. It chanced that at this time the Lacedaemonians held the outer guard, and were seen by the spy, some of them engaged in gymnastic exercises, others combing their long hair. At this the spy greatly marvelled, but he counted their number, and when he had taken accurate note of everything, he rode back quietly; for no one pursued after him, nor paid any heed to his visit. So he returned, and told Xerxes all that he had seen.

Upon this, Xerxes, who had no means of surmising the truth — namely, that the Spartans were preparing to do or die manfully — but thought it laughable that they should be engaged in such employments, sent and called to his presence Demaratus the son of Ariston, who still remained with the army. When he appeared, Xerxes told him all that he had heard, and questioned him concerning the news, since he was anxious to understand the meaning of such behaviour on the part of the Spartans. Then Demaratus said: —

"I spake to thee, O King, concerning these men long since, when we had but just begun our march upon Greece; thou, however, didst only laugh at my words, when I told thee of all this, which I saw would come to pass. Earnestly do I struggle at all times to speak truth to thee, sire; and now listen to it once more. These men have come to dispute the pass with us; and it is for this that they are now making ready. 'Tis their custom, when they are about to hazard their lives, to adorn their heads with care. Be assured, however, that if thou canst subdue the men who are here and the Lacedaemonians who remain in Sparta, there is no other nation in the world which will venture to lift a hand in their defence. Thou hast now to deal with the first kingdom and town in Greece, and with the bravest men."

Then Xerxes, to whom what Demaratus said seemed altogether to surpass belief, asked further, "how it was possible for so small an army to contend with his?"

"O King!" Demaratus answered, "let me be treated as a liar, if matters fall not out as I say."

But Xerxes was not persuaded any the more. Four whole days he suffered to go by,[13] expecting that the Greeks would run away. When, however, he found on the fifth that they were not gone, thinking that their firm stand was mere impudence and recklessness, he grew wroth, and sent against them the Medes and Cissians, with orders to take them alive and bring them into his presence. Then the Medes rushed forward and charged the Greeks, but fell in vast numbers: others, however, took the places of the slain, and would not be beaten off, though they suffered terrible losses. In this way it became clear to all, and especially to the king, that though he had plenty of combatants, he had but very few warriors. The struggle, however, continued during the whole day.

[13] Xerxes may have been awaiting the cooperation of his fleet without avail.

Then the Medes, having met so rough a reception, withdrew from the fight; and their place was taken by the band of Persians under Hydarnes, whom the king called his Immortals: they, it was thought, would soon finish the business. But when they joined battle with the Greeks, it was with no better success than the Median detachment — things went much as before — the two armies fighting in a narrow space, and the barbarians using shorter spears than the Greeks, and having no advantage from their numbers. The Lacedaemonians fought in a way worthy of note, and showed themselves far more skilful in fight than their adversaries, often turning their backs, and making as though they were all flying away, on which the barbarians would rush after them with much noise and shouting, when the Spartans at their approach would wheel round and face their pursuers, in this way destroying vast numbers of the enemy. Some Spartans likewise fell in these encounters, but only a very few. At last the Persians, finding that all their efforts to gain the pass availed nothing, and that whether they attacked by divisions or in any other way, it was to no purpose, withdrew to their own quarters.

During these assaults, it is said that Xerxes, who was watching the battle, thrice leaped from the throne on which he sat, in terror for his army.

Next day the combat was renewed, but with no better success on the part of the barbarians. The Greeks were so few that the barbarians hoped to find them disabled, by reason of their wounds, from offering any further resistance; and so they once more attacked them. But the Greeks were drawn up in detachments according to their cities, and bore the brunt of the battle in turns, all except the Phocians, who had been stationed on the mountain to guard the pathway. So when the Persians found no difference between that day and the preceding, they again retired to their quarters.

Now, as the king was in a great strait, and knew not how he should deal with the emergency, Ephialtes, the son of Eurydemus, a man of Malis, came to him and was admitted to a conference. Stirred by the hope of receiving a rich reward at the king's hands, he had come to tell him of the pathway which led across the mountain to Thermopylae; by which disclosure he brought destruction on the band of Greeks who had there withstood the barbarians. . . . (VII, 205–213) . . .

Great was the joy of Xerxes on this occasion; and as he approved highly of the enterprise which Ephialtes undertook to accomplish, he forthwith sent upon the errand Hydarnes, and the Persians under him. The troops left the camp about the time of the lighting of the lamps. The pathway along which they went was first discovered by the Malians of these parts, who soon afterwards led the Thessalians by it to attack the Phocians, at the time when the Phocians fortified the pass with a wall, and so shielded themselves from danger.

And ever since, the path has always been put to an ill use by the Malians. (VII, 215) . . .

The Persians took this path, and, crossing the Asopus, continued their march through the whole of the night, having the mountains of Oeta on their right hand, and on their left those of Trachis. At dawn of day they found themselves close to the summit. Now the hill was guarded, as I have already said, by a thousand Phocian men-at-arms, who were placed there to defend the pathway, and at the same time to secure their own country. They had been given the guard of the mountain path, while the other Greeks defended the pass below, because they had volunteered for the service, and had pledged themselves to Leonidas to maintain the post.

The ascent of the Persians became known to the Phocians in the following manner: During all the time that they were making their way up, the Greeks remained unconscious of it, inasmuch as the whole mountain was covered with groves of oak; but it happened that the air was very still, and the leaves which the Persians stirred with their feet made, as it was likely they would, a loud rustling, whereupon the Phocians jumped up and flew to seize their arms. In a moment the barbarians came in sight, and perceiving men arming themselves, were greatly amazed; for they had fallen in with an enemy when they expected no opposition. Hydarnes, alarmed at the sight, and fearing lest the Phocians might be Lacedaemonians, inquired of Ephialtes to what nation these troops belonged. Ephialtes told him the exact truth, whereupon he arrayed his Persians for battle. The Phocians, galled by the shower of arrows to which they were exposed, and imagining themselves the special object of the Persian attack, fled hastily to the crest of the mountain, and there made ready to meet death; but while their mistake continued, the Persians, with Ephialtes and Hydarnes, not thinking it worth their while to delay on account of Phocians, passed on and descended the mountain with all possible speed.

The Greeks at Thermopylae received the first warning of the destruction which the dawn would bring on them from the seer Megistias, who read their fate in the victims as he was sacrificing. After this deserters came in, and brought the news that the Persians were marching round by the hills: it was still night when these men arrived. Last of all, the scouts came running down from the heights, and brought in the same accounts, when the day was just beginning to break. Then the Greeks held a council to consider what they should do, and here opinions were divided: some were strong against quitting their post while others contended to the contrary. So when the council had broken up, part of the troops departed and went their ways homeward to their several states; part, however, resolved to remain, and to stand by Leonidas to the last.

It is said that Leonidas himself sent away the troops who departed, because he tendered their safety, but thought it unseemly that either he or his Spartans should quit the post which they had been especially sent to guard. For my own part, I incline to think that Leonidas gave the order, because he perceived the allies to be out of heart and unwilling to encounter the danger to which his own mind was made up. He therefore commanded them to retreat, but said that he himself could not draw back with honour; knowing that, if he stayed, glory awaited him, and that Sparta in that case would not lose her prosperity. . . . (VII, 217–220) . . .

At sunrise Xerxes made libations, after which he waited until the time when the forum is wont to fill, and then began his advance. Ephialtes had instructed him thus, as the descent of the mountain is much quicker and the distance much shorter than the way round the hills and the ascent. So the barbarians under Xerxes began to draw nigh; and the Greeks under Leonidas, as they now went forth determined to die, advanced much further than on previous days, until they reached the more open portion of the pass. Hitherto they had held their station within the wall, and from this had gone forth to fight at the point where the pass was the narrowest. Now they joined battle beyond the defile, and carried slaughter among the barbarians, who fell in heaps. Behind them the captains of the squadrons, armed with whips, urged their men forward with continual blows. Many were thrust into the sea, and there perished; a still greater number were trampled to death by their own soldiers; no one heeded the dying. For the Greeks, reckless of their own safety and desperate, since they knew that, as the mountain had been crossed, their destruction was nigh at hand, exerted themselves with the most furious valour against the barbarians.

By this time the spears of the greater number were all shivered, and with their swords they hewed down the ranks of the Persians; and here, as they strove, Leonidas fell fighting bravely, together with many other famous Spartans, whose names I have taken care to learn on account of their great worthiness, as indeed I have those of all the three hundred. There fell too at the same time very many famous Persians: among them, two sons of Darius, Abrocomes and Hyperanthes, his children by Phratagune, the daughter or Artanes. Artanes was brother of King Darius, being a son of Hystaspes, the son of Arsames; and when he gave his daughter to the king, he made him heir likewise of all his substance; for she was his only child.

Thus two brothers of Xerxes here fought and fell. And now there arose a fierce struggle between the Persians and the Lacedaemonians over the body of Leonidas, in which the Greeks four times drove back the enemy, and at last by their great bravery succeeded in bearing off the body. This combat was scarcely ended when the Persians with Ephialtes approached; and the Greeks, informed that they drew nigh, made a change in the manner of their fighting.

Drawing back into the narrowest part of the pass, and retreating even behind the cross wall, they posted themselves upon a hillock, where they stood all drawn up together in one close body, except only the Thebans. The hillock whereof I speak is at the entrance of the straits, where the stone lion stands which was set up in honour of Leonidas. Here they defended themselves to the last, such as still had swords using them, and the others resisting with their hands and teeth; till the barbarians, who in part had pulled down the wall and attacked them in front, in part had gone round and now encircled them upon every side, overwhelmed and buried the remnant which was left beneath showers of missile weapons.

Thus nobly did the whole body of Lacedaemonians and Thespians behave; but nevertheless one man is said to have distinguished himself above all the rest, to wit, Dieneces the Spartan. A speech which he made before the Greeks engaged the Medes, remains on record. One of the Trachinians told him, "Such was the number of the barbarians, that when they shot forth their arrows the sun would be darkned by their multitude." Dieneces, not at all frightened at these words, but making light of the numbers, answered, "Our Trachinian friend brings us excellent tidings. If the Medes darken the sun, we shall have our fight in the shade." Other sayings too of a like nature are said to have been left on record by this same person.

Next to him two brothers, Lacedaemonians, are reputed to have made themselves conspicuous: they were named Alpheus and Maro, and were the sons of Orsiphantus. There was also a Thespian who gained greater glory than any of his countrymen: he was a man called Dithyrambus, the son of Harmatidas.

The slain were buried where they fell; and in their honour, nor less in honour of those who died before Leonidas sent the allies away, an inscription was set up, which said: —

> Here did four thousand men from Pelops' land
> Against three hundred myriads bravely stand.

This was in honour of all. Another was for the Spartans alone: —

> Go, stranger, and to Lacedaemon tell
> That here, obeying her behests, we fell.

This was for the Lacedaemonians. The seer had the following: —

> The great Megistias' tomb you here may view,
> Whom slew the Medes, fresh from Spercheius' fords.
> Well the wise seer the coming death foreknew,
> Yet scorned he to forsake his Spartan lords.

These inscriptions, and the pillars likewise, were all set up by the Amphictyons, except that in honour of Megestias, which was inscribed to him (on account of their sworn friendship) by Simonides, the son of Leoprepes.[14] (VII, 223-228) . . .

There came now[15] a few deserters from Arcadia to join the Persians — poor men who had nothing to live on, and were in want of employment. The Persians brought them into the king's presence, and there inquired of them, by a man who acted as their spokesman, what the Greeks were doing. The Arcadians answered, "They are holding the Olympic games, seeing the athletic sports and the chariot races." "And what," said the man, "is the prize for which they contend?" "An olive-wreath," returned the others, "which is given to the man who wins." On hearing this, Tritantaechmes, the son of Artabanus, uttered a speech which was in truth most noble, but which caused him to be taxed with cowardice by King Xerxes. Hearing the men say the prize was not money but a wreath of olive, he could not forbear from exclaiming before them all, "Good heavens, Mardonius, what manner of men are these against whom thou hast brought us to fight — men who contend with one another, not for money, but for honour!" (VIII, 26) . . .

Meanwhile, the Grecian fleet, which had left Artemisium,[16] proceeded to Salamis, at the request of the Athenians, and there cast anchor. The Athenians had begged them to take up this position, in order that they might convey their women and children out of Attica,[17] and further might deliberate upon the course which it now behoved them to follow. Disappointed in the hopes which they had previously entertained, they were about to hold a council concerning the present posture of their affairs. For they had looked to see the Peloponnesians drawn up in full force to resist the enemy in Boeotia, but found nothing of what they had expected; nay, they learnt that the Greeks of those parts, only concerning themselves about their own safety, were building a wall across the Isthmus, and intended to guard the Peloponnese, and let the rest of Greece take its chance. These tidings caused them to make the request whereof I spoke, that the combined fleet should anchor at Salamis.

---

[14] Other writers attribute all three inscriptions to Simonides. His special friend, Megestias, was the Greek seer who had accompanied the army and declined to depart although he sent back his only son in the face of impending doom.

[15] As Xerxes and his army proceeded southward on their march toward Athens.

[16] The Greek fleet had originally taken up a position by Artemisium to the north of Euboea to hold the Persians at this point, but after the Persian navy was damaged by a storm and the Persian land army forced the pass of Thermopylae, the Greek ships withdrew southward to the islands off the shores of Attica.

[17] On the advice of Themistocles and his interpretation of the Delphic oracle, the Athenians had meanwhile decided to put their trust in the "wooden walls" of their ships by forsaking the mainland and withdrawing to the neighboring islands of Salamis, Egina, and Troezen.

So while the rest of the fleet lay to off this island, the Athenians cast anchor along their own coast. Immediately upon their arrival, proclamation was made, that every Athenian should save his children and household as he best could; whereupon some sent their families to Egina, some to Salamis, but the greater number to Troezen. This removal was made with all possible haste, partly from a desire to obey the advice of the oracle, but still more for another reason. The Athenians say that they have in their Acropolis a huge serpent, which lives in the temple, and is the guardian of the whole place. Nor do they only say this, but, as if the serpent really dwelt there, every month they lay out its food, which consists of a honey-cake. Up to this time the honey-cake had always been consumed; but now it remained untouched. So the priestess told the people what had happened; whereupon they left Athens the more readily, since they believed that the goddess had already abandoned the citadel. As soon as all was removed, the Athenians sailed back to their station.

And now, the remainder of the Grecian sea-force, hearing that the fleet which had been at Artemisium, was come to Salamis, joined it at that island from Troezen — orders having been issued previously that the ships should muster at Pogon, the port of the Troezenians. The vessels collected were many more in number than those which had fought at Artemisium, and were furnished by more cities. The admiral was the same who had commanded before, Eurybiades, the son of Eurycleides, who was a Spartan, but not of the family of the kings; the city, however, which sent by far the greatest number of ships, and the best sailors, was Athens. (VII, 40–42) . . .

Since the passage of the Hellespont and the commencement of the march upon Greece, a space of four months had gone by; one while the army made the crossing, and delayed about the region of the Hellespont; and three while they proceeded thence to Attica, which they entered in the archonship of Calliades. They found the city forsaken; a few people only remained in the temple, either keepers of the treasures, or men of the poorer sort. These persons having fortified the citadel[18] with planks and boards, held out against the enemy. It was in some measure their poverty which had prevented them from seeking shelter in Salamis; but there was likewise another reason which in part induced them to remain. They imagined themselves to have discovered the true meaning of the oracle uttered by the priestess, which promised that "the wooden wall" should never be taken — the wooden wall, they thought, did not mean the ships, but the place where they had taken refuge.

The Persians encamped upon the hill over against the citadel, which is called the Hill of Ares by the Athenians, and began the

---

[18] Situated on an eminence dominating the surrounding plain, the Acropolis or sacred citadel was historically the final place of refuge and last stronghold of resistance for the Athenians.

siege of the place, attacking the Greeks with arrows whereto pieces of lighted tow were attached, which they shot at the barricade. And now those who were within the citadel found themselves in a most woeful case, for their wooden rampart betrayed them; still, however, they continued to resist. It was in vain that the Pisistratidae came to them and offered terms of surrender — they stoutly refused all parley, and among their other modes of defence, rolled down huge masses of stone upon the barbarians as they were mounting up to the gates: so that Xerxes was for a long time very greatly perplexed, and could not contrive any way to take them.

At last, however, in the midst of these many difficulties, the barbarians made discovery of an access. For verily the oracle had spoken truth; and it was fated that the whole mainland of Attica should fall beneath the sway of the Persians. Right in front of the citadel, but behind the gates and the common ascent — where no watch was kept, and no one would have thought it possible that any foot of man could climb — a few soldiers mounted from the sanctuary of Aglaurus, Cecrops' daughter, notwithstanding the steepness of the precipice. As soon as the Athenians saw them upon the summit, some threw themselves headlong from the wall, and so perished; while others fled for refuge to the inner part of the temple. The Persians rushed to the gates and opened them, after which they massacred the suppliants. When all were slain, they plundered the temple, and fired every part of the citadel.

Xerxes, thus completely master of Athens, dispatched a horseman to Susa, with a message to Artabanus, informing him of his success hitherto. The day after, he collected together all the Athenian exiles who had come into Greece in his train, and bade them go up into the citadel, and there offer sacrifice after their own fashion. I know not whether he had had a dream which bade him give this order, or whether he felt some remorse on account of having set the temple on fire. However this may have been, the exiles were not slow to obey the command given them.

I will now explain why I have made mention of this circumstance: there is a temple of Erechtheus, the Earth-born, as he is called, in this citadel, containing within it an olive-tree and a sea.[19] The tale goes among the Athenians, that they were placed there as witnesses by Poseidon and Athena, when they had their contention about the country. Now this olive-tree had been burnt with the rest of the temple when the barbarians took the place. But when the Athenians, whom the king had commanded to offer sacrifice, went up into the temple for the purpose, they found a fresh shoot, a foot and one-half in length, thrown out from the old trunk. Such at least was the account which these persons gave.

Meanwhile, at Salamis, the Greeks no sooner heard what had be-

[19] A salt-water pool or well.

fallen the Athenian citadel, than they fell into such alarm that some of the captains did not even wait for the council to come to a vote, but embarked hastily on board their vessels, and hoisted sail as though they would take to flight immediately. The rest, who stayed at the council board, came to a vote that the fleet should give battle at the Isthmus. Night now drew on, and the captains, dispersing from the meeting, proceeded on board their respective ships. (VIII, 51–56) . . .

So the Greeks at the Isthmus[1] toiled unceasingly as though in the greatest peril; since they never imagined that any great success would be gained by the fleet. The Greeks at Salamis, on the other hand, when they heard what the rest were about, felt greatly alarmed; but their fear was not so much for themselves as for the Peloponnese. At first they conversed together in low tones, each man with his fellow, secretly, and marvelled at the folly shown by Eurybiades; but presently the smothered feeling broke out, and another assembly was held; whereat the old subjects provoked much talk from the speakers, one side maintaining that it was best to sail to the Peloponnese and risk battle for that, instead of abiding at Salamis and fighting for a land already taken by the enemy; while the other, which consisted of the Athenians, Eginetans, and Megarians, was urgent to remain and have the battle fought where they were.

Then Themistocles, when he saw that the Peloponnesians would carry the vote against him, went out secretly from the council, and instructing a certain man what he should say, sent him on board a merchant ship to the fleet of the Medes. The man's name was Sicinnus; he was one of Themistocles' household slaves, and acted as tutor to his sons; in after times, when the Thespians were admitting persons to citizenship, Themistocles made him a Thespian, and a rich man to boot. The ship brought Sicinnus to the Persian fleet, and there he delivered his message to the leaders in these words: —

"The Athenian commander has sent me to you privily, without the knowledge of the other Greeks. He is a well-wisher to the king's cause, and would rather success should attend on you than on his countrymen; wherefore he bids me tell you that fear has seized the Greeks and they are meditating a hasty flight. Now then it is open to you to achieve the best work that ever ye wrought, if only ye will hinder their escaping. They no longer agree among themselves, so that they will not now make any resistance — nay, 'tis likely ye may see a fight already begun between such as favour and such as oppose your cause." The messenger, when he had thus expressed himself, departed and was seen no more.

Then the captains, believing all that the messenger had said, proceeded to land a large body of Persian troops on the islet of Psyttaleia,

[1] The Isthmus of Corinth, joining the Peloponnesus with the rest of Greece, where the Spartans and others had decided to make their stand against the Persians.

which lies between Salamis and the mainland; after which, about the hour of midnight, they advanced their western wing toward Salamis, so as to enclose the Greeks. At the same time the force stationed about Ceos and Cynosura moved forward, and filled the whole strait as far as Munychia with their ships. This advance was made to prevent the Greeks from escaping by flight, and to block them up in Salamis, where it was thought that vengeance might be taken upon them for the battles fought near Artemisium. The Persian troops were landed on the islet of Psyttaleia, because, as soon as the battle began, the men and wrecks were likely to be drifted thither, as the isle lay in the very path of the coming fight, and they would thus be able to save their own men and destroy those of the enemy. All these movements were made in silence, that the Greeks might have no knowledge of them; and they occupied the whole night, so that the men had no time to get their sleep.

I cannot say that there is no truth in prophecies, or feel inclined to call in question those which speak with clearness, when I think of the following: —

When they shall make a bridge with their ships to the sacred strand
   of the goddess
Girt with the golden falchion, and eke to marine Cynosura,
Mad hope swelling their hearts at the downfall of beautiful Athens —
Then shall godlike Right extinguish haughty Presumption,
Insult's furious offspring, who thinketh to overthrow all things.
Brass with brass shall mingle, and Ares with blood shall empurple
Ocean's waves. Then — then shall the day of Hellas' freedom
Come from Victory fair, and Cronus' son all-seeing.

When I look to this, and perceive how clearly Bacis spoke, I neither venture myself to say anything against prophecies, nor do I approve of others impugning them.

Meanwhile, among the captains at Salamis, the strife of words grew fierce. As yet they did not know that they were encompassed, but imagined that the barbarians remained in the same places where they had seen them the day before.

In the midst of their contention, Aristides, the son of Lysimachus, who had crossed from Egina, arrived in Salamis. He was an Athenian, and had been ostracized by the commonalty;[2] yet I believe, from what I have heard concerning his character, that there was not in all Athens a man so worthy or so just as he. He now came to the council, and standing outside, called for Themistocles. Now Themistocles was not his friend, but his most determined enemy. However, under the

---

[2] Although Themistocles had been influential in the earlier banishment of Aristides for three years (483 B.C.), he later, when Xerxes was approaching, sponsored the recall of all exiles whose banishment was only for a term of years.

pressure of the great dangers impending, Aristides forgot their feud, and called Themistocles out of the council, since he wished to confer with him. He had heard before his arrival of the impatience of the Peloponnesians to withdraw the fleet to the Isthmus. As soon therefore as Themistocles came forth, Aristides addressed him in these words: —

"Our rivalry at all times, and especially at the present season, ought to be a struggle as to who shall most advantage our country. Let me then say to thee, that so far as regards the departure of the Peloponnesians from this place, much talk and little will be found precisely alike. I have seen with my own eyes that which I now report; that, however much the Corinthians or Eurybiades himself may wish it, they cannot now retreat; for we are enclosed on every side by the enemy. Go in to them, and make this known."

"Thy advice is excellent," answered the other, "and thy tidings are also good. That which I earnestly desire to happen, thine eyes have beheld accomplished. Know that what the Medes have now done was at my instance; for it was necessary, as our men would not fight here of their own free will, to make them fight whether they would or no. But come now, as thou hast brought the good news, go in and tell it. For if I speak to them, they will think it a feigned tale, and will not believe that the barbarians have enclosed us around. Therefore do thou go to them, and inform them how matters stand. If they believe thee, it will be for the best; but if otherwise, it will not harm. For it is impossible that they should now flee away, if we are indeed shut in on all sides, as thou sayest."

Then Aristides entered the assembly, and spoke to the captains: he had come, he told them, from Egina, and had but barely escaped the blockading vessels — the Greek fleet was entirely enclosed by the ships of Xerxes — and he advised them to get themselves in readiness to resist the foe. Having said so much, he withdrew. And now another contest arose; for the greater part of the captains would not believe the tidings.

But while they still doubted, a Tenian trireme, commanded by Panaetius the son of Sosimenes, deserted from the Persians and joined the Greeks, bringing full intelligence. For this reason the Tenians were inscribed upon the tripod at Delphi among those who overthrew the barbarians. With this ship, which deserted to their side at Salamis, and the Lemnian vessel which came over before at Artemisium, the Greek fleet was brought to the full number of 380 ships; otherwise it fell short by two of that amount.

The Greeks now, not doubting what the Tenians told them, made ready for the coming fight. At the dawn of day, all the men-at-arms were assembled together, and speeches were made to them, of which the best was that of Themistocles; who throughout contrasted what was noble with what was base, and bade them, in all that came within the range of man's nature and constitution, always to make choice of the nobler part. Having thus wound up his discourse, he told them to go at once on board their ships, which they accordingly did; and about this time the trireme, that had been sent to Egina for the Aeacidae, returned; whereupon the Greeks put to sea with all their fleet.[3] (VIII, 74-83) . . .

Against the Athenians, who held the western extremity of the line towards Eleusis, were placed the Phoenicians; against the Lacedaemonians, whose station was eastward towards the Piraeus, the Ionians. Of these last a few only followed the advice of Themistocles, to fight backwardly; the greater number did far otherwise. I could mention here the names of many trierarchs who took vessels from the Greeks, but I shall pass over all excepting Theomestor the son of Androdamus, and Phylacus the son of Histiaeus, both Samians. I show this preference to them, inasmuch as for this service Theomestor was made tyrant of Samos by the Persians, while Phylacus was enrolled among the king's benefactors, and presented with a large estate in land. In the Persian tongue the king's benefactors are called Orosangs.

Far the greater number of the Persian ships engaged in this battle were disabled — either by the Athenians or by the Eginetans. For as the Greeks fought in order and kept their line, while the barbarians were in confusion and had no plan in anything that they did, the issue of the battle could scarce be other than it was. Yet the Persians fought far more bravely here than at Euboea, and indeed surpassed themselves; each did his utmost through fear of Xerxes, for each thought that the king's eye was upon himself. (VIII, 85-86) . . .

When the rout of the barbarians began, and they sought to make their escape to Phalerum, the Eginetans, awaiting them in the channel, performed exploits worthy to be recorded. Through the whole of the confused struggle the Athenians employed themselves in destroying such ships as either made resistance or fled to shore, while the Eginetans dealt with those which endeavoured to escape down the strait; so that the Persian vessels were no sooner clear of the Athenians than forthwith they fell into the hands of the Eginetan squadron. (VIII, 91) . . .

As soon as the sea-fight was ended, the Greeks drew together to Salamis all the wrecks that were to be found in that quarter, and prepared themselves for another engagement, supposing that the king would renew the fight with the vessels which still remained to him. Many of the wrecks had been carried away by a westerly wind to the coast of Attica, where they were thrown upon the strip of shore called Colias. Thus not only were the prophecies of Bacis and Musaeus concerning this battle fulfilled completely, but likewise, by the place to which the wrecks were drifted, the prediction of Lysistratus, an Athenian soothsayer, uttered many years before these events, and

---

[3] The ensuing decisive naval battle of Salamis was fought in 480 B.C.

quite forgotten at the time by all the Greeks, was fully accomplished. The words were:

> Then shall the sight of the oars fill Colian dames with amazement.

Now this must have happened as soon as the king was departed.

Xerxes, when he saw the extent of his loss, began to be afraid lest the Greeks might be counselled by the Ionians, or without their advice might determine to sail straight to the Hellespont and break down the bridges there; in which case he would be blocked up in Europe, and run great risk of perishing. He therefore made up his mind to fly; but as he wished to hide his purpose alike from the Greeks and from his own people, he set to work to carry a mound across the channel to Salamis,[4] and at the same time began fastening a number of Phoenician merchant ships together, to serve at once for a bridge and a wall. He likewise made many warlike preparations, as if he were about to engage the Greeks once more at sea. Now, when these things were seen, all grew fully persuaded that the king was bent on remaining, and intended to push the war in good earnest. Mardonius, however, was in no respect deceived; for long acquaintance enabled him to read all the king's thoughts. Meanwhile, Xerxes, though engaged in this way, sent off a messenger to carry intelligence of his misfortune to Persia.

Nothing mortal travels so fast as these Persian messengers. The entire plan is a Persian invention; and this is the method of it. Along the whole line of road there are men (they say) stationed with horses, in number equal to the number of days which the journey takes, allowing a man and horse to each day; and these men will not be hindered from accomplishing at their best speed the distance which they have to go, either by snow, or rain, or heat, or by the darkness of night.[5] The first rider delivers his despatch to the second, and the second passes it to the third; and so it is borne from hand to hand along the whole line, like the light in the torch-race, which the Greeks celebrate to Hephaestus. The Persians give the riding post in this manner the name of "Angarum."

At Susa, on the arrival of the first message, which said that Xerxes was master of Athens, such was the delight of the Persians who had remained behind, that they forthwith strewed all the streets with myrtle boughs, and burnt incense, and fell to feasting and merriment. In like manner, when the second message reached them, so sore was their dismay, that they all with one accord rent their garments, and cried aloud, and wept and wailed without stint. They laid the blame of the disaster on Mardonius;[6] and their grief on the occasion was

---

[4] Other authors place this project earlier, before the battle.
[5] Cf. the inscription on the Main Post Office, New York City: "Neither snow, nor rain, nor heat, nor gloom of night stays these couriers from the swift completion of their appointed rounds."
[6] Xerxes' leading general.

less on account of the damage done to their ships, than owing to the alarm which they felt about the safety of the king. Hence their trouble did not cease till Xerxes himself, by his arrival, put an end to their fears. (VIII, 96–99) . . .

. . . The Athenians returned this answer to Alexander[7]: —

"We know, as well as thou dost, that the power of the Mede is many times greater than our own; we did not need to have *that* cast in our teeth. Nevertheless, we cling so to freedom that we shall offer what resistance we may. Seek not to persuade us into making terms with the barbarian — say what thou wilt, thou wilt never gain our assent. Return rather at once, and tell Mardonius that our answer to him is this: — 'So long as the sun keeps his present course, we will never join alliance with Xerxes. Nay, we shall oppose him unceasingly, trusting in the aid of those gods and heroes whom he has lightly esteemed, whose houses and whose images he has burnt with fire.' And come not thou again to us with words like these; nor, thinking to do us a service, persuade us to unholy actions. Thou art the guest and friend of our nation — we would not that thou shouldst receive hurt at our hands."

Such was the answer which the Athenians gave to Alexander. To the Spartan envoys they said: —

"It was natural no doubt that the Lacedaemonians should be afraid we might make terms with the barbarian; but nevertheless it was a base fear in men who knew so well of what temper and spirit we are. Not all the gold that the whole earth contains — not the fairest and most fertile of all lands — would bribe us to take part with the Medes and help them to enslave our countrymen. Even could we anyhow have brought ourselves to such a thing, there are many very powerful motives which would now make it impossible. The first and chief of these is the burning and destruction of our temples and the images of our gods, which forces us to make no terms with their destroyer, but rather to pursue him with our resentment to the uttermost. Again, there is our common brotherhood with the Greeks: our common language, the altars and the sacrifices of which we all partake, the common character which we bear — did the Athenians betray all these, of a truth it would not be well. Know then now, if ye have not known it before, that while one Athenian remains alive, we will never join alliance with Xerxes. . . ."[8] (VIII, 143–144)

[7] The Macedonian Alexander was the head of a mission sent (in 479 B.C.) by the Persian commander in Greece, Mardonius, to try to persuade the hard-pressed Athenians to make a separate and favorable peace with Xerxes.

[8] After learning of the Athenian answer, Mardonius marched against Athens, but was decisively defeated by a combined Greek army in the ensuing battle of Plataea (479 B.C.), thus ending the Persian menace to Greece. The Greek victory at Mycale, on the Asiatic coast, on the same day, destroyed the Persian fleet and further freed the Greeks of Asia Minor.

2

Transition from Republic to Empire Among the Practical Romans

SUETONIUS

Although the Greeks excelled in the domain of ideas, the remarkable empire that was organized throughout the lands surrounding the blue Mediterranean was a Roman one. For the theoretical Greeks met temporary political shipwreck through their insistence on preserving their local self-determination undiminished, whereas the practical Romans gradually adapted their institutions to the needs of an expanding international imperialism.

Transitional between republican and imperial forms of government, as well as a principal agent in the overthrow of the first and the substitution of the second, was Julius Caesar. And the qualities which underlie the Roman contribution to Western civilization are exemplified not only in Caesar but also in his biographer, Suetonius; for both, in their very different walks of life, were typical Romans.

The life of the biographer stands in marked contrast to that of his subject. Gaius Suetonius Tranquillus (c. A.D. 70–c. 160) lived when the Roman Empire was at its height. Personally he seems to have been quiet, studious, and retiring. About his life only a few facts are known, many of them gleaned from certain letters of his friend Pliny the Younger. Well-educated in the manner of his time, Suetonius taught rhetoric for a while, and also pled as a lawyer at the bar. A high point in his career was his service (c. A.D. 121–122) as secretary to the Emperor Hadrian. But Suetonius did not hold this position very long. As Aelianus Spartianus tells it, "Although [Hadrian] had often complained of his wife Sabina's difficult and cross-grained humor, and said that if he had been a private person he would have divorced her, he dismissed Septicius Clarus, Prefect of the Guard, and Suetonius Tranquillus, his Secretary, together with several others for having behaved towards her with less ceremony than was required by court etiquette." After this, Suetonius disappeared from the public eye, but he is believed to have lived to a ripe old age.

Suetonius, who was an industrious writer, is credited with over fifteen books on numerous subjects, ranging from Roman institutions to children's games, and from grammatical problems to lives of famous courtesans. But his only surviving works are his Lives of the Caesars (on which rests his claim to fame) and some fragments of his Illustrious Men: lives of literary figures such as Horace, Terence, and Pliny the Elder. The Lives of the Caesars cover twelve rulers of the Roman Empire, beginning with Julius Caesar and closing with Domitian (died A.D. 96). For this imperial span, Suetonius provides us with much valuable information and numerous details not found in such writers as Dio Cassius, Tacitus, and Plutarch. He is one of our leading sources for the life of Julius Caesar, and useful also for the eleven other "Caesars" who succeeded Julius.

With his Lives of the Caesars, Suetonius inaugurated a new style of biography that was to have a profound influence on this genre. It was a welcome break-away from the older Greek types of formal biography, such as the "moralistic," which was designed to edify the reader; the "panegyrical," which extolled its subject and concealed his faults; and the "grammatical," which was intended as an introduction to the study of a person's works. The biographies written by Suetonius were very popular during the Middle Ages and the Renaissance, and their technique still flourishes in present-day biographical writing.

The Lives by Suetonius are vivid and interesting as well as informative. He has been accused of an excessive taste for gossip and an undue willingness to give credence to salacious tales. While there is some truth in these criticisms, it should be remembered that there actually was a superabundance of both gossip and vice in high places in contemporary Roman society, and that Suetonius does not recount tongue-wagging and scandal indiscriminately or without qualification. A more serious charge is that he lacks the ability to generalize and evaluate: that he fails, for instance, to estimate the relative importance of events like Caesar's conquest of Gaul, to which he gives little more attention than he does to the purported affairs of Caesar with Nicomedes and of Pompeia with Publius Clodius. Yet there may be other reasons for this neglect, such as the fact that Caesar himself had already written of his conquests in Gaul. Still it cannot be denied that Suetonius shows more aptitude and affinity for the personal, the concrete, and the indiscriminate, than for the universal, the abstract, and the evaluative. In this he shows himself a typical Roman writing for like-minded fellow Romans: particular and realistic rather than general and idealistic, lacking to a certain degree in profound intellectual acumen, more imitative of the Greek than truly original, more down-to-earth than speculative, with a firm grip on practical reality in all its multiple and colorful details. His biographies remind us of the highly realistic portrait-sculpture of the Romans, which sought close adherence to the actual model rather than representation of a generalized type or ideal.

Suetonius' life of Julius Caesar is a mirror reflecting important aspects of Roman life at a crucial period in the history of Western civilization. Roman rule has encircled the Mediterranean and is extending itself to Egypt in the southeast and to Gaul in the northwest. The growing inadequacy of the Republic is accentuated by the fierce struggles between the aristocratic Senatorial party and the democratic Popular party. Both sides are invoking successful generals and resorting to force. The weakness and indecision of the Senate in time of crisis is manifest. We watch as Caesar makes his way, within the framework of the Republic, through office-holding, political deals, and military victories to absolute power. His success sounds the death-knell of the Republic and the advent of imperial monarchy, based on the backing and might of the invincible Roman legions.

In his "virtues," or manly qualities, Julius Caesar represents the classical ideal of the "universal man," highly competent in many fields, cast in a Roman mold: energetic, self-confident, practical, efficient; a victorious general, a constructive statesman, a gifted administrator, an unexcelled war-correspondent; renowned alike for his political showmanship and his social graces so devastating with the opposite sex. At the same time, however, we see the poverty of contemporary Roman morals in his frank lack of concern for the fulfilment of contracts, agreements, and financial responsibilities, his resort to extortion, his sexual incontinence, and his light treatment of the marital bond; and the weakness of contemporary Roman religion in his rather calloused skepticism and open incredulity. Caesar's attitude seems to be shared by Suetonius. The moral and religious defects of classical civilization are apparent.

The rising level of Roman culture, drawing liberally from the Greek, is evident in Suetonius' account. Yet so is the typically Roman concentration on the particular, the personal, and the practical, as contrasted with the Greek delight in knowledge and abstract principles for their own sake. Already the assimilative Romans are pursuing liberal studies, including grammar, rhetoric, and literature, in imitation of their Greek teachers, and composing history, poetry, and drama in the Greek manner. In his life of Caesar, Suetonius shows us Rome on the threshold of its Golden Age.

G. Suetonius Tranquillus

FROM *The Lives of the Caesars: Julius Caesar* *

In his sixteenth year[1] Caesar lost his father. During the next consulate, having been nominated high-priest of Jupiter,[2] he broke his engagement with Cossutia, a lady of only equestrian rank but very wealthy, engaged to him since his childhood, and married Cornelia, the daughter of Cinna, four times Consul,[3] by whom he afterwards had a daughter, Julia. In resisting the efforts of Sulla, the Dictator, to force him to divorce Cornelia, he suffered the loss of his sacerdotal office, his wife's dowry, all his family inheritance, and was held to be of the opposition. He was accordingly forced to leave Rome, and although suffering from a quartan ague, to shift from one hiding-place to another almost every night. He saved himself from Sulla's detectives by bribes, until by the mediation of the Vestal Virgins and of his near kinsmen, Aemilius Mamercus and Aurelius Cotta, he obtained a pardon. Every one knows that Sulla, after he had long denied the requests of the most devoted and eminent men of his own party who interceded for Caesar, and they obstinately persisted, at last yielded and cried out, either through divine inspiration or shrewd conjecture: "Have your way and take him. But, bear this in mind: the man you are so eager to save will one day be the ruin of the nobles, whose side you have upheld with me; for in this Caesar there is more than one Marius."[4]

He first served in the wars in Asia[5] on the personal staff of Marcus Thermus, Governor of the province, by whom he was sent to Bithynia[6] to bring out a fleet. He loitered there so long at the court of Nicomedes as to give occasion to rumors that he prostituted his body to the use of the King. He augmented this rumor by a hasty return to Bithynia under the pretext of collecting a debt for a freedman, one of his dependents. The rest of the campaign was more favorable to his reputation, and, after the successful assault of Mytilene, Thermus honored him with a civic garland.[7]

---

* From *The Lives of the Twelve Caesars*, by Suetonius, ed. by Joseph Gavorse. Copyright 1931 and renewed 1959 by The Modern Library, Inc. Reprinted by permission of Random House, Inc.
[1] At the age of fifteen (85–84 B.C.).
[2] More a political than a religious office.
[3] This marriage had marked political and social advantages.
[4] Marius' wife, Julia, was Caesar's aunt. Marius was leader of the "Popular" party of the masses; Sulla, of the aristocratic "Senatorial" party.
[5] Asia was a Roman province in western Asia Minor.
[6] South of the Black Sea in northwestern Asia Minor.
[7] A crown of oak leaves usually given to civilians but sometimes to officers.

He also served in Cilicia[8] under Servilius Isauricus, but only for a short time. For, upon learning of the death of Sulla, and at the same time with the hope of profiting by the new dissensions which Marcus Lepidus was instigating, he hastily returned to Rome. But, although he was offered highly favorable terms, he did not join up with Lepidus, through lack of confidence in that leader's capacity and in the outlook, which he found much less favorable than he had expected.

After this civil discord had been composed, he preferred a charge of extortion against Cornelius Dolabella, an ex-Consul who had been honored with a triumph. On the acquittal of the accused, Caesar determined to retire to Rhodes,[9] as well to escape the ill-will he had incurred, as to rest and have leisure to study under Apollonius Molo, the most renowned teacher of oratory in those days.

On his voyage there, the winter season having already begun, he was taken by pirates near the island of Pharmacussa, and, burning with indignation, held captive by them for nearly forty days, accompanied only by a physician and two body-servants. For his traveling companions and the rest of his attendants he had sent off at the outset, to procure money for his ransom. Once they released him on shore, upon payment of fifty talents,[10] he did not delay but at once collected some ships, put to sea again, and did not cease pursuing them till he had overtaken them. No sooner were they in his power than he inflicted on them the punishment with which he had often threatened them in jest. He then proceeded to Rhodes.

At that time Mithridates was ravaging the adjoining regions. Because he would not be thought to sit still and do nothing when the confederate nations and allies of Rome were in this dangerous situation, he crossed over in Asia, gathered a power of auxiliaries, drove the King's Governor from the province, and so held the wavering and irresolute states to their allegiance.

While serving as Military Tribune,[11] the first office conferred on him by the vote of the people after his return to Rome, he zealously supported those leaders who stood out for the restitution of the authority of the Tribunes of the Commons,[12] the extent of which Sulla had curtailed. Furthermore, through a bill proposed by one Plotius, he effected the recall of Lucius Cinna, his wife's brother, as well as that of the others who had been adherents of Lepidus in his insurrec-

---

[8] In southwestern Asia Minor.

[9] Famous as a Greek center of learning.

[10] A huge sum. There is no point in trying to calculate present-day values, because of inflation and greatly changed times; but a talent today, all things considered, would probably correspond to from $1000 to $5000.

[11] Caesar was elected a Military Tribune of the People.

[12] The Tribunes, who enjoyed the veto power, had the function of protecting the interests of the commoners or masses against the otherwise dominant patricians, who controlled the Senate and other offices.

tion and who, after that Consul's death, had fled to Sertorius.[13] He himself supported the measure in a speech.

When Quaestor,[14] he pronounced the customary orations from the rostra in praise of his aunt Julia and his wife Cornelia, both deceased. And in the eulogy of his aunt he spoke in the following terms of her paternal and maternal ancestry and that of his own father: "My aunt Julia is descended on her mother's side from the Kings, and on her father's side is akin to the immortal Gods: for the Marcii Reges, from whom comes the name of her mother's family, are derived from Ancus Marcius, and the Julii, the family of which ours is a branch, from Venus.[15] Our stock therefore has at once the sanctity of Kings, who among men are most powerful, and the claim to reverence which attaches to the Gods, to whom Kings themselves are subject."

In place of Cornelia he then wedded Pompeia, daughter of Quintus Pompeius and granddaughter of Lucius Sulla. But he afterward divorced her, suspecting her of adultery with Publius Clodius. As a matter of fact the report was so persistent that Clodius, disguised in woman's apparel, had secretly gained access to her at the celebration of a public religious ceremony[16] the Senate by decree directed that this pollution of sacred rites be judicially investigated.

While he was Quaestor it fell to him by lot to serve in Farther Spain. While there, as he rode his circuit of the assize-towns to hold court under order of the Praetor,[17] he came to Gades,[18] where he noticed a statue of Alexander the Great in the temple of Hercules. At the sight of it he drew a deep sigh, as one displeased with his own shortcomings, in that he had as yet performed no memorable act, whereas at his age Alexander had already conquered the whole world.[19]

He soon after made earnest suit for his discharge, in order to seize the first opportunity to compass greater enterprises at home within the city. The following night he was much disquieted by a dream in which he imagined he had carnal company with his own mother. But hopes of most glorious achievement were kindled in him by the soothsayers, who interpreted the dream to mean that he was destined to have sovereignty over all the world, his mother whom he saw under him signifying none other than the earth, which is counted the mother of all things.

Leaving Spain, therefore, before the expiration of the accustomed

---

[13] Sertorius led a popular revolution in Spain.
[14] Originally the two Quaestors or Inquisitors were deputies of the Consuls to investigate and try more serious crimes.
[15] Supposedly from Aeneas through his son Julius.
[16] The nocturnal rites of the Good Goddess, from which men were excluded.
[17] Or provincial governor.
[18] Cadiz.
[19] Alexander the Great died at the age of 33.

term, he went to the Latin colonies,[1] which were then in a state of unrest, and meditating a demand for citizenship. He might have excited them to some rash act, but that the Consuls,[2] anticipating this very danger, detained there the legions which had been enrolled for service in Cilicia.

And yet, for all that, he soon after entertained more daring designs in Rome. For only a few days before he entered upon his aedileship,[3] he was suspected of having conspired with Marcus Crassus, an ex-consul, together with Publius Sulla and Lucius Autronius, who, after they had been elected Consuls, had been convicted of bribery. The plan of the conspirators was to fall upon the Senate at the opening of the new year and, after they had massacred as many as they thought necessary, Crassus was to usurp the Dictatorship and appoint Caesar Master of Horse.[4] When they had reorganized the state to their wishes, the consulship was to be restored to Autronius. Mention is made of this conspiracy by Tanusius Geminus in his History, by Marcus Bibulus[5] in his edicts, and by Gaius Curio the elder in his speeches. Cicero, too, seems to imply as much in a letter to Axius, where he says that Caesar in his consulship secured for himself that arbitrary power which he had contemplated when Aedile. Tanusius adds that Crassus, either from remorse or from fear, did not appear on the day appointed for the massacre, and that therefore Caesar did not give the signal, which it had been agreed he should give. This signal, Curio says, was that Caesar should let his toga fall from his shoulder. We have the authority of the same Curio, as well as that of Marcus Actorius Naso, that Caesar also conspired with Gnaeus Piso, a youth to whom the province of Spain was assigned unsought and out of regular order,[6] because he was suspected of conspiring in the city; that they had agreed to stir up insurrection simultaneously, Piso abroad and Caesar at Rome, using as their instruments the Ambrani and the tribes beyond the Po; but that the death of Piso frustrated both their designs.

When Caesar was Aedile, he decorated not only the Comitium[7] and the Forum with its adjacent halls, but also the Capitol, building temporary galleries for the purpose of displaying some part of the abundant paraphernalia he had collected for the amusement of the people. He exhibited combats with wild beasts, and stage-plays, too, both jointly with his companion in office and independently. The result was that, although the charges were borne in common by them

---

[1] Of northern Italy.
[2] The supreme power in the Roman republic was vested in two Consuls.
[3] The Aedile was commissioner of buildings.
[4] Or Commander of Cavalry.
[5] Caesar's colleague in office.
[6] As a mild form of banishment.
[7] A building where assemblies of the people were held.

both, Caesar alone obtained all the credit. Nor did his colleague, Marcus Bibulus, dissemble the matter, but openly said that he served in the manner of Pollux; that just as the temple erected in the Forum to both the twin brothers bore the name of Castor alone, even so the joint munificence of Caesar and himself was credited to Caesar alone. Caesar gave a gladiatorial show besides, but not with so many pairs of combatants as he had intended. He had assembled from all quarters such a huge band his enemies became alarmed, and a decree was made restricting the number of gladiators which any one was permitted to retain in Rome.

Having won the favor of the populace,[8] Caesar endeavored, through his association with some of the Tribunes, to obtain, by a decree of the Commons, Egypt assigned him as a province. The opportunity he seized for asking so irregular an appointment was that the Alexandrians had deposed their King[9] whom the Senate had named an ally and friend of the Roman people, and this was generally resented. Nevertheless, there was so much opposition from the party of the nobles,[10] he failed to carry his point. Wishing, therefore, to impair their influence by every means in his power he restored the trophies erected to commemorate the victories of Gaius Marius over Jugurtha, the Cimbri, and Teutoni, which had long before been demolished by Sulla. Furthermore, when sitting in judgment upon murders, he treated as assassins even those who, in the late proscription,[11] had received money from the public treasury for bringing in the heads of Roman citizens, although they were expressly excepted by the Cornelian laws....

After renouncing all hope of obtaining Egypt for his province, he announced himself candidate for the office of Chief Priest, having recourse to the most profuse bribery. Thinking about the enormous debts he had thus contracted, he is reported to have said to his mother, when she kissed him as he was going out in the morning to the assembly for the election, that he would never return home except as Pontiff. And indeed, he so decisively defeated his two most powerful competitors, both his superiors in age and rank, that he had more votes in their tribes than were cast for both of them in all the tribes together.

After he was chosen Praetor,[12] the conspiracy of Catilline was discovered. And while every other member of the Senate voted for inflicting capital punishment on the accomplices in the plot, he alone proposed that their property be confiscated, and that each be imprisoned in a separate town....

---

[8] Like his uncle Marius, Caesar became identified with the Popular party.
[9] Father of Cleopatra.
[10] The Senatorial party.
[11] Sulla had outlawed partisans of the Popular cause and given bounties for their heads.
[12] Praetor at Rome, where the office was judicial.

On the first day of his praetorship, he called upon Quintus Catulus to render an account to the people respecting the restoration of the Capitol, proposing a bill for transferring the office of curator to another. But he withdrew the measure, since he could not cope with the united opposition of the aristocrats, who, he perceived, had at once dropped attendance on the newly elected Consuls, and hastily gathered in throngs resolved on obstinate resistance.

Nevertheless, when Caecilius Metellus, Tribune of the Commons, brought forward some bills of a highly seditious nature in spite of all the opposition of his colleagues, Caesar abetted him and espoused his cause in the most stubborn manner, until at last both were suspended from the exercise of their public functions by a decree of the Senate. Yet in spite of this, Caesar had the audacity to continue in office and to hold court. But when he learned that some were ready to stop him by force of arms, he dismissed his Lictors,[13] laid aside his robe of office, and slipped off privily to his house, intending to remain in retirement because of the state of the times. Indeed, when the populace on the following day flocked to him quite of their own accord, and with riotous demonstrations offered him their aid in recovering his position, he held them in check. Since this action of his was wholly unexpected, the Senate, which had been hurriedly convoked to take action about that very gathering, publicly thanked him through its leading men. Then, summoning him to the House and lauding him in the strongest terms, they rescinded their former decree and restored him to his office.

He again fell into danger by being named among the accomplices of Catiline, both before the commissioner Novius Niger by an informer called Lucius Vettius, and in the Senate by Quintus Curius, who had been voted a sum of money from the public funds for having first discovered the designs of the conspirators. Curius alleged that his information came directly from Catiline, while Vettius actually offered to produce a letter to Catiline in Caesar's handwriting. As this was an indignity Caesar knew intolerable, he showed by appealing to Cicero's testimony that he had of his own accord reported to the Consul certain details of the plot, and thus prevented Curius from getting the reward. As for Vettius, after his bond was declared forfeit and his goods seized, he was roughly handled by the populace assembled before the rostra, and all but torn to pieces. Caesar then put him in prison, and Novius the commissioner went there, too, for allowing an official of superior rank to be arraigned before his tribunal.

Being allotted the province of Farther Spain after his praetorship, Caesar got rid of his creditors, who tried to detain him, by means of sureties,[14] and, contrary to both law and precedent, was on his way

[13] Official attendants.
[14] During the earlier part of his career, Caesar was chronically in debt, and his debts seemed to become ever greater.

before his appointment was confirmed by the Senate and funds and equipment provided. It is uncertain whether this precipitancy arose through fear of some judicial proceeding against him as a private person, or that he might the more promptly respond to the entreaties of our allies for help. After restoring order in his province, he made as great haste to leave it, not waiting for the arrival of his successor, and to sue at the same time for a triumph and the consulship. But inasmuch as the day for the elections had already been announced and no account could be taken of Caesar's candidacy unless he entered the city as a private citizen, and since his intrigues to gain exemption from the laws met with general protest, he was forced to forego the triumph, to avoid losing the consulship.

Of the two competing candidates for this office, Lucius Lucceius and Marcus Bibulus, Caesar joined forces with the former, making a bargain with him that since Lucceius had less influence but more funds, he should in their common name promise largess to the electors from his own pocket. When this became known, the aristocracy authorized Bibulus to promise the same amount, being seized with fear that Caesar would stick at nothing when he became chief magistrate, if he had a colleague who was heart and soul with him. Many of them contributed to the fund, and even Cato did not deny that bribery under such circumstances was for the good of the commonwealth.[15]

So Caesar was chosen Consul with Bibulus. With the same motives the aristocracy took care that provinces of the smallest importance should be assigned to the newly elected Consuls, that is, mere woods and pastures.[16] Thereupon Caesar, especially incensed by this slight, by every possible attention courted the goodwill of Gnaeus Pompeius, who was at odds with the Senate because of its tardiness in ratifying his acts after his victory over King Mithridates. He also patched up a peace between Pompeius and Marcus Crassus, who had been enemies since their consulship, which had been one of constant wrangling. Then he made an agreement with them, that no step should be taken in public affairs which did not suit any one of the three.

Caesar's very first enactment after becoming Consul was, that the proceedings both of the Senate and of the people should day by day be compiled and published. He also revived a by-gone custom, that during the months when he did not have the fasces[17] an orderly should walk before him, while the Lictors followed him. He brought forward an agrarian law, too, and when his colleague announced adverse omens, he resorted to arms and drove him from the Forum; and when next day Bibulus made complaint in the Senate and no one could

---

[15] Although there were strict laws against bribery at elections.
[16] The Senate was afraid of entrusting Caesar with a province involving command of an army, a fear which later proved well-founded.
[17] Rods of office.

be found who ventured to make a motion, or even to express an opinion about so high-handed a proceeding (although decrees had often been passed touching less serious breaches of the peace), Caesar's conduct drove him to such a pitch of desperation, that from that time until the end of his term he did not leave his house, but merely issued proclamations announcing adverse omens.

From that time on Caesar managed all the affairs of state alone and according to his own pleasure; so that sundry witty fellows, pretending by way of jest to sign and seal testamentary documents, wrote "Done in the consulship of Julius and Caesar," instead of "Bibulus and Caesar," writing down the same man twice, by name and by surname. Presently too the following verses were on every one's lips: —

> "Caesar of late did many things, but Bibulus not one;
> For naught by Consul Bibulus can I remember done."

The plain called Stellas, which had been devoted to the Gods by the men of by-gone days, and the Campanian territory,[18] which had been reserved to pay revenues for the aid of the government, he divided,[19] without casting lots, among twenty thousand citizens who had three or more children each. . . .

At about the same time he took to wife Calpurnia, daughter of Lucius Piso, who was to succeed him in the consulship, and affianced his own daughter Julia to Gnaeus Pompeius, breaking a previous engagement with Servilius Caepio, although the latter had shortly before rendered him conspicuous service in his contest with Bibulus. After this new alliance he began to call upon Pompey first to give his opinion in the Senate, although it had been his habit to begin with Crassus, and it was the rule for the Consul in calling for opinions to continue throughout the year the order which he had established on the Kalends of January.[1]

Backed therefore by his father-in-law and son-in-law, out of all the numerous provinces he made the Gauls his choice, as the most likely to enrich him and furnish suitable material for triumphs. At first, it is true, by the bill of Vatinius he received only Cisalpine Gaul[2] with the addition of Illyricum. But presently he was assigned Gallia Comata[3] as well by the Senate, since the members feared that even if they should refuse it, the people would give him this also. Transported with joy at this success, he could not keep from boasting a few

---

[18] I.e., another district in the Campanian region.
[19] By appointing a commission to handle the division.
[1] New Year's Day.
[2] "Gaul this side of the Alps": northern Italy, which had earlier been controlled by Celts, but had now for some time been in Roman hands.
[3] "Long-haired Gaul": Gaul beyond the Alps, except for southeastern Gaul, or Narbonensis, which he also received.

days later before a crowded house, that having gained his heart's desire to the grief and lamentation of his opponents, he would therefore from that time mount on their heads. And when some one insultingly remarked that that would be no easy matter for any woman, he replied in the same vein that Semiramis too had been Queen in Syria and the Amazons in days of old had held sway over a great part of Asia.

When, at the close of his consulship, the Praetors Gaius Memmius and Lucius Domitius moved an inquiry into his conduct during the previous year, Caesar laid the matter before the Senate. When they failed to take it up, and three days had been wasted in fruitless wrangling, he went off to his province. Whereupon his Quaestor was at once arraigned on several counts, as a preliminary to his own impeachment. Presently he himself too was prosecuted by Lucius Antistius, Tribune of the Commons, and it was only by appealing to the whole college that he contrived not to be brought to trial, on the ground that he was absent on public service. Then to secure himself for the future, he took great pains always to put the magistrates for the year under personal obligation, and not to aid any candidates or suffer any to be elected, save such as guaranteed to defend him in his absence. And he did not hesitate in some cases to exact an oath to keep this pledge or even a written contract.

When, however, Lucius Domitius, candidate for the consulship, openly threatened to effect as Consul what he had been unable to do as Praetor, and to take his armies from him, Caesar compelled Pompeius and Crassus to come to Luca, a city in his province, where he prevailed on them to stand for a second consulship, to defeat Domitius; and he also succeeded through their influence in having his term as Governor of Gaul made five years longer. Encouraged by this, he added to the legions which he had received from the state others at his own cost, one actually composed of men of Transalpine Gaul and bearing a Gallic name too (for it was called Alauda),[4] which he trained in the Roman tactics and equipped with Roman arms; and later on he gave every man of it citizenship. After that he did not let slip any pretext for war, however unjust and dangerous it might be, picking quarrels as well with allied, as with hostile and barbarious nations; so that once the Senate decreed that a commission be sent to inquire into the condition of the Gallic provinces, and some even recommended that Caesar be handed over to the enemy. But as his enterprises prospered, supplication days[5] were appointed in his honor oftener and for longer periods than for any one before his time.

During the nine years of his command this is in substance what he did. All that part of Gaul which is bounded by the Pyrenees, the Alps and the Cévennes, and by the Rhine and Rhone rivers, a circuit

[4] "Legion of the Lark."
[5] Thanksgiving days honoring a victorious general.

of some 3,200 miles,[6] not counting some allied states which had rendered him good service, he reduced to the form of a province; and imposed upon it a yearly tribute of 40,000,000 sesterces.[7] He was the first Roman to build a bridge and attack the Germans beyond the Rhine; and he inflicted heavy losses upon them. He invaded the Britons too, a people unknown before, vanquished them, and exacted moneys and hostages. Amid all these successes he met with adverse fortune but three times in all: in Britain, where his fleet narrowly escaped destruction in a violent storm; in Gaul, when one of his legions was routed at Gergovia; and in the land of Germany, when his lieutenants Titurius and Aurunculeius were ambushed and slain.

Within this same space of time he lost first his mother, then his daughter,[8] and soon afterwards his grandson. Meanwhile, as the community was aghast at the murder of Publius Clodius,[9] the Senate had voted that only one Consul should be chosen, and expressly named Gnaeus Pompeius. When the Tribunes planned to make him Pompey's colleague, Caesar urged them rather to propose to the people that he be permitted to stand for a second consulship without coming to Rome, when the term of his governorship drew near its end, to prevent his being forced for the sake of the office to leave his province prematurely and without finishing the war. On the granting of this, aiming still higher and flushed with hope, he neglected nothing in the way of lavish expenditure or of favors to any one, either in his public capacity or privately. He began a Forum[10] with the proceeds of his spoils, the ground for which cost more than a hundred million sesterces. He announced a combat of gladiators and a feast for the people in memory of his daughter, a thing quite without precedent. To raise the expectation of these events to the highest possible pitch, he had the material for the banquet prepared in part by his own household, although he had let contracts to the markets as well. He issued an order too that whenever famous gladiators fought without winning the favor of the people, they should be rescued by force and kept for him.[11] He had the novices trained, not in a gladiatorial school by professionals, but in private houses by Roman Knights and even by Senators who were skilled in arms, earnestly beseeching them, as is shown by his own letters, to give the recruits individual attention and personally direct

---

[6] The Roman mile, about 4860 feet, was slightly shorter than the English and American mile of 5280 feet.

[7] Translated into present-day values, a sesterce would be worth anything from five to twenty-five cents.

[8] Julia, who died in childbirth.

[9] Suspected of adultery with Caesar's former wife, as well as of violating the rites of the Good Goddess (cf. page 36, above).

[10] The old Forum had become too small, with the great increase of population and business which resulted from Roman expansion.

[11] Otherwise they would be put to death.

their exercises. He doubled the pay of the legions for all time. Whenever grain was plentiful, he distributed it to them without stint or measure, and now and then gave each man a slave from among the captives.

Moreover, to retain his relationship and friendship with Pompey, Caesar offered him his sister's granddaughter, Octavia in marriage, although she was already the wife of Gaius Marcellus, and asked for the hand of Pompey's daughter, who was promised to Faustus Sulla. When he had put all Pompey's friends under obligation, as well as the great part of the Senate, through loans made without interest or at a low rate, he lavished gifts on men of all other classes, both those whom he invited to accept his bounty and those who applied to him unasked, including even freedmen and slaves who were special favorites of their masters or patrons. In short, he was the sole and ever ready help of all who were in legal difficulties or in debt and of young spendthrifts, excepting only those whose burden of guilt or of poverty was so heavy, or who were so given up to riotous living, that even he could not save them. And to these he declared in the plainest terms that what they needed was a civil war.

He took no less pains to win the devotion of princes and provinces all over the world, offering prisoners to some by the thousands as a gift, and sending auxiliary troops to the aid of others whenever they wished, and as often as they wished, without the sanction of the Senate or people, besides adorning the principal cities of Asia and Greece with magnificent public works, as well as those of Italy and the provinces of Gaul and Spain. At last, when all were thunderstruck at his actions and wondered what their purpose could be, the Consul Marcus Claudius Marcellus, after first making proclamation that he purposed to bring before the Senate a matter of the highest public moment, proposed that a successor to Caesar be appointed before the end of his term, on the ground that the war was ended, peace was established, and the victorious army ought to be disbanded. He further proposed that no account be taken of Caesar at the elections, unless he were present, as Pompey himself had afterwards not annulled the decree of the people. And it was true that when Pompey proposed a bill touching the privileges of officials, in the clause where he debarred absentees from candidacy for office he forgot[12] to make a special exception in Caesar's case, and did not correct the oversight until the law had been inscribed on a tablet of bronze and deposited in the treasury. Not content with depriving Caesar of his provinces and his privilege, Marcellus also moved that the colonists whom Caesar had settled in Novum Comum[13] by the bill of Vatinius should lose their citizenship, on the ground that it had been given from political motives and was not authorized by the law.

Aroused by these measures, and thinking, as they say he was

[12] Or purposely neglected.
[13] New Como in northern Italy.

often heard to remark, that now that he was the leading man of the state, it would be harder to push him down from the first place to the second than from the second to the lowest, Caesar stoutly resisted Marcellus, partly through vetoes of the Tribunes and partly through the other Consul, Servius Sulpicius. When next year Gaius Marcellus, who had succeeded his cousin Marcus as Consul, tried the same thing, Caesar by means of an immense bribe secured the support of the other Consul, Aemilius Paulus, and of Gaius Curio, the most reckless of the Tribunes. But seeing that everything against him was being pushed most persistently, and that even the Consuls-elect were among the opposition, he sent a written appeal to the Senate, not to take from him the privilege which the people had granted, or else to compel the others in command of armies to resign also; feeling sure, it was thought, that he could more readily muster his veterans as soon as he wished, than Pompey his newly levied troops. He further proposed a compromise to his opponents, that after giving up eight legions and Transalpine Gaul, he be allowed to keep two legions and Cisalpine Gaul, or at least one legion and Illyricum, until he was elected Consul.

But when the Senate declined to interfere, and his opponents declared that they would accept no compromise in a matter affecting the public welfare, he crossed to Hither Gaul,[14] and after holding all the assizes,[15] halted at Ravenna, intending to resort to war if the Senate took any drastic action against the Tribunes of the Commons who interposed vetoes in his behalf.[16] Now this was his excuse for the civil war, but it is believed that he had other motives. Gnaeus Pompeius used to declare that since Caesar's own means were not sufficient to complete the works which he had planned, nor to do all that he had led the people to expect on his return, he desired a state of general unrest and turmoil. Others say that he dreaded the necessity of rendering an account for what he had done in his first consulship contrary to the auspices and the laws, and regardless of vetoes. For Marcus Cato often declared, and took oath too, that he would impeach Caesar the moment he had disbanded his army. It was openly said too that if he was out of office on his return, he would be obliged, like Milo,[17] to make his defense in a court hedged about by armed men. The latter opinion is the more credible one in view of the assertion of Asinius Pollio, that when Caesar at the battle of Pharsalus[18] saw his enemies slain or in flight, he said, word for word: "They would have it so. Even I, Gaius Caesar, after so many great

[14] Nearer or Cisalpine Gaul: northern Italy.
[15] Sessions of court.
[16] The Senate passed a decree that Caesar should disband his army, but the Tribunes Mark Antony and Quintus Cassius vetoed it, whereupon they were obliged to seek safety in flight.
[17] Murderer of Publius Clodius.
[18] At Pharsalus in Thessaly, Caesar defeated the numerically superior forces of Pompey (48 B.C.).

deeds, should have been found guilty, if I had not turned to my army for help." Some think habit had given him a love of power, and that weighing the strength of his adversaries against his own, he grasped the opportunity of usurping the despotism which had been his heart's desire from early youth. Cicero too was seemingly of this opinion, when he wrote in the third book of his *De Officiis* that Caesar ever had upon his lips these lines of Euripides, of which Cicero himself adds a version:

> "Be just, unless a kingdom tempts to break the laws,
> For sovereign power alone can justify the cause."

Accordingly, when word came that the veto of the Tribunes had been set aside and they themselves had left the city, he at once sent on a few cohorts with all secrecy, and then, to disarm suspicion, concealed his purpose by appearing at a public show, inspecting the plans of a gladiatorial school which he intended building, and joining as usual in a banquet with a large company. It was not until after sunset that he set out very privily with a small company, taking the mules from a bakeshop hard by and harnessing them to a carriage. When his lights went out and he lost his way, he was astray for some time, but at last found a guide at dawn and got back to the road on foot by narrow bypaths. Then, overtaking his cohorts at the river Rubicon,[19] which was the boundary of his province, he paused for a while, and realizing what a step he was taking, he turned to those about him and said: "Even yet we may turn back; but once cross yon little bridge, and the whole issue is with the sword."

As he stood in doubt, this sign was given him. On a sudden there appeared hard by a being of wondrous stature and beauty, who sat and played upon a reed. And when not only the shepherds flocked to hear him, but many of the soldiers left their posts, and among them some of the trumpeters, the apparition snatched a trumpet from one of them, rushed to the river, and sounding the warnote with mighty blast, strode to the opposite bank. Then Caesar cried: "Take we the course which the signs of the Gods and the false dealing of our foes point out. The die is cast," said he.

Accordingly, crossing with his army, and welcoming the Tribunes of the Commons, who had come to him after being driven from Rome, he harangued the soldiers with tears, and rending his robe from his breast besought their faithful service. It is even thought that he promised every man a Knight's estate, but that came of a misunderstanding. For, since he often pointed to the finger of his left hand as he addressed them and urged them on, declaring that to

---

[19] To cross the Rubicon from provincial Cisalpine Italy into Italy proper with an army was forbidden by law and was equivalent to a declaration of war on the existing government in Rome.

satisfy all those who helped him to defend his honor he would gladly tear his very ring from his hand, those on the edge of the assembly, who could see him better than they could hear his words, assumed that he said what his gesture seemed to mean; and so the report went about that he had promised them the right of the ring and four hundred thousand sesterces[1] as well.

The sum total of his movements after that is, in their order, as follows: He overran Umbria, Picenum, and Etruria, took prisoner Lucius Domitius, who had been irregularly named his successor and was holding Corfinium with a garrison, let him go free, and then proceeded along the Adriatic to Brundisium, where Pompey and the Consuls had taken refuge, intending to cross the sea as soon as might be. After vainly trying by every kind of hindrance to prevent their sailing, he marched off to Rome, and after calling the Senate together to discuss public business, went to attack Pompey's strongest forces, which were in Spain under command of three of his lieutenants — Marcus Petreius, Lucius Afranius, and Marcus Varro — saying to his friends before he left: "I go to meet an army without a leader, and I shall return to meet a leader without an army." And in fact, though his advance was delayed by the siege of Massilia, which had shut its gates against him, and by extreme scarcity of supplies, he nevertheless quickly gained a complete victory.

Returning thence to Rome, he crossed into Macedonia, and after blockading Pompey for almost four months behind mighty ramparts, finally routed him in the battle of Pharsalus, followed him in his flight to Alexandria, and when he learned that his rival had been slain, made war on King Ptolemy, who he perceived had treacherous designs upon his own life as well; a war in truth of great difficulty, convenient neither in time nor place, but carried on during the winter season, within the walls of a well-provisioned and crafty foeman, while Caesar himself was without supplies of any kind and ill-prepared. Victor in spite of all, he turned over the rule of Egypt to Cleopatra and her younger brother, fearing that if he made a province of it, it might one day under a headstrong Governor be a source of revolution. From Alexandria he crossed to Syria, and from there went to Pontus, spurred on by the news that Pharnaces, son of Mithridates the Great, had taken advantage of the situation to make war, and was already flushed with numerous successes. But Caesar vanquished him in a single battle within five days after his arrival and four hours after getting sight of him, often remarking on Pompey's good luck in gaining his principal fame as a general by victories over such feeble foemen. Then he overcame Scipio and Juba, who were patching up the remnants of their party in Africa, and the sons of Pompey in Spain.

---

[1] Knights, or members of the Equestrian order, had the right to wear a gold ring. They must possess an estate worth at least 400,000 sesterces.

In all the civil wars he suffered not a single disaster except among his lieutenants. . . .

Having ended the wars, he celebrated five triumphs, four in a single month. . . .

He gave entertainments of divers kinds: a combat of gladiators and also stage-plays in every ward all over the city, performed too by actors of all languages, as well as races in the circus, athletic contests, and a sham sea-fight. . . .

Then turning his attention to the reorganization of the state, he reformed the calendar, which the negligence of the pontiffs had long since so disordered, through their privilege of adding months or days at pleasure, that the harvest festivals did not come in summer nor those of the vintage in the autumn. And he adjusted the year to the sun's course by making it consist of three hundred and sixty-five days, abolishing the intercalary month,[2] and adding one day every fourth year. Furthermore, that the correct reckoning of time might begin with the next Kalends of January, he inserted two other months between those of November and December. Hence the year in which these arrangements were made was one of fifteen months, including the intercalary month, which belonged to that year according to the former custom.

He filled the vacancies in the Senate, enrolled additional patricians, and increased the number of Praetors, Aediles, and Quaestors, as well as of the minor officials. He reinstated those who had been degraded by official action of the Censors or found guilty of bribery by verdict of the jurors. He shared the elections with the people on this basis: that except in the case of the consulship, half of the magistrates should be appointed by the people's choice, while the rest should be those whom he had personally nominated. And these he announced in brief notes like the following, circulated in each tribe: "Caesar, the Dictator, to this or that tribe. I commend to you so and so, to hold their positions by your votes." He admitted to office even the sons of those who had been proscribed. He limited the right of serving as jurors to two classes, the equestrian and senatorial orders, disqualifying the third class, the Tribunes of the treasury.

He made the enumeration of the people neither in the usual manner nor place, but from street to street aided by the owners of blocks of houses, and reduced the number of those who received grain at public expense from three hundred and twenty thousand to one hundred and fifty thousand. And to prevent the calling of additional meetings at any future time for purposes of enrollment, he provided that the places of such as died should be filled each year by the Praetors from those who were not on the list.

Moreover, to keep up the population of the city, depleted as it was

[2] A month inserted from time to time after February in order to keep the old Roman year of 355 days in step with the true solar year of about 365¼ days.

by the assignment of eighty thousand citizens to colonies across the sea, he made a law that no citizen older than twenty or younger than forty, unless detained by service in the army, should be absent from Italy for more than three successive years; that no Senator's son should go abroad except as the companion of a magistrate or on his staff; and that those who made a business of grazing should have among their herdsmen at least one-third who were men of free birth. He conferred citizenship on all who practiced medicine at Rome, and on all teachers of the liberal arts, to make them more desirous of living in the city and to induce others to resort to it.

As to debts, he disappointed those who looked for their cancellation, which was often agitated, but finally decreed that the debtors should satisfy their creditors according to a valuation of their possessions at the price which they had paid for them before the civil war, deducting from the principal whatever interest had been paid in cash or pledged through bankers; an arrangement which wiped out about a fourth part of their indebtedness. He dissolved all guilds, except those of ancient foundation. He increased the penalties for crimes; and inasmuch as the rich involved themselves in guilt with less hesitation because they merely suffered exile, without any loss of property, he punished murderers of freemen by the confiscation of all their goods, as Cicero writes, and others by the loss of one-half.

He administered justice with the utmost conscientiousness and strictness. Those convicted of extortion he even dismissed from the senatorial order. He annulled the marriage of an ex-praetor, who had married a woman the very day after her divorce, although there was no suspicion of adultery. He imposed duties on foreign wares. He denied the use of litters and the wearing of scarlet robes or pearls to all except to those of a designated position and age, and on set days. In particular he enforced the law against extravagance, setting watchmen in various parts of the market, to seize and bring to him dainties which were exposed for sale in violation of the law; and sometimes he sent his Lictors and soldiers to take from a dining-room any articles which had escaped the vigilance of his watchmen, even after they had been served.

In particular, for the beautification and convenience of the city, as well as for guarding and extending the bounds of the empire, he formed more projects and more extensive ones every day: first of all, to rear a temple to Mars, greater than any in existence, filling up and leveling the pool in which he had exhibited the sea-fight, and to build a theater of vast size, sloping down from the Tarpeian rock; to reduce the civil code to fixed limits, and of the vast and prolix mass of statutes to include only the best and most essential in a limited number of volumes; to open to the public the greatest possible libraries of Greek and Latin books, assigning to Marcus Varro[3] the charge of

[3] Distinguished Roman scholar and encylopedist.

procuring and classifying them; to drain the Pomptine marshes; to let out the water from Lake Fucinus; to make a highway from the Adriatic across the summit of the Apennines as far as the Tiber; to cut a canal through the Isthmus,[4] to check the Dacians, who had poured into Pontus and Thrace; then to make war on the Parthians by way of Lesser Armenia, but not to risk a battle with them until he had first tested their mettle.

All these enterprises and plans were cut short by his death. But before I speak of that, it will not be amiss to describe briefly his personal appearance, his dress, his mode of life, and his character, as well as his conduct in civil and military life.

He is said to have been tall of stature, with a fair complexion, shapely limbs, a somewhat full face, and keen black eyes; sound of health, except that towards the end he was subject to sudden fainting fits and to nightmare as well. He was twice attacked by the falling sickness[5] during his campaigns. He was somewhat overnice in the care of his person, not only keeping the hair of his head closely cut and his face smoothly shaved, but, as some have charged, even having superfluous hair plucked out. His baldness was a disfigurement which troubled him greatly, since he found that it was often the subject of the gibes of his detractors. Because of it he used to comb forward his scanty locks from the crown of his head, and of all the honors voted him by the Senate and people there was none which he received or made use of more gladly than the privilege of wearing a laurel wreath at all times. They say, too, that he was fantastic in his dress; that he wore a Senator's tunic with fringed sleeves reaching to the wrist, and always had a girdle over it, though rather a loose one; and this, they say, was the occasion of Sulla's *mot*, when he often warned the nobles to keep an eye on the ill-girt boy.[6] . . .

There was no stain on his reputation for chastity[7] except his intimacy with King Nicomedes, but that was a deep and lasting reproach, which laid him open to insults from every quarter. . . .

It is admitted by all that he was much addicted to women, as well as very extravagant in his intrigues with them, and that he seduced many illustrious women, among them Postumia, wife of Servius Sulpicius, Lollia, wife of Aulus Gabinius, Tertulla, wife of Marcus Crassus, and even Gnaeus Pompey's wife Mucia. At all events there is no doubt that Pompey was taken to task by the elder and the younger Curio, as well as by many others, because through a desire for power he had afterwards married the daughter of a man on whose account he divorced a wife who had borne him three children, and whom he

[4] The Isthmus of Corinth.
[5] Epileptic seizures.
[6] Or: "Beware of that boy with the loose clothes!" His manner of dress seemed somewhat effeminate.
[7] From what follows, it is apparent that the current concept of chastity was limited to abstention from sexual relations with persons of the same sex.

had often referred to with a groan as an Aegisthus.⁸ But beyond all others Caesar loved Servilia, the mother of Marcus Brutus, for whom in his first consulship he bought a pearl costing six million sesterces. During the civil war, too, besides other presents, he knocked down some fine estates to her in a public auction at a nominal price, and when some expressed their surprise at the low figure, Cicero wittily remarked: "To let you know the real value of the purchase, between ourselves, Tertia⁹ was deducted." And in fact it was thought that Servilia was prostituting her own daughter Tertia to Caesar.

That he did not refrain from intrigues with married women in the provinces is shown in particular by this distich, which was also shouted by the soldiers in his Gallic triumph:

> "Watch well your wives, O citizens
> A lecher bald we bring.
> In Gaul adultery cost thee gold,
> Here 'tis but borrowing."

He had love affairs with Queens, too, including Eunoe the Moor, wife of Bogudes, on whom, as well as on her husband, he bestowed many splendid presents, as Naso writes. But his greatest favorite was Cleopatra, with whom he often feasted until daybreak, and he would have gone through Egypt with her in her state-barge almost to Aethiopia, had not his soldiers refused to follow him. Finally he called her to Rome and did not let her leave until he had laden her with high honors and rich gifts, and he allowed her to give his name to the child which she bore. In fact, according to certain Greek writers, this child was very like Caesar in looks and carriage. Mark Antony declared to the Senate that Caesar had really acknowledged the boy, and that Gaius Matius, Gaius Oppius, and other friends of Caesar knew this. Of these Gaius Oppius, as if admitting that the situation required apology and defense, published a book, to prove that the child whom Cleopatra fathered on Caesar was not his. Helvius Cinna, Tribune of the Commons, admitted to several that he had a bill drawn up in due form, which Caesar had ordered him to propose to the people in his absence, making it lawful for Caesar to marry what wives he wished, and as many as he wished, "for the purpose of begetting children." To leave no room for doubt of his evil reputation both for sodomy and adultery, Curio the elder, in one of his speeches, calls him "every woman's man and every man's woman."

That he drank very little wine not even his enemies denied. There is a saying of Marcus Cato that Caesar was the only man who under-

---

⁸ Aegisthus committed adultery with Clytemnestra while Agamemnon was off at the Trojan War.
⁹ Besides being a feminine name, Tertia means a third.

took to overthrow the state when sober. Even in the matter of food Gaius Oppius tells us that he was so indifferent, that once when his host served stale oil instead of fresh, and the other guests would have none of it, Caesar partook even more plentifully than usual, that he might not seem to charge his host with carelessness or lack of manners.

But his abstinence did not extend to pecuniary advantages, either when in command of armies or when in civil office. . . .

In eloquence and in the art of war he either equaled or excelled the glory of the very best. After his prosecution of Dolabella, he was indisputably reckoned one of the most distinguished advocates. Cicero, at all events, in reviewing the orators in his *Brutus* says that he does not see that Caesar was inferior to any one of them, maintaining that his style is elegant as well as brilliant, even grand and in a sense noble. Again in a letter to Cornelius Nepos he writes thus of Caesar: "Come now, what orator would you rank above him of those who have devoted themselves to nothing else? Who has more clever or more frequent epigrams? Who is more polished or more elegant in diction?" . . .

He left memoirs too of his deeds in the Gallic War and in the civil strife with Pompey. . . . He left besides a work in two volumes "On Analogy,"[10] the same number of "Speeches in Reply to Cato," in addition to a poem, entitled "The Journey." . . . There are also letters of his to Cicero, as well as to his intimates on private affairs. In the latter, if he had anything confidential to say, he wrote it in cipher, that is, by so changing the order of the letters of the alphabet, that not a word could be made out. . . .

He was highly skilled in arms and horsemanship, and of incredible powers of endurance. On the march he headed his army, sometimes on horseback, but oftener on foot, bareheaded both in the heat of the sun and in rain. He covered great distances with incredible speed, making a hundred miles a day in a hired carriage and with little baggage, swimming the rivers which barred his path or crossing them on inflated skins, and very often arriving before the messengers sent to announce his coming.

In the conduct of his campaigns it is a question whether he was more cautious or more daring, for he never led his army where ambuscades were possible without carefully reconnoitering the country, and he did not cross to Britain without making personal inquiries about the harbors, the course, and the approach to the island. But on the other hand, when news came that his camp in Germany was besieged, he made his way to his men through the enemies' pickets, disguised as a Gaul. He crossed from Brundisium to Dyrrachium[11] in winter time, running the blockade of the enemy's fleets; and when the troops

[10] A grammar.
[11] Durazzo, across the Adriatic from Brindisi; in present-day Albania.

which he had ordered to follow him delayed to do so, and he had sent to fetch them many times in vain, at last in secret and alone he boarded a small boat at night with his head muffled up; and he did not reveal who he was, or suffer the helmsman to give way to the gale blowing in their teeth, until he was all but overwhelmed by the waves.

No regard for religion ever turned him from any undertaking, or even delayed him. Though the victim escaped as he was offering sacrifice, he did not put off his expedition against Scipio and Juba. Even when he had a fall as he disembarked, he gave the omen a favorable turn by crying: "I hold thee fast, Africa." Furthermore, to make the prophecies ridiculous which declared that the stock of the Scipios was fated to be fortunate and invincible in that province, he kept with him in camp a contemptible fellow belonging to the Cornelian family, to whom the nickname Salvito had been given as a reproach for his manner of life.

He joined battle, not only after planning his movements in advance but on a sudden opportunity, often immediately at the end of a march, and sometimes in the foulest weather, when one would least expect him to make a move. It was not until his later years that he became slower to engage, through a conviction that the oftener he had been victor, the less he ought to tempt fate, and that he could not possibly gain as much by success as he might lose by a defeat. He never put his enemy to flight without also driving him from his camp, thus giving him no respite in his panic. When the issue was doubtful, he used to send away the horses, and his own among the first, to impose upon his troops the greater necessity of standing their ground by taking away that aid to flight. . . .

When his army gave way, he often rallied it single-handed, planting himself in the way of the fleeing men, laying hold of them one by one, even seizing them by the throat and turning them to face the enemy; that, too, when they were in such a panic that an eagle-bearer made a pass at him with the point[12] as he tried to stop him, while another left the standard in Caesar's hand when he would hold him back.

His presence of mind was no less renowned and the instances of it will appear even more striking. After the battle of Pharsalus, when he had sent on his troops and was crossing the strait of the Hellespont in a small passenger boat, he met Lucius Cassius, of the hostile party, with ten armored ships, and made no attempt to escape, but went to meet Cassius and actually exhorted him to surrender. Cassius sued for mercy and was taken on board.

At Alexandria, while assaulting a bridge, he was forced by a sudden sally of the enemy to take to a small skiff. When many others threw

---

[12] The eagle, standard of the Roman legion, was mounted on a pole sharply pointed at one end so it could be set in the soil.

themselves into the same boat, he plunged into the sea, and after swimming for two hundred paces, got away to the nearest ship, holding up his left hand all the way, so as not to wet some papers which he was carrying, and dragging his cloak after him with his teeth, to keep the enemy from getting it as a trophy.

He valued his soldiers neither for their personal character nor their fortune, but solely for their prowess, and he treated them with equal strictness and indulgence. For he did not curb them everywhere and at all times, but only in the presence of the enemy. Then he required the strictest discipline, not announcing the time of a march or a battle, but keeping them ready and alert to be led on a sudden at any moment wheresoever he might wish. He often called them out even when there was no occasion for it, especially on rainy days and holidays. Sometimes, giving them orders not to lose sight of him, he would steal away suddenly by day or night and make a longer march than usual, to tire out those who were tardy in following.

When they were in a panic through reports about the enemy's numbers, he used to rouse their courage not by denying or discounting the rumors, but by falsely exaggerating the true danger. For instance, when the anticipation of Juba's coming filled them with terror, he called the soldiers together and said: "Let me tell you that within the next few days the king will be here with ten legions, thirty thousand horsemen, a hundred thousand light-armed troops, and three hundred elephants. Let none of you, therefore, presume to make further inquiry or to indulge in conjectures, but take my word for what I tell you, which I have on good information. Otherwise, I shall surely have them shipped on some worn out craft and carried off to whatever lands the wind may blow them."

He did not take notice of all their offenses or punish them by rule, but he kept a sharp lookout for deserters and mutineers, and chastised them most severely, shutting his eyes to other faults. Sometimes, too, after a great victory he relieved them of all duties and gave them full license to revel, being in the habit of boasting that his soldiers could fight well even when reeking of perfumes. In the assembly he addressed them not as "soldiers," but by the more flattering term "comrades," and he kept them in fine trim, furnishing them with arms inlaid with silver and gold, both for show and to make them hold the faster to them in battle, through fear of the greatness of the loss. Such was his love for them that when he heard of the disaster to Titurius,[13] he let his hair and beard grow long, and would not cut them until he had taken vengeance. In this way he made them most devoted to his interests as well as most valiant. . . .

They did not mutiny once during the ten years of the Gallic war; in the civil wars they did so now and then, but quickly resumed their

---

[13] In 54 B.C. a legion commanded by Titurius was cut to pieces near Aix-la-Chapelle by the Eburones under Ambiorix.

duty, not so much owing to any indulgence of their General as to his authority. For he never gave way to them when they were insubordinate, but always boldly faced them, discharging the entire ninth legion in disgrace before Placentia, though Pompey was still in the field, reinstating them unwillingly and only after many abject entreaties, and insisting on punishing the ringleaders.

Again at Rome, when the men of the tenth legion clamored for their discharge and rewards with terrible threats and no little peril to the city, though the war in Africa was then raging, he did not hesitate to appear before them, against the advice of his friends, and to disband them. But with a single word, calling them "citizens," instead of "soldiers," he easily brought them round and bent them to his will. For they at once replied that they were his "soldiers" and insisted on following him to Africa, although he refused their service. Even then he punished the most insubordinate by the loss of a third part of the booty and of the land intended for them. . . .

Even in avenging wrongs he was by nature most merciful. When he got hold of the pirates who had captured him, having sworn that he would crucify them, he did so indeed, but ordered that their throats be cut first. He could never make up his mind to harm Cornelius Phagites, although when he was sick and in hiding, the man had waylaid him night after night, and even a bribe had barely saved him from being handed over to Sulla. The slave Philemon, his amanuensis, who had promised Caesar's enemies that he would poison him, he merely punished by death, without torture. When summoned as a witness against Publius Clodius, the paramour of his wife Pompeia, who was being prosecuted for desecration of sacred rights,[14] Caesar declared that he had no evidence, although both his mother Aurelia and his sister Julia had given the same jurors a faithful account of the whole affair. When he was then asked why after all he had divorced Pompeia, he replied: "Because I maintain that the members of my family should be free not only from guilt, but from even the suspicion of guilt."

He certainly showed admirable self-restraint and mercy, both in his conduct of the civil war and in the hour of victory. While Pompey threatened to treat as enemies those who did not take up arms for the government, Caesar gave out that those who were neutral and of neither party should be numbered with his friends. He freely allowed all those whom he had made Centurions on Pompey's recommendation to go over to his rival. When conditions of surrender were under discussion at Ilerda, and friendly intercourse between the two parties was constant, Afranius and Petreius, with a sudden change of purpose, put to death all of Caesar's soldiers whom they found in their camp, but Caesar could not bring himself to retaliate in kind. At the battle of Pharsalus he cried out, "Spare your fellow citizens,"

---

[14] Those of the Good Goddess. See pages 36 and 43, above.

and afterwards allowed each of his men to save any one man he pleased of the opposite party. . . . To those who spoke ill of him he thought it enough to give public warning not to persist in their offense, bearing with good nature the attacks on his reputation made by the scurrilous volume of Aulus Caecina and the abusive lampoons of Pitholaus.

Yet after all, his other actions and words so far outweigh all his good qualities that it is thought he abused his power and was justly slain. For not only did he accept excessive honors, such as an uninterrupted consulship, the dictatorship for life, and the censorship of public morals, as well as the forename Imperator, the surname of Father of his Country, a statue among those of the Kings, and a raised couch in the orchestra of the theater. He also allowed honors to be bestowed on him which were too great for mortal man: a golden throne in the House and on the judgment seat; a chariot and litter in the procession at the circus; temples, altars, and statues beside those of the Gods; a special priest, an additional college of the Luperci, and the calling of one of the months by his name. In fact, there were no honors which he did not receive or confer at pleasure.

He held his third and fourth consulships in name only, content with the power of the dictatorship conferred on him at the same time as the consulships. Moreover, in both years he substituted two Consuls for himself for the last three months, in the meantime holding no elections except for Tribunes and plebian Aediles, and appointing Prefects instead of the Praetors, to manage the affairs of the city during his absence. When one of the Consuls suddenly died the day before the Kalends of January, he gave the vacant office for a few hours to a man who asked for it. With the same disregard of law and precedent he named magistrates for several years to come, bestowed the emblems of consular rank on ten ex-Praetors, and admitted to the House men who had been given citizenship, and in some cases even half-civilized Gauls. He assigned the charge of the mint and of the public revenues to his own slaves, and gave the oversight and command of the three legions which he had left at Alexandria to a favorite boy of his called Rufio, son of one of his freedmen.

No less arrogant were his public utterances, which Titus Ampius records: that the Republic was a name only, without substance or reality; that Sulla did not know his A. B. C. when he laid down his dictatorship; that men ought now to be more circumspect in addressing him, and to regard his word as law. So far did he go in his presumption, that when a soothsayer once announced to him the direful omen that a victim offered for sacrifice was without a heart, he said: "The entrails will be more favorable when I please. It ought not to be taken as a miracle if a beast have no heart."

But it was the following action in particular that roused deadly hatred against him. When the Senate approached him in a body with many highly honorary decrees, he received them before the temple of Venus Genetrix without rising. Some think that when he attempted to get up, he was held back by Cornelius Balbus; others, that he made no such move at all, but on the contrary frowned angrily on Gaius Trebatius when he suggested that he should rise. This action of his seemed the more intolerable, because when he himself in one of his triumphal processions rode past the benches of the Tribunes, he was so incensed because one of their number, Pontius Aquila by name, did not rise, that he cried: "Come then, Aquila, mighty Tribune, and take from me the Republic," and for several days afterwards, he would promise a favor to no one without adding, "That is, if Pontius Aquila will give me leave."

To an insult which so plainly showed his contempt for the Senate he added an act of even greater insolence. After the sacred rites of the Latin Festival, as he was returning to the city, amid the extravagant and unprecedented demonstrations of the populace, some one in the press placed on his statue a laurel wreath with a white fillet[15] tied to it. When Epidius Marullus and Caesetius Flavus, Tribunes of the Commons gave orders that the ribbon be removed from the crown and the man taken off to prison, Caesar sharply rebuked and deposed them, either offended that the hint at regal power had been received with so little favor, or, as was said, that he had been robbed of the glory of refusing it. But from that time on he could not rid himself of the odium of having aspired to the title of monarch, although he replied to the Commons, when they hailed him as King, "I am Caesar and not King." At the Lupercalia,[16] when the Consul Antony several times attempted to place a crown upon his head as he spoke from the rostra, he put it aside and at last sent it to the Capitol, to be offered to Jupiter Optimus Maximus. Nay, more, the report had spread in various quarters that he intended to move to Ilium[17] or Alexandria, taking with him the resources of the state, draining Italy by levies, and leaving it and the charge of the city to his friends; also that at the next meeting of the Senate Lucius Cotta would announce as the decision of the Fifteen,[18] that inasmuch as it was written in the books of fate that the Parthians could be conquered only by a King, Caesar should be given that title.

In order to avoid giving assent to this proposal the conspirators hastened the execution of their designs. Therefore the plots which had previously been formed separately, often by groups of two or three, were united in a general conspiracy, since even the populace no

---

[15] Signifying royalty.

[16] A rather wild Roman festival, celebrated in February, during which priests of Pan (Faunus) ran naked through the streets.

[17] The site of ancient Troy. Almost four centuries later Constantine the Great contemplated the same move before deciding on Byzantium (Constantinople, Istanbul) instead.

[18] The college of priests who expounded the Sybilline books.

longer were pleased with present conditions, but both secretly and openly rebelled at his tyranny and cried out for defenders of their liberty. On the admission of foreigners to the Senate, a placard was posted: "God bless the Commonwealth! Let no one consent to point out the House to a newly made Senator." The following verses too were repeated everywhere: —

> "The Gauls he dragged in triumph through the town
> Caesar has brought into the Senate house
> And changed their breeches[19] for the purple gown."

When Quintus Maximus, whom he had appointed Consul in his place for three months, was entering the theater, and his Lictor in the usual manner called attention to his arrival, a general shout was raised: "He's no Consul!" After the removal of Caesetius and Marullus from office as Tribunes, they were bound to have not a few votes at the next elections of Consuls. Some wrote on the base of Lucius Brutus's statue, "Oh, that you were still alive"; and on that of Caesar himself:

> "Because he drove from Rome the royal race
> Brutus was first made Consul in their place.
> This man, because he put the Consuls down,
> Has been rewarded with a royal crown."

More than sixty joined the conspiracy against him, led by Gaius Cassius and Marcus and Decimus Brutus. At first they hesitated whether to form two divisions at the elections in the Campus Martius, so that while some hurled him from the bridge as he summoned the tribes to vote, the rest might wait below and slay him; or to set upon him in the Sacred Way or at the entrance to the theater. When, however, a meeting of the Senate was called for the Ides[1] of March in the Hall of Pompey, they readily gave that time and place the preference.

Now Caesar's approaching murder was foretold to him by unmistakable signs.[2] A few months before, when the settlers assigned to the colony at Capua by the Julian Law were demolishing some tombs of great antiquity, to build country houses, and plied their work with the greater vigor because as they rummaged about they found a quantity of vases of ancient workmanship, there was discovered in a tomb, which was said to be that of Capys, the founder of Capua, a

---

[19] The Celts of Gaul wore trousers instead of the flowing gowns of the Romans.

[1] March 15.

[2] Note in what follows the popular Roman conviction concerning the validity of omens.

bronze tablet, inscribed with Greek words and characters to this effect: "Whenever the bones of Capys shall be discovered, it will come to pass that a descendant of his shall be slain at the hands of his kindred, and presently avenged at heavy cost to Italy." And let no one think this tale a myth or a lie, for it is vouched for by Cornelius Balbus, an intimate friend of Caesar. Shortly before his death, as he was told, the herds of horses which he had dedicated to the river Rubicon when he crossed it, and had let loose without a keeper, stubbornly refused to graze and wept copiously. Again, when he was offering sacrifice, the soothsayer Spurinna warned him to beware of danger, which would come not later than the Ides of March. On the day before the Ides of that month a little bird called the king-bird flew into the Hall of Pompey with a sprig of laurel, pursued by others of various kinds from the grove hard by, which tore it to pieces in the hall. In fact the very night before his murder he dreamt now that he was flying above the clouds, and now that he was clasping the hand of Jupiter; and his wife Calpurnia thought that the pediment of their house fell, and that her husband was stabbed in her arms; and on a sudden the door of the room flew open of its own accord.

Both for these reasons and because of poor health he hesitated for a long time whether to stay at home and put off what he had planned to do in the Senate. But at last, urged by Decimus Brutus not to disappoint the full meeting, which had for some time been waiting for him, he went forth almost at the end of the fifth hour.[3] When a note revealing the plot was handed him by some one on the way, he put it with others which he held in his left hand, intending to read them presently. Then, after many victims had been slain, and he could not get favorable omens, he entered the House in defiance of portents, laughing at Spurinna and calling him a false prophet, because the Ides of March were come without bringing him harm. Spurinna replied that they had of a truth come, but they had not gone.

As he took his seat, the conspirators gathered about him as if to pay their respects, and straightway Tillius Cimber, who had assumed the lead, came nearer as though to ask something. When Caesar with a gesture put him off to another time, Cimber caught his toga by both shoulders. As Caesar cried, "Why, this is violence!" one of the Cascas stabbed him from one side just below the throat. Caesar caught Casca's arm and ran it through with his stylus,[4] but as he tried to leap to his feet, he was stopped by another wound. When he saw that he was beset on every side by drawn daggers, he muffled his head in his robe, and at the same time drew down its lap to his feet with his left hand, in order to fall more decently, with the lower part of his body also covered. And in this wise he was stabbed with three and twenty wounds, uttering not a word, but merely a groan at the

[3] About 11:00 A.M.
[4] A pointed instrument used for writing on wax tablets.

first stroke, though some have written that when Marcus Brutus rushed at him, he said in Greek, "You too, my child?" All the conspirators made off, and he lay there lifeless for some time, until finally three common slaves put him on a litter and carried him home, with one arm hanging down. And of so many wounds none, in the opinion of the physician Antistius, would have proved mortal except the second one in the breast.

The conspirators had intended after slaying him to drag his body to the Tiber, confiscate his property, and revoke his decrees. But they forebore through fear of Marcus Antonius, the Consul, and Lepidus, the master of horse.

At the request of his father-in-law, Lucius Piso, his will was opened and read in Antony's house. He had made it on the Ides of the preceding September at his villa near Lavicum, and committed it to the care of the chief Vestal Virgin. Quintus Tubero states that from his first consulship until the beginning of the civil war it was his wont to write down Gnaeus Pompeius as his heir, and to read this to the assembled soldiers. In his last will, however, he named three heirs, the grandsons of his sisters, namely: Gaius Octavius,[5] to three-fourths of his estate, and Lucius Pinarius and Quintus Pedius to share the remainder. At the end of the will, too, he adopted Gaius Octavius into his family and gave him his name. Several of his assassins were named among the guardians of his son, in case one should be born to him, and Decimus Brutus even among his heirs in the second degree. To the people he left his gardens near the Tiber for their common use and three hundred sesterces to each man.

When the funeral was announced, a pyre was erected in the Campus Martius near the tomb of Julia. On the rostra was placed a gilded shrine, made after the model of the temple of Venus Genetrix. Within was a bier of ivory with coverlets of purple and gold, and at its head a pillar hung with the robe in which he was slain. Since it was clear that the day would not be long enough for those who offered gifts, they were directed to bring them to the Campus by whatsoever streets of the city they wished, regardless of any order of precedence. At the funeral games, to rouse pity and indignation at his death, these words from the "Contest for the Arms" of Pacuvius were sung: —

"Saved I these men that they might murder me?"

and words of a like purport from the "Electra" of Atilius. Instead of a eulogy the Consul Antonius caused a herald to recite the decree of the Senate in which it had voted Caesar all divine and human honors at once, and likewise the oath with which they had all pledged themselves to watch over his personal safety; to which he added a

[5] Who later became Emperor as Augustus and ruled until A.D. 14.

very few words of his own. The bier on the rostra was carried to the Forum by magistrates and ex-magistrates. While some were urging that it be burned in the temple of Jupiter of the Capitol, and others in the Hall of Pompey, on a sudden two beings with swords by their sides and brandishing a pair of darts set fire to it with blazing torches, and at once the throng of bystanders heaped upon it dry branches, the judgment seats with the benches, and whatever else could serve as an offering. Then the musicians and actors tore off their robes, which they had taken from the equipment of his triumphs and put on for the occasion, rent them to bits and threw them into the flames, and the veterans of the legions the arms with which they had adorned themselves for the funeral. Many of the women, too, offered up the jewels which they wore and the amulets and robes of their children.

At the height of the public grief a throng of foreigners went about lamenting each after the fashion of his country, above all the Jews,[6] who even flocked to the place for several successive nights.

The populace, with torches in their hands, ran from the funeral to the houses of Brutus and Cassius, and after being repelled with difficulty, they slew Helvius Cinna when they met him, through a mistake in the name, supposing that he was Cornelius Cinna, who had the day before made a bitter indictment of Caesar and for whom they were looking; and they set his head upon a spear and paraded it about the streets. Afterwards they set up in the Forum a solid column of Numidian marble almost twenty feet high, and inscribed upon it, "To the Father of his Country." At the foot of this they continued for a long time to sacrifice, make vows, and settle some of their disputes by an oath in the name of Caesar.

Caesar left in the minds of some of his friends the suspicion that he did not wish to live any longer and had taken no precautions, because of his failing health; and that therefore he neglected the warnings which came to him from portents and from the reports of his friends. Some think that it was because he had full trust in that last decree of the Senators and their oath that he dismissed even the armed bodyguard of Spanish soldiers that formerly attended him. Others, on the contrary, believe that he elected to expose himself once for all to the plots that threatened him on every hand, rather than to be always anxious and on his guard. Some, too, say that he was wont to declare that it was not so much to his own interest as to that of his country that he remain alive. He had long since had his fill of power and glory. But if aught befell him, the commonwealth would have no peace, and, involved in another civil war, would be in a worse state than before.

About one thing almost all are fully agreed, that his death was in many respects such as he would have chosen. For once when he read

---

[6] Caesar was beloved by the Jews for many acts of kindness.

in Xenophon how Cyrus in his last illness gave directions for his funeral he expressed his horror of such a lingering kind of end and his wish for one which was swift and sudden. And the day before his murder, in a conversation which arose at a dinner at the house of Marcus Lepidus, as to what manner of death was most to be desired, he had given his preference to one which was sudden and unexpected.

He died in the fifty-sixth year of his age,[7] and was numbered among the Gods, not only by a formal decree, but also in the conviction of the vulgar.[8] For at the first of the games which his heir Augustus gave in honor of his apotheosis, a comet shone for seven successive days, rising about the eleventh hour, and was believed to be the soul of Caesar, who had been taken to heaven. This is why a star is set upon the crown of his head in his statue.

It was voted that the hall in which he was slain be walled up, that the Ides of March be called the Day of Parricide, and that a meeting of the Senate should never be called on that day.

Hardly any of his assassins survived him for more than three years, or died a natural death. They were all condemned, and they perished in various ways — some by shipwreck, some in battle; and some took their own lives with the self-same dagger with which they had impiously slain Caesar.

[7] In 44 B.C.
[8] Emperor worship was thus beginning about this time among the Romans.

3

The Divine Salt and Leaven: Christ and His Church

EUSEBIUS

The third basic component of Western civilization — in the long run its most precious and essential element — is Christianity. Just as "Greece took Rome her captor captive," so Christianity, which for three centuries was culturally, socially, and politically spurned, at length assimilated and converted both the Greeks and the Romans.

Even as Herodotus of Halicarnassus is known as "the father of history," so Bishop Eusebius of Caesarea is known as "the father of Church history." Living in the third and fourth centuries, Eusebius witnessed the last and severest persecutions of the Christian Church and then its growing ascendance in the Roman Empire. Born of a noble family in Palestine about A.D. 260, he received a good education, both secular and religious. He was an outstanding student in the Christian school conducted at Caesarea by the presbyter Pamphilus, to whom he became so devoted that he afterwards called himself Eusebius Pamphili (Eusebius of Pamphilus). Pamphilus was a noted scholar, famous in history as the founder of the magnificent library of Caesarea, which Eusebius was to use in his researches. The enthusiasm of Pamphilus for the Scriptures and his admiration for the Christian writer and teacher Origen made a profound impression on Eusebius. Even more so did his martyrdom; for during the rigorous persecution ordered by Diocletian early in the fourth century, Pamphilus was imprisoned, tortured, and at last executed (307–309). Eusebius himself was temporarily imprisoned, but he was released without serious harm. Although he was later chided by an opponent for having escaped unscathed, charges of defection or cowardice were never seriously directed against him. During these final persecutions, Eusebius was a personal witness to many of the sufferings, tortures, and executions which he describes in realistic detail.

About 313, Eusebius was made Bishop of Caesarea, then a leading city in Palestine. In this office, which he retained until his death about A.D. 340, he became one of the leading ecclesiastical figures of his day. He was an intimate of the Emperor

Constantine, to whom contemporary Christians owed so much, and was a frequent guest at the imperial palace. He sat at the emperor's side at the first ecumenical council of Nicaea, where he also delivered an opening address. He composed a panegyrical biography of Constantine in which he told of the emperor's vision of the cross in the sky before the battle of the Milvian Bridge. Eusebius was offered the Patriarchate of Antioch in 331, but he declined this honor.

In his day Eusebius incurred some criticism because of his position on Arianism. At first he was inclined to favor the teachings of Arius, with whom he was friendly. But Arianism was condemned by the Council of Nicaea (325) as heretical in denying the eternal coexistence and equal divinity of Christ the Son with God the Father; and Eusebius withdrew his support, although he never became an extreme foe of the Arians, and indeed continued on friendly terms with many of them.

Eusebius was a prodigious writer. Besides the Ecclesiastical History, at least forty-seven other works are known to have come from his pen. Among these are his Life of Constantine; a book of Martyrs of Palestine; a Chronography of dates, rulers, and important events; apologetical works defending and explaining the Christian faith; theological works refuting heresies; and commentaries on various books of the Bible. Yet it is to his Ecclesiastical History that he owes his fame. If we except the books of the New Testament, this was not only the first but also the most valuable Church history composed in antiquity. As Eusebius explains, his purpose is twofold: (1) historical: to preserve the memory of the Christian past; and (2) apologetic: to argue for the divinity of the Church from its history. Rather arbitrarily divided into ten books, his story of the Church begins with Christ and comes down to about the year 323. One of the greatest services of the History is its liberal quotation from works since lost and hence its preservation of passages today available in no other sources.

The Ecclesiastical History is valuable in reflecting the early Christian viewpoint as well as in recording and highlighting early Christian history. As he states in his introduction, Eusebius stresses the divinity of Christ, the Apostolic office, and the episcopal succession; persecutions and martyrdoms; the spread and triumph of the Church despite all obstacles; the services of great Christian writers and teachers; the errors of heretics and their rejection by the universal Church. Following the Church from its foundation through its trials to the beginning of its triumph in the Empire, the History exemplifies the firm belief of the early Christians in the presence of a force superhuman and divine. It testifies to their trust in the continuing instruction and guidance of Christ, exercised first through the Apostles and then through an unbroken succession of bishops. It especially stresses the episcopal succession in the Apostolic sees or patriarchates of Rome, Alexandria, Jerusalem, and Antioch. Rome, accepted as the final see and scene of martyrdom for Saints Peter and Paul, is accorded pre-eminence and listed first among the patriarchal sees. Christian unity is emphasized, and aversion to heretics is manifested. Christian consciousness of the historical nature and continuity of the Christian religion and traditions is writ large. Christian assimilation of Greek and Roman culture is attested by the work itself, in its organization, approach, and presentation. Christian intellectual interests and concern for scholarship are shown by the fact that leading teachers and writers are singled out for extensive treatment. Contemporary missionary zeal is shown by the work's apologetical bent and propagational purpose. The ferocious cruelty of the persecutions in many parts of the Empire is vividly brought out, as is also the constancy of most Christians in maintaining their faith. And finally, the deep respect of the Christians for their martyrs or "witnesses," who have given "testimony" to their faith, is a pervading theme of this work which, to a singular degree, enables us to recapture the spirit of early Christianity.

Eusebius of Caesarea

from *Ecclesiastical History* *

It is my purpose to record the successions of the holy apostles, together with the times since our Saviour, down to the present, to recount how many and important transactions are said to have occured in ecclesiastical history, what individuals in the most noted places eminently governed and presided over the church, what men also in their respective generations, whether with or without their writings, proclaimed the divine word; to describe the character, times, and number of those who, stimulated by the desire of innovation, and advancing to the greatest errors, announced themselves leaders in the propagation of false opinions, like grievous wolves, unmercifully assaulting the flock of Christ. It is my intention, also, to

* From *The Ecclesiastical History of Eusebius Pamphilus, Bishop of Caesarea in Palestine*, translated by C. F. Cruse (London: 1865).

describe the calamities that swiftly overwhelmed the whole Jewish nation, in consequence of their plots against our Saviour; how often, by what means, and in what times, the word of God has encountered the hostility of the nations; what eminent persons persevered in contending for it through those periods of blood and torture, besides the martyrdoms which have been endured in our own times; and after all, to show the gracious and benign interposition of our Saviour. These being proposed as the subjects of the present work, I shall go back to the very origin and the earliest introduction of the dispensation of our Lord and Saviour, the Christ of God.

But here, acknowledging that it is beyond my power to present the work perfect and unexceptionable, I freely confess it will crave indulgence, especially since, as the first of those that have entered upon the subject, we are attempting a kind of trackless and unbeaten path. . . . (I, 1) . . .

No language is sufficient to express the origin, the dignity, even the substance and nature of Christ. Whence even the divine Spirit in the prophecies says, "Who will declare his generation?" For as no one hath known the Father, but the Son, so no one, on the other hand, can know the Son fully, but the Father alone, by whom he was begotten. For who but the Father hath thoroughly understood that Light which existed before the world was — that intellectual and substantial wisdom, and that living word which in the beginning was with the Father, before all creation and any production visible or invisible, the first and only offspring of God, the prince and leader of the spiritual and immortal host of heaven, the angel of the mighty council, the agent to execute the Father's secret will, the maker of all things with the Father, the second cause of the universe next to the Father, and the true and only Son of the Father, and the Lord and God and King of all created things, who has received power and dominion with divinity itself, and power and honour from the Father.[1] . . . (I, 2) . . .

After the necessary preliminary to the Ecclesiastical History which we have proposed to write, it now remains that we commence our course, invoking God, the Father of the world, and Jesus Christ himself, our revealed Saviour and Lord, the heavenly word of God, as our aid and fellow labourer in the narration of the truth. It was the forty-second year of the reign of Augustus, but the twenty-eighth from the subjugation of Egypt and the death of Antony and Cleopatra, which terminated the dynasty of the Ptolemies, when, according to prophetic prediction, our Lord and Saviour Jesus Christ was born in Bethlehem of Judea; the same year, when the first census was taken, and Quirinius[2] was governor of Syria. — This census is mentioned

---

[1] This passage reflects the controversies over the precise nature of Christ and his relationship to the Father, current in Eusebius' time.

[2] Quirinius is a rendition of the Cyrenius mentioned by St. Luke (2:2). For the birth of Christ, see Matthew 2 and Luke 2.

by Flavius Josephus, the distinguished historian among the Hebrews, who also adds another account respecting the sect of the Galileans, which arose about the same time, of which also mention is made by our Luke in his book of Acts, in the following words — "After this man arose Judas of Galilee, in the days of the taxing (assessment), and drew away much people after him, he also perished; and all, even as many as obeyed him, were dispersed." (Acts v. 37.) . . . (I, 5)

At the time that Herod was king, who was the first foreigner that reigned over the Jewish people, the prophecy recorded by Moses received its fulfilment, viz. "That a prince should not fail of Judah, nor a ruler from his loins, until he should come for whom it is reserved."[3] . . . (I, 6) . . .

Christ, then, having been born, according to the prophecies,[4] in Bethlehem of Judea, about the time that had been revealed, Herod was not a little alarmed at the intelligence. Having ascertained, on the inquiry of the eastern Magi, where the king of the Jews should be born, as they had seen his star, and this had been the cause of so long a journey to them, glowing with zeal to worship the infant as God; he was under great apprehensions, as supposing his own kingdom to be in danger. Having, therefore, inquired of the doctors of the law in the nation, where they expected Christ should be born, and ascertained the prophecy of Micah,[5] announcing that it would be in Bethlehem, in a single edict he ordered the male infants from two years and below to be slain, both in Bethlehem and all its parts, according to the time that he had accurately ascertained from the Magi; thinking at all events, as seemed very probable, that he would carry off Jesus also, in the same destruction with those of his own age. The child, however, anticipated the snare, being carried into Egypt by his parents, who had been informed by the appearance of an angel of what was about to happen. These same facts are also stated in the sacred text of the Gospel.[6]

It is also worth while to observe the reward which Herod received for his criminal audacity against Christ and the infants; how, without the least delay, the Divine justice immediately overtook him; and even before his death, exhibited the prelude to those punishments that awaited him after death. . . . (I, 8) . . .

It was about the fifteenth year of the reign of Tiberius, according to the Evangelist, in the fourth year that Pilate was procurator of Judea, when Herod, Lysanias, and Philip, as tetrarchs, held the government of the rest of Judea, when our Lord and Saviour Jesus Christ was in his thirtieth year, that he came to the baptism of John, and then made the beginning of promulgating his gospel.[7] The holy Scrip-

---

[3] From the Septuagint version of the Bible, which was the one used by Eusebius.
[4] Micheas 5:2.
[5] Micheas 5:2.
[6] Matthew 2.
[7] Luke 3–4.

tures, moreover, relate that he passed the whole time of his public ministry under the high priests Annas and Caiaphas; intimating, that during the years of their priesthood the whole time of his ministry was terminated.[8] For, beginning with the pontificate of Annas, and continuing after that of Caiaphas, the whole of this interval does not even give us four years.... Our Lord and Saviour Jesus Christ, not very long after the commencement of his public ministry, elected the twelve, whom he called Apostles, by way of eminence over the rest of his disciples.[9] He also appointed seventy others beside these, whom he sent, two and two, before him into every place and city whither he himself was about to go.[10] (I, 10)

As it was not long before this that John the Baptist was beheaded by Herod the younger, the holy Scriptures record the fact.[11] This is also confirmed by Josephus, who has expressly made mention of Herodias by name, and the circumstance of her being married to Herod, though she was the wife of his brother; Herod having first divorced his former lawful wife. She was a daughter of Aretas, king of Arabia Petraea. But having forced Herodias from her husband yet living, and on whose account also he slew John, he was involved in a war with Aretas for the disgrace inflicted on his daughter; in which war he relates that, when coming to battle, the army of Herod was completely destroyed; and that he suffered all this on account of the crime that he committed against John....

... After relating these things concerning John, Josephus in the same work also makes mention of our Saviour in the following manner: "About the same time, there was a certain Jesus, a wise man, if indeed it is proper to call him a man. For he was a performer of extraordinary deeds; a teacher of men, that received his doctrine with delight; and he attached to himself many of the Jews, many also of the Greeks. This was Christ. Pilate having inflicted the punishment of the cross upon him, on the accusation of our principal men, those who had been attached to him before did not, however, afterwards cease to love him: for he appeared to them alive again on the third day, according to the holy prophets, who had declared these and innumerable other wonderful things respecting him. The race of the Christians, who derive their name from him, likewise still continues."
... (I, 11) ...

The divinity of our Lord and Saviour Jesus Christ, being famed abroad among all men, in consequence of his wonder-working power, attracted immense numbers, both from abroad and from the remotest parts of Judea, with the hope of being cured of their diseases and various afflictions.... (I, 13) ...

---

[8] Luke 3:2; Matthew 26:3; and Acts 4:6.
[9] Luke 6:13–16; Matthew 10:1–4; Mark 3:13–19. Caiaphas or Caiphas.
[10] Luke 10:1.
[11] Matthew 14:1–10; Mark 6:14–29; Luke 9:7–9.

Whatsoever particulars it was necessary for us to premise in this Ecclesiastical History, both respecting the divinity of the saving word and the antiquity of the doctrines which we teach, as also of the antiquity of that evangelical life which Christians lead, these particulars we have already discussed, together with the circumstances of his late appearance among men, of his sufferings, of the election of his apostles, and have exhibited the proofs in the condensed subjects of the preceding book. Let us now, also, examine the circumstances that followed his ascension, presenting some from the divine Scriptures, and others from such other documents to which we shall have occasion to refer. (II, Pref.)

First then, in the place of Judas the traitor, Matthias was chosen by lot, who, as was shown above, was also one of the disciples of the Lord.[12] There were appointed also, with prayer and the imposition of hands, by the apostles, approved men, unto the office of deacons, for the public service; these were those seven of whom Stephen was one.[13] He was the first, also, after our Lord, who at the time of ordination, as if ordained to this very purpose, was stoned to death by the murderers of the Lord. And thus he first received the crown answering to his name, of the victorious martyrs of Christ.[14] Then also James, called the brother of our Lord, because he is also called the son of Joseph. For Joseph was esteemed the father of Christ, because the Virgin being betrothed to him, "she was found with child by the Holy Ghost before they came together," as the narrative of the holy Gospel shows.[15] This James, therefore, whom the ancients, on account of the excellence of his virtue, surnamed the Just, was the first that received the episcopate of the church at Jerusalem.[16] But Clement, in the sixth book of his Institutions, represents it thus: "Peter, and James, and John, after the ascension of our Saviour, though they had been preferred by our Lord, did not contend for the honour, but chose James, the Just as bishop of Jerusalem." ... (II, 1) ...

Thus, then, under a celestial influence and co-operation, the doctrine of the Saviour, like the rays of the sun, quickly irradiated the whole world. Presently, in accordance with divine prophecy, the sound of his inspired evangelists and apostles had gone throughout all the earth, and their words to the ends of the world. Throughout every city and village, like a replenished barn-floor, churches were rapidly found abounding, and filled with members from every people. Those who, in consequence of the delusions that had descended to them from their ancestors, had been fettered by the ancient disease of idolatrous superstition, were now liberated, by the power of Christ,

[12] Acts 1:12–26; cf. also above.
[13] Acts 6:1–6.
[14] Acts 6:8–15; 7:1–59. According to a tradition, Stephanos was the Greek for his original Aramaic name meaning crown.
[15] Matthew 1:18; Luke 1:26–38.
[16] Acts 12:17; 15:13; 21:18. This James was not an Apostle.

through the teachings and miracles of his messengers. And, as if delivered from dreadful masters, and emancipated from the most cruel bondage, they on the one hand renounced the whole multitude of gods and demons, and on the other, confessed that there was only one true God, the Creator of all things. This same God they now also honoured with the rites of a true piety, under the influence of that inspired and reasonable worship which had been planted among men by our Saviour. But the gratuitous benevolence of God, being now poured out also upon the rest of the nations, Cornelius was the first of Caesarea in Palestine, who, with his whole house, received the faith in Christ, through a divine vision and the agency of Peter; as did also a great number of Greeks at Antioch, to whom the gospel had been preached by those who were scattered by the persecution of Stephen.

The church at Antioch, also, now flourishing and abounding in members, and the greatest number of teachers coming hither from Jerusalem, with whom were Barnabas and Paul, and many other brethren with them, the epithet of Christians first sprung up at that place, as from a grateful and productive soil. Agabus, also, one of the assembled prophets, uttered a prediction respecting the impending famine, and Paul and Barnabas were delegated to proceed to the relief of the necessities of the brethren. (II, 3)

"About this time, (it is manifest he[17] means the reign of Claudius,) Herod the king[18] prepared to afflict some of the church. But he slew James, the brother of John, with the sword."[19] Of this James, Clement adds a narrative worthy of note, in the seventh book of his Institutions, evidently recording it according to the tradition which he had received from his ancestors. He says, that the man who led him to the judgment-seat, seeing him bearing his testimony to the faith, and moved by the fact, confessed himself a Christian. Both therefore, says he, were led away to die. On their way, he entreated James to be forgiven of him, and James, considering a little, replied, "Peace be to thee," and kissed him; and then both were beheaded at the same time. Then also, as the Scriptures say, Herod, at the death of James, seeing that the deed gave pleasure to the Jews, also attacked Peter, and having committed him to prison, had well nigh executed the same murderous intention against him, had he not been wonderfully delivered from his prison by an angel appearing to him at night, and thus liberated to proclaim the gospel. Such was the providence of God in behalf of Peter.[1] (II, 9) . . .

. . . Entering the city of Rome, by the co-operation of that malignant spirit which had fixed its seat there, the attempts of Simon

[17] St. Luke.
[18] Herod Agrippa, a grandson of Herod the Great.
[19] Acts 12:1-2. This James was one of the first Apostles.
[1] Acts 12:3-10.

Magus[2] were soon so far successful, as to be honoured as a god, with the erection of a statue by the inhabitants of that city. This, however, did not continue long; for immediately under the reign of Claudius, by the benign and gracious providence of God, Peter, that powerful and great apostle, who by his courage took the lead of all the rest, was conducted to Rome against this pest of mankind. He, like a noble commander of God, fortified with divine armour, bore the precious merchandise of the revealed light from the east to those in the west, announcing the light itself, and the salutary doctrine of the soul, the proclamation of the kingdom of God. (II, 14)

The divine word having thus been established among the Romans, the power of Simon was soon extinguished and destroyed together with the man.[3] So greatly, however, did the splendour of piety enlighten the minds of Peter's hearers, that it was not sufficient to hear but once, nor to receive the unwritten doctrine of the gospel of God, but they persevered in every variety of entreaties, to solicit Mark as the companion of Peter, and whose Gospel we have, that he should leave them a monument of the doctrine thus orally communicated, in writing. Nor did they cease their solicitations until they had prevailed with the man, and thus become the means of that history which is called the Gospel according to Mark. They say also, that the apostle, (Peter,) having ascertained what was done by the revelation of the Spirit, was delighted with the zealous ardour expressed by these men, and that the history obtained his authority for the purpose of being read in the churches. This account is given by Clement, in the sixth book of his Institutions, whose testimony is corroborated also by that of Papias, bishop of Hierapolis. But Peter makes mention of Mark in the first epistle, which he is also said to have composed at the same city of Rome, and that he shows this fact, by calling the city by an unusual trope, Babylon; thus, "The church at Babylon, elected together with you, saluteth you, as also my son Marcus." (1 Pet. v. 13.) (II, 15) . . .

Festus was sent by Nero as successor to Felix.[4] Under him, Paul, after having pleaded his cause, was sent a prisoner to Rome. But Aristarchus was his companion, whom he also somewhere in his epistles calls his fellow prisoner; and here Luke, that wrote the Acts of the Apostles, after showing that Paul passed two whole years at Rome as a prisoner at large, and that he preached the gospel without restraint, brings his history to a close. After pleading his cause, Paul is said to have been sent again upon the ministry of preaching, and after a second visit to the city, to have finished his life with martyr-

---

[2] Simon Magus, who had unsuccessfully attempted to purchase the power of working miracles from St. Peter (Acts 8:18–24), had subsequently come to Rome, where he had won a large following by his wiles and magic.

[3] It would seem according to this that Simon Magus was discredited and died during the reign of Claudius, though it may have been later under Nero.

[4] As governor of Syria.

dom. Whilst he was a prisoner, he wrote his Second Epistle to Timothy, in which he both mentions his first defence and his impending death. . . . It is indeed probable, that as Nero was more disposed to mildness in the beginning, the defence of the apostle's doctrine would be more easily received; but as he advanced to such criminal excesses as to disregard all right, the apostles also, with others, experienced the effects of the measures pursued against them. (II, 22).

But the Jews, after Paul had appealed to Caesar, and had been sent by Festus to Rome, frustrated in their hope of entrapping him by the snares they had laid, turned themselves against James, brother of the Lord, to whom the episcopal seat at Jerusalem was committed by the apostles. The following were their nefarious measures also against him. Conducting him into a public place, they demanded that he should renounce the faith of Christ before all the people; but contrary to the sentiments of all, with a firm voice, and much beyond their expectation, he declared himself fully before the whole multitude, and confessed that Jesus Christ was the Son of God, our Saviour and Lord. Unable to bear any longer the testimony of the man, who, on account of his elevated virtue and piety, was deemed the most just of men, they seized the opportunity of licentiousness afforded by the prevailing anarchy, and slew him. For as Festus died about this time in Judea, the province was without a governor and head. But, as to the manner of James's death, it has been already stated in the words of Clement, that he was thrown from a wing of the temple, and beaten to death with a club . . . (II, 23) . . .

But Nero now having the government firmly established under him, and henceforth plunging into nefarious projects, began to take up arms against that very religion which acknowledges the one Supreme God. To describe, indeed, the greatness of this man's wickedness, is not compatible with our present object; and as there are many that have given his history in the most accurate narratives,[5] every one may, at his pleasure, in these contemplate the grossness of his extraordinary madness. Under the influence of this, he did not proceed to destroy so many thousands with any calculation, but with such indiscriminate murder as not even to refrain from his nearest and dearest friends. His own mother and wife, with many others that were his near relatives, he killed like strangers and enemies, with various kinds of deaths. And, indeed, in addition to all his other crimes, this too was yet wanting to complete the catalogue, that he was the first of the emperors that displayed himself an enemy of piety towards the Deity. This fact is recorded by the Roman Tertullian, in language like the following: "Examine your records. There you will find that Nero was the first that persecuted this doctrine, particularly then when, after subduing all the East, he exercised his cruelty against all at Rome. Such is the man of whom we boast, as the leader in our punishment. For one that knows who he was, may know

[5] Such as Tacitus in his *Annals*, Bks. XIII–XVI.

also that there could scarcely be any thing but what was great and good, condemned by Nero." Thus Nero publicly announcing himself as the chief enemy of God, was led on in his fury to slaughter the apostles. Paul is therefore said to have been beheaded at Rome, and Peter to have been crucified under him. And this account is confirmed by the fact that the names of Peter and Paul still remain in the cemeteries of that city even to this day. But likewise, a certain ecclesiastical writer, Caius by name, who was born about the time of Zephyrinus, bishop of Rome, disputing with Proclus, the leader of the Phrygian sect, gives the following statement respecting the places where the earthly tabernacles of the aforesaid apostles are laid. "But I can show," says he, "the trophies of the apostles. For if you will go to the Vatican, or to the Ostian road, you will find the trophies of those who have laid the foundation of this church.[6] And that both suffered martyrdom about the same time, Dionysius, bishop of Corinth, bears the following testimony, in his discourse addressed to the Romans. 'Thus, likewise, you, by means of this admonition, have mingled the flourishing seed that had been planted by Peter and Paul at Rome and Corinth. For both of these, having planted us at Corinth, likewise instructed us; and having in like manner taught in Italy, they suffered martyrdom about the same time.'" This testimony I have superadded, in order that the truth of the history might be still more confirmed. (II, 25) ...

Such, then, was the state of the Jews at this time. But the holy apostles and disciples of our Saviour, being scattered over the whole world, Thomas, according to tradition, received Parthia[7] as his allotted region; Andrew received Scythia,[8] and John, Asia[9]; where, after continuing for some time, he died at Ephesus. Peter appears to have preached through Pontus, Galatia, Bithynia, Cappadocia, and Asia,[10] to the Jews that were scattered abroad. Peter also, finally coming to Rome, was crucified with his head downward, having requested of himself to suffer in this way. Why should we speak of Paul, spreading the gospel of Christ from Jerusalem to Illyricum, and finally suffering martyrdom at Rome, under Nero? This account is given by Origen, in the third book of his Exposition of Genesis. (III, 1)

After the martyrdom of Paul and Peter, Linus was the first that received the episcopate at Rome. Paul makes mention of him in his epistle from Rome to Timothy, in the address at the close of the epistle, saying, "Eubulus and Pudens, and Linus, and Claudia, salute thee."[11] (III, 2) .....

---

[6] According to tradition, Peter was buried on the Vatican Hill, Paul on the *Via Ostia*.
[7] Parthia proper was northeast of Persia proper, but the Parthian Empire replaced the Persian Empire for some time, including the first century A.D.
[8] Region north of the Black Sea in southern Russia.
[9] I.e., the province of Asia in western Asia Minor.
[10] As above. Peter thus preached throughout Asia Minor.
[11] II Timothy 4:21.

That Paul preached to the Gentiles, and established churches from Jerusalem and around as far as Illyricum, is evident both from his own expressions,[12] and from the testimony of Luke in the book of Acts. And in what provinces Peter also proclaimed the doctrine of Christ, the doctrine of the New Covenant, appears from his own writings, and may be seen from that epistle we have mentioned as admitted in the canon, and which he addressed to the Hebrews in the dispersion throughout Pontus, Galatia, Cappadocia, Asia, and Bithynia. But how many and which of these, actuated by a genuine zeal, were judged suitable to feed the churches established by these apostles, it is not easy to say, any further than may be gathered from the writings of Paul. For he, indeed, had innumerable fellow labourers, or as he himself calls them, fellow soldiers in the church. Of these, the greater part are honoured with an indelible remembrance by him in his epistles, where he gives a lasting testimony concerning them. Luke also, in his Acts, speaking of his friends, mentions them by name. Timothy, indeed, is recorded as having first received the episcopate at Ephesus, as Titus also was appointed over the churches in Crete. But Luke, who was born at Antioch, and by profession a physician, being for the most part connected with Paul, and familiarly acquainted with the rest of the apostles, has left us two inspired books, the institutes of that spiritual healing art which he obtained from them. One of these is his Gospel, in which he testifies that he has recorded, "as those who were from the beginning eye-witnesses, and ministers of the word," delivered to him, whom also, he says, he has in all things followed. The other is his Acts of the Apostles, which he composed, not from what he had heard from others, but from what he had seen himself. It is also said, that Paul usually referred to Luke's Gospel whenever in his epistles he spoke of some particular gospel of his own, saying, "according to my gospel." But of the rest that accompanied Paul, Crescens is mentioned by him as sent to Gaul (Gallia).[13] Linus, whom he has mentioned in his Second Epistle to Timothy as his companion at Rome,[14] has been before shown to have been the first after Peter that obtained the episcopate at Rome. Clement also, who was appointed the third bishop of this church is proved by him to have been a fellow labourer and fellow soldier with him. Beside, the Areopagite, called Dionysius, whom Luke has recorded in his Acts, after Paul's address to the Athenians in the Areopagus, as the first that believed, is mentioned by Dionysius, another of the ancients, and pastor of the church at Corinth, as the first bishop of the church at Athens. But the manner and times of the

---

[12] Including the addressees of his several epistles (the Ephesians, Philippians, Colossians, Galatians, Thessalonians, Corinthians, Hebrews, and Romans), as well as various statements therein.

[13] II Timothy 4:10, where the reading in Eusebius' time was *Gallia* or Gaul, whereas the corrected reading in our own day is *Galatia*.

[14] II Timothy 4:21.

apostolic succession shall be mentioned by us as we proceed in our course. Now let us pursue the order of our history. (III, 4) . . .

Domitian,[15] indeed, having exercised his cruelty against many, and unjustly slain no small number of noble and illustrious men at Rome, and having, without cause, punished vast numbers of honourable men with exile and the confiscation of their property, at length established himself as the successor of Nero, in his hatred and hostility to God. He was the second that raised a persecution against us, although his father Vespasian[16] had attempted nothing to our prejudice. (III, 17)

In this persecution, it is handed down by tradition, that the apostle and evangelist John, who was yet living, in consequence of his testimony to the divine word, was condemned to dwell on the island of Patmos. Irenaeus, indeed, in his fifth book against the heresies, where he speaks of the calculation formed on the epithet of Antichrist, in the above-mentioned Revelation of John, speaks in the following manner respecting him. "If, however, it were necessary to proclaim his name (i.e. Antichrist) openly at the present time, it would have been declared by him who saw the revelation, for it is not long since it was seen, but almost in our own generation, at the close of Domitian's reign." To such a degree, indeed, did the doctrine which we profess flourish, that even historians that are very far from befriending our religion, have not hesitated to record this persecution and its martyrdoms in their histories. These, also, have accurately noted the time, for it happened, according to them, in the fifteenth year of Domitian. At the same time, for professing Christ, Flavia Domitilla, the niece of Flavius Clemens, one of the consuls of Rome at that time, was transported with many others, by way of punishment, to the island of Pontia. (III, 18) . . .

So great a persecution was then commenced against our faith, in most places, that Plinius Secundus, one of the most distinguished governors, moved by the number of martyrs, communicated with the emperor respecting the multitudes that were put to death for their faith. At the same time he informed him, that as far as he had ascertained, they did nothing wicked or contrary to the laws; except that they rose with the morning sun, and sang a hymn to Christ as to a god. But that adultery, and murder, and criminal excesses like these, were totally abhorred by them; and that in all things they acted according to the laws. To this Trajan, in reply, issued a decree, the purport of which was that no search should be made after those that were Christians, but when they presented themselves they should be punished.[17] On this, the persecution in some measure seemed abated

[15] Domitian ruled as emperor A.D. 81–96.
[16] Vespasian ruled as emperor 69–79, being succeeded first by his son Titus, 79–81, and then by his second son, Domitian.
[17] The texts of both the letter of Pliny the Younger, Governor of Bithynia, and the rescript of Emperor Trajan (A.D. 113) are still preserved.

in its extreme violence, but there were no less pretexts left for those that wished to harass us. Sometimes the people, sometimes the rulers of different places, would waylay us to insnare us. So that without an obvious persecution, there were partial persecutions in the provinces, and many of the faithful endured martyrdoms of various kinds. . . (III, 33) . . .

. . . Others, indeed, that compose historical narratives, would record nothing but victories in battle, the trophies of enemies, the warlike achievements of generals, the bravery of soldiers, sullied with blood and innumerable murders, for the sake of children, and country, and property. But our narrative embraces that conversation and conduct which is acceptable to God; the wars and conflicts of a most pacific character, whose ultimate tendency is to establish the peace of the soul; those, also, that have manfully contended for the truth, rather than for their country, and who have struggled for piety, rather than their dearest friends. Such as these our narrative would engrave on imperishable monuments. The firmness of the champions for the true religion, their fortitude in the endurance of innumerable trials, their trophies erected over daemoniacal agencies, and their victories over their invisible antagonists, and the crowns that have been placed upon all these, it would proclaim and perpetuate by an everlasting remembrance. (V, Pref.)

Gaul was the place where the arena was prepared for the above-mentioned conflict.[18] Of these the two distinguished capitals are celebrated as surpassing all the rest, viz., Lyons and Vienne. Through both of these the river Rhone passes, traversing the whole region with a mighty stream. The account, however, of the martyrs, was sent by the most illustrious churches there, to those of Asia and Phrygia, by whom the events that took place among them, are related in the following manner — I will subjoin their own declarations: "The servants of Christ dwelling at Lyons and Vienne, in Gaul, to those brethren in Asia and Phrygia, having the same faith and hope with us, peace and grace and glory from God the Father and Christ Jesus our Lord." Then, premising some other matters, they commence their subject in the following words:

The greatness, indeed, of the tribulation, and the extent of the madness exhibited by the heathen against the saints, and the sufferings which the martyrs endured in this country, we are not able fully to declare, nor is it, indeed, possible to describe them. For the adversary assailed us with his whole strength, giving us already a prelude of how unbridled his future movements among us would be. And, indeed, he resorted to every means, to accustom and exercise his own servants against those of God, so that we should not only be excluded from houses, and baths, and markets, but every thing belonging to us was prohibited from appearing in any place whatever.

[18] The persecution under Marcus Aurelius, who ruled A.D. 161–180.

But the grace of God contended for us, and rescued the weak, and prepared those who, like firm pillars, were able, through patience, to sustain the whole weight of the enemy's violence against them. These coming in close conflict, endured every species of reproach and torture. Esteeming what was deemed great as but little, they hastened to Christ, showing in reality, "that the sufferings of this time are not worthy to be compared with the glory that shall be revealed in us." And first, they nobly sustained all the evils that were heaped upon them by the populace, clamours and blows, plundering and robberies, stonings and imprisonments and whatsoever a savage people delight to inflict upon enemies. After this they were led to the forum, and when interrogated by the tribune and the authorities of the city, in the presence of the multitude, they were shut up in prison until the arrival of the governor. Afterwards, they were led away to be judged by him, from whom we endured all manner of cruelty. . . . Those, indeed, that were worthy to fill up the number of the martyrs, were seized from day to day, so that all the zealous members of the two churches, and those by whose exertions the church had been there established, were collected. Some domestics that were heathen, belonging to our brethren, were also seized, as the governor had publicly commanded search to be made for all of us. But these, at the instigation of Satan, fearing the tortures which they saw the saints suffering, and the soldiers beside this urging them, charged us with feasts of Thyestes,[19] and the incests of Oedipus,[1] and such crimes as are neither lawful for us to speak nor to think; and such, indeed, as we do not even believe were committed by men. These things being spread abroad among the people, all were so savage in their treatment of us, that, if before some had restrained themselves on account of some affinity, they now carried their cruelty and rage against us to a great excess. Then was fulfilled the declaration of our Lord, "that the day would come when every one that slayeth you will think he is doing God a service." The holy martyrs, after this, finally endured tortures, beyond all description; Satan striving with all his power, that some blasphemy might be uttered by them. Most violently did the collective madness of the mob, the governor, and the soldiers, rage against the holy deacon of Vienne, and against Maturus, a new convert, indeed, but a noble champion of the faith. Also against Attalus, a native of Pergamus, who was a pillar and foundation of the church there. Against Blandina, also, in whom Christ made manifest that the things that appear mean, and deformed, and contemptible among men, are esteemed of great glory with God, on account of love to him, which is really and powerfully displayed, and glories not in mere appearance. For whilst we were all trembling, and

---

[19] Thyestes, according to mythology, ate part of his own son, whom his brother had slain.
[1] Oedipus slew his father and married his own mother.

her earthly mistress, who was herself one of the contending martyrs, was apprehensive lest through the weakness of the flesh she should not be able to profess her faith with sufficient freedom, Blandina was filled with such power, that her ingenious tormentors, who relieved and succeeded each other from morning till night, confessed that they were overcome, and had nothing more than they could inflict upon her. Only amazed that she still continued to breathe after her whole body was torn asunder and pierced, they gave their testimony that one single kind of the torture inflicted was of itself sufficient to destroy life, without resorting to so many and such excruciating sufferings as these.

But this blessed saint, as a noble wrestler, in the midst of her confession itself renewed her strength, and to repeat, "I am a Christian, no wickedness is carried on by us," was to her rest, refreshment, and relief from pain.[2] But Sanctus himself, also nobly sustaining beyond all measure and human powers, the various torments devised by men, whilst the wicked tormentors hoped that, by the continuance and the greatness of the tortures, they would get to hear something from him that he ought not to say, withstood them with so much firmness, that he did not even declare his name, nor that of his nation, nor the city whence he was, nor whether he was a slave or a freeman, but to all the questions that were proposed, he answered in the Roman tongue, "I am a Christian." For this he confessed instead of his name, his city, his race, and instead of every thing. No other expression did the heathen hear from him. Whence, also, an ambitious struggle in torturing arose between the governor and the tormentors against him; so that when they had nothing farther that they could inflict, they at last fastened red-hot plates of brass to the most tender parts of his body. But he continued unsubdued and unshaken, firm in his confession, refreshed and strengthened by the celestial fountain of living water that flows from Christ. But the corpse itself was evidence of his sufferings, as it was one continued wound, mangled and shrivelled, that had entirely lost the form of man to the external eye. Christ suffering in him exhibited wonders; defeating the adversary, and presenting a kind of model to the rest, that there is nothing terrific where the love of the Father, nothing painful where the glory of Christ, prevails.[3] ... (V, 1) ...

But when Severus[4] raised a persecution against the churches, there were illustrious testimonies given by the combatants of religion in all the churches every where. They particularly abounded in Alexandria,

[2] To avoid threatened torture, the servants of the Christians confessed that their masters were guilty of various crimes, such as infanticide and incest; then the judges tried, by the same devices, to get the Christians to confess these same crimes.

[3] The *Ecclesiastical History* is filled with descriptions of excruciating torments, of which we give only a few instances.

[4] Septimus Severus, Emperor A.D. 193–211.

whilst the heroic wrestlers from Egypt and Thebais were escorted thither as to a mighty theatre of God, where, by their invincible patience under various tortures and modes of death, they were adorned with crowns from heaven. Among these was Leonides, said to be the father of Origen, who was beheaded, and left his son behind yet very young. His early predilection for the divine word, as instructed by his father, it is not out of place here briefly to state, so much the more especially as his fame is celebrated by many. (VI, 1) . . .

. . . It was in the tenth year of the reign of Severus, when Alexandria and the rest of Egypt were under the government of his viceroy Laetus, and the churches there were under the episcopal administration of Demetrius, the successor of Julian, that the kindled flame of persecution blazed forth mightily, and many thousands were crowned with martyrdom.

It was then, too, that the love of marytrdom so powerfully seized the soul of Origen, though yet an almost infant boy, that he advanced so close to encounter danger, and was eager to leap forward and rush upon the conflict. And, indeed, there had been now but little wanting, and the termination of his life had not been far off, unless the heavenly providence of God, for the benefit of vast numbers, had, by means of his mother, interposed an impediment to his eager desire. She, indeed, at first, implored and entreated him to spare a mother's tenderness regarding him, but seeing him only the more vehemently bent upon it, as he understood that his father was taken and kept a prisoner, and he was wholly borne away by the desire of becoming a martyr, his mother concealed his clothes in order to compel him to remain at home.[5] . . . (VI, 2) . . .

In the mean time, also, that madman Manes,[6] as he was called, well agreeing with his name, for his daemoniacal heresy, armed himself by the perversion of his reason, and at the instigation of Satan, to the destruction of many. He was a barbarian in his life, both in speech and conduct, but in his nature as one possessed and insane. Accordingly, he attempted to form himself into a Christ, and then also proclaimed himself to be the very Paraclete[7] and the Holy Spirit, and with all this was greatly puffed up with his madness. Then, as if he were Christ, he selected twelve disciples, the partners of his new religion, and after patching together false and ungodly doctrines, collected from a thousand heresies long since extinct, he swept them off like a deadly poison from Persia upon this part of the world. Hence the impious name of the Manichees, spreading among many, even to the present day. Such then was the occasion of this knowledge, as

[5] Eusebius scatters an extended account of the life of Origen through various chapters of this book (VI).

[6] The oriental name Mani or Manes is here equated to the Greek *maneis* (madman) for effect.

[7] The name "Paraclete," meaning Comforter or Advocate, was an epithet of the Holy Spirit, assumed by such heretics as Montanus and Manes.

it was falsely called, that sprouted up in these times. (VII, 21) . . .

It was the nineteenth year of the reign of Diocletian,[8] and the month of Dystrus, called by the Romans March, in which the festival of our Saviour's passion was at hand, when the imperial edicts were everywhere published, to tear down the churches to the foundations, and to destroy the sacred Scriptures by fire; and which commanded, also, that those who were in honourable stations should be degraded, but those who were freedmen should be deprived of their liberty, if they persevered in their adherence to Christianity. The first edict against us was of this nature; but it was not long before other edicts were also issued, in which it was ordered that all the prelates in every place should first be committed to prison, and then by every artifice constrained to offer sacrifice to the gods. (VIII, 2)

Then, indeed, vast numbers of the prelates of the church endured with a noble resolution the most appalling trials, and exhibited instances of illustrious conflicts for the faith. Vast numbers, however, of others, broken and relaxed in spirit, by timidity before the contest, voluntarily yielded at the first onset. But of the rest, each encountered various kinds of torments. Here was one that was scourged with rods, there another tormented with the rack and excruciating scrapings, in which some at the time endured the most terrible death; others again passed through other torments in the struggle. . . . (VIII, 3) . . .

I know not how it happened, but there was a fire that broke out in the imperial palace at Nicomedia, in these days,[9] which, by a false suspicion reported abroad, was attributed to our brethren as the authors; in consequence of which, whole families of the pious here were slain in masses at the imperial command, some with the sword, some also with fire. Then it is said that men and women, with a certain divine and inexpressible alacrity, rushed into the fire. But the populace binding another number upon planks, threw them into the depths of the sea. But the imperial domestics, also, who after death had been committed to the earth with proper burial, their legal masters thought necessary to have dug up again from their sepulchres, and likewise cast into the sea, lest any, reasoning like themselves, should worship them in their graves, as if they were gods. And such, then, was the complexion of things in the commencement of the persecution at Nicomedia.

But, ere long, as there were some in the region called Melitina and others, again, in Syria, that attempted to usurp the government, it was commanded, by an imperial edict, that the heads of the churches every where should be thrust into prison and bonds. And the spec-

---

[8] Diocletian ruled from 284 to 305, and began to persecute the Christians in 303. A series of edicts was issued against the Christians in 303–304.

[9] In the period 302–303 there seem to have been not merely one but two mysterious fires in the imperial palace at Nicomedia.

tacle of affairs after these events exceeds all description. Innumerable multitudes were imprisoned in every place, and the dungeons, formerly destined for murderers and the vilest criminals, were then filled with bishops, and presbyters, and deacons, readers and exorcists, so that there was no room left for those condemned for crime. But when the former edict was followed by another,[10] in which it was ordered that the prisoners should be permitted to have their liberty if they sacrificed, but persisting, they should be punished with the most excruciating tortures, who could tell the number of those martyrs in every province, and particularly in Mauritania, Thebais, and Egypt, that suffered death for their religion? (VIII, 6)

. . . Who can behold, without amazement, all this: their conflicts, after scourging, with bloody beasts of prey, when they were cast as food to leopards and bears, wild boars and bulls, goaded with fire, and branded with glowing iron against them? And in each of these, who can fail to admire the wonderful patience of these noble martyrs? At these scenes we have been present ourselves, when we also observed the divine power of our Lord and Saviour Jesus Christ himself present, and effectually displayed in them; when, for a long time, the devouring wild beasts would not dare either to touch or to approach the bodies of these pious men, but directed their violence against others that were any where stimulating them from without. . . . (VIII, 7)

. . . Some, after being tortured with scrapings and the rack, and the most dreadful scourgings, and other innumerable agonies, which one might shudder to hear, were finally committed to the flames; some plunged and drowned in the sea, others voluntarily offering their own heads to the executioners, others dying in the midst of their torments, some wasted away by famine, and others again fixed to the cross. Some, indeed, were executed as malefactors usually were; others, more cruelly, were nailed with the head downwards, and kept alive until they were destroyed by starving on the cross itself. (VIII, 8)

But it would exceed all power of detail to give an idea of the sufferings and tortures which the martyrs of Thebais endured. These, instead of hooks, had their bodies scraped with shells, and were mangled in this way until they died. Women tied by one foot, and then raised on high in the air by certain machines, with their naked bodies and wholly uncovered, presented this most foul, cruel, and inhuman spectacle to all beholders: others again perished, bound to trees and branches. For, drawing the stoutest of the branches together by machines for this purpose, and binding the limbs of the martyrs to each of these, they then let loose the boughs to resume

---

[10] By a series of edicts (303–304), it was successively ordered that all Christian churches should be destroyed; all Christian books burnt; all Christians dismissed from public service and deprived of privileges; all bishops, priests, and deacons imprisoned and forced to sacrifice; and finally all Christians, lay as well as clerical, compelled to sacrifice to the pagan gods.

their natural position, designing thus to produce a violent action, to tear asunder the limbs of those they had thus treated. ... (VII, 9) ...

Why should I now mention the names of others, or number the multitude of men, or picture the various torments of the admirable martyrs of Christ; some of whom were slain with the axe, as in Arabia; some had their limbs fractured, as in Cappadocia; and some were suspended by the feet, and a little raised from the ground, with their heads downward, were suffocated with the ascending smoke of a gentle fire kindled below, as was done to those in Mesopotamia; some were mutilated by having their noses, ears, and hands cut off, and the rest of their limbs and parts of their body cut to pieces, as was the case at Alexandria? Why should we revive the recollection of those at Antioch, who were roasted on grates of fire, not to kill immediately, but torture them with a lingering punishment? Others, again, rather resolved to thrust their arm into the fire, than touch the unholy sacrifice; some shrinking from the trial, sooner than be taken and fall into the hands of their enemies, cast themselves headlong from the lofty houses, considering death an advantage compared with the malignity of these impious persecutors. A certain holy and admirable female, admirable for her virtue, and illustrious above all at Antioch for her wealth, family, and reputation, had educated her two daughters, who were now in the bloom of life, noted for their beauty, in the principles of piety. As they had excited great envy among many, every measure was tried to trace them in their concealment; but when it was discovered that they were abroad, they were, with a deep-laid scheme, called to Antioch. They were now caught in the toils of the soldiery. The mother, therefore, being at a loss for herself and daughters, knowing what dreadful outrages they would suffer from the men, represented their situation to them, and, above all, the threatened violation of their chastity, an evil more to be dreaded than any other, to which neither she nor they should even listen for a moment, at the same time declaring, that to surrender their souls to the slavery of daemons was worse than death and destruction. From all these, she suggested there was only one way to be delivered, to betake themselves to the aid of Christ. After this, all agreeing to the same thing, and having requested the guards a little time to retire on the way, they decently adjusted their garments, and cast themselves into the flowing river. These, then, destroyed themselves. ... Others, at Pontus, endured torments that are too horrible to relate. Some had their fingers pierced with sharp reeds thrust under their nails. Others, having masses of melted lead, bubbling and boiling with heat, poured down their backs, and roasted, especially in the most sensitive parts of the body. Others, also, endured insufferable torments on their bowels and other parts, such as decency forbids to describe, which those generous and equitable judges, with a view to display their own cruelty, devised as some pre-eminence in wisdom, deserving their ambition. Thus constantly inventing new tortures, they vied with one another, as if there were prizes proposed in the contest, who should invent the greatest cruelties. But as to the last of these calamities, when the judges now had despaired of inventing any thing more effectual, and were weary with slaughter, and had surfeited themselves with shedding of blood, they then applied themselves to what they considered kindness and humanity, so that they seemed disposed to exercise no further cruelty against us. For, said they, the cities should not be polluted with blood any more, and the government of the sovereigns, which was so kind and merciful toward all, should not be defamed for excessive cruelty: it was more proper that the benefits afforded by their humane and imperial Majesties, should be extended to all, and that we should no longer be punished with death. For we were liberated from this punishment by the great elemency of the emperors. After this, therefore, they were ordered only to tear out our eyes, or to deprive us of one of our legs. Such was their kindness, and such the lightest kind of punishment against us; so that in consequence of this humanity of theirs, it was impossible to tell the great and incalculable number of those that had their right eye dug out with the sword first, and were then branded with a red-hot iron; those, too, whose left foot was maimed with a searing iron; after them, those who in different provinces were condemned to the copper mines, not so much for their service as for the contumely and misery they should endure. Many, also, endured conflicts of other kinds, which it would be impossible to detail; for their noble fortitude surpasses all power of description. In this the magnanimous confessors of Christ that shone conspicuous throughout the whole world, every where struck the beholders with astonishment, and presented the obvious proofs of our Saviour's divine interposition in their own persons. And hence, to mention each by name, would be at least a long and tedious work, not to say impossible. (VIII, 12) ...

During the whole ten years of the persecution,[11] there was no cessation of plots and civil wars among the persecutors themselves.[12] For the sea indeed was impassable to the mariner, nor could any set sail from any port, without being exposed to every kind of torment, either scourged, or racked in their limbs, or lacerated and galled with torturing instruments in their sides, to ascertain whether they had come from the enemy of the opposite party, and at last were subjected either to the punishment of the cross or of fire. Besides these things, one saw every where shields and coats of mail preparing, darts and javelins and other implements of war; and in every place, also, were collections of galleys and naval armour. Neither was there any thing

[11] As Caesar in the East under Diocletian, Galerius ushered in the persecution by a purge of the Christians from the army in 302.
[12] The period 305–313 was filled with civil wars over the succession.

expected any where but the attacks of enemies from day to day. Besides this, famine and pestilence were superadded, of which we shall relate what is most important in its proper place. (VIII, 15)

... Though it had been necessary that these things should occur by some divine judgment, yet it is declared. "Woe to him through whom the offence cometh!" Hence he[13] was visited by a judgment sent from God, which beginning in his flesh proceeded to his very soul. For a sudden tumour appeared about the middle of the body, then a spongy fistula in these parts, which continued to extend and penetrate with its ulcerations to the inmost parts of the bowels. Hence sprung an immense multitude of worms, hence also an insufferable death-like effluvia exhaled, as his whole body before his disease, by reason of his gluttony, had been changed into an excessive mass of fat, which then becoming putrid, exhibited a dreadful and intolerable spectacle to those that drew near. Some, indeed, of the physicians, totally unable to endure the excessively offensive smell, were slain; others again, as the swelling had penetrated every where, and they were unable to give any relief, despaired of safety, and were put to death without mercy. (VIII, 16)

Thus struggling with so many miseries, he[14] had some compunctions for the crimes that he had committed against the pious. Turning, therefore, his reflections upon himself, first of all he confessed his sin to the Supreme God; then summoning his officers, he immediately ordered that, without delay, they should stop the persecution against the Christians, and by an imperial ordinance and decree, commanded that they should hasten to rebuild the churches, that they might perform their accustomed devotions, and offer up prayers for the emperor's safety. This decree was immediately followed by its effects; the imperial decrees were published in the cities, embracing the following revocation with regard to us.

"The Emperors Caesar Galerius Valerius Maximianus, Invictus, Augustus, Pontifex Maximus, Germanicus Maximus, Aegyptiacus Maximus, Thebaicus Maximus, Sarmaticus Maximus, the fifth time, Persicus Maximus, Carpicus Maximus, second time, Armeniacus Maximus, sixth time, Medicus Maximus, Adiabenicus Maximus, Tribune of the People XX., Emperor XIX., Consul VIII., Father of his country, Proconsul: and the Emperor Caesar Flavius Valerius Constantinus, Pius, Felix, Invictus, Augustus, Pontifex Maximus, Tribune of the People, and Emperor V., Consul, Father of his country, Proconsul: also, the Emperor Caesar Valerius Licinianus, Pius, Felix, Invictus, Augustus; Pontifex Maximus, Tribune of the People IV., Emperor III.,

---

[13] Galerius, a prime mover in the Diocletian persecution, first was Caesar in the East under Diocletian (293–305) and then was Eastern Augustus (305–311) after the retirement of Diocletian.

[14] Galerius, as above.

Consul, Father of his country, Proconsul;[15] to their subjects in the provinces, send greeting:

"Among other matters which we have devised for the benefit and common advantage of our people, we have first determined to restore all things according to the ancient laws and the public institutions of the Romans. And to make provision for this, that also the Christians, who have left the religion of their fathers, should return again to a good purpose and resolution. For by some means, such arrogance had overtaken, and such stupidity had beset them, that they would not follow the principles anciently prescribed to them, which in all probability their ancestors had established, but they began to make and follow laws, each one according to his own purpose and his own will, and thus different multitudes assembled with different opinions and of different sects. Hence, when a decree of this kind was issued by us, that they should return again to the established usages of their forefathers, vast numbers were subjected to danger, many, when threatened, endured various kinds of death. But though we saw the great mass still persevering in their folly, and that they neither gave the honour that was due to the immortal gods, nor heeded that of the Christians, still having a regard to our clemency and our invariable practice, according to which we are wont to grant pardon to all, we most cheerfully have resolved to extend our indulgence in this matter also: that there may be Christians again, and that they may restore their houses in which they were accustomed to assemble, so that nothing be done by them contrary to their profession. In another episode we shall point out to the judges, what they will be required to observe; whence, according to this condescension of ours, they are obligated to implore their God for our safety, as well as that of the people and their own. That in every place the public welfare may be preserved, and they may live unmolested in their respective homes and fire-hearths." Such was the purport of this ordinance.[16] (VIII, 17)

But the author of this edict, after this acknowledgment, soon after was liberated from his pains, and terminated his life. It is agreed he was the original cause of the miseries of the persecution, as he had, long before the movements of the other emperors, attempted to seduce the Christian soldiers of his own house from their faith, degrading some from their military rank, and insulting others in the most abusive manner, even punishing some with death, and at last exciting his associate emperors to a general persecution against all. Nor have I thought proper that the death of these emperors should be passed

---

[15] Note that the edict is jointly issued in the names of Galerius, Constantine, and Licinian.

[16] What purports to be the original Latin edict is preserved in Lactantius, *De mortibus persecutorum*, 34.

over in silence. As there were four,[17] therefore, that held the sovereignty divided among them, those that were advanced in years and honours, after nearly two years from the persecution, abdicated the government,[18] as we have already shown; and thus passing their days in common and retired life, ended their life in the following manner. —The one,[19] indeed, who preceded the others in honour and age, was at length overpowered by a long and distressing disease, but the next to him in dignity[1] destroyed himself by strangling, suffering thus according to certain daemoniacal prognostics, on account of the innumerable crimes that he had committed. But of the two after these, the last,[2] whom we have mentioned as the leader of the whole persecution, suffered such things as we have already stated. But he that surpassed them all in kindness and condescension, the emperor Constantius,[3] who had conducted his government the whole time consistently with the imperial dignity, and who exhibited himself a most gracious and benevolent prince in other respects, also had no hand in raising the persecution against us, but even protected and patronized those pious persons that were under him. He neither demolished the buildings of the churches, nor devised any thing in opposition to us; and finally enjoyed a death really happy and blessed, being the only one of the four that in the midst of a tranquil and glorious reign, at his death transmitted the government to his own son as his successor,[4] a prince most eminent in all respects for his wisdom and piety. He, at the very beginning, was proclaimed supreme emperor and Augustus, by the armies,[5] and exhibited himself a generous rival of his father's piety, with regard to us. Such, then, was the issue of the life of the four emperors, at different times.[6] (VIII, 17, App.) . . .

. . . But Constantine, who was first both in dignity and imperial rank, first took compassion upon those who were oppressed at Rome, invoking the God of heaven, and his Son and Word, our Lord Jesus Christ, the Saviour of all, as his aid, advanced with his whole army, purporting to restore the Romans to that liberty which they had derived from their ancestors.[7] Maxentius, however, relying more upon

---

[17] Diocletian, Maximian, Constantius, and Galerius.
[18] According to prior agreement, Diocletian and Maximian both retired in 305.
[19] Diocletian.
[1] Maximian.
[2] Galerius.
[3] Constantius, father of Constantine the Great, was Caesar in the West from 293 to 305, and Western Augustus for a short while (305–306) after the resignation of Maximian.
[4] Constantine the Great.
[5] In 306, Constantine's army declared him Caesar or Augustus. Galerius, Eastern Augustus, recognized Constantine as Caesar, and Maximian recognized him as Western Augustus in 307.
[6] The foregoing, from "But the author of this edict . . . ," is found appended to Chapter 17 of Book VIII in some copies.
[7] Eusebius now describes the crucial battle between Constantine and his rival in the West, Maxentius, the son of Maximian, in 312.

the arts of juggling than the affection of his subjects, did not venture to advance beyond the gates of the city, but fortified every place and region and city, with vast numbers of soldiers and innumerable bands and garrisons in all places of Rome and Italy that were enslaved by him. But the emperor, (Constantine,) stimulated by the divine assistance, proceeded against the tyrant, and defeating him without difficulty in the first, second, and third engagements, he advanced through the greatest part of Italy, and came almost to the very gates of Rome. Then, however, that he might not be forced to wage war with the Romans for the sake of the tyrant, God himself drew the tyrant, as if bound in fetters, to a considerable distance from the gates;[8] and here he confirmed those miraculous events performed of old against the wicked, and which have been discredited by so many, as if belonging to fiction and fable, but which have been established in the sacred volume, as credible to the believer. He confirmed them, I say, as true, by an immediate interposition of his power, addressed alike I may say to the eyes of believers and unbelievers. As, therefore, anciently in the days of Moses, and the religious people of the Hebrews, the chariots of Pharaoh and his forces were cast into the Red Sea, and his chosen triple combatants were overwhelmed in it; thus, also, Maxentius, and his combatants and guards about him sunk into the depths like a stone, when he fled before the power of God that was with Constantine, and passed through the river in his way, over which he had formed a bridge by joining boats, and thus prepared the means of his own destruction. Here, one might say, "he digged a pit and opened it, and he fell into the ditch that he made. His mischief shall fall upon his own head, and his iniquity descend upon his own pate." Thus, then, the bridge of boats over the river being broken, the crossing began to cease, and immediately the vessels with the men sunk, and were destroyed, and the most impious tyrant himself first of all, then the guards that he had around him, just as the divine oracles declare, sunk like lead in the swelling floods. . . . (IX, 9)

Now let us, also, subjoin translations from the Latin, of the imperial ordinances of Constantine and Licinius.

Copy of the imperial ordinances, translated from the Latin language.[9]

"As we long since perceived that religious liberty should not be denied, but that it should be granted to the opinion and wishes of each one to perform divine duties according to his own determination, we had given orders, that each one, and the Christians among the rest,

[8] To the vicinity of the Milvian Bridge across the Tiber.

[9] Eusebius wrote his *Ecclesiastical History* in Greek, into which language he translated the text or sense of such edicts as the present one, originally issued in Latin. What is apparently the original of the present edict is preserved in Lactantius, *De mortibus persecutorum*, and begins, "When we, Emperors Constantine and Licinius, met under happy circumstances at Milan. . . ."

have the liberty to observe the religion of his choice, and his peculiar mode of worship. But as there plainly appeared to be many and different sects added in that edict,[10] in which this privilege was granted them, some of them perhaps, after a little while, on this account shrunk from this kind of attention and observance. Wherefore, as I, Constantine Augustus, and I, Licinius Augustus, came under favourable auspices to Milan,[11] and took under consideration all affairs that pertained to the public benefit and welfare, these things among the rest appeared to us to be most advantageous and profitable to all. We have resolved among the first things to ordain those matters by which reverence and worship to the Deity might be exhibited. That is, how we may grant likewise to the Christians, and to all, the free choice to follow that mode of worship which they may wish. That whatsoever divinity and celestial power may exist, may be propitious to us and to all that live under our government. Therefore, we have decreed the following ordinance, as our will, with a salutary and most correct intention, that no freedom at all shall be refused to Christians, to follow or to keep their observances or worship. But that to each one power may be granted to devote his mind to that worship which he may think adapted to himself. That the Deity may in all things exhibit to us his accustomed favour and kindness. It was just and consistent that we should write that this was our pleasure. That all exceptions respecting the Christians being completely removed, which were contained in the former epistle, that we sent to your fidelity, and whatever measures were wholly sinister and foreign to our mildness, that these should be altogether annulled; and now that each one of the Christians may freely and without molestation pursue and follow that course and worship which he has proposed to himself: which, indeed, we have resolved to communicate most fully to your care and diligence, that you may know we have granted liberty and full freedom to the Christians, to observe their own mode of worship; which as your fidelity understands absolutely granted to them by us, the privilege is also granted to others to pursue that worship and religion they wish. Which it is obvious is consistent with the peace and tranquillity of our times; that each may have the privilege to select and to worship whatsoever divinity he pleases. But this has been done by us, that we might not appear in any manner to detract any thing from any manner of religion, or any mode of worship. And this we further decree, with respect to the Christians, that the places in which they were formerly accustomed to assemble, concerning

---

[10] The edict here mentioned is lost, unless reference is made to the Edict of Galerius, whose reading as rendered above (and in Lactantius) does not seem to fit.

[11] The present ordinance, a milestone in the history of Christianity, is popularly known as the Edict of Milan (313), although it may more properly be called a rescript. Its principal author was Constantine, and Licinius again took to discriminating against the Christians.

which also we formerly wrote to your fidelity, in a different form, that if any persons have purchased these, either from our treasury, or from any other one, these shall restore them to the Christians, without money and without demanding any price, without any super-added value, or augmentation, without delay, or hesitancy. And if any have happened to receive these places as presents, that they shall restore them as soon as possible to the Christians, so that if either those that purchased or those that received them as presents, have anything to request of our munificence, they may go to the provincial governor, as the judge; that provision may also be made for them by our clemency. All which, it will be necessary to be delivered up to the body of Christians, by your care, without any delay. And since the Christians themselves are known to have had not only those places where they were accustomed to meet, but other places also, belonging not to individuals among them, but to the right of the whole body of Christians, you will also command all these, by virtue of the law before mentioned, without any hesitancy, to be restored to these same Christians, that is, to their body, and to each conventicle respectively. The aforesaid consideration, to wit, being observed; namely, that they who as we have said restore them without valuation and price, may expect their indemnity from our munificence and liberality. In all which it will be incumbent on you, to exhibit your exertions as much as possible to the aforesaid body of Christians, that our orders may be most speedily accomplished, that likewise in this provision may be made by our clemency, for the preservation of the common and public tranquillity. For by these means, as before said, the divine favour with regard to us, which we have already experienced in many affairs, will continue firm and permanent at all times. But that the purpose of this our ordinance and liberality may be extended to the knowledge of all, it is expected that these things written by us, should be proposed and published to the knowledge of all. That this act of our liberality and kindness may remain unknown to none."[12] (X, 5)

[12] Eusebius goes on to quote further ordinances in favor of the Christians granted by Constantine, and the latter's victory over Licinius in 324, whereby the Empire was reunited.

SECTION II

The Early Middle Ages: Western Civilization Gets a New Start

☙

WITH THE dissolution of its original matrix, the old Roman Empire, Western civilization was compelled in effect to make a new start in the Early Middle Ages. Although this was at first difficult and trying, it was eventually beneficial, since in the process much that was dross was sloughed off. Western civilization now began its new phase in a frontier area, the western half of Europe, that soon ceased to be Mediterranean-centered. And it worked with fresh material that included the new blood and outlook of former Celtic, Slavic, and especially Teutonic barbarians. These latter elements, described for us by Tacitus in his *Germania*, fused with elements from Roman civilization, vivified and enlightened by Christianity, to produce Germanic successor states, such as that of the Franks. The Empire of Charlemagne, presented in Einhard's *Life of Charlemagne*, was the glorious if ephemeral culmination of this process, both transitional to feudalism and foreshadowing stronger states of the future. The chief catalyst and agent in the process of combination as well as of reformation was the Christian Church. And in the Church the principal means of conversion, instruction, nutriment, and survival in those violent times was monasticism, unfolded for us in the *Rule* drawn up by that greatest of monastic legislators, St. Benedict.

4

Uncivilized Indo-Europeans: The Germanic Barbarians Before the Invasions

Tacitus

A new component of Western civilization as it developed during the Middle Ages was the Germanic addition. Even when the Roman Empire was at its height, about two-thirds of Europe was still occupied by barbarians, mainly Caucasoid (white) Indo-Europeans. Although these barbarians included groups such as Celts and Slavs, the most important and probably the most numerous were those who spoke the Teutonic languages: the "Germans." The latter bordered the Empire on the Rhine-Danube frontier and, by the fourth century, inhabited the lands between the Rhine and the Vistula and between the Danube and the Don. These Teutonic barbarians invaded and overthrew the Roman Empire in the West, and set up on former Roman soil their own kingdoms, some of which also came to include territory in the old Germanic homeland.

What manner of people were these uncivilized Indo-Europeans? Fortunately we have a description of the as yet "unspoiled" Germans, written in the first century A.D. by the Roman historian Tacitus. Tacitus was a Roman of aristocratic lineage, born about A.D. 54. His first name, Caius or Cornelius, is uncertain. He moved in the highest circles, was a friend of various emperors, and married the daughter of a Roman governor of Britain. From the combined points of view of style, insight, and objectivity, Tacitus is considered by many to be the greatest of Roman historians. He is certainly our leading authority for Rome in the first century, with his Annals and Histories which cover the periods A.D. 14–69 and 69–96 respectively. Although a friend of emperors, Tacitus was critical of the Empire and lamented the passing of the Republic. He had, however, a senatorial and aristocratic as well as a republican bias. He was also critical of the moral laxity of his day as opposed to the old Roman virtues. His style is notable for its compactness in marked contrast to the prolixity of contemporary rhetoric. As a historian, Tacitus not only had the advantage of moving in the society of those who were making history, but he himself rose through the customary cursus honorum from lower to higher offices in the Roman public service.

The Germania, published about A.D. 98, testifies to the continuing popular interest in the "origins, geography, institutions, and tribes" of the barbarians beyond the frontiers. After a brief opening section on the geography of "Germany" (section 1), Tacitus divides his work into two main parts. The first (sections 2–27) discusses the Germans in general: their reputed origins, economy and technology, military and political organization, religious beliefs, popular assemblies and courts, social classes and customs, housing, clothing, marriage customs, morality, education of the young, recreations, serfs, and miscellaneous features of their society. The second part (sections 28–46) locates and comments on the various tribes of the Germans and a few neighboring peoples. In discussing the tribes Tacitus proceeds down the Rhineland from the upper (southern) to the lower (northern) Rhine and the North Sea, to the Elbe region, and along the Baltic to the Vistula; finally he follows the Danube Valley eastward, concluding with some of the peoples separated from the Germans "by mountains and mutual fear."

As portrayed by Tacitus, the Germans in the first century A.D. were a bundle of paradoxes. Semi-democratic yet semi-monarchical, semi-equalitarian yet semi-aristocratic, semi-nomadic yet semi-agricultural, bellicose yet hospitable, extremely moral in some ways yet wholly amoral in others, maintaining private property-rights in animals yet owning land collectively, they were technologically in the Iron Age yet otherwise halfway between the Old and New Stone Ages.

Already, when Tacitus wrote of them, the Germans were learning from the Romans trade techniques, the use of coins, and military tactics. By the time of the migrations or Volkerwanderung, three centuries later, the Germans had advanced far beyond what they were at the time of Tacitus. This was largely a result of their contacts and competition with the Romans. Their territory was almost doubled. Various groups had been united into "nations" or permanent federations. These peoples were ruled by monarchs whose office had become hereditary and whose powers were much more extensive than those of earlier chiefs. They had larger, better organized, more disciplined armies than the Germans of the first century. They had progressed in agriculture and had improved their technology. Many had even become Christians, for Arian Christianity had spread among the East Germans, following the missionary labors of

Ulfilas, "Apostle of the Goths." And with Christianity had come the beginnings of a written literature.

Except for such differences, the fourth-century Germanic invaders of the Roman Empire were, in their basic characteristics, probably much as described by Tacitus. Tacitus has been accused of writing the Germania for propaganda purposes: in order, by exaggerating the virtues of the early Germans, and the "democratic" features of barbarian institutions, to shame his fellow Romans for their careless surrender of political liberty and their flagrant immorality. It is true that Tacitus does not miss the opportunity to moralize; but if he seems at times to underline the virtues of the Germans, he also points out their vices and shortcomings. And in considering their institutions, he does not overlook the marked class structure of their society. Another charge made against Tacitus is that he got his information about the Germans at second hand. This may not be entirely so, since he seems to have spent some time, in the course of his public career, in the partly Germanic provinces to the west of the Rhine known as Upper and Lower Germany (c. A.D. 90–94). But even when he derives his information from other sources, such as Julius Caesar, Pomponius Mela, and Pliny the Elder, this in itself need not disprove its accuracy, for Tacitus appears to have been judicious with his materials. If we keep in mind that his picture of the Germans in general does not necessarily and equally apply to all of them, that Roman knowledge of the more remote tribes was less distinct than of the nearer ones, and, finally, that the leaven of contact with Roman ways was already at work among the barbarians, we may gain from Tacitus some valuable insights into the nature and mores of these vigorous folk who were so profoundly to affect the course of Western civilization.

C. Tacitus

Germania: The Origins, Geography, Institutions, and Tribes of the Germans *

1. Germany is separated from the Galli,[1] the Rhaeti,[2] and Pannonii,[3] by the rivers Rhine and Danube; mountain ranges, or the fear which each feels for the other, divide it from the Sarmatae[4] and Daci.[5] Elsewhere ocean girds it, embracing broad peninsulas and islands of unexplored extent, where certain tribes and kingdoms are newly known to us, revealed by war. The Rhine springs from a precipitous and inaccessible height of the Rhaetian Alps,[6] bends slightly westward, and mingles with the Northern Ocean.[7] The Danube pours down from the gradual and gently rising slope of Mount Abnoba,[8] and visits many nations, to force its way at last through six channels into the Pontus;[9] a seventh mouth is lost in marshes.

2. The Germans themselves I should regard as aboriginal, and not mixed at all with other races through immigration or intercourse. For, in former times, it was not by land but on shipboard that those who sought to emigrate would arrive; and the boundless and, so to speak, hostile ocean beyond us, is seldom entered by a sail from our world. And, besides the perils of rough and unknown seas, who would leave Asia, or Africa, or Italy for Germany, with its wild country, its inclement skies, its sullen manners and aspect, unless indeed it were his home? In their ancient songs, their only way of remembering or recording the past, they celebrate an earth-born god, Tuisco, and his son Mannus, as the origin of their race, as their founders. To Mannus they assign three sons, from whose names, they say, the coast tribes are called Ingaevones; those of the interior, Herminones; all the rest, Istaevones.[10] Some, with the freedom of conjecture permitted by

---

* Translated by Alfred J. Church and William J. Brodribb.

[1] Inhabitants of Gaul, the Gauls.

[2] Inhabitants of Rhaetia, located in eastern Switzerland, western Austria, and northern Italy.

[3] Inhabitants of Pannonia, in the territory south and west of the middle Danube, including western Hungry.

[4] The Sarmatians, located east of the Vistula and north of the lands adjacent to the Black Sea, in eastern Poland and western Russia.

[5] The Dacians, to the north of the lower Danube in present-day Rumania and vicinity.

[6] The Alps in the area of Rhaetia.

[7] Baltic Sea.

[8] In the Black Forest area of southwestern Germany.

[9] Black Sea.

[10] An old classification.

antiquity, assert that the god had several descendants, and the nation several appellations, as Marsi, Gambrivii, Suevi, Vandilii,[11] and that these are genuine old names. The name Germany, on the other hand, they say, is modern and newly introduced, from the fact that the tribes which first crossed the Rhine and drove out the Gauls, and are now called Tungrians,[12] were then called Germans. Thus what was the name of a tribe, and not of a race, gradually prevailed, till all called themselves by this self-invented name of Germans, which the conquerors had first employed to inspire terror.

3. They say that Hercules,[13] too, once visited them; and when going into battle, they sing of him first of all heroes. They have also these songs of theirs, by the recital of which ("baritus," they call it), they rouse their courage, while from the note they augur the result of the approaching conflict. For, as their line shouts, they inspire or feel alarm. It is not so much an articulate sound, as a general cry of valour. They aim chiefly at a harsh note and a confused roar, putting their shields to their mouth, so that, by reverberation, it may swell into a fuller and deeper sound. Ulysses, too, is believed by some, in his long legendary wanderings, to have found his way into this ocean, and, having visited German soil, to have founded and named the town of Asciburgium,[14] which stands on the bank of the Rhine, and is to this day inhabited. They even say that an altar dedicated to Ulysses, with the addition of the name of his father, Laertes, was formerly discovered on this same spot, and that certain monuments and tombs, with Greek inscriptions, still exist on the borders of Germany and Rhaetia. These statements I have no intention of sustaining by proof, or of refuting; every one may believe or disbelieve them as he feels inclined.

4. For my own part, I agree with those who think that the tribes of Germany are free from all taint of intermarriages with foreign nations, and that they appear as a distinct, unmixed race, like none but themselves. Hence, too, the same physical peculiarities throughout so vast a population. All have fierce blue eyes, red hair, huge frames, fit only for a sudden exertion. They are less able to bear laborious work. Heat and thirst they cannot in the least endure; to cold and hunger their climate and their soil inure them.

5. Their country, though somewhat various in appearance, yet generally either bristles with forests or reeks with swamps; it is more rainy on the side of Gaul, bleaker on that of Noricum[15] and Pannonia. It is productive of grain, but unfavourable to fruit-bearing trees; it is rich in flocks and herds, but these are for the most part undersized,

---

[11] Discussed later.
[12] Located in the vicinity of Tongres in noreastern Belgium.
[13] Tacitus equates Latin and Teutonic gods. Hercules may be Thor or Donar.
[14] Asburg, or Asberg, on the left bank of the lower (northern) Rhine.
[15] South of the Danube, between Rhaetia and Pannonia, Noricum included much of present-day Austria and Bavaria.

and even the cattle have not their usual beauty or noble head. It is number that is chiefly valued; they are in fact the most highly prized, indeed the only riches of the people. Silver and gold the gods have refused to them, whether in kindness or in anger I cannot say. I would not, however, affirm that no vein of German soil produces gold or silver, for who has ever made a search? They care but little to possess or use them. You may see among them vessels of silver, which have been presented to their envoys and chieftains, held as cheap as those of clay. The border population, however, value gold and silver for their commercial utility, and are familiar with, and show preference for, some of our coins. The tribes of the interior use the simpler and more ancient practice of the barter of commodities. They like the old and well-known money, coins milled, or showing a two-horse chariot. They likewise prefer silver to gold, not from any special liking, but because a large number of silver pieces is more convenient for use among dealers in cheap and common articles.

6. Even iron is not plentiful with them,[16] as we infer from the character of their weapons. But few use swords or long lances. They carry a spear (*framea* is their name for it), with a narrow and short head, but so sharp and easy to wield that the same weapon serves, according to circumstances, for close or distant conflict. As for the horse-soldier, he is satisfied with a shield and spear; the foot-soldiers also scatter showers of missiles, each man having several and hurling them to an immense distance, and being naked or lightly clad with a little cloak. There is no display about their equipment: their shields alone are marked with very choice colours. A few only have corslets,[17] and just one or two here and there a metal or leathern helmet. Their horses are remarkable neither for beauty nor for fleetness. Nor are they taught various evolutions after our fashion, but are driven straight forward, or so as to make one wheel to the right in such a compact body that none is left behind another. On the whole, one would say that their chief strength is in their infantry, which fights along with the cavalry; admirably adapted to the action of the latter is the swiftness of certain foot-soldiers, who are picked from the entire youth of their country, and stationed in front of the line. Their number is fixed, — a hundred from each canton,[18] and from this they take their name among their countrymen, so that what was originally a mere number has now become a title of distinction. Their line of battle is drawn up in a wedge-like formation. To give ground, provided you return to the attack, is considered prudence rather than cowardice. The bodies of their slain they carry off even in indecisive

---

[16] Although iron deposits were plentiful in Germany, they were not yet exploited.
[17] Body armor.
[18] A district similar to the German *gau*, the Latin *pagus*, the French county, and the English shire. Among the Germans, each state was divided into cantons and each canton into hundreds, according to Caesar.

engagements. To abandon your shield is the basest of crimes; nor may a man thus disgraced be present at the sacred rites, or enter their council; many, indeed, after escaping from battle, have ended their infamy with the halter.

7. They choose their kings by birth, their generals for merit. These kings have not unlimited or arbitrary power, and the generals do more by example than by authority. If they are energetic, if they are conspicuous, if they fight in the front, they lead because they are admired. But to reprimand, to imprison, even to flog, is permitted to the priests alone, and that not as a punishment, or at the general's bidding, but, as it were, by the mandate of the god whom they believe to inspire the warrior. They also carry with them into battle certain figures and images taken from their sacred groves. And what most stimulates their courage is that their squadrons or battalions, instead of being formed by chance or by a fortuitous gathering, are composed of families and clans. Close by them, too, are those dearest to them, so that they hear the shrieks of women, the cries of infants. *They* are to every man the most sacred witnesses of his bravery — *they* are his most generous applauders. The soldier brings his wounds to mother and wife, who shrink not from counting or even demanding them, and who administer both food and encouragement to the combatants.

8. Tradition says that armies already wavering and giving way have been rallied by women who, with earnest entreaties and bosoms laid bare, have vividly represented the horrors of captivity, which the Germans fear with such extreme dread on behalf of their women, that the strongest tie by which a state can be bound is the being required to give, among the number of hostages, maidens of noble birth. They even believe that the sex has a certain sanctity and prescience, and they do not despise their counsels, or make light of their answers. In Vespasian's days we saw Veleda, long regarded by many as a divinity. In former times, too, they venerated Aurinia, and many other women, but not with servile flatteries, or with sham deification.

9. Mercury[19] is the deity whom they chiefly worship, and on certain days they deem it right to sacrifice to him even with human victims. Hercules[1] and Mars[2] they appease with more lawful offerings. Some of the Suevi also sacrifice to Isis.[3] Of the occasion and origin of this foreign rite I have discovered nothing, but that the image, which is fashioned like a light galley, indicates an imported worship. The Germans, however, do not consider it consistent with the grandeur of celestial beings to confine the gods within walls, or

---

[19] Mercury: Woden, whence Wednesday (Woden's day) for the Roman Mercury's day.

[1] Hercules: perhaps Thor or Donar.

[2] Mars: Tiu or Ziu, whence Tuesday (Tiu's day) for the Roman Mars' day.

[3] Interesting instance of the importation of religious ideas, perhaps even a mystery-religion, from the East.

to liken them to the form of any human countenance. They consecrate woods and groves, and they apply the names of deities to the abstraction which they see only in spiritual worship.

10. Augury and divination by lot no people practise more diligently. The use of the lots is simple. A little bough is lopped off a fruit-bearing tree, and cut into small pieces; these are distinguished by certain marks, and thrown carelessly and at random over a white garment. In public questions the priest of the particular state, in private the father of the family, invokes the gods, and, with his eyes towards heaven, takes up each piece three times, and finds in them a meaning according to the mark previously impressed on them. If they prove unfavourable, there is no further consultation that day about the matter; if they sanction it, the confirmation of augury is still required. For they are also familiar with the practice of consulting the notes and the flight of birds. It is peculiar to this people to seek omens and monitions from horses.[4] Kept at the public expense, in these same woods and groves, are white horses, pure from the taint of earthly labour; these are yoked to a sacred car, and accompanied by the priest and the king, or chief of the tribe, who note their neighings and snortings. No species of augury is more trusted, not only by the people and by the nobility, but also by the priests, who regard themselves as the ministers of the gods, and the horses as acquainted with their will. They have also another method of observing auspices, by which they seek to learn the result of an important war. Having taken, by whatever means, a prisoner from the tribe with whom they are at war, they pit him against a picked man of their own tribe, each combatant using the weapons of their country. The victory of the one or the other is accepted as an indication of the issue.

11. About minor matters the chiefs deliberate, about the more important the whole tribe. Yet even when the final decision rests with the people, the affair is always thoroughly discussed by the chiefs. They assemble, except in the case of a sudden emergency, on certain fixed days, either at new or at full moon; for this they consider the most auspicious season for the transaction of business. Instead of reckoning by days as we do, they reckon by nights, and in this manner fix both their ordinary and their legal appointments. Night they regard as bringing on day. Their freedom has this disadvantage, that they do not meet simultaneously or as they are bidden, but two or three days are wasted in the delay of assembling. When the multitude think proper, they sit down armed. Silence is proclaimed by the priests, who have on these occasions the right of keeping order. Then the king or the chief, according to age, birth, distinction in war, or eloquence, is heard, more because he has influence to persuade than because he has power to command. If his sentiments displease them,

---

[4] A superstition also found among the Persians; monitions: warnings.

they reject them with murmurs; if they are satisfied, they brandish their spears. The most complimentary form of assent is to express approbation with their weapons.

12. In their councils an accusation may be preferred or a capital crime prosecuted. Penalties are distinguished according to the offence. Traitors and deserters are hanged on trees; the coward, the unwarlike, the man stained with abominable vices, is plunged into the mire of the morass, with a hurdle put over him. This distinction in punishment means that crime, they think, ought in being punished, to be exposed, while infamy ought to be buried out of sight. Lighter offences, too, have penalties proportioned to them; he who is convicted, is fined in a certain number of horses or of cattle. Half of the fine is paid to the king or to the state, half to the person whose wrongs are avenged and to his relatives. In these same councils they also elect the chief magistrates, who administer law in the cantons and the towns. Each of these has a hundred associates chosen from the people, who support him with their advice and influence.

13. They transact no public or private business without being armed. It is not, however, usual for anyone to wear arms till the state has recognised his power to use them. Then in the presence of the council, one of the chiefs, or the young man's father, or some kinsman, equips him with a shield and a spear.[5] These arms are what the "toga" is with us, the first honour with which youth is invested. Up to this time he is regarded as a member of a household, afterwards as a member of the commonwealth. Very noble birth or great services rendered by the father secure for lads the rank of a chief; such lads attach themselves to men of mature strength and of long approved valour. It is no shame to be seen among a chief's followers. Even in his escort there are gradations of rank, dependent on the choice of the man to whom they are attached. These followers vie keenly with each other as to who shall rank first with his chief, the chiefs as to who shall have the most numerous and the bravest followers. It is an honour as well as a source of strength to be thus always surrounded by a large body of picked youths; it is an ornament in peace and a defence in war. And not only in his own tribe but also in the neighbouring states it is the renown and glory of a chief to be distinguished for the number and valour of his followers, for such a man is courted by embassies, is honoured with presents, and the very prestige of his name often settles a war.

14. When they go into battle, it is a disgrace for the chief to be surpassed in valour, a disgrace for his followers not to equal the valour of the chief. And it is an infamy and a reproach for life to have survived the chief, and returned from the field. To defend, to protect him, to ascribe one's own brave deeds to his renown, is the

[5] This practice evidently influenced the ceremony of knighting in medieval chivalry.

height of loyalty. The chief fights for victory; his vassals fight for their chief. If their native state sinks into the sloth of prolonged peace and repose, many of its noble youths voluntarily seek those tribes which are waging some war, both because inaction is odious to their race, and because they win renown more readily in the midst of peril, and cannot maintain a numerous following except by violence and war. Indeed, men look to the liberality of their chief for their war-horse and their blood-stained and victorious lance. Feasts and entertainments, which, though inelegant, are plentifully furnished, are their only pay. The means of this bounty come from war and rapine. Nor are they as easily persuaded to plough the earth and to wait for the year's produce as to challenge an enemy and earn the honour of wounds. Nay, they actually think it tame and stupid to acquire by the sweat of toil what they might win by their blood.

15. Whenever they are not fighting, they pass much of their time in the chase, and still more in idleness, giving themselves up to sleep and to feasting, the bravest and the most warlike doing nothing, and surrendering the management of the household, of the home, and of the land, to the women, the old men, and all the weakest members of the family. They themselves lie buried in sloth, a strange combination in their nature that the same men should be so fond of idleness, so averse to peace. It is the custom of the states to bestow by voluntary and individual contribution on the chiefs a present of cattle or of grain, which, while accepted as a compliment, supplies their wants. They are particularly delighted by gifts from neighbouring tribes, which are sent not only by individuals but also by the state, such as choice steeds, heavy armour, trappings, and neckchains. We have now taught them to accept money also.

16. It is well known that the nations of Germany have no cities, and that they do not even tolerate closely contiguous dwellings. They live scattered and apart, just as a spring, a meadow, or a wood has attracted them. Their villages they do not arrange in our fashion, with the buildings connected and joined together, but every person surrounds his dwelling with an open space, either as a precaution against the disasters of fire, or because they do not know how to build. No use is made by them of stone or tile; they employ timber for all purposes, rude masses without ornament or attractiveness. Some parts of their buildings they stain more carefully with a clay so clear and bright that it resembles painting, or a coloured design. They are wont also to dig out subterranean caves, and pile on them great heaps of dung, as a shelter from winter and as a receptacle for the year's produce, for by such places they mitigate the rigour of the cold. And should an enemy approach, he lays waste the open country, while what is hidden and buried is either not known to exist, or else escapes him from the very fact that it has to be searched for.

17. They all wrap themselves in a cloak which is fastened with a

clasp, or, if this is not forthcoming, with a thorn, leaving the rest of their persons bare. They pass whole days on the hearth by the fire. The wealthiest are distinguished by a dress which is not flowing, like that of the Sarmatae and Parthi,[6] but is tight, and exhibits each limb. They also wear the skins of wild beasts; the tribes on the Rhine and the Danube in a careless fashion, those of the interior with more elegance, as not obtaining other clothing by commerce. These select certain animals, the hides of which they strip off and vary them with the spotted skins of beasts, the produce of the outer ocean, and of the seas unknown to us. The women have the same dress as the men, except that they generally wrap themselves in linen garments, which they embroider with purple, and do not lengthen out the upper part of their clothing into sleeves. The upper and lower arm is thus bare, and the nearest part of the bosom is also exposed.

18. Their marriage code, however, is strict, and indeed no part of their manners is more praiseworthy. Almost alone among barbarians they are content with one wife, except a very few among them, and these not from sensuality, but because their noble birth procures for them many offers of alliance. The wife does not bring a dower to the husband, but the husband to the wife. The parents and relatives are present, and pass judgment on the marriage-gifts, gifts not meant to suit a woman's taste, nor such as a bride would deck herself with, but oxen, a caparisoned steed, a shield, a lance, and a sword. With these presents the wife is espoused, and she herself in turn brings her husband a gift of arms. This they count their strongest bond of union, these their sacred mysteries, these their gods of marriage. Lest the woman should think herself to stand apart from aspirations after noble deeds and from the perils of war, she is reminded by the ceremony which inaugurates marriage that she is her husband's partner in toil and danger, destined to suffer and to dare with him alike both in peace and in war. The yoked oxen, the harnessed steed, the gift of arms, proclaim this fact. She must live and die with the feeling that she is receiving what she must hand down to her children neither tarnished nor depreciated, what future daughters-in-law may receive, and may be so passed on to her grand-children.

19. Thus with their virtue protected they live uncorrupted by the allurements of public shows or the stimulant of feastings. Clandestine correspondence is equally unknown to men and women. Very rare for so numerous a population is adultery, the punishment for which is prompt, and in the husband's power. Having cut off the hair of the adulteress and stripped her naked, he expels her from the house in the presence of her kinsfolk, and then flogs her through the whole village. The loss of chastity meets with no indulgence; neither beauty, youth, nor wealth will procure the culprit a husband. No one in

[6] Parthians; or perhaps Persians. Parthia was an ancient district northeast of Persia, subsequently conquered by the Persians.

Germany laughs at vice, nor do they call it the fashion to corrupt and to be corrupted. Still better is the condition of those states in which only maidens are given in marriage, and where the hopes and expectations of a bride are then finally terminated. They receive one husband, as having one body and one life, that they may have no thoughts beyond, no further-reaching desires, that they may love not so much the husband as the married state. To limit the number of their children or to destroy any of their subsequent offspring is accounted infamous, and good habits are here more effectual than good laws elsewhere.

20. In every household the children, naked and filthy, grow up with those stout frames and limbs which we so much admire. Every mother suckles her own offspring, and never entrusts it to servants and nurses. The master is not distinguished from the slave by being brought up with greater delicacy. Both live amid the same flocks and lie on the same ground till the freeborn are distinguished by age and recognised by merit. The young men marry late, and their vigour is thus unimpaired. Nor are the maidens hurried into marriage; the same age and a similar stature is required; well-matched and vigorous they wed and the offspring reproduce the strength of the parents.[7] Sisters' sons are held in as much esteem by their uncles as by their fathers; indeed, some regard the relation as even more sacred and binding, and prefer it in receiving hostages, thinking thus to secure a stronger hold on the affections and a wider bond for the family. But every man's own children are his heirs and successors, and there are no wills. Should there be no issue, the next in succession to the property are his brothers and his uncles on either side. The more relatives he has, the more numerous his connections, the more honoured is his old age; nor are there any advantages in childnessness.

21. It is a duty among them to adopt the feuds as well as the friendships of a father or a kinsman. These feuds are not implacable; even homicide is expiated by the payment of a certain number of cattle and of sheep, and the satisfaction is accepted by the entire family, greatly to the advantage of the state, since feuds are dangerous in proportion to a people's freedom.

No nation indulges more profusely in entertainments and hospitality. To exclude any human being from their roof is thought impious; every German, according to his means, receives his guest with a well-furnished table. When his supplies are exhausted, he who was but now the host becomes the guide and companion to further hospitality, and without invitation they go to the next house. It matters not; they are entertained with like cordiality. No one distinguishes between an acquaintance and a stranger, as regards the rights of

---

[7] Some anthropologists allege that later maturation and marriage are a likely reason for the difference of stature between members of the Nordic and Mediterranean races, both long-headed and possibly of common descent.

hospitality. It is usual to give the departing guest whatever he may ask for, and a present in return is asked with as little hesitation. They are greatly charmed with gifts, but they expect no return for what they give, nor feel any obligation for what they receive.

22. On waking from sleep, which they generally prolong to a late hour of the day, they take a bath, oftenest of warm water, which suits a country where winter is the longest of the seasons. After their bath they take their meal, each having a separate seat and table of his own. Then they go armed to business, or no less often to their festal meetings. To pass an entire day and night in drinking disgraces no one. Their quarrels, as might be expected with intoxicated people, are seldom fought out with mere abuse, but commonly with wounds and bloodshed. Yet it is at their feasts that they generally consult on the reconciliation of enemies, on the forming of matrimonial alliances, on the choice of chiefs, finally even on peace and war, for they think that at no time is the mind more open to simplicity of purpose or more warmed to noble aspirations. A race without either natural or acquired cunning, they disclose their hidden thoughts in the freedom of the festivity. Thus the sentiments of all having been discovered and laid bare, the discussion is renewed on the following day, and from each occasion its own peculiar advantage is derived. They deliberate when they have no power to dissemble; they resolve when error is impossible.

23. A liquor for drinking is made out of barley or other grain, and fermented into a certain resemblance to wine.[8] The dwellers on the river-bank also buy wine. Their food is of a simple kind, consisting of wild-fruit, fresh game, and curdled milk.[9] They satisfy their hunger without elaborate preparation and without delicacies. In quenching their thirst they are not equally moderate. If you indulge their love of drinking by supplying them with as much as they desire, they will be overcome by their own vices as easily as by the arms of an enemy.

24. One and the same kind of spectacle is always exhibited at every gathering. Naked youths who practise the sport bound in the dance amid swords and lances that threaten their lives. Experience gives them skill, and skill again gives grace; profit or pay are out of the question; however reckless their pastime, its reward is the pleasure of the spectators. Strangely enough they make games of hazard a serious occupation even when sober, and so venturesome are they about gaining or losing, that, when every other resource has failed, on the last and final throw they stake the freedom of their own persons. The loser goes into voluntary slavery: though the younger and stronger, he suffers himself to be bound and sold. Such is their stubborn persistency in a bad practice; they themselves call it honour. Slaves of

[8] Beer?
[9] Or cheese.

this kind the owners part with in the way of commerce, and also to relieve themselves from the scandal of such a victory.

25. The other slaves are not employed after our manner with distinct domestic duties assigned to them, but each one has the management of a house and home of his own. The master requires from the slave a certain quantity of grain, of cattle, and of clothing, as he would from a tenant, and this is the limit of subjection. All other household functions are discharged by the wife and children. To strike a slave or to punish him with bonds or with hard labour is a rare occurrence. They often kill them, not in enforcing strict discipline, but on the impulse of passion, as they would an enemy, only it is done with impunity. The freedmen do not rank much above slaves, and are seldom of any weight in the family, never in the state, with the exception of those tribes which are ruled by kings. There indeed they rise above the freeborn and the noble; elsewhere the inferiority of the freedman marks the freedom of the state.

26. Of lending money on interest and increasing it by compound interest they know nothing, — a more effectual safeguard than if it were prohibited.

Land proportioned to the number of inhabitants is occupied by the whole community in turn, and afterwards divided among them according to rank. A wide expanse of plains makes the partition easy. They till fresh fields every year, and they have still more land than enough; with the richness and extent of their soil, they do not laboriously exert themselves in planting orchards, inclosing meadows, and watering gardens. Corn[10] is the only produce required from the earth; hence even the year itself is not divided by them into as many seasons as with us. Winter, spring, and summer have both a meaning and a name; the name and the blessings of autumn are alike unknown.

27. In their funerals there is no pomp; they simply observe the custom of burning the bodies of illustrious men with certain kinds of wood. They do not heap garments or spices on the funeral pile. The arms of the dead man and in some cases his horse are consigned to the fire. A turf mound forms the tomb. Monuments with their lofty elaborate splendour they reject as oppressive to the dead. Tears and lamentations they soon dismiss; grief and sorrow but slowly. It is thought becoming for women to bewail, for men to remember, the dead.

Such on the whole is the account which I have received of the origin and manners of the entire German people. I will now touch on the institutions and religious rites of the separate tribes,[11] pointing out

---

[10] Grain.
[11] Tacitus locates the tribes as they were situated in his own day. Many later moved, or were amalgamated with other tribes. The locations given in our notes are often probable rather than positive.

how far they differ, and also what nations have migrated from Germany into Gaul.

28. That highest authority, the great Julius,[12] informs us that Gaul was once more powerful than Germany. Consequently we may believe that Gauls even crossed over into Germany. For what a trifling obstacle would a river be to the various tribes, as they grew in strength and wished to possess in exchange settlements which were still open to all, and not partitioned among powerful monarchies! Accordingly the country between the Hercynian forest and the rivers Rhine and Moenus,[13] and that which lies beyond, was occupied respectively by the Helvetii and Boii, both tribes of Gaul. The name Boiemum[14] still survives marking the old tradition of the place, though the population has been changed. Whether however the Aravisci[15] migrated into Pannonia from the Osi,[16] a German race, or whether the Osi came from the Aravisci into Germany, as both nations still retain the same language, institutions, and customs, is a doubtful matter; for as they were once equally poor and equally free, either bank has the same attractions, the same drawbacks. The Treveri and Nervii[17] are even eager in their claims of a German origin, thinking that the glory of this descent distinguishes them from the uniform level of Gallic effeminacy. The Rhine bank itself is occupied by tribes unquestionably German, — the Vangiones, the Triboci, and the Nemetes.[18] Nor do even the Ubii,[19] though they have earned the distinction of being a Roman colony and prefer to be called Agrippinenses,[1] from the name of their founder, blush to own their origin. Having crossed the sea in former days, and given proof of their allegiance, they were settled on the Rhine-bank itself, as those who might guard it, but need not be watched.

29. Foremost among all these nations in valour, the Batavi occupy an island within the Rhine[2] and but a small portion of the bank. Formerly a tribe of the Chatti,[3] they were forced by internal dissension to migrate to their present settlements and there become a part of the Roman Empire. They yet retain the honourable badge of an

---

[12] Julius Caesar describes the Germans briefly in his *Gallic Wars*.
[13] Main River.
[14] Bohemia: land of the Boii, a Celtic people.
[15] A people of southwestern Hungary or Pannonia.
[16] The Osi apparently dwelt in Galicia, north of the former.
[17] The Treveri dwelt in the region of Treves; the Nervii, in Belgium in the region of Cambrai.
[18] These three tribes were located on the left (west) bank of the Rhine: the Vangiones in the vicinity of Worms; the Triboci, of Strassburg; and the Nemetes, of Speyer.
[19] The Ubii were on the left bank of the Rhine in the area of Cologne.
[1] Colonia Agrippinenses: Cologne.
[2] An island or delta of the lower Rhine in the region of the Dutch Netherlands. The Batavi were early *foederati*.
[3] The Chatti or Hessians were in Hesse, to the east of the middle Rhine, in the region of the upper Weser River.

ancient allegiance; for they are not insulted by tribute, nor ground down by the tax-gatherer. Free from the usual burdens and contributions, and set apart for fighting purposes, like a magazine of arms, we reserve them for our wars. The subjection of the Mattiaci[4] is of the same character. For the greatness of the Roman people has spread reverence for our empire beyond the Rhine and the old boundaries. Thus this nation, whose settlements and territories are on their own side of the river, are yet in sentiment and purpose one with us; in all other respects they resemble the Batavi, except that they still gain from the soil and climate of their native land a keener vigour. I should not reckon among the German tribes the cultivators of the tithe-lands,[5] although they are settled on the further side of the Rhine and Danube. Reckless adventurers from Gaul, emboldened by want, occupied this land of questionable ownership. After a while, our frontier having been advanced, and our military positions pushed forward, it was regarded as a remote nook of our empire and a part of a Roman province.

30. Beyond them are the Chatti, whose settlements begin at the Hercyian forest,[6] where the country is not so open and marshy as in the other cantons into which Germany stretches. These are found where there are hills, and with them grow less frequent, for the Hercynian forest keeps close till it has seen the last of its native Chatti. Hardy frames, close-knit limbs, fierce countenances, and a peculiarly vigorous courage, mark the tribe. For Germans, they have much intelligence and sagacity; they promote their picked men to power, and obey those whom they promote; they keep their ranks, note their opportunities, check their impulses, portion out the day, intrench themselves by night, regard fortune as a doubtful, valour as an unfailing, resource; and what is most unusual, and only brought by systematic discipline, they rely more on the general than on the army. Their whole strength is in their infantry, which, in addition to its arms, is laden with iron tools and provisions. Other tribes you see going to battle, the Chatti to a campaign. Seldom do they engage in mere raids and casual encounters. It is indeed the peculiarity of a cavalry force quickly to win and as quickly to yield a victory. Fleetness and timidity go together; deliberateness is more akin to steady courage.

31. A practice, rare among the other German tribes, and simply characteristic of individual prowess, has become general among the Chatti, of letting the hair and beard grow as soon as they have attained manhood, and not till they have slain a foe laying aside that

---

[4] Apparently a branch of the Chatti, located in the region of Nassau-Hesse, to the east of the middle Rhine, between the latter and the Lahn and Fulda rivers.
[5] The tithe-lands or *Agri Decumates* were in the triangular area between the upper Rhine and Danube rivers.
[6] In the Harz Mountains region.

peculiar aspect which devotes and pledges them to valour. Over the spoiled and bleeding enemy they show their faces once more, then, and not till then, proclaiming that they have discharged the obligations of their birth, and proved themselves worthy of their country and of their parents. The coward and the unwarlike remain unshorn. The bravest of them also wear an iron ring (which otherwise is a mark of disgrace among the people) until they have released themselves by the slaughter of a foe. Most of the Chatti delight in these fashions. Even hoary-headed men are distinguished by them, and are thus conspicuous alike to enemies and to fellow-countrymen. To begin the battle always rests with *them; they* form the first line, an unusual spectacle. Nor even in peace do they assume a more civilised aspect. They have no home or land or occupation; they are supported by whomsoever they visit, as lavish of the property of others as they are regardless of their own, till at length the feebleness of age makes them unequal to so stern a valour.

32. Next to the Chatti on the Rhine, which has now a well-defined channel, and serves as a boundary, dwell the Usipii and Tencteri.[7] The latter, besides the more usual military distinctions, particularly excel in the organisation of cavalry, and the Chatti are not more famous for their foot-soldiers than are the Tencteri for their horsemen. What their forefathers originated, posterity maintain. This supplies sport to their children, rivalry to their youths: even the aged keep it up. Horses are bequeathed along with the slaves, the dwelling-house, and the usual rights of inheritance; they go to the son, not to the eldest, as does the other property, but to the most warlike and courageous.

33. After the Tencteri came, in former days, the Bructeri;[8] but the general account now is, that the Chamavi and Angrivarii entered their settlements, drove them out and utterly exterminated them with the common help of the neighbouring tribes, either from hatred of their tyranny, or from the attractions of plunder, or from heaven's favourable regard for us. It did not even grudge us the spectacle of the conflict. More than sixty thousand fell, not beneath the Roman arms and weapons, but, grander far, before our delighted eyes. May the tribes, I pray, ever retain if not love for us, at least hatred for each other; for while the destinies of empire hurry us on, fortune can give no greater boon than discord among our foes.

34. The Angrivarii and Chamavi[9] are bounded in the rear by the

[7] The Usipii were located to the east of the lower Rhine, in the vicinity of Dusseldorf and the Ruhr River basin; the Tencteri were to the east of the Rhine south of the Usipii, between the Ruhr and Sieg rivers.
[8] The Bructeri were located to the east of the lower Rhine in the basins of the Lippe and upper Ems rivers.
[9] The Angrivarii established themselves in Westphalia in the region of the Weser River and towards the Elbe River; the Chamavi were in the Ems River region in a fluctuating area.

Dulgubini and Chasuarii,[10] and other tribes not equally famous. Towards the river are the Frisii,[11] distinguished as the Greater and Lesser Frisii, according to their strength. Both these tribes, as far as the ocean, are skirted by the Rhine, and their territory also embraces vast lakes which Roman fleets have navigated. We have even ventured on the ocean itself in these parts. Pillars of Hercules, so rumour commonly says, still exist; whether Hercules really visited the country, or whether we have agreed to ascribe every work of grandeur, wherever met with, to his renown. Drusus Germanicus[12] indeed did not lack daring; but the ocean barred the explorer's access to itself and to Hercules. Subsequently no one has made the attempt, and it has been thought more pious and reverential to believe in the actions of the gods than to inquire.

35. Thus far we have taken note of Western Germany. Northwards the country takes a vast sweep. First comes the tribe of the Chauci,[13] which, beginning at the Frisian settlements, and occupying a part of the coast, stretches along the frontier of all the tribes which I have enumerated, till it reaches with a bend as far as the Chatti. This vast extent of country is not merely possessed, but densely peopled, by the Chauci, the noblest of the German races, a nation who would maintain their greatness by righteous dealing. Without ambition, without lawless violence, they live peaceful and secluded, never provoking a war or injuring others by rapine and robbery. Indeed, the crowning proof of their valour and their strength is, that they keep up their superiority without harm to others. Yet all have their weapons in readiness, and an army if necessary, with a multitude of men and horses; and even while at peace they have the same renown of valour.

36. Dwelling on one side of the Chauci and Chatti, the Cherusci[14] long cherished, unassailed, an excessive and enervating love of peace. This was more pleasant than safe, for to be peaceful is self-deception among lawless and powerful neighbours. Where the strong hand decides, moderation and justice are terms applied only to the more powerful; and so the Cherusci, ever reputed good and just, are now called cowards and fools, while in the case of the victorious Chatti success has been identified with prudence. The downfall of the Cherusci brought with it also that of the Fosi,[15] a neighbouring tribe,

[10] The Dulgubini may have been located south or southwest of the Angrivarii; the Chasuarii may have been between the Ruhr and Lippe rivers to the east of the Rhine.
[11] The Frisians dwelt along the North Sea between the Rhine and the Ems.
[12] Drusus, a younger stepson of Augustus, temporarily expanded Roman holdings as far as the Elbe and won the title *Germanicus*.
[13] The Chauci were located along the North Sea coast between the Ems and the Elbe.
[14] The Cherusci were in the Brunswick area from the middle Weser to the Elbe.
[15] A small tribe in the Brunswick or Hanover region.

which shared equally in their disasters, though they had been inferior to them in prosperous days.

37. In the same remote corner of Germany, bordering on the ocean dwell the Cimbri,[16] a now insignificant tribe, but of great renown. Of their ancient glory widespread traces yet remain; on both sides of the Rhine are encampments of vast extent, and by their circuit you may even now measure the warlike strength of the tribe, and find evidence of that mighty emigration. Rome was in her 640th year when we first heard of the Cimbrian invader in the consulship of Caecilius Metellus and Papirius Carbo, from which time to the second consulship of the Emperor Trajan we have to reckon about 210 years. So long have we been in conquering Germany. In the space of this long epoch many losses have been sustained on both sides. Neither Samnite nor Carthaginian, neither Spain nor Gaul, not even the Parthians,[17] have given us more frequent warnings. German independence truly is fiercer than the despotism of an Arsaces.[18] What else, indeed, can the East taunt us with but the slaughter of Crassus, when it has itself lost Pacorus, and been crushed under a Ventidius? But Germans, by routing or making prisoners of Carbo, Cassius, Scaurus Aurelius, Servilius Caepio, and Marcus Manlius, deprived the Roman people of five consular armies,[19] and they robbed even a Caesar[1] of Varus and his three legions. Not without loss to us were they discomfited by Marius in Italy, by the great Julius in Gaul, and by Drusus, Nero, and Germanicus, on their own ground. Soon after, the mighty menaces of Caius Caesar were turned into a jest. Then came a lull, until on the occasion of our discords and the civil war, they stormed the winter camp of our legions, and even designed the conquest of Gaul. Again were they driven back; and in recent times we have celebrated triumphs rather than won conquests over them.

38. I must now speak of the Suevi,[2] who are not one nation as are the Chatti and Tencteri, for they occupy the greater part of Germany, and have hitherto been divided into separate tribes with names of their own, though they are called by the general designation of "Suevi." A national peculiarity with them is to twist their hair back,

---

[16] Apparently located in the Jutland peninsula (Denmark).

[17] Or Persians. See above, n. 6, p. 102.

[18] Or: "is more formidable (or dangerous) than the despotism of the Arsacids." The Arsacae or Arsacids were a dynasty of Parthian rulers, established about 250 B.C. by Arsaces, who overthrew Seleucid domination and set up an empire in the area of the old Persian Empire, which lasted until about A.D. 226.

[19] The Cimbri and Teutones in the later second century B.C., before they were stopped by Marius.

[1] Augustus, as a result of the disastrous battle of the Teutoberg Forest in A.D. 9.

[2] The Suevi, Suevians, or Suabians: designating a large part of the population of ancient Germany, centered about the basin or the Elbe, and between it and the Danube, and including the Hermunduri, Lombards, Semnones, Marcomanni, and other tribes.

and fasten it in a knot. This distinguishes the Suevi from the other Germans, as it also does their own freeborn from their slaves. With other tribes, either from some connection with the Suevic race, or, as often happens, from imitation, the practice is an occasional one, and restricted to youth. The Suevi, till their heads are grey, affect the fashion of drawing back their unkempt locks, and often they are knotted on the very top of the head. The chiefs have a more elaborate style, so much do they study appearance, but in perfect innocence, not with any thoughts of love-making; but arranging their hair when they go to battle, to make themselves tall and terrible, they adorn themselves, so to speak, for the eyes of the foe.

39. The Semnones[3] give themselves out to be the most ancient and renowned branch of the Suevi. Their antiquity is strongly attested by their religion. At a stated period, all the tribes of the same race assemble by their representatives in a grove consecrated by the auguries of their forefathers, and by immemorial associations of terror. Here, having publicly slaughtered a human victim, they celebrate the horrible beginning of their barbarous rite. Reverence also in other ways is paid to the grove. No one enters it except bound with a chain, as an inferior acknowledging the might of the local divinity. If he chance to fall, it is not lawful for him to be lifted up or to rise to his feet; he must crawl out along the ground. All this superstition implies the belief that from this spot the nation took its origin, that here dwells the supreme and all-ruling deity, to whom all else is subject and obedient. The fortunate lot of the Semnones strengthens this belief; a hundred cantons are in their occupation, and the vastness of their community makes them regard themselves as the heads of the Suevic race.

40. To the Langobardi,[4] on the contrary, their scanty numbers are a distinction. Though surrounded by a host of most powerful tribes, they are safe, not by submitting, but by daring the perils of war. Next come the Reudigni, the Aviones,[5] the Anglii,[6] the Varini, the Eudoses,[7] the Suardones, and Nuithones who are fenced in by rivers or forests. None of these tribes have any noteworthy feature, except their common worship of Ertha,[8] or mother-Earth, and their belief that she interposes in human affairs, and visits the nations in her car. In an island of the ocean there is a sacred grove, and within it a consecrated chariot, covered over with a garment. Only one priest

---

[3] The Semnones were apparently in the Brandenburg or Anhalt area by the middle Elbe and Oder.

[4] Lombards or "Long-beards": west of the middle and lower Elbe, north of the Saale River.

[5] Apparently in the Mecklenburg area.

[6] May have been dwelling at this time in the interior of Germany, in the vicinity of the Elbe, or, as we later find them, in Schleswig-Holstein.

[7] The Eudoses or Endoses may have been located in Denmark.

[8] Ertha or Nertha, Earth-Mother, who seems to have had various forms: Frigga, Freya, Holde, and Helda, according to her various functions.

is permitted to touch it. *He* can perceive the presence of the goddess in this sacred recess, and walks by her side with the utmost reverence as she is drawn along by heifers. It is a season of rejoicing, and festivity reigns wherever she deigns to go and be received. They do not go to battle or wear arms; every weapon is under lock; peace and quiet are known and welcomed only at these times, till the goddess, weary of human intercourse, is at length restored by the same priest to her temple. Afterwards the car, the vestments, and, if you like to believe it, the divinity herself, are purified in a secret lake. Slaves perform the rite, who are instantly swallowed up by its waters. Hence arises a mysterious terror and a pious ignorance concerning the nature of that which is seen only by men doomed to die. This branch indeed of the Suevi stretches into the remoter regions of Germany.

41. Nearer to us is the state of the Hermunduri[9] (I shall follow the course of the Danube as I did before that of the Rhine), a people loyal to Rome. Consequently they, alone of the Germans, trade not merely on the banks of the river, but far inland, and in the most flourishing colony of the province of Raetia. Everywhere they are allowed to pass without a guard; and while to the other tribes we display only our arms and our camps, to them we have thrown open our houses and country-seats, which they do not covet. It is in their lands that the Elbe takes its rise, a famous river known to us in past days; now we only hear of it.

42. The Narisci border on the Hermunduri, and then follow the Marcomanni and Quadi.[10] The Marcomanni stand first in strength and renown, and their very territory, from which the Boii were driven in a former age, was won by valour. Nor are the Narisci and Quadi inferior to them. This I may call the frontier of Germany, so far as it is completed by the Danube. The Marcomanni and Quadi have, up to our time, been ruled by kings of their own nation, descended from the noble stock of Maroboduus and Tudrus. They now submit even to foreigners; but the strength and power of the monarch depend on Roman influence. He is occasionally supported by our arms, more frequently by our money, and his authority is none the less.

43. Behind them the Marsigni, Gotini, Osi, and Buri, close in the rear of the Marcomanni and Quadi. Of these, the Marsigni and Buri,[11] in their language and manner of life, resemble the Suevi. The

---

[9] A large and powerful Suevian tribe between the Main and Danube rivers, occupying parts of Bavaria, Swabia, and Bohemia.

[10] The Narisci were located east of the Hemunduri and north of the Danube, between the latter and the Sudeten Mountains; the Marcomanni or "Men of the Marches" were in Bohemia by the first century A.D.; the Quadi were north of the Danube in Moravia and vicinity and about the source of the Elbe.

[11] The Marsigni were probably in northern Bohemia and southern Silesia on the upper Elbe; the Buri or Burii were in the region of the upper Vistula in the vicinity of Cracow.

Gotini and Osi[12] are proved by their respective Gallic and Panonian tongues, as well as by the fact of their enduring tribute, not to be Germans. Tribute is imposed on them as aliens, partly by the Sarmatae,[13] partly by the Quadi. The Gotini, to complete their degradation, actually work iron mines. All these nations occupy but little of the plain country, dwelling in forests and on mountain-tops. For Suevia is divided and cut in half by a continuous mountain-range,[14] beyond which live a multitude of tribes. The name of Ligii,[15] spread as it is among many states, is the most widely extended. It will be enough to mention the most powerful, which are the Harii,[16] the Helvecones,[17] the Manimi, the Helisii[18] and the Nahanarvali. Among these last is shown a grove of immemorial sanctity. A priest in female attire has the charge of it. But the deities are described in Roman language as Castor and Pollux. Such, indeed, are the attributes of the divinity, the name being Alcis. They have no images, or, indeed, any vestige of foreign superstition, but it is as brothers and as youths that the deities are worshipped. The Harii, besides being superior in strength to the tribes just enumerated, savage as they are, make the most of their natural ferocity by the help of art and opportunity. Their shields are black, their bodies dyed. They choose dark nights for battle, and, by the dread and gloomy aspect of their death-like host, strike terror into the foe, who can never confront their strange and almost infernal appearance. For in all battles it is the eye which is first vanquished.

44. Beyond the Ligii are the Gothones,[19] who are ruled by kings, a little more strictly than the other German tribes, but not as yet inconsistently with freedom. Immediately adjoining them, further from the coast, are the Rugii and Lemovii,[1] the badge of all these tribes being the round shield, the short sword, and servile submission to their kings.

And now begin the states of the Suiones,[2] situated on the Ocean[3] itself, and these, besides men and arms, are powerful in ships. The

12 The Gotini were in the region of Silesia; the Osi were apparently in Galicia.
13 The Sarmatae or Sarmatians were in eastern Poland and western Russia in a wide arc extending from the Vistula to the Volga.
14 The mountains which today separate Moravia, Hungary, Silesia, and Bohemia.
15 Ligii, Lugii, or Lugi: in the vicinity of the upper Oder and Vistula rivers in northeastern Germany and northwestern Poland. Also known as Lygians.
16 The Harii seem to have been located in Polish Prussia.
17 The Helevecones were apparently in northwestern Poland or northeastern Germany to the west of the Vistula.
18 The Helisii or Helusii or Elysians seem also to have been in Poland.
19 The Gothones dwelt in northeastern Pomerania and far northwestern Poland towards the mouth of the Vistula.
1 The Rugii or Rugians were probably in Pomerania in northeastern Germany along the Baltic Sea; the Lemovii or Lemovians seem also to have been situated in Pomerania, along the Baltic coast.
2 The Suiones or Swedes apparently occupied Sweden and the Danish isles to its southwest.
3 The Baltic Sea.

form of their vessels is peculiar in this respect, that a prow at either extremity acts as a forepart, always ready for running into shore. They are not worked by sails, nor have they a row of oars attached to their sides; but, as on some rivers, the apparatus of rowing is unfixed, and shifted from side to side as circumstances require. And they likewise honour wealth, and so a single ruler holds sway with no restrictions, and with no uncertain claim to obedience. Arms are not with them, as with the other Germans, at the general disposal, but are in the charge of a keeper, who is actually a slave; for the ocean forbids the sudden inroad of enemies, and, besides, an idle multitude of armed men is easily demoralized. And indeed it is by no means the policy of a monarch to place either a nobleman, a freeborn citizen, or even a freedman, at the head of an armed force.

45. Beyond the Suiones is another sea,[4] sluggish and almost motionless, which, we may certainly infer, girdles and surrounds the world, from the fact that the last radiance of the setting sun lingers on till sunrise, with a brightness sufficient to dim the light of the stars. Even the very sound of his rising, as popular belief adds, may be heard, and the forms of gods and the glory round his head may be seen. Only thus far (and here rumour seems truth) does the world extend.

At this point the Suevic sea,[5] on its eastern shore, washes the tribes of the Aestii,[6] whose rites and fashions and style of dress are those of the Suevi, while their language is more like the British. They worship the mother of the gods, and wear as a religious symbol the device of a wild boar. This serves as armour, and as a universal defence, rendering the votary of the goddess safe even amidst enemies. They often use clubs, iron weapons but seldom. They are more patient in cultivating corn and other produce than might be expected from the general indolence of the Germans. But they also search the deep, and are the only people who gather amber (which they call "glesum"), in the shallows, and also on the shore itself. Barbarians as they are, they have not investigated or discovered what natural cause or process produces it. Nay, it even lay amid the sea's other refuse, till our luxury gave it a name. To them it is utterly useless; they gather it in its raw state, bring it to us in shapeless lumps, and marvel at the price which they receive. It is however a juice from trees, as you may infer from the fact that there are often seen shining through it, reptiles, and even winged insects, which, having become entangled in the fluid, are gradually enclosed in the substance as it hardens. I am therefore inclined to think that the islands and countries of the West, like the remote recesses of the East, where frank-incense and

[4] Evidently the Arctic Ocean.
[5] The Baltic Sea.
[6] The Aestii or Aestui were apparently located in Prussia and Courland, east and southeast of the Baltic. Or they may have been the Ests of Esthonia.

balsam exude, contain fruitful woods and groves; that these productions, acted on by the near rays of the sun, glide in a liquid state into the adjacent sea, and are thrown up by the force of storms on the opposite shores. If you test the composition of amber by applying fire, it burns like pinewood, and sends forth a rich and fragrant flame; it is soon softened into something like pitch or resin.

Closely bordering on the Suiones are the tribes of the Sitones,[7] which, resembling them in all else, differ only in being ruled by a woman. So low have they fallen, not merely from freedom, but even from slavery itself. Here Suevia ends.

46. As to the tribes of the Peucini, Veneti,[8] and Fenni,[9] I am in doubt whether I should class them with the Germans or the Sarmatae, although indeed the Peucini, called by some Bastarnae, are like Germans in their language, mode of life, and in the permanence of their settlements. They all live in filth and sloth, and by the intermarriages of the chiefs they are becoming in some degree debased into a resemblance to the Sarmatae. The Veneti have borrowed largely from the Sarmatian character; in their plundering expeditions they roam over the whole extent of forest and mountain between the Peucini and Fenni. They are however to be rather referred to the German race, for they have fixed habitations, carry shields, and delight in strength and fleetness of foot, thus presenting a complete contrast to the Sarmatae, who live in waggons and on horseback. The Fenni are strangely beastlike and squalidly poor; neither arms nor homes have they; their food is herbs, their clothing skins, their bed the earth. They trust wholly to their arrows, which, for want of iron, are pointed with bone. The men and the women are alike supplied by the chase; for the latter are always present, and demand a share of the prey. The little children have no shelter from wild beasts and storms but a covering of interlaced boughs. Such are the homes of the young, such the resting place of the old. Yet they count this greater happiness than groaning over field-labour, toiling at building, and poising the fortunes of themselves and others between hope and fear. Heedless of men, heedless of gods, they have attained that hardest of results, the not needing so much as a wish. All else is fabulous, as that the Hellusii and Oxiones have the faces and expressions of men, with the bodies and limbs of wild beasts. All this is unauthenticated, and I shall leave it open.

---

[7] Some believe that the Sitones were located in Finland; others place them in Norway.
[8] The Veneti or Wends seem to have been Slavonic tribes to the east of the lower Vistula River.
[9] The Fenni or Finns were apparently northeast of the Vistula.

5

The Frankish Empire: An Amalgam of Christian, Roman, and German Elements

EINHARD

Just as the glory of the Greeks was their fifth century B.C. and the Persian Wars, and the pride of the Romans was the Augustan Age and the Pax Romana (c. 31 B.C.–A.D. 180), so the zenith of the kingdoms established by the German barbarians upon Roman soil was the Era of Charlemagne and the Carolingian Renaissance. For of the Germanic kingdoms, that of the Franks, which reached its apogee at the time of Charlemagne (A.D. 768–814), was the most successful and had the most enduring influence: political, military, social, religious, and cultural. Our principal source for the Carolingian era is Einhard's Life of Charlemagne.

An example of the contemporary spread of civilization and learning beyond the Rhine, the German Einhard was born of humble parents in the valley of the Main River, some time between 770 and 775. As a youth, he studied at the famous monastery of Fulda, which had been established by St. Boniface in Thuringia about seventy miles northeast of Frankfort-on-Main. Einhard displayed such promise that in 791 or 792 the Abbot of Fulda sent him to the court of Charlemagne. There, under the tutelage of the scholarly Saxon monk, Alcuin of York, he continued to progress in learning. Thus later the aging Alcuin referred Charlemagne to Einhard on a question concerning the classics, after he himself had retired to the monastery of Tours.

Einhard soon became Charlemagne's secretary and one of his most trusted counsellors. He was compared to "a busy ant" by a contemporary. His nickname in court circles was "Bezeleel," who is mentioned in Exodus (31:2) as having been a skilled builder of the Tabernacle of the Jews. He thus seems to have been something of an architect, and to have become Charlemagne's superintendent of construction. Some think that Einhard advised Charlemagne to crown Louis the Pious co-Emperor in 813. At any rate, Einhard's influence at the court of Louis, who succeeded his father in 814, was great.

It was evidently some time between 817 and 830 that Einhard wrote his Life of Charlemagne. About 828 or 830, rewarded with the titular (lay) abbacy of several monasteries, he retired from court life. He resided at the Abbey of Seligenstadt, not far from Fulda, where he sent his son to study and where he maintained contacts with famous scholars. He died in 840.

Einhard's life of Charles the Great bears certain similarities to Tacitus' Germania. It is our principal source concerning its subject; it is admirably concise, yet presents within its narrow compass an extraordinarily complete picture; it is carefully planned and logically organized. Although the author is frankly prejudiced in favor of his subject, most of his account has stood the test of time and historical criticism. But Einhard is on firmer ground than Tacitus, since he was an intimate associate of his subject for many years, whereas Tacitus had to rely largely on second-hand information. Tacitus pictures the "unspoiled" pagan and barbarous Germans; Einhard gives us a portrait of a great German who lived centuries later: one who personified that fusion of Teutonic, Roman, and Christian elements which constituted Western civilization in the Carolingian period.

Einhard wrote his Life of Charlemagne partly as a monument to the great achievements of his beloved benefactor, partly no doubt as a "blueprint" for Charlemagne's descendants, partly perhaps to satisfy a certain nostalgia for the "good old days." In the translation given here, the work is prefaced by a Prologue written by Walafrid Strabo, who was tutor to Charles the Bald from 829 to 838 and subsequently Abbot of Reichenau. After a brief preface by Einhard himself, the Life begins with a review of the Carolingian succession to 771, when Charlemagne became sole monarch on the death of his brother (sections 1-4). Next comes an account of the wars of Charlemagne and the resultant expansion of his realms (5-15), followed by a discussion of Charlemagne's diplomatic relations with foreign powers, his building program, and his measures for the defense of Frankland (16-17). After describing Charlemagne's private life (18-20), character and habits (21-24), and cultural interests and activities (25-29), the Life concludes with his last days, death, burial, and will (30-33).

Einhard gives us an excellent summary of the life and achievements of Charlemagne, and at the same time sheds considerable light on the life and customs of the time. Charlemagne's strong points are clearly delineated: his prodigious energy, his intelligence and versatility, his temperance in food and drink and his healthful habits in exercise, and above all his magnetic leadership. Nor does Einhard gloss over Charlemagne's strong sexuality: his numerous successive queens and mistresses (or morganatic wives), and his selfish, overprotective devotion to his daughters. The strength of the Church and of Christianity is evidenced in Charlemagne's personal piety, his numerous gifts to the Church, and his reverence for the Papacy. From beginning to end, Church and Churchmen play a prominent part in the narrative, from the papal approval of the Carolingian succession in 741 to the wording and terms of Charlemagne's last testament. The classical heritage of Carolingian culture is shown in Charlemagne's construction of imposing palaces and his church at Aachen, in his respect for Rome, his attempted revival of the Western Empire, and his personal coronation of his son as Imperator and Augustus. This classical heritage is reflected in another way in Einhard's biography — in the very language and structure of the work itself, written in Latin, modeled on Suetonius' life of Augustus in the Lives of the Caesars, and borrowing therefrom many appropriate expressions.

In general, Einhard's work is regarded as highly accurate, although there are a few errors concerning events which took place before he came to the court of Charlemagne and of which he had no first-hand knowledge. The Life of Charlemagne was very popular during the Middle Ages, and it remains one of the most prized biographies of all time. Subsequent lives of Charlemagne have drawn heavily on this original one by Einhard.

Einhard

Life of Charlemagne *

THE PROLOGUE OF WALAFRID[1]

THE following account of that most glorious Emperor Charles[2] was written, as is well known, by Einhard, who amongst all the palace officials of that time had the highest praise not only for learning but also for his generally high character; and, as he was himself present at nearly all the events that he describes, his account has the further advantage of the strictest accuracy.

* Translated by A. J. Grant (London: Chatto and Windus, 1907).
[1] Walafrid Strabo, one of the leading scholars and poets of the ninth century, was Abbot of Reichenau in the 840's.
[2] Charlemagne: co-King of the Franks, from 768; sole King, from 771; Emperor, from 800 until his death in 814.

He was born in eastern Frankland,[3] in the district that is called Moingewi, and it was in the monastery of Fulda, in the school of Saint Boniface the Martyr,[4] that his boyhood received its first training. Thence he was sent by Baugolf, the abbot of the monastery, to the palace of Charles, rather on account of his remarkable talents and intelligence, which even then gave bright promise of his wisdom that was to be so famous in later days, than because of any advantage of birth. Now, Charles was beyond all kings most eager in making search for wise men and in giving them such entertainment that they might pursue philosophy in all comfort. Whereby, with the help of God, he rendered his kingdom, which, when God committed it to him, was dark and almost wholly blind (if I may use such an expression), radiant with the blaze of fresh learning, hitherto unknown to our barbarism. But now once more men's interests are turning in an opposite direction, and the light of wisdom is less loved, and in most men is dying out.

And so this little man[5] — for he was mean of stature — gained so much glory at the Court of the wisdom-loving Charles by reason of his knowledge and high character that among all the ministers of his royal Majesty there was scarce anyone at that time with whom that most powerful and wise King discussed his private affairs more willingly. And, indeed, he deserved such favour, for not only in the time of Charles, but even more remarkably in the reign of the Emperor Lewis,[6] when the commonwealth of the Franks was shaken with many and various troubles, and in some parts was falling into ruin, he so wonderfully and providentially balanced his conduct, and, with the protection of God, kept such a watch over himself, that his reputation for cleverness, which many had envied and many had mocked at, did not untimely desert him nor plunge him into irremediable dangers.

This I have said that all men may read his words without doubting, and may know that, while he has given great glory to his great leader, he has also provided the curious reader with the most unsullied truth.

I, Strabo, have inserted the headings and the decorations as seemed well to my own judgement that he who seeks for any point may the more easily find what he desires.

Here ends the Prologue

[3] Austrasia, the older, more German, and more eastward part of Frankland, in the Rhineland.

[4] Fulda, long the leading monastery of Germany, by the Fulda River in Old Saxony, was jointly founded by Sts. Boniface and Sturm (its first abbot) about 744. Baugulf was Abbot of Fulda about 779–802. St. Boniface the Martyr, originally named Winfrid, was the missionary "Apostle of the Germans," 719–755. He was slain in 755, on a mission to the Frisians.

[5] Einhard became secretary to Charlemagne, as well as royal superintendent of construction, and an adviser of the monarch.

[6] Louis the Pious (814–840), son and successor of Charlemagne.

THE LIFE OF THE EMPEROR CHARLES
WRITTEN BY EINHARD

Having made up my mind to write an account of the life and conversation, and to a large extent of the actions of my lord and patron King Charles, of great and deservedly glorious memory, I have compressed my task within the narrowest possible limits. My aim has been on the one hand to insert everything of which I have been able to find an account; and on the other to avoid offending the fastidious by telling each new incident at wearisome length. Above all, I have tried to avoid offending in this new book those who look down upon even the monuments of antiquity written by learned and eloquent men.

There are, I do not doubt, many men of learning and leisure who feel that the life of the present day must not be utterly neglected, and that the doings of our own time should not be devoted to silence and forgetfulness as wholly unworthy of record; who, therefore, have such love of fame that they would rather chronicle the great deeds of others in writings, however poor, than, by abstaining from writing, allow their name and reputation to perish from the memory of mankind. But, even so, I have felt that I ought not to hold my hand from the composition of this book, for I knew that no one could write of these events more truthfully than I could, since I was myself an actor in them, and, being present, knew them from the testimony of my own eyes; while I could not certainly know whether anyone else would write them or no. I thought it better, therefore, to join with others in committing this story to writing for the benefit of posterity rather than to allow the shades of oblivion to blot out the life of this King, the noblest and greatest of his age, and his famous deeds, which the men of later times will scarcely be able to imitate.

Another reason, and not, I think, a foolish one, occurred to me, which even by itself would have been strong enough to persuade me to write — the care, I mean, that was taken with my upbringing, and the unbroken friendship which I enjoyed with the King himself and his children from the time when first I began to live at his Court. For in this way he has so bound me to himself, and has made me his debtor both in life and death, that I should most justly be considered and condemned as ungrateful if I were to forget all the benefits that he conferred upon me and were to pass over in silence the great and glorious deeds of a man who was so kind to me; if I were to allow his life to remain as unchronicled and unpraised, as if he had never lived, when that life deserves not merely the efforts of my poor talents, which are insignificant, small and almost non-existent, but all the eloquence of a Cicero.

So here you have a book containing the life of that great and glorious man. There is nothing for you to wonder at or admire except his deeds; unless, indeed, it be that I, a barbarian, and little versed in the Roman tongue, have imagined that I could write Latin inoffensively and usefully, and have become so swollen with impudence as to despise Cicero's words when, speaking about Latin writers in the first book of the Tusculans, he says: "If a man commits his thoughts to paper when he can neither arrange them well nor write them agreeably, nor furnish pleasure of any kind to the reader, he is recklessly misusing both his leisure and his paper." The great orator's opinion would, perhaps, have deterred me from writing if I had not fortified myself with the reflection that I ought to risk the condemnation of men, and bring my poor talents into peril by writing, rather than spare my reputation and neglect this great man's memory.

The Preface[7] ends: the Book begins

THE race of the Merovings,[8] from which the Franks were accustomed to choose their kings, is reckoned as lasting to King Hilderich,[9] who, by the order of Stephen,[10] the Roman Pontiff, was deposed, tonsured, and sent into a monastery. But this race, though it may be regarded as finishing with him, had long since lost all power, and no longer possessed anything of importance except the empty royal title. For the wealth and power of the kingdom was in the hands of the Praefects of the Court, who were called Mayors of the Palace, and exercised entire sovereignty. The King, contented with the mere royal title, with long hair and flowing beard, used to sit upon the throne and act the part of a ruler, listening to ambassadors, whencesoever they came, and giving them at their departure, as though of his own power, answers which he had been instructed or commanded to give. But this was the only function that he performed, for besides the empty royal title and the precarious life income which the Praefect of the Court allowed him at his pleasure, he had nothing of his own except one estate with a very small revenue, on which he had his house, and from which he drew the few servants who performed such services as were necessary and made him a show of deference. Wherever he had to go he travelled in a waggon, drawn in rustic style by a pair of oxen, and driven by a cowherd. In this fashion he used to go to the palace and to the general meetings of the people, which were held yearly for the affairs of the kingdom; in this fashion he returned home. But the Praefect of the Court looked after the

---

[7] Einhard's.

[8] Merovings or Merovingians, so called from Merovech, grandfather of Clovis, reigned in Frankland from 481 to 751.

[9] Hilderich or Childeric III, deposed by Pepin the Short in 751.

[10] Here Einhard is obviously mistaken. It was not Pope Stephen II (752) nor Stephen III (II) (752–757), but Pope Zachary (741–752) who approved the Carolingian accession to the Frankish crown.

administration of the kingdom and all that had to be done or arranged at home or abroad.

2. When Hilderich was deposed, Pippin,[11] the father of King Charles, was performing the duties of Mayor of the Palace as if by hereditary right. For his father Charles,[12] who put down the tyrants who were claiming dominion for themselves through all Frankland, and so crushed the Saracens, when they were attempting to conquer Gaul, in two great battles (the one in Aquitania, near the city of Poitiers,[13] the other near Narbonne, on the river Birra,) that he forced them to return into Spain — his father Charles had nobly administered the same office, and had inherited it from his father Pippin.[14] For the people did not usually give this honour except to such as were distinguished for the renown of their family and the extent of their wealth.

This office, then, was handed down from his father and his grandfather to Pippin, the father of King Charles, and to his brother Carloman.[15] He exercised it for some years conjointly with his brother Carloman on terms of the greatest harmony, still in nominal subordination to the above-mentioned King Hilderich. But then his brother Carloman, for some unknown cause, but probably fired with love of the contemplative life, abandoned the toilsome administration of a temporal kingdom and retired to Rome in search of peace. There he changed his dress, and, becoming a monk in the monastery upon Mount Soracte, built near the church of the blessed Silvester, enjoyed for some years the quiet that he desired, with many brethren, who joined themselves to him for the same purpose. But as many of the nobles of Frankland came on pilgrimage to Rome to perform their vows, and, unwilling to pass by one who had once been their lord, interrupted the peace that he most desired by frequent visits, he was compelled to change his abode. For, seeing that the number of his visitors interfered with his purpose, he left Mount Soracte and retired to the monastery of Saint Benedict, situated in the camp of Mount Cassino, in the province of Samnium. There he occupied what remained to him of this temporal life in religious exercises.

3. But Pippin, after he was made King instead of Mayor of the Palace by the authority of the Roman Pontiff, exercised sole rule over the Franks for fifteen years, or rather more.[16] Then, after finishing the Aquitanian war, which he had undertaken against Waifar, Duke

---

[11] Pippin or Pepin III, Charlemagne's father, was Mayor of the Palace, 741–751; King, 751–758.
[12] Charles Martel was Mayor of the Palace, 714–741.
[13] In the famous battle of Tours-Poitiers (732).
[14] Pepin II of Heristal, father of Charles Martel, ruled over East Frankland from 678, and over a united Frankland from 687. He died in 714.
[15] Carolman ruled jointly as Mayor with his brother Pepin III, the Short, until 747, when he retired to a monastery.
[16] Pepin III, the Short, Mayor from 741, ruled as King from 751 to 768.

EINHARD: *Life of Charlemagne*

of Aquitania, and had carried on for nine consecutive years, he died at Paris of the dropsy, and left behind him two sons, Charles[17] and Carloman,[18] to whom by divine will the succession of the kingdom came. For the Franks called a solemn public assembly, and elected both of them to be kings, on the understanding that they should equally divide the whole kingdom, but that Charles should receive for his special administration that part which his father Pippin had held, while Carloman received the territories ruled by their uncle Carloman.[19] The conditions were accepted and each received the share of the kingdom that was allotted to him. Harmony was maintained between the two brothers, though not without difficulty; for many partisans of Carloman tried to break their alliance, and some even hoped to engage them in war. But the course of events proved that the danger to Charles was imaginary rather than real. For, upon the death of Carloman, his wife with her sons and some of the leading nobles fled to Italy, and, for no obvious reason, passed over her husband's brother, and placed herself and her children under the protection of Desiderius, King of the Lombards. Carloman, after ruling the kingdom for two years conjointly with Charles, died of disease, and Charles, upon the death of Carloman, was made sole king with the consent of all the Franks.

4. It would be foolish of me to say anything about his birth and infancy, or even about his boyhood, for I can find nothing about these matters in writing, nor does anyone survive who claims to have personal knowledge of them. I have decided, therefore, to pass on to describe and illustrate his acts and his habits and the other divisions of his life without lingering over the unknown. I shall describe first his exploits both at home and abroad, then his habits and interests, and lastly the administration of the kingdom and the end of his reign, omitting nothing that demands or deserves to be recorded.

PART I
His Exploits at Home and Abroad

5. Of all the wars that he waged, that in Aquitania, begun, but not finished, by his father, was the first that he undertook, because it seemed easy of accomplishment. His brother was still alive, and was

---

[17] Charlemagne (Charles the Great).

[18] Carloman, Charlemagne's brother, ruled jointly with him from 768 to 771, but died in the latter year.

[19] This was not exactly the case. In 741, the dividing line ran more north and south; in 768, it ran more east and west. In 741, Carloman, the elder brother, received most of Austrasia, Alemannia (Swabia), and Thuringia (with Bavaria as a possible dependency); in 768, Carloman, the younger brother, received Burgundy, Provence, Septimannia, and Alemannia (with Bavaria as a possible dependency). Only Alemannia (with Bavaria as a possible dependency) is the same in both cases, so that differences exceed similarities.

called upon for assistance, and, though he failed to provide the help that he promised, Charles prosecuted the enterprise that he had undertaken with the utmost energy, and would not desist or slacken in his task before, by perseverance and continuous effort, he had completely reached the end after which he strove. For he forced Hunold, who after the death of Waifar had attempted to occupy Aquitania and renew the almost finished war, to abandon Aquitania and retire into Gascony. Even there he did not allow him to remain, but crossed the Garonne, and sent ambassadors to Lupus, Duke of the Gascons, ordering him to surrender the fugitive, and threatening him with war unless he did so at once. Lupus, more wisely, not only surrendered Hunold, but also submitted himself and the province over which he presided to the power of Charles.

6. When the Aquitanian trouble was settled and the war finished, when, too, his partner in the kingdom had withdrawn from the world's affairs, he undertook a war against the Lombards, being moved thereto by the entreaties and the prayers of Hadrian,[1] Bishop of the City of Rome. Now, this war, too, had been undertaken by his father at the supplication of Pope Stephen,[2] under circumstances of great difficulty, inasmuch as certain of the chiefs of the Franks, whose advice he was accustomed to ask, so strongly resisted his wishes that they openly declared that they would leave their King to return home. But now Charles undertook the war against King Haistulf,[3] and most swiftly brought it to an end. For, though his reasons for undertaking the war were similar to, and, indeed, the same as those of his father, he plainly fought it out with a very different energy, and brought it to a different end. For Pippin, after a siege of a few days at Pavia,[4] forced King Haistulf to give hostages, and restore to the Romans the towns and fortresses that he had taken from them, and to give a solemn promise that he would not attempt to regain what he had surrendered. But King Charles, when once he had begun the war, did not stop until he had received the surrender of King Desiderius, whom he had worn down after a long siege;[5] until he had forced his son Adalgis, in whom the hopes of his people seemed to be centred, to fly not only from his kingdom but from Italy; until he had restored to the Romans all that had been taken from them; until he had crushed Hruodgausus, Praefect of the Duchy of Friuli, who was attempting a revolution;[6] until, in fine, he had brought all Italy under

---

[1] Pope Hadrian I (772–795).
[2] Pope Stephen III (II) (752–757).
[3] This is a slip, since it is a chronological impossibility. For Haistulf or Aistulf, King of the Lombards 749–756, should obviously be substituted Desiderius, King of the Lombards 756–774.
[4] In 754.
[5] 773–774.
[6] Hrodgausus or Hrodgaud, Lombard Duke of Friuli in northeastern Italy, rose in revolt in 775, but was defeated in a battle in 776, in which he was slain.

his rule, and placed his son Pippin as king over the conquered country.[7] I should describe here the difficulties of the passage of the Alps and the vast toil with which the Franks found their way through the pathless mountain ridges, the rocks that soared to heaven, and the sharply-pointed cliffs, if it were not that my purpose in the present work is rather to describe Charles's manner of life than to chronicle the events of the wars that he waged. The sum of this war was the conquest of Italy, the transportation and perpetual exile of King Desiderius, the expulsion of his son Adalgis from Italy, power taken from the kings of the Lombards and restored to Hadrian, the Ruler of the Roman Church.[8]

7. When this war was ended, the Saxon war, which seemed dropped for a time, was taken up again. Never was there a war more prolonged nor more cruel than this, nor one that required greater efforts on the part of the Frankish peoples. For the Saxons, like most of the races that inhabit Germany, are by nature fierce, devoted to the worship of demons, and hostile to our religion, and they think it no dishonour to confound and transgress the laws of God and man. There were reasons, too, which might at any time cause a disturbance of the peace. For our boundaries and theirs touch almost everywhere on the open plain, except where in a few places large forests or ranges of mountains are interposed to separate the territories of the two nations by a definite frontier; so that on both sides murder, robbery, and arson were of constant occurrence. The Franks were so irritated by these things that they thought it was time no longer to be satisfied with retaliation but to declare open war against them.

So war was declared, and was fought for thirty years continuously[9] with the greatest fierceness on both sides, but with heavier loss to the Saxons than the Franks. The end might have been reached sooner had it not been for the perfidy of the Saxons. It is hard to say how often they admitted themselves beaten and surrendered as suppliants to King Charles; how often they promised to obey his orders, gave without delay the required hostages, and received the ambassadors that were sent to them. Sometimes they were so cowed and broken that they promised to abandon the worship of devils and willingly to submit themselves to the Christian religion. But though sometimes ready to bow to his commands, they were always eager to break their promise, so that it is impossible to say which course seemed to come more natural to them, for from the beginning of the war there

---

[7] Charlemagne's second son Pepin, originally called Carloman, became King of Italy about 780. He is not to be confused with Charlemagne's illegitimate son, Pepin the Hunchback, who later rose in unsuccessful revolt.

[8] The Donation of Charlemagne of the Papal States to the Pope in 774 renewed and confirmed the Donations made by his father, Pepin III, the Short, in 754 and 765, with minor modifications.

[9] Actually thirty-two to thirty-three years, 772–804. The term "continuously" is here used in a loose sense.

was scarcely a year in which they did not both promise and fail to perform.

But the high courage of the King and the constancy of his mind, which remained unshaken by prosperity and adversity, could not be conquered by their changes nor forced by weariness to desist from his undertakings. He never allowed those who offended in this way to go unpunished, but either led an army himself, or sent one under the command of his counts, to chastise their perfidy and inflict a suitable penalty. So that at last, when all who had resisted had been defeated and brought under his power, he took ten thousand of the inhabitants of both banks of the Elbe, with their wives and children, and planted them in many groups in various parts of Germany and Gaul. And at last the war, protracted through so many years, was finished on conditions proposed by the King and accepted by them; they were to abandon the worship of devils, to turn from their national ceremonies, to receive the sacraments of the Christian faith and religion, and then, joined to the Franks, to make one people with them.

8. In this war, despite its prolongation through so many years, he did not himself meet the enemy in battle more than twice — once near the mountain called Osning, in the district of Detmold, and again at the river Hasa — and both these battles were fought in one month, with an interval of only a few days. In these two battles the enemy were so beaten and cowed that they never again ventured to challenge the King nor to resist his attack unless they were protected by some advantage of ground.

In this war many men of noble birth and high office fell on the side both of the Franks and Saxons. But at last it came to an end in the thirty-third year, though in the meanwhile so many and such serious wars broke out against the Franks in all parts of the world, and were carried on which such skill by the King, that an observer may reasonably doubt whether his endurance of toil or his good fortune deserves the greater admiration. For the war in Italy began two years before the Saxon war, and though it was prosecuted without intermission, no enterprise in any part of the world was dropped, nor was there anywhere a truce in any struggle, however difficult. For this King, the wisest and most high-minded of all who in that age ruled over the nations of the world, never refused to undertake or prosecute any enterprise because of the labour involved, nor withdrew from it through fear of its danger. He understood the true character of each task that he undertook or carried through, and thus was neither broken by adversity nor misled by the false flatteries of good fortune.

9. Whilst the war with the Saxons was being prosecuted constantly and almost continuously, he placed garrisons at suitable places on the frontier, and attacked Spain with the largest military expedition that he could collect. He crossed the Pyrenees, received

the surrender of all the towns and fortresses that he attacked, and returned with his army safe and sound, except for a reverse which he experienced through the treason of the Gascons on his return through the passes of the Pyrenees. For while his army was marching in a long line, suiting their formation to the character of the ground and the defiles, the Gascons placed an ambuscade on the top of the mountain — where the density and extent of the woods in the neighbourhood rendered it highly suitable for such a purpose — and then, rushing down into the valley beneath, threw into disorder the last part of the baggage train and also the rearguard which acted as a protection to those in advance. In the battle which followed the Gascons slew their opponents to the last man. Then they seized upon the baggage, and under cover of the night, which was already falling, they scattered with the utmost rapidity in different directions. The Gascons were assisted in this feat by the lightness of their armour and the character of the ground where the affair took place. In this battle Eggihard, the surveyor of the royal table; Anselm, the Count of the Palace; and Roland, Praefect of the Breton frontier, were killed along with very many others.[10] Nor could this assault be punished at once, for when the deed had been done the enemy so completely disappeared that they left behind them not so much as a rumour of their whereabouts.

10. He conquered the Bretons, too, who dwelt in the extreme west of France by the shores of the ocean. They had been disobedient, and he, therefore, sent against them an expedition, by which they were compelled to give hostages and promise that they would henceforth obey his orders.

Then later he himself entered Italy with an army, and, passing through Rome, came to Capua, a city of Campania. There he pitched his camp, and threatened the men of Beneventum with war unless they surrendered. But Aragis, Duke of that people, prevented this war by sending his sons Rumold and Grimold to meet the King with a large sum of money. He asked the King to receive his children as hostages, and promised that he and his people would obey all the commands of the King, except only that he would not come himself into the King's presence. Charles, considering rather the advantage of the people than their Duke's obstinacy, received the hostages who were offered him, and as a great favour consented to forego a personal interview. He kept the younger of the two children as a hostage and sent back the elder one to his father. Then he sent ambassadors to require and receive oaths of fidelity from the Beneventans and from Aragis, and so came back to Rome. There he spent some days in the veneration of the holy places, and then returned to Gaul.

11. Then the Bavarian war broke out suddenly, and was swiftly

---

[10] It was apparently this event and reference which gave rise to the much-embellished *Song of Roland,* in which the Moslems rather than the Gascons attack the Frankish rearguard at Roncesvalles.

ended. It was caused by the pride and folly of Tassilo, Duke of Bavaria; for upon the instigation of his wife, who thought that she might revenge through her husband the banishment of her father Desiderius, King of the Lombards, he made an alliance with the Huns,[11] the eastern neighbours of the Bavarians, and not only refused obedience to King Charles but even dared to challenge him in war. The high courage of the King could not bear his overweening insolence, and he forthwith called a general levy for an attack on Bavaria, and came in person with a great army to the river Lech, which separates Bavaria from Germany. He pitched his camp upon the banks of the river, and determined to make trial of the mind of the Duke before he entered the province. But Duke Tassilo saw no profit either for himself or his people in stubborness, and threw himself upon the King's mercy. He gave the hostages who were demanded, his own son Theodo among the number, and further promised upon oath that no one should ever persuade him again to fall away from his allegiance to the King. And thus a war which seemed likely to grow into a very great one came to a most swift ending. But Tassilo was subsequently summoned into the King's presence, and was not allowed to return, and the province that he ruled was for the future committed to the administration not of dukes but of counts.

12. When these troubles had been settled he waged war against the Slavs, whom we are accustomed to call Wilzi, but who properly — that is, in their own tongue — are called Welatabi.[12] Here the Saxons fought along with the other allied nations who followed the King's standards, though their loyalty was feigned and far from sincere. The cause of the war was that the Wilzi were constantly invading and attacking the Abodriti, the former allies of the Franks, and refused to obey the King's commands to desist from their attacks. There is a gulf stretching from the western sea towards the East, of undiscovered length, but nowhere more than a hundred miles in breadth, and often much narrower. Many nations occupy the shores of this sea.[13] The Danes and the Swedes, whom we call the Northmen, called its northern shore and all the islands in it. The Slavs and the Aisti[14] and various other nations inhabit the eastern shore, amongst whom the chief are these Welatabi against whom then the King waged war. He so broke and subdued them in a single campaign, conducted by himself, that they thought it no longer wise to refuse to obey his commands.

13. The greatest of all his wars, next to the Saxon war, followed this one — that, namely which he undertook against the Huns and

---

[11] Actually the Avars, a people very similar to the Huns.
[12] Wilzi, Wiltzi, Weltzi, or Weltzes: located between the Elbe and the Baltic.
[13] Obviously the Baltic Sea.
[14] Or Ests, who gave their name to Esthonia.

the Avars.[15] He prosecuted this with more vigour than the rest and with a far greater military preparation. However, he conducted in person only one expedition into Pannonia, the province then occupied by the Avars; the management of the rest he left to his son Pippin, and the governors of the provinces, and in some cases to his counts and lieutenants. These carried on the war with the greatest energy, and finished it after eight years of fighting. How many battles were fought there and how much blood was shed is still shown by the deserted and uninhabited condition of Pannonia, and the district in which stood the palace of the Kagan[16] is so desolate that there is not so much as a trace of human habitation. All the nobles of the Huns were killed in this war, all their glory passed away; their money and all the treasures that they had collected for so long were carried away. Nor can the memory of man recall any war waged against the Franks by which they were so much enriched and their wealth so increased. Up to this time they were regarded almost as a poor people, but now so much gold and silver were found in the palace, such precious spoils were seized by them in their battles, that it might fairly be held that the Franks had righteously taken from the Huns what they unrighteously had taken from other nations. Only two of the nobles of the Franks were killed in this war. Eric, the Duke of Friuli, was caught in an ambuscade laid by the townsmen of Tharsatica, a maritime town of Liburnia. And Gerold, the Governor of Bavaria, when he was marshalling his army to fight with the Huns in Pannonia, was killed by an unknown hand, along with two others, who accompanied him as he rode along the line encouraging the soldiers by name. For the rest, the war was almost bloodless so far as the Franks were concerned, and most fortunate in its result although so difficult and protracted.

14. After this the Saxon war ended in a settlement as lasting as the struggle had been protracted. The wars with Bohemia and Luneburg which followed were soon over; both of them were swiftly settled under the command of the younger Charles.

The last war of all that Charles undertook was against those Northmen, who are called Danes, who first came as pirates, and then ravaged the coasts of Gaul and Germany with a greater naval force. Their King, Godofrid,[17] was puffed up with the vain confidence that he would make himself master of all Germany. He looked upon Frisia and Saxony as his own provinces. He had already reduced his neighbours the Abodriti to obedience, and had forced them to pay him tribute. Now he boasted that he would soon come to Aix,[18] the

---

[15] Einhard here, as earlier, uses the terms "Huns" and "Avars" interchangeably. As Einhard has related, the Avars had allied with Tassilo against Charlemagne.
[16] Khagan or King of the Avars.
[17] Godofrid or Godefrid, King of the Danes, died about 810.
[18] Aix-la-Chapelle or Aachen in Western Germany, by the Belgian border.

seat of the King's Court, with a mighty force. His boast, however idle, found some to believe it; it was thought that he would certainly have made some such attempt if he had not been prevented by a sudden death. For he was killed by one of his own followers, and so ended both his life and the war that he had begun.

15. These, then, are the wars which this mighty King waged during the course of forty-seven years — for his reign extended over that period — in different parts of the world with the utmost skill and success. By these wars he so nobly increased the kingdom of the Franks, which was great and strong when he inherited it from his father Pippin, that the additions he made almost doubled it. For before his time the power of the Frankish kingdom extended only over that part of Gaul which is bounded by the Rhine, the Loire, and the Balearic Sea[19]; and that part of Germany which is inhabited by the so-called eastern Franks, and which is bounded by Saxony, the Danube, the Rhine, and the river Saal, which stream separates the Thuringians and the Sorabs; and, further, over the Alamanni and the Bavarians. But Charles, by the wars that have been mentioned, conquered and made tributary the following countries: — First, Aquitania and Gascony, and the whole Pyrenean range, and the country of Spain as far as the Ebro, which, rising in Navarre and passing through the most fertile territory of Spain, falls into the Balearic Sea, beneath the walls of the city of Tortosa; next, all Italy from Augusta Praetoria[20] as far as lower Calabria, where are the frontiers of the Greeks and Beneventans, a thousand miles and more in length; next, Saxony, which is a considerable portion of Germany, and is reckoned to be twice as broad and about as long as that part of Germany which is inhabited by the Franks; then both provinces of Pannonia and Dacia, on one side of the river Danube, and Histria and Liburnia and Dalmatia, with the exception of the maritime cities which he left to the Emperor of Constantinople on account of their friendship and the treaty made between them; lastly, all the barbarous and fierce nations lying between the Rhine, the Vistula, the Ocean, and the Danube, who speak much the same language, but in character and dress are very unlike. The chief of these last are the Welatabi, the Sorabi,[1] the Abodriti, and the Bohemians; against these he waged war, but the others, and by far the larger number, surrendered without a struggle.

16. The friendship, too, which he established with certain kings and peoples increased the glory of his reign.

Adlefonsus, King of Gallaecia and Asturica,[2] was joined in so close an alliance with him that whenever he sent letters or ambassadors to

[19] The northwestern Mediterranean.
[20] In far northwestern Italy.
[1] The Sorabi or Sorbs were in the middle Elbe Valley, beyond Thuringia and between the Wiltzi and the Bohemians.
[2] Ildefonse or Ildefonso or Alfonso II (c. 790–842), King of Galicia and Asturias, a small Christian kingdom in far northwestern Spain.

Charles he gave instructions that he should be called "the man"[3] of the Frankish King.

Further, his rich gifts had so attached the kings of the Scots to his favour that they always called him their lord and themselves his submissive servants. Letters are still in existence sent by them to Charles in which those feelings towards him are clearly shown.

With Aaron, the King of the Persians,[4] who ruled over all the East, with the exception of India, he entertained so harmonious a friendship that the Persian King valued his favour before the friendship of all the kings and princes in the world, and held that it alone deserved to be cultivated with presents and titles. When, therefore, the ambassadors of Charles, whom he had sent with offerings to the most holy sepulchre of our Lord and Saviour and to the place of His resurrection, came to the Persian King and proclaimed the kindly feelings of their master, he not only granted them all they asked but also allowed that sacred place of our salvation to be reckoned as part of the possessions of the Frankish King. He further sent ambassadors of his own along with those of Charles upon the return journey, and forwarded immense presents to Charles — robes and spices, and the other rich products of the East — and a few years earlier he had sent him at his request an elephant, which was then the only one he had.

The Emperors of Constantinople, Nicephorus, Michael, and Leo,[5] too, made overtures of friendship and alliance with him, and sent many ambassadors. At first Charles was regarded with much suspicion by them, because he had taken the imperial title, and thus seemed to aim at taking from them their empire; but in the end a very definite treaty was made between them, and every occasion of quarrel on either side thereby avoided. For the Romans and the Greeks always suspected the Frankish power; hence there is a well-known Greek proverb: "the Frank is a good friend but a bad neighbour."

17. Though he was so successful in widening the boundaries of his kingdom and subduing the foreign nations, he, nevertheless, put on foot many works for the decoration and convenience of his kingdom, and carried some to completion. The great church dedicated to Mary, the holy Mother of God, at Aix, and the bridge, five hundred feet in length, over the great river Rhine near Mainz, may fairly be regarded as the chief of his works. But the bridge was burnt down a year before his death, and though he had determined to rebuild it of stone instead of wood, it was not restored, because his death so speedily followed. He began also to build palaces of splendid workmanship — one not far from the city of Mainz, near a town called Ingelheim; another at Nimeguen, on the river Waal, which flows along the south of the

---

[3] Or vassal.
[4] Harun al-Rashid or Aaron the Just, Caliph of Bagdad (786–809).
[5] The Byzantine emperors Nicephorus I, Michael I, and Leo V reigned successively in the period 802–820.

Batavian island.⁶ And he gave special orders to the bishops and priests who had charge of sacred buildings that any throughout his realm which had fallen into ruin through age should be restored, and he instructed his agents to see that his orders were carried out.

He built a fleet, too, for the war against the Northmen,⁷ constructing ships for this purpose near those rivers which flow out of Gaul and Germany into the northern ocean. And because the Northmen laid waste the coasts of Gaul and Germany by their constant attacks, he planted forts and garrisons in all harbours and at the mouths of all navigable rivers, and prevented in this way the passage of the enemy. He took the same measures in the South, on the shore of Narbonne and Septimania, and also along the coasts of Italy as far as Rome, to hold in check the Moors, who had lately begun to make piratical excursions. And by reason of these precautions Italy suffered no serious harm from the Northmen, in the days of Charles; except that Centumcellae, a city of Etruria, was betrayed into the hands of the Moors and plundered, and in Frisia certain islands lying close to Germany were ravaged by the Northmen.

PART II

Private Life and Character of Charlemagne

18. I have shown, then, how Charles protected and expanded his kingdom and also what splendour he gave to it. I shall now go on to speak of his mental endowments, of his steadiness of purpose under whatever circumstances of prosperity or adversity, and of all that concerns his private and domestic life.

As long as, after the death of his father, he shared the kingdom with his brother, he bore so patiently the quarrelling and restlessness of the latter as never even to be provoked to wrath by him. Then, having married at his mother's bidding the daughter of Desiderius, King of the Lombards, he divorced her, for some unknown reason, a year later. He took in marriage, Hildigard,⁸ of the Suabian race, a woman of the highest nobility, and by her he had three sons — viz. Charles and Pippin and Ludovicus,⁹ and three daughters — Hrotrud and Bertha and Gisla. He had also three other daughters — Theoderada and Hiltrud and Hruodhaid. Two of these were the children of his wife Fastrada, a woman of the eastern Franks or Germans; the third was the daughter of a concubine,¹⁰ whose name has escaped my

⁶ Nimeguen, Nimuegen, or Nimwegan, in the Dutch Netherlands.
⁷ The Northmen or Vikings, piratical raiders from Scandinavia.
⁸ Or Hildegard.
⁹ Pippin or Pepin: at first called Carloman, was King of Italy from 781 to 810. Ludovicus or Louis the Pious had a twin brother Lothar, who died in infancy, and is omitted, as are also two daughters of Charlemagne who died very young.
¹⁰ Some believe that by a "concubine" (here) and "concubines" (in the next sentence) Einhard has reference to legally married but morganatic wives, who did not share the throne or have a right to succession on the part of their progeny.

memory. On the death of Fastrada he married Liutgard, of the Alemannic race, by whom he had no children. After her death he had four concubines — namely Madelgarda, who bore him a daughter of the name of Ruothild; Gersuinda, of Saxon origin, by whom he had a daughter of the name of Adolthrud; Regina, who bore him Drogot and Hugo; and Adallinda, who was the mother of Theoderic.

His mother Bertrada lived with him to old age in great honour. He treated her with the utmost reverence, so that no quarrel of any kind ever arose between them — except in the matter of the divorce of the daughter of King Desiderius, whom he had married at her bidding. Bertrada died after the death of Hildigard, having lived to see three grandsons and as many granddaughters in her son's house. Charles had his mother buried with great honour in the same great church of St. Denys in which his father lay.

He had only one sister, Gisla, who from childhood was dedicated to the religious life. He treated her with the same affectionate respect as his mother. She died a few years before Charles's own death in the monastery in which she had passed her life.

19. In educating his children he determined to train them, both sons and daughters, in those liberal studies to which he himself paid great attention. Further, he made his sons, as soon as their age permitted it, learn to ride like true Franks, and practise the use of arms and hunting. He ordered his daughters to learn wool work and devote attention to the spindle and distaff, for the avoidance of idleness and lethargy, and to be trained to the adoption of high principles.

He lost two sons and one daughter before his death — namely, Charles, his eldest; Pippin, whom he made King of Italy; and Hruotrud, his eldest daughter, who had been betrothed to Constantine, the Emperor of the Greeks. Pippin left one son, Bernard, and five daughters — Adalheid, Atula, Gundrada, Berthaid, and Theoderada. In his treatment of them Charles gave the strongest proof of his family affection, for upon the death of his son he appointed his grandson Bernard to succeed him,[11] and had his granddaughters brought up with his own daughters.

He bore the deaths of his two sons and of his daughters with less patience than might have been expected from his usual stoutness of heart, for his domestic affection, a quality for which he was as remarkable as for courage, forced him to shed tears. Moreover, when the death of Hadrian, the Roman Pontiff, whom he reckoned as the chief of his friends, was announced to him, he wept for him as though he had lost a brother or a very dear son. For he showed a very fine disposition in his friendships: he embraced them readily and maintained them faithfully, and he treated with the utmost respect all whom he had admitted into the circle of his friends.

He had such care of the upbringing of his sons and daughters that

---

[11] As King of Italy (810–817). In 817, as punishment for revolting against Louis the Pious (814–840), Bernard was blinded and died as a consequence.

he never dined without them when he was at home, and never travelled without them. His sons rode along with him, and his daughters followed in the rear. Some of his guards, chosen for this very purpose, watched the end of the line of march where his daughters travelled. They were very beautiful, and much beloved by their father, and, therefore, it is strange that he would give them in marriage to no one, either among his own people or of a foreign state. But up to his death he kept them all at home, saying that he could not forego their society. And hence the good fortune that followed him in all other respects was here broken by the touch of scandal and failure. He shut his eyes, however, to everything, and acted as though no suspicion of anything amiss had reached him, or as if the rumour of it had been discredited.

20. He had by a concubine a son called Pippin — whom I purposely did not mention along with the others — handsome, indeed, but deformed.[12] When Charles, after the beginning of the war against the Huns, was wintering in Bavaria, this Pippin pretended illness, and formed a conspiracy against his father with some of the leaders of the Franks, who had seduced him by a vain promise of the kingdom. When the design had been detected and the conspirators punished, Pippin was tonsured and sent to the monastery of Prumia, there to practise the religious life, to which in the end he was of his own will inclined.

Another dangerous conspiracy had been formed against him in Germany at an earlier date. The plotters were some of them blinded and some of them maimed, and all subsequently transported into exile. Not more than three lost their lives, and these resisted capture with drawn swords, and in defending themselves killed some of their opponents. Hence, as they could not be restrained in any other way, they were cut down.

The cruelty of Queen Fastrada is believed to be the cause and origin of these conspiracies. Both were caused by the belief that, upon the persuasion of his cruel wife, he had swerved widely from his natural kindness and customary leniency. Otherwise his whole life long he so won the love and favour of all men both at home and abroad that never was the slightest charge of unjust severity brought against him by anyone.

21. He had a great love for foreigners, and took such pains to entertain them that their numbers were justly reckoned to be a burden not only to the palace but to the kingdom at large. But, with his usual loftiness of spirit, he took little note of such charges, for he found in the reputation of generosity and in the good fame that followed such actions a compensation even for grave inconveniences.

22. His body was large and strong; his stature tall but not ungainly,

---

[12] Pepin (or Pippin) the Hunchback, who conspired against his father in 792, was retired to the monastery of Prum, where he died in 811.

for the measure of his height was seven times the length of his own feet. The top of his head was round; his eyes were very large and piercing. His nose was rather larger than is usual; he had beautiful white hair; and his expression was brisk and cheerful; so that, whether sitting or standing, his appearance was dignified and impressive. Although his neck was rather thick and short and he was somewhat corpulent, this was not noticed owing to the good proportions of the rest of his body. His step was firm and the whole carriage of his body manly; his voice was clear, but hardly so strong as you would have expected. He had good health, but for four years before his death was frequently attacked by fevers, and at last was lame of one foot. Even then he followed his own opinion rather than the advice of his doctors, whom he almost hated, because they advised him to give up the roast meat to which he was accustomed, and eat boiled instead. He constantly took exercise both by riding and hunting. This was a national habit; for there is hardly any race on earth that can be placed on equality with the Franks in this respect. He took delight in the vapour of naturally hot waters, and constantly practised swimming, in which he was so proficient that no one could be fairly regarded as his superior. Partly for this reason he built his palace at Aix, and lived there continuously during the last years of his life up to the time of his death. He used to invite not only his sons to the bath but also his nobles and friends, and at times even a great number of his followers and bodyguards.

23. He wore the national — that is to say, the Frankish dress. His shirts and drawers were of linen, then came a tunic with a silken fringe, and hose. His legs were cross-gartered and his feet enclosed in shoes. In winter-time he defended his shoulders and chest with a jerkin made of the skins of otters and ermine. He was clad in a blue cloak, and always wore a sword, with the hilt and belt of either gold or silver. Occasionally, too, he used a jewelled sword, but this was only on the great festivals or when he received ambassadors from foreign nations. He disliked foreign garments, however beautiful, and would never consent to wear them, except once at Rome on the request of Pope Hadrian, and once again upon the entreaty of his successor, Pope Leo,[13] when he wore a long tunic and cloak, and put on shoes made after the Roman fashion. On festal days he walked in procession in a garment of gold cloth, with jewelled boots and a golden girdle to his cloak, and distinguished further by a diadem of gold and precious stones. But on other days his dress differed little from that of the common people.

24. He was temperate in eating and drinking, but especially so in drinking; for he had a fierce hatred of drunkenness in any man, and especially in himself or in his friends. He could not abstain so easily from food, and used often to complain that fasting was injurious to

[13] Leo III (795–816).

his health. He rarely gave large banquets, and only on the high festivals, but then he invited a large number of guests. His daily meal was served in four courses only, exclusive of the roast, which the hunters used to bring in on spits, and which he ate with more pleasure than any other food. During the meal there was either singing or a reader for him to listen to. Histories and the great deeds of men of old were read to him. He took delight also in the books of Saint Augustine, and especially in those which are entitled the City of God. He was so temperate in the use of wine and drink of any kind that he rarely drank oftener than thrice during dinner.

In summer, after his midday meal, he took some fruit and a single draught, and then, taking off his clothes and boots, just as he was accustomed to do at night, he would rest for two or three hours. At night he slept so lightly that he would wake, and even rise, four or five times during the night.

When he was putting on his boots and clothes he not only admitted his friends, but if the Count of the Palace told him there was any dispute which could not be settled without his decision he would have the litigants at once brought in, and hear the case, and pronounce on it just as if he were sitting on the tribunal. He would, moreover, at the same time transact any business that had to be done that day or give any orders to his servants.

25. In speech he was fluent and ready, and could express with the greatest clearness whatever he wished. He was not merely content with his native tongue but took the trouble to learn foreign languages. He learnt Latin so well that he could speak it as well as his native tongue; but he could understand Greek better than he could speak it. His fluency of speech was so great that he even seemed sometimes a little garrulous.

He paid the greatest attention to the liberal arts, and showed the greatest respect and bestowed high honours upon those who taught them. For his lessons in grammar he listened to the instruction of Deacon Peter of Pisa, an old man; but for all other subjects Albinus, called Alcuin, also a deacon, was his teacher — a man from Britain, of the Saxon race, and the most learned man of his time. Charles spent much time and labour in learning rhetoric and dialectic, and especially astronomy, from Alcuin. He learnt, too, the art of reckoning,[14] and with close application scrutinised most carefully the course of the stars. He tried also to learn to write, and for this purpose used to carry with him and keep under the pillow of his couch tablets and writing-sheets that he might in his spare moments accustom himself to the formation of letters. But he made little advance in this strange task,[15] which was begun too late in life.

[14] Arithmetic or mathematics.
[15] Or: "unaccustomed pursuit." Some authorities feel that this does not mean that Charlemagne did not know how to write, but that he was trying, without success, to master the calligraphy, or art of ornate and beautiful writing, practiced by contemporary scribes.

26. He paid the most devout and pious regard to the Christian religion, in which he had been brought up from infancy. And, therefore, he built the great and most beautiful church at Aix,[16] and decorated it with gold and silver and candelabras and with wicket-gates and doors of solid brass. And, since he could not procure marble columns elsewhere for the building of it, he had them brought from Rome and Ravenna. As long as his health permitted it, he used diligently to attend the church both in the morning and evening, and during the night, and at the time of the Sacrifice. He took the greatest care to have all the services of the church performed with the utmost dignity, and constantly warned the keepers of the building not to allow anything improper or dirty either to be brought into or to remain in the building. He provided so great a quantity of gold and silver vessels, and so large a supply of priestly vestments, that at the religious services not even the doorkeepers, who form the lowest ecclesiastical order, had to officiate in their ordinary dress. He carefully reformed the manner of reading and singing; for he was thoroughly instructed in both, though he never read publicly himself, nor sang except in a low voice, and with the rest of the congregation.

27. He was most devout in relieving the poor and in those free gifts which the Greeks call alms. For he gave it his attention not only in his own country and in his own kingdom, but he also used to send money across the sea to Syria, to Egypt, to Africa — to Jerusalem, Alexandria, and Carthage — in compassion for the poverty of any Christians whose miserable condition in those countries came to his ears.[17] It was for this reason chiefly that he cultivated the friendship of kings beyond the sea, hoping thereby to win for the Christians living beneath their sway some succour and relief.

Beyond all other sacred and venerable places he loved the church of the holy Apostle Peter at Rome, and he poured into its treasury great wealth in silver and gold and precious stones. He sent innumerable gifts to the Pope; and during the whole course of his reign he strove with all his might (and, indeed, no object was nearer to his heart than this) to restore to the city of Rome her ancient authority, and not merely to defend the church of Saint Peter but to decorate and enrich it out of his resources above all other churches. But although he valued Rome so much, still, during all the forty-seven years that he reigned, he only went there four times to pay his vows and offer up his prayers.

28. But such were not the only objects of his last visit; for the Romans had grievously outraged Pope Leo, had torn out his eyes and cut off his tongue, and thus forced him to throw himself upon the protection of the King. He, therefore came to Rome to restore the condition of the church, which was terribly disturbed, and spent the

---

[16] The central part of the domed, polygonal church built by Charlemagne still stands at Aachen, where it has been incorporated into the present cathedral.
[17] The Christians in this area were under Moslem sway.

whole of the winter there. It was then that he received the title of Emperor and Augustus, which he so disliked at first that he affirmed that he would not have entered the church on that day[18] — though it was the chief festival of the church — if he could have forseen the design of the Pope. But when he had taken the title, he bore very quietly the hostility that it caused and the indignation of the Roman emperors. He conquered their ill-feeling by his magnanimity, in which, doubtless, he far excelled them, and sent frequent embassies to them, and called them his brothers.

29. When he had taken the imperial title he noticed many defects in the legal systems of his people; for the Franks have two legal systems,[19] differing in many points very widely from one another, and he, therefore, determined to add what was lacking, to reconcile the differences, and to amend anything that was wrong or wrongly expressed. He completed nothing of all his designs beyond adding a few capitularies, and those unfinished. But he gave orders that the laws and rules of all nations comprised within his dominions which were not already written out should be collected and committed to writing.[1]

He also wrote out the barbarous and ancient songs, in which the acts of the kings and their wars were sung, and committed them to memory. He also began a grammar of his native language.

He gave the months names in his own tongue, for before his time they were called by the Franks partly by Latin and partly by barbarous names. He also gave names to the twelve winds, whereas before not more than four, and perhaps not so many, had names of their own. Of the months, he called January Winter-month, February Mud-month,[2] March Spring-month, April Easter-month, May Joy-month,[3] June Plough-month, July Hay-month, August Harvest-month,[4] September Wind-month, October Vintage-month, November Autumn-month,[5] December Holy-month. The following are the names which he gave to the winds: — The Subsolanus (east) he called East Wind; the Eurus (east by south) East-South Wind; the Euroaster (south by east) South-East Wind; the Auster (south) South Wind; the Austro-Afric (south by west) South-West Wind; the Afric (west by south) West-South Wind; the Zephyr (west) West Wind; the Corus (west by north) West-North Wind; the Circius (north by west) North-West Wind; the Septentrion (north) North Wind; the Aquilon (north by east) North-East Wind; the Vulturnus (east by north) East-North Wind.

30. At the very end of his life, when already he was feeling the

---

[18] On Christmas Day, A.D. 800.
[19] The Salian and Ripuarian laws.
[1] Thus the laws of the Frisians, **Thuringians, and Saxons.**
[2] Or Horn-shedding-month.
[3] Or Pasture-month.
[4] Or Ears (of grain)-month.
[5] Or Harvest-month.

pressure of old age and sickness,[6] he summoned his own son Lewis,[7] King of Aquitania, the only surviving son of Hildigard, and then solemnly called together the Frankish nobles of his whole kingdom. He then, with the consent of all, made Lewis partner in the whole kingdom and heir to the imperial title. After that, putting the diadem on Lewis' head, he ordered them to salute him "Imperator" and Augustus. This decision of his was received by all present with the greatest favour, for it seemed to them a divine inspiration for the welfare of the realm. It added to his dignity at home and increased the terror of his name abroad.

He then sent his son back to Aquitania, and himself, though broken with old age, proceeded to hunt, as his custom was, not far from the palace of Aix, and after spending the rest of the autumn in this pursuit he came back to Aix about the beginning of November. Whilst he was spending the winter there he was attacked by a sharp fever, and took to his bed. Then, following his usual habit, he determined to abstain from food, thinking that by such self-discipline he would be able either to cure or alleviate the disease. But the fever was complicated by a pain in the side which the Greeks call pleurisy; and, as Charles still persisted in fasting, and only very rarely drank something to sustain his strength, seven days after he had taken to his bed he received holy communion, and died, in the seventy-second year of his life and in the forty-seventh year of his reign, on the fifth day before the Kalends of February, at the third hour of the day.

31. His body was washed and treated with the usual ceremonies, and then, amidst the greatest grief of the whole people, taken to the church and buried. At first there was some doubt as to where he should rest, since he had given no instructions during his lifetime. But at length all were agreed that he could be buried nowhere more honourably than in the great church which he had built at his own expense in the same town, for the love of our Lord God Jesus Christ and the honour of His holy and ever-virgin Mother. There he was buried on the same day on which he died. A gilded arch was raised above the tomb, with his statue, and an inscription. The inscription ran as follows: —

> "Beneath this tomb lies the body of Charles, the great and orthodox Emperor, who nobly expanded the kingdom of the Franks and reigned prosperously for forty-seven years. He departed this life, more than seventy years of age, in the eight hundred and fourteenth year of our Lord, in the seventh indiction, on the fifth day before the Kalends of February."

32. There were many prodigies to show that his end drew near, and he as well as others understood the meaning of their warnings.

[6] In 813.
[7] Lewis or Louis the Pious, sole survivor of Charlemagne's legitimate sons, who succeeded his father as Emperor, 814–840.

During all the three last years of his life there were constant eclipses of sun and moon, and a black coloured spot appeared in the sun for the space of seven days. The gallery which he had built, of great size and strength, between the palace and the church, suddenly, on Ascension Day, fell in ruins down even to the foundations. Also, the wooden bridge over the Rhine near Mainz, which he had built with wonderful skill, and the labour of ten years, so that it seemed as though it would last for ever, was accidentally set on fire, and in three hours burnt so far that not a plank remained except those that were covered by the water. Further, when he was making his last expedition in Saxony against Godofrid, King of the Danes, as he was moving out of camp and beginning his march before sunrise, he suddenly saw a meteor rush across the heavens with a great blaze and pass from right to left through the clear sky. Whilst all were wondering what this sign meant, suddenly the horse that he was riding fell head foremost, and threw him so violently to the ground that the girdle of his cloak was broken, and his sword belt slipped from it. When his attendants ran up to help him they found him disarmed and disrobed. His javelin, too, which he was holding in his hand at the time of his fall, fell twenty paces and more away from him. Moreover, the palace at Aix was frequently shaken, and in houses where he lived there was a constant creaking in the fretted ceilings. The church in which he was afterwards buried was struck by lightning, and the golden apple that adorned the summit of the roof was thrown down by a thunderstroke, and fell upon the Bishop's house, which adjoined the church. In the same church an inscription was written on the edge of the circular space which ran round the inside of the church between the upper and lower arches, saying by whom the sacred edifice had been built. And in the last line occurred the words: "Carolus Princeps." Some noticed that in the very year in which Charles died, and a few months before his death, the letters of the word "princeps" were so destroyed as to be quite invisible. But he either refused to notice or despised all these omens as though they had no connection at all with anything that concerned him.

33. He had determined to draw out wills in order to make his daughters and the sons whom his concubines had borne to him heirs to some part of his property; but he took up this design too late, and could not carry it out. But some three years before he died he divided his treasures, his money and his robes, and all his other moveable property, in presence of his friends and ministers, and appealed to them to ratify and maintain by their support this division after his death. He also stated in a document how he wished to have the property which he had divided disposed of.[8] . . .

---

[8] Einhard now gives the terms of Charlemagne's will and the names of witnessing dignitaries, and concludes with the observation that Louis the Pious faithfully fulfilled his father's wishes.

6

Benedictine Monasticism: A Corporate Attempt to Realize Christ's Counsels

St. Benedict

The leading institution and leaven in early medieval Europe was the Christian Church, and the leading institution and leaven in the Church was monasticism: an organized, cooperative endeavor to put into practice the Christian counsels of perfection in the fullest, most sustained way possible. Like Christianity itself, monasticism originated in the eastern Mediterranean area, its principles and practices being eventually formulated by St. Basil of Caesarea, in the middle of the fourth century, into a commonly accepted Rule. Thence monasticism spread to the West, where it was at first practiced in various forms largely based on eastern models. In the early sixth century a sound and sane Rule adapted to Western habits and ideals was drawn up by St. Benedict of Nursia, and it was in the Benedictine form that monasticism spread throughout the West.

Because of the tremendous influence of his Rule, St. Benedict has been called "the Patriarch of Western Monasticism." He was born in the town of Nursia in north central Italy about A.D. 480. While still young, he went to Rome to study, but was so shocked by the prevailing licentiousness in this cosmopolitan center that he soon withdrew to the hilly country about forty miles east of the city to become a hermit. At Subiaco, in the vicinity of an old abandoned villa and artificial lakes of Nero, he found a cave, and there he lived for three years, praying and practicing extreme austerities. At the end of this time he was invited to become the head of a neighboring body of monks, who had recently lost their superior, but his efforts to enforce discipline and conformity to their rule so incited their anger that he narrowly escaped death by poisoning.

Benedict now returned to the region of Subiaco. His reputation for sanctity, wisdom, and miracle-working so spread that he attracted numerous disciples, whom he instructed, governed, and organized into some twelve monasteries. It was probably at this time, or very shortly thereafter, that he drew up his Rule. Because of the jealousy and animosity of a local priest, Benedict decided to withdraw from Subiaco, leaving his monasteries in charge of their own superiors; this was about 525-528. He journeyed southward to the vicinity of Cassino, about half way between Rome and Naples; and on a steep and rocky eminence overlooking the town, he founded the famous monastery of Monte Cassino. Benedict died about 543-545, having founded fourteen monasteries.

Whether Benedict composed his monastic Rule at the request of the Pope or of other abbots, or on his own initiative, there are indications that it was intended as a general guide for monasteries in various places. He specifically states that it is meant only as an elementary formulation of minimum essentials, obligatory for all in a monastic life, and this is probably all that a common Rule could be. Just as Basil of Caesarea had broken away from the hermitic life while retaining much of its spirit and many of its principles, so Benedict of Nursia departed from many features of Eastern monasticism while retaining its essential purpose and many of its aspects. In other words, Benedict formulated a new Rule, based on his experience with Western monks and his own good judgment, as well as on pre-existing monastic rules and ascetical literature. Benedict's sources in composing his Rule included the Rules of Sts. Basil, Pachomius, Macarius, and Caesarius of Arles, the Institutes and Conferences of Abbot John Cassian of Marsailles, and the Lives of the Egyption Fathers of the desert, as well as the writings of such Western Church Fathers as Sts. Augustine, Jerome, and Gregory the Great. Finally, a principal source, and the one Benedict quotes most frequently (about two hundred times), is the Bible.

Benedict's plan for monasticism was eminently successful. By the close of the sixth century, in the time of Pope Gregory I, it seems to have been generally followed in Italy, and had been introduced as far north as England. By the close of the eighth century, it was practically universal throughout Western Europe (outside of the Celtic lands: Ireland, Scotland, and Wales), so that Charlemagne could inquire whether there had ever been any other monastic rule.

The Rule of St. Benedict, the greater part of which is here given, is divided into 73 chapters, each with its own number and heading. The first seven chapters concern general principles of the monastic life; the next thirteen relate to recitation of the Divine Office: the common prayer of the monks. Chapters 21-67, the bulk of the text, have to do with various aspects of monastic organization, administration, and discipline. The concluding six chapters return to general principles.

The Rule of St. Benedict exhibits to us the way of life of what was in its day the most dynamic institution in the Western world. In it, Roman genius for social organization and Western realism are applied to Christian counsels of perfection and Eastern asceticism. The Rule retains highest ideals but tempers them with practicality. It is firm, yet flexible; imperative, yet patient; simple in conception, yet sufficiently detailed for workability. It is permeated by a spirit of faith and a trust in the word of God as found in the Bible and the teachings of the Church. More positive than negative, it breathes a spirit of love rather than one of fear. It reverences ecclesiastical traditions as transmitted in the writings of the Church Fathers and the great monastics, yet it exercises a rational discretion concerning them. It has confidence in the supreme efficacy of prayer, especially the common prayer of the Divine Office. Its ideal of monastic society is a divine family, in which God the Father is represented by the Abbot, and Christ is present in every brother. Benedict's pursuit of perfection is cooperative rather than individualistic, and the monastery is "a school of the divine service," in which the monks are trained to be soldiers of Christ and spiritual workmen.

Among particular means whereby monks are to effect their purposes are obedience, stability, prayer, reading, humility, moderation, prudence, and a definite, balanced schedule. In the Benedictine system, obedience to the Rule and the Abbot as to God is the key virtue. It is reinforced by the oath of stability, whereby a monk pledges himself to stay in the same monastery, and is not free to pick up and leave when he wishes. The chief external function of the monk is recitation of the Divine Office, the public prayer of the Church. Humility is his main armor, for it expresses his submission to God and his observance of the key virtue of obedience. The natural virtues of prudence and moderation are not obviated by the life of grace, but are raised to a supernatural plane. Just as individual repetition of good acts creates praiseworthy habits or virtues, so the social repetition of the regular daily schedule provided by the Rule makes an orderly and pious monastery. The twenty-four hours from sunrise to sunrise are, on the average, almost equally divided into (1) prayer and reading (4 plus 4, or 8 hours), (2) manual labor or some equivalent (7 hours), and (3) sleep and meals (8 plus 1, or 9 hours). Benedict's stress on reading implies prior education and represents a continuation of the same. An average of four hours daily, or about a fourth of the waking day, is set aside for private reading, in addition to the reading connected with the common recitation of the Divine Office, which occupies another fourth of the waking day.

In the Benedictine Rule we see the plan of spiritual training and religious life which came to be accepted in most of the monasteries of Western Europe. We see the system which made the monks who lived according to it the backbone of the medieval Church, the principal missionaries and teachers, and the moral inspiration and pattern for medieval society, as well as a leading source for zealous and able bishops, popes, and saints. It is estimated that by the thirteenth century there were more than 30,000 monasteries following the Benedictine way of life. But the continuing influence of the Rule extended far beyond monastic cloisters to society at large, and it affected virtually all subsequent religious orders and ascetic regimens, which retained most of its principles and many of its precepts.

St. Benedict of Nursia

The Rule of St. Benedict *

Prologue. . . .[1] We are about to found a training school for the Lord's service; in the organization of which we trust that we shall ordain nothing severe and nothing burdensome. But even if, the demands of justice dictating it, something a little irksome shall be the result, for the purpose of amending vices or preserving charity; — thou shalt not therefore, struck by fear, flee the way of salvation, which can not be entered upon except through a narrow entrance. But as one's way of life and one's faith progresses, the heart becomes broadened, and, with the unutterable sweetness of love, the way of the mandates of the Lord is traversed. Thus, never departing from His guidance, continuing in the monastery in His teaching until death, through patience we are made partakers in Christ's passion, in order that we may merit to be companions in His kingdom.

---

* Adapted from *Select Historical Documents of the Middle Ages*, translated and edited by Ernest F. Henderson, Bohn's Antiquarian Library (London: Bell and Sons, 1896), with the exception of numbers 4 and 7.

[1] Preceding this in the Prologue are pious exhortations and considerations calculated to inspire the reader and based on the Scriptural texts: "It is now the hour to rise from sleep"; "Turn from evil and do good"; "Lord, who shall dwell in thy tabernacle? He that walketh without stain and doth what is right"; "Not to us, O Lord, but to thy name give glory"; "By the grace of God I am what I am"; and "The Lord saith, 'I seek not the death of the sinner, but that he be converted and live.'"

1. *Concerning the kinds of monks and their manner of living.* It is manifest that there are four kinds of monks. The cenobites[2] are the first kind; that is, those living in a monastery, serving under a rule or an abbot. Then the second kind is that of the anchorites;[3] that is, the hermits, — those who, not by the new fervour of a conversion, but by the long probation of life in a monastery, have learned to fight against the devil, having already been taught by the solace of many. They, having been well prepared in the army of brothers for the solitary fight of the hermit, being secure now without the consolation of another, are able, God helping them, to fight with their own hand or arm against the vices of the flesh or of their thoughts.

But a third very bad kind of monks are the sarabaites,[4] approved by no rule, experience being their teacher, as with the gold which is tried in the furnace. But, softened after the manner of lead, keeping faith with the world by their works, they are known through their tonsure to lie to God. These, being shut up by twos or threes, or indeed, alone, without a shepherd, not in the Lord's but in their own sheep-folds, — their law is the satisfaction of their desires. For whatever they think good or choice, this they call holy; and what they do not wish, this they consider unlawful. But the fourth kind of monks is the kind which is called gyratory.[5] During their whole life they are guests, for three or four days at a time, in the cells of the different monasteries, throughout the various provinces; always wandering and never stationary, given over to the services of their own pleasures and the joys of the palate, and in every way worse than the sarabaites. Concerning the most wretched way of living of all of such monks it is better to be silent than to speak. These things therefore being omitted, let us proceed, with the aid of God, to treat of the best kind, the cenobites.

2. *What the Abbot[6] should be like.* An abbot who is worthy to preside over a monastery ought always to remember what he is called, and carry out with his deeds the name of a Superior. For he is believed to be Christ's representative, since he is called by His name, the apostle saying: "Ye have received the spirit of adoption of sons, whereby we call Abba, Father."[7] and so the abbot should not — grant that he may not — teach, or decree, or order, any thing apart from the precept of the Lord; but his order or teaching should be sprinkled with the ferment of divine justice in the minds of his disciples. Let the abbot always be mindful that, at the tremendous

---

[2] Term derived from Greek *koinos* (common) and *bios* (life); that is, those who live in a monastic community.
[3] From Greek *ana* (back) and *choreo* (retire); those who practice monasticism as individuals, by themselves.
[4] The etymology of this word, possibly of Egyptian origin, is uncertain. Without a rule or obedience, the sarabaites confused self-will with God's will.
[5] From Greek *gyros* (circle); wandering monks, rolling stones.
[6] From Semitic *abba* or *abbas* (father).
[7] Romans 8:15.

judgment of God, both things will be weighed in the balance: his teaching and the obedience of his disciples. And let the abbot know that whatever the father of the family finds of less utility among the sheep is laid to the fault of the shepherd. Only in a case where the whole diligence of their pastor shall have been bestowed on an unruly and disobedient flock, and his whole care given to their morbid actions, shall that pastor, absolved in the judgment of the Lord, be free to say to the Lord with the prophet: "I have not hid Thy righteousness within my heart, I have declared Thy faithfulness and Thy salvation,[8] but they despising have scorned me."[9] And then at length let the punishment for the disobedient sheep under his care be death itself prevailing against them. Therefore, when any one receives the name of abbot, he ought to rule over his disciples with a double teaching; that is, let him show forth all good and holy things by deeds more than by words. So that to ready disciples he may propound the mandates of God in words; but, to the hard-hearted and the more simple-minded, be may show forth the divine precepts by his deeds. But as to all the things that he has taught to his disciples to be wrong, he shall show by his deeds that they are not to be done; lest, preaching to others, he himself shall be found worthy of blame,[10] and lest God may say at some time to him a sinner: "What hast thou to do to declare my statutes or that thou should'st take my covenant in thy mouth. Seeing that thou hatest instruction and casteth my words behind thee;[11] and why beholdest thou the mote that is in thy brother's eye, but considerest not the beam that is in thine own eye?"[12] He shall make no distinction of persons in the monastery. One shall not be more cherished than another, unless it be the one whom he finds excelling in good works or in obedience. A freeborn man shall not be preferred to one coming from servitude, unless there be some other reasonable cause. But if, justice demanding that it should be thus, it seems good to the abbot, he shall do this no matter what the rank shall be. But otherwise they shall keep their own places; for whether we be bond or free we are all in one Christ;[13] and, under one God, we perform an equal service of subjection; for God is no respecter of persons.[14] Only in this way is a distinction made by Him concerning us: if we are found humble and surpassing others in good works. Therefore let him (the abbot) have equal charity for all: let the same discipline be administered in all cases according to merit.[15] In his teaching indeed the abbot ought always to ob-

[8] Psalms 39:11.
[9] Isaias 1:2.
[10] I Corinthians 9:27.
[11] Psalms 49:16–17.
[12] Matthew 7:3.
[13] I Corinthians 12:13.
[14] Ephesians 6:9.
[15] Note monastic democracy.

serve that form laid down by the apostle when he says: "reprove, rebuke, exhort."[16] That is, mixing seasons with seasons, blandishments with terrors, let him display the feeling of a severe yet devoted master. He should, namely, rebuke more severely the unruly and the turbulent. The obedient, moreover, and the gentle and the patient, he should exhort, that they may progress to higher things. But the negligent and scorners, we warn him to admonish and reprove. Nor let him conceal the sins of the erring: but, in order that he may prevail, let him pluck them out by the roots as soon as they begin to spring up; being mindful of the danger of Eli the priest of Shiloh.[17] And the more honest and intelligent minds, indeed, let him rebuke with words, with a first or second admonition; but the wicked and the hard-hearted and the proud, or the disobedient, let him restrain at the very beginning of their sin by castigation of the body, as it were, with whips: knowing that it is written: "A fool is not bettered by words."[18] And again: "Strike thy son with the rod and thou shalt deliver his soul from death."[19] The abbot ought always to remember what he is, to remember what he is called, and to know that from him to whom more is committed, the more is demanded. And let him know what a difficult and arduous thing he has undertaken, — to rule the souls and aid the morals of many. And in one case indeed with blandishments, in a second with rebukes, in another with persuasion — according to the quality or intelligence of each one, — he shall so conform and adapt himself to all, that not only shall he not suffer detriment to come to the flock committed to him, but shall rejoice in the increase of a good flock. Above all things, let him not, dissimulating or undervaluing the safety of the souls committed to him, give more heed to transitory and earthly and passing things: but let him always reflect that he has undertaken to rule souls for which he is to render account. And, lest perchance he enter into strife for a lesser matter, let him remember that it is written: "Seek ye first the kingdom of God and His righteousness; and all these things shall be added unto you."[1] And again: "They that fear Him shall lack nothing."[2] And let him know that he who undertakes to rule souls must prepare to render account. And, whatever number of brothers he knows that he has under his care, let him know for certain that at the day of judgment he shall render account to God for all their souls; his own soul without doubt being included. And thus, always fearing the future interrogation of the shepherd concerning the flocks entrusted to him, while keeping free from foreign interests, he

---

[16] II Timothy 4:2.
[17] I Kings 2:11–36. Eli and his family were severely punished for the sacrilegious sins of his sons.
[18] Proverbs 23:9; 23:19.
[19] Proverbs 23:14.
[1] Matthew 6:33.
[2] Psalms 111:1–3.

is rendered careful for his own. And when, by his admonitions, he administers correction to others, he is himself cleansed from his vices.

3. *About calling in the brethren to take council.* As often as anything especial is to be done in the monastery, the abbot shall call together the whole congregation, and shall himself explain the question at issue. And, having heard the advice of the brethren, he shall think it over by himself, and shall do what he considers most advantageous. And for this reason, moreover, we have said that all ought to be called to take counsel: because often it is to a younger person that God reveals what is best. The brethren, moreover, with all subjection of humility, ought to give their advice, that they do not presume boldly to defend what seems good to them; but it should rather depend on the judgment of the abbot; so that whatever he decides to be the more salutary, they should all agree to it. But even as it behooves the disciples to obey the master, so it is fitting that he should providently and justly arrange all matters. In all things, indeed, let all follow the Rule as their guide; and let no one rashly deviate from it. Let no one in the monastery follow the inclination of his own heart; and let no one boldly presume to dispute with his abbot, within or without the monastery. But, if he should so presume, let him be subject to the discipline of the Rule. The abbot, on the other hand, shall do all things fearing the Lord and observing the Rule; knowing that he, without a doubt shall have to render account to God as to a most impartial judge, for all his decisions. But if any lesser matters for the good of the monastery are to be decided upon, he shall employ the counsel of the elder members alone, since it is written: "Do all things with counsel, and after it is done thou wilt not repent."[3]

4. *What are the instruments of good works.* The instruments of good works are:[4]

> First of all, to love the Lord God with all our heart, with all our soul, and with all our strength.
> Next, to love our neighbour as ourself.
> Then, not to kill.
> Not to commit adultery.
> Not to steal.
> Not to be covetous.
> Not to bear false witness.
> To respect all men.
> Not to do to another what one would not like to have done to oneself.
> To deny oneself in order to follow Christ.
> To chastise the body.

---

[3] Ecclesiasticus 32:24.

[4] The following seventy-two commandments and counsels are drawn from the New and Old Testaments.

Not to be avid for pleasures.
To love fasting.
To feed the poor.
To clothe the naked.
To visit the sick.
To bury the dead.
To assist those in trouble.
To comfort those in sadness.
To become a stranger to the ways of the world.
To prefer nothing to the love of Christ.
Not to give way to wrath.
Not to harbour anger for any time.
Not to nurse deceit in the heart.
Not to make false peace.
Not to depart from charity.
Not to swear, lest perhaps one perjure oneself.
To bear the truth upon one's heart and lips.
Not to return evil for evil.
Not to do injustice, but to suffer injustice with patience.
To love one's enemies.
Not to speak ill of those who revile one; but rather to speak well of them.
To suffer persecution for the sake of what is right.
Not to be proud.
Not to be given to wine.
Not to be a great eater.
Not to be given to too much sleep.
Not to be slothful.
Not to be a murmurer.
Not to be a detractor.
To put one's hope in God.
When one sees any good in oneself, to attribute it to God rather than oneself.
On the other hand to recognize that evil is one's own doing, and to blame oneself.
To fear the judgment of God.
To dread the pains of Hell.
To long for life eternal with the full desire of one's soul.
To have the thought of death before one's eyes each day.
To keep watch over one's actions every hour of the day.
To know for certain that God sees one everywhere.
To dash against Christ (as against a rock) evil thoughts as soon as they arise in one's mind.
And to reveal all such to one's spiritual superior.
To guard one's mouth from uttering evil or wicked speech.
Not to be fond of much talking.
Not to talk without purpose or in such a way as to rouse laughter.
Not to be fond of great or excessive laughter.

Willingly to hear holy reading.
Often to devote oneself to prayer.
To confess to God in prayer one's past offences each day with sighs and tears, and to amend one's life in the future.
Not to follow the lusts of the flesh, and to hate one's own will.
In all things to obey the commands of the Abbot, even though he himself, which God forbid, act otherwise, mindful of our Lord's precept: "Do what they say, but do not do as they do."
Not to wish to be called holy before one is really holy, but to be holy first so that one may be more truly called such.
To fulfil God's commandments each day by one's actions.
To love chastity.
To hate no one.
Not to be jealous or vengeful.
Not to be fond of wrangling.
To avoid arrogance.
To reverence one's elders.
To love one's juniors.
To pray for one's enemies for the love of Christ.
To make peace with one's adversary before the sun sets.
And never to despair of God's mercy.

Behold these are the instruments of our spiritual craft. When we have made incessant use of them both day and night, and this is recognized on the day of judgment, our Lord will give us that reward which He promised, "Which eye hath not seen, nor ear heard, neither hath it entered into the heart of man to conceive what God hath prepared for those who love Him."[5] The workshops where we may diligently employ all of these are the cloisters of the monastery and stability in the community.[6]

5. *Concerning obedience.* The first grade of humility is obedience without delay. This becomes those who, on account of the holy service which they have professed, or on account of the fear of hell or the glory of eternal life, consider nothing dearer to them than Christ: so that, so soon as anything is commanded by their superior, they may not know how to suffer delay in doing it, even as if it were a divine command. Concerning whom the Lord said: "As soon as he heard me he obeyed me."[7] And again he said to the learned men: "He who heareth you heareth me."[8] Therefore let all such, straightway leaving their own affairs and giving up their own will, with unoccupied hands and leaving incomplete what they were doing — the

[5] I Corinthians 2:9.
[6] Stability in a monastic community was a key feature of the Benedictine Rule, since it gave the monk an opportunity to practice these virtues to the utmost.
[7] Psalms 17:45. Benedict made submission to God's will, expressed by obedience, the key monastic virtue.
[8] Luke 10:16.

foot of obedience being foremost, — follow with their deeds the voice of him who orders. And, as it were, in the same moment, let the aforesaid command of the master and the perfected work of the disciple — both together in the swiftness of the fear of God, — be called into being by those who are possessed with a desire of advancing to eternal life. And therefore let them seize the narrow way of which the Lord says: "Narrow is the way which leadeth unto life."[9] Thus, not living according to their own judgment nor obeying their own desires and pleasures, but walking under another's judgment and command, passing their time in monasteries, let them desire an abbot to rule over them. Without doubt all such live up to that precept of the Lord in which he says: "I am not come to do my own will but the will of him that sent me."[10] . . .

6. *Concerning silence.* Let us do as the prophet says: "I said, I will take heed to my ways that I sin not with my tongue, I have kept my peace even from good; and my sorrow was stirred."[11] Here the prophet shows that if one ought at times, for the sake of silence, to refrain from good sayings; how much more, as a punishment for sin, ought one to cease from evil words. . . . And therefore, if anything is to be asked of the prior, let it be asked with all humility and subjection of reverence; lest one seem to speak more than is fitting. Scurrilities, however, or idle words and those exciting laughter, we condemn in all places with a lasting prohibition: nor do we permit a disciple to open his mouth for such sayings.

7. *Concerning humility.* The divine writings cry out to us, brothers, saying: "Every one who exalts himself shall be humbled, and he who humbleth himself shall be exalted."[12] . . . Wherefore, brothers, if we would scale the summit of humility, and swiftly gain the heavenly height which is attained by lowliness in this present life, we must set up a ladder of ascending deeds like that which Jacob saw in his dreams.[13] . . . The first step of humility is reached when a man with the fear of God always before his eyes, does not permit himself to forget but is ever conscious of God's commandments. . . . The second step of humility is reached when one, denying his own will, takes no heed to satisfy his own desires, but copies in his life what our Lord says: "I came not to do my own will, but that of Him who sent me."[14] . . . The third step of humility is reached when a man, for the love of God, submits himself with all obedience to a superior. . . . The fourth step of humility is reached when one in the exercise of obedience bears patiently and with quiet mind all that is

---

9 Matthew 7:14.
10 John 5:30.
11 Psalms 38:2–3. Or: "I was dumb, and was humbled, and refrained from speaking about good things, and my sorrow was renewed."
12 Luke 14:11.
13 Genesis 28:12.
14 John 6:38.

imposed upon him, even harsh and contrary things and injustices. . . . The fifth step of humility is reached when a monk manifests to his abbot by humble confession all the evil thoughts that occur to his heart and his secret faults. . . . The sixth step of humility is reached when a monk is content with all that is meanest and lowest, and with regard to all that he is assigned to do, accounts himself a poor and worthless workman. . . . The seventh step of humility is reached when one not only confesses with his tongue that he is most lowly and inferior to others, but in his inmost heart believes so. . . . The eighth step of humility is reached when a monk does nothing but what the common rule of the monastery or the example of his elders enjoins. The ninth step of humility is reached when a monk refrains from talking, and, observing silence, does not speak until a question is asked of him. . . . The tenth step of humility is reached when one is not easily and quickly moved to laughter. . . . The eleventh step of humility is reached when a monk in speaking does so quietly and without laughter. . . . The twelfth step of humility is reached when a monk not only has humility in his heart, but also shows it exteriorly to all who sees him. . . .[15]

8. *Concerning the divine offices*[16] *at night.* In the winter time, that is from the Calends of November[17] until Easter, according to what is reasonable, they must rise at the eighth hour of the night,[18] so that they rest a little more than half the night, and rise when they have already digested.[19] But let the time that remains after vigils[1] be kept for meditation by those brothers who are in any way behind hand with the psalter or lessons.[2] From Easter, moreover, until the aforesaid Calends of November,[3] let the hour of keeping vigils be so

---

[15] To a considerable extent Benedict identifies the practice of humility with the exercise of his key virtue of obedience. It would seem that the number of "steps" in humility is somewhat stretched to bring them to twelve and thus to stress the virtue. We are told that in the first seven chapters, of which the present is the last, Benedict gives the general principles of his monastic Rule.

[16] The Divine Office, or Work of God, as St. Benedict called this oral common prayer of the Church, was considered the principal external work of the monk.

[17] From November 1 until Easter, or in winter. In Mediterranean countries there are really two seasons: the colder, wetter winter, and the warmer, dryer summer, as in our California.

[18] Day and night were divided into twelve "hours" each, with sunrise and sunset as the termini. Since the duration of daylight and darkness varied through the year, the day hours and the night hours were never of equal length except at the equinoxes, at which sunrise and sunset would be at about 6:00 A.M. and 6:00 P.M. respectively. The eighth hour, really the close of the eighth hour (like our hours "o'clock"), would thus come at about 2:00 A.M. at an equinox.

[19] Or: "are already refreshed."

[1] After Vigils or the night office (later known as Matins), there were about one and a half hours for spiritual reading, private prayer, or study, until Matins at dawn.

[2] The Psalter contained the 150 psalms which were to be recited by the monks at the night offices each week; the lessons were readings from the Scriptures and the Fathers.

[3] In the summer or warmer half of the Mediterranean year the nights would be shorter and each of their "hours" correspondingly briefer.

arranged that, a short interval being observed in which the brethren may go out for the necessities of nature, the matins, which are always to take place with the dawning light,[4] may straightway follow.[5]

10. *How in summer the nocturnal praise shall be carried on.* From Easter moreover until the Calends of November, the whole quantity of psalmody, as has been said above, shall be observed: except that the lessons from the Scripture, on account of the shortness of the nights, shall not be read at all.[6] But in place of those three lessons, one from the old Testament shall be said by memory, and a short response shall follow it. And everything else shall be carried out as has been said; that is, so that never less than the number of twelve psalms shall be said at nocturnal vigils; excepting the third and ninety-fourth psalm.

16. *How Divine Services shall be held through the day.* As the prophet says: "Seven times in the day do I praise Thee."[7] Which sacred number of seven will thus be fulfilled by us if, at matins, at the first, third, sixth, ninth hours, at vesper time, and at "completorium"[8] we perform the duties of our service; for it is of these hours of the day that he said: "Seven times in the day do I praise Thee." For, concerning nocturnal vigils, the same prophet says: "At midnight I arose to confess unto thee."[9] Therefore, at these times, let us give thanks to our Creator concerning the judgments of his righteousness; that is, at matins, and at night we will rise and confess to him.

18. *In what order the psalms are to be said.*[10] . . . The order of the daily psalmody having been arranged, all the rest of the psalms that remain shall be equally divided among the vigils[11] of the seven nights, separating, indeed, the psalms that are the longest among them; and twelve shall be appointed for each night. Laying great stress upon this fact, however, that if this distribution of psalms be not pleasing to any one, he shall arrange it otherwise if he think best; provided he sees to it under all circumstances that every week the entire psalter, to the number of 150 psalms, is said. And on Sunday at Vigils it shall always be begun anew. For those monks show a too scanty proof of their devotion, who, during the course of a week, sing less than the Psalter with its customary canticles: inasmuch as we read that

---

[4] Dawn was about an hour before sunrise, or at about 5:00 A.M. at the equinox.
[5] Matins (later known as Lauds) would thus come at about 5:00 A.M. at the equinox.
[6] Since the monks got less sleep in the shorter summer nights, with their briefer hours, the deficiency was made up by the customary Mediterranean siesta which lasted for about an hour after dinner.
[7] Psalms 118:164.
[8] Later: lauds, prime, terce, sext, none, vespers, and compline; said approximately at dawn, the end of the first hour after sunrise, the third hour, the sixth hour, the ninth hour, the eleventh hour (dusk), and the twelfth hour (sunset).
[9] Psalms 118:62.
[10] Benedict here gives a long list of psalms for the day offices.
[11] Later Matins.

our holy Fathers in one day rigidly fulfilled that, which would that we — lukewarm as we are — might perform in an entire week.

19. *Concerning the art of prayerful singing.* Whereas we believe that there is a divine presence, and that the eyes of the Lord look down everywhere upon the good and the evil: chiefly then, without any doubt, we may believe that this is the case when we are assisting at divine service. Therefore let us always be mindful of what the prophet says: "Serve the Lord in all fear";[12] and again, "Sing wisely";[13] and, "in the sight of the angels I will sing unto thee."[14] Therefore let us consider how we ought to conduct ourselves before the face of the divinity and his angels; and let us so stand and sing that our voice may accord with our intention.

20. *Concerning reverence for prayer.* If when to powerful men we wish to suggest anything, we do not presume to do it unless with reverence and humility: how much more should we supplicate with all humility, and devotion of purity, God who is the Lord of all. And let us know that we are heard, not for much speaking, but for purity of heart and compunction of tears. And, therefore, prayer ought to be brief and pure; unless perchance it be prolonged by the influence of the inspiration of the divine grace. When assembled together, then, let the prayer be altogether brief; and, the sign being given by the prior, let all rise together.

22. *How the monks shall sleep.* They shall sleep separately in separate beds. They shall receive positions for their beds, after the manner of their characters, according to the dispensation of their abbot. If it can be done, they shall all sleep in one place. If, however, their number do not permit it, they shall rest by tens or twenties, with elders who will concern themselves about them. A candle shall always be burning in that same cell until early in the morning. They shall sleep clothed, and girt with belts or with ropes; and they shall not have their knives at their sides while they sleep, lest perchance in a dream they should wound the sleepers.[15] And let the monks be always on the alert; and, when the signal is given, rising without delay, let them hasten to mutually prepare themselves for the service of God — with all gravity and modesty, however. The younger brothers shall not have beds by themselves, but interspersed among those of the elder ones.[16] And when they rise for the service of God, they shall exhort each other mutually with moderation, on account of the excuses that those who are sleepy are inclined to make.

23. *Concerning excommunication for faults.* If any one is found to be a scorner — being contumacious or disobedient, or a mur-

---

[12] Psalms 2:11.
[13] Psalms 46:8.
[14] Psalms 137:1.
[15] Note the rusticity and roughness suggested.
[16] A practical safeguard for discipline and morals.

murer,[17] or one acting in any way contrary to the holy Rule, and to the precepts of his elders: let such a one, according to the teaching of our Lord, be admonished once, and a second time, secretly, by his elders. If he do not amend his ways, he shall be rebuked publicly in the presence of all. But if, even then, he do not better himself — if he understands how great the penalty is — he shall be subject to excommunication. But, if he is a wicked man, he shall be given over to corporal punishment.

24. *What ought to be the measure of the excommunication.* According to the amount of the fault the measure of the excommunication or of the discipline ought to be extended:[18] which amount of the faults shall be determined by the judgment of the abbot. If any brother, however, be taken in lighter faults, he shall be prevented from participating at table. With regard to one deprived of participation at table, moreover, this shall be the regulation: that he shall not start a psalm or a chant in the oratory, or recite a lesson, until he has atoned. The refreshment of food, moreover, he shall take alone, after the refreshment of the brothers. So that if, for example, the brothers eat at the sixth hour, that brother shall do so at the ninth; if the brothers at the ninth, then he at Vespers; until by suitable satisfaction he gains pardon.

25. *Concerning graver faults.* That brother, moreover, who is held guilty of a graver fault shall be suspended at the same time from table and from the oratory. None of the brothers may in any way consort with him, or have speech with him. He shall be alone at the labour enjoined upon him, persisting in the struggle of penitence; knowing that terrible sentence of the Apostle who said that such a man was given over to the destruction of the flesh in order that his soul might be saved at the day of the Lord.[19] The refection of food moreover he shall take alone, in the measure and at the time that the abbot shall appoint as suitable for him. Nor shall he be blessed by any one who passes by, nor shall any food be given him.

27. *What care the abbot should exercise with regard to the excommunicated.* With all solicitude the abbot shall exercise care with regard to delinquent brothers: "They that be whole need not a physician, but they that are sick."[1] And therefore he ought to use every means, as a wise physician, to send in as it were secret consolers — that is, wise elders brothers who, as it were secretly, shall console the wavering brother and lead him to the atonement of humility. And they shall comfort him lest he be swallowed up by overmuch sorrow. On the contrary, as the same apostle says, charity shall be confirmed in him, and he shall be prayed for by all.[2] For the abbot should greatly

---

17 A complainer, criticizer, gossiper.
18 Note the prudence and moderation, yet decision and firmness.
19 I Corinthians 5:5.
1 Matthew 9:12.
2 II Corinthians 2:8.

exert his solicitude, and take care with all sagacity and industry, lest he lose any of the sheep entrusted to him. For he should know that he has undertaken the care of weak souls, not the tyranny over sound ones. And he shall fear the threat of the prophet through whom the Lord says: "Ye did take that which ye saw to be strong, and that which was weak ye did cast out."[3] And let him imitate the pious example of the good Shepherd, who, leaving the ninety and nine sheep upon the mountains, went out to seek the one sheep that had gone astray: and He had such compassion upon its infirmity, that He deigned to place it upon His sacred shoulders, and thus to carry it back to the flock.[4]

28. *Concerning those who, being often rebuked, do not amend.* If any brother, having frequently been rebuked for any fault, do not amend even after he has been excommunicated, a more severe rebuke shall fall upon him; — that is, the punishment of the lash shall be inflicted upon him. But if he do not even then amend; or, if perchance — which God forbid, — swelled with pride, he try even to defend his works: then the abbot shall act as a wise physician. If he have applied the fomentations and ointments of exhortation, the medicaments of the Divine Scriptures; if he have proceeded to the final cautery of excommunication, or to blows with rods, and if he see that his efforts avail nothing: let him also — what is greater — call in the prayer of himself and all the brothers for him: that God who can do all things may work a cure upon an infirm brother. But if he be not healed even in this way, then at last the abbot may use the pruning knife, as the apostle says: "Remove evil from you."[5] And again: "If the faithless one depart, let him depart."[6] lest one diseased sheep contaminate the whole flock.

29. *Whether brothers who leave the monastery ought again to be received.* A brother who goes out, or is cast out, of the monastery for his own fault, if he wish to return, shall first promise all amends for the fault on account of which he departed; and thus he shall be received into the lowest degree — so that thereby his humility may be proved. But if he again depart, up to the third time he shall be received. Knowing that after this every opportunity of return is denied to him.

30. *Concerning boys under age, how they shall be corrected.* Every age or intelligence ought to have its proper bounds. Therefore as often as boys or youths, or those who are less able to understand how great is the punishment of excommunication: as often as such persons offend, they shall either be afflicted with excessive fasts, or coerced with severe blows, that they may be healed.

[3] Ezechiel 34:3–5.
[4] Luke 15:4–6.
[5] I Corinthians 5–13.
[6] I Corinthians 7:15.

31. *Concerning the cellarer[7] of the monastery, what sort of a person he shall be.* As cellarer of the monastery there shall be elected from the congregation one who is wise, mature in character, sober, not given to much eating, not proud, not turbulent, not an upbraider, not tardy, not prodigal, but fearing God: a father, as it were, to the whole congregation. He shall take care of every thing, he shall do nothing without the order of the abbot. He shall have charge of what things are ordered: he shall not rebuff the brethren. If any brother by chance demand anything unreasonably from him, he shall not, by spurning, rebuff him; but reasonably, with humility, shall deny to him who wrongly seeks.

Let him guard his soul, mindful always of that saying of the apostle, that he who ministers well purchases to himself a good degree.[8] He shall care with all solicitude for the infirm and youthful, for guests and for the poor; knowing without doubt that he shall render account for all of these at the day of judgment. All the utensils of the monastery, and all its substance, he shall look upon as though they were the sacred vessels of the altar. He shall deem nothing worthy of neglect; nor shall he give way to avarice; nor shall he be prodigal or a squanderer of the substance of the monastery; but he shall do everything with moderation and according to the order of the abbot. He shall have humility above all things: and when there is nothing substantial for him to give, let a good word of reply be offered, as it is written: "a good word is above the best gift."[9] Every thing which the abbot orders him to have, let him have under his care; what he prohibits let him refrain from. To the brethren he shall offer the fixed measure of food without any haughtiness or delay, in order that they be not offended; being mindful of the divine saying as to what he merits "who offends one of these little ones."[10] If the congregation is rather large, assistants shall be given him; by whose aid he himself, with a calm mind, shall fill the office committed to him. At suitable hours those things shall be given which are to be given, and those things shall be asked for which are to be asked for: so that no one may be disturbed or rebuffed in the house of God.

32. *Concerning the utensils or property of the monastery.* For the belongings of the monastery in utensils, or garments, or property of any kind, the abbot shall provide brothers of whose life and morals he is sure; and to them as he shall see fit he shall consign the different things to be taken care of and collected. Concerning which the abbot shall keep a list, so that when in turn the brothers succeed each other in the care of the things assigned, he may know what he gives

---

[7] The cellarer had charge of food and drink, usually stored in the cellars for refrigeration purposes.
[8] I Timothy 3:13.
[9] Ecclesiasticus 18:17.
[10] Matthew 18:6.

or what he receives.¹¹ If moreover any one have soiled or treated negligently the property of the monastery, he shall be rebuked; but if he do not amend, he shall be subjected to the discipline of the Rule.

33. *Whether the monks should have any thing of their own.* More than any thing else is this special vice to be cut off root and branch from the monastery, that one should presume to give or receive anything without the order of the abbot, or should have anything of his own. He should absolutely not have anything: neither a book, nor tablets, nor a pen — nothing at all. — For indeed it is not allowed to the monks to have their own bodies or wills in their own power. But all things necessary they must expect from the Father of the monastery; nor is it allowable to have anything which the abbot did not give or permit. All things shall be common to all, as it is written: "Let not any man presume or call anything his own."¹² But if any one shall have been discovered delighting in this most evil vice: being warned once and again, if he do not amend, let him be subjected to punishment.

34. *Whether all ought to receive necessaries equally.* As it is written: "It was divided among them singly, according as each had need":¹³ whereby we do not say — far from it — that there should be an excepting of persons, but a consideration for infirmities. Wherefore he who needs less, let him thank God and not be dismayed; but he who needs more, let him be humiliated on account of his infirmity, and not exalted on account of the mercy that is shown him. And thus all members will be in peace. Above all, let not the evil of murmuring¹⁴ appear, for any cause, through any word or sign whatever. But, if such a murmurer is discovered, he shall be subjected to stricter discipline.

35. *Concerning the weekly officers of the kitchen.* The brothers shall so serve each other in turn that no one shall be excused from the duty of cooking,¹⁵ unless either through sickness, or because he is occupied in some important work of utility. For, by this means, charity and a greater reward are acquired. Moreover assistants shall be provided for the weak, so that they may not do this as a burden, but may all have helpers according to the size of the congregation or the nature of the place. If the congregation is a large one, the cellarer, or any who, as we have said, are occupied with matters of greater utility, shall be excused from cooking. The rest shall serve each other in turn with all charity. At the end of the week he (the weekly cook) shall, on Saturday, do the cleansing. . . .

36. *Concerning infirm brothers.* Before all, and above all, attention

¹¹ An inventory. Note the care for practical details.
¹² Acts 4:32.
¹³ Acts 4:35.
¹⁴ Complaining.
¹⁵ Note the democracy: even the scion of a noble or a king was not exempt from work in the kitchen.

shall be paid to the care of the sick; so that they shall be served as if it were actually Christ. For He himself said: "I was sick and ye visited me."[16] And: "Inasmuch as ye have done it unto one of the least of these ye have done it unto me."[17] But let the sick also consider that they are being served to the honour of God; and let them not offend by their abundance the brothers who serve them: which (offences) nevertheless are patiently to be borne, for, from such, a greater reward is acquired. Wherefore let the abbot take the greatest care lest they suffer neglect. And for these infirm brothers a cell by itself shall be set apart, and a servitor, God-fearing, and diligent and careful. The use of baths shall be offered to the sick as often as it is necessary: to the healthy, and especially to youths, it shall not be so readily conceded.[18] But also the eating of flesh shall be allowed to the sick, and altogether to the feeble, for their rehabilitation. But when they have grown better, they shall all, in the usual manner, abstain from flesh. The abbot, moreover, shall take the greatest care lest the sick are neglected by the cellarer or by the servitors: for whatever fault is committed by the disciples rebounds upon him.

37. *On the old and the young.* Although human nature itself is prone to have pity for these ages — that is, old age and infancy, — nevertheless the authority of the Rule also has regard for them. Their weakness shall always be considered, and in the matter of food, the strict tenor of the Rule shall by no means be observed, as far as they are concerned; but they shall be treated with pious consideration, and may anticipate the canonical hours.

38. *Concerning the weekly reader.* At the tables of the brothers when they eat, the reading should not fail; nor may any one at random dare to take up the book and begin to read there; but he who is about to read for the whole week shall begin his duties on Sunday. And, entering upon his office after mass and communion, he shall ask all to pray for him, that God may avert from him the spirit of elation. And this verse shall be said in the oratory three times by all, he however beginning it: "O Lord open Thou my lips and my mouth shall show forth Thy praise."[19] And thus, having received the benediction, he shall enter upon his duties as reader. And there shall be the greatest silence at table, so that the muttering or the voice of no one shall be heard there, except that of the reader alone. But whatever things are necessary to those eating and drinking, the brothers shall so furnish them to each other in turn, that no one shall need to ask for anything. But if, nevertheless, something is wanted, it shall rather be sought by the employment of some sign than by the voice. . . .

[16] Matthew 25:36.
[17] Matthew 25:40.
[18] Bathing was considered something of a luxury and an indulgence of the senses, not to be permitted too often.
[19] Psalms 50:17.

39. *Of the amount of food.* We believe, moreover, that, for the daily refection of the sixth as well as of the ninth hour, two cooked dishes, on account of the infirmities of the different ones, are enough for all tables: so that whoever, perchance, can not eat of one may partake of the other. Therefore let two cooked dishes suffice for all the brothers: and, if it is possible to obtain apples or growing vegetables, a third may be added. One full pound of bread shall suffice for a day, whether there be one refection, or a breakfast and a supper. But if they are going to have supper, the third part of that same pound shall be reserved by the cellarer, to be given back to those who are about to sup. But if, perchance, some greater labour shall have been performed, it shall be in the will and the power of the abbot, if it is expedient, to increase anything; surfeiting[1] above all things being guarded against, so that indigestion may never seize a monk: for nothing is so contrary to every Christian as surfeiting, as our Lord says: "Take heed to yourselves, lest your hearts be overcharged with surfeiting." But to younger boys the same quantity shall not be served, but less than that to the older ones; moderation being observed in all things. But the eating of the flesh of quadrupeds[2] shall be abstained from altogether by every one, excepting alone the weak and the sick.

40. *Concerning the amount of drink.* Each one has his own gift from God, the one in this way, the other in that.[3] Therefore it is with some hesitation that the amount of daily sustenance for others is fixed by us. Nevertheless, in view of the weakness of the infirm we believe that a hemina[4] of wine a day is enough for each one. Those moreover to whom God gives the ability of bearing abstinence shall know that they will have their own reward. But the prior shall judge if either the needs of the place, or labour or the heat of summer, requires more; considering in all things lest satiety or drunkenness creep in. Indeed we read that wine is not suitable for monks at all. But because, in our day, it is not possible to persuade the monks of this, let us agree at least as to the fact that we should not drink till we are sated, but sparingly.[5] For wine can make even the wise to go astray. Where, moreover, the necessities of the place are such that the amount written above can not be found, — but much less or nothing at all, — those who live there shall bless God and shall not murmur. And we admonish them as to this above all: that they be without murmuring.

41. *At what hours the brothers ought to take their refection.* From

---

[1] Over-eating or "stuffing oneself": gluttony.

[2] The flesh of four-legged animals, which would include beef, pork, mutton, and venison, was forbidden; but not that of poultry and other birds. Exception was made, however, for the sick.

[3] I Corinthians 7:7.

[4] About a pint.

[5] This passage permitting the temperate use of wine is often cited as an example of the moderation of Benedict's Rule.

the holy Easter time until Pentecost[6] the brothers shall have their refection at the sixth hour;[7] and at evening they shall sup.[8] From Pentecost, moreover, through the whole summer, — if the monks do not have hard labour in the fields, or the extreme heat of the summer does not prevent them, — they shall fast on the fourth and sixth day until the ninth hour;[9] but on the other days they shall have their repast at the sixth hour. Which sixth hour, if they have ordinary work in the fields, or if the heat of summer is not great, shall be kept to for the repast; and it shall be for the abbot to decide. And he shall so temper and arrange all things, that their souls may be saved on the one hand; and that, on the other, what the brothers do they shall do without any justifiable murmuring. Moreover, from the ides of September until the beginning of Lent, they shall always have their refection at the ninth hour.[10] But in Lent, until Easter, they shall have their refection at Vesper time.[11] And that same Vesper meal shall be so arranged that those who take their repast may not need the light of a lantern; but everything shall be consumed while it is still daylight. But indeed at all times, the hour, whether of supper or of refection, shall be so arranged, that everything may be done while it is still light.

42. *That after "completorium"*[12] *no one shall speak.* At all times the monks ought to practise silence, but most of all in the nocturnal hours. And thus at all times, whether of fasting or of eating: if it be meal-time, as soon as they have risen from the table, all shall sit together and one shall read selections or lives of the Fathers, or indeed anything which will edify the hearers. But not the Pentateuch or Kings; for, to weak intellects, it will be of no use at that hour to hear this part of Scripture; but they shall be read at other times. But if the days are fast days, when Vespers have been said, after a short interval they shall come to the reading of the selections as we have said; and four or five pages, or as much as the hour permits having been read, they shall all congregate, upon the cessation of the reading. If, by chance, any one is occupied in a task assigned to him, he shall nevertheless approach. All therefore being gathered together, they shall say the completing prayer; and, going out from the "completorium,"

---

[6] Easter came between March 22 and April 25, and usually fell in April.

[7] Dinner at noon.

[8] A lighter supper was taken before sunset during this time.

[9] During the summer, after Pentecost or Whitsunday, they did not eat dinner until about 2:30 P.M. on Wednesdays and Fridays, on which day they had no supper.

[10] From the fifteenth of September until the beginning of Lent (which commenced about 46 days before Easter), that is, during the winter half of the year, the monks did not eat dinner until the ninth hour, about 2:30 or 3:00 P.M., and had no supper.

[11] During Lent the monks ate their sole meal at about 5:00 P.M.

[12] Completorium or Compline was the final day office said before retiring. Thus in Lent it was said at about 6:00 P.M. (sunset) and lasted about half an hour.

there shall be no further opportunity for any one to say anything. But if any one be found acting contrary to this rule of silence, he shall be subjected to a very severe punishment. Unless a necessity in the shape of guests should arise, or the abbot, by chance, should give some order. But even this, indeed, he shall do most seriously, with all gravity and moderation.

45. *Concerning those who make mistakes in the oratory.* If any one, in saying a psalm, response, or antiphone or lesson, make a mistake: unless he humble himself there before all, giving satisfaction, he shall be subjected to greater punishment, as one who was unwilling to correct by humility that in which he had erred by neglect. But children, for such a fault, shall be whipped.[13]

46. *Concerning those who err in any other matters.* If any one commit any fault while at any labour, in the kitchen, in the cellar, in the offices, in the bakery, while labouring at any art, or in any place; or shall break or lose anything, or commit any excess wherever he may be; and do not himself, coming before the abbot or the congregation, of his own accord give satisfaction and declare his error: if it become known through another, he shall be subjected to greater amends. But if the cause of his sin lie hidden in his soul, he may declare it to the abbot alone or to his spiritual elders; who may know how to cure his wounds, and not to uncover and make public those of another.

48. *Concerning the daily manual labour.* Idleness is the enemy of the soul. And therefore, at fixed times, the brothers ought to be occupied in manual labour; and again, at fixed times, in sacred reading. Therefore we believe that, according to this disposition, both seasons ought to be arranged; so that, from Easter until the Calends of October, going out early, from the first until the fourth hour they shall do what labour may be necessary. Moreover, from the fourth hour until about the sixth, they shall be free for reading. After the meal of the sixth hour, moreover, rising from table, they shall rest in their beds with all silence; or, perchance, he that wishes to read may so read to himself that he do not disturb another. And the ninth hour of the office (none) shall be said a bit earlier about the middle of the eighth hour;[14] and again they shall work at what is to be done until Vespers.[15] But, if the exigency or poverty of the place demands that they be occupied by themselves in picking fruits, they shall not be

---

[13] Benedict believed in the adage, "Spare the rod and spoil the child." It was believed that moderate corporal punishment was a "means of communication" with the young.

[14] About 1:30 P.M.

[15] Thus during the summer season, including our late spring and early fall, the monks were to be occupied in manual labor or some equivalent work from about 7:00 to 10:00 A.M. and about 2:00 to 5:00 P.M.; and with reading from about 10:00 A.M. to 12:00 noon and, if they wished, during siesta time from about 12:30 to 1:30 P.M.

dismayed: for then they are truly monks if they live by the labours of their hands; as did also our fathers and the apostles. Let all things be done with moderation, however, on account of the fainthearted. From the Calends of October, moreover, until the beginning of Lent they shall be free for reading until the second full hour. At the end of which, terce shall be said, following which all shall labour at the task which is enjoined upon them until the ninth. The first signal, moreover, of the ninth hour having been given, they shall each one leave off his work; and be ready when the second signal strikes. Moreover after the refection they shall be free for their readings or for psalms.[16] But in the days of Lent, from dawn until the third full hour, they shall be free for their readings; and, until the tenth full hour, they shall do the labour that is enjoined on them.[17] In which days of Lent they shall all receive separate books from the library;[18] which they shall read entirely through in order. These books are to be given out on the first day of Lent. Above all there shall certainly be appointed one or two elders, who shall go round the monastery at the hours in which the brothers are engaged in reading, and see to it that no troublesome brother chance to be found who is open to idleness and trifling, and is not intent on his reading; being not only of no use to himself, but also stirring up others. If such a one — may it not happen — be found, he shall be admonished once and a second time. If he do not amend, he shall be subject under the Rule to such punishment that the others may have fear. Nor shall brother join brother at unsuitable hours. Moreover on Sunday all shall engage in reading: excepting those who are deputed to various duties. But if anyone be so negligent and lazy that he will not or can not read, some task shall be imposed upon him which he can do; so that he be not idle. On feeble or delicate brothers such a labour or art is to be imposed, that they shall neither be idle, nor shall they be so oppressed by the violence of labour as to be driven to take flight. Their weakness is to be taken into consideration by the abbot.

49. Although at all times the life of the monk should be such as though Lent were being observed: nevertheless, since few have that virtue, we urge that, on those said days of Lent, he shall keep his life in all purity; and likewise wipe out, in those holy days, the negligencies of other times. This is then worthily done if we refrain from all vices, if we devote ourselves to prayer with weeping, to reading and

[16] Thus during the winter season, including late fall and early spring, the monks were to be occupied with manual labor or some equivalent work from about 8:30 A.M. to 2:30 P.M.; and with reading from about 6:00 to 8:30 A.M. and from about 3:00 to 4:30 P.M.

[17] In Lent the monks were occupied with reading from about 5:00 to 9:00 A.M.; and with manual labor or some equivalent from about 9:30 A.M. to 4:00 P.M. Time out was taken only for the recitation of brief hours of the Divine Office such as terce, sext, and none.

[18] It may readily be seen how this encouraged and even necessitated the copying of manuscripts.

compunction of heart, and to abstinence. Therefore, on these days, let us add of ourselves something to the ordinary amount of our service: special prayers, abstinence from food and drink; — so that each one, over and above the amount allotted to him, shall offer of his own will something to God with rejoicing of the Holy Spirit. That is, he shall restrict his body in food, drink, sleep, talkativeness, and merry-making; and, with the joy of a spiritual desire, shall await the holy Easter. The offering, moreover, that each one makes, he shall announce to his abbot; that it may be done with his prayers and by his will. For what is done without the permission of the spiritual Father, shall be put down to presumption and vain glory, and not to a monk's credit. Therefore all things are to be done according to the will of the abbot.[19]

50. *Concerning brothers who labour far from the oratory, or who are on a journey.* Brothers who are at work very far off, and cannot betake themselves at the proper hour to the oratory, shall, if the abbot deem this to be the case, celebrate the Divine Service there where they are at work; bending their knees in the fear of God. Likewise as to those who are sent on a journey: the established hours shall not escape them; but, according as they can, they shall perform of themselves, and not neglect to render, the rightful amount of service. . . .

53. *Concerning the reception of guests.* All guests who come shall be received as though they were Christ: for He Himself said: "I was a stranger and ye took me in."[1] And to all, fitting honour shall be shown; but, most of all, to servants of the faith and to pilgrims. When, therefore, a guest is announced, the prior or the brothers shall run to meet him, with every office of love.[2] And first they shall pray together; and thus they shall be joined together in peace. Which kiss of peace shall not first be offered, unless a prayer have preceded; on account of the wiles of the devil. In the salutation itself, moreover, all humility shall be exhibited. In the case of all guests arriving or departing: with inclined head, or with prostrating of the whole body upon the ground, Christ, who is also received in them, shall be adored. The guests moreover, having been received, shall be conducted to prayer; and afterwards the prior, or one whom he himself orders, shall sit with them. The law of God shall be read before the guest that he may be edified; and, after this, every kindness shall be exhibited. A fast may be broken by the prior on account of a guest; unless, perchance, it be a special day of fast which can not be violated. The brothers, moreover, shall continue their customary fasts. The

---

[19] Austerities other than those prescribed by the Rule were to be approved by the monk's superior.

[1] Matthew 25:35.

[2] Medieval monasteries were proverbial for their hospitality and served as hostels in out-of-the-way places.

abbot shall give water into the hands of his guests; and the abbot as well as the whole congregation shall wash the feet of all guests. This being done, they shall say this verse: "We have received, oh Lord, Thy loving-kindness in the midst of Thy temple."[3] Chiefly in the reception of the poor and of pilgrims shall care be most anxiously exhibited: for in them Christ is received the more. For the very fear of the rich exacts honour for them. The kitchen of the abbot and the guests shall be by itself; so that guests coming at uncertain hours, as is always happening in a monastery, may not disturb the brothers. . . .

55. *Of clothing and shoes.* Vestments shall be given to the brothers according to the quality of the places where they dwell, or the temperature of the air. For in cold regions more is required; but in warm, less. This, therefore, is a matter for the abbot to decide. We nevertheless consider that for ordinary places there suffices for the monks a cowl and gown apiece — the cowl, in winter hairy, in summer plain or old, — and a working garment, on account of their labours. As clothing for the feet, shoes and boots. Concerning the colour and size of all of which things the monks shall not talk; but they shall be such as can be found in the province where they are or as can be bought the most cheaply. The abbot, moreover, shall provide, as to the measure, that those vestments be not short for those using them; but of suitable length. And, when new ones are received, they shall always straightway return the old ones, to be kept in the vestiary on account of the poor. It is enough, moreover, for a monk to have two gowns and two cowls; on account of the nights, and on account of washing the things themselves. Every thing, then, that is over this is superfluous, and ought to be removed. And the shoes, and whatever is old, they shall return when they receive something new. And those who are sent on a journey shall receive cloths for the loins from the vestiary; which on their return they shall restore, having washed them. And there shall be cowls and gowns somewhat better than those which they have ordinarily: which, when they start on a journey, they shall receive from the vestiary, and, on returning, shall restore. As trappings for the beds, moreover, shall suffice a mat, a woollen covering, a woollen cloth under the pillow, and the pillow. . . .

56. *Concerning the table of the abbot.* The table of the abbot shall always be with the guests and pilgrims. As often, however, as guests are lacking, it shall be in his power to summon those of the brothers whom he wishes. He shall see, nevertheless, that one or two elders are always left with the brothers, for the sake of discipline.

57. *Concerning the artificers[4] of the monastery.* Artificers, if there are any in the monastery, shall practise with all humility their special arts, if the abbot permit it. But if any one of them becomes in-

---

[3] Psalms 47:10.
[4] Craftsmen: shoemakers, smiths, cabinetmakers, etc.

flated with pride on account of knowledge of his art, to the extent that he seems to be conferring something on the monastery: such a one shall be plucked away from that art; and he shall not again return to it unless the abbot perchance again orders him to, he being humiliated. But, if anything from the works of the artificers is to be sold, they themselves shall take care through whose hands they (the works) are to pass, lest they (the intermediaries) presume to commit some fraud upon the monastery. They shall always remember Ananias and Sapphira;[5] lest, perchance, the death that they suffered with regard to the body, these, or all those who have committed any fraud as to the property of the monastery, may suffer with regard to the soul. In the prices themselves, moreover, let not the evil of avarice crop out: but let the object always be given a little cheaper than it is given by other and secular persons; so that, in all things, God shall be glorified.

58. *Concerning the manner of receiving brothers.* When any new comer applies for conversion, an easy entrance shall not be granted him: but, as the apostle says, "Try the spirits if they be of God."[6] Therefore, if he who comes perseveres in knocking, and is seen after four or five days to patiently endure the insults inflicted upon him, and the difficulty of ingress, and to persist in his demand: entrance shall be allowed him, and he shall remain for a few days in the cell of the guests. After this, moreover, he shall be in the cell of the novices, where he shall meditate and eat and sleep. And an elder[7] shall be detailed off for him who shall be capable of saving souls, who shall altogether intently watch over him, and make it a care to see if he reverently seek God, if he be zealous in the service of God, in obedience, in suffering shame. And all the harshness and roughness of the means through which God is approached shall be told him in advance. If he promise perseverance in his steadfastness, after the lapse of two months this Rule shall be read to him in order, and it shall be said to him: Behold the law under which thou dost wish to serve; if thou canst observe it, enter; but if thou canst not, depart freely. If he have stood firm thus far, then he shall be led into the aforesaid cell of the novices; and again he shall be proven with all patience. And, after the lapse of six months, the Rule shall be read to him; that he may know upon what he is entering. And, if he stand firm thus far, after four months the same Rule shall again be re-read to him. And if, having deliberated with himself, he shall promise to keep everything, and to obey all the commands that are laid upon him: then he shall be received in the congregation; knowing that it is decreed, by the law of the Rule, that from that day he shall not be allowed to depart from the monastery,[8] nor to shake free his neck from the

---

[5] Acts 5:1–10.
[6] I John 4:1.
[7] This "elder" came to be known as "the Master of Novices."
[8] Note Benedictine "stability."

yoke of the Rule, which, after such tardy deliberation, he was at liberty either to refuse or receive. He who is to be received, moreover, shall, in the oratory, in the presence of all, make promise concerning his steadfastness and the change in his manner of life and his obedience to God and to His saints; so that if, at any time, he act contrary, he shall know that he shall be condemned by Him whom he mocks. Concerning which promise he shall make a petition in the name of the saints whose relics are there, and of the abbot who is present. Which petition he shall write with his own hand. Or, if he really be not learned in letters, another, being asked by him, shall write it. And that novice shall make his sign; and with his own hand shall place it (the petition) above the altar. And when he has placed it there, the novice shall straightway commence this verse: "Receive me oh Lord according to thy promise and I shall live, and do not cast me down from my hope."[9] Which verse the whole congregation shall repeat three times, adding: "Glory be to the Father." Then that brother novice shall prostrate himself at the feet of each one, that they may pray for him. And, already, from that day, he shall be considered as in the congregation. If he have any property, he shall either first present it to the poor, or, making a solemn donation, shall confer it on the monastery, keeping nothing at all for himself: as one, forsooth, who from that day, shall know that he shall not have power even over his own body. Straightway, therefore in the oratory, he shall take off his own garments in which he was clad, and shall put on the garments of the monastery. Moreover those garments which he has taken off shall be placed in the vestiary to be preserved; so that if, at any time, the devil persuading him, he shall consent to go forth from the monastery — may it not happen, — then, taking off the garments of the monastery, he may be cast out. That petition of his, nevertheless, which the abbot took from above the altar, he shall not receive again; but it shall be preserved in the monastery. . . .

60. *Concerning priests who may chance to wish to dwell in the monastery.* If anyone of the order of priests ask to be received in the monastery, assent indeed, shall not too quickly be given him. Nevertheless, if he altogether persist in this supplication, he shall know that he must observe all the discipline of the Rule; nor shall anything be relaxed unto him, that it may be as it is written: "Friend, wherefore art thou come?" Nevertheless it shall be allowed to him to stand after the abbot, and to give the benediction, or to hold mass; if, however, the abbot order him to.[10] . . .

61. *Concerning pilgrim monks, how they shall be received.* If any pilgrim monk come from distant parts, — if he wish as a guest to dwell in the monastery, and will be content with the customs which he finds in the place, and do not perchance by his lavishness disturb

[9] Psalms 108:116.
[10] In earlier times most monks were not priests.

the monastery, but is simply content with what he finds: he shall be received for as long a time as he desires. If, indeed, he find fault with anything, or expose it, reasonably, and with the humility of charity: the abbot shall discuss it prudently, lest perchance God had sent him for this very thing. But if, afterwards, he wish to establish himself lastingly, such a wish shall not be refused: and all the more, since, in the time of his sojourn as guest, his manner of life could have become known. But, if he have been found lavish or vicious in the time of his sojourn as guest, — not only ought he not to be joined to the body of the monastery, but also it shall be said to him, honestly, that he must depart; lest, by sympathy with him, others also become contaminated. But, if he be not such a one as to merit being cast out: not only if he ask it, shall he be received and associated with the congregation, but he shall also be urged to remain; that by his example others may be instructed. For in every place one God is served, and one King is warred for. And if the abbot perceive him to be such a one, he may be allowed to place him in a somewhat higher position. For the abbot can place not only a monk, but also one from the above grades of priests or clergy, in a greater place than that in which he enters; if he perceive their life to be such a one as to demand it. Moreover the abbot must take care lest, at any time, he receive a monk to dwell (with him) from another known monastery, without the consent of his abbot or letters of commendation. For it is written: "Do not unto another what thou wilt not that one do unto thee."[11]

62. *On the priests of the monastery.* If any abbot seek to ordain for himself a priest or deacon, he shall elect from among his fold one who is worthy to perform the office of a priest. He who is ordained, moreover, shall beware of elation or pride. Nor shall he presume to do anything at all unless what he is ordered to by the abbot; knowing that he is all the more subject to the Rule. Nor, by reason of the priesthood, shall he forget obedience and discipline; but he shall advance more and more towards God. But he shall always expect to hold that position which he had when he entered the monastery: except when performing the service of the altar, and if, perchance, the election of the congregation and the will of the abbot inclines to promote him on account of his merit of life. . . .

63. *Concerning rank in the congregation.* They shall preserve their rank in the monastery according as the time of their conversion and the merit of their life decrees; and as the abbot ordains. And the abbot shall not perturb the flock committed to him; nor using as it were an arbitrary power, shall he unjustly dispose anything. But he shall always reflect that he is to render account to God for all his judgments and works. Therefore, according to the order which he has decreed, or which the brothers themselves have held: thus they shall go to the absolution, to the communion, to the singing of the psalm, to their place in the choir. And in all places altogether, age

[11] Matthew 7:12.

does not decide the rank or affect it; for Samuel and Daniel, as boys, judged the priests.[12] Therefore excepting those who, as we have said, the abbot has, for a higher reason, preferred, or, for certain causes, degraded: all the rest, as they are converted, so they remain. Thus, for example, he who comes to the monastery at the second hour of the day, may know that he is younger than he who came at the first hour of the day, of whatever age or dignity he be. And, in the case of boys, discipline shall be observed in all things by all. The juniors, therefore, shall honour their seniors; the seniors shall love their juniors. In the very calling of names, it shall be allowed to no one to call another simply by his name: but the seniors shall call their juniors by the name of brothers. The juniors, moreover, shall call their seniors "nonni," which indicates paternal reverence. The abbot, moreover, because he is believed to be Christ's representative, shall be called Master and Abbot: not by his assumption, but through honour and love for Christ. His thoughts moreover shall be such, and he shall show himself such, that he may be worthy of such honour. Moreover, wherever the brothers meet each other, the junior shall seek a blessing from the senior. When the greater one passes, the lesser one shall rise and give him a place to sit down. Nor shall the junior presume to sit unless his senior bid him; so that it shall be done as is written: "Vying with each other in honour."[13] Boys, little ones or youths, shall obtain their places in the oratory or at table with discipline as the end in view. Out of doors, moreover, or wherever they are, they shall be guarded and disciplined; until they come to an intelligent age.

66. *Concerning the doorkeepers and location of the monastery.* At the door of the monastery shall be placed a wise old man who shall know how to receive a reply and to return one; whose ripeness of age will not permit him to trifle. Which doorkeeper ought to have a cell next to the door; so that those arriving may always find one present from whom they may receive a reply. And straightway, when any one has knocked, or a poor man has called out, he shall answer, "Thanks be to God!" or shall give the blessing; and with all the gentleness of the fear of God he shall hastily give a reply with the fervour of charity. And if this doorkeeper need assistance he may receive a younger brother.

A monastery, moreover, if it can be done, ought so to be arranged that everything necessary, — that is, water, a mill, a garden, a bakery, — may be made use of, and different arts be carried on, within the monastery; so that there shall be no need for the monks to wander about outside. For this is not at all good for their souls. We wish, moreover, that this Rule be read very often in the congregation; lest any of the brothers excuse himself on account of ignorance.

68. *If impossiblities are enjoined on a brother.* If on any brother

[12] I Kings 7:15. Cf. Daniel 13:45ff.
[13] Romans 12:10.

by chance any burdensome or impossible tasks are enjoined, he shall receive indeed the command of him who orders with all gentleness and obedience. But if he shall see that the weight of the burden altogether exceeds the measure of his strength, he shall patiently and in due season suggest to him who is in authority the causes of the impossibility, but not with pride, or resisting, or contradicting. But if, after his suggestion, the command of the superior continue according to his first opinion, the junior shall know that thus it is expedient for him; and in all love, trusting in the aid of God, he shall obey.

70. *That no one shall presume to strike promiscuously.* — Every ground for presumption shall be forbidden in the monastery. We decree that it shall be allowed to no one to excommunicate or to strike any of his brothers, unless he be one to whom power is given by his abbot. Sinners, moreover, shall be called to account in the presence of all: so that the others may have fear. The care of disciplining, and the custody of children up to fifteen years of age, however, shall belong to all. But this also with all moderation and reason. For he who presumes in any way against one of riper age, without precept of the abbot; or who, even against children, becomes violent without discretion, — shall be subject to the discipline of the Rule; for it is written: "Do not unto another what thou wilt not that one do unto thee."[14]

72. *Concerning the good zeal which the monks ought to have.* — As there is an evil zeal of bitterness, which separates from God and leads to Hell; so there is a good zeal, which separates from vice and leads to God and to eternal life. Let the monks therefore exercise this zeal with the most fervent love: that is, let them mutually surpass each other in honour.[15] Let them most patiently tolerate their weaknesses, whether of body or character; let them vie with each other in showing obedience. Let no one pursue what he thinks useful for himself, but rather what he thinks useful for another. Let them love the brotherhood with a chaste love; let them fear God; let them love their abbot with a sincere and humble love; let them prefer nothing whatever to Christ, who leads us alike to eternal life.

73. *Concerning the fact that not every just observance is decreed in this Rule.* — We have written out this Rule, indeed, that we may show those observing it in the monasteries how to have some honesty of character, or beginning of conversion. But for those who hasten to the perfection of living, there are the teachings of the holy Fathers: the observance of which leads a man to the heights of perfection. For what page, or what discourse, of Divine authority of the Old or the New Testament is not a most perfect rule for human life? Or what book of the holy Catholic Fathers does not trumpet forth how by the right path we shall come to our Creator? Also the reading aloud of the

---

[14] Tobias 4:16.
[15] Romans 12:10.

Collations of the Fathers, and their *Institutes* and their *Lives;* also the Rule of our holy Father Basil — what else are they except instruments of virtue for well-living and obedient monks? We, moreover, blush with confusion for the idle, and the evilly living and the negligent. Thou, therefore, whoever doth hasten to the celestial fatherland, perform with Christ's aid this Rule written out as the least of beginnings: and then at length, under God's protection, thou wilt come to the greater things that we have mentioned, to the summits of learning and virtue.

SECTION III

The High Middle Ages: The Blossoming of a Church-Centered Civilization

ઙ૰

WESTERN CIVILIZATION reached its medieval zenith during the High Middle Ages — the eleventh to thirteenth centuries. This "Age of Faith" was dynamic, enterprising, and progressive. A commercial revolution both promoted and was promoted by the overseas movement known as the Crusades, a series of remarkable undertakings which were launched under papal leadership, and which utilized the military skills developed by feudalism. With revived communications and trade, national states began to consolidate under monarchical direction. The Church was renewed and strengthened by a reform movement which began in the monasteries and ultimately reached the Papacy and the secular clergy. Marvelous progress was made in education and learning. Universities were established for the first time in history. Scholastic philosophy and theology engaged in a cooperative project to unite reason and faith, and in the process stimulated great advances in numerous fields of learning.

In the following selections, Fulcher of Chartres' *Chronicle of the First Crusade* exemplifies the strong faith prevalent in the era, the influence and leadership of Church and Papacy, and the enterprise and daring of a vigorous young Europe just coming of age. The *Chronicle* of William of Malmesbury tells the story of the "conquest" and resultant consolidation of England under its first Norman kings, and thus recounts the early unification and centralization of a strong and progressive European state. Finally Peter Abelard's *Story of My Misfortunes* shows the meeting of reason and faith, flesh and spirit, world and Christianity in the life of a brilliant, self-centered man, who, for all his reverses and "calamities," was a heroic trail-blazer in the intellectual progress of the High Middle Ages.

7

The Church Militant and Overseas Expansion in the Near East

FULCHER OF CHARTRES

A leading manifestation of the growing wealth, strength, and enterprise as well as of the faith of Western Europe, in the High Middle Ages, was the Crusades. Perhaps better than any other development, the Crusades illustrate high medieval religious fervor, feudalism, militarism, energy, vitality, varied interests, growing prosperity, and budding creativity. The direct result of the Crusades was that Western Europeans won, and for two centuries maintained a foothold on the mainland of the Near East. But, in one way or another, the Crusades influenced almost every aspect of European life. Although historians number several Crusades, only the first one (1096–1099), the subject of our present selection, was fully successful; indeed, most of the others were downright failures.

Our chronicler, Fulcher (or Foucher) of Chartres, was born about 1058. He received a good education, probably at the already famous cathedral school of Chartres. As a priest in his mid-thirties, Fulcher attended the council convoked by the reforming pope, Urban II, at Clermont in southern France in 1095. Here he heard Urban's famous speech calling for an expedition to the East. Fulcher decided to take the cross, and participated in the First Crusade, first in the company of Count Stephen of Blois and Duke Robert of Normandy, who headed contingents of northern Frenchmen, and then as chaplain of the shrewd Count Baldwin, who set up a principality at Edessa and later succeeded his brother Godfrey of Bouillon as ruler of the Kingdom of Jerusalem. Fulcher followed Baldwin in his adventures and campaigns, both in the region of Edessa and in Jerusalem. After King Baldwin's demise in 1118, Fulcher remained in the Holy Land, possibly as Prior of the Mount of Olives, until his own death at the ripe age of about seventy years.

Fulcher's chronicle, the full title of which is *Jerusalem-Story: The Deeds of the Franks on Their Pilgrimage to Jerusalem*, runs from the Council of Clermont in 1095 to about the time of his own death, in 1127 or 1128. It is divided into three books. The first book, most of which is given here, tells of the origins, course, and immediate aftermath of the First Crusade from 1095 to 1100. Whether Fulcher did any writing during these years, or started about 1101 and covered them retrospectively, is a matter of conjecture. He tells us that he was urged on by his associates, and that he composed his history of the "deeds of brave men" both for the entertainment and edification of the living and for the benefit of departed souls through remembrance and prayer. Most of the work was written during the period when the Crusaders' kingdom was at its height and in the first flush of its success and prosperity.

Fulcher's chronicle reflects the essential elements of Western civilization in its eleventh-century phase: energy, enterprise, and perseverance shining forth in an atmosphere of adventure and suspense; a widening outlook, as Western provincialism was tempered by new sights and experiences; an emergent nationalism stimulated by contacts with diverse strangers. Above all, the chronicle attests to the spirit of faith and the ascendance of the Church in the High Middle Ages. Sin is considered worse than physical misfortune, and temporal suffering is regarded as divine chastisement; thus the Crusades present an opportunity to expiate the one through undergoing the other. A high confidence in ultimate success, with God's assistance, is undimmed by reverses. Such faith and hope make possible the endurance of extreme hardships and appalling casualties. Many paradoxes appear: simultaneous piety and cruelty, charity and intolerance, high ideals and sullied realities. There is ecstasy in beholding the holy places sanctified by Christ's life, but oblivion of the forgiveness and mercy which Christ would have extended to the inhabitants. The primacy of the Pope is accepted, but the northern French are scandalized by the venality of the supporters of Antipope Wibert. Fulcher manifests shrewdness and intelligence in recognizing the insecurity of the Crusaders in the East and the need for Byzantine cooperation. Yet there is an artless simplicity in his apparent unawareness of intrigue and duplicity among the great lords, as in his naïve accounts of such matters as Baldwin's accession at Edessa and Bohemund's gaining entrance into Antioch.

Fulcher is generally accurate and highly informative concerning places and events, but inclined to exaggerate with regard to numbers of persons. He seems to have been unable to estimate the size of any assemblage with any correctness. That he has received a good education is evidenced by his ability to express himself clearly and forcibly in Latin, and by his familiarity with the classics, the Bible, and the writings of the Church Fathers. If we detect a certain credulity in matters astrological, that too is in the spirit of his time. There are other contemporary accounts of the First Crusade, likewise written to stir up European interest in this new and costly Eastern venture; but Fulcher's work is generally regarded as the most balanced, impartial, reliable, and representative.

FULCHER OF CHARTRES

FROM *Chronicle of the First Crusade* *

THE DEEDS OF THE FRANKS ON THEIR PILGRIMAGE TO JERUSALEM

Prologue

1. It is especially pleasing to the living, and it is even beneficial to the dead, when the deeds of brave men, (particularly of those serving as soldiers of God), are either read from writings or soberly recounted from memory among the faithful. For, after hearing of the deeds of faithful predecessors who rejected the beauties and pleasures of the world and clung to God, and in accordance with the precept of the Gospel, left their parents and wives and possessions, however great, to follow Him, those here on earth are inspired to serve Him more eagerly in that same spirit. It is beneficial to the dead, especially to those dead in the Lord, when the living, upon hearing of their good and devoted works, bless their faithful souls, and out of love bestow alms with prayers on their behalf whether they were known to them, or not.

2. Therefore, induced by the promptings of certain of my companions on several occasions, I carefully arranged the deeds, most distinguished in the Lord, of the armies of the Franks who, by God's ordination, made a pilgrimage to Jerusalem. I have recorded in my unpolished style, as truthfully as possible, what is worth remembering and what I saw with my own eyes on that journey.[1]

---

* From Fulcher of Chartres, *Chronicle of the First Crusade,* translated by Martha Evelyn McGinty (Philadelphia: University of Pennsylvania Press, 1941); reprinted by permission.

[1] The First Crusade is presented as primarily a religious venture or pilgrimage, and such it was for most.

I
The Council of Clermont

1. In the year 1095 from the Lord's Incarnation, with Henry reigning in Germany as so-called emperor,[2] and with Philip as king in France,[3] manifold evils were growing in all parts of Europe because of wavering faith. In Rome ruled Pope Urban II,[4] a man distinguished in life and character, who always strove wisely and actively to raise the status of the Holy Church above all things.

2. He saw that the faith of Christianity was being destroyed to excess by everybody, by the clergy as well as by the laity. He saw that peace was altogether discarded by the princes of the world, who were engaged in incessant warlike contention and quarreling among themselves. He saw the wealth of the land being pillaged continuously. He saw many of the vanquished, wrongfully taken prisoner and very cruelly thrown into foulest dungeons, either ransomed for a high price or, tortured by the triple torments of hunger, thirst, and cold, blotted out by a death hidden from the world. He saw holy places violated; monasteries and villas burned. He saw that no one was spared of any human suffering, and that things divine and human alike were held in derision.

3. He heard, too, that the interior regions of Romania,[5] where the Turks ruled over the Christians, had been perniciously subjected in a savage attack.[6] Moved by long-suffering compassion and by love of God's will, he descended the mountains to Gaul, and in Auvergne he called for a council to congregate from all sides at a suitable time at a city called Clermont.[7] Three hundred and ten bishops and abbots,[8] who had been advised beforehand by messengers, were present.

4. Then, on the day set aside for it, he called them together to himself and, in an eloquent address, carefully made the cause of the meeting known to them. In the plaintive voice of an aggrieved Church, he expressed great lamentation, and held a long discourse with them about the raging tempests of the world, which have been mentioned, because faith was undermined.

5. One after another, he beseechingly exhorted them all, with re-

---

[2] Henry IV (1056–1106) was not recognized as emperor by either Gregory VII or Urban II, because of his insistence on lay investiture and simony.
[3] Philip I (1060–1108). One of the reasons for the Council was to excommunicate the French king for his illicit relations with Bertrade de Montfort.
[4] Urban II (1088–99), former Bishop of Ostia and Cluniac monk.
[5] The former lands of the East Romans or Byzantines in Asia.
[6] Asia Minor or Anatolia had been taken by the Seljuk Turks after their victory over the Byzantines at Manzikert in 1071.
[7] At Clermont-Ferrand in Auvergne, Nov. 18–28, 1095.
[8] Estimates of the number of prelates present range from 190 to 463; Ferdinand Chalandon favors about 200.

newed faith, to spur themselves in great earnestness to overcome the Devil's devices and to try to restore the Holy Church, most unmercifully weakened by the wicked, to its former honorable status.[9]

II
The Decree of Pope Urban in the Council

1. "Most beloved brethren," he said, "by God's permission placed over the whole world with the papal crown, I, Urban, as the messenger of divine admonition, have been compelled by an unavoidable occasion to come here to you servants of God. I desired those whom I judged to be stewards of God's ministries to be true stewards and faithful, with all hypocrisy rejected.[10]

2. "But with temperance in reason and justice being remote, I, with divine aid, shall strive carefully to root out any crookedness or distortion which might obstruct God's law. For the Lord appointed you temporarily as stewards over His family to serve it nourishment seasoned with a modest savor. Moreover, blessed will you be if at last the Overseer find you faithful.[11]

3. "You are also called shepherds; see that you are not occupied after the manner of mercenaries. Be true shepherds, always holding your crooks in your hands; and sleeping not, guard on every side the flock entrusted to you.

4. "For if through your carelessness or negligence, some wolf seizes a sheep, you doubtless will lose the reward prepared for you by our Lord.[12] Nay, first most cruelly beaten by the whips of the lictors, you afterwards will be angrily cast into the keeping of a deadly place.

5. "Likewise, according to the evangelical sermon, you are the 'salt of the earth'.[13] But if you fail, it will be disputed wherewith it was salted. O how much saltiness, indeed, is necessary for you to salt the people in correcting them with the salt of wisdom, people who are ignorant and panting with desire after the wantonness of the world; so that they might not be unsalted and rotten with sins, and stink whenever the Lord might wish to exhort them.

6. "For if because of the sloth of your management, He should find in them worms, that is, sin, straightway, He will order that they, despised, be cast into the dungheap. And because you could not make restoration for such a great loss, He will banish you, utterly condemned in judgment, from the familiarity of His love.

[9] Urban II was continuing the Cluniac-Gregorian reform movement, promoted by Leo IX and Hildebrand, and implemented by Councils such as that of Clermont.
[10] I Corinthians 4:1–2.
[11] Matthew 24:45–46.
[12] John 10:12–16.
[13] Matthew 5:13.

7. "It behooves saltiness of this kind to be wise, provident, temperate, learned, peace-making, truth-seeking, pious, just, equitable, pure. For how will the unlearned be able to make men learned, the intemperate make them temperate, the impure make them pure? If one despises peace, how will he appease? Or if one has dirty hands, how will he be able to wipe the filth off another one defiled? For it is read, 'If the blind lead the blind, both shall fall into a ditch.'[14]

8. "Set yourselves right before you do others, so that you can blamelessly correct your subjects. If you wish to be friends of God, gladly practise those things which you feel will please Him.

9. "Especially establish ecclesiastical affairs firm in their own right, so that no simoniac heresy will take root among you.[15] Take care lest the vendors and moneychangers, flayed by the scourges of the Lord, be miserably driven out into the narrow streets of destruction.[16]

10. "Uphold the Church in its own ranks altogether free from all secular powers.[17] See that the tithes of all those who cultivate the earth are given faithfully to God; let them not be sold or held back.[18]

11. "Let him who has seized a bishop be considered an outlaw. Let him who has seized or robbed monks, clerics, nuns and their servants, pilgrims, or merchants, be excommunicated. Let the robbers and burners of homes and their accomplices, banished from the Church, be smitten with excommunication.[19]

12. "It must be considered very carefully, as Gregory says, by what penalty he must be punished who seizes other men's property, if he who does not bestow his own liberally is condemned to Hell. For so it happened to the rich man in the well-known Gospel, who on that account was not punished because he had taken away the property of others, but because he had misused that which he had received.

13. "And so by these iniquities, most beloved, you have seen the world disturbed too long; so long, as it was told to us by those reporting, that perhaps because of the weakness of your justice in some parts of your provinces, no one dares to walk in the streets with safety, lest he be kidnapped by robbers by day or thieves by night, either by force or trickery, at home or outside.

14. "Wherefore the Truce,[1] as it is commonly called, now for a long time established by the Holy Fathers, must be renewed. In admonition, I entreat you to adhere to it most firmly in your own

---

[14] Matthew 15:14.
[15] One of the objectives of reform was to eliminate purchase of church offices.
[16] John 2:15.
[17] Another objective of reform was to eliminate lay-control in the Church.
[18] Overlords often diverted revenues of the Church by various means.
[19] Here and below, reference is made to feudal anarchy.
[1] The Truce of God, or abstinence from warfare for stated intervals on religious grounds, which was proclaimed anew at the Council of Clermont.

FULCHER OF CHARTRES: *The First Crusade*

bishopric. But if anyone affected by avarice or pride breaks it of his own free will, let him be excommunicated by God's authority and by the sanction of the decrees of this Holy Council."

III
The Pope's Exhortation Concerning The Expedition to Jerusalem

1. These and many other things having been suitably disposed of, all those present, both clergy and people, at the words of Lord Urban, the Pope, voluntarily gave thanks to God and confirmed by a faithful promise that his decrees would be well kept. But straightway he added that another thing not less than the tribulation already spoken of, but even greater and more oppressive, was injuring Christianity in another part of the world, saying:[2]

2. "Now that you, O sons of God, have consecrated yourselves to God to maintain peace among yourselves more vigorously and to uphold the laws of the Church faithfully, there is work to do, for you must turn the strength of your sincerity, now that you are aroused by divine correction, to another affair that concerns you and God. Hastening to the way, you must help your brothers living in the Orient, who need your aid for which they have already cried out many times.[3]

3. "For, as most of you have been told, the Turks, a race of Persians,[4] who have penetrated within the boundaries of Romania[5] even to the Mediterranean to that point which they call the Arm of Saint George,[6] in occupying more and more of the lands of the Christians, have overcome them, already victims of seven battles, and have killed and captured them, have overthrown churches, and have laid waste God's kingdom. If you permit this supinely for very long, God's faithful ones will be still further subjected.

4. "Concerning this affair, I, with suppliant prayer — not I but the Lord — exhort you, heralds of Christ, to persuade all of whatever class, both knights and footmen, both rich and poor in numerous edicts, to strive to help expel that wicked race from our Christian lands before it is too late.

5. "I speak to those present, I send word to those not here; moreover, Christ commands it. Remission of sins will be granted for

---

[2] There are varying accounts of Urban's famous speech; Fulcher's is one of the best.

[3] The Byzantines had been appealing for help for some time. Gregory VII had projected a crusade to aid them, until he became preoccupied with the investiture controversy.

[4] The Seljuk Turks.

[5] Anatolia and other former Byzantine lands.

[6] The Hellespont or Bosporus.

those going thither, if they end a shackled life either on land or in crossing the sea, or in struggling against the heathen. I, being vested with that gift from God, grant this to those who go.

6. "O what a shame, if a people, so despised, degenerate, and enslaved by demons would thus overcome a people endowed with the trust of almighty God, and shining in the name of Christ! O how many evils will be imputed to you by the Lord Himself, if you do not help those who, like you, profess Christianity![7]

7. "Let those," he said, "who are accustomed to wage private wars wastefully even against Believers,[8] go forth against the Infidels in a battle worthy to be undertaken now and to be finished in victory. Now, let those, who until recently existed as plunderers, be soldiers of Christ; now, let those who formerly contended against brothers and relations, rightly fight barbarians; now, let those, who recently were hired for a few pieces of silver, win their eternal reward. Let those, who wearied themselves to the detriment of body and soul, labor for a twofold honor. Nay, more, the sorrowful here will be glad there, the poor here will be rich there, and the enemies of the Lord here will be His friends there.

8. "Let no delay postpone the journey of those about to go, but when they have collected the money owed to them and the expenses for the journey, and when winter has ended and spring has come, let them enter the crossroads courageously with the Lord going on before."[9]

IV

The Bishop of Puy and the Events After the Council

1. After these words were spoken, the hearers were fervently inspired. Thinking nothing more worthy than such an undertaking, many in the audience solemnly promised to go, and to urge diligently those who were absent. There was among them one Bishop of Puy, Ademar by name,[10] who afterwards, acting as vicar-apostolic, ruled the whole army of God wisely and thoughtfully, and spurred them to complete their undertaking vigorously.

2. So, the things that we have told you were well established and confirmed by everybody in the Council. With the blessing of absolu-

---

[7] Although schismatics in Western eyes, the Byzantines were still Christians.
[8] Reference is made to local feudal warfare.
[9] For various versions of the speech, see D. C. Munro, "The Speech of Pope Urban II at Clermont, 1095," *American Historical Review*, XI (1906), 231–242.
[10] Ademar de Monteil, Bishop of Puy, was the only person of any repute and experience to take the cross at this time, and hence Urban appointed him leader of the expedition, November 27, 1095. He appointed him as his representative in December, 1095.

tion given, they departed; and after returning to their homes, they disclosed to those not knowing, what had taken place. As it was decreed far and wide throughout the provinces, they established the peace, which they call the Truce, to be upheld mutually by oath.

3. Many, one after another, of any and every occupation, after confession of their sins and with purified spirits, consecrated themselves to go where they were bidden.

4. Oh, how worthy and delightful to all of us who saw those beautiful crosses, either silken or woven of gold, or of any material, which the pilgrims sewed on the shoulders of their woolen cloaks or cassocks by the command of the Pope, after taking the vow to go.[11] To be sure, God's soldiers, who were making themselves ready to battle for His honor, ought to have been marked and fortified with a sign of victory. And so by embroidering the symbol [of the cross] on their clothing in recognition of their faith, in the end they won the True Cross itself. They imprinted the ideal so that they might attain the reality of the ideal.

5. It is plain that good meditation leads to doing good work and that good work wins salvation of the soul. But, if it is good to mean well, it is better, after reflection, to carry out the good intention. So, it is best to win salvation through action worthy of the soul to be saved. Let each and everyone, therefore, reflect upon the good, that he makes better in fulfillment, so that, deserving it, he might finally receive the best, which does not diminish in eternity.

6. In such a manner Urban, a wise man and reverenced,
   Meditated a labor, whereby the world florescenced.

For he renewed peace and restored the laws of the Church to their former standards; also he tried with vigorous instigation to expel the heathen from the lands of the Christians. And since he strove to exalt all things of God in every way, almost everyone gladly surrendered in obedience to his paternal care.

V

The Departure of the Christians and The Names of the Chief Pilgrims

1. In March of the year 1096 from the Lord's Incarnation, after Pope Urban had held the Council, which has been described, at Auvergne in November, some people, earlier prepared than others, hastened to begin the holy journey. Others followed in April or May, June or July, and also in August, September, or October, whenever the opportunity of securing expenses presented itself.

2. In that year, with God disposing, peace and a vast abundance of grain and wine overflowed through all the regions of the earth, so

[11] Hence the name "Crusaders" — marked with the cross.

that they who chose to follow Him with their crosses according to His commands did not fail on the way for lack of bread.

3. Since it is appropriate that the names of the leaders of the pilgrims at that time be remembered, I name Hugh the Great,[12] brother of Philip, King of France. The first of the heroes crossing the sea, he landed at the city of Durazzo in Bulgaria[13] with his own men, but having imprudently departed with a scant army, he was seized by the citizens there and brought to the Emperor of Constantinople,[14] where he was detained for a considerable time not altogether free.

4. After him, Bohemond,[15] an Apulian of Norman race, the son of Robert Guiscard,[16] went along the same route with his army.

5. Next, Godfrey, Duke of Lorraine,[17] went through Hungary with many people.

6. Raymond, Count of the Provençals,[18] with Goths and Gascons; also, Ademar, Bishop of Puy, crossed through Dalmatia.

7. A certain Peter the Hermit,[19] after many people on foot and a few knights had joined him, first made his way through Hungary. Afterwards, Walter, called the Penniless,[1] certainly a very good soldier, who later with many of his companions was slain by the Turks between Nicomedia and Nicaea, was the commander of these people.

8. In October, Robert, Count of the Normans,[2] son of William, King of the English, began the journey, after collecting a great army composed of people of Normandy, England, and Brittany; and with him went Stephen, the noble Count of Blois,[3] his brother-in-law, and Robert, Count of Flanders, with many other nobles.[4]

9. So with such a great band proceeding from western parts, gradually from day to day on the way there grew armies of innumerable people coming together from everywhere. Thus a countless multitude speaking many languages and coming from many regions was to be seen. However, all were not assembled into one army until we arrived at the city of Nicaea.

10. What more shall I tell? The islands of the seas and all the kingdoms of the earth were so agitated that one believed that the

---

[12] Count Hugh of Vermandois, younger son of Henry I, and leader of the northern Franks. His brother, Philip I, was excommunicated at the time.

[13] Durazzo was not in Bulgaria but in the Byzantine Empire.

[14] Alexius Comnenus, Emperor of Constantinople, 1081–1118.

[15] Son of Robert Guiscard by Alberade.

[16] Founder of the Norman principality in Apulia.

[17] Godfrey, Duke of Lower Lorraine, was accompanied by his brothers, Baldwin and Eustace.

[18] Raymond of St. Gilles, Count of Toulouse.

[19] Peter of Amiens preached the Crusade, and was one of the leaders of the Peasants' Crusade.

[1] Walter of Perejo.

[2] Robert Curthose, Duke of Normandy.

[3] Stephen, husband of Adele of Normandy (daughter of William the Conqueror), father of Stephen of Boulogne who became King of England.

[4] Fulcher went on this expedition.

prophecy of David was fulfilled, who said in his Psalm: "All nations whom Thou hast made shall come and worship before Thee, O Lord",⁵ and what those going all the way there, later said with good reason: "We shall worship in the place where His feet have stood."⁶ We have read much about this in the Prophets which it is tedious to repeat.

11. Oh, how much grief there was! How many sighs! How much sorrow! How much weeping among loved ones, when the husband left his wife so dear to him, as well as his children, father and mother, brothers and grandparents, and possessions however great!

12. But however so many tears those remaining shed for those going, these were not swayed by such tears from leaving all that they possessed; without doubt believing that they would receive an hundredfold what the Lord promised to those loving him.

13. Then the wife reckoned the time of her husband's return, because if God permitted him to live, he would come home to her. He commended her to the Lord, kissed her, and promised as she wept that he would return. She, fearing that she would never see him again, not able to hold up, fell senseless to the ground; mourning her living beloved as though he were dead. He, having compassion, it seems, neither for the weeping of his wife, nor feeling pain for the grief of any friends, and yet having it, for he secretly suffered severely, unchanging, went away with a determined mind.

14. Sadness to those remaining, however, was joy to those going away. What, then, can we say? "This is the Lord's doing; it is marvelous in our eyes."⁷

VII

The Journey of the Count of Normandy, and the Events at Rome at that Time

1. After leaving Gaul⁸ and going through Italy, we Western Franks⁹ came as far as Lucca,¹⁰ most renowned city. Near there we met Pope Urban;¹¹ and Robert the Norman and Stephen, Count of Blois, and others of us who wished spoke with him. Having received his blessing,¹² we went on our way joyfully to Rome.

2. When he had entered the Church of Saint Peter, we met, before

5 Psalms 86:9.
6 Psalms 132:7.
7 Psalms 118:23.
8 France.
9 Frenchmen.
10 In northern Tuscany.
11 Pope Urban II was then in exile from Rome, which was held by the antipope supported by Henry IV.
12 October 26, 1096.

the altar, men of Wibert, the pseudo-Pope,[13] who, with swords in their hands, wrongly snatched the offerings placed on the altar. Others ran up and down on the roof of the church itself, and from there threw stones at us as we were prostrate praying. For when they saw anyone faithful to Urban, they straightway wished to slay him.

3. In one of the towers of the church were Lord Urban's men, who carefully guarded it in fidelity to him, and withstood their adversaries as well as they could. We were very grieved when we saw such a great atrocity committed there, but we earnestly wished for nothing to be done except as punishment by the Lord. Thereupon, without hesitation, many who had came this far with us, now weak with cowardice, returned to their homes.

VIII

The Drowning of the Pilgrims and The Divinely Manifest Miracle

1. In the year of the Lord 1097, with spring weather accompanying March, immediately Robert the Norman and Count Stephen of Blois, who had been waiting for favorable weather, accompanied by their men, again turned seaward. The fleet was prepared, and on the Nones of April, which at the time fell on the Holy Day of Easter, they embarked at the port of Brindisi.[14]

2. "How unsearchable are His judgments, and His ways past finding out!"[15] For we saw one boat among the others, which, while near the shore and apparently unhindered, suddenly cracked apart in the middle. Whereby four hundred of both sexes perished by drowning, concerning whom joyful praise to God immediately sounded.

3. For when those who were standing around had collected as many of the dead bodies as they could, they discovered crosses actually imprinted in the flesh on the shoulders of some of them. For what those living bore on their garments, it was fitting, with the Lord willing, that the same victorious sign remain with them thus preoccupied in His service under a pledge of faith. And at the same time, reason made it plain to those reflecting on it, that it was appropriate that, by such a miracle, those dead had already by God's mercy obtained the peace of everlasting life in the clearly evident fulfillment of the prophecy which had been written: "The just, though taken prematurely by death, shall find peace."[16]

---

[13] Antipope Guibert or Wibert, raised by Henry IV against Gregory VII, had taken the name of Clement III and held Rome at this time.
[14] In southeast Italy, opposite Durazzo.
[15] Romans 11:33.
[16] Wisdom 4:7.

4. Of the others now wrestling with death, only a few lived. Horses and mules were destroyed by the waves, and much money was lost, too. When we saw this misfortune, we were confused with so great a fear that very many of the weak-hearted ones, not yet aboard the vessels, went back to their homes, having abandoned the pilgrimage, and saying that never would they place themselves on the deceptive water.[17]

5. But placing our hope on almighty God deep within us, with topsails raised again, and with a great trumpet sound, we thrust ourselves upon the sea, when the wind was blowing slightly. After we had been detained on the high seas for three days by the failing wind, on the fourth day we reached land about ten miles, I judge, from the city of Durazzo. Two harbors received our fleet.[18] Then, joyfully we resumed our dry-land journey, and we approached the aforementioned city.

6–8. We proceeded over the land of the Bulgars, over mountain precipices and rather desert places . . . to Constantinople.[19] After stretching our tents before this city, we rested for fourteen days. . . .

9. Because we were not able to enter that city, since it was not pleasing to the emperor (for he feared that by chance we might plot some injury to him), it was necessary that we buy outside the walls our daily supplies, which the citizens brought to us by his order. Only five or six of us at the same time were permitted to go into the city each hour; thus some were coming out and others were going in to pray in the churches.

IX

The City of Constantinople and the Journey of the Pilgrims to Nicaea

1. Oh, what an excellent and beautiful city! How many monasteries, and how many palaces there are in it, of wonderful work skilfully fashioned! How many marvelous works are to be seen in the streets and districts of the town! It is a great nuisance to recite what an opulence of all kinds of goods are found there; of gold, of silver, of many kinds of mantles, and of holy relics. In every season, merchants, in frequent sailings, bring to that place everything that man might need. Almost twenty thousand eunuchs, I judge, are kept there continuously.

2. When we had sufficiently refreshed our fatigued selves, then

[17] Note unfamiliarity with the sea.
[18] The harbors of Durazzo and Epidamnus, both in modern Albania.
[19] After traveling across the Balkans (account here omitted), Fulcher's contingent, headed by Stephen of Blois and Robert of Normandy, arrived at Constantinople in May, 1097.

our leaders, after counsel, agreed upon a contract under oath with the Emperor, upon his demand. Already Lord Bohemond and Duke Godfrey, who had preceded us, had taken it. However, Count Raymond at that time refused to do so. The Count of Flanders, just as the others did, took that same oath.[1]

3. It was necessary for all to confirm friendship with the Emperor, without whose counsel and aid we could not have completed our journey, nor could those who were to follow us on that same road. To these, then, the Emperor himself offered as many coins and silken garments as he pleased; also some horses and some money, which they needed to complete such a great journey.

4. After this was completed, we crossed the sea which they call the Arm of Saint George.[2] We hastened then to the city of Nicaea, which Lord Bohemond, Duke Godfrey, Count Raymond, and the Count of Flanders had already surrounded in siege by the middle of May. The Oriental Turks,[3] very keen archers and bowmen, then possessed this city. These Turks from Persia, after they had crossed the Euphrates River fifty years before, subjugated the whole land of Romania[4] for themselves as far as the city of Nicomedia.[5]

5. Oh, how many severed heads and bones of the dead lying on the plains did we then find beyond Nicodemia near that sea! In the preceding year, the Turks destroyed those who were ignorant of and new to the use of the arrow. Moved to compassion by this, we shed many tears there.[6]

X

The Siege of Nicaea[7] and the Surrender of That City

1. When those who were besieging Nicaea had heard, as it was told, that our princes, the Count of the Normans and Stephen of Blois, had come,[8] they came joyfully to meet them and us on the way, and escorted us to the place where we stretched our tents before the city on the south side.

2. Once already, the Turks had gathered in force and had prepared

---

[1] Bohemond or Bohemund took the oath November 1096; Godfrey, January 1097; and Raymond's refusal but assurance of peace was given April 1097.
[2] The Hellespont or Bosporus.
[3] The Seljuk Turks: a reference to their eastern origin.
[4] Anatolia or Asia Minor; former Byzantine holdings in Asia.
[5] In their conquest, the Seljuks crossed the Euphrates in 1047, reached Nicomedia in 1081.
[6] Here members of the Peasants' Crusade had met disaster in October, 1096.
[7] In far northwestern Asia Minor, about 30 miles inland, across the Sea of Marmora from Constantinople.
[8] The siege of Nicaea was begun in mid-May, and the northern French contingent arrived in early June, 1097.

either to break the blockade if they could, or to better fortify the city with their soldiers. But repulsed fiercely by our men, almost two hundred of theirs were killed. When they had seen the Franks so furious and mighty in strength, they fled into the interior of Romania, until they should feel that the time was opportune to attack them.

3. We, who were the last to come, arrived at the siege in the first week of June.

4. Then the many armies there were united into one, which those who were skilled in reckoning estimated at six hundred thousand strong for war. Of these, there were one hundred thousand full-armed with corselets and helmets, not counting the unarmed, that is, the clerics, monks, women, and little children.[9] . . .

7. Truly, you would have grieved and sighed with compassion, to see them let down iron hooks, which they lowered and raised by ropes, and seize the body of any of our men that they had slaughtered in some way near the wall. None of our men dared, nor could, take the body from them. Having robbed the corpse, they threw the carcass outside.

8. Then we drew some large skiffs overland with oxen and ropes from Civetot as far as Nicaea.[10] We placed them on a lake[11] near the city to guard the entrance, so that the city might not be supplied with food.

9. We had harassed the city in siege for five weeks,[12] and many times had terrified the Turks by assaults. Meanwhile, they parleyed with the Emperor through mediators, and slyly returned the city to him, when already it had been greatly encompassed by force and cleverness.

10. Then the Turks let in the Turcoples,[13] sent there by the Emperor, who guarded the city with the money in it on behalf of the Emperor just as he had commanded them. Because he kept all of that money in his possession, the Emperor gave some of his own gold and silver and mantles to our nobles; he also distributed some of his copper coins, which they call *tartarons*,[14] to the footsoldiers.

---

[9] These numbers are apparently exaggerated. Stephen Runciman, in his excellent *History of the Crusades*, Volume I (Cambridge: University, 1953), says: "The actual size of the Crusading armies can only be conjectured. Medieval estimates are always exaggerated, but Peter the Hermit's rabble, including its many non-combatants, probably approached twenty thousand. The chief Crusading armies, Raymond's, Godfrey's, and the northern French, each numbered well over ten thousand, including non-combatants. Bohemund's was a little smaller, and there were other lesser groups. But in all from sixty to a hundred thousand persons must have entered the Empire from the West between the summer of 1096 and the spring of 1097."

[10] June 17, 1097.

[11] Lake Isnik.

[12] May 14 to June 18.

[13] Greek mercenary soldiers, light-armed cavalry, recruited from halfbreeds and natives.

[14] Eastern cheap copper coins of varying value.

11. The summer solstice came on the day in June when Nicaea was thus seized or restored.[15]

XI

The Fatal Battle of the Christians with the Turks[16]

1. When our soldiers had received permission from the Emperor to leave, three days before the Kalends of July,[17] we left Nicaea to go into the interior regions of Romania. But when we had proceeded on our journey for two days, it was announced that the Turks, after laying ambushes for us on the plains over which they thought we would go, awaited battle.

2. When we had heard this, we lost no courage. But on that evening, when our scouts had seen many of them from a distance, they immediately warned us; because of that, we had our tents guarded on all sides that night by watchmen. In the early morning, which fell on the Kalends of July, after arms were taken up, and being arranged in wings facing them and the tribunes and centurions properly leading the cohorts and centuries, with a warning horn and with banners flying, we began to advance in battle formation.

3. In the second hour of the day, lo, their advance guards approached our scouts! When we heard this, we pitched our tents near a certain marsh, so that having removed the pack saddles, we should be more readily prepared for fighting.

4. After this was done, behold! there were the Turks whose emir[18] and prince was Sulaiman[19] who held Nicaea and Romania under his power. The Turks, heathen Persians, who commanded by him, had come for a journey of thirty days and more to his aid, were with him; also many emirs or princes, namely, Admircaradigum and Miriathos, and many others.[1] All of these together numbered three hundred and sixty thousand warriors, that is archers.[2] For it is their custom to use such arms. They were all cavalry. We, on the other hand, were both infantry and cavalry.

5. At that time, Duke Godfrey and Count Raymond and Hugh the Great were not with us. For two days, I know not for what reason, they, with a large number of our people, had withdrawn from us at a forked crossroad. On account of this, irreparable harm befell us, because our men were slain, and because the Turks were not killed

---

[15] June 19, 1097.
[16] Battle of Dorylaeum.
[17] Kalends of July: July 1.
[18] Commander.
[19] Sulaiman II, Sultan of Iconium or Rum or Asia Minor, 1092–1107.
[1] Admircaradigum: Al Amir Koradja. Miriathos: Mir Atsiz.
[2] Mounted archers or *Askar*. Note the customary exaggeration.

nor repulsed. Since they received our messengers late, they brought aid to us late.

6. The Turks, with clashing of weapons and shrieking, fiercely let loose a shower of arrows. Stunned and almost dead and with many injured, we straightway turned our backs in flight. Nor is this to be wondered at since such fighting was unknown to any of us.

7. Directly from another part of the marsh, a large band of them fiercely forced their way as far as our tents. Having entered, they were snatching our things and were killing some of our people, when, with God arranging, the advance guards of Hugh the Great, of Count Raymond, and of Duke Godfrey came upon this disaster from the rear. When our men had retreated to our tents, the Turks, who had entered them, left, for they thought our men had returned to fight them. But what they took for boldness and courage, was, if they had been able to know, really great fear.

8. What shall I tell next? All of us, huddled together like sheep in a fold, trembling and terrified, were fenced in by the enemy on all sides, so that we could not turn in any direction.[3] It was evident that this had befallen us because of our sins. For dissipation had polluted certain ones, and avarice or some other iniquity had corrupted others. There was a vast cry smiting the heavens, of men and women and little children, and also of the heathens who rushed in upon us. No hope of life remained.

9. Then we confessed that we were culprits and sinners humbly begging mercy from God. The Bishop of Puy, our Protector, and four other bishops were there. There were many priests present, clothed in white vestments, who besought the Lord most humbly to overthrow the strength of our enemy and pour gifts of His mercy on us. They sang weeping; they wept singing. Many, fearing immediate death, ran to them and confessed their sins.

10. Our leaders, Robert, Count of Normandy, Stephen, Count of Blois, Robert, Count of Flanders, and also Bohemond, resisted them with all their might, and often strove to attack them. These, likewise, were strongly assailed by the Turks.

XII

The Flight of the Turks and the Victory of the Christians

1. The Lord does not give victory to the pomp of nobility nor to brilliance in arms, but out of pity He aids the pure in heart who are fortified by divine strength in time of need. Therefore the Lord, perhaps pleased with our supplication, little by little restored vigor

---

[3] Fulcher evidently had neither an active part nor a very good view.

to us, and more and more weakened the Turks. When our allies, who were hastening to help us, were seen, praising God we resumed our courage and in troops and cohorts we strove to resist further.

2. Alas! How many of our men straggling slowly behind us did they kill that day! Even from the first hour of the day, as I have said, up to the sixth, difficulties encompassed us; but then, little by little, after we were spurred on and strengthened by union with some of our allies, divine grace was miraculously present. Suddenly, we saw the backs of the Turks as they turned in flight.

3. Shouting fiercely, we pursued them over mountains and through valleys. Nor did we cease to rout them, until our swiftest men came to their tents. There, some of them loaded camels and many horses with the Turk's possessions and the tents themselves which they, out of fright, had left. Others followed the fleeing Turks until nightfall. Because our horses were hungry and tired, we kept a few of theirs.

4. It was a great miracle of God that on the morrow and on the third day they never stopped their flight, although no one except God put them to flight any longer.

5. Happy over this outcome, we unloosed our thanks to God, because He was not willing that our journey be altogether brought to nought, but had indicated that it would succeed more honorably than usual and would bring honor to His Christianity. As a result, the story shall sound from East to West forever.

6. Then, we pressed on our journey carefully. One day, we endured a very severe thirst, which so oppressed some men and women that they died. The Turks, fleeing before us in troops, sought hiding places for themselves all over Romania.

XIII

The Want of the Christians

1. Then we came to Antioch, which they called the Lesser, in the province of Pisidia; thence to Iconium.[4] We very often suffered the lack of enough bread and other food in these places; for we found Romania, which is very good land and especially fertile for all crops, excessively devastated and ravaged by the Turks.

2. Yet ever so many times, you would see such a great multitude of people well refreshed by what was found on the scattered farms, which we found here and there in this region, with the aid of God who fed five thousand men with two loaves and five fishes.[5] We were very glad for this and, rejoicing, acknowledged that these were gifts of the mercy of God.

3. Truly, either you would laugh or perhaps shed tears out of

---

[4] Antioch (Lesser Antioch): located in the interior (near the middle) of Asia Minor. Iconium: located to the southeast of Lesser Antioch in the interior of Asia Minor. July 31, 1097.

[5] Matthew 15:32–39; Mark 6:34–44; Luke 9:12–17.

compassion, when many of our people lacking beasts of burden, because many had died, loaded wethers, she-goats, sows, or dogs with their possessions, such as garments, loaves of bread, or whatever pack is necessary for the use of pilgrims. We saw the backs of these small beasts chafed by the heavy loads. Occasionally armed knights even used oxen as mounts.

4. Who ever heard of such a mixture of languages in one army, since there were French, Flemings, Frisians, Gauls, Allobroges, Lotharingians, Allemani, Bavarians, Normans, English, Scots, Aquitanians, Italians, Dacians, Apulians, Iberians, Bretons, Greeks, and Armenians? If any Breton or Teuton wished to question me, I could neither understand nor answer.[6]

5. But we who were diverse in languages, nevertheless seemed to be brothers in the love of God and very close to being of one mind. For if one lost any of his possessions, he who found it would keep it carefully for many days, until by inquiry he found the loser and returned the article to him. This is fit and proper for those who make the pilgrimage in the right spirit.[7]

XV

The Arrival of the Franks at Antioch and the Siege of That City

1. In the month of October,[8] after crossing the river which they call the Fernus or Orontes, the Franks came to Antioch in Syria, the city which Seleucus,[9] son of Antiochus, founded and made the capital of Syria. It was formerly called Reblata.[10] Tents were ordered to be pitched within the first milestone before the city, where later fierce encounters were often made by both sides. For when the Turks darted forth from that city, they killed many of our men. But retaliation having been made, they mourned for the men they had lost also.

2. Antioch is an extensive city, has a strong wall, and is well situated for defense. It could never be captured by outside enemies if the inhabitants, supplied with bread, wished to defend it long enough. In the city there is a church worthy to be revered, dedicated to the Apostle Peter. Elevated to the episcopate, he sat on the throne here after he had received dominion of the Church and the keys of the Kingdom of Heaven from the Lord Jesus.

[6] The Crusade fostered a feeling of nationalism among those with similar speech.
[7] Chapter XIV, here omitted, concerns Baldwin and his taking of Edessa. Fulcher accompanied Baldwin.
[8] October 20, 1097.
[9] Antioch, a leading Near Eastern city, was founded on the Orontes about 300 B.C. by Seleucus Nicator, the general of Alexander the Great.
[10] Reblata or Ribleth was confused with Antioch by St. Jerome in his *Onomastikon*, and Fulcher followed Jerome in this error.

3. Also there is another church, round in form, built in honor of the Blessed Mary, and several others fittingly constructed. Although these had long been under the Turks, yet God, knowing all things beforehand, saved them intact for us, so that at some time or other He would be magnified by us in them.

4. The sea is about thirteen miles, I judge, from Antioch. Since the Fernus [Orontes] River happens to flow into the sea, boats loaded with all goods come from far distant parts almost to Antioch through the channel of this river. Thus the city, fortified by sea as well as by land, abounds in manifold riches.

5. When our princes had seen the great difficulty of overcoming it, they swore mutually by oath to work together in siege until, with God favoring, they would capture it either by force or by ruse.[11]

6. They found some boats on the aforementioned river, which they seized, and out of them fashioned a bridge for themselves. They were able to cross over this to carry on their work, whereas before they had to wade over with difficulty.

7. When the Turks saw that they were besieged by such a great Christian multitude, they feared that they could in no way shake them off. After a plan was mutually formed, Aoxian,[12] prince and emir of Antioch, sent his son, Sensadolus by name,[13] to the Sultan,[14] that is, the emperor, of Persia, to get his help most quickly, since they held hope for aid from no other except Mohammed, their advocate. Thus directed, he conducted this legation there very hastily.

8. Meanwhile, those who remained, awaiting the requested aid, guarded the city, and frequently plotted many kinds of harm to the Franks. Nevertheless the Franks resisted their cunning with all their power.

9. It happened on a certain day that the Franks killed seven hundred Turks; and the Turks, who set ambushes for the Franks, were overcome by the Franks lying in ambush. The strength of God was present there. All of our men retreated uninjured, with the exception of one whom they wounded.

10. Alas! how many Christians, Greeks, Syrians, and Armenians, who lived in the city, were killed by the maddened Turks. With the Franks looking on, they threw outside the walls the heads of those killed, with their petrariae[15] and slings. This especially grieved our people. Holding these Christians in hatred, the Turks feared lest by some chance they give the Franks information to their own detriment.

11. When the Franks had besieged the city for some time, and had pillaged the surrounding region for food necessary for themselves and had devastated it on all sides, bread could be bought nowhere,

[11] The siege of Antioch lasted from October 1097 to June 1098.
[12] Aoxian: Yagi Siyan of Antioch (1086–1098).
[13] Sensadolous: Shams ad Daula.
[14] Bark Yarok, Seljuk Sultan of Persia (1094–1104), son of Malik Shah.
[15] Rock-casters or catapults.

and they endured excessive hunger. As a result, everybody was especially desolate and many secretly considered withdrawal from the siege in flight, either by land or by sea.

12. They had no supplies on which they could live. It was with great fear that they sought food far away, in going distances of forty or fifty miles from the siege, that is, in the mountains, where they were often killed by the Turks lying in ambush.

13. We believed that these misfortunes befell the Franks, and that they were not able for so long a time to take the city because of their sins. Not only dissipation, but also avarice or pride or rapaciousness corrupted them.

14. After holding council, they drove out the women from the army, both married and unmarried, lest they, stained by the defilement of dissipation, displease the Lord. Those women then found places to live in the neighboring camps.

XVI

The Wretched Poverty of the Christians and the Flight of the Count of Blois

1. In the year of the Lord 1098, after the region all around Antioch had been wholly devasted by the multitude of our people, the strong as well as the weak were more and more harassed by famine.

2. At that time, the famished ate the shoots of beanseeds growing in the fields and many kinds of herbs unseasoned with salt; also thistles, which, being not well cooked because of the deficiency of firewood, pricked the tongues of those eating them; also horses, asses, and camels, and dogs, and rats. The poorer ones ate even the skins of the beasts and seeds of grain found in manure.

3. They endured winter's cold, summer's heat, and heavy rains for God.[16] Their tents became old and torn and rotten from the continuation of rains. Because of this, many of them were covered by only the sky.

4. So like gold thrice proved and purified sevenfold by fire, long predestined by God, I believe, and weighed by such a great calamity, they were cleansed of their sins. For even if the assassin's sword had not failed, many, long agonizing, would have voluntarily completed a martyr's course. . . .

6. So what then? There were some of our men, as you heard before, who left the siege because it brought so much anguish; others, because of poverty; others, because of cowardice; others, because of fear of death; first the poor and then the rich.

7. Stephen, Count of Blois, withdrew from the siege and returned

---

[16] Note religious motive here and elsewhere.

home to France by sea. Therefore all of us grieved, since he was a very noble man and valiant in arms. On the day following his departure, the city of Antioch was surrendered to the Franks.[17] If he had persevered, he would have rejoiced much in the victory with the rest. This act disgraced him. For a good beginning is not beneficial to anyone unless it be well consummated.[18] I shall cut short many things in the Lord's affairs lest I wander from the truth, because lying about them must be especially guarded against.

8. The siege lasted continuously from this same month of October, as it was mentioned, through the following winter and spring until June. The Turks and Franks alternately staged many attacks and counter-attacks; they overcame and were overcome. Our men, however, triumphed more often than theirs. . . .

XVII
The Surrender of the City of Antioch

1. When it pleased God that the labor of His people should be consummated, perhaps pleased by the prayers of those who daily poured out supplications and entreaties to Him, out of His compassion He granted that through a fraud of the Turks the city be returned to the Christians in a secret surrender. Hear, therefore, of a fraud, and yet not a fraud.

2. Our Lord appeared to a certain Turk,[19] chosen beforehand by His grace, and said to him: "Arise, thou who sleepest! I command thee to return the city to the Christians." The astonished man concealed that vision in silence.

3. However, a second time, the Lord appeared to him: "Return the city to the Christians," He said, "for I am Christ who command this of thee." Meditating what to do, he went away to his ruler, the prince of Antioch, and made that vision known to him. To him the ruler responded: "You do not wish to obey the phantom, do you, stupid?" Returning, he was afterwards silent.

4. The Lord again appeared to him, saying: "Why hast thou not fulfilled what I ordered thee? Thou must not hesitate, for I, who command this, am Lord of all." No longer doubting, he discreetly negotiated with our men, so that by his zealous plotting they might receive the city.

5. He finished speaking, and gave his son as hostage to Lord Bohemond, to whom he first directed that discourse, and whom he

---

[17] June 3, 1098.
[18] Fulcher here ignores Stephen's return in 1101 when he met martyrdom.
[19] Pirus or Firouz whom the Christian sources call a Turk, the Moslems an Armenian.

first persuaded.[1] On a certain night, he sent twenty of our men over the wall by means of ladders made of ropes. Without delay, the gate was opened. The Franks, already prepared, entered the city. Forty of our soldiers, who had previously entered by ropes, killed sixty Turks found there, guards of the tower. In a loud voice, altogether the Franks shouted: "God wills it! God wills it!" For this was our signal cry, when we were about to press forward on any enterprise.

6. After hearing this, all the Turks were extremely terrified. Then, when the redness of dawn had paled, the Franks began to go forward to attack the city. When the Turks had first seen Bohemond's red banner on high, furling and unfurling, and the great tumult aroused on all sides, and the Franks running far and wide through the streets with their naked swords and wildly killing people, and had heard their horns sounding on the top of the wall, they began to flee here and there, bewildered. From this scene, many who were able fled into the citadel situated on a cliff.

7. Our rabble wildly seized everything that they found in the streets and houses. But the proved soldiers kept to warfare, in following and killing the Turks.

8. The fleeing emir of Antioch, Aoxian, was beheaded by a certain rustic Armenian.

He, thereupon, brought the severed head to the Franks.

XIX

The Siege of the Christians by the Turks in the City of Antioch

1. On the day after Antioch had been taken, as has been told, an innumerable multitude of Turks surrounded the city in siege. The Sultan, that is, the King of the Persians, had been told by a legation that the Franks were besieging Antioch, and after collecting many people, immediately he sent an army against the Franks. Corbagath[2] was the leader and commander of this people.

2. He had besieged the city of Edessa, which Lord Baldwin possessed at that time, for three weeks;[3] but accomplishing nothing there, he hastened to Antioch to aid Prince Aoxian.

3. Seeing this army, the Franks were more desolate than ever, because punishment for their sins was doubled. For when they had

---

[1] The foregoing account is extremely questionable. According to other accounts, Bohemund contacted Firouz and bribed him to hand over the towers he commanded.

[2] Kerboga or Kerbogha, Atabeg of Mosul, who seems to have exercised some suzerainty over neighboring Turkish emirs.

[3] May 4–25, 1098.

entered the city, many of them had sought out unlawful women without delay.

4. Almost sixty thousand Turks entered by way of a fort on the top of a cliff. These exerted pressure on our men most fiercely in repeated attacks. There was not a pause; filled with great trembling, after leaving the city, they went forth to the siege. The Franks, shut in, remained unbelievably anxious.[4]

XXI
The Battle Which the Franks Asked of the Turks

1. Meanwhile, after holding council, they announced to the Turks through a certain Peter the Hermit, that unless they peacefully evacuated the region which at one time belonged to the Christians, they would surely begin war against them on the following day. But if they wished it to be done otherwise, war could be waged by five or ten or twenty or by one hundred soldiers chosen from each side, so that with not all fighting at the same time, such a great multitude of people would not die, and the party which overcame the other would take the city and kingdom freely without controversy.

2. This was proposed, but not accepted by the Turks, who, confident in the large number of their people and in their courage, thought that they could overcome and destroy ours.

3. In number, they were estimated to be three hundred thousand[5] altogether, both cavalry and infantry. They knew our knights had been forced to become footmen, weak and helpless.

4. After Peter, the ambassador, returned, the answer was given. After they heard it, the Franks prepared to fight, stopping at nothing, but placing their hope wholly in God.

5. There were many Turkish princes whom they called emirs present. These are: Corbagath, Maleducat,[6] Amisoliman,[7] and many others whom it takes too long to name.

XXII
The Preparation for Battle

1. The Frankish princes were: Hugh the Great, Robert, Count of the Normans, Robert, Count of Flanders, Duke Godfrey, Count Raymond, Bohemond, and others of lesser rank. May God bless the soul of Ademar, Bishop of Puy, an apostolic man, who always kindly comforted the people and strengthened them in the Lord.

---

[4] The terror of the Turks and Franks was enhanced by the appearance of a meteor.
[5] Obviously a greatly exaggerated number.
[6] El Muluk Dukak of Damascus.
[7] Emir Sulaiman of Aleppo.

2. Oh, pious circumstance! On the preceding evening, he ordered by heralds to all the soldiers of the army of God, that each one lay out as much grain as he could, considering the dearness of it, to supply his horse, so that those carrying the riders on the morrow might not become weak from hunger in the hour of battle. It was ordered, and it was done.

3. All having been thus prepared, they went forth to battle from the city in the early morning, which fell four days before the Kalends of July.[8] The banners of the squadrons and lines, conveniently divided into troops and phalanges, went first. Among these were the priests clothed in white vestments, who, weeping for all the people, sang hymns to God, and poured out many prayers devoutly.

4. When a certain Turk, Amirdal by name,[9] a well-proven soldier, had seen our people with standards raised coming forth against them, he was exceedingly astonished. And when he had carefully regarded our nobles' standards, which he saw advancing one by one in order, he supposed that the battle would shortly ensue.

5. He had reconnoitred frequently in Antioch, where he had learned this about the Franks. He immediately hastened to Corbagath, and informed him what he had seen, saying: "Why do you amuse yourself with chess? Behold, the Franks are coming!" Corbagath responded to him: "Are they coming to fight?" Amirdal responded: "Up to the present time, I do not know, but wait a little while."

6. When Corbagath also saw the banners of our nobles carried before them in order and the divisions of men, properly ordered, following them, returning quickly, he said: "Behold, the Franks! What do you think?" Amirdal responded: "It is war, I believe, but it is still doubtful. I shall soon recognize to whom these standards, which I see, belong."

7. Looking more closely, he recognized the standard of the Bishop of Puy advancing in the third squadron.

Without waiting any longer, he told Corbagath:

"Behold, the Franks are coming: either flee now, or fight well; for I see the standard of the great Pope advancing. Today you may fear to be overcome by those whom you thought could be entirely annihilated."

8. Corbagath said: "I shall send word to the Franks, that what they asked of me yesterday, today I shall grant." Amirdal said: "You have spoken too late." Although he demanded it, he did not obtain what he asked. Amirdal presently

> Withdrawing from that place, drove his horse with spurs.
> He reflected whether or not to flee; yet he told his comrades
> That everybody should fight bravely and hurl arrows.

[8] June 28, 1098.
[9] Probably an emir or leader not personally identifiable.

XXIII
The Battle and the Victory of the Christians and the Flight of the Turks

1. Behold, Hugh the Great and Count Robert the Norman, and also Robert, Count of Flanders, were stationed in the first line of battle for the attack. In the second, Duke Godfrey followed with the Germans and Lotharingians. After those marched the Bishop of Puy and the people of Count Raymond, Gascons and Provençals. Count Raymond himself remained in the city to guard it. Bohemond skilfully led the last division.

2. When the Turks saw that they were being fircely attacked by the whole army of the Franks, they began to dart out in a scattered fashion, as was their custom, and to hurl arrows. But fear having been let loose from heaven against them, as if the whole world had fallen, all of them took to unrestrained flight, and the Franks chased them with all their might.

3. But because the Franks had few horses and these weak from hunger, they did not take as much booty as they should have. Nevertheless, all the tents remained on the plains, and they found many kinds of things in them, such as gold, silver, coverlets, clothing, utensils, and many other things, which the Turks, in great flight, had left or flung away in their flight, namely, horses, mules, camels, asses, the best helmets, and bows and arrows with quivers.

4. Corbagath, who had slain the Franks many times with such cruel words and threats, fled more swiftly than a deer. But why did he, who had a people so great and so well equipped with horses, flee? Because he strove to fight against God, and the Lord seeing him afar, entirely broke his pomp and strength.

5. Because they had good and swift horses, they escaped, although the slower ones fell into the hands of the Franks. Many of them and of the Saracen infantry were killed. A few of ours were injured. When their women were found in the tents, the Franks did nothing evil to them except pierce their bellies with their lances.[10]

6. Everybody, placed in such great need and distress, blessed and glorified God in a voice of exultation, God, who in the righteousness of His compassion liberated those trusting in Him from such a savage enemies. He powerfully scattered them in defeat, after the Christians were almost conquered first. Made wealthy with the substance of those people, they returned pleased to the city.

7. When the venerable city of Antioch was taken
   Eleven times a hundred, if you subtract therefrom twice one,
   Then so many were the years of our Lord born of the Virgin
   Under the star of Phoebus, twice nine times risen from Gemini.

---

[10] Fulcher apparently means that the Franks abstained from mistreating the Moslem women sexually.

8. At that time Ademar the Bishop, may his soul enjoy eternal rest, died on the Kalends of August.[11] Amen! Also Hugh the Great, with the good will of the princes, went away to Constantinople; thence to France.[12]

XXV

The Invasion of the Cities. The Siege Undertaken at Archas and the Journey and Arrival of the Franks at Jerusalem

1. When our men and their horses, who had been wearied by much labor for many days, were refreshed by food and rest for four months at Antioch, they resumed their former strength. Having arranged a plan, one part of the army went into inner Syria, desiring to delay the march to Jerusalem. In this, Bohemond and Count Raymond were the leaders.[13] Other princes remained in the vicinity of Antioch.

2. These two men, with their people, seized Barra[14] and Marra,[15] by a courageous attack. After the former city had been captured quickly and completely depopulated by the slaughter of its citizens and everything which they found there had been seized, they hastened to the other city. Here, when the siege had lasted twenty days,[16] our people suffered excessive hunger. I shudder to tell that many of our people, harassed by the madness of excessive hunger, cut pieces from the buttocks of the Saracens already dead there, which they cooked, but when it was not yet roasted enough by the fire, they devoured it with savage mouth. So the besiegers rather than the besieged were tormented.

3. Meanwhile, after they had made what machines they could, and moved them to the wall, in an assault of great boldness, with God favoring, the Franks entered over the top of the wall. On that day and the following, they killed all the Saracens from the greatest to the least, and plundered all their substance.

4. This city having been thus destroyed, Bohemond returned to Antioch, from which he drove out the men whom Count Raymond had left there to guard his section of the city. Afterwards he possessed this city with the whole province. For he said that it was through his promises and through his negotiations that it had been acquired.

---

[11] August 1, 1098.
[12] At the beginning of July, 1098.
[13] According to the *Gesta*, this expedition was begun by Raymond Pilet, one of Count Raymond's men, but Count Raymond had to rescue him.
[14] Barra (Albara) was taken September 25, 1098.
[15] The Franks arrived at Marra November 27, 1098.
[16] The siege ended December 11, 1098. The Franks remained there until January 13, 1099.

5. Count Raymond, after Tancred joined him, continued the journey to Jerusalem already begun. Also the Norman Count joined this army on the second day after the departure from captured Marra.

6. In the year 1099 from the Incarnation of the Lord, they set out to the aforementioned town of Archas,[17] situated at the foot of Mount Lebanon, which Aracaeus, the son of Canaan, the nephew of Noah,[18] founded. But because it was most difficult to take, after laboring for almost five weeks in its siege, they accomplished nothing.

7. Duke Godfrey and Robert, Count of Flanders, followed not far after the army. They were besieging Gibellum,[19] when, upon the arrival of messengers, they had to hasten to the others. For this reason, they left Gibellum immediately, and because of the call for aid, they hastened to join the army. But the battle for which they had been summoned did not materialize. They stayed to take part in the siege [of Archas].[1]

8. In that siege, Anselm of Ribemont, a vigorous soldier, died of a blow from a stone.

9. Having held council, they decided that to stay there and not take the town would do great harm to the whole army. It would be advantageous, some said, to abandon the siege and take up the march at a time when the road was not crowded with merchants, and during the harvest season. For as they marched along, they could live on the ripened harvests prepared for their subsistence by God, under Whose leadership they would reach the much desired end of their pilgrimage. This plan was accepted and undertaken.

10. The tents having been packed, they went away and crossed through the city of Tripoli. After they had passed through this city, they came to the town of Gibelet.[2] It was April, and already they were living off the harvests. Thence, going forward and passing near the city of Beirut, they came upon another city which we read as Sidon by its name in the land of Phoenicia; which Sidon, a son of Canaan, founded, whence came the Sidonians. From Sidon to Sarepta. From here, they came to Tyre, a very excellent city, from which Apollo came, about whom we have read. About these two cities, the Gospel says: "into the provinces of Tyre and Sidon."[3] Now, the inhabitants of the region called the former Sagitta, and the other Sur. For it was called Soor in Hebrew.

11. Thence to the fortress named Ziph, in the sixth mile from Ptolemais. After this, they crossed over to Ptolemais, formerly called

---

[17] February 14, 1099.
[18] Genesis 10:15–17.
[19] Gibellum: Gabala, port in northern Syria near St. Simeon.
[1] While besieging Archas, Raymond and Robert of Normandy heard that a Turkish army was coming to attack them; so they requested Godfrey to come to their aid.
[2] Gibelet (Djubail): ancient Byblos (whence Bible).
[3] Matthew 15:21.

Accon,⁴ which certain mistaken ones of our men thought to be Acharon. But the city of Acharon is in the land of the Philistines near Ascalon, between Jamnia⁵ and Azot. In truth Accon, that is Ptolemais, has Mount Carmel on the south. Crossing next to it, they left to the right the city called Caypha.⁶ After these, we came close to Dora, then to Caesarea of Palestine, which in ancient times was called by another name of Turris Stratonis. Here Herod, named Agrippa, the nephew of that Herod in whose time Christ was born, died unhappily, consumed by worms.

12. Then they left the maritime region on the right and the town of Arsur, and they proceeded through a city, Rama or Aramathea by name, from which the Saracen inhabitants had fled on the day before the Franks arrived. Here they found much grain which they loaded on their beasts of burden and carried all the way to Jerusalem.

13. After a delay of four days there,⁷ when they had appointed the bishop of the Church of Saint George,⁸ and had placed men on guard in the citadels of the city, they went forward on their journey to Jerusalem. On that day they marched as far as the fortress, which was called Emmaus,⁹ near which was Modin, the city of the Maccabees.

14. On the following night, one hundred of the truest soldiers mounted their horses. When the dawn grew bright, they came close to Jerusalem, and hastened all the way to Bethlehem. Of these, one was Tancred, and another one was Baldwin.¹⁰ When the Christians, evidently Greeks and Syrians, who frequently reconnoitred there, found that the Franks had come, they were especially filled with great joy. Yet at first they did not know what race they were, thinking them to be either Turks or Arabs.

15. But when they looked at them more closely face to face, they did not doubt that they were Franks. Immediately, when they had gladly taken up their crosses and banners they proceeded to meet the Franks with weeping and pious singing: with weeping, because they feared lest such a small number of people at one time or other would be very easily slain by such a great multitude of heathen, whom they knew to be in their own land; with singing, because they wished joy to those whom they had desired to come for a long time, those who they knew would raise Christianity again to its proper and former honor, after it had been ruined by the wicked for such a long time.

16. A consecrated public thanksgiving to God was performed there

[4] The Franks stayed May 24–25 in Acre (Accon), St. Jean d'Acre, ancient Ptolemais.
[5] Ibelin.
[6] Haifa.
[7] The Franks remained from June 2 to June 6, 1099, in Rama (Ramleh), which Fulcher errs in identifying as Aramathea.
[8] Robert de Rouen.
[9] Emmaus: Amwas.
[10] Baldwin de Bourg, cousin to Godfrey, later became King Baldwin II.

in the Church of the Blessed Mary. When they had visited the place where Christ was born, and after they had given the kiss of peace to the Syrians, they returned quickly to the holy city of Jerusalem.

17. Behold! there was the army following. Gabaon,[11] which was about five and three-quarters miles from Jerusalem, had been passed on the left. Here Joshua had commanded the sun and the moon. They approached the city. When the advance guard bearing the banners aloft had shown them to the citizens, straightway the enemy within came out against them. But those who had so hastily come out, were soon driven hastily back into the city.

June was now warmed by the heat of its seventh sun,
When the Franks surrounded Jerusalem in siege.

XXVI
The Situation of Jerusalem

1. The city of Jerusalem is situated in a mountainous region, lacking in streams, woods, and springs, with the exception of the Pool of Siloam, which is a bowshot from the city. Here there is sufficient water sometimes, but occasionally the supply is reduced by drawing off the water. This little pool is in the valley at the foot of Mount Zion, in the course of the brook Cedron which, in the winter time, is accustomed to flow through the middle of the Valley of Jehosophat.

2. Many cisterns in the city, which are reserved for winter rains, are kept filled with an abundance of water. Many, from which man and beast are refreshed, are found outside the city also.

3. This city was made of modest size in its extent, so that neither because of its smallness nor because of its magnitude does it offend anyone. Within, it is as wide from wall to wall as a bow can shoot an arrow four times. On the west there is the Tower of David, at the angle of two walls of the city; on the south is Mount Zion, a little closer than a bowshot; to the east is the Mount of Olives, a mile from the city.

4. The Tower of David is of solid masonry up to the middle, constructed of large square stones sealed with molten lead. If it were well supplied with rations for soldiers, fifteen or twenty men could defend it from every attack of the enemy.

5. In this city is the Temple of the Lord, a round structure, at the place where Solomon had formerly built one which was more wonderful. Although in no wise can this Temple be compared to that former one, yet it is most beautifully made and of marvelous workmanship.

6. The Church of the Lord's Sepulchre, also round in form, was never covered, but through a wide opening which was skilfully devised by a wise architect, the Sepulchre can always be seen from above.

[11] Gibeon.

7. I am not able, nor do I dare to assert, nor am I wise enough to tell many things that are kept therein, some of which are there now, and others already gone, lest I mislead those who hear of or read about these things. In the middle of the Temple, when we first entered it, and for almost fifteen years afterwards, we saw kept a certain native rock. They claimed to know by divination that the Ark of the Covenant of the Lord with the urn and with the tablets of Moses were inclosed and sealed in it. Josiah, King of Judah, ordered it to be placed there, saying: "You will in no wise carry it from that place." For he saw its future captivity.

8. But that is contrary to what we read in the writings of Jeremiah in the second book of the Maccabees, because Jeremiah himself hid it in Arabia, saying that it was in no wise to be found, until many nations were gathered together. He was a contemporary of the King Josiah; although the king's life came to an end before Jeremiah died.

9. They also said that an Angel of the Lord had stood on the aforementioned rock and that people had perished because of an enumeration foolishly made by David and displeasing to the Lord. Since that rock disfigured the Temple of the Lord, afterwards it was entirely covered and encased in marble. Its present position is under the altar where the priest performs the rituals. All the Saracens had greatly revered this Temple of the Lord. Here they made their prayers more gladly than elsewhere, although they wasted them, since in idolatry they made them in the name of Mohammed. They permitted no Christian to enter there.

10. Another temple, which is said to be Solomon's, is large and marvelous. However, it is not that same one which Solomon built. Because of our poverty, it could not be maintained in the state in which we found it; and because of this, it is now destroyed in great part.

11. They had gutters in the streets of the city, in which all dirt was washed away in the rainy season.

12. The Emperor Aelius Hadrian decorated this city wonderfully, and adorned the streets beautifully with pavements. Jerusalem was called Aelia in his honour. Because of these and other such things, it is a venerated and glorious city.

XXVII

The Siege of the City of Jerusalem

1. When the Franks viewed the city, and saw that it would be difficult to take, our princes ordered wooden ladders to be made. By erecting them against the wall they hoped to scale it, and by a fierce attack enter the city, with God helping.

2. After they had done this, when the leaders gave the signal and

the trumpets sounded, in morning's bright light of the seventh day following[12] they rushed upon the city from all sides in an astonishing attack. But when they had rushed upon it until the sixth hour of the day, and were unable to enter by means of the scaling ladders because there were few of them, they sadly abandoned the assault.

3. After consultation, craftsmen were ordered to make machines, so that by moving them to the walls they might, with God's aid, obtain the desired end. So this was done.

4. Meanwhile they suffered lack of neither bread nor meat; but, because that place was dry, unirrigated, and without rivers, both the men and the beasts of burden were very much in need of water to drink. This necessity forced them to seek water at a distance, and daily they laboriously carried it in skins from four or five miles to the siege.

5. After the machines were prepared, namely, the battering rams and the sows, they again prepared to assail the city. In addition to other kinds of siege craft, they constructed a tower from small pieces of wood, because large pieces could not be secured in those regions. When the order was given, they carried the tower piecemeal to a corner of the city. Early in the same morning, when they had gathered the machines and other auxiliary weapons, they very quickly erected the tower in compact shape not far from the wall. After it was set up and well covered by hides on the outside, by pushing it they slowly moved it nearer to the wall.

6. Then a few but brave soldiers, at a signal from the horn, climbed on the tower. Nevertheless the Saracens defended themselves from these soldiers and, with slings, hurled firebrands dipped in oil and grease at the tower and at the soldiers, who were in it. Thereafter death was present for many on both sides.

7. From their position on Mount Zion, Count Raymond and his men likewise made a great assault with their machines. From another position, where Duke Godfrey, Robert, Count of the Normans, and Robert of Flanders, were situated, an even greater assault was made on the wall. This was what was done on that day.

8. On the following day, at the blast of the trumpets, they undertook the same work more vigorously, so that by hammering in one place with the battering-rams, they breached the wall. The Saracens had suspended two beams before the battlement and secured them by ropes as a protection against the stones hurled at them by their assailants. But what they did for their advantage later turned to their detriment, with God's providence. For when the tower was moved to the wall, the ropes, by which the aforesaid beams were suspended, were cut by falchions, and the Franks constructed a bridge for themselves out of the same timber, which they cleverly extended from the tower to the wall.

[12] June 13, 1099.

9. Already one stone tower on the wall, at which those working our machines had thrown flaming firebrands, was afire. The fire, little by little replenished by the wooden material in the tower, produced so much smoke and flame that not one of the citizens on guard could remain near it.

10. Then the Franks entered the city magnificently at the noonday hour on Friday,[13] the day of the week when Christ redeemed the whole world on the cross. With trumpets sounding and with everything in an uproar, exclaiming: "Help, God!" they vigorously pushed into the city, and straightway raised the banner on the top of the wall. All the heathen, completely terrified, changed their boldness to swift flight through the narrow streets of the quarters. The more quickly they fled, the more quickly were they put to flight.

11. Count Raymond and his men, who were bravely assailing the city in another section, did not perceive this until they saw the Saracens jumping from the top of the wall. Seeing this, they joyfully ran to the city as quickly as they could, and helped the others pursue and kill the wicked enemy.

12. Then some, both Arabs and Ethiopians, fled into the Tower of David; others shut themselves in the Temple of the Lord and of Solomon, where in the halls a very great attack was made on them. Nowhere was there a place where the Saracens could escape the swordsmen.

13. On the top of Solomon's Temple, to which they had climbed in fleeing, many were shot to death with arrows and cast down headlong from the roof. Within this Temple about ten thousand[14] were beheaded. If you had been there, your feet would have been stained up to the ankles with the blood of the slain. What more shall I tell? Not one of them was allowed to live. They did not spare the women and children.

XXVIII

The Spoils Which the Christians Took

1. After they had discovered the cleverness of the Saracens, it was an extraordinary thing to see our squires and poorer people split the bellies of those dead Saracens, so that they might pick out besants[15] from their intestines, which they had swallowed down their horrible gullets while alive. After several days, they made a great heap of their bodies and burned them to ashes, and in these ashes they found the gold more easily.

[13] July 15, 1099.
[14] Albert of Aix says three hundred. Hagenmeyer accepts this estimate, not Fulcher's.
[15] Gold coins, so called because they were originally Byzantine. Saracen besants were dinars of the same value.

2. Tancred rushed into the Temple of the Lord, and seized much of the gold and silver and precious stones. But he restored it, and returned everything or something of equal value to its holy place. I say "holy," although nothing divine was practised there at the time when the Saracens exercised their form of idolatry in religious ritual and never allowed a single Christian to enter.

3. With drawn swords, our people ran through the city;
Nor did they spare anyone, not even those pleading for mercy.
The crowd was struck to the ground, just as rotten fruit
Falls from shaken branches, and acorns from a windblown oak.

XXX

The Creation of King and Patriarch of Jerusalem and the Finding of the Lord's Cross

1. In the thousand and one hundred year less one
From the illustrious Lord's birth of the Virgin,
When Phoebus had lighted July fifteen times,[16]
The Franks captured Jerusalem by strength of power;
And soon made Godfrey the ruler of the land.[17]

All the people of the army of the Lord elected him because of his noble excellence, the proven worth of his military service, his patient temperance, and also the elegance of his manners, as the ruler of the kingdom in the Holy City, to preserve and govern it.

2. At that time canons were appointed to serve in the Church of the Lord's Sepulchre and in His Temple. Then they decided not to elect a patriarch until they had asked the Roman Pope whom he wished to nominate.[18]

3. Meanwhile about five hundred Turks, Arabs, and black Ethiopians, who had fled into the Tower of David, requested Count Raymond, who sojourned near that tower, to permit as many as were alive to go away provided they leave their money in the tower. He granted this, and from that place they went to Ascalon.

4. It was pleasing to God at that time, that a small piece of the Lord's Cross was found in a hidden place. From ancient times until now it had been concealed by religious men, and now, God being willing, it was revealed by a certain Syrian. He, with his father as conspirator, had carefully concealed and guarded it there. This particle, reshaped in the style of the cross and artistically decorated with gold and silver, was first carried to the Lord's Sepulchre and

---

[16] July 15, 1099.
[17] July 22, 1099.
[18] Arnulf of Chocques, Duke Robert of Normandy's chaplain, was elected patriarch *pro tem.*

then to the Temple joyfully, with singing and giving thanks to God, who for so many days had preserved this treasure, His own and ours.[19]

[19] The remaining six chapters have to do with the defeat of a Moslem army from Egypt at Ascalon (August, 1099), the return of various princes to their homes, the death of Godfrey of Bouillon, and the capture of Bohemund (July–August, 1100).

8

The Making of England: Norman Conquest and Consolidation

WILLIAM OF MALMESBURY

Among many progressive features of the High Middle Ages were increased consolidation of states, marked growth of monarchial power, notable advances in learning, and a rising interest in history. These and many other aspects of the period are well illustrated in William of Malmesbury's Chronicle of the Kings of England. If the Venerable Bede was the original "father of English historiography," William of Malmesbury, who proposes to resume Bede's work almost four centuries later, is its second father.

William was born in southern England about 1090. His mother was English; his father was a French knight of some learning, for he taught his son to read and inculcated in him a taste for literature. Eventually the studious William became a monk in the famous old Wessex abbey of Malmesbury, which had a reputation for learning as early as the seventh century. William received a good education, and was particularly attracted to history, which he considered a branch of moral philosophy. He became librarian of the Abbey of Malmesbury, in which capacity he not only obtained numerous works of history, but also undertook to continue the work of Bede and bring English history down to his own time. By 1125, when he was still in his thirties, William had completed his dual Chronicles or "Histories" or "Deeds" of the kings and prelates of England. He then continued with a New (Modern) History, which carried on the account of England's history from 1125 to late 1142, which was probably the year before he died. He also wrote several other historical, biographical, and exegetical works. He had friends in high places in the English church and state; but although he was offered the position of Abbot of Malmesbury on more than one occasion, he preferred to remain librarian in order to pursue his scholarly researches.

William was well qualified for his historical work, which has enjoyed an almost undiminished popularity from medieval to modern times. An erudite, cultured lover of history, he was intelligent and perceptive, shrewd in his appraisals, canny in his estimates, and devoted to the truth. He was also a born storyteller and a skillful writer, with an engaging and familiar approach. Sometimes, it is true, his love of a good tale overcomes his critical judgment, while his unquestioning acceptance of extraordinary signs and prodigies reflects the credulity of his age. But he is generally acclaimed as the best historian of his day — and by some, as the best of the entire medieval period.

Like most medieval works of its type, the Chronicle of the Kings of England is divided into books. Of these, the first two trace English history to the Norman Conquest in 1066, with the story down to 731 based largely on Bede. The remaining three books bring the account to the twentieth year of Henry I (1120), subsequently extended to 1125. The selections given here begin with the accession of Edward the Confessor in 1042 and run through the reigns of Edward, William I, William II, and Henry I.

William of Malmesbury's Chronicle reveals the cultural trend of the High Middle Ages: with thought and learning encompassing the classical and secular as well as the Christian and Scriptural, the scientific and historical as well as the literary and philosophical, and, increasingly, the laic as well as the ecclesiastical. Historical writing now becomes not only more abundant but also more logical and connected; it is concerned with causes, interrelationships, and results, not merely with simple events. And it is presented in a more polished Latin than earlier medieval chroniclers had commanded, and with improved literary style.

The cosmopolitan interests and outlook of the day are evidenced by William's inclusion, in this English chronicle, of information and events relative to Danish, French, Scottish, Italian, German, Papal, Byzantine, and Moslem history. At the same time, a nascent English patriotism and sense of national identity is indicated in the attitude assumed towards other peoples: the "lice-ridden" Scots, the "hunt-loving" Welsh, the "alcohol-addicted" Danes, the "fish-devouring" Norwegians, the "free-spending" French, the "unscrupulous" Italians, and so on. The influence and power of the clergy and Papacy are evident at every hand: William the Conqueror secures papal approval of his invasion of England, and Henry I carefully defends to the Pope his treatment of Robert of Normandy.

Although William's evaluation of conflicting claims to the English crown is obviously pro-Norman, his accounts of the

Conquest and subsequent events seem relatively fair. Clearly drawn are the contrasting characters and modes of operation of successive English kings in this critical period: the gentle piety of Edward the Confessor; the heroism and the naïveté of Harold; the determined leadership of William the Conqueror; the progressive corruption of William II; and the shrewd capability of Henry I.

If our American history and culture are essentially transplanted continuations of the English, then these extracts from William of Malmesbury should be of particular interest and concern to us. For the Norman Conquest started England on the road to consolidation as a strong nation-state and irreversibly set the future course of English history.

WILLIAM OF MALMESBURY

FROM *Chronicle of the Kings of England* *

A LONG period has elapsed since, as well through the care of my parents as my own industry, I became familiar with books. This pleasure possessed me from my childhood: this source of delight has grown with my years. Indeed I was so instructed by my father, that, had I turned aside to other pursuits, I should have considered it as jeopardy to my soul and discredit to my character. Wherefore mindful of the adage "covet what is necessary," I constrained my early age to desire eagerly that which it was disgraceful not to possess. I gave, indeed, my attention to various branches of literature, but in different degrees. Logic, for instance, which gives arms to eloquence, I contented myself with barely hearing. Medicine, which ministers to the health of the body, I studied with somewhat more attention. But now, having scrupulously examined the several branches of Ethics,[1] I bow down to its majesty, because it spontaneously unveils itself to those who study it, and directs their minds to moral practice; History more especially, through an agreeable recapitulation of past events, excites its readers, by example, to frame their lives to the pursuit of good, or to aversion from evil.[2] When, therefore, at my own expense, I had procured some historians of foreign nations, I proceeded, during

---

* Translated by J. A. Giles (London, Bohn, 1847).

[1] Ethics (or practical, applied philosophy) included such subjects as political and economic theory, in addition to personal morals.

[2] Note the practical and moral purpose ascribed to history in the Middle Ages as in antiquity.

my domestic leisure, to inquire if any thing concerning our own country could be found worthy of handing down to posterity. Hence it arose, that, not content with the writings of ancient times, I began, myself, to compose: not indeed to display my learning, which is comparatively nothing, but to bring to light events lying concealed in the confused mass of antiquity. . . . (II, Prol.).

In the year of our Lord's incarnation 1042, St. Edward,[3] the son of Ethelred, assumed the sovereignty, and held it not quite twenty-four years; he was a man from the simplicity of his manners little calculated to govern; but devoted to God, and in consequence directed by him. For while he continued to reign, there arose no popular commotions, which were not immediately quelled; no foreign war; all was calm and peaceable both at home and abroad; which is the more an object of wonder, because he conducted himself so mildly, that he would not even utter a word of reproach to the meanest person. For when he had once gone out to hunt, and a countryman had overturned the standings by which the deer are driven into the toils, struck with noble indignation he exclaimed, "By God and his mother, I will serve you just such a turn, if ever it come in my way." Here was a noble mind, who forgot that he was a king, under such circumstances, and could not think himself allowed to injure a man even of the lowest condition. In the meantime, the regard his subjects entertained for him was extreme, as was also the fear of foreigners; for God assisted his simplicity, that he might be feared, for he knew not how to be angry. . . . Edward, receiving the mournful intelligence of the death of Hardecanute,[4] was lost in uncertainty what to do, or whither to betake himself. While he was revolving many things in his mind, it occurred as the better plan to submit his situation to the opinion of Godwin.[5] To Godwin therefore he sent messengers, requesting, that he might in security have a conference with him. Godwin, though for a long time hesitating and reflecting, at length assented, and when Edward came to him and endeavoured to fall at his feet, he raised him up; and when relating the death of Hardecanute, and begging his assistance to effect his return to Normandy, Godwin made him the greatest promises. He said, it was better for him to live with credit in power, than to die ingloriously in exile: that he was the son of Ethelred,[6] the grandson of Edgar: that the kingdom was his due: that he was come to mature age, disciplined by difficulties, conversant in the art of well-governing from his years, and knowing, from his

[3] King Edward the Confessor (1042–66).
[4] Hardecanute or Harthacanute, King of England 1040–42, the dissolute, wayward, and incompetent younger son of Canute (d. 1035).
[5] Godwin, powerful Earl of Wessex (d. 1053), father of Harold who became king in 1066.
[6] Ethelred "the Redeless" or "Unready," King of England 979–1016, overthrown by Sweyn and Canute.

former poverty, how to feel for the miseries of the people: if he thought fit to rely on him[7] there could be no obstacle; for his authority so preponderated in England, that wherever he inclined, there fortune was sure to favour: if he assisted him, none would dare to murmur; and just so was the contrary side of the question: let him then only covenant a firm friendship with himself; undiminished honours for his sons, and a marriage with his daughter, and he who was now shipwrecked almost of life and hope, and imploring the assistance of another, should shortly see himself a king.

There was nothing which Edward would not promise, from the exigency of the moment: so, pledging fidelity on both sides, he confirmed by oath every thing which was demanded. Soon after convening an assembly at Gillingham, Godwin, unfolding his reasons, caused him to be received as king, and homage was paid to him by all. He[8] was a man of ready wit, and spoke fluently in the vernacular tongue; powerful in speech, powerful in bringing over the people to whatever he desired. Some yielded to his authority; some were influenced by presents; others admitted the right of Edward; and the few who resisted in defiance of justice and equity were carefully marked, and afterwards driven out of England.

Edward was crowned with great pomp at Winchester, on Easter-day, and was instructed by Eadsine,[9] the archbishop, in the sacred duties of governing. This, at the time, he treasured up with readiness in his memory, and afterwards displayed in the holiness of his conduct. The above-mentioned Eadsine, in the following year, falling into an incurable disease, appointed as his successor Siward, abbat of Abingdon; communicating his design only to the king and the earl, lest any improper person should aspire to so great an eminence, either by solicitation of by purchase. Shortly after, the king took Edgitha, the daughter of Godwin, to wife; a woman whose bosom was the school of every liberal art, though little skilled in earthly matters: on seeing her, if you were amazed at her erudition, you must absolutely languish for the purity of her mind, and the beauty of her person. Both in her husband's life-time, and afterwards, she was not entirely free from suspicion of dishonour; but when dying, in the time of king William, she voluntarily satisfied the by-standers of her unimpaired chastity, by an oath. When she became his wife, the king acted towards her so delicately, that he neither removed her from his bed, nor knew her after the manner of men. I have not been able to discover, whether he acted thus from dislike to her family, which he prudently dissembled from the exigency of the times, or out of pure regard to chastity; yet it is most notoriously affirmed, that he never violated his purity by connexion with any woman. . . .

[7] Godwin.
[8] Godwin.
[9] The *Anglo-Saxon Chronicle* says that Eadsine, Archbishop of Canterbury since 1038, consecrated Edward at Winchester on Easter of 1042, and "before all people well admonished him."

King Edward declining into years, as he had no children himself, and saw the sons of Godwin growing in power, despatched messengers to the king of Hungary, to send over Edward, the son of his brother Edmund, with all his family: intending, as he declared, that either he, or his sons, should succeed to the hereditary kingdom of England, and that his own want of issue should be supplied by that of his kindred. Edward came in consequence, but died almost immediately at St. Paul's[10] in London: he was neither valiant, nor a man of abilities. He left three surviving children; that is to say, Edgar, who, after the death of Harold, was by some elected king; and who, after many revolutions of fortune, is now living wholly retired in the country, in extreme old age: Christina, who grew old at Romsey in the habit of a nun: Margaret, whom Malcolm king of the Scots espoused. Blessed with a numerous offspring, her sons were Edgar, and Alexander, who reigned in Scotland after their father in due succession: for the eldest, Edward, had fallen in battle with his father; the youngest, David, noted for his meekness and discretion, is at present king of Scotland.[11] Her daughters were, Matilda, whom in our time king Henry has married, and Maria, whom Eustace the younger, earl of Boulogne, espoused. The king, in consequence of the death of his relation, losing his first hope of support, gave the succession of England to William earl of Normandy.[12] He was well worthy of such a gift, being a young man of superior mind, who had raised himself to the highest eminence by his unwearied exertion: moreover, he was his nearest relation by consanguinity, as he was the son of Robert, the son of Richard the second, whom we have repeatedly mentioned as the brother of Emma, Edward's mother. Some affirm that Harold himself was sent into Normandy by the king for this purpose: others, who knew Harold's more secret intentions, say, that being driven thither against his will, by the violence of the wind, he imagined this device, in order to extricate himself. This, as it appears nearest the truth, I shall relate. Harold being at his country-seat at Boseham,[13] went for recreation on board a fishing boat, and, for the purpose of prolonging his sport, put out to sea; when a sudden tempest arising, he was driven with his companions on the coast of Ponthieu.[14] The people of that district, as was their native custom, immediately assembled from all quarters; and Harold's company, unarmed and few in number, were, as it easily might be, quickly overpowered by an armed multitude, and bound hand and foot. Harold, craftily meditating a remedy for this mischance, sent a person, whom he had

---

[10] According to the *Anglo-Saxon Chronicle*, this Edward died in 1057 and was buried at St. Paul's.
[11] David I, King of Scotland, 1107/24–1153.
[12] Duke William of Normandy, "the Conqueror," King of England 1066–87. This concession is disputed. Note that William of Malmesbury was a supporter of the Norman line.
[13] Near Chichester in southern England.
[14] Across the Channel in northwestern France.

allured by very great promises, to William[15] to say that he had been sent into Normandy by the king, for the purpose of expressly confirming, in person, the message which had been imperfectly delivered by people of less authority; but that he was detained in fetters by Guy, earl of Ponthieu, and could not execute his embassy: that it was the barbarous and inveterate custom of that country, that such as had escaped destruction at sea, should meet with perils on shore: that it well became a man of his dignity not to let this pass unpunished: that to suffer those to be laden with chains, who appealed to his protection, detracted somewhat from his own greatness: and that if his captivity must be terminated by money, he would gladly give it to earl William, but not to the contemptible Guy. By these means, Harold was liberated at William's command, and conducted to Normandy by Guy in person. The earl entertained him with much respect, both in banqueting and in vesture, according to the custom of his country; and the better to learn his disposition, and at the same time to try his courage, took him with him in an expedition he at that time led against Brittany. There, Harold, well proved both in ability and courage, won the heart of the Norman; and, still more to ingratiate himself, he of his own accord, confirmed to him by oath the castle of Dover, which was under his jurisdiction, and the kingdom of England, after the death of Edward. Wherefore, he was honoured both by having his[16] daughter, then a child, betrothed to him, and by the confirmation of his ample patrimony, and was received into the strictest intimacy. Not long after his return home, the king was crowned[17] at London on Christmas-day, and being there seized with the disorder of which he was sensible he should die, he commanded the church of Westminster to be dedicated on Innocents-day.[18] Thus, full of years and of glory, he surrendered his pure spirit to heaven, and was buried on the day of the Epiphany, in the said church, which he, first in England, had erected after that kind of style which, now, almost all attempt to rival at enormous expense.[19] The race of the West Saxons, which had reigned in Britain five hundred and seventy-one years, from the time of Cerdic, and two hundred and sixty-one from Egbert, in him ceased altogether to rule.[1] For while the grief for the king's death was yet fresh, Harold, on the very day of the Epiphany, seized the diadem, and extorted[2] from the nobles their consent;

[15] Duke William of Normandy, as above.
[16] Duke William's.
[17] It was customary for the king to wear his crown at solemn festivals.
[18] Westminster Abbey was built by Edward the Confessor and consecrated on Dec. 28, 1065. Building was continued after his death.
[19] The Romanesque: specifically Norman Romanesque, introduced by Edward.
[1] According to William of Malmesbury, Cerdic led the West Saxon invasion of England in 495. The strong Egbert (Ecgbert) of Wessex began to rule in 802 (William's 261 would suppose 805, but he says 800 earlier) and became Bretwalda by about 829. Edward the Confessor died on Jan. 5, 1066.
[2] Note Malmesbury's bias: the election was apparently free.

though the English say that it was granted him by the king: but I conceive it alleged, more through regard to Harold, than through sound judgment, that Edward should transfer his inheritance to a man of whose power he had always been jealous. Still, not to conceal the truth, Harold would have governed the kingdom with prudence and with courage, in the character he had assumed, had he undertaken it lawfully. Indeed, during Edward's lifetime, he had quelled, by his valour, whatever wars were excited against him; wishing to signalize himself with his countrymen, and looking forward with anxious hope to the crown. He first vanquished Griffin king of the Welsh, as I have before related, in battle; and afterwards, when he was again making formidable efforts to recover his power, deprived him of his head; appointing as his successors, two of his own adherents, that is, the brothers of this Griffin, Blegent and Rivallo, who had obtained his favour by their submission. The same year Tosty arrived on the Humber, from Flanders, with a fleet of sixty ships, and infested with piratical depredations those parts which were adjacent to the mouth of the river; but being quickly driven from the province by the joint force of the brothers, Edwin and Morcar, he set sail towards Scotland; where meeting with Harold Harfager king of Norway, then meditating an attack on England with three hundred ships, he put himself under his command. Both, then, with united forces, laid waste the country beyond the Humber; and falling on the brothers, reposing after their recent victory and suspecting no attack of the kind, they first routed, and then shut them up in York. Harold, on hearing this, proceeded thither with all his forces, and, each nation making every possible exertion, a bloody encounter followed: but the English obtained the advantage, and put the Norwegians to flight. Yet, however reluctantly posterity may believe it, one single Norwegian for a long time delayed the triumph of so many, and such great men. For standing on the entrance of the bridge, which is called Standford Brigge,[3] after having killed several of our party, he prevented the whole from passing over. Being invited to surrender, with the assurance that a man of such courage should experience the amplest clemency from the English, he derided those who entreated him; and immediately, with stern countenance, reproached the set of cowards who were unable to resist an individual. No one approaching nearer, as they thought it unadvisable to come to close quarters with a man who had desperately rejected every means of safety, one of the king's followers aimed an iron javelin at him from a distance; and transfixed him as he was boastfully flourishing about, and too incautious from his security, so that he yielded the victory to the English. The army immediately passing over without opposition, destroyed the dispersed and flying Norwegians. King Harfager and Tosty were slain; the king's son, with all the ships, was kindly sent back to his own

[3] Harold's forces won the victory of Stamford Bridge on Sept. 25, 1066.

country. Harold, elated by his successful enterprise, vouchsafed no part of the spoil to his soldiers. Wherefore many, as they found opportunity, stealing away, deserted the king, as he was proceeding to the battle of Hastings. For with the exception of his stipendiary and mercenary soldiers, he had very few of the people[4] with him. . . . Nor in saying this, do I at all derogate from the valour of the Normans, to whom I am strongly bound, both by my descent, and for the privileges I enjoy. Still those persons appear to me to err, who augment the numbers of the English, and underrate their courage; who, while they design to extol the Normans, load them with ignominy.[5] A mighty commendation indeed! that a very warlike nation should conquer a set of people who were obstructed by their multitude, and fearful through cowardice! On the contrary, they were few in number and brave in the extreme; and sacrificing every regard to their bodies, poured forth their spirit for their country. (II, 13)

When king Edward had yielded to fate, England fluctuating with doubtful favour, was uncertain to which ruler she should commit herself: to Harold, William, or Edgar: for the king had recommended him also to the nobility, as nearest to the sovereignty in point of birth; concealing his better judgment from the tenderness of his disposition. Wherefore, as I have said above, the English were distracted in their choice, although all of them openly wished well to Harold. He, indeed, once dignified with the diadem, thought nothing of the covenant between himself and William: he said that he was absolved from his oath, because his daughter, to whom he had been betrothed, had died before she was marriageable. For this man, though possessing numberless good qualities, is reported to have been careless about abstaining from perfidy, so that he could, by any device, elude the reasonings of men on this matter. Moreover, supposing that the threats of William would never be put into execution, because he was occupied in wars with neighbouring princes, he had, with his subjects, given full indulgence to security. For indeed, had he not heard that the king of Norway was approaching, he would neither have condescended to collect troops, nor to array them. William, in the meantime, began mildly to address him by messengers; to expostulate on the broken covenant; to mingle threats with entreaties; and to warn him, that ere a year expired, he would claim his due by the sword, and that he would come to that place, where Harold supposed he had firmer footing than himself. Harold again rejoined what I have related, concerning the nuptials of his daughter, and added, that he had been

[4] Due to the rapidity with which he struck at his enemies, first at Stamford Bridge and then at Hastings, Harold could not have had much time to recruit very large forces or replenish his losses, for which after-the-fact critics blame him.

[5] William of Poitiers, for example, asserts that Harold had collected large forces from England and also had auxiliaries from Denmark, but it seems certain that he is exaggerating.

precipitate on the subject of the kingdom, in having confirmed to him by oath another's right, without the universal consent and edict of the general meeting and of the people: again, that a rash oath ought to be broken; for if the oath, or vow, which a maiden, under her father's roof, made concerning her person, without the knowledge of her parents, was adjudged invalid; how much more invalid must that oath be, which he had made concerning the whole kingdom, when under the king's authority, compelled by the necessity of the time, and without the knowledge of the nation.[6] Besides it was an unjust request, to ask him to resign a government which he had assumed by the universal kindness of his fellow subjects, and which would neither be agreeable to the people, nor safe for the military.

. . . But at that time the prudence of William, seconded by the providence of God, already anticipated the invasion of England; and that no rashness might stain his just cause, he sent to the pope, formerly Anselm, bishop of Lucca, who had assumed the name of Alexander,[7] alleging the justice of the war which he meditated with all the eloquence he was master of. Harold omitted to do this, either because he was proud by nature, or else distrusted his cause; or because he feared that his messengers would be obstructed by William and his partisans, who beset every port. The pope, duly examining the pretensions of both parties, delivered a standard to William, as an auspicious presage of the kingdom: on receiving which, he summoned an assembly of his nobles, at Lillebourne, for the purpose of ascertaining their sentiments on this attempt. And when he had confirmed, by splendid promises, all who approved his design, he appointed them to prepare shipping, in proportion to the extent of their possessions. Thus they departed at that time; and, in the month of August, re-assembled in a body at St. Vallery,[8] for so that port is called by its new name. Collecting, therefore, ships from every quarter, they awaited the propitious gale which was to carry them to their destination. When this delayed blowing for several days, the common soldiers, as is generally the case, began to mutter in their tents, "that the man must be mad, who wished to subjugate a foreign country; that God opposed him, who withheld the wind; that his father purposed a similar attempt, and was in like manner frustrated; that it was the fate of that family to aspire to things beyond their reach, and find God for their adversary." In consequence of these things, which were enough to enervate the force of the brave, being publicly noised abroad, the duke held a council with his chiefs, and ordered the body of St. Vallery to be brought forth, and to be exposed to the open air, for the purpose of imploring a wind. No

[6] Evidently the Great Council had never formally settled the crown on Duke William.
[7] Pope Alexander II (1061–73).
[8] Evidently the St. Valeri at the mouth of the Somme River in Picardy.

delay now interposed, but the wished-for gale filled their sails. A joyful clamour then arising, summoned every one to the ships. The earl himself first launching from the continent into the deep, awaited the rest, at anchor, nearly in mid-channel. All then assembled round the crimson sail of the admiral's ship; and, having first dined, they arrived, after a favourable passage, at Hastings. As he disembarked he slipped down, but turned the accident to his advantage; a soldier who stood near calling out to him, "you hold England,[9] my lord, its future king." He then restrained his whole army from plundering; warning them, that they should now abstain from what must hereafter be their own;[10] and for fifteen successive days he remained so perfectly quiet, that he seemed to think of nothing less than of war.

In the meantime Harold returned from the battle with the Norwegians; happy, in his own estimation, at having conquered; but not so in mine, as he had secured the victory by parricide.[11] When the news of the Norman's arrival reached him, reeking as he was from battle, he proceeded to Hastings, though accompanied by very few forces. No doubt the fates urged him on, as he neither summoned his troops, nor, had he been willing to do so, would he have found many ready to obey his call; so hostile were all to him, as I have before observed, from his having appropriated the northern spoils entirely to himself. He sent out some persons, however, to reconnoitre the number and strength of the enemy: these, being taken within the camp, William ordered to be led amongst the tents, and, after feasting them plentifully, to be sent back uninjured to their lord. On their return, Harold inquired what news they brought: when, after relating at full, the noble confidence of the general, they gravely added, that almost all his army had the appearance of priests, as they had the whole face, with both lips, shaven. For the English leave the upper lip unshorn, suffering the hair continually to increase; which Julius Caesar, in his treatise on the Gallic War,[12] affirms to have been a national custom with the ancient inhabitants of Britain. The king smiled at the simplicity of the relators, observing, with a pleasant laugh, that they were not priests, but soldiers, strong in arms, and invincible in spirit. His brother, Girth, a youth, on the verge of manhood, and of knowledge and valour surpassing his years, caught up his words: "Since," said he, "you extol so much the valour of the Norman, I think it ill-advised for you, who are his inferior in strength and desert, to contend with him. Nor can you deny being bound to him, by oath, either willingly, or by compulsion. Wherefore you will act wisely if, yourself withdrawing from this pressing emergency, you allow us to

---

[9] In feudal investiture, delivery of lands or an office was accomplished by handing over a visible symbol, such as a clod of earth, a twig, a branch, or the like.
[10] If the Conqueror gave such orders, they seem to have been of little avail.
[11] Or fratricide? Harold's brother, Tostig, was slain in battle.
[12] Book V, Ch. 14.

try the issue of a battle. We, who are free from all obligation, shall justly draw the sword in defence of our country. It is to be apprehended, if you engage, that you will be either subjected to flight or to death: whereas, if we only fight, your cause will be safe at all events: for you will be able both to rally the fugitives, and to avenge the dead."

His[13] unbridled rashness yielded no placid ear to the words of his adviser, thinking it base, and a reproach to his past life, to turn his back on danger of any kind; and, with similar impudence, or to speak more favourably, imprudence, he drove away a monk, the messenger of William, not deigning him even a complacent look; imprecating only that God would decide between him and the earl. He was the bearer of three propositions: either that Harold should relinquish the kingdom, according to his agreement; or hold it of William; or decide the matter by single combat in the sight of either army. For William[14] claimed the kingdom on the ground that king Edward, by the advice of Stigand, the archbishop, and of the earls Godwin and Siward, had granted it to him, and had sent the son and nephew of Godwin to Normandy, as sureties of the grant. If Harold should deny this, he would abide by the judgment of the pope, or by battle: on all which propositions, the messenger being frustrated by the single answer I have related, returned, and communicated to his party fresh spirit for the conflict.

The courageous leaders mutually prepared for battle, each according to his national custom. The English, as we have heard, passed the night without sleep, in drinking and singing, and, in the morning, proceeded without delay towards the enemy; all were on foot, armed with battle-axes, and covering themselves in front by the junction of their shields, they formed an impenetrable body, which would have secured their safety that day, had not the Normans, by a feigned flight, induced them to open their ranks, which till that time, according to their custom, were closely compacted. The king himself on foot, stood, with his brother, near the standard; in order that, while all shared equal danger, none might think of retreating. This standard William sent, after the victory, to the pope; it was sumptuously embroidered, with gold and precious stones, in the form of a man fighting.

On the other side, the Normans passed the whole night in confessing their sins, and received the sacrament in the morning: their infantry, with bows and arrows, formed the vanguard, while their cavalry, divided into wings, were thrown back. The earl, with serene countenance, declaring aloud, that God would favour his, as being the righteous side, called for his arms; and presently, when, through the hurry of his attendants, he had put on his hauberk the

---

[13] Harold's.
[14] The following, evidently from William of Poitiers, is obviously false.

hind part before, he corrected the mistake with a laugh; saying, "My dukedom shall be turned into a kingdom." Then beginning the song of Roland,[15] that the warlike example of that man might stimulate the soldiers, and calling on God for assistance, the battle commenced on both sides. They fought with ardour, neither giving ground, for a great part of the day. Finding this, William gave a signal to his party, that, by a feigned flight, they should retreat. Through this device, the close body of the English, opening for the purpose of cutting down the straggling enemy, brought upon itself swift destruction; for the Normans, facing about, attacked them thus disordered, and compelled them to fly. In this manner, deceived by a stratagem, they met an honourable death in avenging their country; nor indeed were they at all wanting to their own revenge, as, by frequently making a stand, they slaughtered their pursuers in heaps: for, getting possession of an eminence, they drove down the Normans, when roused with indignation and anxiously striving to gain the higher ground, into the valley beneath, where, easily hurling their javelins and rolling down stones on them as they stood below, they destroyed them to a man. Besides, by a short passage, with which they were acquainted, avoiding a deep ditch, they trod under foot such a multitude of their enemies in that place, that they made the hollow level with the plain, by the heaps of carcasses. This vicissitude of first one party conquering, and then the other, prevailed as long as the life of Harold continued; but when he fell, from having his brain pierced with an arrow, the flight of the English ceased not until night. The valour of both leaders was here eminently conspicuous. . . .

This was a fatal day to England, a melancholy havoc of our dear country, through its change of masters. For it had long since adopted the manners of the Angles, which had been very various according to the times: for in the first years of their arrival, they were barbarians in their look and manners, warlike in their usages, heathens in their rites; but, after embracing the faith of Christ, by degrees, and in process of time, from the peace they enjoyed, regarding arms only in a secondary light, they gave their whole attention to religion. I say nothing of the poor, the meanness of whose fortune often restrains them from overstepping the bounds of justice: I omit men of ecclesiastical rank, whom sometimes respect to their profession, and sometimes the fear of shame, suffer not to deviate from the truth: I speak of princes, who from the greatness of their power might have full liberty to indulge in pleasure; some of whom, in their own country, and others at Rome, changing their habit, obtained a heavenly kingdom, and a saintly intercourse. Many during their whole lives in outward appearance only embraced the present world, in order that they might exhaust their treasures on the poor, or divide them amongst monasteries. What shall I say of the multitudes of bishops, hermits,

---

[15] Note the popularity of the *Chanson de Roland*.

and abbats? Does not the whole island blaze with such numerous relics of its natives, that you can scarcely pass a village of any consequence but you hear the name of some new saint, besides the numbers of whom all notices have perished through the want of records? Nevertheless, in process of time, the desire after literature and religion had decayed for several years before the arrival of the Normans. The clergy, contented with a very slight degree of learning, could scarcely stammer out the words of the sacraments; and a person who understood grammar, was an object of wonder and astonishment. The monks mocked the rule of their order by fine vestments, and the use of every kind of food. The nobility, given up to luxury and wantonness, went not to church in the morning after the manner of Christians, but merely, in a careless manner, heard matins and masses from a hurrying priest in their chambers, amid the blandishments of their wives. The commonalty, left unprotected, became a prey to the most powerful, who amassed fortunes, by either seizing on their property, or by selling their persons into foreign countries; although it be an innate quality of this people, to be more inclined to revelling, than to the accumulation of wealth. There was one custom, repugnant to nature, which they adopted; namely, to sell their female servants, when pregnant by them and after they had satisfied their lust, either to public prostitution, or foreign slavery. Drinking in parties was a universal practice, in which occupation they passed entire nights as well as days. They consumed their whole substance in mean and despicable houses; unlike the Normans and French, who, in noble and splendid mansions, lived with frugality. The vices attendant on drunkenness, which enervate the human mind, followed; hence it arose that engaging William, more with rashness, and precipitate fury, than military skill, they doomed themselves, and their country to slavery, by one, and that an easy, victory. "For nothing is less effective than rashness; and what begins with violence, quickly ceases, or is repelled." In fine, the English at that time, wore short garments reaching to the mid-knee; they had their hair cropped; their beards shaven; their arms laden with golden bracelets; their skin adorned with punctured designs. They were accustomed to eat till they became surfeited, and to drink till they were sick. These latter qualities they imparted to their conquerors; as to the rest, they adopted their manners. I would not, however, have these bad propensities universally ascribed to the English. I know that many of the clergy, at that day, trod the path of sanctity, by a blameless life; I know that many of the laity, of all ranks and conditions, in this nation, were well-pleasing to God. Be injustice far from this account; the accusation does not involve the whole indiscriminately. "But, as in peace, the mercy of God often cherishes the bad and the good together; so, equally, does his severity, sometimes, include them both in captivity."

Moreover, the Normans, that I may speak of them also, were at that time, and are even now, proudly apparelled, delicate in their food, but not excessive. They are a race inured to war, and can hardly live without it; fierce in rushing against the enemy; and where strength fails of success, ready to use strategem, or to corrupt by bribery. As I have related, they live in large edifices with economy; envy their equals; wish to excel their superiors; and plunder their subjects, though they defend them from others; they are faithful to their lords, though a slight offence renders them perfidious.[16] They weigh treachery by its chance of success, and change their sentiments with money. They are, however, the kindest of nations, and they esteem strangers worthy of equal honour with themselves. They also intermarry with their vassals. They revived, by their arrival, the observances of religion, which were everywhere grown lifeless in England. You might see churches rise in every village, and monasteries in the towns and cities, built after a style unknown before; you might behold the country flourishing with renovated rites; so that each wealthy man accounted that day lost to him, which he had neglected to signalize by some magnificent action. But having enlarged sufficiently on these points, let us pursue the transactions of William.

When his victory was complete, he[17] caused his dead to be interred with great pomp; granting the enemy the liberty of doing the like, if they thought proper. He sent the body of Harold to his mother, who begged it, unransomed; though she proffered large sums by her messengers. She buried it, when thus obtained, at Waltham; a church which he had built at his own expense, in honour of the Holy Cross, and had endowed for canons. William then, by degrees proceeding, as became a conqueror, with his army, not after an hostile, but a royal manner, journeyed towards London, the principal city of the kingdom; and shortly after, all the citizens came out to meet him with gratulations. Crowds poured out of every gate to greet him, instigated by the nobility, and principally by Stigand, archbishop of Canterbury, and Aldred, of York. For, shortly before, Edwin and Morcar, two brothers of great expectation, hearing, at London, the news of Harold's death, solicited the citizens to exalt one of them to the throne: failing, however, in the attempt, they had departed for Northumberland, conjecturing, from their own feelings, that William would never come thither. The other chiefs would have chosen Edgar, had the bishops supported them; but, danger and domestic broils closely impending, neither did this take effect. Thus the English, who, had they united in one opinion, might have repaired the ruin of their country, introduced a stranger, while they were unwilling to choose a native, to govern them. Being now decidedly hailed king, he was crowned on Christmas-day by archbishop Aldred; for he was

[16] Mark the catch in the feudal system based on gentlemanly contractual oaths and moral obligations.
[17] William.

careful not to accept this office from Stigand, as he was not canonically an archbishop.[18]

Of the various wars which he carried on, this is a summary. Favoured by God's assistance, he easily reduced the city of Exeter, when it had rebelled; for part of the wall fell down accidentally, and made an opening for him. Indeed he had attacked it with the more ferocity, asserting that those irreverent men would be deserted by God's favour, because one of them, standing upon the wall, had bared his posteriors, and had broken wind, in contempt of the Normans. He almost annihilated the city of York, that sole remaining shelter for rebellion, and destroyed its citizens with sword and famine. For there Malcolm, king of the Scots,[19] with his party; there Edgar,[1] and Morcar, and Waltheof, with the English and Danes, often brooded over the nest of tyranny; there they frequently killed his generals; whose deaths, were I severally to commemorate, perhaps I should not be superfluous, though I might risk the peril of creating disgust; while I should be not easily pardoned as an historian, if I were led astray by the falsities of my authorities. . . .

On this account perhaps the conduct of the king may reasonably be excused, if he was at any time rather severe against the English; for he scarcely found any one of them faithful. This circumstance so exasperated his ferocious mind, that he deprived the more powerful, first of their wealth, next of their estates, and finally, some of them of their lives. Moreover, he followed the device of Caesar, who drove out the Germans, concealed in the vast forest of Ardennes, whence they harassed his army with perpetual irruptions, not by means of his own countrymen, but by the confederate Gauls; that, while strangers destroyed each other, he might gain a bloodless victory. Thus, I say, William acted towards the English. For, allowing the Normans to be unemployed, he opposed an English army, and an English commander, to those, who, after the first unsuccessful battle, had fled to Denmark and Ireland, and had returned at the end of three years with considerable force: forseeing that whichever side might conquer, it must be a great advantage to himself. Nor did this device fail him; for both parties of the English, after some conflicts between themselves, without any exertion on his part, left a victory for the king; the invaders being driven to Ireland, and the royalists purchasing the empty title of conquest, at their own special loss, and that of their general. . . .

[18] One of the principal causes of papal support of William had been that the Anglo-Saxon party had deposed the legitimate Archbishop of Canterbury, Robert of Jumieges, and installed their own candidate, Stigand, whom they obstinately supported.

[19] Malcolm III, Canmore (1058–93), brother-in-law of Edgar Aetheling since 1068.

[1] Edgar Aetheling, grandson of Edmund Ironside, English king who died in 1016.

Now, king William conducting himself with mildness towards the obedient but with severity to the rebellious, possessed the whole of England in tranquillity, holding all the Welsh tributary to him. At this time too, beyond sea, being never unemployed, he nearly annihilated the county of Maine, leading thither an expedition composed of English; who, though they had been easily conquered in their own, yet always appeared invincible in a foreign country. He lost multitudes of his men at Dol, a town of Brittany, whither, irritated by some broil, he had led a military force. He constantly found Philip king of France, the daughter of whose aunt he had married, unfaithful to him; because he was envious of the great glory of a man who was vassal both to his father and to himself. But William did not the less actively resist his attempts, although his first-born son Robert, through evil counsel, assisted him in opposition to his father. Whence it happened, that in an attack at Gerborai, the son became personally engaged with his father; wounded him and killed his horse: William, the second son, departed with a hurt also, and many of the king's party were slain. In all other respects, during the whole of his life, he was so fortunate, that foreign and distant nations feared nothing more than his name. He had subdued the inhabitants so completely to his will, that without any opposition, he first caused an account to be taken of every person; compiled a register of the rent of every estate throughout England,[2] and made all free men, of every description, take the oath of fidelity to him. . . .

The king of Denmark then, as I have said, was the only obstacle to William's uninterrupted enjoyment: on whose account he enlisted such an immense multitude of stipendiary soldiers out of every province on this side of the mountains, that their numbers oppressed the kingdom. But he, with his usual magnaminity, not regarding the expense, had engaged even Hugo the Great, brother to the king of France, with his bands to serve in his army. He was accustomed to stimulate and incite his own valour, by the remembrance of Robert Guiscard;[3] saying it was disgraceful to yield, in courage, to him whom he surpassed in rank. For Robert, born of middling parentage in Normandy, that is, neither very low nor very high, had gone, a few years before William's arrival in England, with fifteen knights, into Apulia, to remedy the narrowness of his own circumstances, by entering into the service of that inactive race of people. Not many years elapsed, ere, by the stupendous assistance of God, he reduced the whole country under his power. For where his strength failed, his ingenuity was alert: first receiving the towns, and after, the cities into confederacy with him. Thus he became so successful, as to make himself duke of Apulia and Calabria; his brother Richard, prince of Capua; and his other brother, Roger, earl of Sicily. At last, giving

[2] Domesday Book.
[3] Robert Guiscard, "the Crafty": noted Norman conqueror of southern Italy.

Apulia to his son Roger, he crossed the Adriatic with his other son Boamund,[4] and taking Durazzo, was immediately proceeding against Alexius, emperor of Constantinople, when a messenger from pope Hildebrand[5] stopped him in the heat of his career. For Henry,[6] emperor of Germany, son of that Henry[7] we have before mentioned, being incensed against the pope, for having excommunicated him on account of the ecclesiastical investitures, led an army against Rome; besieged it; expelled Hildebrand, and introduced Guibert of Ravenna.[8] Guiscard learning this by the letter of the expelled pope, left his son Boamund, with the army, to follow up his designs, and returned to Apulia; where quickly getting together a body of Apulians and Normans, he proceeded to Rome. Nor did Henry wait for a messenger to announce his approach; but, affrighted at the bare report, fled with his pretended pope. Rome, freed from intruders, received its lawful sovereign; but soon after again lost him by similar violence. Then too, Alexius, learning that Robert was called home by the urgency of his affairs, and hoping to put a finishing hand to the war, rushed against Boamund, who commanded the troops which had been left. The Norman youth, however, observant of his native spirit, though far inferior in number, turned to flight, by dint of military skill, the undisciplined Greeks[9] and the other collected nations. At the same time, too, the Venetians, a people habituated to the sea, attacking Guiscard, who having settled the object of his voyage was now sailing back, met with a similar calamity: part were drowned or killed, the rest put to flight. He, continuing his intended expedition, induced many cities, subject to Alexius, to second his views. The emperor took off, by crime, the man he was unable to subdue by arms: falsely promising his wife an imperial match. By her artifices, he drank poison, which she had prepared, and died; deserving, had God so pleased, a nobler death: for he was unconquerable by the sword of an enemy, but fell a victim to domestic treachery.[10] He was buried at Venusium in Apulia, having the following epitaph:

> Here Guiscard lies, the terror of the world,
> Who from the Capitol Rome's sovereign hurl'd.
> No band collected could Alexis free,
> Flight only; Venice, neither flight nor sea.

On the death of Alexander, therefore, Hildebrand, called Gregory the Seventh, succeeded.[11] He openly asserted what others had whis-

---

[4] Bohemund, Robert's natural son, famous fighter and participant in the First Crusade, who became Prince of Antioch.
[5] Hildebrand became Pope Gregory VII.
[6] Henry IV.
[7] Son of Henry III.
[8] As Antipope Clement III.
[9] I.e., Byzantines.
[10] Guiscard died of an apparent fever in 1085.
[11] Pope Gregory VII (1073–85).

pered, excommunicating those persons who, having been elected, should receive the investiture of their churches, by the ring and staff, through the hands of the laity. On this account Henry,[12] emperor of Germany, being incensed that he should so far presume without his concurrence, expelled him from Rome, as I observed, after the expiration of eleven years, and brought in Guibert.[13] Not long after, the pope, being seized with that fatal disease which he had no doubt would be mortal, was requested by the cardinals to appoint his successor; referring him to the example of St. Peter, who, in the church's earliest infancy, had, while yet living, nominated Clement. He refused to follow this example, because it had anciently been forbidden by councils: he would advise, however, that if they wished a person powerful in worldly matters, they should choose Desiderius, abbat of Cassino,[14] who would quell the violence of Guibert successfully and opportunely by a military force; but if they wanted a religious and eloquent man, they should elect Odo bishop of Ostia.[15] Thus died a man, highly acceptable to God, though perhaps rather too austere towards men. Indeed it is affirmed, that in the beginning of the first commotion between him and the emperor, he would not admit him within his doors, though barefooted, and carrying shears and scourges,[16] despising a man guilty of sacrilege, and of incest with his own sister. The emperor, thus excluded, departed, vowing that this repulse should be the death of many a man. And immediately doing all the injury he was able to the Roman see, he excited thereby the favourers of the pope, on every side, to throw off their allegiance to himself; for one Rudolph,[17] revolting at the command of the pope, who had sent him a crown in the name of the apostles, he was immersed on all sides in the tumult of war. But Henry, ever superior to ill fortune, at length subdued him and all others faithlessly rebelling. At last, driven from his power, not by a foreign attack, but the domestic hatred of his son, he died miserably. To Hildebrand succeeded Desiderius, called Victor, who at his first mass fell down dead, though from what mischance is unknown; the cup, if it be possible to credit such a thing, being poisoned. The election then fell upon Odo, a Frenchman by birth, first archdeacon of Rheims, then prior of Clugny, afterwards bishop of Ostia, lastly pope by the name of Urban. . . .

William, following up the design he had formerly begun in Nor-

[12] Henry IV (1056–1106).
[13] Antipope Clement III.
[14] Became Hildebrand's first successor as Victor III (1087).
[15] Became Hildebrand's second successor as Urban II (1088–99); preached the First Crusade at Clermont (1095).
[16] This evidently has reference to Henry's penitence at Canossa. William is not always accurate on such faraway events.
[17] Anti-king Rudolph, set up by several German princes opposed to Henry IV, and eventually supported by Gregory VII.

mandy, permitted Stigand, the pretended and false archbishop, to be deposed by the Roman cardinals and by Ermenfred bishop of Sion.[18] Walkelin succeeded him at Winchester, whose good works, surpassing fame, will resist the power of oblivion, as long as the episcopal see shall there continue. In Kent[19] succeeded Lanfranc, of whom I have before spoken, who was, by the gift of God, as resplendent in England,

> As Lucifer,[1] who bids the stars retire,
> Day's rosy harbinger with purple fire;

so much did the monastic germ sprout by his care, so strongly grew the pontifical power while he survived. The king was observant of his advice in such wise that he deemed it proper to concede whatever Lanfranc asserted ought to be done. At his instigation also was abolished the infamous custom of those ill-disposed people who used to sell their slaves into Ireland. . . .

His[2] sons were Robert, Richard, William, and Henry. The two last reigned after him successively in England: Robert, irritated that Normandy was refused him during his father's life-time, went indignantly to Italy, that by marrying the daughter of Boniface the marquis, he might procure assistance in those parts, to oppose the king: but failing of this connexion, he excited Philip[3] king of France against his father.[4] Wherefore, disappointed of his paternal blessing and inheritance, at his death, he missed England, retaining with difficulty the duchy of Normandy: and pawning even this, at the expiration of nine years, to his brother William, he joined the expedition into Asia, with the other Christians.[5] From thence, at the end of four years, he returned with credit for his military exploits; and without difficulty sat himself down in Normandy, because his brother William[6] being recently dead, king Henry,[7] unsettled on account of his fresh-acquired power, deemed it enough to retain England under his command: but as I must speak of this in another place, I will here pursue the relation I had begun concerning the sons of William the Great.

Richard afforded his noble father hopes of his future greatness; a fine youth and of aspiring disposition, considering his age: but an untimely death quickly withered the bud of this promising flower.

---

[18] William's promise to depose Stigand, who had usurped the see of Canterbury, was one of the papal reasons for approving the Norman invasion.
[19] As Archbishop of Canterbury, chief city of Kent.
[1] The morning star.
[2] William's.
[3] Philip I (1060–1108).
[4] Against William the Conqueror.
[5] The First Crusade (1096–99).
[6] William II was killed in 1100, while hunting.
[7] Henry I (1100–1135) immediately siezed the throne.

They relate that while hunting deer in the New-forest, he contracted a disorder from a stream of infected air. This is the place which William his father, desolating the towns and destroying the churches for more than thirty miles, had appropriated for the nurture and refuge of wild beasts;[8] a dreadful spectacle, indeed, that where before had existed human intercourse and the worship of God, there deer, and goats, and other animals of that kind, should now range unrestrained, and these not subjected to the general service of mankind. Hence it is truly asserted that, in this very forest, William his son, and his grandson Richard, son of Robert, earl of Normandy, by the severe judgment of God, met their deaths, one by a wound in the breast by an arrow, the other by a wound in the neck, or as some say, from being suspended by the jaws on the branch of a tree, as his horse passed beneath it.

His daughters were five; first, Cecilia, abbess of Caen, who still survives: the second, Constantia, married to Alan Fergant, earl of Brittany, excited the inhabitants, by the severity of her justice, to administer a poisonous potion to her; the third, Adela, the wife of Stephen, earl of Blois, a lady celebrated for secular industry, lately took the veil at Marcigny. The names of the two others have escaped me.[9] One of these, as we have said, was betrothed to Harold, and died ere she was marriageable: the other was affianced, by messengers, to Alphonso, king of Gallicia, but obtained, from God, a virgin death. . . .

King William kindly admitted foreigners to his friendship; bestowed honours on them without distinction, and was attentive to almsgiving; he gave many possessions in England to foreign churches, and scarcely did his own munificence, or that of his nobility, leave any monastery unnoticed, more especially in Normandy, so that their poverty was mitigated by the riches of England. This, in his time, the monastic flock increased on every side; monasteries arose, ancient in their rule, but modern in building: but here I perceive the muttering of those who say it would have been better that the old should have been preserved in their original state, than that new ones should have been erected from their plunder.

He[10] was of just stature, extraordinary corpulence, fierce countenance; his forehead bare of hair: of such great strength of arm, that it was often matter of surprise, that no one was able to draw his bow, which himself could bend when his horse was on full gallop: he was majestic, whether sitting or standing, although the protuberance of his belly deformed his royal person: of excellent health, so that he was never confined with any dangerous disorder, except at the last:

---

[8] Some manuscripts have a milder reading for the following to the end of the paragraph.
[9] Agatha and Adeliza, according to Ordericus Vitalis.
[10] William I.

so given to the pleasure of the chase, that as I have before said, ejecting the inhabitants, he let a space of many miles grow desolate, that, when at liberty from other avocations, he might there pursue his pleasures. He gave sumptuous and splendid entertainments, at the principal festivals; passing, during the years he could conveniently remain in England, Christmas at Gloucester; Easter at Winchester; Pentecost at Westminster. At these times a royal edict summoned thither all the principal persons of every order, that the ambassadors from foreign nations might admire the splendour of the assemblage, and the costliness of the banquets. Nor was he at any time more affable or indulgent; in order that the visitants might proclaim universally, that his generosity kept pace with his riches. This mode of banqueting was constantly observed by his first successor;[11] the second[12] omitted it.

His anxiety for money[13] is the only thing for which he can deservedly be blamed. This he sought all opportunities of scraping together, he cared not how; he would say and do some things, and, indeed, almost any thing, unbecoming such great majesty, where the hope of money allured him. I have here no excuse whatever to offer, unless it be, as one has said, that, "Of necessity, he must fear many, whom many fear." For, through dread of his enemies, he used to drain the country of money, with which he might retard or repel their attacks; very often, as it happens in human affairs, where strength failed, purchasing the forbearance of his enemies with gold. This disgraceful calamity is still prevalent, and every day increases; so that both towns and churches are subjected to contributions: nor is this done with firm-kept faith on the part of the imposers, but whoever offers more, carries the prize; all former agreements being disregarded.

Residing in his latter days in Normandy, when enmity had arisen between him and the king of France, he, for a short period, was confined to the house: Philip, scoffing at this forbearance, is reported to have said, "The king of England is lying-in at Rouen, and keeps his bed, like a woman after her delivery;" jesting on his belly, which he had been reducing by medicine. Cruelly hurt at this sarcasm, he replied, "When I go to mass, after my confinement, I will make him an offering of a hundred thousand candles."[14] He swore this, "by the Resurrection and Glory of God:" for he was wont purposely to swear such oaths as, by the very form of his mouth, would strike terror into the minds of his hearers.

Not long after, in the end of the month of August, when the corn was ripe on the ground, the clusters on the vines, and the orchards

[11] William II.
[12] Henry I.
[13] Some manuscripts have a different, milder reading from here to "I have."
[14] A reference to the ritual whereby a woman after childbirth was readmitted to the Church bearing a candle in her hand. William evidently alluded to the burnings he planned to perpetrate in the lands of Philip I.

laden with fruit in full abundance, collecting an army, he entered France in a hostile manner, trampling down, and laying every thing waste: nothing could assuage his irritated mind, so determined was he to revenge this injurious taunt at the expense of multitudes. At last he set fire to the city of Mantes, where the church of St. Mary was burnt, together with a recluse who did not think it justifiable to quit her cell even under such an emergency; and the whole property of the citizens was destroyed. Exhilarated by this success, while furiously commanding his people to add fuel to the conflagration, he approached too near the flames, and contracted a disorder from the violence of the fire and the intenseness of the autumnal heat. Some say, that his horse leaping over a dangerous ditch, ruptured his rider, where his belly projected over the front of the saddle. Injured by this accident, he sounded a retreat, and returning to Rouen, as the malady increased he took to his bed. His physicians, when consulted, affirmed, from an inspection of his urine, that death was inevitable. On hearing this, he filled the house with his lamentations, because death had suddenly seized him, before he could effect that reformation of life which he had long since meditated. Recovering his fortitude, however, he performed the duties of a Christian in confession and receiving the communion. Reluctantly, and by compulsion, he bestowed Normandy on Robert; to William he gave England; while Henry received his maternal possessions. He ordered all his prisoners to be released and pardoned: his treasures to be brought forth, and distributed to the churches: he gave also a certain sum of money to repair the church which had been burnt. Thus rightly ordering all things, he departed on the eighth of the ides of September,[15] in the fifty-ninth year of his age: the twenty-second of his reign: the fifty-second of his duchy: and in the year of our Lord 1087. (III)

William[16] then, the son of William, was born in Normandy many years before his father came to England; and being educated with extreme care by his parents, as he had naturally an ambitious mind, he at length reached the summit of dignity. He would no doubt have been a prince incomparable in our time, had not his father's greatness eclipsed him; and had not the fates cut short his years too early for his maturer age to correct errors contracted by the licentiousness of power and the impetuosity of youth. When childhood was passed, he spent the period of youth in military occupations; in riding, throwing the dart, contending with his elders in obedience, and with those of his own age in action: and he esteemed it injurious to his reputation, if he was not the foremost to take arms in military commotions; unless he was the first to challenge the adversary, or when challenged, to overcome him. To his father he was ever dutiful; always exerting

[15] The eighth day of or before the ides of September (Sept. 13) would be Sept. 6, since the Romans counted both the initial and final days. Actually William I died on Sept. 9, 1087.
[16] William II, Rufus (1087–1100).

himself in his sight in battle, ever at his side in peace. His hopes gradually expanding, he already aspired after the succession, especially on the rejection of his elder brother,[17] while the tender age of the younger[18] gave him no uneasiness. Thus, adopted as his successor by his father during his last illness, he set out to take possession of the kingdom ere the king had breathed his last: where being gladly received by the people, and obtaining the keys of the treasury, he by these means subjected all England to his will. Archbishop Lanfranc, the grand mover of every thing, had educated him, and made him a knight,[19] and now he favoured his pretensions to the throne; by his authority and assistance William was crowned on the day of the saints Cosmas and Damian,[20] and passed the remainder of the winter quietly and with general favour. . . .

Greatness of soul was pre-eminent in the king, which in process of time, he obscured by excessive severity; vices, indeed, in place of virtues, so insensibly crept into his bosom, that he could not distinguish them. The world doubted, for a long time, whither he would incline; what tendency his disposition would take. At first, as long as archbishop Lanfranc survived, he abstained from every crime; so that it might be hoped he would be the very mirror of kings. After his death, for a time, he showed himself so variable, that the balance hung even betwixt vices and virtues. At last, however, in his latter years, the desire after good grew cold, and the crop of evil increased to ripeness: his liberality became prodigality; his magnanimity pride; his austerity cruelty. I may be allowed, with permission of the royal majesty, not to conceal the truth; for he feared God but little, man not at all. If any one shall say this is undiscerning, he will not be wrong; because wise men should observe this rule, "God ought to be feared at all times; man, according to circumstances." He was, when abroad, and in public assemblies, of supercilious look, darting his threatening eye on the by-stander; and with assumed severity and ferocious voice, assailing such as conversed with them. From apprehension of poverty, and of the treachery of others, as may be conjectured, he was too much given to lucre, and to cruelty. . . .

The fame of his generosity pervaded all the West, and reached even to the East. Military men came to him out of every province on this side of the mountains, whom he rewarded most profusely. In consequence, when he had no longer aught to bestow, poor and exhausted, he turned his thoughts to rapine. The rapacity of his disposition was seconded by Ralph,[21] the inciter of his covetousness; a

---

[17] Robert, who became Duke of Normandy.
[18] Henry Beauclerc, later Henry I.
[19] There was at this time a custom of receiving knighthood from bishops and abbots.
[20] September 27, 1087.
[21] Ralph or Ranulph or Ranulf Flambard, Bishop of Durham, unpopular chief minister of William II.

clergyman of the lowest origin, but raised to eminence by his wit and subtilty. If at any time a royal edict issued, that England should pay a certain tribute, it was doubled by this plunderer of the rich, this exterminator of the poor, this confiscator of other men's inheritance. He was an invincible pleader, as unrestrained in his words as in his actions; and equally furious against the meek or the turbulent. Wherefore some people used to laugh,[1] and say, that he was the only man who knew how to employ his talents in this way, and cared for no one's hatred, so that he could please his master. At this person's suggestion, the sacred honours of the church, as the pastors died, were exposed to sale: for whenever the death of any bishop or abbat was announced, directly one of the king's clerks was admitted, who made an inventory of every thing, and carried all future rents into the royal exchequer. In the meantime some person was sought out fit to supply the place of the deceased; not from proof of morals, but of money; and, at last, if I may so say, the empty honour was conferred, and even that purchased, at a great price. These things appeared the more disgraceful, because, in his father's time, after the decease of a bishop or abbat, all rents were reserved entire, to be given up to the succeeding pastor; and persons truly meritorious, on account of their religion, were elected. But in the lapse of a very few years, every thing was changed. There was no man rich except the moneychanger; no clerk, unless he was a lawyer; no priest, unless (to use a word which is hardly Latin) he was a farmer.[2] Men of the meanest condition, or guilty of whatever crime, were listened to, if they could suggest any thing likely to be advantageous to the king: the halter was loosened from the robber's neck, if he could promise any emolument to the sovereign. All military discipline being relaxed, the courtiers preyed upon the property of the country people, and consumed their substance, taking the very meat from the mouths of these wretched creatures.[3] Then was there flowing hair and extravagant dress; and then was invented the fashion of shoes with curved points; then the model for young men was to rival women in delicacy of person, to mince their gait, to walk with loose gesture, and half naked. Enervated and effeminate, they unwillingly remained what nature had made them; the assailers of others' chastity, prodigal of their own. Troops of pathics, and droves of harlots, followed the court; so that it was said, with justice, by a wise man, that England would be fortunate if Henry could reign; led to such an opinion, because he abhorred obscenity from his youth.

Here, were it necessary, I could add, that archbishop Anselm attempted to correct these abuses; but failing of the co-operation of his

---

[1] Some manuscripts here read, "The king used to laugh" etc.
[2] *firmarius.*
[3] Many of those who followed the court were wont to plunder the countryside without restraint wherever they went.

suffragans, he voluntarily quitted the kingdom, yielding to the depravity of the times....

The day before the king died, he dreamed that he was let blood by a surgeon; and that the stream, reaching to heaven, clouded the light, and intercepted the day. Calling on St. Mary for protection, he suddenly awoke, commanded a light to be brought, and forbade his attendants to leave him. They then watched with him several hours until daylight. Shortly after, just as the day began to dawn, a certain foreign monk told Robert Fitz Hamon, one of the principal nobility, that he had that night dreamed a strange and fearful dream about the king: "That he had come into a certain church, with menacing and insolent gesture, as was his custom, looking contemptuously on the standers by; then violently seizing the crucifix, he gnawed the arms, and almost tore away the legs: that the image endured this for a long time, but at length struck the king with its foot in such a manner that he fell backwards: from his mouth, as he lay prostrate, issued so copious a flame that the volumes of smoke touched the very stars." Robert, thinking that this dream ought not to be neglected, as he was intimate with him, immediately related it to the king. William, repeatedly laughing, exclaimed, "He is a monk, and dreams for money like a monk: give him a hundred shillings." Nevertheless, being greatly moved, he hesitated a long while whether he should go out to hunt, as he had designed: his friends persuading him not to suffer the truth of the dreams to be tried at his personal risk. In consequence, he abstained from the chase before dinner, dispelling the uneasiness of his unregulated mind by serious business. They relate, that, having plentifully regaled that day, he soothed his cares with a more than usual quantity of wine. After dinner he went into the forest, attended by few persons; of whom the most intimate with him was Walter, surnamed Tirel, who had been induced to come from France by the liberality of the king. This man alone had remained with him, while the others, employed in the chase, were dispersed as chance directed. The sun was now declining, when the king, drawing his bow and letting fly an arrow, slightly wounded a stag which passed before him; and, keenly gazing, followed it, still running, a long time with his eyes, holding up his hand to keep off the power of the sun's rays. At this instant Walter, conceiving a noble exploit, which was while the king's attention was otherwise occupied to transfix another stag which by chance came near him, unknowingly, and without power to prevent it, Oh, gracious God! pierced his breast with a fatal arrow.[4] On receiving the wound, the king uttered not a word; but breaking off the shaft of the weapon where it projected from his body, fell upon the wound, by which he accelerated his death. Walter immediately ran up, but as he found him senseless and speechless, he

---

[4] There is serious reason to doubt the generally received story that it was an arrow of Sir Walter Tirel that killed William II.

leaped swiftly upon his horse, and escaped by spurring him to his utmost speed. Indeed there was none to pursue him: some connived at his flight; others pitied him; and all were intent on other matters. Some began to fortify their dwellings; others to plunder; and the rest to look out for a new king. A few countrymen conveyed the body, placed on a cart, to the cathedral at Winchester; the blood dripping from it all the way. Here it was committed to the ground within the tower, attended by many of the nobility, though lamented by few. . . . He was a man much to be pitied by the clergy, for throwing away a soul which they could not save; to be beloved by stipendiary soldiers, for the multitude of his gifts; but not to be lamented by the people, because he suffered their substance to be plundered. I remember no council being held in his time, wherein the health of the church might be strengthened through the correction of abuses. He hesitated a long time ere he bestowed ecclesiastical honours, either for the sake of emolument, or of weighing desert. So that on the day he died, he held in his own hands three bishoprics, and twelve vacant abbeys.[5] Besides, seeking occasion from the schism between Urban in Rome and Guibert at Ravenna, he forbade the payment of the tribute to the holy see: though he was more inclined to favour Guibert; because the ground and instigation of the discord between himself and Anselm was, that this man, so dear to God, had pronounced Urban to be pope, the other an apostate.

In his time began the Cistercian order, which is now both believed and asserted to be the surest road to heaven.[6] To speak of this does not seem irrelevant to the work I have undertaken, since it redounds to the glory of England to have produced the distinguished man who was the author and promoter of that rule. To us he belonged, and in our schools passed the earlier part of his life. Wherefore, if we are not envious, we shall embrace his good qualities the more kindly in proportion as we knew them more intimately. And, moreover, I am anxious to extol his praise, "because it is a mark of an ingenuous mind to approve that virtue in others, of which in yourself you regret the absence." He was named Harding, and born in England of no very illustrious parents. From his early years, he was a monk at Sherborne; but when secular desires had captivated his youth, he grew disgusted with the monastic garb, and went first to Scotland, and afterwards to France. Here, after some years' exercise in the liberal arts, he became awakened to the love of God. . . . (IV, 1)

Henry,[7] the youngest son of William the Great, was born in England the third year after his father's arrival;[8] a child, even at that time, fondly cherished by the joint good wishes of all, as being the only one

---

[5] During the vacancy of an ecclesiastical benefice, both its administration and its revenues reverted to the king as overlord.
[6] Juvenal, *Satires*, i, 37.
[7] Henry I (1100–1135).
[8] Henry was born in 1068. His mother was Matilda of Flanders.

of William's sons born in royalty, and to whom the kingdom seemed to pertain. The early years of instruction he passed in liberal arts, and so thoroughly imbibed the sweets of learning,[9] that no warlike commotions, no pressure of business, could ever erase them from his noble mind: although he neither read much openly, nor displayed his attainments except sparingly. His learning, however, to speak the truth, though obtained by snatches, assisted him much in the science of governing; according to that saying of Plato, "Happy would be the commonwealth, if philosophers governed, or kings would be philosophers." Not slenderly tinctured by philosophy, then, by degrees, in process of time, he learned how to restrain the people with lenity; nor did he ever suffer his soldiers to engage but where he saw a pressing emergency. In this manner, by learning, he trained his early years to the hope of the kingdom; and often in his father's hearing made use of the proverb, that "An illiterate king is a crowned ass." They relate, too, that his father, observing his disposition, never omitted any means of cherishing his lively prudence; and that once, when he had been ill-used by one of his brothers, and was in tears, he spirited him up, by saying, "Weep not, my boy, you too will be a king."

In the twenty-first year,[10] then, of his father's reign, when he was nineteen years of age, he was knighted by him at Westminster during Pentecost; and then accompanying him to Normandy, was, shortly after, present at his funeral; the other brothers departing whither their hopes led them, as my former narrative has related. Wherefore, supported by the blessing of his father, together with his maternal inheritance and immense treasures, he paid little regard to the haughtiness of his brothers; assisting or opposing each of them as they merited. More attached, however, to Robert for his mildness, he took every means of stimulating his remissness by his own spirit. . . .

On the violent death of king William, after the solemnization of the royal funeral, he[11] was elected king; though some trifling dissensions had first arisen among the nobility which were allayed chiefly through the exertions of Henry earl of Warwick, a man of unblemished integrity, with whom he had long been in the strictest intimacy. He immediately promulgated an edict throughout England, annulling the illegal ordinances of his brother, and of Ranulph; he remitted taxes; released prisoners; drove the flagitious from court; restored the nightly use of lights within the palace, which had been omitted in his brother's time; and renewed the operation of the ancient laws, confirming them with his own oath, and that of the nobility, that they might not be eluded. A joyful day then seemed to dawn on the people, when the light of fair promise shone forth after such repeated clouds of distress.

---

[9] Henry was known as "Beauclerc," or fine cleric or scholar.
[10] In 1087, according to William; 1086, according to others.
[11] Henry I, who had been in the hunting train of Rufus on that fatal day, occupied the throne in the absence of Robert, his elder brother.

And that nothing might be wanting to the aggregate of happiness, Ranulf, the dregs of iniquity, was cast into the gloom of a prison, and speedy messengers were despatched to recall Anselm. Wherefore, all vying in joyous acclamation, Henry was crowned king at London, on the nones of August, four days after his brother's death. These acts were the more sedulously performed, lest the nobility should be induced to repent their choice; as a rumour prevailed, that Robert earl of Normandy, returning from Apulia, was just on the point of arriving. Soon after, his friends, and particularly the bishops, persuading him to give up meretricious pleasures and adopt legitimate wedlock, he married, on St. Martin's day, Matilda, daughter of Malcolm king of Scotland, to whom he had long been greatly attached; little regarding the marriage portion, provided he could possess her whom he so ardently desired.

In the meantime, Robert, arriving in Normandy,[12] recovered his earldom without any opposition; on hearing which, almost all the nobility of this country violated the fealty which they had sworn to the king: some without any cause; some feigning slight pretences, because he would not readily give them such lands as they coveted. Robert Fitz-Haymon, and Richard de Rivers, and Roger Bigod, and Robert earl of Mellent, with his brother Henry, alone declared on the side of justice. But all the others either secretly sent for Robert to make him king, or openly branded their lord with sarcasms; calling him, Godric, and his consort, Goddiva.[13] Henry heard these taunts, and, with a terrific grin, deferring his anger, he repressed the contemptuous expressions cast on him by the madness of fools, by a studied silence; for he was a calm dissembler of his enmities, but, in due season, avenged them with fierceness. This tempest of the times was increased by the subtlety of Ranulf. For, concerting with his butler, he procured a rope to be sent him. The deceitful servant, who was water-bearer, carried him a very long one in a cask; by which he descended from the wall of the tower, but whether he hurt his arms, or grazed the skin off his hands, is a matter of no importance. Escaping thence to Normandy, he stimulated the earl, already indignant and ripe for war, to come to England without a moment's delay.

In the second year, then, of Henry's reign, in the month of August, arriving at Portsmouth, he landed, divided and posted his forces over the whole district.[14] Nor did the king give way to indolence, but collected an innumerable army over against him, to assert his dignity, should it be necessary. For, though the nobility deserted him, yet

[12] Robert, known as "Curthose" or "Shortlegs," returning from the First Crusade, arrived back in Normandy in September of 1100 to find his younger brother Henry in possession of the English throne.

[13] Evidently intended as sneers at the regular life or studied "godliness" of Henry and his queen, Edith Matilda, daughter of Malcolm III of Scotland.

[14] Robert crossed over to England to dispute Henry's title in July, 1101.

was his party strong; being espoused by archbishop Anselm, with his brother bishops, and all the English. In consequence, grateful to the inhabitants for their fidelity, and anxious for their safety, he frequently went through the ranks, instructing them how to elude the ferocity of the cavalry by opposing their shields, and how to return their strokes. By this he made them voluntarily demand the fight, perfectly fearless of the Normans. Men, however, of sounder counsel interfering, who observed, that the laws of natural affection must be violated should brothers meet in battle, they shaped their minds to peace; reflecting, that, if one fell, the other would be the weaker, as there was no surviving brother. Besides, a promise of three thousand marks deceived the easy credulity of the earl; who imagined that, when he had disbanded his army, he might gratify his inclinations with such an immense sum of money; which, the very next year, he cheerfully surrendered to the queen's pleasure, because she desired it. . . .

The torch of war now lighted up in Normandy, receiving fresh fuel by the arrival of traitors, and blazed forth and seized every thing within its reach. Normandy, indeed, though not very wide in its extent, is a convenient and patient fosterer of the abandoned.[15] . . .

King Henry, however, felt deeply for his brother's infamy, carried to the highest pitch by the sufferings of the country;[16] aware, that it was the extreme of cruelty, and far from a good king's duty, to suffer abandoned men to riot on the property of the poor. In consequence, he once admonished his brother, whom he had sent for into England, with fair words; but afterwards, arriving in Normandy, he severely reminded him, more than once, by arms, to act the prince rather than the monk. He also despoiled William,[17] the instigator of these troubles, of every thing he had in England; razing his castles to the ground. But when he could, even thus, make no progress towards peace, the royal majesty long anxiously employed its thoughts, whether, regardless of fraternal affection, it should rescue the country from danger, or through blind regard, suffer it to continue in jeopardy. And indeed the common weal, and sense of right, would have yielded to motives of private affection, had not pope Paschal,[18] as they say,[19] urged him, when hesitating, to the business by his letters: averring, with his powerful eloquence, that it would not be a civil war, but a signal benefit to a noble country. In consequence, passing over,[1] he,

[15] Unsuccessful rebels in England fled to loosely governed Normandy, itself a breeding place for rebels.
[16] I.e., Normandy.
[17] This William, called Clito, was the son of Duke Robert of Normandy.
[18] Pope Paschal II (1099–1118).
[19] This seems to be mere rumor. There is no trace of this severe advice in any surviving letter of Pope Paschal, who is known, on the other hand, to have attempted to effect a reconciliation of the two brothers through Archbishop Anselm.
[1] In 1106.

in a short time, took, or more properly speaking, received, the whole of Normandy; all flocking to his dominion, that he might provide, by his transcendent power, for the good of the exhausted province. Yet he achieved not this signal conquest without bloodshed; but lost many of his dearest associates.[2] ...

The king, thus splendidly successful, returned triumphant to his kingdom, having established such peace in Normandy as it had never known before; and such as even his father himself, with all his mighty pomp of words and actions, had never been able to accomplish. Rivalling his father also, in other respects, he restrained, by edict, the exactions of the courtiers, thefts, rapine, and the violation of women; commanding the delinquents to be deprived of sight, as well as of their manhood. He also displayed singular diligence against the mintmasters, commonly called moneyers: suffering no counterfeiter, who had been convicted of deluding the ignorant by the practice of his roguery, to escape, without losing his hand.[3]

Adopting the custom of his brother, he soothed the Scottish kings by his affability. For William made Duncan, the illegitimate son of Malcolm,[4] a knight; and, on the death of his father, appointed him king of Scotland. When Duncan[5] was taken off by the wickedness of his uncle Donald, he promoted Edgar[6] to the kingdom; the above-mentioned Donald being despatched by the contrivance of David, the youngest brother, and the power of William. Edgar yielding to fate, Henry made affinity with Alexander,[7] his successor, giving him his illegitimate daughter in marriage, by whom he had no issue that I know of; and when she died, he did not much lament her loss: for there was, as they affirm, some defect about the lady, either in correctness of manners, or elegance of person. Alexander resting with his ancestors, David[8] the youngest of Malcolm's sons, whom the king had made a knight and honoured with the marriage of a woman of quality, ascended the throne of Scotland. A youth more courtly than the rest, and who, polished, from a boy, by intercourse and familiarity with us, had rubbed off all the rust of Scottish barbarism. Finally, when he obtained the kingdom, he released from the payment of taxes, for three years, all such of his countrymen as would pay more attention to their dwellings, dress more elegantly, and feed more nicely. No history has ever recorded three kings, and at the same time

[2] Henry defeated Robert in the battle of Tinchebrai in 1106, and took him prisoner to England, where he held him captive for 28 years in various castles until his death in 1134.
[3] Henry I is called "the Lion of Justice" by John of Salisbury.
[4] Malcolm III, Canmore (1058–93), whose second wife, the sister of the English Edgar Aetheling, became St. Margaret of Scotland.
[5] Duncan II (1093–94), Malcom's first son, born of his first wife.
[6] Edgar (c. 1094–1107) established the line of his mother, Margaret, by putting out the eyes of his uncle, Donald Ban, as by other unsaintly expedients.
[7] Alexander I (1107–24).
[8] David I (1124–35), who had been educated by Normans, spread many of their practices in Scotland. Throughout the aforesaid period, as later, Scottish politics were in turmoil partly as a result of English meddling.

brothers, who were of equal sanctity, or savoured so much of their mother's piety; for independently of their abstemiousness, their extensive charity, and their frequency in prayer, they so completely subdued the domestic vice of kings, that no report, even, prevailed that any entered their bed except their legitimate wives, or that either of them had ever been guilty of any unlawful intercourse.

The Welsh, perpetually rebelling, were subjugated by the king in repeated expeditions, who, relying on a prudent expedient to quell their tumults, transported thither all the Flemings then resident in England. For that country contained such numbers of these people, who, in the time of his father, had come over from national relationship to his mother, that, from their numbers, they appeared burdensome to the kingdom. In consequence he settled them, with all their property and connexions, at Ross, a Welsh province, as in a common receptacle, both for the purpose of cleansing the kingdom, and repressing the brutal temerity of the enemy. Still, however, he did not neglect leading his expeditions thither, as circumstances required: in one of which, being privily aimed at with an arrow from a distance, though by whose audacity is unknown, he opportunely and fortunately escaped, by the interposition of his firmly mailed hauberk, and the counsel of God at the same time frustrating this treachery. . . .

Henry was inferior in wisdom to no king of modern time, and, as I may almost say, he clearly surpassed all his predecessors in England, and preferred contending by counsel, rather than by the sword. If he could, he conquered without bloodshed; if it was unavoidable, with as little as possible. He was free, during his whole life, from impure desires; for, as we have learned from those who were well informed, he was led by female blandishments, not for the gratification of incontinency, but for the sake of issue; nor condescended to casual intercourse, unless where it might produce that effect; in this respect the master of his natural inclinations, not the passive slave of lust. He was plain in his diet, rather satisfying the calls of hunger, than surfeiting himself by variety of delicacies. He never drank but to allay thirst; execrating the least departure from temperance, both in himself and in those about him. He was heavy to sleep, which was interrupted by frequent snoring. His eloquence was rather unpremeditated than laboured; not rapid, but deliberate.

His piety towards God was laudable, for he built monasteries in England and in Normandy. . . . He yielded up the investiture of the churches to God and St. Peter, after much controversy between him and archbishop Anselm, scarcely induced, even at last, to consent, through the manifold grace of God, by an inglorious victory over his brother.[9] The tenor of these disputes Edmer has recorded at great length. . . .

[9] The settlement of the investiture controversy in England, arrived at in the Concordat of London (1107), was actually a compromise, although the physical investiture was performed by ecclesiastics.

By Matilda king Henry had a son named William,[10] educated and destined to the succession, with the fondest hope, and surpassing care. For to him, when scarcely twelve years of age, all the free men of England and Normandy, of every rank and condition, and under fealty to whatever lord, were obliged to submit themselves by homage, and by oath. When a boy, too, he was betrothed to and received in wedlock, the daughter of Fulco earl of Anjou,[11] who was herself scarcely marriageable; his father-in-law bestowing on him the county of Maine as her dower. Moreover, Fulco, proceeding to Jerusalem, committed his earldom to the king, to be restored, should he return, but otherwise, to go to his son-in-law. Many provinces, then, looked forward to the government of this boy: for it was supposed that the prediction of king Edward would be verified in him; and it was said, that now might be expected, that the hopes of England, like the tree cut down, would, through this youth, again blossom and bring forth fruit, and thus put an end to her sufferings: but God saw otherwise; for this illusion vanished into air, as an early day was hastening him to his fate. Indeed, by the exertions of his father-in-law, and of Theobald the son of Stephen, and of his aunt Adala,[12] Lewis[13] king of France conceded the legal possession of Normandy to the lad, on his doing him homage. The prudence of his truly careful father so arranged and contrived, that the homage, which he, from the extent of his empire, disdained to perform, should not be refused by his son, a youth of delicate habit, and not very likely to live. In discussing and peaceably settling these matters, the king spent the space of four years; continuing the whole of that time in Normandy. Nevertheless, the calm of this brilliant, and carefully concerted peace, this anxious, universal hope, was destroyed in an instant by the vicissitudes of human estate. For, giving orders for returning to England, the king set sail from Barfleur just before twilight on the seventh before the kalends of December;[14] and the breeze which filled his sails conducted him safely to his kingdom and extensive fortunes. But the young man, who was now somewhat more than seventeen years of age, and, by his father's indulgence, possessed everything but the name of king, commanded another vessel to be prepared for himself; almost all the young nobility flocking around him, from similarity of youthful pursuits. The sailors, too, immoderately filled with wine, with that seaman's hilarity which their cups excited, exclaimed, that those who were now a-head must soon be left astern; for the ship was of the best construction, and recently fitted with new materials. When, therefore, it was now dark night, these imprudent youths, overwhelmed

[10] Known as "the Aetheling."
[11] Fulk V, "the Young," Count of Anjou (1109–29).
[12] Adala or Adela or Adele, daughter of the Conqueror, married the Count of Blois, and their son Stephen later became King of England (1135–54).
[13] Louis VI (1108–37) of France.
[14] November 25, 1120. See note 15, page 232, on Roman reckoning.

with liquor, launched the vessel from the shore. She flies swifter than the winged arrow, sweeping the rippling surface of the deep: but the carelessness of the intoxicated crew drove her on a rock, which rose above the waves not far from shore. In the greatest consternation, they immediately ran on deck, and with loud outcry got ready their boat-hooks, endeavouring, for a considerable time, to force the vessel off: but fortune resisted and frustrated every exertion. The oars, too, dashing, horribly crashed against the rock,[15] and her battered prow hung immoveably fixed. Now, too, the water washed some of the crew overboard, and, entering the chinks, drowned others; when the boat having been launched, the young prince was received into it, and might certainly have been saved by reaching the shore, had not his illegitimate sister, the countess of Perche, now struggling with death in the larger vessel, implored her brother's assistance; shrieking out that he should not abandon her so barbarously. Touched with pity, he ordered the boat to return to the ship, that he might rescue his sister; and thus the unhappy youth met his death through excess of affection: for the skiff, overcharged by the multitudes who leaped into her, sank, and buried all indiscriminately in the deep. One rustic alone escaped; who, floating all night upon the mast, related in the morning, the dismal catastrophe of this tragedy. No ship was ever productive of so much misery to England; none ever so widely celebrated throughout the world....

His daughter Matilda, by Matilda, king Henry gave in marriage to Henry emperor of Germany,[16] son of that Henry mentioned in the third book. Henry was the fifth emperor of the Germans of this name; who, although he had been extremely incensed at his father for his outrages against the holy see, yet, in his own time, was the rigid follower of, and stickler for, the same sentiments. For when Paschal,[17] a man possessed of every virtue, had succeeded pope Urban, the question again arose concerning the investiture of the churches, together with all the former contentions and animosities: as neither party would give way. The emperor had in his favour all the bishops and abbats of his kingdoms situated on this side of the mountains; because Charles the Great,[18] to keep in check the ferocity of those nations, had conferred almost all the country on the churches:[19] most wisely considering, that the clergy would not so soon cast off their fidelity to their lord as the laity; and, besides, if the laity were to rebel, they might be restrained by the authority of their excommunication, and the weight of their power. The pope had brought over to his

---

[15] Virgil, *Aeneid*, v, 206.
[16] Henry V of Germany and the Empire (1106–25).
[17] Pope Paschal II (1099–1118).
[18] Not only Charlemagne, but also various subsequent Ottonian and Franconian rulers.
[19] Malmesbury gives us a good analysis of the origins of the church-state conflict in the Empire.

side the churches beyond the mountains, and the cities of Italy scarcely acknowledged the dominion of Henry; thinking themselves exonerated from servitude after the death of his brother Conrad, who, being left by his father as king of Lombardy, had died at Arezzo. But Henry, rivalling the ancient Caesars in every noble quality, after tranquillizing his German empire, extended his thoughts to his Italian kingdom: purposing to quell the revolt of the cities, and decide the question of investitures, according to his own pleasure. This progress to Rome,[1] accomplished by great exertion of mind, and much painful labour of body, hath been described by David, bishop of Bangor,[2] a Scot; though far more partially to the king than becomes an historian. Indeed he commends highly even his unheard-of violence in taking the pope captive,[3] though he held him in free custody; citing the example of Jacob's holding the angel fast till he extorted a blessing. Moreover, he labours to establish that the saying of the apostle, "No servant of God embroils himself in worldly business," is not repugnant to the desires of those bishops, who are invested by the laity, because the doing homage to a layman, by a clergyman, is not a secular business. How frivolous such arguments are, any person's consideration may decide. In the meantime, that I may not seem to bear hard on a good man by my judgment, I determine to make allowances for him, since he has not written a history, but a panegyric....

All France made no scruple of considering the emperor as accursed by the power of ecclesiastical zeal hurled against him. Roused at this, in the seventeenth year of pope Paschal,[4] he proceeded to Rome, to inflict signal vengeance on him. But he, by a blessed departure,[5] had avoided all earthly molestation, and from his place of repose on high, laughed at the threats of the angry emperor; who having heard of his death, quickened his journey, in order that ejecting John Gaitan, chancellor to the late pope, who had been already elected and called Gelasius,[6] he might intrude Maurice, bishop of Brague, surnamed Bourdin, on the See.[7] ...

Gelasius after his expulsion, embarking at Salerno, came thence to Genoa, and afterwards proceeded by land to Clugny, where he died.[8] Then, that is A.D. 1119, the cardinals who had accompanied him, together with the whole Cisalpine church, elevating with great pomp

---

[1] Henry V's first "progress to Rome" took place in 1110–11.
[2] The *History of Henry V* written by David of Bangor has since been lost.
[3] Henry V invaded Italy with a large army in 1110, and took Paschal II a prisoner in 1111, extorting from the Pope both imperial coronation and recognition of his right of investiture.
[4] Henry V again invaded Italy in 1116 and advanced to Rome in 1118.
[5] Pope Paschal II died in January, 1118.
[6] Pope Gelasius II (1118–19).
[7] Maurice Bourdin, Archbishop of Braga, Henry's antipope elected in 1118, took the name of Gregory VIII.
[8] Gelasius II died at Cluny on Jan. 29, 1119.

Guido, archbishop of Vienne, to the papacy, called him Calixtus,[9] hoping, from the consideration of his piety and energy, that through his power, as he possessed great influence, they might be able to withstand the force of the emperor. Nor did he deceive their confidence: for soon after calling a council at Rheims, he separated from the churches,[10] such as had been, or should be, invested by the laity, including the emperor also, unless he should recant. Thus continuing for some time in the hither districts, to strengthen his party, and having settled all affairs in Gaul, he came to Rome, and was gladly received by the citizens, as the emperor had now departed. Bourdin then, deserted, fled to Sutri, determining to nurture his power by many a pilgrim's loss. . . .

In his[11] time there were no snares laid for the traveller in the neighborhood of Rome; no assaults on him when he arrived within the city. The offerings to St. Peter, which, through insolence, and for their lusts, the powerful used to pillage, basely injuring such preceding popes as dared to complain, Calixtus brought back to their proper use; that is to say, for the public service of the ruler of the holy see. Neither could the desire of amassing money, nor the love of it when collected, produce in his breast any thing repugnant to justice: so that he admonished the English pilgrims, on account of the length of the journey, rather to go to St. David's[12] than to Rome; allowing the benefit of the same benediction to such as went twice to that place, as resulted to those who went once to Rome. Moreover that inveterate controversy between the empire and the priesthood, concerning investiture, which for more than fifty years had created commotions, to such a degree, that, when any favourer of this heresy was cut off by disease or death, immediately, like the hydra's heads, many sprouted up afresh; this man by his diligence cut off, brought low, rooted out, or plucked up: beating down the crest of German fierceness by the vigorous stroke of the papal hatchet.[13] . . . (V)

9 Pope Calixtus II or Callistus II (1119–24).
10 I.e., excommunicated.
11 Callistus'.
12 The shrine of St. David, the sixth-century British saint, in Wales. Callistus formally canonized St. David at the request of Henry I in 1120.
13 William of Malmesbury evidently has reference to the Concordat of Worms (1122) which, like that of London, was a compromise and something of a papal victory in view of earlier practices. William's *Chronicle* and *New History* carry the account to 1142.

9

The Scholastic Union of Faith and Reason

ABELARD

The breathtaking cultural blossoming of the High Middle Ages is epitomized in the "twelfth-century renaissance" and in the career of Peter Abelard. Recognized as a founding father of both the medieval universities and Scholastic philosophy, Abelard was a champion of the rights of reason against the attacks of mystics and ultra-conservatives, as well as hero and victim of a famous and tragic romance. In a sense, what Joan of Arc was to the fifteenth century, Abelard was to the twelfth. Both were "martyrs," in their individual ways; both were faithful children of the Church, invincibly persuaded of their "mission." But whereas Joan's objectives were nationalistic and humanitarian, Abelard's were intellectual and educational. Both became heroes of the French, as well as universal symbols.

Pierre Abelard was born in Brittany of noble parents in 1079. After being trained in letters from an early date through his father's solicitude, Abelard gave up his right of succession to his father's estate as first-born to become a knight-errant of philosophy. Like many another "wandering scholar" of his day, he followed the road of learning from place to place in quest of famous masters: to Loches to study logic and perhaps grammar under the nominalist Roscellin; to Chartres for science and mathematics under Master Thierry; to Paris for dialectics and philosophy under the noted William of Champeaux; to Laon for theology and scriptural studies under the venerable Anselm. And like many other brilliant young men, he soon felt that he had learned all his plodding pedagogues had to offer. He aroused the hostility of William of Champeaux by his challenging refutations; that of Anselm of Laon by his undisguised boredom; that of both by his decision to teach on his own without having completed their courses.

The bitter feelings of Abelard's former masters, and the general professorial criticisms aimed at the unconventional upstart, were sharpened by the crowds of students he attracted, as well as by the fact that he openly questioned old tenets and adopted new methods. Scorning hostility, Abelard advanced in his scholastic campaign from Melun to Corbeil and finally to Paris, where he returned again and again, despite recurrent retreats forced upon him. Overweeningly self-confident and inflamed with passion, as he himself acknowledges, he now engaged in an affair with the niece of Fulbert, a canon of Notre Dame in Paris. His calculated liberties with the enchanted Heloise set in train a series of events — the birth of their child, their secret marriage, and the mutilation wreaked upon him by Heloise's vengeful relatives — which ended in driving him into the prolonged retirement of monastic life, and Heloise to a convent.

But Abelard was unable to find peace and quiet, even within the cloister. He succeeded neither as a monk in the large and sophisticated urban abbey of St. Denis, nor as abbot of the small and sequestered monastery of St. Gildas in remote Brittany. His haughty manner, critical temper, intellectual sword-play, and tactless blindness to other men's views and feelings brought him into repeated conflicts. As a result, shortly after writing his Historia Calamitatum (some time between 1131 and 1135), he fled the "nightmare" of St. Gildas.

By 1136, at least, he was back in Paris again, teaching on Mont Ste. Geneviève: "a famed and learned master admired by all," as his student John of Salisbury describes him. But his critics, led by the fiery Cistercian, St. Bernard of Clairvaux, would allow him no respite, and brought him before the Council of Sens in 1140, which in effect judged him guilty before he was heard. In an attempt to avoid the coup, Abelard appealed to the Pope and set out for Rome. Still he was condemned not only by the Council but also by Pope Innocent II on the advice of the Council and of St. Bernard. Making his way toward Rome, Abelard stopped off at the monastery of Cluny, where he was befriended by Peter the Venerable and admitted to the community. Physically worn out as well as mentally discouraged, Abelard became fatally ill. The kindly Peter transferred him to the priory of Châlons-sur-Saone, where he died in 1142, meanwhile reconciled, through Peter's offices, with both St. Bernard and the Pope. He was buried at the Paraclete, the monastery he had founded, where Heloise was now abbess of a sisterhood; and twenty-two years later she was laid beside him. The remains of both were ultimately transferred to Paris.

Although Abelard wrote several works on various subjects — dialectical, ethical, theological, scriptural, apologetic, poetic, and epistolary — they are more important for their approach and method, which became that of Scholasticism, than for their specific content. Equally important was his contribution to the rise of the University of Paris, through the crowds of students he attracted and the intellectual interests he aroused.

Abelard's "story of his misfortunes" was really a letter written to console a friend. Although the original addressee is unknown, the letter eventually came into the hands of Heloise, for whom Abelard seems in fact to have intended it as a pièce justificative for his impending departure from St. Gildas. The letter was composed in the early 1130's; and though obviously prejudiced and exaggerated, it is our principal source concerning the life of Abelard.

Valuable as an account of the origins of the University of Paris and Scholasticism, the Historia Calamitatum brings into relief the restless and paradoxical nature of its author: his brilliance and impracticality, pride and self-criticism, ambition and resignation, and his capacity for inspiring to an unusual degree both enthusiastic admiration and implacable enmity. It also reveals qualities of typical contemporaries; his father's respect for learning; the narrow righteousness of Abbot Bernard of Clairvaux; the gentle kindness of the Prior of St. Ayoul at Provins; the greed of Canon Fulbert; the persecuting zeal of William of Champeaux and Alberic of Rheims; the confusion of ordinary bishops confronted with theological abstrusities; the conciliatory efforts of practical administrators such as Bishop Geoffrey of Chartres and the papal legate, Conon of Praeneste.

On a broader scale, this autobiography of Abelard's is illustrative of the growing twelfth-century conflicts between the old and the new, faith and reason, Christian other-worldly values and the blandishments of this world, conservatives and liberals. We note the mounting enthusiasm for logic and the dialectical method; the eager concourse of students to noted masters, and especially those in Paris; the juxtaposition of humanistic and Aristotelian learning with Scriptural and Patristic quotations; the clerical affiliations of most scholars; the coercive power of Church officials; the deficiencies in the secular administration of justice; and the academic proclivity to foment tempests in teapots.

The conflict over "universals," in which Abelard participated, concerned the nature of general ideas, such as justice and injustice, or human and animal. Extreme realists, like William of Champeaux, taught, with Plato, that such universal concepts are substantial realities. Nominalists, like Roscellin, maintained that general ideas are nothing more than names or verbal sounds. Conceptualists, like Abelard, also known as moderate realists, held that universals, while lacking in substance, are real in the sense that they represent resemblances and common traits actually existing in individual substances.

Through Abelard's account we gain some idea of the power, influence, and implementation of the Church and of the Christian faith in the twelfth century. On the one hand, we see human imperfections, the petty jealousies and animosities of some churchmen, the narrow outlook of others, the latitudinarian morals of a few, the laxity of life in certain monasteries. On the other hand, we glimpse the breadth of speculative interests among clerics, their intellectual zest, the evidences of some democracy in Church governmental circles, and above all the strength of the faith that inspires and ennobles such diverse personalities as the ardent, loving Heloise and the brilliant, egotistical Abelard.

PETER ABELARD

The Story of My Misfortunes *

CHAPTER I

Of the Birthplace of Pierre Abélard and of His Parents[1]

KNOW that I am come from a certain town which was built on the way into lesser Brittany, distant some eight miles, as I think, eastward from the city of Nantes, and in its own tongue called Palets.[2] Such is the nature of that country, or, it may be, of them who dwell there — for in truth they are quick in fancy — that my mind bent itself easily to the study of letters. Yet more, I had a father[3] who had won some smattering of letters before he had girded on the soldier's belt. And so it came about that long afterwards his love thereof was so strong that he saw to it that each son of his should be taught in letters[4] even earlier than in the management of arms. Thus indeed did it come to pass. And because I was his first born, and

---

* From Peter Abelard, *Historia Calamitatum (The Story of My Misfortunes): An Autobiography*, translated by Henry Adams Bellows (St. Paul, Minn.: Thomas A. Boyd, 1922. Also Glencoe, Ill.: The Free Press, 1958).

[1] These and following chapter divisions and headings have been inserted by the translator.

[2] Palets, Pallets, Palais, or Palatium ("Palace"), about 12 miles east of Nantes in the Loire Valley of Brittany. Abelard was the first-born (1079) of a noble Breton family.

[3] Abelard's father was named Berengarius; his mother, Lucia.

[4] An evidence of lay education among the upper classes in the later eleventh century.

for that reason the more dear to him, he sought with double diligence to have me wisely taught. For my part, the more I went forward in the study of letters, and ever more easily, the greater became the ardour of my devotion to them, until in truth I was so enthralled by my passion for learning that, gladly leaving to my brothers the pomp of glory in arms, the right of heritage and all the honours that should have been mine as the eldest born, I fled utterly from the court of Mars that I might win learning in the bosom of Minerva.[5] And since I found the armory of logical reasoning more to my liking than the other forms of philosophy, I exchanged all other weapons for these, and to the prizes of victory in war I preferred the battle of minds in disputation. Thenceforth, journeying through many provinces, and debating as I went, going whithersoever I heard that the study of my chosen art most flourished, I became such an one as the Peripatetics.[6]

CHAPTER II

Of the Persecution He Had from His Master William of Champeaux — Of His Adventures at Melun, at Corbeil and at Paris — Of His Withdrawal from the City of the Parisians to Melun, and His Return to Mont Ste. Geneviève — Of His Journey to His Old Home

I came at length to Paris, where above all in those days the art of dialectics was most flourishing, and there did I meet William of Champeaux,[7] my teacher, a man most distinguished in his science both by his renown and by his true merit. With him I remained for some time, at first indeed well liked of him; but later I brought him great grief, because I undertook to refute certain of his opinions, not infrequently attacking him in disputation, and now and then in these debates I was adjudged victor. Now this, to those among my fellow students who were ranked foremost, seemed all the more insufferable because of my youth and the brief duration of my studies.

Out of this sprang the beginning of my misfortunes, which have

---

[5] I.e., he turned from military pursuits to the quest of knowledge and wisdom.
[6] John of Salisbury refers to Abelard as "the Peripatetic from Palais" or "the Palatine Peripatetic" (*Metalogicon*, i, 5). Aristotle's disciples were known as "peripatetics" from their habit of walking about while discussing philosophy, and Abelard was both an ardent student of Aristotle and an avid philosopher.
[7] William of Champeaux, who was teaching in the Cathedral School of Notre Dame at Paris, was one of the leading logicians of the day and an extreme realist (see *infra*). Abelard does not mention his earlier studies, such as, it seems, those under the chastened nominalist Roscellin, at Loches in Brittany, or science and mathematics under Thierry of Chartres. Abelard may have gone to Loches about 1094.

followed me even to the present day; the more widely my fame was spread abroad, the more bitter was the envy that was kindled against me. It was given out that I, presuming on my gifts far beyond the warranty of my youth, was aspiring despite my tender years to the leadership of a school; nay, more, that I was making ready the very place in which I would undertake this task, the place being none other than the castle of Melun, at that time a royal seat.[8] My teacher himself had some foreknowledge of this, and tried to remove my school as far as possible from his own. Working in secret, he sought in every way he could before I left his following to bring to nought the school I had planned and the place I had chosen for it. Since, however, in that very place he had many rivals, and some of them men of influence among the great ones of the land, relying on their aid I won to the fulfillment of my wish; the support of many was secured for me by reason of his own unconcealed envy. From this small inception of my school, my fame in the art of dialectics began to spread abroad, so that little by little the renown, not alone of those who had been my fellow students, but of our very teacher himself, grew dim and was like to die out altogether. Thus it came about, that, still more confident in myself, I moved my school as soon as I well might to the castle of Corbeil,[9] which is hard by the city of Paris, for there I knew there would be given more frequent chance for my assaults in our battle of disputation.

No long time thereafter I was smitten with a grievous illness, brought upon me by my immoderate zeal for study. This illness forced me to turn homeward to my native province, and thus for some years I was as if cut off from France. And yet, for that very reason, I was sought out all the more eagerly by those whose hearts were troubled by the lore of dialectics. But after a few years had passed, and I was whole again from my sickness, I learned that my teacher, that same William, Archdeacon of Paris, had changed his former garb and joined an order of the regular clergy.[10] This he had done, or so men said, in order that he might be deemed more deeply religious, and so might be elevated to a loftier rank in the prelacy, a thing which, in truth, very soon came to pass, for he was made bishop of Châlons. Nevertheless, the garb he had donned by reason of his conversion did nought to keep him away either from the city of Paris or from his wonted study of philosophy; and in the very monastery wherein he had shut himself up for the sake of religion he straightway set to teaching again after the same fashion as before.[11]

[8] About 1101–02. One of several residences of Philip I, Melun is about 30 miles south of Paris.
[9] A few miles south of Paris.
[10] The time is about 1110. William had meanwhile become a canon (1103) as well as archdeacon; but in 1108 had withdrawn to the abbey of St. Victor, Paris.
[11] William is reckoned as founder of the famous school of St. Victor's in Paris.

To him did I return, for I was eager to learn more of rhetoric from his lips; and in the course of our many arguments on various matters, I compelled him by most potent reasoning first to alter his former opinion on the subject of the universals, and finally to abandon it altogether. Now, the basis of this old concept of his regarding the reality of universal ideas was that the same quality formed the essence alike of the abstract whole and of the individuals which were its parts: in other words, that there could be no essential differences among these individuals, all being alike save for such variety as might grow out of the many accidents of existence.[12] Thereafter, however, he corrected this opinion, no longer maintaining that the same quality was the essence of all things, but that, rather, it manifested itself in them through diverse ways. This problem of universals is ever the most vexed one among logicians, to such a degree, indeed, that even Porphyry, writing in his "Isagoge"[13] regarding universals, dared not attempt a final pronouncement thereon, saying rather: "This is the deepest of all problems of its kind." Wherefore it followed that when William had first revised and then finally abandoned altogether his views on this subject, his lecturing sank into such a state of negligent reasoning that it could scarce be called lecturing on the science of dialectics at all; it was as if all his science had been bound up in this one question of the nature of universals.

Thus it came about that my teaching won such strength and authority that even those who before had clung most vehemently to my former master, and most bitterly attacked my doctrines, now flocked to my school.[14] The very man who had succeeded to my master's chair in the Paris school offered me his post, in order that he might put himself under my tutelage along with all the rest, and this in the very place where of old his master and mine had reigned. And when, in so short a time, my master saw me directing the study of dialectics there, it is not easy to find words to tell with what envy he was consumed or with what pain he was tormented. He could not long, in truth, bear the anguish of what he felt to be his wrongs, and shrewdly he attacked me that he might drive me forth. And because there was nought in my conduct whereby he could come at me openly, he tried to steal away the school by launching the vilest calumnies against him who had yielded his post to me, and by putting in his place a certain rival of mine. So then I returned to Melun, and set up my school there as before; and the more openly his envy pur-

---

[12] This may also be translated: "For he held the position on the common existence of universals that the same thing exists wholly and essentially in all individuals of a class, and that there is no distinction of essence in them but only variety through multiplicity of accidents." (*The Story of Abelard's Adversities*, tr. J. T. Muckle; Toronto, Pontifical Institute, 1954, p. 16.)

[13] The *Isagoge* or *Introduction* to Aristotle's *Categories*, composed by Porphyry (third century A.D.), translated by Boethius (sixth century).

[14] Abelard was now teaching in connection with the Parisian cathedral school of Notre Dame.

sued me, the greater was the authority it conferred upon me. Even so held the poet: "Jealousy aims at the peaks; the winds storm the loftiest summits."[15]

Not long thereafter, when William became aware of the fact that almost all his students were holding grave doubts as to his religion, and were whispering earnestly among themselves about his conversion, deeming that he had by no means abandoned this world, he withdrew himself and his brotherhood, together with his students, to a certain estate far distant from the city. Forthwith I returned from Melun to Paris, hoping for peace from him in the future. But since, as I have said, he had caused my place to be occupied by a rival of mine, I pitched the camp, as it were, of my school outside the city on Mont Ste. Geneiève.[16] Thus I was as one laying siege to him who had taken possession of my post. No sooner had my master heard of this than he brazenly returned post haste to the city, bringing back with him such students as he could, and reinstating his brotherhood in their former monastery, much as if he would free his soldiery, whom he had deserted, from my blockade.[17] In truth, though, if it was his purpose to bring them succour, he did nought but hurt them. Before that time my rival had indeed had a certain number of students, of one sort and another, chiefly by reason of his lectures on Priscian, in which he was considered of great authority.[18] After our master had returned, however, he lost nearly all of these followers, and thus was compelled to give up the direction of the school. Not long thereafter, apparently despairing further of worldly fame, he was converted to the monastic life.

Following the return of our master to the city, the combats in disputation which my scholars waged both with him himself and with his pupils, and the successes which fortune gave to us, and above all to me, in these wars, you have long since learned of through your own experience. The boast of Ajax, though I speak it more temperately, I still am bold enough to make:

". . . if fain you would learn now
How victory crowned the battle, by him was I never vanquished."[19]

But even were I to be silent, the fact proclaims itself, and its outcome reveals the truth regarding it.[1]

While these things were happening, it became needful for me again to repair to my old home, by reason of my dear mother, Lucia, for after the conversion of my father, Berengarius, to the monastic life,

---

[15] Ovid, *Remedy for Love*, i, 369.
[16] Abelard, at the zenith of his popularity, taught at Ste. Geneviève on the heights overlooking Paris (c. 1108).
[17] Note the feudal military figures.
[18] The *Institutes of Grammar* by Priscian (c. A.D. 500), a large and exhaustive work, was a standard medieval textbook on Latin grammar.
[19] Ovid, *Metamorphoses*, xiii, 89.
[1] Abelard's pride and boastfulness need no comment.

she so ordered her affairs as to do likewise.[2] When all this had been completed, I returned to France, above all in order that I might study theology, since now my oft-mentioned teacher, William, was active in the episcopate of Châlons.[3] In this field of learning Anselm of Laon,[4] who was his teacher therein, had for long years enjoyed the greatest renown.

CHAPTER III
Of How He Came to Laon to Seek Anselm as Teacher

I sought out, therefore, this same venerable man, whose fame, in truth, was more the result of long-established custom than of the potency of his own talent or intellect.[5] If any one came to him impelled by doubt on any subject, he went away more doubtful still. He was wonderful, indeed, in the eyes of these who only listened to him, but those who asked him questions perforce held him as nought. He had a miraculous flow of words, but they were contemptible in meaning and quite void of reason. When he kindled a fire, he filled his house with smoke and illumined it not at all. He was a tree which seemed noble to those who gazed upon its leaves from afar, but to those who came nearer and examined it more closely was revealed its barrenness. When, therefore, I had come to this tree that I might pluck the fruit thereof, I discovered that it was indeed the fig tree which Our Lord cursed,[6] or that ancient oak to which Lucan likened Pompey, saying:

". . . he stands, the shade of a name once mighty,
Like to the towering oak in the midst of the fruitful field."[7]

It was not long before I made this discovery, and stretched myself lazily in the shade of that same tree. I went to his lectures less and less often, a thing which some among his eminent followers took sorely to heart, because they interpreted it as a mark of contempt for so illustrious a teacher.[8] Thenceforth they secretly sought to influence him against me, and by their vile insinuations made me hated of him. It chanced, moreover, that one day, after the exposition of certain texts,[9] we scholars were jesting among ourselves, and one of

[2] After their children were raised, it was permissible for a husband and wife to retire to a monastery, if both agreed to do so.
[3] William became Bishop of Châlons-sur-Marne in 1113, died in 1121.
[4] Anselm, who with his brother Ralph conducted the Cathedral school at Laon, was one of the most famous theologians and scriptural scholars of his day.
[5] Since Anselm died not long afterward (1117), he may have been weakening with age.
[6] Matthew 21:19; Mark 11:13.
[7] Lucan, *Pharsalia*, iv, 35.
[8] And so it was. So apparently Anselm thought.
[9] Muckle translates this: "after a session of Sentences" (the latter being truths of conclusions from revelation).

them, seeking to draw me out, asked me what I thought of the lectures on the Books of Scripture. I, who had as yet studied only the sciences, replied that following such lectures seemed to me most useful in so far as the salvation of the soul was concerned, but that it appeared quite extraordinary to me that educated persons should not be able to understand the sacred books simply by studying them themselves, together with the glosses thereon, and without the aid of any teacher. Most of those who were present mocked at me, and asked whether I myself could do as I had said, or whether I would dare to undertake it. I answered that if they wished, I was ready to try it. Forthwith they cried out and jeered all the more. "Well and good," said they; "we agree to the test. Pick out and give us an exposition of some doubtful passage in the Scriptures, so that we can put this boast of yours to the proof." And they all chose that most obscure prophecy of Ezekiel.[10]

I accepted the challenge, and invited them to attend a lecture on the very next day. Whereupon they undertook to give me good advice, saying that I should by no means make undue haste in so important a matter, but that I ought to devote a much longer space to working out my exposition and offsetting my inexperience by diligent toil. To this I replied indignantly that it was my wont to win success, not by routine, but by ability. I added that I would abandon the test altogether unless they would agree not to put off their attendance at my lecture. In truth at this first lecture of mine only a few were present, for it seemed quite absurd to all of them that I, hitherto so inexperienced in discussing the Scriptures, should attempt the thing so hastily. However, this lecture gave such satisfaction to all those who heard it that they spread its praises abroad with notable enthusiasm, and thus compelled me to continue my interpretation of the sacred text. When word of this was bruited about, those who had stayed away from the first lecture came eagerly, some to the second and more to the third, and all of them were eager to write down the glosses which I had begun on the first day, so as to have them from the very beginning.

CHAPTER IV

Of the Persecution He Had from His Teacher Anselm

Now this venerable man of whom I have spoken was acutely smitten with envy,[11] and straightway incited, as I have already mentioned, by the insinuations of sundry persons, began to persecute me

---

[10] Abelard believed that scriptural texts could be interpreted mainly by natural reason, without much help from tradition.

[11] This need not have been envy so much as indignation. If it appeared presumptuous and out of order for a person to lecture on dialectics without having been passed or certified by a master, would it not be even more so to lecture on sacred doctrine?

for my lecturing on the Scriptures no less bitterly than my former master, William, had done for my work in philosophy. At that time there were in this old man's school two who were considered far to excel all the others: Alberic of Rheims and Lotulphe the Lombard.[12] The better opinion these two held of themselves, the more they were incensed against me. Chiefly at their suggestion, as is afterwards transpired, yonder venerable coward had the impudence to forbid me to carry on any further in his school the work of preparing glosses which I had thus begun. The pretext he alleged was that if by chance in the course of this work I should write anything containing blunders — as was likely enough in view of my lack of training — the thing might be imputed to him. When this came to the ears of his scholars, they were filled with indignation at so undisguised a manifestation of spite, the like of which had never been directed against any one before. The more obvious this rancour became, the more it redounded to my honour, and his persecution did nought save to make me more famous.

CHAPTER V

Of How He Returned to Paris and Finished the Glosses Which He Had Begun at Laon

And so, after a few days, I returned to Paris, and there for several years I peacefully directed the school which formerly had been destined for me, nay, even offered to me, but from which I had been driven out.[13] At the very outset of my work there, I set about completing the glosses on Ezekiel which I had begun at Laon. These proved so satisfactory to all who read them that they came to believe me no less adept in lecturing on theology than I had proved myself to be in the field of philosophy. Thus my school was notably increased in size by reason of my lectures on subjects of both these kinds, and the amount of financial profit as well as glory which it brought me cannot be concealed from you, for the matter was widely talked of.[14] But prosperity always puffs up the foolish, and worldly comfort enervates the soul, rendering it an easy prey to carnal temptations. Thus I, who by this time had come to regard myself as the only philosopher remaining in the whole world, and had ceased to fear any further disturbance of my peace, began to loosen the rein on my desires,

[12] In 1113–14 Alberic became Archdeacon of Rheims, where he and Lutolph the Lombard conducted a school. In 1137 Alberic became Archbishop of Bourges, in central France, a leading see. Lutolph or Lotulphe is also referred to as "of Novara."

[13] Abelard now obtained a chair at the Cathedral School of Notre Dame (c. 1113 or 1115), and he may have been made a canon of the cathedral.

[14] The twelfth-century dialectician seems to have enjoyed a fame and popularity comparable to that of the Renaissance artist or the twentieth-century movie star.

although hitherto I had always lived in the utmost continence. And the greater progress I made in my lecturing on philosophy or theology, the more I departed alike from the practice of the philosophers and the spirit of the divines in the uncleanness of my life. For it is well known, methinks, that philosophers, and still more those who have devoted their lives to arousing the love of the sacred study, have been strong above all else in the beauty of chastity.

Thus did it come to pass that while I was utterly absorbed in pride and sensuality, divine grace, the cure for both diseases, was forced upon me, even though I, forsooth, would fain have shunned it.[15] First was I punished for my sensuality, and then for my pride. For my sensuality I lost those things whereby I practiced it; for my pride, engendered in me by my knowledge of letters — and it is even as the Apostle said: "Knowledge puffeth itself up"[16] — I knew the humiliation of seeing burned the very book in which I most gloried. And now it is my desire that you should know the stories of these two happenings, understanding them more truly from learning the very facts than from hearing what is spoken of them, and in the order in which they came about. Because I had ever held in abhorrence the foulness of prostitutes, because I had diligently kept myself from all excesses and from association with the women of noble birth who attended the school,[17] because I knew so little of the common talk of ordinary people,[18] perverse and subtly flattering chance gave birth to an occasion for casting me lightly down from the heights of my own exaltation. Nay, in such case not even divine goodness could redeem one who, having been so proud, was brought to such shame, were it not for the blessed gift of grace.

CHAPTER VI

Of How, Brought Low by His Love for Héloïse, He Was Wounded in Body and Soul

Now there dwelt in that same city of Paris a certain young girl named Héloïse,[19] the niece of a canon[1] who was called Fulbert. Her uncle's love for her was equalled only by his desire that she should have the best education which he could possibly procure for her. Of no mean beauty, she stood out above all by reason of her abundant knowledge of letters. Now this virtue is rare among women, and for that very reason it doubly graced the maiden, and made her the most

---

[15] Note the spirit of faith with which Abelard regarded his adversities as salutary punishments from God.
[16] I Corinthians 8:1.
[17] Note feminine education in the 12th century.
[18] The supercilious scholar speaks.
[19] Heloise was born about 1101.
[1] Of the Cathedral of Notre Dame.

worthy of renown in the entire kingdom. It was this young girl whom I, after carefully considering all those qualities which are wont to attract lovers, determined to unite with myself in the bonds of love, and indeed the thing seemed to me very easy to be done. So distinguished was my name, and I possessed such advantages of youth and comeliness, that no matter what woman I might favour with my love, I dreaded rejection of none. Then, too, I believed that I could win the maiden's consent all the more easily by reason of her knowledge of letters and her zeal therefor; so, even if we were parted, we might yet be together in thought with the aid of written messages. Perchance, too, we might be able to write more boldly than we could speak, and thus at all times could we live in joyous intimacy.

Thus, utterly aflame with my passion for this maiden, I sought to discover means whereby I might have daily and familiar speech with her, thereby the more easily to win her consent. For this purpose I persuaded the girl's uncle, with the aid of some of his friends, to take me into his household — for he dwelt hard by my school — in return for the payment of a small sum.[2] My pretext for this was that the care of my own household was a serious handicap to my studies, and likewise burdened me with an expense far greater than I could afford. Now, he was a man keen in avarice, and likewise he was most desirous for his niece that her study of letters should ever go forward, so, for these two reasons, I easily won his consent to the fulfillment of my wish, for he was fairly agape for my money, and at the same time believed that his niece would vastly benefit by my teaching. More even than this, by his own earnest entreaties he fell in with my desires beyond anything I had dared to hope, opening the way for my love; for he entrusted her wholly to my guidance, begging me to give her instruction whensoever I might be free from the duties of my school, no matter whether by day or by night, and to punish her sternly if ever I should find her negligent of her tasks. In all this the man's simplicity was nothing short of astounding to me; I should not have been more smitten with wonder if he had entrusted a tender lamb to the care of a ravenous wolf. When he had thus given her into my charge, not alone to be taught but even to be disciplined, what had he done save to give free scope to my desires, and to offer me every opportunity, even if I had not sought it, to bend her to my will with threats and blows if I failed to do so with caresses? There were, however, two things which particularly served to allay any foul suspicion: his own love for his niece, and my former reputation for continence.

Why should I say more? We were united first in the dwelling that sheltered our love, and then in the hearts that burned with it. Under the pretext of study we spent our hours in the happiness of love, and learning held out to us the secret opportunities that our passion craved.

[2] By way of rent.

Our speech was more of love than of the books which lay open before us; our kisses far outnumbered our reasoned words. Our hands sought less the book than each other's bosoms; love drew our eyes together far more than the lesson drew them to the pages of our text. In order that there might be no suspicion, there were, indeed, sometimes blows, but love gave them, not anger; they were the marks, not of wrath, but of a tenderness surpassing the most fragrant balm in sweetness. What followed? No degree in love's progress was left untried by our passion, and if love itself could imagine any wonder as yet unknown, we discovered it. And our inexperience of such delights made us all the more ardent in our pursuit of them, so that our thirst for one another was still unquenched.

In measure as this passionate rapture absorbed me more and more, I devoted ever less time to philosophy and to the work of the school. Indeed it became loathsome to me to go to the school or to linger there; the labour, moreover, was very burdensome, since my nights were vigils of love and my days of study. My lecturing became utterly careless and lukewarm; I did nothing because of inspiration, but everything merely as a matter of habit. I had become nothing more than a reciter of my former discoveries, and though I still wrote poems, they dealt with love, not with the secrets of philosophy. Of these songs you yourself well know how some have become widely known and have been sung in many lands, chiefly, methinks, by those who delighted in the things of this world. As for the sorrow, the groans, the lamentations of my students when they perceived the preoccupation, nay, rather the chaos, of my mind, it is hard even to imagine them.

A thing so manifest could deceive only a few: no one, methinks, save him whose shame it chiefly bespoke, the girl's uncle, Fulbert. The truth was often enough hinted to him, and by many persons, but he could not believe it, partly, as I have said, by reason of his boundless love for his niece, and partly because of the well-known continence of my previous life. Indeed we do not easily suspect shame in those whom we most cherish, nor can there be the blot of foul suspicion on devoted love. Of this St. Jerome in his epistle to Sabinianus[3] says: "We are wont to be the last to know the evils of our own households, and to be ignorant of the sins of our children and our wives, though our neighbours sing them aloud." But no matter how slow a matter may be in disclosing itself, it is sure to come forth at last, nor is it easy to hide from one what is known to all. So, after the lapse of several months, did it happen with us. Oh, how great was the uncle's grief when he learned the truth, and how bitter was the sorrow of the lovers when we were forced to part! With what shame was I overwhelmed, with what contrition smitten because of the blow which had fallen on her I loved, and what a

---

[3] Epistle 147.

tempest of misery burst over her by reason of my disgrace! Each grieved most, not for himself, but for the other. Each sought to allay, not his own sufferings, but those of the one he loved. The very sundering of our bodies served but to link our souls closer together; the plentitude of the love which was denied to us inflamed us more than ever. Once the first wildness of shame had passed, it left us more shameless than before, and as shame died within us the cause of it seemed to us ever more desirable. And so it chanced with us as, in the stories that the poets tell, it once happened with Mars and Venus when they were caught together.[4]

It was not long after this that Héloïse found that she was pregnant, and of this she wrote to me in the utmost exultation, at the same time asking me to consider what had best be done. Accordingly, on a night when her uncle was absent, we carried out the plan we had determined on, and I stole her secretly away from her uncle's house, sending her without delay to my own country.[5] She remained there with my sister until she gave birth to a son, whom she named Astrolabe.[6] Meanwhile her uncle, after his return, was almost mad with grief; only one who had then seen him could rightly guess the burning agony of his sorrow and the bitterness of his shame. What steps to take against me, or what snares to set for me, he did not know. If he should kill me or do me some bodily hurt, he feared greatly lest his dear-loved niece should be made to suffer for it among my kinsfolk. He had no power to seize me and imprison me somewhere against my will, though I make no doubt he would have done so quickly enough had he been able or dared, for I had taken measures to guard against any such attempt.

At length, however, in pity for his boundless grief, and bitterly blaming myself for the suffering which my love had brought upon him through the baseness of the deception I had practiced, I went to him to entreat his forgiveness, promising to make any amends that he himself might decree. I pointed out that what had happened could not seem incredible to any one who had ever felt the power of love, or who remembered how, from the very beginning of the human race, women had cast down even the noblest men to utter ruin.[7] And in order to make amends even beyond his extremest hope, I offered to marry her whom I had seduced, provided only the thing could be kept secret, so that I might suffer no loss of reputation thereby.[8] To this he gladly assented, pledging his own faith and that of his kindred, and sealing with kisses the pact which I had sought of him — and all this that he might the more easily betray me.

[4] Ovid, *Ars Amatoria*, ii, 561 ff.; *Metamorphoses*, iv, 169–189.
[5] Brittany.
[6] This name, perhaps meaning "taker of the stars" or "measure of the stars" in an ecstatic sense, was rather common as a proper name at the time.
[7] It is difficult to see how Canon Fulbert would be mollified by the latter argument, which seems to cast the blame on Heloise.
[8] Or hope of ecclesiastical preferment.

CHAPTER VII

Of the Arguments of Héloïse against Wedlock — Of How None the Less He Made Her His Wife

Forthwith I repaired to my own country, and brought back thence my mistress, that I might make her my wife. She, however, most violently disapproved of this, and for two chief reasons: the danger thereof, and the disgrace which it would bring upon me. She swore that her uncle would never be appeased by such satisfaction as this, as, indeed, afterwards proved only too true. She asked how she could ever glory in me if she should make me thus inglorious, and should shame herself along with me. What penalties, she said, would the world rightly demand of her if she should rob it of so shining a light![9] What curses would follow such a loss to the Church, what tears among the philosophers would result from such a marriage! How unfitting, how lamentable it would be for me, whom nature had made for the whole world, to devote myself to one woman solely, and to subject myself to such humiliation! She vehemently rejected this marriage, which she felt would be in every way ignominious and burdensome to me.

Besides dwelling thus on the disgrace to me, she reminded me of the hardships of married life, to the avoidance of which the Apostle[10] exhorts us, saying: "Art thou loosed from a wife? seek not a wife. But and if thou marry, thou hast not sinned; and if a virgin marry, she hath not sinned. Nevertheless such shall have trouble in the flesh: but I spare you." And again: "But I would have you to be free from cares." But if I would heed neither the counsel of the Apostle nor the exhortations of the saints regarding this heavy yoke of matrimony, she bade me at least consider the advice of the philosophers, and weigh carefully what had been written on this subject either by them or concerning their lives. Even the saints themselves have often and earnestly spoken on this subject for the purpose of warning us. Thus St. Jerome, in his first book *Against Jovinianus*,[11] makes Theophrastus set forth in great detail the intolerable annoyances and the endless disturbances of married life, demonstrating with the most convincing arguments that no wise man should ever have a wife, and concluding his reasons for this philosophic exhortation with these words: "Who among Christians would not be overwhelmed by such arguments as these advanced by Theophrastus?"

Then, turning from the consideration of such hindrances to the study of philosophy, Héloïse bade me observe what were the conditions of honourable wedlock. What possible concord could there be

---

[9] Heloise evidently shared Abelard's grand idea of himself.
[10] St. Paul in I Corinthians 7:27, 28, and 32.
[11] Chapter 47.

between scholars and domestics, between authors and cradles, between books or tablets and distaffs, between the stylus or the pen and the spindle? What man, intent on his religious or philosophical meditations, can possibly endure the whining of children, the lullabies of the nurse seeking to quiet them, or the noisy confusion of family life? Who can endure the continual untidiness of children? The rich, you may reply, can do this, because they have palaces or houses containing many rooms, and because their wealth takes no thought of expense and protects them from daily worries. But to this the answer is that the condition of philosophers is by no means that of the wealthy, nor can those whose minds are occupied with riches and worldly cares find time for religious or philosophical study.[12] . . .

Now, she added, if laymen and gentiles, bound by no profession of religion, lived after this fashion, what ought you, a cleric and a canon, to do in order not to prefer base voluptuousness to your sacred duties, to prevent this Charybdis from sucking you down headlong, and to save yourself from being plunged shamelessly and irrevocably into such filth as this? If you care nothing for your privileges as a cleric, at least uphold your dignity as a philosopher. If you scorn the reverence due to God, let regard for your reputation temper your shamelessness. Remember that Socrates was chained to a wife, and by what a filthy accident he himself paid for this blot on philosophy, in order that others thereafter might be made more cautious by his example. Jerome thus mentions this affair, writing about Socrates in his first book *Against Jovinianus:*[13] "Once when he was withstanding a storm of reproaches which Xantippe was hurling at him from an upper story, he was suddenly drenched with foul slops; wiping his head, he said only, 'I knew there would be a shower after all that thunder.' "

Her final argument was that it would be dangerous for me to take her back to Paris, and that it would be far sweeter for her to be called my mistress than to be known as my wife; nay, too, that this would be more honourable for me as well. In such case, she said, love alone would hold me to her, and the strength of the marriage chain would not constrain us. Even if we should by chance be parted from time to time, the joy of our meetings would be all the sweeter by reason of its rarity. But when she found that she could not convince me or dissuade me from my folly by these and like arguments, and because she could not bear to offend me, with grievous sighs and tears she made an end of her resistance, saying: "Then there is no more left but this, that in our doom the sorrow yet to come shall be no less than the love we two have already known." Nor in this, as now the whole world knows, did she lack the spirit of prophecy.

---

[12] Heloise goes on to quote and cite Seneca, the Nazarites and other Jewish sects, the Apostles, Pythagoras, and St. Augustine.
[13] I, 48.

So, after our little son was born, we left him in my sister's care, and secretly returned to Paris. A few days later, in the early morning, having kept our nocturnal vigil of prayer unknown to all in a certain church, we were united there in the benediction of wedlock, her uncle and a few friends of his and mine being present. We departed forthwith stealthily and by separate ways, nor thereafter did we see each other save rarely and in private, thus striving our utmost to conceal what we had done. But her uncle and those of his household, seeking solace for their disgrace, began to divulge the story of our marriage, and thereby to violate the pledge they had given me on this point. Héloïse, on the contrary, denounced her own kin and swore that they were speaking the most absolute lies. Her uncle, aroused to fury thereby, visited her repeatedly with punishments. No sooner had I learned this than I sent her to a convent of nuns at Argenteuil,[14] not far from Paris, where she herself had been brought up and educated as a young girl. I had them make ready for her all the garments of a nun, suitable for the life of a convent, excepting only the veil,[15] and these I bade her put on.

When her uncle and his kinsmen heard of this, they were convinced that now I had completely played them false and had rid myself forever of Héloïse by forcing her to become a nun.[16] Violently incensed, they laid a plot against me, and one night, while I, all unsuspecting, was asleep in a secret room in my lodgings, they broke in with the help of one of my servants, whom they had bribed. There they had vengeance on me with a most cruel and most shameful punishment, such as astounded the whole world, for they cut off those parts of my body with which I had done that which was the cause of their sorrow. This done, straightway they fled, but two of them were captured, and suffered the loss of their eyes and their genital organs. One of these two was the aforesaid servant, who, even while he was still in my service, had been led by his avarice to betray me.

CHAPTER VIII

Of the Suffering of His Body — Of How He Became a Monk in the Monastery of St. Denis and Héloïse a Nun at Argenteuil

When morning came the whole city was assembled before my dwelling. It is difficult, nay, impossible, for words of mine to describe the amazement which bewildered them, the lamentations they uttered, the uproar with which they harassed me, or the grief with which they increased my own suffering. Chiefly the clerics, and above

---

[14] About 20 miles northwest of Paris.
[15] Heloise took the veil later, when she formally became a nun.
[16] It would appear that he had.

all my scholars, tortured me with their intolerable lamentations and outcries, so that I suffered more intensely from their compassion than from the pain of my wound. In truth I felt the disgrace more than the hurt to my body, and was more afflicted with shame than with pain. My incessant thought was of the renown in which I had so much delighted, now brought low, nay, utterly blotted out, so swiftly by an evil chance. I saw, too, how justly God had punished me in that very part of my body whereby I had sinned. I perceived that there was indeed justice in my betrayal by him whom I had myself already betrayed; and then I thought how eagerly my rivals would seize upon this manifestation of justice, how this disgrace would bring bitter and enduring grief to my kindred and my friends, and how the tale of this amazing outrage would spread to the very ends of the earth.

What path lay open to me thereafter? How could I ever again hold up my head among men, when every finger should be pointed at me in scorn, every tongue speak my blistering shame, and when I should be a monstrous spectacle to all eyes? I was overwhelmed by the remembrance that, according to the dread letter of the law, God holds eunuchs in such abomination that men thus maimed are forbidden to enter a church, even as the unclean and filthy;[17] nay, even beasts in such plight were not acceptable as sacrifices. Thus in Leviticus[18] is it said: "Ye shall not offer unto the Lord that which hath its stones bruised, or crushed, or broken, or cut." And in Deuteronomy,[19] "He that is wounded in the stones, or hath his privy member cut off, shall not enter into the congregation of the Lord."

I must confess that in my misery it was the overwhelming sense of my disgrace rather than any ardour for conversion to the religious life that drove me to seek the seclusion of the monastic cloister. Héloïse had already, at my bidding, taken the veil and entered a convent. Thus it was that we both put on the sacred garb, I in the abbey of St. Denis,[1] and she in the convent of Argenteuil, of which I have already spoken. She, I remember well, when her fond friends sought vainly to deter her from submitting her fresh youth to the heavy and almost intolerable yoke of monastic life, sobbing and weeping replied in the words of Cornelia:

". . . O husband most noble,
Who ne'er shouldst have shared my couch! Has fortune such power
To smite so lofty a head? Why then was I wedded
Only to bring thee to woe? Receive now my sorrow,
The price I so gladly pay."[2]

[17] Leviticus 21:21.
[18] Leviticus 22:24.
[19] Deuteronomy 23:1.
[1] The famous favorite royal abbey at Paris, where kings were buried and the French royal banner or oriflamme was kept.
[2] Lucan, *Pharsalia*, viii, 94.

With these words on her lips did she go forthwith to the altar, and lifted therefrom the veil, which had been blessed by the bishop, and before them all she took the vows of the religious life. For my part, scarcely had I recovered from my wound when clerics sought me in great numbers, endlessly beseeching both my abbot and me myself that now, since I was done with learning for the sake of gain or renown, I should turn to it for the sole love of God. They bade me care diligently for the talent which God had committed to my keeping,[3] since surely He would demand it back from me with interest. It was their plea that, inasmuch as of old I had laboured chiefly in behalf of the rich, I should now devote myself to the teaching of the poor. Therein above all should I perceive how it was the hand of God that had touched me, when I should devote my life to the study of letters in freedom from the snares of the flesh and withdrawn from the tumultuous life of this world. Thus, in truth, should I become a philosopher less of this world than of God.

The abbey, however, to which I had betaken myself[4] was utterly worldly and in its life quite scandalous. The abbot himself was as far below his fellows in his way of living and in the foulness of his reputation as he was above them in priestly rank. This intolerable state of things I often and vehemently denounced, sometimes in private talk and sometimes publicly, but the only result was that I made myself detested of them all. They gladly laid hold of the daily eagerness of my students to hear me as an excuse whereby they might be rid of me; and finally, at the insistent urging of the students themselves, and with the hearty consent of the abbot and the rest of the brotherhood, I departed thence to a certain hut, there to teach in my wonted way. To this place such a throng of students flocked that the neighbourhood could not afford shelter for them, nor the earth sufficient sustenance.

Here, as befitted my profession, I devoted myself chiefly to lectures on theology, but I did not wholly abandon the teaching of the secular arts, to which I was more accustomed, and which was particularly demanded of me. I used the latter, however, as a hook, luring my students by the bait of learning to the study of the true philosophy, even as the Ecclesiastical History[5] tells of Origen, the greatest of all Christian philosophers. Since apparently the Lord had gifted me with no less persuasiveness in expounding the Scriptures than in lecturing on secular subjects, the number of my students in these two courses began to increase greatly, and the attendance at all the other schools was correspondingly diminished. Thus I aroused the envy and hatred of the other teachers. Those who sought to belittle me in every pos-

---

[3] Matthew 25:15.
[4] I.e., that of St. Denis (or Dionysius).
[5] Or: "as it is recorded by Eusebius" (Muckle); Eusebius, *Ecclesiastical History*, vi, 8.

sible way took advantage of my absence to bring two principal charges against me: first, that it was contrary to the monastic profession to be concerned with the study of secular books;[6] and, second, that I had presumed to teach theology without ever having been taught therein myself. This they did in order that my teaching of every kind might be prohibited, and to this end they continually stirred up bishops, archbishops, abbotts and whatever other dignitaries of the Church they could reach.

CHAPTER IX

Of His Book on Theology and His Persecution at the Hands of His Fellow Students — Of the Council Against Him

It so happened that at the outset I devoted myself to analysing the basis of our faith through illustrations based on human understanding, and I wrote for my students a certain tract on the unity and trinity of God.[7] This I did because they were always seeking for rational and philosophical explanations, asking rather for reasons they could understand than for mere words, saying that it was futile to utter words which the intellect could not possibly follow, that nothing could be believed unless it could first be understood, and that it was absurd for any one to preach to others a thing which neither he himself nor those whom he sought to teach could comprehend. Our Lord Himself maintained this same thing when He said: "They are blind leaders of the blind."[8]

Now, a great many people saw and read this tract, and it became exceedingly popular, its clearness appealing particularly to all who sought information on this subject. And since the questions involved are generally considered the most difficult of all, their complexity is taken as the measure of the subtlety of him who succeeds in answering them. As a result, my rivals became furiously angry, and summoned a council[9] to take action against me, the chief instigators therein being my two intriguing enemies of former days, Alberic and Lotulphe. These two, now that both William and Anselm, our erstwhile teachers, were dead, were greedy to reign in their stead, and, so to speak, to succeed them as heirs. While they were directing the school at Rheims, they managed by repeated hints to stir up their archbishop, Rodolphe,[10] against me, for the purpose of holding a

---

[6] Obviously false. Cf. Jean Leclercq, *The Love of Learning and the Desire for God: A Study of Monastic Culture* (Fordham: 1961).
[7] *De Unitate et Trinitate Dei*, sometimes referred to simply as *De Trinitate*.
[8] Matthew 15:14.
[9] The Provincial Council of Soissons (1121).
[10] Rodolphe, Archbishop of Rheims since 1114, a leader among the French clergy.

meeting, or rather an ecclesiastical council, at Soissons, provided they could secure the approval of Conon, Bishop of Praeneste, at that time papal legate in France.[11] Their plan was to summon me to be present at this council, bringing with me the famous book I had written regarding the Trinity. In all this, indeed, they were successful, and the thing happened according to their wishes.

Before I reached Soissons,[12] however, these two rivals of mine so foully slandered me with both the clergy and the public that on the day of my arrival the people came near to stoning me and the few students of mine who had accompanied me thither. The cause of their anger was that they had been led to believe that I had preached and written to prove the existence of three gods. No sooner had I reached the city, therefore, than I went forthwith to the legate; to him I submitted my book for examination and judgment, declaring that if I had written anything repugnant to the Catholic faith, I was quite ready to correct it or otherwise to make satisfactory amends. The legate directed me to refer my book to the archbishop and to those same two rivals of mine, to the end that my accusers might also be my judges. So in my case was fulfilled the saying: "Even our enemies are our judges."[13]

These three, then, took my book and pawed it over and examined it minutely, but could find nothing therein which they dared to use as the basis for a public accusation against me. Accordingly they put off the condemnation of the book until the close of the council, despite their eagerness to bring it about. For my part, every day before the council convened I publicly discussed the Catholic faith in the light of what I had written, and all who heard me were enthusiastic in their approval alike of the frankness and the logic of my words. When the public and the clergy had thus learned something of the real character of my teaching, they began to say to one aonther: "Behold, now he speaks openly, and no one brings any charge against him. And this council, summoned, as we have heard, chiefly to take action upon his case, is drawing toward its end. Did the judges realize that the error might be theirs rather than his?" . . .

On the last day of the council, before the session convened, the legate and the archbishop deliberated with my rivals and sundry others as to what should be done about me and my book, this being the chief reason for their having come together. And since they had discovered nothing, either in my speech or in what I had hitherto written, which would give them a case against me, they were all reduced to silence, or at the most to maligning me in whispers. Then Geoffroi, Bishop of Chartres,[14] who excelled the other bishops alike

[11] Conon, Bishop of Praeneste, represented Pope Paschal II at three French councils in 1115, and Pope Callistus II at the present council.
[12] About 60 miles northeast of Paris.
[13] Deuteronomy 32:31.
[14] Geoffroi or Geoffrey, Bishop of Chartres from 1116 to 1149, was widely respected.

in the sincerity of his religion and in the importance of his see, spoke thus:

"You know, my lords, all who are gathered here, the doctrine of this man, what it is, and his ability, which has brought him many followers in every field to which he has devoted himself. You know how greatly he has lessened the renown of other teachers, both his masters and our own, and how he has spread as it were the offshoots of his vine[15] from sea to sea. Now, if you impose a lightly considered judgment on him, as I cannot believe you will, you well know that even if mayhap you are in the right there are many who will be angered thereby, and that he will have no lack of defenders. Remember above all that we have found nothing in this book of his that lies before us whereon any open accusation can be based. Indeed it is true, as Jerome says: 'Fortitude openly displayed always creates rivals, and the lightning strikes the highest peaks.'[16] Have a care, then, lest by violent action you only increase his fame, and lest we do more hurt to ourselves through envy than to him through justice. A false report, as that same wise man reminds us, is easily crushed, and a man's later life gives testimony as to his earlier deeds.[17] If, then, you are disposed to take canonical action against him, his doctrine or his writings must be brought forward as evidence, and he must have free opportunity to answer his questioners. In that case, if he is found guilty or if he confesses his error, his lips can be wholly sealed. Consider the words of the blessed Nicodemus, who, desiring to free Our Lord Himself, said: 'Doth our law judge any man before it hear him and know what he doeth?' "[18]

When my rivals heard this they cried out in protest, saying: "This is wise counsel, forsooth, that we should strive against the wordiness of this man, whose arguments, or rather, sophistries, the whole world cannot resist!" And yet, methinks, it was far more difficult to strive against Christ Himself, for Whom, nevertheless, Nicodemus demanded a hearing in accordance with the dictates of the law. When the bishop could not win their assent to his proposals, he tried in another way to curb their hatred, saying that for the discussion of such an important case the few who were present were not enough, and that this matter required a more thorough examination. His further suggestion was that my abbot, who was there present, should take me back with him to our abbey, in other words to the monastery of St. Denis, and that there a large convocation of learned men should determine, on the basis of a careful investigation, what ought to be done. To this last proposal the legate consented, as did all the others.

Then the legate arose to celebrate mass before entering the council,

---

[15] Psalms 79:12.
[16] Jerome, in his *Lib. Hebr. Quaest.*, quoting Horace, *Carmina*, ii, 167.
[17] Epist. 14:13.
[18] John 7:51.

and through the bishop sent me the permission which had been determined on, authorizing me to return to my monastery and there await such action as might be finally taken. But my rivals, perceiving that they would accomplish nothing if the trial were to be held outside of their own diocese, and in a place where they could have little influence on the verdict, and in truth having small wish that justice should be done, persuaded the archbishop that it would be a grave insult to him to transfer this case to another court, and that it would be dangerous for him if by chance I should thus be acquitted. They likewise went to the legate, and succeeded in so changing his opinion that finally they induced him to frame a new sentence, whereby he agreed to condemn my book without any further inquiry, to burn it forthwith in the sight of all, and to confine me for a year in another monastery. The argument they used was that it sufficed for the condemnation of my book that I had presumed to read it in public without the approval either of the Roman pontiff or of the Church, and that, furthermore, I had given it to many to be transcribed.[19] Methinks it would be a notable blessing to the Christian faith if there were more who displayed a like presumption. The legate, however, being less skilled in law than he should have been, relied chiefly on the advice of the archbishop, and he, in turn, on that of my rivals. When the Bishop of Chartres got wind of this, he reported the whole conspiracy to me, and strongly urged me to endure meekly the manifest violence of their enmity. He bade me not to doubt that this violence would in the end react upon them and prove a blessing to me, and counseled me to have no fear of the confinement in a monastery, knowing that within a few days the legate himself, who was now acting under compulsion, would after his departure set me free. And thus he consoled me as best he might, mingling his tears with mine.

· · · · ·

[CH. X] The very cruelty and heartlessness of my punishment, however, made every one who heard the story vehement in censuring it, so that those who had a hand therein were soon eager to disclaim all responsibility, shouldering the blame on others. Nay, matters came to such a pass that even my rivals denied that they had had anything to do with the matter, and as for the legate, he publicly denounced the malice with which the French had acted. Swayed by repentance for his injustice, and feeling that he had yielded enough to satisfy their rancour, he shortly freed me from the monstery whither I had been taken, and sent me back to my own. Here, however, I found almost as many enemies as I had in the former days of which I have already spoken, for the vileness and shamelessness of their way of living made them realize that they would again have to endure my censure.

[19] Cf. G. B. Flahiff, "Ecclesiastical Censorship of Books in the Twelfth Century," *Mediaeval Studies,* IV (1942), 2 ff.

After a few months had passed, chance gave them an opportunity by which they sought to destroy me. It happened that one day, in the course of my reading, I came upon a certain passage of Bede,[1] in his commentary on the Acts of the Apostles, wherein he asserts that Dionysius the Areopagite was the bishop, not of Athens, but of Corinth.[2] Now, this was directly counter to the belief of the monks, who were wont to boast that their Dionysius, or Denis, was not only the Areopagite but was likewise proved by his acts to have been the Bishop of Athens. Having thus found this testimony of Bede's in contradiction of our own tradition, I showed it somewhat jestingly to sundry of the monks who chanced to be near. Wrathfully they declared that Bede was no better than a liar, and that they had a far more trustworthy authority in the person of Hilduin,[3] a former abbot of theirs, who had travelled for a long time throughout Greece for the purpose of investigating this very question. He, they insisted, had by his writings removed all possible doubt on the subject, and had securely established the truth of the traditional belief.

One of the monks went so far as to ask me brazenly which of the two, Bede or Hilduin, I considered the better authority on this point. I replied that the authority of Bede, whose writings are held in high esteem by the whole Latin Church, appeared to me the better. Thereupon in a great rage they began to cry out that at last I had openly proved the hatred I had always felt for our monastery, and that I was seeking to disgrace it in the eyes of the whole kingdom, robbing it of the honour in which it had particularly gloried, by thus denying that the Areopagite was their patron saint. To this I answered that I had never denied the fact, and that I did not much care whether their patron was the Areopagite or some one else, provided only he had received his crown from God. Thereupon they ran to the abbot and told him of the misdemeanour with which they charged me.

The abbot[4] listened to their story with delight, rejoicing at having found a chance to crush me, for the greater vileness of his life made him fear me more even than the rest did. Accordingly he summoned his council, and when the brethren had assembled he violently threatened me, declaring that he would straightway send me to the

---

[1] "The Venerable Bede," eighth-century English monastic scholar and historian.

[2] There was much confusion concerning the Dionysius the Areopagite mentioned as having become a convert of St. Paul (in Acts 17:34). A second-century Dionysius who was Bishop of Corinth said he had become Bishop of Athens. Various mystical works of the fourth or fifth century were also attributed to him.

[3] Hilduin, Abbot of St. Denis from 814 to 840, was commissioned by Louis the Pious in 834 to write a *Life of St. Denis,* still extant, in which he identified their patron saint with the Areopagite.

[4] Abbot Adam, succeeded in 1122 by Suger. This trouble must accordingly have occurred in 1121–22.

king, by him to be punished for having thus sullied his crown and the glory of his royalty. And until he should hand me over to the king, he ordered that I should be closely guarded.[5] In vain did I offer to submit to the customary discipline if I had in any way been guilty. Then, horrified at their wickedness, which seemed to crown the ill fortune I had so long endured, and in utter despair at the apparent conspiracy of the whole world against me, I fled secretly from the monastery by night, helped thereto by some of the monks who took pity on me, and likewise aided by some of my scholars.

I made my way to a region where I had formerly dwelt, hard by the lands of Count Theobald (of Champagne).[6] He himself had some slight acquaintance with me, and had compassion on me by reason of my persecutions, of which the story had reached him. I found a home there within the walls of Provins, in a priory of the monks of Troyes,[7] the prior of which had in former days known me well and shown me much love. In his joy at my coming he cared for me with all diligence. It chanced, however, that one day my abbot came to Provins to see the count on certain matters of business. As soon as I had learned of this, I went to the count, the prior accompanying me, and besought him to intercede in my behalf with the abbot. I asked no more than that the abbot should absolve me of the charge against me, and give me permission to live the monastic life wheresoever I could find a suitable place. The abbot, however, and those who were with him took the matter under advisement, saying that they would give the count an answer the day before they departed. It appeared from their words that they thought I wished to go to some other abbey, a thing which they regarded as an immense disgrace to their own. They had, indeed, taken particular pride in the fact that, upon my conversion, I had come to them, as if scorning all other abbeys, and accordingly they considered that it would bring great shame upon them if I should now desert their abbey and seek another. For this reason they refused to listen either to my own plea or to that of the count. Furthermore, they threatened me with excommunication unless I should instantly return; likewise they forbade the prior with whom I had taken refuge to keep me longer, under pain of sharing my excommunication. When we heard this, both the prior and I were stricken with fear. The abbot went away still obdurate, but a few days thereafter he died.

As soon as his successor[8] had been named, I went to him, accompanied by the Bishop of Meaux,[9] to try if I might win from him the

---

[5] Note the external jurisdiction exercised by the abbot.
[6] Theobald II, Count of Blois, Meaux, and Champagne from the 1120's to 1152, and one of the most powerful figures in France.
[7] In the county of Champagne, about 90 miles southeast of Paris.
[8] The famous Suger, who became Abbot of St. Denis in 1122, and who was a leading counsellor of King Louis VII, as he had been of Louis VI.
[9] Bishop Burchard of Meaux.

permission I had vainly sought of his predecessor. At first he would not give his assent, but finally, through the intervention of certain friends of mine, I secured the right to appeal to the king and his council, and in this way I at last obtained what I sought. The royal seneschal, Stephen,[10] having summoned the abbot and his subordinates that they might state their case, asked them why they wanted to keep me against my will. He pointed out that this might easily bring them into evil repute, and certainly could do them no good, seeing that their way of living was utterly incompatible with mine. I knew it to be the opinion of the royal council that the irregularities in the conduct of this abbey would tend to bring it more and more under the control of the king, making it increasingly useful and likewise profitable to him, and for this reason I had good hope of easily winning the support of the king and those about him.

Thus, indeed, did it come to pass. But in order that the monastery might not be shorn of any of the glory which it had enjoyed by reason of my sojourn there, they granted me permission to betake myself to any solitary place I might choose, provided only I did not put myself under the rule of any other abbey. This was agreed upon and confirmed on both sides in the presence of the king and his councellors. Forthwith I sought out a lonely spot known to me of old in the region of Troyes,[11] and there, on a bit of land which had been given to me, and with the approval of the bishop of the district, I built with reeds and stalks my first oratory in the name of the Holy Trinity. And there concealed, with but one comrade, a certain cleric, I was able to sing over and over again to the Lord: "Lo, then would I wander far off, and remain in the wilderness."[12]

CHAPTER XI

Of His Teaching in the Wilderness

No sooner had scholars learned of my retreat than they began to flock thither from all sides, leaving their towns and castles to dwell in the wilderness. In place of their spacious houses they built themselves huts; instead of dainty fare they lived on the herbs of the field and coarse bread; their soft beds they exchanged for heaps of straw and rushes, and their tables were piles of turf. In very truth you may well believe that they were like those philosophers of old of whom Jerome tells us in his second book *Against Jovinianus*.[13] . . .

Such a life, likewise, the sons of the prophets who were the followers of Eliseus are reported to have led. Of these Jerome also tells

[10] Stephen de Garland, archdeacon, and chief steward of the royal household.
[11] In the parish of Quincey.
[12] Psalms 54:8.
[13] Chap. 8 ff.

us, writing thus to the monk Rusticus as if describing the monks of those ancient days: "The sons of the prophets, the monks of whom we read in the Old Testament, built for themselves huts by the waters of the Jordan, and forsaking the throngs and the cities, lived on pottage and the herbs of the field."[14]

Even so did my followers build their huts above the waters of the Arduzon,[15] so that they seemed hermits rather than scholars. And as their number grew ever greater, the hardships which they gladly endured for the sake of my teaching seemed to my rivals to reflect new glory on me, and to cast new shame on themselves. Nor was it strange that they, who had done their utmost to hurt me, should grieve to see how all things worked together for my good, even though I was now, in the words of Jerome,[16] afar from cities and the market place, from controversies and the crowded ways of men. And so, as Quintilian[17] says, did envy seek me out even in my hiding place. Secretly my rivals complained and lamented one to another, saying: "Behold now, the whole world runs after him, and our persecution of him has done nought save to increase his glory. We strove to extinguish his fame, and we have but given it new brightness. Lo, in the cities scholars have at hand everything they may need, and yet, spurning the pleasures of the town, they seek out the barrenness of the desert, and of their own free will they accept wretchedness."

The thing which at that time chiefly led me to undertake the direction of a school was my intolerable poverty, for I had not strength enough to dig, and shame kept me from begging.[18] And so, resorting once more to the art with which I was familiar, I was compelled to substitute the service of the tongue for the labour of my hands. The students willingly provided me with whatsoever I needed in the way of food and clothing, and likewise took charge of the cultivation of the fields and paid for the erection of buildings, in order that material cares might not keep me from my studies. Since my oratory was no longer large enough to hold even a small part of their number, they found it necessary to increase its size, and in so doing they greatly improved it, building it of stone and wood. Although this oratory had been founded in honour of the Holy Trinity, and afterwards dedicated thereto, I now named it the Paraclete, mindful of how I had come there a fugitive and in despair, and had breathed into my soul something of the miracle of divine consolation.

Many of those who heard of this were greatly astonished, and some violently assailed my action, declaring that it was not permissible to dedicate a church exclusively to the Holy Spirit rather than to God

---

[14] Epist. 125:7.
[15] A small river in the area.
[16] *Liber Heb. Quaest. in Genesim.*
[17] Declamations, xiii, 2; quoted by Jerome.
[18] Luke 16:3.

the Father. They held, according to an ancient tradition, that it must be dedicated either to the Son alone or else to the entire Trinity.[19] ...

CHAPTER XII

Of the Persecution Directed against Him by Sundry New Enemies or, as it Were, Apostles

And so I dwelt in this place, my body indeed hidden away, but my fame spreading throughout the whole world, till its echo reverberated mightily — echo, that fancy of the poet's, which has so great a voice, and nought beside. My former rivals, seeing that they themselves were now powerless to do me hurt, stirred up against me certain new apostles in whom the world put great faith. One of these took pride in his position as canon of a regular order;[1] the other made it his boast that he had revived the true monastic life.[2] These two ran hither and yon preaching and shamelessly slandering me in every way they could, so that in time they succeeded in drawing down on my head the scorn of many among those having authority, among both the clergy and the laity. They spread abroad such sinister reports of my faith as well as of my life that they turned even my best friends against me, and those who still retained something of their former regard for me were fain to disguise it in every possible way by reason of their fear of these two men.

God is my witness that whensoever I learned of the convening of a new assemblage of the clergy, I believed that it was done for the express purpose of my condemnation. Stunned by this fear like one smitten with a thunderbolt, I daily expected to be dragged before their councils or assemblies as a heretic or one guilty of impiety. Though I seem to compare a flea with a lion, or an ant with an elephant, in very truth my rivals persecuted me no less bitterly than the heretics of old hounded St. Athanasius.[3] Often, God knows, I sank so deep in despair that I was ready to leave the world of Christendom and go forth among the heathen, paying them a stipulated tribute in order that I might live quietly a Christian life among the enemies of Christ. It seemed to me that such people might indeed be kindly disposed toward me, particularly as they would doubtless suspect me of being no good Christian, imputing my flight to some crime I had committed, and would therefore believe that I might perhaps be won over to their form of worship.

[19] Abelard's action was novel. A considerable defense follows, but is here omitted.
[1] Or: "claimed it as his glory that he had revived the life of Regular Canons." (Muckle). Abelard seems to refer to St. Norbert of Prémontré, founder of the Premonstratensians, though this is disputed.
[2] This seems to refer to St. Bernard of Clairvaux, although there are no other surviving indications that Bernard began his campaign against Abelard this early.
[3] Early defender of orthodoxy against Arianism, several times exiled from his see of Alexandria.

CHAPTER XIII

Of the Abbey to Which He Was Called and of the Persecution He Had from His Sons, that is to Say the Monks, and from the Lord of the Land

While I was thus afflicted with so great perturbation of the spirit, and when the only way of escape seemed to be for me to seek refuge with Christ among the enemies of Christ, there came a chance whereby I thought I could for a while avoid the plottings of my enemies. But thereby I fell among Christians and monks who were far more savage than heathens and more evil of life. The thing came about in this wise. There was in lesser Brittany, in the bishopric of Vannes, a certain abbey of St. Gildas at Ruits, then mourning the death of its shepherd.[4] To this abbey the elective choice of the brethren called me, with the approval of the prince of that land, and I easily secured permission to accept the post from my own abbot and brethren. Thus did the hatred of the French drive me westward, even as that of the Romans drove Jerome toward the East. Never, God knows, would I have agreed to this thing had it not been for my longing for any possible means of escape from the sufferings which I had borne so constantly.

The land was barbarous and its speech was unknown to me; as for the monks, their vile and untameable way of life was notorious almost everywhere. The people of the region, too, were uncivilized and lawless. Thus, like one who in terror of the sword that threatens him dashes headlong over a precipice, and to shun one death for a moment rushes to another, I knowingly sought this new danger in order to escape from the former one. And there, amid the dreadful roar of the waves of the sea, where the land's end left me no further refuge in flight, often in my prayers did I repeat over and over again: "From the end of the earth will I cry unto Thee, when my heart is overwhelmed."[5]

No one, methinks, could fail to understand how persistently that undisciplined body of monks, the direction of which I had thus undertaken, tortured my heart day and night, or how constantly I was compelled to think of the danger alike to my body and to my soul. I held it for certain that if I should try to force them to live according to the principles they had themselves professed, I should not survive. And yet, if I did not do this to the utmost of my ability, I saw that my damnation was assured. Moreover, a certain lord who was ex-

---

[4] According to tradition, this abbey of St. Gildas was the oldest in Brittany, reputedly dating back to the fifth century. At any rate, it had a long authentic history. Abelard became abbot there in 1125, and "endured" the life for about ten years. The *Historia Calamitatum* was apparently written shortly before his flight.

[5] Psalms 60:3.

ceedingly powerful in that region had some time previously brought the abbey under his control, taking advantage of the state of disorder within the monastery to seize all the lands adjacent thereto for his own use, and he ground down the monks with taxes heavier than those which were extorted from the Jews themselves.[6]

The monks pressed me to supply them with their daily necessities, but they held no property in common which I might administer in their behalf, and each one, with such resources as he possessed, supported himself and his concubines, as well as his sons and daughters. They took delight in harassing me on this matter, and they stole and carried off whatsoever they could lay their hands on, to the end that my failure to maintain order might make me either give up trying to enforce discipline or else abandon my post altogether. Since the entire region was equally savage, lawless and disorganized, there was not a single man to whom I could turn for aid, for the habits of all alike were foreign to me. Outside the monastery, the lord and his henchmen ceaselessly hounded me, and within its walls the brethren were forever plotting against me, so that it seemed as if the Apostle had had me and none other in mind when he said: "Without were fightings, within were fears."[7]

I considered and lamented the uselessness and the wretchedness of my existence, how fruitless my life now was, both to myself and to others; how of old I had been of some service to the clerics whom I had now abandoned for the sake of these monks, so that I was no longer able to be of use to either; how incapable I had proved myself in everything I had undertaken or attempted, so that above all others I deserved the reproach, "This man began to build, and was not able to finish."[8] My despair grew still deeper when I compared the evils I had left behind with those to which I had come, for my former sufferings now seemed to me as nought. Full often did I groan: "Justly has this sorrow come upon me because I deserted the Paraclete, which is to say the Consoler, and thrust myself into sure desolation; seeking to shun threats I fled to certain peril."

The thing which tormented me most was the fact that, having abandoned my oratory, I could make no suitable provision for the celebration there of the divine office, for indeed the extreme poverty of the place would scarcely provide the necessities of one man. But the true Paraclete Himself[9] brought me real consolation in the midst of this sorrow of mine, and made all due provision for His own oratory. For it chanced that in some manner or other, laying claim to it as having legally belonged in earlier days to his monastery, my abbot

[6] An example of a defect of feudalism in action. As to the Jews: in several areas of Europe the Jews had to pay special taxes. Anti-Jewish sentiment was stimulated by the Crusades.
[7] II Corinthians 7:5.
[8] Luke 14:30.
[9] The Holy Ghost or Holy Spirit, Third Person of the Holy Trinity.

of St. Denis got possession of the abbey of Argenteuil,[10] of which I have previously spoken, wherein she who was now my sister in Christ rather than my wife, Héloïse, had taken the veil. From this abbey he expelled by force all the nuns who had dwelt there, and of whom my former companion had become the prioress. The exiles being thus dispersed in various places, I perceived that this was an opportunity presented by God himself to me whereby I could make provision anew for my oratory. And so, returning thither, I bade her come to the oratory, together with some others from the same convent who had clung to her.[11]

On their arrival there I made over to them the oratory, together with everything pertaining thereto, and subsequently, through the approval and assistance of the bishop of the district,[12] Pope Innocent II[13] promulgated a decree confirming my gift in perpetuity to them and their successors. And this refuge of divine mercy, which they served so devotedly, soon brought them consolation, even though at first their life was one of want, and for a time of utter destitution. But the place proved itself a true Paraclete to them, making all those who dwelt round about feel pity and kindliness for the sisterhood. So that, methinks, they prospered more through gifts in a single year than I should have done if I had stayed there a hundred. True it is that the weakness of womankind makes their needs and sufferings appeal strongly to people's feelings, as likewise it makes their virtue all the more pleasing to God and man. And God granted such favour in the eyes of all to her who was now my sister, and who was in authority over the rest, that the bishops loved her as a daughter, the abbots as a sister, and the laity as a mother. All alike marvelled at her religious zeal, her good judgment and the sweetness of her incomparable patience in all things. The less often she allowed herself to be seen, shutting herself up in her cell to devote herself to sacred meditations and prayers, the more eagerly did those who dwelt without demand her presence and the spiritual guidance of her words.

CHAPTER XIV

Of the Evil Report of His Iniquity

Before long all those who dwelt thereabouts began to censure me roundly, complaining that I paid far less attention to their needs[14] than I might and should have done, and that at least I could do

---

10 Suger based his claim on a charter from the reign of Pepin, purportedly showing ownership. Ownership was transferred and the nuns dispossessed in 1128–29.

11 Double monasteries of men and women located in the same vincinity were not uncommon.

12 Bishop Hatto of Troyes, who not only befriended Abelard but also seems to have ordained him a priest.

13 In 1131.   14 The spiritual needs of the nuns.

something for them through my preaching. As a result, I returned thither frequently, to be of service to them in whatsoever way I could. Regarding this there was no lack of hateful murmuring, and the thing which sincere charity induced me to do was seized upon by the wickedness of my detractors as the subject of shameless outcry. They declared that I, who of old could scarcely endure to be parted from her I loved, was still swayed by the delights of fleshly lust. Many times I thought of the complaint of St. Jerome in his letter to Asella regarding those women whom he was falsely accused of loving, when he said:[15] "I am charged with nothing save the fact of my sex, and this charge is made only because Paula is setting forth to Jerusalem." And again: "Before I became intimate in the household of the saintly Paula, the whole city was loud in my praise, and nearly every one deemed me deserving of the highest honours of priesthood. But I know that my way to the kingdom of Heaven lies through good and evil report alike."

When I pondered over the injury which slander had done to so great a man as this, I was not a little consoled thereby. If my rivals, I told myself, could but find an equal cause for suspicion against me, with what accusations would they persecute me! But how is it possible for such suspicion to continue in my case, seeing that divine mercy has freed me therefrom by depriving me of all power to enact such baseness? How shameless is this latest accusation! In truth that which had happened to me so completely removes all suspicion of this iniquity among all men that those who wish to have their women kept under close guard employ eunuchs for that purpose, even as sacred history tells regarding Esther and the other damsels of King Ahasuerus.[16] . . .

CHAPTER XV

Of the Perils of His Abbey and of the Reasons for the Writing of This His Letter

Reflecting often upon all these things, I determined to make provision for those sisters and to undertake their care in every way I could. Furthermore, in order that they might have the greater reverence for me, I arranged to watch over them in person. And since now the persecution carried on by my sons was greater and more incessant than that which I formerly suffered at the hands of my brethren, I returned frequently to the nuns, fleeing the rage of the tempest as to a haven of peace. There, indeed, could I draw breath for a little in quiet, and among them my labours were fruitful, as they never were

---

[15] Epist. 95:2.
[16] Esther 2:3. A lengthy defense of his ministrations to the nuns follows, mostly based on the authority of the Scriptures and the Fathers.

among the monks. All this was of the utmost benefit to me in body and soul, and it was equally essential for them by reason of their weakness.[17]

But now has Satan beset me to such an extent that I no longer know where I may find rest or even so much as live. I am driven hither and yon, a fugitive and a vagabond, even as the accursed Cain.[18] I have already said that "without were fightings, within were fears,"[19] and these torture me ceaselessly, the fears being indeed without as well as within, and the fightings wheresoever there are fears. Nay, the persecution carried on by my sons rages against me more perilously and continuously than that of my open enemies, for my sons I have always with me, and I am ever exposed to their treacheries. The violence of my enemies I see in the danger to my body if I leave the cloister; but within it I am compelled incessantly to endure the crafty machinations as well as the open violence of those monks who are called my sons, and who are entrusted to me as their abbot, which is to say their father.

Oh, how often have they tried to kill me with poison, even as the monks sought to slay St. Benedict! Methinks the same reason which led the saint to abandon his wicked sons might encourage me to follow the example of so great a father[1]...

And now, most dear brother in Christ and comrade closest to me in the intimacy of speech,[2] it should suffice for your sorrows and the hardships you have endured that I have written this story of my own misfortunes, amid which I have toiled almost from the cradle. For so, as I said in the beginning of this letter, shall you come to regard your tribulation as nought, or at any rate as little, in comparison with mine, and so shall you bear it more lightly in measure as you regard it as less. Take comfort ever in the saying of Our Lord, what he foretold for his followers at the hands of the followers of the devil: "If they have persecuted me, they will also persecute you,[3] If the world hate you, ye know that it hated me before it hated you. If ye were of the world, the world would love his own."[4] And the apostle says: "All that will live godly in Christ Jesus shall suffer persecution."[5] And elsewhere he says: "I do not seek to please men.

---

[17] It is well to remember that by this time Abelard was in his fifties, and pretty well worn down, physically and mentally, by his misfortunes. There is no reason to doubt his sincerity and purity.

[18] Genesis 4:14.

[19] II Corinthians 7:5.

[1] Early in his career, St. Benedict of Nursia had similar troubles with a group of monks who had elected him as their abbot, but resisted his reforming efforts. He eventually left them, as Abelard later fled this community.... Abelard now proceeds to expatiate on his trials.

[2] It is a common opinion that this letter was intended ultimately for Heloise, into whose hands it eventually did come. It may well have been a sort of justification for his impending decision to leave the Abbey of St. Gildas.

[3] John 15:20.

[4] John 15:18–19.

[5] II Timothy 3:12.

For if I yet pleased men, I should not be the servant of Christ."[6] And the Psalmist says: "They who have been pleasing to men have been confounded, for that God hath despised them."[7]

And since all things are done in accordance with the divine ordering, let every one of true faith console himself amid all his afflictions with the thought that the great goodness of God permits nothing to be done without reason, and brings to a good end whatsoever may seem to happen wrongfully. Wherefore rightly do all men say: "Thy will be done." And great is the consolation to all lovers of God in the word of the Apostle when he says: "We know that all things work together for good to them that love God."[8] The wise man of old had this in mind when he said in his Proverbs: "There shall no evil happen to the just."[9] By this he clearly shows that whosoever grows wrathful for any reason against his sufferings has therein departed from the way of the just, because he may not doubt that these things have happened to him by divine dispensation. Even such are those who yield to their own rather than to the divine purpose, and with hidden desires resist the spirit which echoes in the words, "Thy will be done," thus placing their own will ahead of the will of God. Farewell.

[6] Galatians 1:10.
[7] Psalms 52:6.
[8] Romans 8:28.
[9] Proverbs 12:21.

SECTION IV

The Renaissance: Revision and Transition

෯

THE LATER MIDDLE AGES (roughly, the fourteenth and fifteenth centuries), often called the "Age of Transition" or the "Epoch of the Italian Renaissance," was a period of stress and strain, revision and change. The old order of feudalism, agrarianism, and church-centered culture was passing away, and a new era of urban-centered life, commercialism, and lay culture was emerging. Although the process had begun in the High Middle Ages, its revolutionary effects became much more pronounced in the Later Middle Ages.

The Italian Renaissance was the most dramatic and dynamic manifestation of this period. Italy temporarily became the leader of Europe. The Late Gothic development north of the Alps was essentially a final phase before dissolution, whereas the Italian Renaissance was a positive harbinger of the modern era. Whether or not it represented improvement and progress may be debated, but it held the key to the future.

Three of the most salient and influential aspects of the Italian Renaissance were its humanism, its artistic achievements, and its new social and political *mores*. These provide focal points for the following selections: Renaissance humanism is epitomized in the life, work, and views of Petrarch, as reflected in some of his *Correspondence;* the return to classical models and standards in art is mirrored in Vasari's *Lives* of contemporary artists; and the "new politique," with its altered concepts of social and political ethics, is displayed in *The Prince*, a guidebook for rulers composed by the Florentine statesman Machiavelli.

10

The Birth of Renaissance Humanism in Italy

Petrarch

Petrarch was the earliest trail-blazer of a movement whose doctrines and ideals he himself most fully represented and most effectively propagated. As a result of a long life of single-minded dedication, tireless study, unflagging literary production, and continuous propaganda for the "cause," he has become for posterity the personification of Italian humanism during the Renaissance.

Although of a Florentine family, Francesco Petrarch (di Petracco, or Petrarca) was born in 1304 at Arezzo, his father having been exiled from Florence two years earlier, for political reasons, along with Dante and others of the unsuccessful "White Guelf" faction. Petrarch's mother, however, obtained permission for herself and her son to return to Florentine territory, and for six or seven years they lived in the small village of Ancisa, about fourteen miles north of Florence, where the boy was able to imbibe the Tuscan dialect. After a year at Pisa, the family moved in 1312 or 1313 to Avignon, where opportunities of employment for Petrarch's father as a lawyer and notary were greater because the papal court had recently taken up residence there.

Petrarch received his basic general education in the humanities from Convennole of Prato at Carpentras, just east of Avignon, during the years 1315-19. He demonstrated great fondness and aptitude for Latin grammar and literature. But his father wanted him to become a lawyer, so he studied law, first at the University of Montepellier (1319-23) in southern France, and then at the University of Bologna in Italy (1323-26).

On his father's death in 1326, Petrarch forsook law and entered the clergy, partly because of straitened family circumstances and partly so that he could devote himself more fully to literary pursuits. He was greatly aided by the friendship and patronage of the wealthy and powerful Colonna family, as extended first by Giacomo, who became Bishop of Lombez, and then by Cardinal Giovanni. Although Petrarch enjoyed the status and income of a cleric, he seems never to have engaged seriously in the pastoral ministry.

It was in 1327, in church in Avignon, that Petrarch first saw Laura, the idealized married beauty who was to inspire his finest poems. Although he continued to cherish his vision of her, he apparently maintained a mistress who bore him a son in 1337 and a daughter in 1343.

To escape the bustle of worldly affairs and concentrate on scholarship and literature, Petrarch established himself in 1337 at sylvan Vaucluse, in the picturesque valley of the Sorgue, about fifteen miles from Avignon. This became his beloved retreat and recurrent residence for some sixteen years, and here he did much writing in what he describes as the most productive period of his life. One of his principal concerns was the composition of an epic poem, Africa, describing the exploits of Scipio Africanus and the launching of Rome on the course of empire.

During the Vaucluse years, Petrarch made several trips and maintained contacts with many prominent persons. In tribute to his literary successes, he was entertained by King Robert of Naples and was crowned poet laureate by the Senate at Rome. His equanimity was evidently upset by the ravages of the Black Death (in 1348 and following years) which carried off many of his friends, including Laura. In 1353 Petrarch left Vaucluse, never to return.

Away from Vaucluse, Petrarch lived as the guest of various despots, who seem to have vied for his presence. Besides enjoying the hospitality of the Correggios of Parma, the Gonzagas of Mantua, the d'Estes of Ferrara, and the Malatestas of Rimini, he resided for about a decade (c. 1353-62) with the Visconti of Milan, for whom he went on important embassies. The remaining years of his life he spent as an honored guest of the Republic of Venice and finally of the Carraras of Padua. He died in 1374, in his library, in the village of Arqua, near Padua.

Petrarch was not a philosopher or a theologian, nor was he a practical man of affairs. He was avowedly patriotic and pious, yet he oscillated in his politics and was lukewarm in his religion. He urged the unification of Italy and demanded that the popes return from Avignon to Rome, but did little else for either cause. It is as a literary scholar and a writer that Petrarch stars, and he is one of the great figures of the Italian Renaissance.

He was the author of numerous works. Although as a humanist he urged the use of classical Latin, he condescended to write several poems in the vernacular, notably those to Laura, who knew no Latin. Such poems, included in his Canzoniere, are recognized as his masterpieces. His prolific writings in Latin include his incomplete Africa, a pastoral Bucolic of twelve eclogues, several metrical epistles, an Epitome of Roman History, his Lives of Illustrious Men, orations, essay-like moral treatises, and, finally, over 550 prose letters.

The seven letters given here — one to posterity, one to an abbot, one to a cardinal, two to Cicero, and two to Boccaccio — bring out the essence of his humanism: an effective appreciation and enjoyment of classical literature, as well as of its spirit and values. They show how the humanistic temper finds expression in the avid study and enthusiastic imitation of classical models, in zeal to implant in others this reverence for the classical writers, in a feeling of intimacy with them and their world, in the use of classical allusions and examples, in the collection of a classical library and the search for old manuscripts. Classical ideals and concerns are becoming ascendant: patriotism, appreciation of nature, interest in geography, love of travel, absorption with man and the works of man as well as man's past, and desire for posthumous fame. These letters of Petrarch's also reveal some "negative" aspects of humanism: depreciation of the vernacular, aversion alike for metaphysical abstractions and scientific details, and a certain verbiage resulting from excessive attention to style. We note, too, a relative inattention to religion, as compared with writings from the Early and High Middle Ages. And indeed, humanism, with its homocentric focus, its premium on individuality, and its rediscovery of the ideals of classical civilization, reinforced the emergent secular tendencies of the Later Middle Ages. In becoming acquainted with the "Father of Renaissance Humanism" through his own writings, we may better understand both Petrarch the man and the movement he promoted.

Francesco Petrarch

A Selection from His Correspondence *

His Letter to Posterity[1]

Greeting. — It is possible that some word of me may have come to you, though even this is doubtful, since an insignificant and obscure name will scarcely penetrate far in either time or space. If, however,

---

* From *Petrarch: The First Modern Scholar and Man of Letters. A Selection from his Correspondence...*, translated and edited by James Harvey Robinson and Henry W. Rolfe (New York: G. P. Putnam's Sons, 1909).

[1] This "Letter to Posterity," which takes Petrarch's life from 1304 to 1351, when it abruptly breaks off, was worked on as late as the 1370's.

you should have heard of me, you may desire to know what manner of man I was, or what was the outcome of my labours, especially those of which some description or, at any rate, the bare titles may have reached you.

To begin with myself then, the utterances of men concerning me will differ widely, since in passing judgment almost every one is influenced not so much by truth as by preference, and good and evil report alike know no bounds. I was, in truth, a poor mortal like yourself, neither very exalted in my origin, nor, on the other hand, of the most humble birth, but belonging, as Augustus Caesar says of himself, to an ancient family. As to my disposition, I was not naturally perverse or wanting in modesty; however the contagion of evil associations may have corrupted me. My youth was gone before I realised it; I was carried away by the strength of manhood; but a riper age brought me to my senses and taught me by experience the truth I had long before read in books: that youth and pleasure are vanity — nay, that the Author of all ages and times permits us miserable mortals, puffed up with emptiness, thus to wander about, until finally, coming to a tardy consciousness of our sins, we shall learn to know ourselves. In my prime I was blessed with a quick and active body, although not exceptionally strong; and while I do not lay claim to remarkable personal beauty, I was comely enough in my best days. I was possessed of a clear complexion, between light and dark, lively eyes, and for long years a keen vision, which however deserted me, contrary to my hopes, after I reached my sixtieth birthday, and forced me, to my great annoyance, to resort to glasses.[2] Although I had previously enjoyed perfect health, old age brought with it the usual array of discomforts.

My parents were honourable folk, Florentine in their origin, of medium fortune, or, I may as well admit it, in a condition verging upon poverty. They had been expelled from their native city,[3] and consequently I was born in exile, at Arezzo,[4] in the year 1304 of this latter age which begins with Christ's birth, on July the twentieth, a Monday, at dawn. I have always possessed an extreme contempt for wealth; not that riches are not desirable in themselves, but because I hate the anxiety and care which are invariably associated with them. I certainly do not long to be able to give gorgeous banquets. I have, on the contrary, led a happier existence with plain living and ordinary fare than all the followers of Apicius,[5] with their elaborate dainties. So-called *convivia*,[6] which are but vulgar bouts, sinning against sobriety and good manners, have always been repugnant to me. I have

---

[2] Eyeglasses were a somewhat new invention at this time.
[3] Petrarch's father and Dante, both officers in the overthrown White Guelf government, were banished from Florence by the same decree of Jan. 27, 1302.
[4] Arezzo was a Ghibelline city about 40 miles south of Guelphic Florence. The Guelphs and the Ghibellines were the two major opposing political factions in Italy in the Middle Ages, around which local feuds and parties crystallized.
[5] A celebrated Roman epicure.
[6] Feasts, especially drinking bouts.

ever felt that it was irksome and profitless to invite others to such affairs, and not less so to be bidden to them myself. On the other hand, the pleasure of dining with one's friends is so great that nothing has ever given me more delight than their unexpected arrival, nor have I ever willingly sat down to table without a companion. Nothing displeases me more than display, for not only is it bad in itself, and opposed to humility, but it is troublesome and distracting.

I struggled in my younger days with a keen but constant and pure attachment, and would have struggled with it longer had not the sinking flame been extinguished by death — premature and bitter, but salutary.[7] I should be glad to be able to say that I had always been entirely free from irregular desires, but I should lie if I did so. I can, however, conscientiously claim that, although I may have been carried away by the fire of youth or by my ardent temperament, I have always abhorred such sins from the depths of my soul. As I approached the age of forty, while my powers were unimpaired and my passions were still strong, I not only abruptly threw off my bad habits, but even the recollection of them, as if I had never looked upon a woman. This I mention as among the greatest of my blessings, and I render thanks to God, who freed me, while still sound and vigorous, from a disgusting slavery which had always been hateful to me.[8] But let us turn to other matters.

I have taken pride in others, never in myself, and however insignificant I may have been, I have always been still less important in my own judgment. My anger has very often injured myself, but never others. I have always been most desirous of honourable friendships, and have faithfully cherished them. I make this boast without fear, since I am confident that I speak truly. While I am very prone to take offence, I am equally quick to forget injuries, and have a memory tenacious of benefits. In my familiar associations with kings and princes, and in my friendship with noble personages, my good fortune has been such as to excite envy. But it is the cruel fate of those who are growing old that they can commonly only weep for friends who have passed away. The greatest kings of this age have loved and courted me. They may know why; I certainly do not. With some of them I was on such terms that they seemed in a certain sense my guests rather than I theirs; their lofty position in no way embarrassing me, but, on the contrary, bringing with it many advantages.[9] I fled, however, from many of those to whom I was greatly attached; and such was my innate longing for liberty, that I studiously avoided those whose very name seemed incompatible with the freedom that I loved.

I possessed a well-balanced rather than a keen intellect, one prone

[7] Apparently a veiled reference to Laura.
[8] Petrarch's daughter Francesca, his second and last child, was born in 1343 when he was on the brink of forty.
[9] One somehow gets the idea that Petrarch is boasting! Note his patent pride, despite protestations of humility.

to all kinds of good and wholesome study, but especially inclined to moral philosophy and the art of poetry. The latter, indeed, I neglected as time went on, and took delight in sacred literature. Finding in that a hidden sweetness which I had once esteemed but lightly, I came to regard the works of the poets as only amenities. Among the many subjects which interested me, I dwelt especially upon antiquity, for our own age has always repelled me, so that, had it not been for the love of those dear to me, I should have preferred to have been born in any other period than our own. In order to forget my own time, I have constantly striven to place myself in spirit in other ages, and consequently I delighted in history;[10] not that the conflicting statements did not offend me, but when in doubt I accepted what appeared to me most probable, or yielded to the authority of the writer.

My style, as many claimed, was clear and forcible; but to me it seemed weak and obscure. In ordinary conversation with friends, or with those about me, I never gave any thought to my language, and I have always wondered that Augustus Caesar should have taken such pains in this respect. When, however, the subject itself, or the place or listener, seemed to demand it, I gave some attention to style, with what success I cannot pretend to say; let them judge in whose presence I spoke. If only I have lived well, it matters little to me how I talked. Mere elegance of language can produce at best but an empty renown.

My life up to the present has, either through fate or my own choice, fallen into the following divisions. A part only of my first year was spent at Arezzo, where I first saw the light. The six following years were, owing to the recall of my mother from exile, spent upon my father's estate at Ancisa, about fourteen miles above Florence.[11] I passed my eighth year at Pisa,[12] the ninth and following years in Farther Gaul, at Avignon, on the left bank of the Rhone, where the Roman Pontiff holds and has long held the Church of Christ in shameful exile.[13] It seemed a few years ago as if Urban V was on the point of restoring the Church to its ancient seat, but it is clear that nothing is coming of this effort, and, what is to me the worst of all, the Pope seems to have repented him of his good work, for failure came while he was still living. Had he lived but a little longer, he would certainly have learned how I regarded his retreat. My pen was in my hand when he abruptly surrendered at once his exalted office and his life.[14] Unhappy man, who might have died before the

---

[10] Petrarch, like Cicero, is a great booster for history.

[11] Ancisa (or Incisa) was in Florentine territory, and Petrarch's father could not join them there because of his perpetual exile.

[12] Petrarch's father prepared a home for them at Pisa, but they did not stay there long for lack of legal business.

[13] The papal seat was at Avignon from 1309 to 1378, and there were more opportunities here.

[14] Urban V returned to Rome, but directly came back to Avignon because of difficulties, only to die almost immediately in December, 1370.

altar of Saint Peter and in his own habitation! Had his successors remained in their capital he would have been looked upon as the cause of this benign change, while, had they left Rome, his virtue would have been all the more conspicuous in contrast with their fault.[15]

But such laments are somewhat remote from my subject. On the windy banks of the river Rhone I spent my boyhood, guided by my parents, and then, guided by my own fancies, the whole of my youth. Yet there were long intervals spent elsewhere, for I first passed four years at the little town of Carpentras,[16] somewhat to the east of Avignon: in these two places I learned as much of grammar, logic, and rhetoric as my age permitted, or rather, as much as it is customary to teach in school: how little that is, dear reader, thou knowest. I then set out for Montpellier to study law, and spent four years there,[17] then three at Bologna.[18] I heard the whole body of the civil law, and would, as many thought, have distinguished myself later, had I but continued my studies. I gave up the subject altogether, however, so soon as it was no longer necessary to consult the wishes of my parents.[19] My reason was that, although the dignity of the law, which is doubtless very great, and especially the numerous references it contains to Roman antiquity, did not fail to delight me, I felt it to be habitually degraded by those who practise it. It went against me painfully to acquire an art which I would not practise dishonestly, and could hardly hope to exercise otherwise. Had I made the latter attempt, my scrupulousness would doubtless have been ascribed to simplicity.

So at the age of two and twenty[1] I returned home. I call my place of exile home, Avignon, where I had been since childhood; for habit has almost the potency of nature itself. I had already begun to be known there, and my friendship was sought by prominent men; wherefore I cannot say. I confess this is now a source of surprise to me, although it seemed natural enough at an age when we are used to regard ourselves as worthy of the highest respect. I was courted first and foremost by that very distinguished and noble family, the Colonnesi, who, at that period, adorned the Roman Curia with their presence. However it might be now, I was at that time certainly quite unworthy of the esteem in which I was held by them. I was especially honoured by the incomparable Giacomo Colonna, then Bishop of Lombez,[2] whose peer I know not whether I have ever seen or ever shall see, and was taken by him to Gascony; there I spent such a divine

---

[15] Petrarch vociferously opposed the papal residence at Avignon, which he dubbed "the Babylonian Captivity" of the Church.
[16] 1315–19.
[17] 1319–23.
[18] 1323–26.
[19] The news of their father's death recalled Petrarch and his brother from Bologna in April, 1326.
[1] Evidently in 1326.
[2] In southwestern France about 30 miles southwest of Toulouse.

summer among the foot-hills of the Pyrenees, in happy intercourse with my master and the members of our company, that I can never recall the experience without a sigh of regret.[3]

Returning thence, I passed many years in the house of Giacomo's brother, Cardinal Giovanni Colonna, not as if he were my lord and master, but rather my father, or better, a most affectionate brother — nay, it was as if I were in my own home.[4] About this time, a youthful desire impelled me to visit France and Germany. While I invented certain reasons to satisfy my elders of the propriety of the journey, the real explanation was a great inclination and longing to see new sights. I first visited Paris, as I was anxious to discover what was true and what fabulous in the accounts I had heard of that city.[5] On my return from this journey, I went to Rome,[6] which I had since my infancy ardently desired to visit. There I soon came to venerate Stephano, the noble head of the family of the Colonnesi, like some ancient hero, and was in turn treated by him in every respect like a son. The love and good-will of this excellent man toward me remained constant to the end of his life, and lives in me still, nor will it cease until I myself pass away.

On my return, since I experienced a deep-seated and innate repugnance to town life, especially in that disgusting city of Avignon which I heartily abhorred, I sought some means of escape. I fortunately discovered, about fifteen miles from Avignon, a delightful valley, narrow and secluded, called Vaucluse, where the Sorgue, the prince of streams, takes its rise. Captivated by the charms of the place, I transferred thither myself and my books.[7] Were I to describe what I did there during many years, it would prove a long story. Indeed, almost every bit of writing which I have put forth was either accomplished or begun, or at least conceived, there, and my undertakings have been so numerous that they still continue to vex and weary me. My mind, like my body, is characterised by a certain versatility and readiness, rather than by strength, so that many tasks that were easy of conception have been given up by reason of the difficulty of their execution. The character of my surroundings suggested the composition of a sylvan or bucolic song.[8] I also dedicated a work in two books upon *The Life of Solitude,* to Philip, now exalted to the Cardinal-bishopric of Sabina. Although always a great man, he was, at the time of which I speak, only the humble Bishop of Cavaillon.[9] He is

---

[3] It was on this occasion that Petrarch formed his lifelong acquaintance and friendship with his Roman "Laelius" and his Netherland-born "Socrates."

[4] Petrarch became a commensal (table-sharing) chaplain or honored companion in the house of the Cardinal.

[5] Evidently in 1333.

[6] Apparently in 1336.

[7] In 1337 Petrarch acquired what was to be his recurrent home address until 1351.

[8] Petrarch's works include a *Carmen Bucolicum* (bucolic song) in 12 eclogues.

[9] Close by the valley of the Sorgue.

the only one of my old friends who is still left to me, and he has always loved and treated me not as a bishop (as Ambrose did Augustine), but as a brother.

While I was wandering in those mountains upon a Friday in Holy Week, the strong desire seized me to write an epic in an heroic strain, taking as my theme Scipio Africanus the Great, who had, strange to say, been dear to me from my childhood. But although I began the execution of this project with enthusiasm, I straightway abandoned it, owing to a variety of distractions. The poem was, however, christened *Africa,* from the name of its hero, and, whether from his fortunes or mine, it did not fail to arouse the interest of many before they had seen it.

While leading a leisurely existence in this region, I received, remarkable as it may seem, upon one and the same day,[10] letters both from the Senate at Rome and the Chancellor of the University of Paris, pressing me to appear in Rome and Paris, respectively, to receive the poet's crown of laurel. In my youthful elation I convinced myself that I was quite worthy of this honour; the recognition came from eminent judges, and I accepted their verdict rather than that of my own better judgment. I hesitated for a time which I should give ear to, and sent a letter to Cardinal Giovanni Colonna, of whom I have already spoken, asking his opinion. He was so near that, although I wrote late in the day, I received his reply before the third hour on the morrow. I followed his advice, and recognised the claims of Rome as superior to all others. My acceptance of his counsel is shown by my twofold letter to him on that occasion, which I still keep. I set off accordingly; but although, after the fashion of youth, I was a most indulgent judge of my own work, I still blushed to accept in my own case the verdict even of such men as those who summoned me, despite the fact that they would certainly not have honoured me in this way, had they not believed me worthy.

So I decided, first to visit Naples, and that celebrated king and philosopher, Robert, who was not more distinguished as a ruler than as a man of culture.[11] He was, indeed, the only monarch of our age who was the friend at once of learning and of virtue, and I trusted that he might correct such things as he found to criticise in my work. The way in which he received and welcomed me is a source of astonishment to me now, and, I doubt not, to the reader also, if he happens to know anything of the matter. Having learned the reason of my coming, the King seemed mightily pleased. He was gratified, doubtless, by my youthful faith in him, and felt, perhaps, that he shared in a way the glory of my coronation, since I had chosen him from all others as the only suitable critic. After talking over a great

[10] Sept. 1, 1340. These were not unsolicited.
[11] Robert of Naples, grandson of Charles of Anjou, was Petrarch's suzerain, as overlord of Avignon. In 1348 Queen Joanna sold Avignon to Pope Clement VI.

many things, I showed him my *Africa*, which so delighted him that he asked that it might be dedicated to him in consideration of a handsome reward.[12] This was a request that I could not well refuse, nor, indeed, would I have wished to refuse it, had it been in my power. He then fixed a day upon which we could consider the object of my visit. This occupied us from noon until evening, and the time proving too short, on account of the many matters which arose for discussion, we passed the two following days in the same manner. Having thus tested my poor attainments for three days, the King at last pronounced me worthy of the laurel. He offered to bestow that honour upon me at Naples, and urged me to consent to receive it there, but my veneration for Rome prevailed over the insistence of even so great a monarch as Robert. At length, seeing that I was inflexible in my purpose, he sent me on my way accompanied by royal messengers and letters to the Roman Senate, in which he gave enthusiastic expression to his flattering opinion of me. This royal estimate was, indeed, quite in accord with that of many others, and especially with my own, but to-day I cannot approve either his or my own verdict. In this case, affection and the natural partiality to youth were stronger than his devotion to truth.

On arriving at Rome, I continued, in spite of my unworthiness, to rely upon the judgment of so eminent a critic, and, to the great delight of the Romans who were present, I who had been hitherto a simple student received the laurel crown.[13] This occasion is described elsewhere in my letters, both in prose and verse. The laurel, however, in no way increased my wisdom, although it did arouse some jealousy — but this is too long a story to be told here.

On leaving Rome, I went to Parma, and spent some time with the members of the house of Correggio,[14] who, while they were most kind and generous towards me, agreed but ill among themselves. They governed Parma, however, in a way unknown to that city within the memory of man, and the like of which it will hardly again enjoy in this present age.

I was conscious of the honour which I had but just received, and fearful lest it might seem to have been granted to one unworthy of the distinction; consequently, as I was walking one day in the mountains, and chanced to cross the river Enza to a place called Selva Piana, in the territory of Reggio,[15] struck by the beauty of the spot, I began to write again upon the *Africa*, which I had laid aside. In my

[12] This may also be translated: "he asked that it might be dedicated to him as a great favor," since the Latin is *"magno pro munere."*
[13] Petrarch's coronation as poet laureate at Rome made him a celebrity and the recipient of many invitations from those desirous of display.
[14] Petrarch was an old friend of the tricky Azzo Correggio, who had just seized control of Parma, which he governed as a wily despot.
[15] About 30 miles southeast of Parma.

enthusiasm, which had seemed quite dead, I wrote some lines that very day, and some each day until I returned to Parma. Here I happened upon a quiet and retired house, which I afterwards bought, and which still belongs to me. I continued my task with such ardour, and completed the work in so short a space of time, that I cannot but marvel now at my despatch.[16] I had already passed my thirty-fourth year when I returned thence to the Fountain of the Sorgue and to my Transalpine solitude.[17] I had made a long stay both in Parma and Verona,[18] and everywhere I had, I am thankful to say, been treated with much greater esteem than I merited.

Some time after this, my growing reputation procured for me the good-will of a most excellent man, Giacomo the Younger, of Carrara,[19] whose equal I do not know among the rulers of his time. For years he wearied me with messengers and letters when I was beyond the Alps, and with his petitions whenever I happened to be in Italy, urging me to accept his friendship. At last, although I anticipated little satisfaction from the venture, I determined to go to him and see what this insistence on the part of a person so eminent, and at the same time a stranger to me, might really mean. I appeared, though tardily, at Padua,[20] where I was received by him of illustrious memory, not as a mortal, but as the blessed are greeted in heaven — with such delight and such unspeakable affection and esteem, that I cannot adequately describe my welcome in words, and must, therefore, be silent. Among other things, learning that I had led a clerical life from boyhood, he had me made a canon of Padua, in order to bind me the closer to himself and his city. In fine, had his life been spared, I should have found there an end to all my wanderings. But alas! nothing mortal is enduring, and there is nothing sweet which does not presently end in bitterness. Scarcely two years was he spared to me, to his country, and to the world. God, who had given him to us, took him again.[21] Without being blinded by my love for him, I feel that neither I, nor his country, nor the world was worthy of him. Although his son, who succeeded him, was in every way a prudent and distinguished man, who, following his father's example, always loved and honoured me, I could not remain after the death of him with whom, by reason especially of the similarity of our ages, I had been much more closely united.

I returned to Gaul, not so much from a desire to see again what

[16] His *Africa* was never really completed.
[17] To Vaucluse, evidently in 1342.
[18] The sequence of events seems a bit mixed here as to minor details.
[19] I.e., of the Carrara family, petty despots who ruled Padua.
[20] Apparently in 1349. Petrarch omits mention of the dire events of the Black Death of 1348 which carried off many of his friends, including the beloved Laura.
[21] Giacomo was murdered by his nephew in December, 1350.

I had already beheld a thousand times, as from the hope, common to the afflicted, of coming to terms with my misfortunes by a change of scene.[22] . . .

The Humanist
TO THE ABBOT OF ST. BENIGNO

Strangely enough I long to write, but do not know what or to whom. This inexorable passion has such a hold upon me that pen, ink, and paper, and work prolonged far into the night, are more to my liking than repose and sleep. In short, I find myself always in a sad and languishing state when I am not writing, and, anomalous though it seems, I labour when I rest, and find my rest in labour. My mind is hard as rock, and you might well think that it really sprang from one of Deucalion's stones.[1] Let this tireless spirit pore eagerly over the parchment, until it has exhausted both fingers and eyes by the long strain, yet it feels neither heat nor cold, but would seem to be reclining upon the softest down. It is only fearful that it may be dragged away, and holds fast the mutinous members. Only when sheer necessity has compelled it to quit, does it begin to flag. It takes a recess as a lazy ass takes his pack when he is ordered up a sharp hill, and comes back again to its task as a tired ass to his well-filled manger. My mind finds itself refreshed by prolonged exercise, as the beast of burden by his food and rest. What then am I to do, since I cannot stop writing, or bear even the thought of rest? I write to you, not because what I have to say touches you nearly, but because there is no one so accessible just now who is at the same time so eager for news, especially about me, and so intelligently interested in strange and mysterious phenomena, and ready to investigate them.

I have just told you something of my condition and of my indefatigable brain, but I will tell you now an incident which may surprise you even more, and will at the same time prove the truth of what I have said. It happened at a time when, after a long period of neglect, I had just taken up my *Africa* again, and that with an ardour like that of the African sun itself. This is the task which, if anything will help me, I trust may some time moderate or assuage my insatiable thirst for work. One of my very dearest friends, seeing that I was almost done for with my immoderate toil, suddenly asked me to grant him a very simple favour. Although I was unaware of the nature of his

---

[22] Petrarch's "Letter to Posterity" breaks off abruptly with his return to Vaucluse in 1351. Since he was writing in his old age, perhaps he tired of the account, or even forgot about it. The "misfortunes" he here mentions, that he is trying to forget, perhaps include the toll of the plague as well as other disappointments. Petrarch died 23 years later, in 1374. The present letter was written in the early 1370's.

[1] According to mythology, stones thrown by Deucalion, King of Sicily, who survived the flood, became men, to repopulate the earth.

request, I could not refuse one who I knew would ask nothing except in the friendliest spirit. He thereupon demanded the key of my cabinet. I gave it to him, wondering what he would do, when he proceeded to gather together and lock up carefully all my books and writing materials. Then, turning away, he prescribed ten days of rest, and ordered me, in view of my promise, neither to read nor write during that time. I saw his trick; to him I now seemed to be resting, although in reality I felt as if I were bound hand and foot. That day passed wearily, seeming as long as a year. The next day I had a headache from morning till night. The third day dawned and I began to feel the first signs of fever, when my friend returned, and seeing my plight gave me back the keys. I quickly recovered, and perceiving that I lived on work, as he expressed it, he never repeated his request.

Is it then true that this disease of writing, like other malignant disorders, is, as the Satirist claims, incurable, and, as I begin to fear, contagious as well? How many, do you reckon, have caught it from me? Within our memory, it was rare enough for people to write these things.[2] But now there is no one who does not write them; few indeed write anything else. Some think that the fault, so far as our contemporaries are concerned, is largely mine. I have heard this from many, but I solemnly declare, as I hope some time to be granted immunity from the other ills of the soul — for I look for none from this — that I am now at last suddenly awakened for the first time by warning signs to a consciousness that this may perhaps be true; while intent only upon my own welfare, I may have been unwittingly injuring, at the same time, myself and others. I fear that the reproaches of an aged father, who unexpectedly came to me, with a long face and almost in tears, may not be without foundation. "While I," he said, "have always honoured your name, see the return you make in compassing the ruin of my only son!" I stood for a time in embarrassed silence, for the age of the man and the expression of his face, which told of great sorrow, went to my heart. Then, recovering myself, I replied, as was quite true, that I was unacquainted either with him or his son. "What matters it," the old man answered, "whether you know him or not? He certainly knows you. I have spent a great deal in providing instruction for him in the civil law, but he declares that he wishes to follow in your footsteps. My fondest hopes have been disappointed, and I presume that he will never be either a lawyer or a poet." At this neither I nor the others present could refrain from laughter, and he went off none the better humoured. But now I recognise that this merriment was ill-timed, and that the poor old man deserved our consolation, for his complaints and his reproaches were not ungrounded. Our sons formerly employed themselves in preparing such papers as might be useful to themselves or their friends, relating to

[2] *Haec,* here translated "these things," may mean "verses."

family affairs, business, or the wordy din of the courts. Now we are all engaged in the same occupation, and it is literally true, as Horace says, "learned or unlearned, we are all writing verses alike."[3]

It is after all but a poor consolation to have companions in misery. I should prefer to be ill by myself. Now I am involved in others' ill-fortune as well as in my own, and am hardly given time to take breath. For every day letters and poems from every corner of our land come showering down upon my devoted head. Nor does this satisfy my foreign friends. I am overwhelmed by floods of missives, no longer from France alone, but from Greece, from Germany, from England.[4] I am unable to judge even my own work, and yet I am called upon to be the universal critic of others. Were I to answer the requests in detail, I should be the busiest of mortals. If I condemn the composition, I am a jealous carper at the good work of others; if I say a good word for the thing, it is attributed to a mendacious desire to be agreeable; if I keep silence altogether, it is because I am a rude, pert fellow. They are afraid, I infer, that my disease will not make way with me promptly enough. Between their goading and my own madness I shall doubtless gratify their wishes.

But all this would be nothing if, incredible as it may seem, this subtle poison had not just now begun to show its effects in the Roman Curia itself. What do you think the lawyers and doctors are up to? Justinian[5] and Aesculapius[6] have palled upon them. The sick and the litigious cry in vain for their help, for they are deafened by the thunder of Homer's and Virgil's names,[7] and wander oblivious in the woody valleys of Cirrha, by the purling waters of the Aonian fountain.[8] But it is hardly necessary to speak of these lesser prodigies. Even carpenters, fullers, and ploughmen leave the implements of their calling to talk of Apollo[9] and the Muses.[10] I cannot say how far the plague, which lately was confined to a few, has now spread.

If you would find an explanation for all this, you must recollect that although the delights of poetry are most exquisite, they can be fully understood only by the rarest geniuses, who are careless of wealth and possess a marked contempt for the things of this world, and who are by nature especially endowed with a peculiar elevation and freedom of soul.[11] Consequently, as experience and the authority of the

[3] Petrarch's effect on his contemporaries can hardly be exaggerated.
[4] An earlier Transalpine spread of the influence of Petrarch and the Italian Renaissance than is commonly accepted may be here suggested.
[5] Justinian's *Corpus Juris Civilis* was a standard text for the study of law.
[6] Aesculapius: the god of medicine.
[7] Representative of epic poets.
[8] The region of the Muses.
[9] Apollo was considered the god of eloquence, poetry, and music, as well as of beauty and youth.
[10] Nine goddesses reputedly representing various facets of learning, literature, and the arts.
[11] A soul able to disengage itself from the literal and penetrate to the allegorical meaning.

most learned writers agree, in no branch of art can mere industry and application accomplish so little. Hence — and you may find it comical, although it disgusts me — all the poets are nowadays to be found on the street corner, and we can descry scarcely one on Helion[12] itself. They are all nibbling at the Pierian[13] honeycomb, but no one can manage to digest it. How delightful indeed must this gift be to those who really possess it, when it can exercise such a fascination over sluggish minds, and in our vain and degenerate age can induce even the most avaricious to leave the pursuit of gain! On one thing, at least, our country may be congratulated: in spite of all the tares and sterile stalks which cumber the earth, some signs of true youthful genius are to be discovered. Some, if I am not misled by my hopes, will not drink in vain of the Castalian spring. — I felicitate thee, Mantua,[14] beloved of the Muses, thee, Padua,[15] thee, Verona,[16] thee, Cimbria,[17] thee, Sulmo,[18] and thee, Parthenope,[19] home of Maro,[20] when I see elsewhere the thirsty herd of upstart poetasters wandering drearily among uncertain byways!

It pricks my conscience that I should be responsible in great part for fostering all these forms of literary madness, and should have misled others through my example, — by no means the least of offences. I fear lest those laurel leaves, which in my eagerness I tore prematurely from the branch, may in a way be answerable for the trouble. While, as many believe, they have been the means of bringing true dreams to me, they have caused in others a multitude of delusive visions, which were allowed to escape while all the world was asleep, through the ivory gates, into the autumnal air. But never mind, I suffer for my sins, for I am in a rage if I stay at home, and yet hardly dare nowadays to venture into the street. If I do, wild fellows rush up from every side and seize upon me, asking advice, giving me suggestions, disputing and fighting among themselves. They discover meanings in the poets of which the Mantuan shepherd,[21] or the old blind man of Moeonia[22] never dreamed. I become more and more irritated, and at last begin to fear that I may be dragged off before a magistrate for breaking the peace.

But how I am running on! I have spun a whole letter out of mere

[12] Mt. Helicon in Boeotia was the reputed abode of Apollo and the Muses.
[13] I.e., poetic.
[14] Virgil was born near Mantua.
[15] Livy was born in the vicinity of Padua, birthplace of various Roman writers.
[16] The Poet Catullus was born at Verona.
[17] The reference to Cimbria is not clear. Might this be a slip for Chios or Cyprus, conjectured birthplaces of Homer?
[18] Ovid was a native of Sulmo.
[19] Virgil's final home and resting place was Parthenope, poetic for Naples.
[20] Virgil (Publius Vergilius Maro).
[21] Virgil, born near Mantua and composer of pastoral eclogues.
[22] Homer, believed to have been blind.

trifles....[23] I have just arrived here,[24] and will await you as long as I possibly can. I know not whether it be that the air here renders the mind less susceptible to foreign impressions, or whether this "closed valley" does, as its name indicates, shut out alien preoccupations, but certain it is that, although I have from my earliest manhood spent many years here, none of the inhabitants have yet become poets through contagious contact with me, with the sole exception of one of my farm-hands. Although advanced in years, he, as Persius hath it, is beginning to dream on the two-peaked Parnassus.[25] If the disease spreads I am undone. Shepherds, fishermen, hunters, ploughboys, — all would be carried away, even the cows would low in numbers and ruminate sonnets. Do not forget me. Farewell.

FOUNTAIN OF THE SORGUE.

To Marcus Tullius Cicero[1]

Your letters I sought for long and diligently; and finally, where I least expected to, I found them.[2] At once I read them, over and over, with the utmost eagerness. And as I read, I seemed to hear your bodily voice, O Marcus Tullius, saying many things, uttering many lamentations, ranging through many phases of thought and feeling. I long had known how excellent a guide you have proved for others; as last I was to learn what sort of guidance you gave yourself.

Now it is your turn to be the listener. Hearken, wherever you are, to the words of advice, or rather of sorrow and regret, that fall, not unaccompanied by tears, from the lips of one of your successors, who loves you faithfully and cherishes your name. O spirit ever restless and perturbed! in old age — I am but using your own words — self-involved in calamities and ruin! what good could you think would come from your incessant wrangling, from all this wasteful strife and enmity? Where were the peace and quiet that befitted your years, your profession, your station in life? What Will-o'-the-wisp tempted you away, with a delusive hope of glory; involved you, in your declining years, in the wars of younger men; and, after exposing you to every form of misfortune, hurled you down to a death that it was

---

[23] A section of the letter concerning an appointment some of his friends wanted to obtain for him is here omitted.

[24] At Vaucluse, his "valley enclosed."

[25] A mountain in central Greece, regarded as sacred to the Muses. There was a legend that one could become a prophet or poet by sleeping overnight on Mt. Parnassus or drinking from the Castalian spring.

[1] In addition to hundreds of letters to his contemporaries, Petrarch wrote a number to his favorite authors, including Cicero, Virgil, Horace, Livy, Quintilian, Homer, and St. Augustine. It is to be remembered that such letters were meant to be published and preserved for posterity.

[2] The present letter to his beloved and admired Cicero was written soon after the delighted Petrarch found at Verona certain letters of Cicero to Atticus and Quintus Brutus.

unseemly for a philosopher to die?[3] Alas! the wise counsel that you gave your brother, and the salutary advice of your great masters, you forgot. You were like a traveller in the night, whose torch lights up for others the path where he himself has miserably fallen.

Of Dionysius I forbear to speak; of your brother and nephew, too; of Dolabella even, if you like. At one moment you praise them all to the skies; at the next fall upon them with sudden maledictions. This, however, could perhaps be pardoned. I will pass by Julius Caesar, too, whose well-approved clemency was a harbour of refuge for the very men who were warring against him. Great Pompey, likewise, I refrain from mentioning. His affection for you was such that you could do with him what you would. But what insanity led you to hurl yourself upon Antony?[4] Love of the republic, you would probably say. But the republic had fallen before this into irretrievable ruin, as you had yourself admitted. Still, it is possible that a lofty sense of duty, and love of liberty, constrained you to do as you did, hopeless though the effort was. That we can easily believe of so great a man. But why, then, were you so friendly with Augustus?[5] What answer can you give to Brutus? If you accept Octavius, said he, we must conclude that you are not so anxious to be rid of all tyrants as to find a tyrant who will be well-disposed toward yourself. Now, unhappy man, you were to take the last false step, the last and most deplorable. You began to speak ill of the very friend whom you had so lauded, although he was not doing any ill to you, but merely refusing to prevent others who were. I grieve, dear friend, at such fickleness. These shortcomings fill me with pity and shame. Like Brutus, I feel no confidence in the arts in which you are so proficient. What, pray, does it profit a man to teach others, and to be prating always about virtue, in high-sounding words, if he fails to give heed to his own instructions? Ah! how much better it would have been, how much more fitting for a philosopher, to have grown old peacefully in the country, meditating, as you yourself have somewhere said, upon the life that endures forever, and not upon this poor fragment of life; to have known no *fasces*, yearned for no triumphs, found no Catilines to fill the soul with ambitious longings![6] — All this, however, is vain. Farewell, forever, my Cicero.

3 In a somewhat wavering and compromising manner, Cicero had defended the cause of the Republic against the dictatorial encroachments of Caesar, Antony, Lepidus, and Octavian. He was eventually proscribed and met death at the port of Formiae, to which he had fled, in 43 B.C.

4 Mark Antony, at first Julius Caesar's principal successor, against whom Cicero mainly directed his *Philippics*.

5 Octavian, or Octavius, Caesar's nephew, who eventually became Augustus, first Roman Emperor. Cicero, a confirmed political optimist, long trusted that Octavian was trying to save the Republic.

6 Petrarch is convinced that Cicero should have stuck to literature and abstained from politics, at least in his old age. His criticism does not appear justified, since Cicero's defense of freedom and his death in its cause constitute one of his chief claims to reverence by posterity.

Written in the land of the living; on the right bank of the Adige, in Verona, a city of Transpadane[7] Italy; on the 16th of June, and in the year of that God whom you never knew[8] the 1345th.

To Marcus Tullius Cicero[9]

If my earlier letter gave you offence, — for, as you often have remarked, the saying of your contemporary in the *Andria* is a faithful one, that 'compliance begets friends, truth only hatred,'[10] — you shall listen now to words that will soothe your wounded feelings and prove that the truth need not always be hateful. For, if censure that is true angers us, true praise, on the other hand, gives us delight.

You lived then, Cicero, if I may be permitted to say it, like a mere man, but spoke like an orator, wrote like a philosopher. It was your life that I criticised; not your mind, nor your tongue; for the one fills me with admiration, the other with amazement. And even in your life I feel the lack of nothing but stability, and the love of quiet that should go with your philosophic professions, and abstention from civil war, when liberty had been extinguished and the republic buried and its dirge sung.

See how different my treatment of you is from yours of Epicurus, in your works at large, and especially in the *De Finibus*. You are continually praising his life, but his talents you ridicule. I ridicule in you nothing at all. Your life does awaken my pity, as I have said; but your talents and your eloquence call for nothing but congratulation. O great father of Roman eloquence! not I alone but all who deck themselves with the flowers of Latin speech render thanks unto you. It is from your well-springs that we draw the streams that water our meads. You, we freely acknowledge, are the leader who marshals us; yours are the words of encouragement that sustain us; yours is the light that illumines the path before us. In a word, it is under your auspices that we have attained to such little skill in this art of writing as we may possess.

You have heard what I think of your life and your genius. Are you hoping to hear of your books also; what fate has befallen them, how they are esteemed by the masses and among scholars? They still are in existence, glorious volumes, but we of today are too feeble a folk to read them, or even to be acquainted with their mere titles. Your fame extends far and wide; your name is mighty, and fills the ears of men; and yet those who really know you are very few, be it

---

[7] Across or beyond the Po River, looking north from Rome.
[8] Jesus Christ.
[9] This is a second letter addressed directly to Cicero. It accurately expresses Petrarch's obvious feelings of reverence for the great master.
[10] Terence in his *Andria*, 68. Petrarch's earlier letter, as we have seen, had chided Cicero for his ill-starred political activities. Compliance may also be translated obsequiousness or flattery.

because the times are unfavourable, or because men's minds are slow and dull, or, as I am the more inclined to believe, because the love of money forces our thoughts in other directions. Consequently right in our own day, unless I am much mistaken, some of your books have disappeared, I fear beyond recovery.[11] It is a great grief to me, a great disgrace to this generation, a great wrong done to posterity. The shame of failing to cultivate our own talents, thereby depriving the future of the fruits that they might have yielded, is not enough for us; we must waste and spoil, through our cruel and insufferable neglect, the fruits of your labours too, and of those of your fellows as well, for the fate that I lament in the case of your own books has befallen the works of many another illustrious man.

It is of yours alone, though, that I would speak now. Here are the names of those among them whose loss is most to be deplored: the *Republic*, the *Praise of Philosophy*, the treatises on the *Care of Property*, on the *Art of War*, on *Consolation*, on *Glory*, — although in the case of this last my feeling is rather one of hopeful uncertainty than of certain despair. And then there are huge gaps in the volumes that have survived. It is as if indolence and oblivion had been worsted in a great battle, but we had to mourn noble leaders slain, and others lost or maimed. This last indignity very many of your books have suffered, but more particularly the *Orator*, the *Academics*, and the *Laws*. They have come forth from the fray so mutilated and disfigured that it would have been better if they had perished outright.

Now, in conclusion, you will wish me to tell you something about the condition of Rome and the Roman republic: the present appearance of the city and whole country, the degree of harmony that prevails, what classes of citizens possess political power, by whose hands and with what wisdom the reins of empire are swayed, and whether the Danube, the Ganges, the Ebro, the Nile, the Don, are our boundaries now, or in very truth the man has arisen who 'bounds our empire by the ocean-stream, our fame by the stars of heaven,' or 'extends our rule beyond Garama and Ind,' as your friend the Mantuan[12] has said. Of these and other matters of like nature I doubt not you would very gladly hear. Your filial piety tells me so, your well-known love of country, which you cherished even to your own destruction. But indeed it were better that I refrained. Trust me, Cicero, if you were to hear of our condition to-day you would be moved to tears, in whatever circle of heaven above, or Erebus[13] below, you may be dwelling. Farewell, forever.

Written in the world of the living; on the left bank of the Rhone,[14]

---

[11] A leading activity of humanists was the quest for lost works of classical authors.
[12] Virgil, *Aeneid*, i, 286–8; vi, 794–5.
[13] A mythical place of darkness, located between the earth and Hades.
[14] Looking north from Italy and Rome, as befitted a humanist.

in Transalpine Gaul; in the same year, but in the month of December, the 19th day.

An Excursion to Paris, the Netherlands, and the Rhineland[1]
TO CARDINAL GIOVANNI COLONNA[2]

I have lately been travelling through France, not on business, as you know, but simply from a youthful curiosity to see the country. I finally penetrated into Germany, to the banks of the Rhine itself. I have carefully noted the customs of the people, and have been much interested in observing the characteristics of a country hitherto unknown to me, and in comparing the things I saw with those at home. While I found much to admire in both countries, I in no way regretted my Italian origin. Indeed, the more I travel, the more my admiration for Italy grows. If Plato, as he himself says, thanked the immortal gods, among other things, for making him a Greek and not a barbarian, why should not we too thank the Lord for the land of our birth, unless to be born a Greek be considered more noble than to be born an Italian. This, however, would be to assert that the slave was above the master.[3] No Greekling, however shameless, would dare to make such a claim, if he but recollected that long before Rome was founded and had by superior strength established her sway, long before the world yet knew of the Romans, "men of the toga, lords of the earth," a beggarly fourth part of Italy, a region desert and uninhabited, was nevertheless styled by its Greek colonists "Greater Greece." If that scanty area could then be called great, how very great, how immense, must the Roman power have seemed after Corinth had fallen, after Aetolia had been devastated and Argos, Mycenae, and other cities had been taken, after the Macedonian kings had been captured, Pyrrhus vanquished, and Thermopylae a second time drenched with Asiatic blood! Certainly no one can deny that it is a trifle more distinguished to be an Italian than a Greek. This, however, is a matter which we may perhaps take up elsewhere.

To revert to my travels in France, — I visited the capital of the kingdom, Paris,[4] which claims Julius Caesar as its founder.[5] I must

---

[1] A love of travel and the beauties of nature, as well as the artificial works of man, was a humanist trait exemplified by Petrarch.

[2] Actually we have two letters here, given together as a unit; both are addressed to Cardinal Giovanni Colonna, who was one of Petrarch's principal benefactors. The first was written from Aix-la-Chapelle in June, 1333; the second, from Lyons in August of the same year.

[3] Petrarch is living in the past.

[4] Paris at the time is supposed to have had a population approaching 200,000, making it perhaps the largest city in western Europe.

[5] Julius Caesar had of course conquered Gaul for the Romans, so that it was asserted that various cities had been founded by him.

have felt much the same upon entering the town as did Apuleius when he wandered about Hypata in Thessaly. I spent no little time there, in open-mouthed wonder; and I was so full of interest and eagerness to know the truth about what I had heard of the place that when daylight failed me I even prolonged my investigations into the night. After loitering about for a long time, gaping at the sights, I at last satisfied myself that I had discovered the point where truth left off and fiction began. But it is a long story, and not suited for a letter, and I must wait until I see you and can rehearse my experiences at length.

To pass over the intervening events, I also visited Ghent, which proudly claims the same illustrious founder as Paris, and I saw something of the people of Flanders and Brabant, who devote themselves to preparing and weaving wool.[6] I also visited Liége, which is noted for its clergy,[7] and Aix-la-Chapelle, Charles's capital, where in a marble church I saw the tomb of that great prince, which is very properly an object of veneration to the barbarian nations.[8] ...

AIX-LA-CHAPELLE, June 21 [1333]

I did not leave Aix-la-Chapelle until I had bathed in the waters, which are warm like those at Baiae.[9] It is from them that the town is said to derive its name.[10] I then proceeded to Cologne, which lies on the left bank of the Rhine, and is noted for its situation, its river, and its inhabitants. I was astonished to find such a degree of culture in a barbarous land. The appearance of the city, the dignity of the men, the attractiveness of the women, all surprised me. The day of my arrival happened to be the feast of St. John the Baptist. It was nearly sunset when I reached the city. On the advice of the friends whom my reputation, rather than any true merit, had won for me even there, I allowed myself to be led immediately from the inn to the river, to witness a curious sight. And I was not disappointed, for I found the river-bank lined with a multitude of remarkably comely women. Ye gods, what faces and forms! And how well attired! One whose heart was not already occupied[11] might well have met his fate here.

I took my stand upon a little rise of ground where I could easily follow what was going on. There was a dense mass of people, but no

---

[6] The textile industry predominated in the Low Countries.

[7] Liége was a famous old ecclesiastical center.

[8] Note that the Transalpine countries, especially the German ones, are "barbarian nations" to Petrarch. The first letter closes with a legend concerning Charlemagne, here omitted. The second, to the same Cardinal, about the same trip, written from Lyons in August, directly follows.

[9] Aix had been a favorite residence for Charlemagne because of its excellent waters for bathing, while Baia was a famous and popular Italian bathing resort, about 5 miles west of Naples.

[10] Aix: derived from *aquae* (Latin, "waters").

[11] Apparently a reference to Laura.

disorder of any kind. They knelt down in quick succession on the bank, half hidden by the fragrant grass, and turning up their sleeves above the elbow they bathed their hands and white arms in the eddying stream. As they talked together, with an indescribably soft foreign murmur, I felt that I had never better appreciated Cicero's remark, which, like the old proverb, reminds us that we are all deaf and dumb when we have to do with an unknown tongue. I, however, had the aid of kind interpreters, for — and this was not the least surprising thing I noted there — these skies, too, give nurture to Pierian[12] spirits. So when Juvenal wonders that

> Fluent Gaul has taught the British advocate,[13]

let him marvel, too, that

> Learned Germany many a clear-voiced bard sustained.

But, lest you should be misled by my words, I hasten to add that there are no Virgils here, although many Ovids,[14] so that you would say that the latter author was justified in his reliance upon his genius or the affection of posterity, when he placed at the end of his *Metamorphoses* that audacious prophecy where he ventures to claim that as far as the power of Rome shall extend, — nay, as far as the very name of Roman shall penetrate in a conquered world, — so widely shall his works be read by enthusiastic admirers.

When anything was to be heard or said, I had to rely upon my companions to furnish both ears and tongue. Not understanding the scene, and being deeply interested in it, I asked an explanation from one of my friends, employing the Virgilian lines:

> . . . What means the crowded shore?
> What seek these eager spirits?[15]

He told me that this was an old custom among the people, and that the lower classes, especially the women, have the greatest confidence that the threatening calamities of the coming year can be washed away by bathing on this day in the river, and a happier fate be so assured. Consequently this annual ablution has always been conscientiously performed, and always will be.[16] I smiled at this explanation, and replied, "Those who dwell by Father Rhine are fortunate indeed if he washes their misfortunes away with him; I fear that neither Po nor Tiber could ever free us of ours. You send your ills to the Britons, by the river; we would gladly ship ours off to the Afri-

---

[12] I.e., poetic.
[13] Juvenal, *Satires*, xv, 111.
[14] Judging from the context, Petrarch seems to refer to copies of the works of Virgil and Ovid rather than to epic and lyric poets.
[15] Virgil, *Aeneid*, vi, 318.
[16] An evidence of vestiges of paganism surviving in the 14th century?

cans or Illyrians." But I was given to understand that our rivers were too sluggish. There was a great laugh over this, and then, as it was getting late, we left the spot and returned home.

During the few days following I wandered about the city, under the guidance of my friends, from morning until night. I enjoyed these rambles not so much for what I actually saw as on account of the reminiscences of our ancestors, who have left such extraordinary monuments to the Roman power in this far-distant country. Marcus Agrippa came, perhaps, most prominently before me. He was the founder of this colony, to which, in preference to all his other great works, whether at home or abroad, he gave his own name.[17] He was a great builder as well as a distinguished warrior. His fame was such that he was chosen by Augustus as the most desirable son-in-law in the world. His wife,[18] whatever else we may say of her, was at least a remarkable woman, the Emperor's only child and very dear to him. I beheld the bodies of the thousands of holy virgins who had suffered together, and the ground dedicated to these noble relics — ground which they say will of its own accord reject an unworthy corpse. I beheld the Capitol, which is an imitation of ours. But in place of our senate, meeting to consider the exigencies of peace and war, here one finds beautiful boys and girls ever lifting up together their harmonious voices in nightly hymns of praise to God. There one might hear the rattle of arms, the rolling chariots and the groans of captives; but here are peace and happiness and the voice of mirth. There it was the warrior who made his triumphal entry; here it is the Prince of Peace.

I saw, too, the great church in the very centre of the town.[19] It is very beautiful, although still uncompleted, and is not unjustly regarded by the inhabitants as the finest building of its kind in the world. I looked with reverence upon the relics of the Three Kings, who, as we read, came once upon a time, bringing presents, to worship at the feet of a Heavenly King as he lay wailing in the manger. Their bodies were brought from the East to the West in three great leaps.[20]

You may perhaps think, noble father, that I have gone too far just here, and dwelt upon unimportant details. I readily admit it, but it is because I have nothing more at heart than to obey your commands. Among the many instructions which you gave me, as I was leaving, the last one was that I should write to you as fully about the countries I visited and the various things I saw and heard as I should tell about them, were we face to face. I was not to spare the pen, nor to strive

---

[17] Cologne or *Colonia Agrippina* was actually founded as a Roman colony by the Emperor Claudius in A.D. 50 on the request of his wife Agrippina (the younger), who was the granddaughter of Marcus Agrippa.
[18] Julia, wayward daughter of Augustus.
[19] The great *Dom* or Gothic cathedral of Cologne, begun in the 13th century.
[20] From the Near East via Constantinople and Milan to Cologne.

for elegance or terseness of expression. Everything was to be included, not simply the more picturesque incidents. In Cicero's words, you told me to write "whatever might come into the cheek."[21] I promised to do this, and from the numerous letters which I have despatched on the way, it would seem that I had kept my engagement. If you had desired me to treat of higher things I should have done what I could; but it seems to me in the present case that the object of my letter should be rather to instruct the reader than to give consequence to the writer. If you and I wish to appear before the public we can do so in books, but in our letters let us just talk with one another.

But to continue, I left Cologne June 30, in such heat and dust that I sighed for Virgil's "Alpine snows and the rigours of the Rhine." I next passed through the Forest of Ardennes, alone, and, as you will be surprised to hear, in time of war. But God, it is said, grants especial protection to the unwary. I had long known something of this region from books; it seemed to me a very wild and dismal place indeed. However, I will not undertake with my pen a journey which I have but just completed with my horse. After many wanderings I reached Lyons to-day. It, too, is a noble Roman colony, a little older even than Cologne. From this point two well known rivers flow together into our ocean, — the Rhone here joining the Arar, or, as the inhabitants now call it, the Saône. But I need not tell you more about them, for they are hurrying on, one led by the other, down to Avignon, where the Roman pontiff detains you and the whole human race.

This morning when I arrived here I ran across one of your servants by accident, and plied him, as those newly arrived from foreign parts are wont to do, with a thousand questions. He knew nothing, however, except that your noble brother, whom I was hastening to join, had gone on to Rome without me. On hearing this, my anxiety to proceed suddenly abated. It is now my purpose to wait here until the heat too shall abate somewhat, and until I regain my vigour by a little rest. I had not realised that I had suffered from either source until I met your servant; no kind of weariness indeed is so keenly felt as that of the mind. If the journey promises to seem tedious to me, I shall float down the Rhone. In the meantime I am glad to know that your faithful servant will see that this reaches you, and that you will know where I am. As for your brother, who was to be my guide, and who now (my disappointment must be my excuse for saying it) has deserted me, I feel that my expostulations must be addressed to him directly. I beg that you will see that the enclosed message[22] reaches him as soon as may be. Farewell. Remember your friend.

Lyons, August 9 [1333].

21 I.e., whatever might come to mind.
22 The letter to Giacomo Colonna, Bishop of Lombez, is preserved, but is not quoted here.

The Charms of Pavia
TO BOCCACCIO[1]

You have done well to visit me by letter, since you either would not or could not come to see me in person. On hearing that you had crossed the Alps to see the Babylon of the West,[2] worse than the ancient city of that name because nearer to us, I was in a constant state of anxiety until I learned of your safe return. For I well know the difficulties of the route, having traversed it frequently, and I thought, too, of your heaviness of body, and of your seriousness of mind, so favourable to scholarly leisure and so averse to the responsibilities which you had assumed. Worried by these considerations, I enjoyed no peace, day or night, and I thank God that you are back safe and sound. The greater the perils of the sea that you have escaped, the greater is my gratitude for your return.

But, unless you were in a very great hurry, it would have been very easy for you, on reaching Genoa, to have turned this way. It would have required but two days to come to see me — whom indeed you see always and wherever you go, — and you would also have seen this city of Ticinum, on the banks of the Ticino, which I believe you have never visited It is now called Pavia, which the grammarians tell us means admirable, or wonderful. It was long the celebrated capital of the Lombards. Still earlier than their time, I find that Caesar Augustus took up his quarters here, on the eve of the German war. I suppose he wished to be nearer the scene of action. He had sent his step-son[3] on into Germany, where he was performing the most glorious deeds of prowess. From here Augustus could observe the campaign as from a watch-tower, stimulating the leader, and ready, should one of the reverses so common in war occur, to bring to his succour all the imperial forces, as well as the majesty of his own name.

You would have seen where the Carthaginian leader[4] gained his first victory over our generals, in a conflict during which the Roman commander[5] was snatched from the enemy's weapons and saved from imminent death by his son,[6] scarcely more than a boy, — a striking presage that the lad would himself one day become a great leader. You would have seen where St. Augustine is buried,[7] and where Boethius found a fitting place of exile in which to spend his old age

---

1 This letter to his "convert" and "disciple," the brilliant Boccaccio, was probably written in 1365, the year Boccaccio undertook an embassy to Avignon.
2 Avignon.
3 Nero Claudius Drusus Germanicus, usually known as Drusus Germanicus.
4 Hannibal in 218 B.C.
5 Publius Cornelius Scipio.
6 Publius Cornelius Scipio Africanus, son of the aforesaid, ultimately brought the Second Punic War to a successful conclusion.
7 St. Augustine of Hippo, who died during its siege by the Vandals.

and to die.[8] They now repose together in two urns, under the same roof with King Liutprand, who transferred the body of St. Augustine[9] from Sardinia to this city. This is indeed a pious and devout concourse of illustrious men. One might think that Boethius followed in the footsteps of St. Augustine, during his life, by his spirit and writings, especially those on the Trinity,[10] which he composed after the example of Augustine, and in death, because his remains share the same tomb. You would wish that your mortal remains might have been destined to lie near such good and learned men. Finally, you would have seen a city famous in the mouths of men for its age. It is true that no reference to it occurs, so far as I can recollect, earlier than the period of the second Punic war, of which I just spoke. Indeed if my memory does not play me false, even in connection with that period, Livy only mentions the river and not the town. However, the similarity of the names — the river, *Ticinus,* and the town, *Ticinum —* might easily lead to the confusion of one with the other.[11]

But I will leave to one side all such doubtful matters and confine myself to what is certain. You would find the air of the place very salubrious. I have now spent three summers here, and I do not remember to have experienced ever anywhere else such frequent and plentiful showers with so little thunder and lightning, such freedom from heat, and such steady, refreshing breezes. You would find the city beautifully situated. The Ligurians, of old a notable race, and to this day a very powerful people, occupy the greater part of northern Italy, and the city lies in the midst of their territory. Commandingly situated on a slight elevation, and on the margin of gently sloping banks, it raises its crown of towers into the clouds, and enjoys a wide and free prospect on all sides, one which, so far as I know, is not exceeded in extent or beauty by that of any town which lies thus in a plain. By turning one's head ever so little, one can see in one direction the snowy crest of the Alps, and in the other the wooded Apennines. The Ticino itself, descending in graceful curves and hastening to join the Po, flows close by the walls, and, as it is written, makes glad the city by its swift waters.[12] Its two banks are joined by as fine a bridge as you would wish to see. It is the clearest of streams, both in reputation and in fact, and flows very rapidly, although just here, as if tired after its long journey and perturbed by the neighbourhood of a more famous river, it moves more deliberately, and has been deprived of some of its natural purity by the brooks

---

[8] Boethius was executed without a trial and on insufficient evidence by Theodoric, King of the Ostrogoths; his remains are at Pavia.

[9] Robinson and Rolfe say that it was the body of Boethius rather than that of St. Augustine which was brought from Sardinia to Pavia by Liutprand.

[10] For some time the authorship of this work by Boethius was doubted, but it is again generally accepted.

[11] Observe the careful study of the classics indicated.

[12] Note the appreciation of nature.

which join it. It is, in short, very much like my Transalpine Sorgue, save that the Ticino is larger, while the Sorgue, on account of the nearness of its source, is cooler in summer and warmer in winter.

You would see, also, one of those works in which you have such an interest, and in which I, too, take the greatest delight, — an equestrian statue in gilded bronze. It stands in the middle of the marketplace, and seems to be just on the point of reaching, with a spirited bound, the summit of an eminence. The figure is said to have been carried off from your dear people of Ravenna. Those best trained in sculpture and painting declare it to be second to none.[13]

Lastly, in order of time, though not of importance, you would see the huge palace, situated on the highest point of the city; an admirable building, which cost a vast amount. It was built by the princely Galeazzo, the younger of the Visconti,[14] the rulers of Milan, Pavia, and many neighbouring towns, a man who surpasses others in many ways, and in the magnificence of his buildings fairly excels himself. I am convinced, unless I be misled by my partiality for the founder, that, with your good taste in such matters, you would declare this to be the most noble production of modern art.

So if you had come, you would not only have seen your friend, which I hope, and indeed know, would have been most agreeable to you, but you would have been delighted also by the spectacle, not, as Virgil says, of wonderful little things, but of a multitude of great and glorious objects. I must confess that in my own case these objects are a source of supreme pleasure, and would keep me here, were it not that other interests call me away. I leave here shortly, but will very gladly return to pass the summer months — if fate grant me more summer months.[15] . . .

Finale: His Intention to Work Until the Last
TO BOCCACCIO[1]

. . . I certainly will not reject the praise you bestow upon me for having stimulated in many instances, not only in Italy, but perhaps beyond its confines also, the pursuit of studies such as ours, which have suffered neglect for so many centuries; I am, indeed, almost the oldest of those among us who are engaged in the cultivation of these subjects. But I cannot accept the conclusion you draw from this, namely, that I should give place to younger minds, and, interrupting

---

13 Note also the appreciation of the arts of man.
14 Galeazzo shared the rule with his elder brother, Bernabo.
15 The description of Pavia closes here in the letter.
1 This letter was written to Boccaccio on April 28, 1373. Petrarch died a little over a year later, on July 18, 1374. In a sense, the letter may be considered a general biographical supplement to the "Letter to Posterity," pages 285–294.

the plan of work on which I am engaged, give others an opportunity to write something, if they will, and not seem longer to desire to reserve everything for my own pen. How radically do our opinions differ, although, at bottom, our object is the same! I seem to you to have written everything, or at least a great deal, while to myself I appear to have produced almost nothing.

But let us admit that I have written much, and shall continue to write; — what better means have I of exhorting those who are following my example to continued perseverance? Example is often more potent than words. The aged veteran Camillus,[2] going into battle like a young man, assuredly aroused more enthusiasm in the younger warriors than if, after drawing them up in line of battle and telling them what was to be done, he had left them and withdrawn to his tent. The fear you appear to harbour, that I shall cover the whole field and leave nothing for others to write, recalls the ridiculous apprehensions which Alexander of Macedon is reported to have entertained, lest his father, Philip, by conquering the whole world, should deprive him of any chance of military renown. Foolish boy! He little realised what wars still remained for him to fight, if he lived, even though the Orient were quite subjugated; he had, perhaps, never heard of Papirius Cursor, or the Marsian generals. Seneca has, however, delivered us from this anxiety, in a letter to Lucilius, where he says, "Much still remains to be done; much will always remain, and even a thousand years hence no one of our descendants need be denied the opportunity of adding his something."

You, my friend, by a strange confusion of arguments, try to dissuade me from continuing my chosen work by urging, on the one hand, the hopelessness of bringing my task to completion, and by dwelling, on the other, upon the glory which I have already acquired. Then, after asserting that I have filled the world with my writings, you ask me if I expect to equal the number of volumes written by Origen or Augustine. No one, it seems to me, can hope to equal Augustine. Who, nowadays, could hope to equal one who, in my judgment, was the greatest in an age fertile in great minds?[3] As for Origen, you know that I am wont to value quality rather than quantity, and I should prefer to have produced a very few irreproachable works rather than numberless volumes such as those of Origen, which are filled with grave and intolerable errors.[4] It is certainly impossible, as you say, for me to equal either of these, although for very different reasons in the two cases. And yet you contradict yourself, for, though your pen invites me to repose, you cite the names of certain active old men, —

[2] Marcus Furius Camillus, spirited Roman soldier and statesman in the later fifth and early fourth centuries B.C.
[3] The humanistic idea of "golden ages" in the past.
[4] These errors were some unwitting deviations from orthodoxy, which hardly spoil his great contributions. Present-day authorities are much less severe on Origen than Petrarch was.

Socrates, Sophocles, and, among our own people, Cato the Censor, — as if you had some quite different end in view. How many more names you might have recalled, except that one does not consciously argue long against himself! Searching desperately for some excuse for your advice and my weakness, you urge that perhaps their temperaments differed from mine. I readily grant you this, although my constitution has sometimes been pronounced very vigorous by those who claim to be experienced in such matters; still, old age will triumph.

You assert, too, that I have sacrificed a great deal of time in the service of princes. But that you may no longer labour under a delusion in this matter, here is the truth. I have lived nominally with princes, in reality, the princes lived with me. I was present sometimes at their councils, and, very rarely, at their banquets. I should never have submitted to any conditions which would, in any degree, have interfered with my liberty or my studies. When everyone else sought the palace, I hied me to the woods, or spent my time quietly in my room, among my books. To say that I have never lost a day would be false. I have lost many days (please God, not all) through inertia, or sickness, or distress of mind, — evils which no one is so fortunate as to escape entirely. What times I have lost in the service of princes you shall hear, for, like Seneca, I keep an account of my outlays.

First, I was sent to Venice to negotiate a peace between that city and Genoa, which occupied me for an entire winter month.[5] Next I betook myself to the extreme confines of the land of the barbarians,[6] and spent three summer months in arranging for peace in Liguria, with that Roman sovereign who fostered — or I had better say deferred, — the hope of restoring a sadly ruined Empire.[7] Finally, I went to France[8] to carry congratulations to King John on his deliverance from an English prison; here three more winter months were lost. Although during these three journeys[9] I dwelt upon my usual subjects of thought, nevertheless, since I could neither write down my ideas nor impress them on my memory, I call those days lost. It is true that when I reached Italy, on my return from the last expedition, I dictated a voluminous letter on the variableness of fortune to a studious old man, Peter of Poitiers; it arrived too late, however, and found him dead. Here, then, are seven months lost in the service of princes; nor is this a trifling sacrifice, I admit, considering the shortness of life. Would that I need not fear a greater loss, incurred long ago by the vanity and frivolous employments of my youth!

You add, further, that possibly the measure of life was different in olden time from what it is in ours, and that nowadays we may regard men as old who were then looked upon as young. But I can

---

[5] In 1353.
[6] He went to Prague in 1356.
[7] Charles IV.   [8] In 1360.
[9] All three of these missions were for the Visconti who ruled Milan.

only reply to you as I did recently to a certain lawyer in this university,[10] who, as I learned, was accustomed to make that same assertion in his lectures, in order to depreciate the industry of the ancients, and excuse the sloth of our contemporaries. I sent by one of his students to warn him against repeating the statement, unless he wished to be considered an ignoramus by scholars. For more than two thousand years there has been no change in the length of human life. Aristotle lived sixty-three years. Cicero lived the same length of time; moreover, although he might have been spared longer had it pleased the heartless and drunken Antony, he had some time before his death written a great deal about his unhappy and premature decline, and had composed a treatise on *Old Age*, for the edification of himself and a friend. Ennius lived seventy years, Horace the same time, while Virgil died at fifty-two, a brief life even for our time. Plato, it is true, lived to be eighty-one; but this, it is said, was looked upon as a prodigy, and because he had attained the most perfect age the Magi decided to offer him a sacrifice, as if he were superior to the rest of mankind. Yet nowadays we frequently see in our cities those who have reached this age: octogenarians and nonagenarians are often to be met with, and no one is surprised, or offers sacrifices to them. If you recall Varro to me, or Cato, or others who reached their hundredth year, or Gorgias of Leontium who greatly exceeded that age, I have other modern instances to set off against them. But as the names are obscure I will mention only one, Romualdo of Ravenna, a very noted hermit, who recently reached the age of one hundred and twenty years, in spite of the greatest privations, suffered for the love of Christ, and in the performance of numerous vigils and fasts such as you are now doing all in your power to induce me to refrain from. I have said a good deal about this matter in order that you may neither believe nor assert that, with the exception of the patriarchs, who lived at the beginning of the world, and who, I am convinced, developed no literary activity whatever, any of our predecessors enjoyed greater longevity than ourselves.[11] They could boast of greater activity, not of a longer life, — if, indeed, life without industry deserves to be called life at all, and not a slothful and useless delay.

By a few cautious words, however, you avoid the foregoing criticism, for you admit that it may not be a question of age after all, but that it may perhaps be temperament, or possibly climate, or diet, or some other cause, which precludes me from doing what the others were all able to do. I freely concede this, but I cannot accept the deduction you draw from it, and which you support with laboriously elaborate arguments; for some of your reasons are, in a certain sense,

---

[10] Of Padua.
[11] Petrarch at his death lacked only two days of living a full seventy-one years.

quite opposed to the thesis you would prove. You counsel me to be contented — I quote you literally — with having perhaps equalled Virgil in verse (as you assert) and Cicero in prose. Oh, that you had been induced by the truth, rather than seduced by friendship, in saying this! You add that, in virtue of a *senatus consultum*, following the custom of our ancestors, I have received the most glorious of titles, and the rare honour of the Roman laurel.[12] Your conclusion from all this is that, with the happy results of my studies, in which I rival the greatest, and with my labours honoured by the noblest of prizes, I should leave off importuning God and man, and rest content with my fate and the fulfilment of my fondest wishes. Certainly I could make no objection to this if what your affection for me has led you to believe were true, or were even accepted by the rest of the world; I should gladly acquiesce in the opinions of others, for I should always rather trust their judgment than my own. But your view is not shared by others, and least of all by myself, who am convinced that I have rivalled no one, except, perhaps, the common herd, and rather than be like it I should choose to remain entirely unknown.

As for the laurel wreath, it encircled my brow when I was as immature in years and mind as were its leaves. Had I been of riper age I should not have desired it. . . .

. . . Continued work and application form my soul's nourishment. So soon as I commenced to rest and relax I should cease to live. I know my own powers. I am not fitted for other kinds of work; but my reading and writing, which you would have me discontinue, are easy tasks, nay, they are a delightful rest, and relieve the burden of heavier anxieties. There is no lighter burden, nor more agreeable, than a pen. Other pleasures fail us, or wound us while they charm; but the pen we take up rejoicing and lay down with satisfaction, for it has the power to advantage, not only its lord and master, but many others as well, even though they be far away, — sometimes, indeed, though they be not born for thousands of years to come. I believe that I speak but the strict truth when I claim that as there is none among earthly delights more noble than literature, so there is none so lasting, none gentler, or more faithful; there is none which accompanies its possessor through the vicissitudes of life at so small a cost of effort or anxiety.[13]

Pardon me then, my brother, pardon me. I am disposed to believe anything that you say, but I cannot accept your opinion in this matter. However you may describe me (and nothing is impossible to the pen of a learned and eloquent writer). I must still endeavour, if I am

---

[12] His coronation as poet laureate by the Roman Senate in 1341.
[13] Such praise and characterization of literature and its rewards was fairly standard. Cicero and Quintilian speak in similar terms in the first centuries B.C. and A.D.; John of Salisbury, in the twelfth century.

a nullity, to become something; if already of some account, to become a little more worthy; and if I were really great, which I am not, I should strive, so far as in me lay, to become greater, even the greatest. May I not be allowed to appropriate the magnificent reply of that fierce barbarian who, when urged to spare himself continued exertions, since he already enjoyed sufficient renown, responded, "The greater I am, the greater shall be my efforts"? Words worthy of another than a barbarian! They are graven on my heart, and the letter which follows this will show you how far I am from following your exhortations to idleness. Not satisfied with gigantic enterprises, for which this brief life of ours does not suffice, and would not if doubled in length, I am always on the alert for new and uncalled-for undertakings, — so distasteful to me is sleep and dreary repose. Do you not know that passage from Ecclesiasticus, "When man has finished his researches, he is but at the beginning, and when he rests, then doth he labour"? I seem to myself to have but begun; whatever you and others may think, this is my verdict. If in the meanwhile the end, which certainly cannot be far off, should come, I would that it might find me still young. But as I cannot, in the nature of things, hope for that, I desire that death find me reading and writing,[14] or, if it please Christ, praying and in tears.

Farewell, and remember me. May you be happy and persevere manfully.

PADUA, April 28 (1373).

[14] Death came to Petrarch in just this way, a little over a year later. According to a letter of a contemporary, "He closed his last days in the library, where he was found leaning over a book as if sleeping."

11

The Artistic Renaissance in Italy

Vasari

In the arts, the product of the Italian Renaissance was even more distinguished than in literature. Here, too, the inspiriting spark was a new enthusiasm for classical antiquity and the natural world. The Italian artistic Renaissance may be divided roughly into three phases: (1) the thirteenth to fourteenth centuries, a transitional period; (2) the fifteenth century, a time of bold experimentation, technical advance, and creative progress; and (3) the High Renaissance, spanning the late fifteenth and early sixteenth centuries, the culmination of all that had gone before, the "Age of the Masters," sometimes referred to as the "Golden Age of Western Art." In many ways the first two periods, the developmental ones, are the most interesting, and it is with these that our selections from Vasari are concerned.

That the Italian Renaissance is so real to us today is due not only to the survival of its masterworks, but also to the fact that the lives and achievements of its artists are so fully and brilliantly recorded by Giorgio Vasari, himself an accomplished painter and architect. Writing from the vantage point of the mid-sixteenth century, Vasari gives an excellent comprehensive account in his Lives of the Most Eminent Painters, Sculptors, and Architects, a classic of art history and a major source for the history of the Italian Renaissance.

Vasari was born in Arezzo, a town in the Florentine state, in 1511. His father, a potter, died when Giorgio was sixteen. His uncle, Luca Signorelli, was a noted painter. At an early age Vasari distinguished himself by his ability to memorize Virgil, with the result that he was taken by Cardinal Passerini to Florence, where he was educated along with members of the Medici family. Meanwhile Vasari demonstrated artistic inclinations and abilities. He studied under Guglielmo da Marsiglia, an artist in stained glass, and later under the gifted painter Andrea del Sarto and the universal genius Michelangelo. At eighteen, with the help of Medicean patronage, Vasari went to Rome, where he intensively studied works of the masters.

Throughout his lifetime (1511-71) Vasari was an indefatigable worker. Much of his work, at Rome, Florence, Naples, Arezzo, Rimini, and elsewhere, consisted in a combination of architecture and painting. He amassed a considerable fortune and built himself a fine house; and he enjoyed the patronage of several successive Medici, as well as of other influential persons, such as Cardinal Farnese. His success, however, was due more to industry and imitation than to genius and originality, for his paintings are somewhat uninspired and his architecture undistinguished. He appears to have been an upright and pleasant man, fair, kindly, and conscientious.

Vasari tells the story of how he came to write his Lives. One night in 1546, when he was dining at Cardinal Farnese's, another guest was Paolo Giovio, possessor of a museum in which he had a gallery of portraits of famous persons. Giovio remarked that he would like to have a treatise telling the history of all those who had been famous in the "arts of design." Vasari commented that to prepare such a work Giovio would need the help of an artist who could understand the technicalities and organize the materials. At the Cardinal's suggestion, Vasari agreed to give Giovio this assistance. He set to work with characteristic energy; but when he presented his material to Giovio, the latter persuaded him to complete the work himself. Vasari had it ready the following year (1547); the first edition was printed in 1550 in three volumes, and a revised and enlarged edition in 1568. English translations of the complete Lives run from four to ten volumes.

Although Vasari did not take long to write the Lives, he apparently had been doing research for many years and had a phenomenal memory. There are some slips in such details as dates, chronology, and collaborations; but by and large, the work is a reliable mine of information, made vivid with details and anecdotes, and distinguished especially by the author's sympathetic appreciation of the activities and works of artists of the past. Vasari was a good historian and a skillful storyteller; moreover, his critical evaluations have generally been confirmed by posterity.

The selections given here are concerned with six leading artists of the Italian Renaissance prior to 1500. In the field of painting, Giotto di Bondone (1266-1337) is credited by Vasari and others with having broken away from the "Byzantine manner" by introducing a "new manner" of realistic representation and narrative in painting. Masaccio (1402-28) completed the transition to the new manner and even anticipated the "grand manner" of the High Renaissance by his use of linear perspective, foreshortening, and chiarioscuro (light and shadow), his dramatic storytelling, psychological insight, and epic spiritual themes. In sculpture, the "Pisanos" (represented here by Andrea, c. 1272-c. 1347) were transitional: they studied and imitated classical models and employed classical realism and composition in their bas-reliefs. Lorenzo Ghiberti (1378-1455), famous for the bas-reliefs of his doors for the Baptistery of Florence, combined naturalism and realistic perspective with fine dramatic insight and aesthetic composition. Donatello (c. 1386-1466), one of the most productive geniuses of the period, emancipated sculpture from architecture, reinstated the nude in art, revived life-size equestrian statuary in bronze, and brought an intense realism to spiritual subjects. Brunelleschi (1377-1446) launched a classical revival in architecture through his study and excavation of classical remains, as well as through his use of classical forms and his daring innovations prompted by classical structures.

Vasari's Lives are windows on the fifteenth century. Florence is the center and undisputed leader of the renaissance in art. Mediccean patronage, along with that of other princes of state and church, figures prominently. Popular interest in and knowledge of the arts is commonplace, while the esteem in which they are held is expressed in the generous recompense of gifted artists. Everywhere the classical inspiration of the Italain Renaissance is evident: the artists, like the humanists, are interested in history, biography, and archaeology; faithfulness to natural reality is stressed; inventiveness and originality are prized.

The widespread activity is amazing. Apprentices learn their craft from master artists in their bottegas or shops. The transmission of skills and techniques is direct: from master to disciple. Journeymen and even apprentices do a great deal of the work of painting and chiseling under the direction of masters. The various arts are interrelated and overlapping; the transfer of skills from one to another is apparent on every hand, and many artists are triple-threat peformers. An intense enthusiasm and an overwhelming energy characterize these men. We see the same individuals undertaking numerous enterprises in many parts of

Italy, sometimes several at one time. They attack practical difficulties with vigor and surmount them courageously, as Brunelleschi demonstrates in solving problems both of engineering and of labor relations in the erection of his famous dome. In Vasari's Lives, the artists of the Italian Renaissance live again for us in all their enthusiasm, ambition, and productivity.

Giorgio Vasari

from *Lives of the Most Eminent Painters, Sculptors, and Architects* *

Giotto,[1] Painter, Sculptor, and Architect, of Florence

The gratitude which the masters in painting owe to Nature — who is ever the truest model of him who, possessing the power to select the brightest parts from her best and loveliest features, employs himself unweariedly in the reproduction of these beauties — this gratitude, I say, is due, in my judgment, to the Florentine painter, Giotto, seeing that he alone — although born amidst incapable artists, and at a time when all good methods in art had long been entombed beneath the ruins of war — yet, by the favour of Heaven, he, I say, alone succeeded in resuscitating art, and restoring her to a path that may be called the true one.[2] And it was in truth a great marvel, that from so rude and inapt an age, Giotto should have had strength to elicit so much, that the art of design, of which the men of those days had

---

* Translated by Mrs. Jonathan Foster (London: Bohn, 1850).
The student will find many of the paintings, sculptures, and edifices mentioned by Vasari reproduced and further discussed in histories of art and especially histories of Renaissance art and arts, such as the following: Bernhard Berenson, *The Italian Painters of the Renaissance* (Oxford, 1952); George H. Chase and R. P. Chandler, *A History of Sculpture* (New York, 1924); Sheldon Cheyney, *World History of Art* (New York, 1937); Banister F. Fletcher, *A History of Architecture* (New York, 1943); L. J. Freeman, *Italian Sculpture of the Renaissance* (New York, 1901); Helen Gardner, *Art Through the Ages* (New York, 1948); Padraic Gregory, *When Painting Was in Glory (1280–1580)* (Milwaukee, 1941); Cecil Gould, *Introduction to Italian Renaissance Painting* (London, 1957); Eric R. Maclagan, *Italian Sculpture of the Renaissance* (Cambridge, Mass., 1935); and Rudolph Whittkower, *Architectural Principles in the Age of Humanism* (London, 1952).

[1] Giotto di Bondone (1266–1337).
[2] The "reform" effected by Giotto in painting was anticipated (c. 1260) by Niccola or Niccolò Pisano in the sister art of sculpture.

little, if any, knowledge, was, by his means, effectually recalled into life.

The birth of this great man took place in the hamlet of Vespignano, fourteen miles from the city of Florence, in the year 1276.[3] His father's name was Bondone, a simple husbandman, who reared the child, to whom he had given the name of Giotto, with such decency as his condition permitted. The boy was early remarked for extreme vivacity in all his childish proceedings, and for extraordinary promptitude of intelligence; so that he became endeared, not only to his father, but to all who knew him in the village and around it. When he was about ten years old, Bondone gave him a few sheep to watch, and with these he wandered about the vicinity — now here and now there. But, induced by Nature herself to the arts of design, he was perpetually drawing on the stones, the earth, or the sand, some natural object that came before him, or some fantasy that presented itself to his thoughts.

It chanced one day that the affairs of Cimabue took him from Florence to Vespignano, when he perceived the young Giotto, who, while his sheep fed around him, was occupied in drawing one of them from life, with a stone slightly pointed, upon a smooth clean piece of rock, — and that without any teaching whatever, but such as Nature herself had imparted. Halting in astonishment, Cimabue inquired of the boy if he would accompany him to his home, and the child replied, he would go willingly, if his father were content to permit it. Cimabue therefore requesting the consent of Bondone, the latter granted it readily, and suffered the artist to conduct his son to Florence, where, in a short time, instructed by Cimabue and aided by Nature, the boy not only equalled his master in his own manner, but became so good an imitator of Nature, that he totally banished the rude Greek manner,[4] restoring art to the better path adhered to in modern[5] times, and introducing the customs of accurately drawing living persons from nature, which had not been used for more than two hundred years. Or, if some had attempted it, as said above, it was not by any means with the success of Giotto. Among the portraits by the artist, and which still remain, is one of his contemporary and intimate friend, Dante Alighieri, who was no less famous as a poet than Giotto as a painter, and whom Messer Giovanni Boccaccio has lauded so highly in the introduction to his story of Messer Forese da Rabatta, and of Giotto the painter himself. This portrait is in the chapel of the palace of the Podestà in Florence;[6] and in the same

---

[3] Actually in 1266, according to most authorities.
[4] The formal, conventional Byzantine mode had dominated Italian painting for centuries. Giotto's master, Cimabue, began a departure but Giotto definitely parted company with this past.
[5] Contemporary: 16th century.
[6] This portrait, along with those of Latini and Donati, was whitewashed later but subsequently restored in a partial and questionable manner.

chapel are the portraits of Ser Brunetto Latini, master of Dante, and of Messer Corso Donati, an illustrious citizen of that day.

The first pictures of Giotto were painted for the chapel of the High Altar in the Abbey of Florence, where he executed many works considered extremely fine. Among these, an Annunciation is particularly admired; the expression of fear and astonishment in the countenance of the Virgin, when receiving the salutation of Gabriel, is vividly depicted; she appears to suffer the extremity of terror, and seems almost ready to take flight. The altar-piece of that chapel is also by Giotto; but this has been, and continues to be, preserved, rather from the respect felt for the work of so distinguished a man, than from any other motive. There are four chapels in Santa Croce also painted by Giotto: three between the Sacristy and the principal chapel, and one on the opposite side of the church. In the first of the three, which belongs to Messer Ridolfi de' Bardi, and wherein are the bell-ropes, is the Life of St. Francis. In this picture are several figures of monks lamenting the death of the saint: the expression of weeping is very natural. In the second chapel, which belongs to the family of Peruzzi, are two passages from the life of St. John the Baptist, to whom the chapel is dedicated, wherein the dancing of Herodias,[7] and the promptitude with which certain servants are performing the service of the table, are depicted with extreme vivacity. Two other paintings in the same chapel, also exceedingly fine, are events from the life of St. John the Evangelist, — that wherein he restores Drusiana to life, and his own ascension into Heaven. The third chapel belongs to the Giugni family: it is dedicated to the Apostles; and Giotto has painted in it various scenes from the martyrdom of many of them. In the fourth chapel, which is on the other side of the church to the north, belonging to the families of Tosinghi and Spinelli, and dedicated to the Assumption of our Lady, he has depicted the following passages from the life of the Virgin: her birth, her marriage, her annunciation, the adoration of the magi, and the presentation of Christ in the Temple. This last is a most beautiful thing; for not only is the warmest expression of love to the child to be perceived on the face of the old man Simeon, but the act of the infant, who, being afraid of him, stretches its arms timidly and turns towards its mother, is depicted in a manner inexpressibly touching and exquisite. The Apostles and Angels, with torches in their hands, who surround the death-bed of the Virgin, in a succeeding picture, are also admirably well done.[8] In the same church, and in the chapel of the Baroncelli family, is a picture in distemper, by the hand of Giotto: it represents the corona-

[7] Giotto confuses Herodias and her daughter Salome. The damaged fresco of Salome was uncovered in 1841.

[8] Although all of these frescoes in the four chapels were later whitewashed, those in the Bardi and Peruzzi chapels have been restored; the rest have been lost to posterity. Whether these Santa Croce frescoes were done earlier or later in Giotto's career is a subject of dispute.

tion of the Virgin, with a great number of small figures, and a choir of saints and angels, very carefully finished. On this work, the name of the master and the date are written in letters of gold.[9] . . . After these works were finished, Giotto departed from Florence, and went to Assisi, to complete the paintings commenced by Cimabue. Passing through Arezzo, he painted one of the chapels of the capitular church, that of St. Francis, which is above the baptistery; and on a round column, which stands beside a very beautiful antique Corinthian capital, are portraits of St. Francis and St. Dominic, by his hand, both taken from nature.[10] In the cathedral without Arezzo, he further executed the Martyrdom of St. Stephen, in one of the larger chapels; of which the composition is fine.[11] Having finished these things, he proceeded to Assisi, a city of Umbria, being invited thither by Fra Giovanni of Muro in the March, who was then general of the fraternity of St. Francis. Here, in the upper church, and under the corridor which traverses the windows, he painted a series of thirty-two frescoes,[12] representing passages from the life and acts of the saint; namely, sixteen on each side; a work which he executed so perfectly as to acquire great fame from it. And, of a truth, there is singular variety in these frescoes; not only in the gestures and attitudes of each figure, but also in the composition of all the stories; the different costumes of those times are also represented; and, in all the accessories, nature is most faithfully adhered to. Among other figures, that of a thirsty man stooping to drink from a fountain, is worthy of perpetual praise: the eager desire with which he bends towards the water is portrayed with such marvellous effect, that one could almost believe him to be a living man actually drinking. There are many other parts of this work that well merit remark, but I refrain from alluding to them, lest I become too discursive. Let it suffice to say, that it added greatly to the fame of Giotto, for the beauty of the figures, the good order, just proportion, and life of the whole, while the facility of execution, which he had received from nature, and afterwards perfected by study, was made manifest in every part of the work. Giotto has indeed well merited to be called the disciple of nature rather than of other masters; having not only studiously cultivated his natural faculties, but being perpetually occupied in drawing fresh stores from nature, which was to him the never-failing source of inspiration.[13]

When the stories above described were finished, Giotto continued

[9] The inscription is OPUS MAGISTRI JOCTI (Work of Master Giotto), but there is no date.

[10] Vasari apparently means using living models, since St. Dominic died in 1221 and St. Francis in 1226.

[11] Destroyed in 1561.

[12] Most of these are still extant. They depict leading events from the Bible stories of (1) Genesis and (2) the New Testament.

[13] Note the repetitious stress on the imitation of nature, rather than the following of conventions.

to labour in the same place, but in the lower church, where he painted the upper part of the walls beside the high altar, together with the four angles of the vault, beneath which the remains of St. Francis repose. All of these display rich and original invention.[14] In the first angle is St. Francis glorified in heaven, and surrounded by those virtues which are essential to him who desires fully to partake of the grace of God. On one side is Obedience, placing a yoke on the neck of a friar who kneels before her, the bands of the yoke being drawn towards heaven by hands above. The figure on the lip of Obedience imposes silence, while her eyes are fixed on Jesus, from whose side the blood is flowing; beside this Virtue, stand Prudence and Humility, to show that where there is true obedience, there are also humility and prudence, directing every action towards the right and good. In the second angle is Chastity, who, firm on a well-defended fortress, refuses to yield to any of the kingdoms, crowns, and glories, that are offered her on all sides. At the feet of Chastity is Purity, washing certain naked figures, while Force is conducting others towards her, to be also washed and purified. On one side of Chastity stands Penitence, driving away Love[15] with the cord of discipline, and putting Incontinence to flight. The third compartment exhibits Poverty walking barefoot amidst thorns: a dog follows her, barking, and a boy throws stones at her, while a second gathers the thorns about her, and presses them into her legs with a stick. This Poverty is here seen to be espoused by St. Francis, while Christ himself is holding her hand; and Hope, not without significance, is present, together with Charity.[16] In the fourth and last of these angles is a St. Francis, also glorified, as in the first compartment. He is dressed in the white tunic of the deacon,[17] and is triumphant in Heaven, attended by a multitude of angels, who form a choir around him; they hold a standard, on which is a cross with seven stars; and over all is the Holy Spirit. In each of these angles are certain Latin words, explanatory of the events depicted. Besides the paintings in these four compartments, those on the walls are extremely fine, and well deserve our admiration, not only for their beauty, but also for the care with which they were executed, which was such that they have retained their freshness even to this day. The portrait of Giotto himself, very well done, may be seen in one of these pictures; and over the door of the sacristy is a fresco, also by him, representing St. Francis at the moment when he receives the stigmata;[18] the expression of the saint being so full of love and devotion,

---

[14] These frescoes in the lower church, representing the Life of St. Francis, still survive. St. Francis, incidentally, is said to have influenced the "new manner" by his love of nature.
[15] Sensual love; passion.
[16] This allegorical fresco possibly reflects the influence of Dante, whose *Paradiso*, xi, describes the espousal of St. Francis and "Holy Poverty."
[17] Although he became a deacon, St. Francis, apparently out of humility, would never become a priest.
[18] The five wounds of the Saviour, reproduced in certain saints.

that to me this seems to be the best picture that Giotto has produced in this work, which is nevertheless all truly beautiful and admirable.[19]

When Giotto had at length completed this St. Francis, he returned to Florence, where, immediately after his arrival, he painted a picture to be sent to Pisa. This is also a St. Francis, standing on the frightful rocks of La Verna; and is finished with extraordinary care: it exhibits a landscape, with many trees and precipices, which was a new thing in those times. In the attitude and expression of St. Francis, who is on his knees receiving the stigmata, the most eager desire to obtain them is clearly manifest, as well as infinite love towards Jesus Christ, who from heaven above, where he is seen surrounded by the seraphim, grants these stigmata to his servant with looks of such lively affection, that it is not possible to conceive any thing more perfect. Beneath this picture are three others, also from the life of St. Francis, and very beautiful. The picture of the Stigmatae, just described, is still in the church of San Francesco[20] in Pisa, close beside the high altar.[1] . . .

After completing these works, and on the 9th of July 1334, Giotto commenced the campanile of Santa Maria del Fiore; the foundations were laid on massive stone, sunk twenty braccia[2] beneath the surface, on a site whence gravel and water had previously been excavated: then having made a good concrete to the height of twelve braccia, he caused the remainder, namely eight braccia, to be formed of masonry. The bishop of the city, with all the clergy and magistrates, were present at the foundation, of which the first stone was solemnly laid by the bishop himself. The edifice then proceeded on the plan before mentioned, and in the Gothic manner of those times; all the historical representations, which were to be the ornaments, being designed with infinite care and diligence by Giotto himself, who marked out on the model all the compartments where the friezes and sculptures were to be placed, in colours of white, black, and red. The lower circumference of the tower is of one hundred braccia, twenty-five that is on each of the four sides. The height is one hundred and forty-four braccia. And if that which Lorenzo di Cione Ghiberti has

[19] The frescoes of the upper and lower churches of Florence rank among Giotto's most famous works, along with the frescoes in the Arena Chapel of Padua. It is certain that Giotto planned, designed, and directed these numerous frescoes, or most of them, but he may not have personally executed them; a work was often entrusted to lesser artists under the supervision and with the correction of the master.

[20] This famous picture is now in the Louvre, Paris. It is inscribed OPUS JOCTI FLORENTINI (Work of Giotto the Florentine). The lower part is divided into three often-reproduced compartments: the vision of Innocent III, Innocent III Receiving St. Francis, and St. Francis Preaching to the Birds. The stigmata were marks corresponding to the wounds of the crucified Christ.

[1] Vasari goes on to discuss numerous paintings, designs, and structures by Giotto in various places.

[2] A braccio (*pl.* braccia) was an Italian measure of length: nearly two English feet.

written be true, as I fully believe it is, Giotto not only made the model of the campanile, but even executed a part of the sculptures and reliefs, those representations in marble, namely, which exhibit the origin of all the arts.[3] Lorenzo also affirms that he saw models in relief from the hand of Giotto, and more particularly those used in these works: an assertion that we can easily believe; for design and invention are the parents of all the arts, and not of one only. This campanile, according to the design of Giotto, was to have been crowned by a spire or pyramid, of the height of fifty braccia; but as this was in the old Gothic manner, the modern architects have always advised its omission: the building appearing to them better as it is. For all these works, Giotto was not only made a citizen of Florence, but also received a pension of a hundred golden florins yearly — a large sum in those times[4] — from the commune of Florence. He was also appointed superintendent of the work, which he did not live to see finished; but which was continued after his death by Taddeo Gaddi. While this undertaking was in progress, Giotto painted a picture for the nuns of San Giorgio, and in the abbey of Florence, within the church, and on an arch over the door, he executed three half-length figures, which were afterwards whitewashed over, *to give more light to the church.*[5] In the great hall of the Podestà in Florence, Giotto painted a picture, the idea of which was afterwards frequently borrowed. In this he represented the Commune seated, in the character of a judge, with a sceptre in the hand, and equally poised scales over the head, to intimate the rectitude of her decisions. The figure is surrounded by four Virtues: these are Force with generosity, Prudence with the laws, Justice with arms, and Temperance with the word. This is a very beautiful picture, of appropriate and ingenious invention.[6]

About this time, Giotto once more repaired to Padua, where he painted several pictures, and adorned many chapels; but more particularly that of the Arena, where he executed various works, from which he derived both honour and profit.[7] In Milan also he produced many paintings, which are scattered throughout that city, and are held in high estimation even to this day. Finally, and no long

---

[3] It is likely that Giotto executed the first and second reliefs on the northern side of the campanile, and designed the remaining reliefs on that side, while all the rest should be credited to Andrea Pisano.

[4] Note the monetary inflation implied.

[5] "Art's little helpers" were already busy whitewashing!

[6] This is now lost. It may have suggested the famous fresco of Lorenzetti at Siena.

[7] The frescoes of the Arena Chapel at Padua were apparently executed intermittently during several years from about 1306 on; the Chapel was built from about 1303. The frescoes represent the mysteries of the Incarnation and Redemption, reflected in various scenes from the lives of Christ and the Virgin Mary. Many art critics would agree with the words of one, that these frescoes are some of the finest things in the whole history of art.

time after he had returned from Milan, having passed his life in the production of so many admirable works, and proved himself a good Christian as well as excellent painter, Giotto resigned his soul to God in the year 1336, not only to the great regret of his fellow citizens, but of all who had known him, or even heard his name.

Giotto ... was of an exceedingly jocund humor and abounded in witty and humorous remarks, which are still remembered in Florence. Examples of these may be found, not only in the writings of Messer Giovanni Boccaccio,[8] but also in the three hundred stories of Franco Sacchetti. ...

It is said that Giotto, when still a boy, and studying with Cimabue, once painted a fly on the nose of a figure on which Cimabue himself was employed, and this so naturally, that when the master returned to continue his work, he believed it to be real and lifted his hand more than once to drive it away before he should go on with his painting.[9]

The memory of Giotto is not only preserved in his own works, but is also consecrated in the writings of the authors of those times,[10] he being the master by whom the true art of painting was recovered, after it had been lost during many years preceding his time. Wherefore, by a public decree, and by command of the elder Lorenzo de' Medici,[11] of glorious memory, who bore him a particular affection, and greatly admired the talent of his distinguished man, his bust was placed in Santa Maria del Fiore, being sculptured in marble by Benedetto de Majano, an excellent sculptor, and verses by that divine poet, Messer Angelo Poliziano, were thereon engraved.

Andrea Pisano,[12] Sculptor and Architect

The art of painting has at no time been flourishing, without the sculptors also making admirable progress in their art at the same moment; and whoever will observe closely, shall find the works of all ages bearing testimony to the truth of this remark. And of a surety these two arts are sisters, born at the same period, nourished and guided by the same spirit. A proof of this is presented by Andrea Pisano, who, devoting himself to sculpture as Giotto did to painting, effected so important an amelioration in the art, both as to practice and theory, that he was esteemed as the best master that the Tuscans had ever possessed. Andrea was most especially celebrated for his castings in bronze, and was, on this account, highly honoured by all, but more particularly by the Florentines, by whom his works were so largely remunerated, that he did not scruple to change his country, his con-

---

[8] Most famous for the hundred tales of his *Decameron*.
[9] Stories of this sort are told of many famous painters.
[10] As by Dante and Petrarch, Boccaccio and Villani.
[11] Lorenzo the Magnificent ruled Florence from 1469 to 1492.
[12] Andrea Pisano or Andrea de Pontadera (c. 1272–c. 1347).

nexions, his property, and his friends. The difficulties encountered by the masters in sculpture who had preceded him, were of infinite advantage to Andrea, since the works of those artists were so rude and common-place, that those of the Pisan were esteemed a miracle.[13] And that these earlier sculptures were indeed coarse, is clearly shown, as we have said elsewhere; by those over the principal door of San Paolo, in Florence, as well as by some in stone, which are in the church of Ognissanti; and are better calculated to excite ridicule, than admiration or pleasure, in those who examine them. It is, however, certain, that if the art of sculpture incur the danger of losing its vitality, there is always less difficulty in its restoration than in that of painting, the former having ever the living and natural model, in the rounded forms which are such as she requires, while the latter cannot so lightly recover the pure outlines and correct manner demanded for her works, and from which alone the labours of the painter derive majesty, beauty, and grace. Fortune was in other respects favourable to Andrea, many relics of antiquity having been collected in Pisa by the fleets of that city, as results of their frequent victories; and from these, which still remain, as we have said, about the cathedral and Campo Santo, the sculptor Andrea obtained such instruction, and derived such light, as could by no means be obtained by the painter Giotto, since the ancient paintings had not been preserved as the sculptures had been.[14] . . .

Periods of Renaissance Art, Especially the Second Period

When I first undertook to write these lives, it was not my purpose to make a mere list of the artists, or to give an inventory, so to speak, of their works. Nor could I by any means consider it a worthy end of my — I will not say satisfactory — but assuredly prolonged and fatiguing labours, that I should content myself with merely ascertaining the number, names, and country of the artists, or with informing my reader in what city or borough precisely, their paintings, sculptures, or buildings, were to be found. This I could have accomplished by a simple register or table, without the interposition of my own judgment in any part. But I have remembered that the writers of history, — such of them, that is to say, as by common consent are admitted to have treated their subject most judiciously, — have in no case contented themselves with a simple narration of the occurrences

---

[13] The fine sculptures of Niccola Pisano and his son Giovanni Pisano (died c. 1320), the latter Andrea's teacher and one-time collaborator, are apparently overlooked at this point.

[14] Vasari goes on to discuss the various sculptures and architectural enterprises of Andrea Pisano. It is certain that the sculptures of the Pisanos were strongly influenced by antique survivals. It is also probable that the sculptures of Niccola and Giovanni influenced Giotto to some extent.

they describe, but have made zealous enquiry respecting the lives of the actors, and sought with the utmost diligence to investigate the modes and methods adopted by distinguished men for the furtherance of their various undertakings. The efforts of such writers have, moreover, been further directed to the examination of the points on which errors have been made, or, on the other hand, by what means successful results have been produced, to what expedients those who govern have had recourse, in what manner they have delivered themselves from such embarrassments as arise in the management of affairs; of all that has been effected, in short, whether sagaciously or injudiciously, whether by the exercise of prudence, piety, and greatness of mind, or by that of the contrary qualities, and with opposite results; as might be expected from men who are persuaded that history is in truth the mirror of human life. These writers have not contented themselves with a mere dry narration of facts and events, occurring under this prince or in that republic, but have set forth the grounds of the various opinions, the motives of the different resolutions, and the character of the circumstances by which the prime movers have been actuated; with the consequences, beneficial or disastrous, which have been the results of all. This is, without doubt, the soul of history. From these details it is that men learn the true government of life; and to secure this effect, therefore, with the addition of the pleasure which may be derived from having past events presented to the view as living and present, is to be considered the legitimate aim of the historian.[1]

Moved by these considerations, I determined, having undertaken to write the history of the noblest masters in our arts, to pursue the method observed by these distinguished writers, so far as my powers would permit; imitating these ingenious men, and desiring, above all things, to honour the arts, and those who labour in them. . . .

. . . To avoid a too minute inquiry, I adopt the division into three parts, or periods — if we so please to call them — from the revival of the arts, down to the present century,[2] and in each of these there will be found a very obvious difference. In the first, and most ancient, of these periods,[3] the three formative arts were very far from their perfection; and that, it must be admitted that they had much in them that was good, yet this was accompanied by so much of imperfection, that those times certainly merit no great share of commendation. Yet, on the other hand, as it is by them that the commencement was made; as it was they who originated the method, and taught the way to the better path, which was afterwards followed, so, if it were but for this, we are bound to say nothing of them but what is good — nay, we

---

[1] An excellent discussion of the method of history-writing — especially for an amateur.
[2] The 16th century.
[3] The 13th to 14th centuries (roughly).

must even accord to them a somewhat larger amount of glory than they might have the right to demand, were their works to be judged rigidly by the strict rules of art.

In the second period,[4] all productions were, obviously, much ameliorated; richer invention was displayed, with more correct drawing, a better manner, improved execution, and more careful finish. The arts were, in a measure, delivered from that rust of old age, and that coarse disproportion, which the rudeness of the previous uncultivated period had left still clinging to them. But who will venture to affirm that there could yet be found an artist perfect at all points? or one who had arrived at that position, in respect of invention, design, and colour, to which we have attained in the present day? Is there any one who has been able so carefully to manage the shadows of his figures, that the lights remain only on the parts in relief? or who has, in like manner, effected those perforations, and secured those delicate results, in sculpture, which are exhibited by the statues and rilievi of our own day? The credit of having effected this is certainly due to the third period[5] only; respecting which it appears to me that we may safely affirm the arts to have effected all that it is permitted to the imitation of nature to perform, and to have reached such a point, that we have now more cause for apprehension lest they should again sink into depression, than ground for hope that they will ever attain to a higher degree of perfection.

Reflecting attentively within myself on all these things, I conclude that it is the peculiar nature, and distinctive characteristic of these arts, that, rising from mean beginnings, they should proceed to elevate themselves, by gradual effort, and should finally attain to the summit of perfection; and I am confirmed in this opinion by the perception of an almost similar mode of progression in others of the liberal arts.[6] And since there is a close relationship between them all,[7] I am strengthened in the conviction that this, my view, is the just one. With respect to painting and sculpture more especially, their fate, in older times, must have been so exactly alike, that we have only to make a certain change in the names, when the same facts might be related of each. For if the writers who lived near to those times, and who could see and judge of their works, be worthy of credit, the statues of Canacus were stiff, hard, without life or movement of any kind, and therefore very unlike the reality. The same thing has been affirmed respecting the works of Calamis, although they are described as possessing somewhat more of softness than those of the first-named artist. Then came Miron, who, if he did not very closely approach to the successful

---

[4] The 15th century (roughly).

[5] The late 15th to the 16th centuries (roughly).

[6] Vasari obviously puts the fine arts among the liberal arts: a Renaissance trend.

[7] Vasari apparently recognizes the interrelationship between the various arts, fine and liberal, and the sciences and philosophy.

imitation of nature, did yet impart to his works such an amount of grace, and correct proportion, that they could be justly called beautiful. In the third degree, there followed Policletus, with the other masters so highly celebrated, and by whom, as is affirmed — and we are bound to believe — the art was carried to its entire perfection.[8] ...

But, to leave these masters, respecting whom we are compelled to confide in the opinions of others, who do not always agree among themselves; nay, what is worse, whose testimony, even as to the periods, is frequently at variance; — let us come to our own times, wherein we have the guidance of our eyes — a much safer and better conductor and judge than hearsay. Do we not clearly see to what extent architecture had been ameliorated, from the Greek Buschetto[9] — to begin with one of the most distinguished masters — to the German Arnolfo,[10] and to Giotto? For our perfect conviction of this truth, we need only to glance at the fabrics of the earlier period: the pilasters, the columns, the bases, the capitals, and the cornices, with their ill-formed members, as we see them, for example, in Santa Maria del Fiore, in Florence; in the exterior incrustations of San Giovanni; at San Miniato al Monte; in the cathedral of Fiesole; the Duomo of Milan; the church of San Vitale at Ravenna; that of Santa Maria Maggiore in Rome; and the Duomo Vecchio, outside the city of Arezzo; wherein, with the exception of those few fragments from the antique, which remain in different parts, there is nothing which deserves to be called good, whether as regards arrangement or execution. But, by the masters above named, architecture was, without doubt, greatly ameliorated, and the art made considerable progress under their influence, since they brought the various parts to more correct proportion, and not only erected their buildings in a manner which imparted strength and durability, but also added the grace of ornament to certain parts of them. ...

The same remarks may be applied to sculpture, which, at the first moment of its revival, had some remains of excellence. Being once freed from the rude Byzantine manner, which was, indeed, so coarse that the works produced in it displayed more of the roughness of the raw material than of the genius of the artist; those statues of theirs being wholly destitute of flexibility, attitude, or movement of any kind, and their draperies entirely without folds, so that they could scarcely be called statues — all this became gradually ameliorated, and when Giotto had improved the art of design, the figures of marble and stone improved also: those of Andrea Pisano, of his son Nino, and of his other disciples, were greatly superior to the statues that had pre-

---

8 Note the familiarity with classical Greek art history.
9 Buschetto was probably an Italian rather than a Greek.
10 Arnolfo di Lapo was probably not a German, as the name Arnulf would suggest, but an Italian.

ceded them; less rigid and stiff, displaying some approach to grace of attitude, and in all respects better.[11] . . . There was, in short, a commencement of effort to reach the better path, but defects still remained in great numbers on every point; the art of design had not yet attained its perfection, nor were there many good models for the artists of those times to imitate. All these impediments and difficulties considered, the masters of those days, and who have been placed by me in the first period, deserve all the praise and credit that can be awarded to their works, since it must not be forgotten that they had received no aid from those who preceded them, but had to find their way by their own efforts. Every beginning, moreover, however insignificant and humble in itself, is always to be accounted worthy of no small praise.[12]

Nor had painting much better fortune during those times; but the devotion of the people called it more frequently into use, and it had more artists employed; by consequence, the progress made by it was more obvious than that of the two sister arts. The Greek, or Byzantine manner, first attacked by Cimabue, was afterwards entirely extinguished by the aid of Giotto, and there arose a new style, which I would fain call the manner of Giotto, since it was discovered by him, continued by his disciples, and finally honoured and imitated by all. By Giotto and his disciples, the hard angular lines by which every figure was girt and bound, the senseless and spiritless eyes, the long pointed feet planted upright on their extremities, the sharp formless hands, the absence of shadow, and every other monstrosity of those Byzantine painters, were done away with, as I have said; the heads received a better grace, and more softness of colour. Giotto himself, in particular, gave more easy attitudes to his figures; he made some approach to vivacity and spirit in his heads, and folded his draperies, which have more resemblance to reality than those of his predecessors; he discovered, to a certain extent, the necessity of foreshortening the figure, and began to give some imitation of the passions and affections, so that fear, hope, anger, and love were, in some sort, expressed by his faces. The early manner had been most harsh and rugged; that of Giotto became softer, more harmonious, and — if he did not give his eyes the limpidity and beauty of life, if he did not impart to them the speaking movement of reality, let the difficulties he had to encounter plead his excuse for this, as well as for the want of ease and flow in the hair and beards: or if his hands have not the articulations and muscles of nature, if his rude figures want the reality of life, let it be remembered that Giotto had never seen the works of any better master than he was himself. And let all reflect on the rectitude of judgment displayed by this artist in his paintings, at a

---

[11] Andrea Pisano (died c. 1347) was actually anticipated by Giovanni Pisano, his teacher, and the latter's father, Niccola Pisano.

[12] Vasari shrewdly observes that the first in any new development rightly obtain preferential historical recognition.

time when art was in so poor a state; on the large amount of ability by which alone he could have produced the results secured; for none will deny that his figures perform the parts assigned to them, or that in all his works are found proofs of a just — if not a perfect — judgment, in matters pertaining to his art. . . .

And now that we have raised these three arts, so to speak, from their cradle, and have conducted them through their childhood, we come to the second period, in which they will be seen to have infinitely improved at all points: the compositions comprise more figures; the accessories and ornaments are richer, and more abundant; the drawing is more correct, and approaches more closely to the truth of nature; and, even where no great facility or practice is displayed, the works yet evince much thought and care; the manner is more free and graceful; the colouring more brilliant and pleasant, insomuch that little is now required to the attainment of perfection in the faithful imitation of nature. By the study and diligence of the great Filippo Brunelleschi, architecture first recovered the measures and proportions of the antique, in the round columns as well as in the square pilasters and the rusticated and plain angles. Then it was that the orders were first distinguished one from another, and that the difference between them was made manifest. Care was taken that all should proceed according to rule; that a fixed arrangement should be adhered to, and that the various portions of the work should each receive its due measure and place. Drawing acquired force and correctness, a better grace was imparted to the buildings erected, and the excellence of the art was made manifest: the beauty and variety of design required for capitals and cornices were restored; and, while we perceive the ground plans of churches and other edifices to have been admirably laid at this period, we also remark that the fabrics themselves were finely proportioned, magnificently arranged, and richly adorned, as may be seen in that astonishing erection, the cupola of Santa Maria del Fiore, in Florence, and in the beauty and grace of its lantern; in the graceful, rich, and variously ornamented church of Santo Spirito; and in the no less beautiful edifice of San Lorenzo; or again, in the fanciful invention of the octangular church of the Angioli; in the light and graceful church and convent belonging to the abbey of Florence; and in the magnificent and lordly commencement of the Pitti Palace, to say nothing of the vast and commodious edifice constructed by Francesco di Giorgio, in the church and palace of the Duomo,[13] at Urbino; of the strong and rich castle of Naples; or of the impregnable fortress of Milan, and many other remarkable erections of that time. . . .

. . . The method adopted by the masters of the second period was so much more efficient, their treatment so much more natural and graceful, their drawing so much more accurate, their proportions so much more correct, that their statues began to assume the appearance

[13] Cathedral.

of living men, and were no longer lifeless images of stone, as were those of the earlier day. Of this there will be found proof in the part we are now about to treat, wherein the works of the Sienese, Jacopo della Quercia, will be remarked as possessing more life and grace, with more correct design, and more careful finish; those of Filippo Brunelleschi exhibit a finer development and play of the muscles, with more accurate proportions, and a more judicious treatment — remarks which are alike applicable to the works produced by the disciples of these masters. Still more was performed by Lorenzo Ghiberti, in his work of the gates of San Giovanni:[14] fertility of invention, judicious arrangement, correct design, and admirable treatment being all alike conspicuous in these wonderful productions, the figures of which seem to move and possess a living soul. Donato[15] also lived at the same period, certain it is, that if we assign him to the second period, we may safely affirm him to be the type and representative of all the other masters of that period; since he united within himself the qualities which were divided among the rest, and which must be sought among many, imparting to his figures a life, movement, and reality which enable them to bear comparison with those of later times — nay even, as I have said, with the ancients themselves.

Similar progress was made at the same time in painting, which the excellent and admirable Masaccio delivered entirely from the manner of Giotto, as regards the heads, the carnations,[16] the draperies, buildings, and colouring; he also restored the practice of foreshortening, and brought to light that modern manner which, adopted in his own time, has been followed by all artists, and is pursued by our own, even to this day; gradually receiving the addition of a better grace, more fertile invention, and richer ornament; embellished and carried forward, in short, as may be seen more particularly set forth in the life of each artist; nor can we fail to remark that a new mode of colouring and foreshortening was introduced, with more natural attitudes, and a much more effectual expression of feeling in the gestures and movements of the body, art seeking to approach the truth of Nature by more correct design, and to exhibit so close a resemblance to the countenance of the living man, that each figure might at once be recognized as the person for whom it was intended. Thus the masters constantly endeavoured to reproduce what they beheld in Nature, and no more; their works became, consequently, more carefully considered and better understood. This gave them courage to impose rules of perspective, and to carry the foreshortenings precisely to the point which gives an exact imitation of the relief apparent in Nature and the real form. Minute attention to the effects of light and shade, and to various difficulties of the art, succeeded, and efforts were

---

[14] The bronze doors of the Baptistery of the Cathedral of Florence.
[15] Donatello.
[16] The flesh-tints of the human face and figure, including nudes.

made to produce a better order of composition. Landscapes, also, were attempted. Tracts of country, trees, shrubs, flowers, the clouds, the air, and other natural objects, were depicted, with some resemblance to the realities represented, insomuch that we may boldly affirm that these arts had not only become ennobled, but had attained to that flower of youth from which the fruit afterwards to follow might reasonably be looked for, and hope entertained that they would shortly reach the perfection of their existence. . . .

The Florentine Sculptor Lorenzo Ghiberti

Lorenzo[1] was the son of Bartoluccio Ghiberti,[2] and in his early youth acquired the art of the goldsmith, under the care of his father,[3] who was an excellent master, and instructed him in such sort that Lorenzo, aided by his natural abilities, became a better goldsmith than his teacher. But delighting still more in the arts of design and sculpture, he sometimes worked in colours, and at other times employed himself in the casting of small figures in bronze, which he finished very gracefully. He also took much pleasure in imitating the dies of ancient coins and medals, besides which he frequently took the portraits of his different friends from the life.

Whilst Lorenzo was thus labouring to acquire the art of goldworking with Bartoluccio, the plague, by which Florence was visited in the year 1400, broke out, as he relates himself in a book written with his own hand, wherein he discourses of matters touching the arts, and which is now in the possession of the venerable Messer Cosimo Bartoli, a Florentine gentleman.[4] To this plague were added civil discords and various troubles in the city, from which Lorenzo was compelled to depart, when he repaired to Romagna, in company with another painter, where they worked together in Rimini, painting a chamber and other works for signor Pandolfo Malatesti,[5] which were all completed by them with great diligence and to the satisfaction of that noble, who, although young, took much pleasure in all things relating to art. Lorenzo meanwhile did not remit the prosecution of his studies in relation to design, but frequently executed rilievi[6] in wax, stucco, and other materials of similar kind, well knowing that such rilievi are the drawing-exercises of sculptors, without

---

[1] Lorenzo Ghiberti (1378–1455).
[2] Bartoluccio Ghiberti was actually the stepfather of Lorenzo, whose real father was Cione di Ser Buonaccorso, also a goldsmith. When Cione died, Lorenzo's mother, Madonna Fiore, married Bartoluccio, another goldsmith.
[3] It is said that both Lorenzo's father and his stepfather instructed him in the goldsmith's art.
[4] The manuscript found its way to the Magliabecchiana Library, Florence.
[5] Pandolfo Malatesta (1370–1427) was lord of Rimini and Fano.
[6] Reliefs.

practice in which they cannot hope to bring any great work to perfection.

But Lorenzo did not long remain absent from his country. After the pestilence had ceased, the Signoria of Florence and the Guild of the Merchants resolved to proceed with the two doors of San Giovanni,[7] one of the oldest and most important churches in the city, concerning which there had already been so much discourse and so many deliberations. The time was favourable for such an undertaking, the art of sculpture then possessing able masters in abundance, foreigners as well as Florentines. Those in authority therefore, considering that the work ought to be done as well as talked of, gave orders that all the artists, masters of eminence throughout Italy, should be given to understand that they might repair to Florence, there to present a specimen of their abilities in a trial of skill, which was to be made by the composition and execution of an historical representation in bronze, similar to those which Andrea Pisano had executed for the first door.

Notice of this determination was sent by Bartoluccio to Lorenzo, who was then working in Pesaro, and whom his father-in-law urged to return to Florence, and show what he could do; saying, that this was an opportunity for making himself known and displaying his abilities, reminding him also that from the occasion now presenting itself, they might derive such advantages that neither one nor the other of them need any longer work at *pear-making*.[8] The words of Bartoluccio roused the spirit of Lorenzo in such a manner, that although the Signor Pandolfo, as well as the other painter, and all the court, were treating him with the most amicable distinction, and entreated him to remain with them, he nevertheless took leave of that noble and of the painter, who were with difficulty persuaded to let him depart, and saw him go with extreme regret; but no promises nor increase of appointments availed to detain him, every minute then seeming to Lorenzo a thousand years, until he found himself on the road to Florence.

Departing from Pesaro, therefore, he arrived safely in his native city. A great concourse of foreign artists had by this time assembled at Florence, and had presented themselves to the syndics or consuls of the Guild, who chose seven masters from the whole number: three of these were Florentines, the remaining four were Tuscans. Each of these artists received a sum of money, and it was commanded that within a year each should produce a story in bronze as a specimen of his powers, all to be of the same size, which was that of one of the compartments in the first door. The subject was chosen by the consuls, and was the Sacrifice of Isaac by his father Abraham, that being selected as presenting sufficient opportunity for the artists

[7] The doors of the Baptistery of St. John the Baptist, Florence.
[8] Making earrings; probably so-called from their favored form.

to display their mastery over the difficulties of their art: this story comprising landscape, with human figures, nude and clothed, as well as those of animals; the foremost of these figures were to be in full-relief, the second in half-relief, and the third in low-relief. The candidates for this work were Filippo di Ser Brunellesco,[9] Donato[10] and Lorenzo di Bartoluccio,[11] who were Florentines, with Jacopo della Quercia,[12] of Siena; Niccolo d'Arezzo, his disciple; Francesco di Valdambrina, and Simone da Colle, called Simon of the Bronzes.[13] All these masters made a promise before the consuls that they would deliver each his specimen completed at the prescribed time, and all set themselves to the work with the utmost care and study, putting forth all their strength, and calling all their knowledge to aid in the hope of surpassing one another. They kept their labours meanwhile entirely secret, one from the other, that they might not copy each other's plans. Lorenzo alone, who had Bartoluccio to guide him, which last suffered him to shrink before no amount of labour, but compelled him to make various models before he resolved on adopting any one of them — Lorenzo only, I say, permitted all the citizens to see his work,[14] inviting them, or any stranger who might be passing and had acquaintance with the art, to say what they thought on the subject; and these various opinions were so useful to the artist, that he produced a model, which was admirably executed and without any defect whatever. He then made the ultimate preparations, cast the work in bronze, and found it succeed to admiration; when Lorenzo, assisted by Bartoluccio his father, completed and polished the whole with such love and patience, that no work could be executed with more care, or finished with greater delicacy.

When the time arrived for comparing the different works, Lorenzo's specimen, with those of all the other masters, were found to be completed, and were given to the Guild of the Merchants for their judgment. Wherefore, all having been examined by the syndics, and by many other citizens, there were various opinions among them touching the matter. Many foreigners had assembled in Florence — some painters, some sculptors, others goldsmiths: these were all invited by the consuls, or syndics, to give judgment on those works, together with the men of the same calling who dwelt in Florence. The number of these persons was thirty-four, all well experienced in their several arts. But although there were divers opinions among them touching various points, and one preferred the manner of this candidate and one of that, yet they all agreed that Filippo di Ser Brunellesco and

---

[9] Brunelleschi. See below, page 346 and note 4 thereon.
[10] Donatello.
[11] Lorenzo Ghiberti.
[12] Jacopo della Quercia (1378–1438): one of the trail-blazers of the "new era" of sculpture, and the most famous sculptor in the history of Siena.
[13] Other noted sculptors of the day.
[14] An argument against Iron Curtains?

Lorenzo di Bartoluccio had presented works of better composition, more richly adorned with figures, and more delicately finished than was that of Donato, although in his specimen also the design was exceedingly good.[15] In the work of Jacopo della Quercia the figures were carefully designed, but wanted delicacy of finish. In the specimen of Francesco da Valdambrina the heads were beautiful and the work well finished, but the composition was confused. That of Simon da Colle was a beautiful specimen of casting, because that was his peculiar branch of art, but the design was not good. The specimen presented by Niccolo d'Arezza showed the hand of the practiced master, but the figures were stunted and the work not well finished. The story executed by Lorenzo only, which is still to be seen in the Hall of Audience, belonging to the Guild of the Merchants,[16] was perfect in all its parts. The whole work was admirably designed and very finely composed: the figures graceful, elegant, and in beautiful attitudes; and all was finished with so much care and to such perfection, that the work seemed not to have been cast and polished with instruments of iron, but looked rather as though it had been blown with the breath.

When Donato and Filippo saw the care and success with which Lorenzo had completed his specimen, they drew aside together, and, conferring with each other, decided that the work ought to be given to him, because it appeared to them that the public advantage, as well as individual benefit, would be thus best secured and promoted, since Lorenzo being very young — for he had not completed his twentieth year — would have the opportunity, while exercising his talents on that magnificent work, of producing those noble fruits of which his beautiful story gave so fair a hope. They declared that, according to their judgment, Lorenzo had executed his specimen more perfectly than any of the other artists, and that it would be a more obvious proof of envy to deprive him of it, than of rectitude to accord it to him.

Lorenzo therefore commenced the works for those doors, beginning with that which is opposite to the house of the wardens, and first he prepared a model, in wood, of the exact size which each compartment was to have in the metal, with the framework and the ornaments of the angles, on each of which was placed a head; and all the decorations by which the stories of every compartment were to be surrounded. After having prepared and dried the mould with infinite care and exactitude in a workshop that he had procured oppo-

[15] Since Donatello was only seventeen at the time, some believe that he could not have competed, and that the confusion is due to a design he made later for the sacristy doors of the Cathedral, which commission he received but never completed.

[16] The panels of Lorenzo Ghiberti and Brunelleschi for the competition of 1401, probably completed in 1402, found their way to the National Museum of Florence.

site to Santa Maria Nuova, where the Weavers' Hospital now stands, and which was called the threshing-floor, he built an immense furnace, which I well remember to have seen, and there cast the portion he had prepared, in metal. But it pleased the fates that this should not succeed; yet Lorenzo, perceiving in what point he had failed, did not lose courage, nor permit himself to despond; but having promptly prepared another mould, without making the occurrence known to any one, he cast the piece again, when it succeeded perfectly. In this manner the artist continued the whole work, casting each story himself; and when he had completed and polished it, he fixed it in place. The arrangement of the stories is similar to that adopted by Andrea Pisano in constructing the first door, which had been designed for him by Giotto. The number of them is twenty; the subjects being taken from the New Testament: beneath these stories, in eight similar compartments, are figures of the four Evangelists, two on each leaf or fold of the door, with the four Doctors of the Church in like manner.[17] All these figures are varied in their attitudes, vestments, and other particulars: one is reading, another writing; some are in deep meditation, and differing thus one from another, all, whether acting or reflecting, are equally lifelike. The framework which encloses each picture is enriched with ornaments of ivy leaves and foliage of other kinds, with mouldings between them, and on each angle is a male or female head in full relief, purporting to represent the Prophets and Sybils. They are very beautiful, and their variety serves to prove the fertility of invention possessed by the master.[18] . . .

This great work was carried forward to its completion without sparing either cost, time, or whatever else could promote the successful termination of the enterprise; the nude figures are in all parts most beautiful, and the draperies, although still retaining some slight trace of the older manner of Giotto's day, have, nevertheless, a direct tendency towards that of more modern times, and this gives to figures of that size a grace of character which is very attractive. The composition of each story is, of a truth, so well arranged, the figures are so judiciously grouped, and so finely executed, that the whole work richly deserves the praise bestowed on it in the commencement by Filippo. The merits of Lorenzo were most honourably acknowledged by his fellow citizens, and from them in general, as well as from the artists in particular, whether compatriots or foreigners, he received the highest commendations. This work, with its exterior ornaments, which are also of metal, representing festoons of fruits, and figures of animals, cost 22,000 florins, and the door weighed 34,000 pounds.

This undertaking being completed,[19] the consuls of the Guild of

---

[17] There are actually two doors with fourteen panels each.
[18] Vasari's description of the panels is omitted here.
[19] In 1424. Ghiberti had been at work 21 years: 1403–1424.

Merchants considered that they had been extremely well served, and hearing the praises given to Lorenzo by all beholders, they determined that he should execute a second work, to be placed in one of the niches outside Or San Michele, and opposite to the building occupied by the cloth-dressers. This was a statue in bronze, four braccia and a half high, to the honour of St. John the Baptist. Lorenzo commenced the work accordingly; nor did he ever leave it until its entire completion: this figure also has been, and still is, highly commended: the name of the artist is engraved on the mantle.[1] . . .

The city of Florence had acquired so much glory and praise from the admirable works of this most ingenious artist, that a resolution was taken by the consuls of the Guild of the Merchants to give him a commission for the third door[2] of San Giovanni, which was also to be of bronze. In the case of the first door,[3] which Lorenzo had made, he had followed the directions of the consuls, as regarded the decoration of the frame-work, by which the figures were surrounded, since they had determined that the general form of all the doors should be similar to that constructed by Andrea Pisano. But having now seen how greatly Lorenzo had surpassed the elder master, the consuls resolved to change the position of the doors, and whereas that of Andrea had previously occupied the centre, they now placed it on the side of the building which stands opposite to the Misericordia,[4] proposing that the new door to be made by Lorenzo should be substituted for it, and should thenceforward occupy the centre; for they fully expected that he would put forth every effort and zealously employ all the resources of his art, insomuch that they now placed themselves in his hands without reserve, referring the whole matter entirely to his care, and declaring that they gave him full permission to proceed with the work as he should think best, and to do whatever might most effectually secure that this third door should be the richest, most highly adorned, most beautiful and most perfect, that he could possibly contrive, or that could be imagined.[5] Nor would they have him spare either time or labour, to the end that, as he had previously surpassed all the sculptors that had lived before him, so he might now eclipse and surpass all his own earlier works.

Lorenzo commenced the undertaking, calling all his knowledge and ability of every kind to aid. He divided his work into ten compartments, or pictures, five on each side,[6] which gave to each compartment one braccio and a third; around the whole and serving as an ornament to the frame-work which encloses the stories, are niches

---

[1] Ghiberti also did statues of St. Matthew and St. Stephen.
[2] Actually doors; read "entrance" or "gate."
[3] Doors, as above.
[4] The Misericordia then stood where the Bigallo now is, on the east side of the Baptistery.
[5] In Ghiberti's own words. The consuls, however, chose or suggested subjects.
[6] Five on each door.

filled with figures in almost full relief, the number of which is twenty, all of exceeding beauty. Among others is the naked form of Sampson, with a jaw-bone in his hand and his arm around a column, and this exhibits a degree of perfection which will bear comparison with that displayed by the ancients in their figures of Hercules, whether in bronze or marble. The same may be said of Joshua, who is in the act of addressing his army, and really seems to speak: there are besides, many prophets and sybils, adorned in a richly-varied manner, and displaying the utmost fertility of invention in draperies, head-dresses, ornaments of the hair, and other decorations.[7] . . .

. . . The justice of the praises bestowed on Lorenzo for this work may be inferred from the words of Michael Angelo Buonarotti, who, standing to look at these doors, and being asked what he thought of them, and whether they were beautiful, replied in these words: — *"They are so beautiful, that they might fittingly stand at the gates of Paradise,"* a truly appropriate tribute, and offered by him who could well judge of the work. Well indeed might Lorenzo complete his undertaking successfully, since, from his twentieth year, wherein he commenced these doors, he laboured at them for forty years with a patience and industry more than extreme, and beyond the power of words to express.[8]

After this most stupendous work, Lorenzo undertook the bronze ornaments of that door of the same church which is opposite to the Misericordia, with those admirably beautiful decorations of foliage which he did not survive to finish, being unexpectedly overtaken by death when he was making his arrangements and had already nearly completed the model for reconstructing the door previously erected by Andrea Pisano.[9] . . .

Masaccio,[1] Painter, of San Giovanni, in Valdarno

When nature has called into existence a genius of surpassing excellence in any vocation, it is not her custom to leave him alone: on the contrary, she for the most part gives life to another, created at the same time and in the same locality, whence the emulation of each is excited and they mutually serve as stimulants one to the other. And this, in addition to the great advantage derived from it by them who, thus united, make their efforts in common, has the further effect of awakening the minds of those who come after them, and who are excited to labour with the utmost zeal and industry for the attain-

[7] Vasari goes on to describe the doors in detail. The stories on the panels were all from the Old Testament.
[8] Vasari is evidently speaking of both pairs of doors, which actually took about 48 years to complete: Ghiberti's first pair 1403–24, and his second pair 1425–52.
[9] Ghiberti died in 1455.
[1] Tommaso Guidi, known as Masaccio (1402–28).

ment of that glorious reputation and those honours which they daily hear ascribed to their distinguished predecessors; and that this is true we find proved by the fact that Florence produced at one and the same time Filippo,[2] Donato,[3] Lorenzo,[4] Paolo Uccello,[5] and Masaccio, each most excellent in his peculiar walk, and all contributing to banish the coarse and hard manner which had prevailed up to the period of their existence; nor was this all, for the minds of those who succeeded these masters were so effectually inflamed by their admirable works, that the modes of production in these arts were brought to that grandeur and height of perfection which are made manifest in the performances of our own times. We then, of a truth, have the greatest obligation to those masters who by their labours first taught us the true path by which to attain the highest summit of perfection; and as touching the good manner in painting, most especially are we indebted to Masaccio, since it was he who, eager for the acquirement of fame, first attained the clear perception that painting is no other than the close imitation, by drawing and colouring simply, of all the forms presented by nature, exhibiting them as they are produced by her, and that whosoever shall most perfectly effect this, may be said to have most nearly approached the summit of excellence. The conviction of this truth formed by Masaccio was the cause, I say, of his attaining to so much knowledge by means of perpetual study, that he may be accounted among the first by whom art was in a great measure delivered from rudeness and hardness: he it was who taught the method of overcoming many difficulties, and led the way to the adoption of those beautiful attitudes and movements never exhibited by any painter before his day, while he also imparted a life and force to his figures with a certain roundness and relief, which render them truly characteristic and natural. Possessing extreme rectitude of judgment, Masaccio perceived that all figures not sufficiently foreshortened to appear standing firmly on the plane whereon they are placed, but reared up on the points of their feet, must needs be deprived of all grace and excellence in the most important essentials, and that those who so represent them prove themselves unacquainted with the art of foreshortening. It is true that Paolo Uccello had given his attention to this subject, and had done something in the matter, which did to a certain extent lessen the difficulty; but Masaccio, differing from him in various particulars, managed his foreshortenings with much greater ability, exhibiting his mastery of this point in every kind and variety of view, and succeeding better than any artist had done before him. He moreover imparted extreme softness and harmony to his paintings, and was careful to have the carnations[6] of the heads and other nude

[2] Brunelleschi.   [3] Donatello.   [4] Ghiberti.
[5] Paolo Uccello (1397–1475), a disciple of Ghiberti, became famous for his development of scientific perspective.
[6] Flesh-tints.

parts in accordance with the colours of the draperies, which he represented with few and simple folds, as they are seen in the natural object. This has been of the utmost utility to succeeding artists, and Masaccio deserves to be considered the inventor of that manner, since it may be truly affirmed that the works produced before his time should be called paintings; but that his performance, when compared with those works, might be designated life, truth, and nature.

The birth-place of this master was Castello San Giovanni, in the Valdarno, and it is said that some figures are still to be seen there which were executed by Masaccio in his earliest childhood.[7] He was remarkably absent and careless of externals, as one who, having fixed his whole mind and thought on art, cared little for himself or his personal interests, and meddled still less with the affairs of others; he could by no means be induced to bestow his attention on the cares of the world and the general interests of life, insomuch that he would give no thought to his clothing, nor was he ever wont to require payment from his debtors, until he was first reduced to the extremity of want; and for all this, instead of being called Tommaso, which was his name, he received from every one the cognomen of Masaccio,[8] by no means for any vice of disposition, since he was goodness itself, but merely from his excessive negligence and disregard of himself; for he was always so friendly to all, so ready to oblige and do service to others, that a better or kinder man could not possibly be desired.

Masaccio's first labours in art were commenced at the time when Masolino da Panicale was working at the chapel of the Brancacci, in the church of the Carmine, at Florence: and he sought earnestly to follow in the track pursued by Donato and Filippo Brunelleschi (although their branch of art, being sculpture, was different from his own), his efforts being perpetually directed to the giving his figures a life and animation which should render them similar to nature. The outlines and colouring of Masaccio are so different from those of the masters preceding him, that his works may be safely brought in comparison with the drawing and colouring of any produced in later times. Studious and persevering in his labours, this artist successfully coped with the difficulties of perspective, which he overcame most admirably and with true artistic skill, as may be seen in a story representing Christ curing a man possessed by a demon, which comprises a number of small figures and is now in the possession of Ridolfo del Ghirlandajo.[9] In this work are buildings beautifully drawn in perspective, and so treated that the inside is seen at the same time. . . .

---

[7] It is said that there was among these a striking, unforgettable picture of an old woman spinning.

[8] Awkward, clumsy, stupid, slovenly, lubberly, or careless, in a mildly chiding sense.

[9] Its fate is unknown.

342   The Renaissance

... Not finding himself at his ease in Florence, and stimulated by
his love and zeal for art, the master resolved to proceed to Rome,
that he might there learn to surpass others, and this he effected. In
Rome Masaccio acquired high reputation, and in a chapel of the
church of San Clemente, he painted a Crucifixion in fresco, with the
thieves on their crosses, and also stories from the life of St. Catherine
the martyr. This work he executed for the cardinal of San Clemente.[10]
He likewise painted many pictures in distemper;[11] but in the troubled
times of Rome these have all been destroyed or lost. There is one
remaining in the church of Santa Maria Maggiore, and in a small chapel
near the sacristy, wherein are four saints so admirably done that they
seem rather to be executed in relief than on the plain surface: in the
midst of these is Santa Maria della Neve. The portrait of Pope
Martin, taken from nature, is also by this master: the pontiff is represented holding a spade in his hand, with which he is tracing out the
foundations of the church; near the pope stands the figure of the
Emperor Sigismund II.[12] I was one day examining that work with
Michael Angelo Buonarotti, when he praised it very highly, remarking at the same time that the two personages depicted had both lived
in Masaccio's day. Whilst this master was in Rome he was appointed
to adorn the walls of the church of San Giovanni in that city, Pisanello
and Gentile da Fabriano being also employed by Pope Martin to
decorate the walls of the same edifice with their paintings.[13] But
Masaccio having received intelligence that Cosmo de Medici, from
whom he had received favour and protection, had been recalled from
exile,[14] again repaired to Florence; there, Masolino da Panicale being
dead,[15] Masaccio was appointed to continue the paintings of the
Brancacci chapel, in the church of the Carmine, left unfinished, as we
have said, by the death[16] of Masolino. Before entering on this work,
our artist painted, as if by way of specimen, and to show to what
extent he had ameliorated his art, that figure of St. Paul[17] which
stands near the place of the bell-ropes; and it is certain that the master
displayed great excellence in this work; for the figure of the saint,
which is the portrait of Bartolo di Angiolino Angiolini,[18] taken from

[10] The Crucifixion of Christ is painted on the wall behind the altar; the
stories from the life of St. Catherine in nine compartments on the lateral walls.
[11] A pigment mixed with a vehicle soluble in water.
[12] Martin V was Pope from 1417 to 1431; Sigismund, Emperor of Germany,
1411–37.
[13] This collaboration is questioned.
[14] This does not seem to have been the reason, since Cosimo de Medici was
exiled in 1433 and returned in 1434, but Masaccio died in 1428.
[15] Masolino da Panicale (1383–c. 1445), Florentine painter, was not dead,
but was apparently absent in Buda, Hungary, from 1423 to 1427.
[16] Absence, rather than death. Masaccio worked in the Brancacci Chapel
from 1422/3 to 1428, and here he did his most famous paintings.
[17] Since lost.
[18] From 1406 to 1432 Bartolo Angiolini held various important offices in the
Florentine Republic.

the life, has something in it so impressive, and is so beautiful and lifelike, that it seems to want nothing but speech; insomuch that he who has not known St. Paul has but to look at this picture, when he will at once behold the noble deportment of him who conjoined the Roman culture and eloquence with that invincible force which distinguished the exalted and devout character of this apostle, whose every care and thought were given to the affairs of the faith. In this picture, Masaccio also afforded further proof of his mastery over the difficulties of foreshortening: the powers of this artist as regards that point were indeed truly wonderful, as may be seen even now in the feet of this apostle, where he has overcome the difficulty in a manner that may well be admired, when we consider the rude ancient fashion of placing all the figures on the points of their feet; and this manner was persisted in even to his day, not having been fully corrected by the older artists; he it was who (earlier than any other master) brought this point of art to the perfection which it has attained in our own times.

While Masaccio was employed on this work, it chanced that the aforesaid church of the Carmine was consecrated,[19] and in memory of that event Masaccio painted the whole ceremony of the consecration as it had occurred, in chiaroscuro, over the door within the cloister which leads into the convent. In this work,[1] which was in "terra-verde," the master painted the portraits of a great number of the citizens who make part of the procession, clothed in hoods and mantles; among these figures were those of Filippo di Ser Brunellesco, in "zoccoli,"[2] Donatello, Masolino da Panicale, who had been his master, Antonio Brancacci, for whom it was that the above-mentioned chapel was painted, Niccolo da Uzzano, Giovanni di Bicci de' Medici, and Bartolommeo Valori, all of whose portraits, painted by the same artist, are also in the house of Simon Corsi, a Florentine gentleman.[3] Masaccio likewise placed the portrait of Lorenzo Ridolfi,[4] who was then ambassador from the Florentine republic to the republic of Venice, among those of the picture of the consecration; and not only did he therein depict the above-named personages from the life, but the door of the convent is also portrayed as it stood, with the porter holding the keys in his hand. . . .

After this Masaccio returned to the works of the Brancacci chapel, wherein he continued the stories from the life of St. Peter, commenced by Masolino da Panicale, of which he completed a certain part.[5] The

[19] April 19, 1422.   [1] Subsequently effaced with whitewash.
[2] Wooden shoes.
[3] Of the fate of these portraits nothing is known.
[4] Ridolfi was twice ambassador to Venice: in 1402 and 1425.
[5] The exact part played by Masolino in the Brancacci paintings is disputed, as is the exact extent of Masaccio's paintings. Filippo Lippi also did some of the painting. But that the masterpieces, such as the "Tribute Money" and the "Baptism by Peter," ascribed to Masaccio are his is certain.

installation of St. Peter as first pontiff, that is to say, the healing of the sick, the raising to life of the dead, and the making the halt sound, by the shadow of the apostle falling on them as he approaches the temple with St. John. But remarkable above all the rest is the story which represents St. Peter, when, by command of Christ, he draws money to pay the tribute from the mouth of the fish; for besides that we have here the portrait of Masaccio himself, in the figure of one of the apostles (the last painted by his own hand, with the aid of a mirror, and so admirably done that it seems to live and breathe); there is, moreover, great spirit in the figure of St. Peter as he looks inquiringly towards Jesus, while the attention given by the apostles to what is taking place, as they stand around their master awaiting his determination, is expressed with so much truth, and their various attitudes and gestures are so full of animation, that they seem to be those of living men. St. Peter, more particularly, bent forward and making considerable effort as he draws the money from the mouth of the fish, has his face reddened with the exertion and position. When he pays the tribute also, the expression of his face as he carefully counts the money, with that of him who receives it, and which last betrays an excessive eagerness to become possessed of it; all this is depicted with the most vivid truth, the latter regarding the coins which he holds in his hand with the greatest pleasure. Masaccio also depicted the restoration to life of the king's son by St. Peter and St. Paul, but this last work remained unfinished at the death of Masaccio, and was afterwards completed by Filippino.[6] In the picture which represents St. Peter administering the rite of Baptism,[7] there is a figure which has always been most highly celebrated: it is that of a naked youth, among those who are baptised, and who is shivering with the cold. This is in all respects so admirable and in so fine a manner, that it has ever since been held in reverence and admiration by all artists, whether of those times or of a later period. This chapel has indeed been continually frequented by an infinite number of students and masters, for the sake of the benefit to be derived from these works, in which there are still some heads so beautiful and life-like, that we may safely affirm no artist of that period to have approached so nearly to the manner of the moderns as did Masaccio. His works do indeed merit all the praise they have received, and the rather as it was by him that the path was opened to the excellent manner prevalent in our own times; to the truth of which we have testimony in the fact that all the most celebrated sculptors and painters since Masaccio's day have become excellent and illustrious by studying their art in this chapel. Among these may be enumerated Fra Gio-

[6] **Filippo** or **Filippino Lippi** (1412–69), also known as Fra Lippo Lippi.
[7] The "Baptism by Peter" is considered an epochal turning point in the history of art.

vanni de Fiesole,[8] Fra Filippo Filippino, who completed the work, Alesso Baldovinetti, Andrea del Castagna, Andrea del Verrocchio, Domenico del Ghirlandajo, Sandro di Botticello, Leonardo da Vinci, Pietro Perugino, Fra Bartolommeo di San Marco, Mariotti Albertinelli, and the sublime[9] Michael Angelo Buonarrotti. Raphael of Urbino also made his first commencement of his exquisite manner in this place, and to these must be added Granaccio, Lorenzo di Credi, Ridolfo del Ghirlandajo, Andrea del Sarto, Rosso, Francia Bigio, or Franciabigio, Baccio Bandinelli, Alonzo Spagnolo, Jacopo da Pontormo, Pierino del Vaga, and Toto del Nunziata; all in short who have sought to acquire their art in its perfection, have constantly repaired to study it in this chapel,[10] there imbibing the precepts and rules necessary to be followed for the ensurance of success, and learning to labour effectually from the figures of Masaccio. And if I have here made mention of but few among the foreigners who have frequented this chapel for purposes of study, let it suffice to say that where the heads go, there the members are certain to follow. But although the works of Masaccio have ever been held in such high estimation, yet it is nevertheless the opinion, or rather the firm belief, of many, that he would have done still greater things for art, had not death, which tore him from us at the age of twenty-six, so prematurely deprived the world of this great master.[11] . . .

The Florentine Sculptor and Architect Filippo Brunelleschi[1]

There are many men who, though formed by nature with small persons and insignificant features, are yet endowed with so much greatness of soul and force of character, that unless they can occupy themselves with difficult — nay, almost impossible undertakings, and carry these enterprises to perfection to the admiration of others, they are incapable of finding peace for their lives. And, however mean or unpromising may be the occasion presented to such persons, however trifling the object to be attained, they find means to make it important, and to give it elevation. Therefore it is that none should

---

[8] Giovanni da Fiesole, or Fra Angelico (1387–1455), a Dominican friar, was already a great painter, but his "Gothic" painting seems to show evidences of the school of Masaccio, according to critics.

[9] Vasari has "the most divine."

[10] The Brancacci Chapel did become a renowned "school of art."

[11] Masaccio apparently died in 1428 at the age of 26 or 27. Possibly to escape his creditors or the prosaic Masolino, he had suddenly left Florence for Rome and promptly disappeared. It is said that he died of a wound or from poison, but this is conjecture.

[1] In this life of Filippo Brunelleschi (1377–1446), Vasari was able to draw on a biography by Antonio Manetti (1423–97).

look with contemptuous glance on any one whom he may encounter, having an aspect divested of that grace and beauty which we might expect that Nature would confer, even from his birth, upon him who is to exhibit distinguished talent, since it is beyond doubt that beneath the clods of earth the veins of gold lie hidden. So much force of mind, and so much goodness of heart, are frequently born with men of the most unpromising exterior, that if these be conjoined with nobility of soul, nothing short of the most important and valuable results can be looked for from them, since they labour to embellish the unsightly form by the beauty and brightness of the spirit. This was clearly exemplified in Filippo di Ser Brunellesco, who was no less diminutive in person than Messer Forete da Rabatta and Giotto,[2] but who was of such exalted genius withal, that we may truly declare him to have been given to us by heaven, for the purpose of imparting a new spirit to architecture, which for hundreds of years had been lost: for the men of those times had badly expended great treasures in the erection of buildings without order, constructed in a wretched manner after deplorable designs, with fantastic inventions, laboured graces, and worse decorations.[3] . . .

Filippo and Donato,[4] who were together, resolved to depart from Florence in company, and to remain in Rome for some years, Filippo proposing to pursue the study of architecture, and Donato that of sculpture. And this Filippo did, desiring to surpass Lorenzo and Donato, in proportion as architecture is more useful to man than are sculpture and paintings, he first sold a small farm which he possessed at Settignano, when both artists departed from Florence and proceeded to Rome, where, when Filippo beheld the magnificence of the buildings and the perfection of the churches, he stood like one amazed, and seemed to have lost his wits.[5] They instantly made preparations for measuring the cornices and taking the ground plans of these edifices, Donato and himself both labouring continually, and sparing neither time nor cost. No place was left unvisited by them, either in Rome or without the city, and in the Campagna; nor did they fail to take the dimensions of any thing good within their reach. And as Filippo was free from all household cares, he gave himself up so exclusively to his studies, that he took no time either to eat or sleep; his every thought was of Architecture, which was then extinct: I mean the good old manner, and not the Gothic and barbarous one, which was much practised at that period. Filippo had two very great purposes in his mind, the one being to restore to light the good manner in architecture, which, if he could effect, he believed that he

[2] Cf. the 5th tale of the 6th day of Boccaccio's *Decameron*.
[3] An obvious exaggeration, but in the spirit of Renaissance Italians.
[4] Donatello. About 1402; following the 1401-2 competition for the Baptistery doors, according to Vasari. Brunelleschi had been the runner-up to Ghiberti, to whom, says Vasari, he had gracefully deferred.
[5] Some enthusiasts hail this as the dawn of modern architecture.

should leave a no less illustrious memorial of himself than Cimabue and Giotto had done; the other was to discover a method for constructing the Cupola of Santa Maria del Fiore in Florence, the difficulties of which were so great, that after the death of Arnolfo Lapi, no one had ever been found of sufficient courage to attempt the vaulting of that Cupola without an enormous expense of scaffolding.[6] He did not impart this purpose, either to Donato or to any living soul, but he never rested while in Rome until he had well pondered on all the difficulties involved in the vaulting of the *Ritonda* in that city (*the Pantheon*), and had maturely considered the means by which it might be effected. He also well examined and made careful drawings of all the vaults and arches of antiquity:[7] to these he devoted perpetual study, and if by chance the artists found fragments of capitals, columns, cornices, or basements of buildings buried in the earth, they set labourers to work and caused them to be dug out, until the foundation was laid open to their view.[8] Reports of this being spread about Rome, the artists were called "treasure-seekers", and this name they frequently heard as they passed, negligently clothed, along the streets, the people believing them to be men who studied geomancy, for the discovery of treasures; the case of which was that they had one day found an ancient vase of earth, full of coins. . . .

In the year 1420, all these foreign masters were at length assembled in Florence, with those of Tuscany, and all the best Florentine artists in design.[9] Filippo likewise then returned from Rome. They all assembled, therefore, in the hall of the wardens of Santa Maria del Fiore, the Syndics[10] and Superintendents, together with a select number of the most capable and ingenious citizens being present, to the end that having heard the opinion of each on the subject, they might at length decide on the method to be adopted for vaulting the tribune.[11] Being called into the audience, the opinions of all were heard one after another, and each architect declared the method which he had thought of adopting. And a fine thing it was to hear the strange and various notions then propounded on that matter: for one said that columns must be raised from the ground up, and that on these they must turn the arches, whereon the woodwork for supporting the weight must rest. Others affirmed that the vault should be turned in cysteolite or sponge-stone, (spugna), thereby to diminish the weight; and several of the masters agreed in the opinion that a column must be erected in the centre, and the cupola raised in the form of a pavilion, like that

[6] The city of Florence voted the new cathedral in 1294. Its first architect, Arnolfo Lapi, died in 1302. Construction had reached the point where it was necessary to decide just how to vault the large space 140–150 feet wide
[7] Many more ancient buildings survived in Rome then than now.
[8] Note these 15th-century archaeologists and their antique inspiration.
[9] There is a question concerning the presence of foreign competitors.
[10] Officials representing the Republic.
[11] The tribune was a raised platform.

of San Giovanni in Florence.[12] Nay, there were not wanting those who maintained that it would be a good plan to fill the space with earth, among which small coins (quatrini) should be mingled, that when the cupola should be raised, they might then give permission that whoever should desire the soil might go to fetch it, when the people would immediately carry it away without expense.[13] Filippo alone declared that the cupola might be erected without so great a mass of wood-work, without a column in the centre, and without the mound of earth; at a much lighter expense than would be caused by so many arches, and very easily, without any frame-work whatever.

Hearing this, the syndics, who were listening in the expectation of hearing some fine method, felt convinced that Filippo had talked like a mere simpleton, as did the superintendents, and all the other citizens; they derided him therefore, laughing at him, and turning away; they bade him discourse of something else, for that this was the talk of a fool or madman, as he was. . . . Filippo, on the other hand, who had spent so many years in close study to prepare himself for this work, knew not to what course to betake himself, and was many times on the poinnt of leaving Florence. Still, if he desired to conquer, it was necessary to arm himself with patience, and he had seen enough to know that the heads of that city seldom remained long fixed to one resolution. He might easily have shown them a small model which he had secretly made, but he would not do so, knowing the imperfect intelligence of the syndics, the envy of the artists, and the instability of the citizens, who favoured now one and now another, as each chanced to please them. And I do not wonder at this, because every one in Florence professes to know as much of these matters as do the most experienced masters, although there are very few who really understand them; a truth which we may be permitted to affirm without offence to those who are well informed on the subject. What Filippo therefore could not effect before the tribunal, he began to attempt with individuals, and talking apart now with a syndic, now with a warden, and again with different citizens, showing moreover certain parts of his design; he thus brought them at length to resolve on confiding the conduct of this work either to him or to one of the foreign architects. Hereupon, the syndics, the wardens, and the citizens, selected to be judges in the matter, having regained courage, gathered together once again, and the architects disputed respecting the matter before them; but all were put down and vanquished on sufficient grounds by Filippo, and here it is said that the dispute of the egg arose, in the manner following. The other architects desired that Filippo should explain his purpose minutely, and show his model as they had shown theirs. This he would not do, but proposed to all the masters, foreigners and compatriots, that he who could make

[12] Not the dome itself, but its external covering has a pavilion-like (or tent-like) form.
[13] Note the poverty of the masses.

an egg stand upright on a piece of smooth marble, should be appointed to build the cupola, since in doing that, his genius would be made manifest. They took an egg accordingly, and all those masters did their best to make it stand upright, but none discovered the method of doing so. Wherefore, Filippo, being told that he might make it stand himself, took it daintily into his hand, gave the end of it a blow on the plane of the marble, and made it stand upright.[14] Beholding this the artists loudly protested, exclaiming, that they could all have done the same; but Filippo replied, laughing, that they might also know how to construct the cupola, if they had seen the model and design. It was thus at length resolved that Filippo should receive the charge of conducting the work, but he was told that he must furnish the syndics and wardens with more exact information. . . .

When Filippo had written the same, he repaired in the morning to the tribunal, and gave his paper to the Syndics and Wardens, who took the whole of it into their consideration; and, although they were not able to understand it all, yet seeing the confidence of Filippo, and finding that the other architects gave no evidence of having better grounds to proceed on, — he moreover showing a manifest security, by constantly repeating the same things in such a manner that he had all the appearance of having vaulted ten Cupolas; — the Syndics, seeing all this, retired apart, and finally resolved to give him the work: they would have liked to see some example of the manner in which he meant to turn this vault without framework, but to all the rest they gave their approbation.[15] And fortune was favourable to this desire: Bartolommeo Barbadori having determined to build a chapel in Santa Felicita, and having spoken concerning it with Filippo, the latter had commenced the work, and caused the chapel, which is on the right of the entrance, where is also the holy water vase (likewise by the hand of Filippo), to be vaulted without any framework. At the same time he constructed another, in like manner, for Stiatta Ridolfi, in the church of Santo Jacopo sopr' Arno; that, namely, beside the chapel of the High Altar; and these works obtained him more credit than was given to his words. The Consuls and wardens feeling at length assured, by the writing that he had given them, and by the works which they had seen, entrusted the Cupola to his care, and he was made principal master of the works by a majority of votes. They would nevertheless not commission him to proceed beyond the height of twelve braccia, telling him that they desired to see how the work would succeed, but that if it proceeded as successfully as he expected, they would not fail to give him the appointment for the remainder. . . .

Drawings and models were meanwhile continually prepared by

---

[14] A similar story is told of Columbus.

[15] The hesitance of the Florentine officials was understandable. Such a dome had not been attempted since that of Sancta (Hagia) Sophia in Constantinople almost nine centuries earlier, and Brunelleschi's proposed methods were daring.

Filippo, for the most minute portions of the building, for the stages or scaffolds for the workmen, and for the machines used in raising the materials. There were nevertheless several malicious persons, friends of Lorenzo,[16] who did not cease to torment him by daily bringing forward models in rivalry of those constructed by him, insomuch that one was made by Maestro Antonio da Verzelli,[17] and other masters who were favoured and brought into notice — now by one citizen and now by another, their fickleness and mutability betraying the insufficiency of their knowledge and the weakness of their judgment, since having perfection within their reach, they perpetually brought forward the imperfect and useless.

The chain-work was now completed around all the eight sides,[18] and the builders, animated by success, worked vigorously; but being pressed more than usual by Filippo, and having received certain reprimands concerning the masonry and in relation to other matters of daily occurrence, discontents began to prevail. Moved by this circumstance and by their envy, the chiefs among them drew together and got up a faction, declaring that the work was a laborious and perilous undertaking, and that they would not proceed with the vaulting of the Cupola, but on condition of receiving large payments, although their wages had already been increased and were much higher than was usual: by these means they hoped to injure Filippo and increase their own gains. This circumstance displeased the wardens greatly, as it did Filippo also; but the latter, having reflected on the matter, took his resolution, and one Saturday evening he dismissed them all. The men seeing themselves thus sent about their business, and not knowing how the affair would turn, were very sullen; but on the following Monday Filippo set ten Lombards to work at the building, and by remaining constantly present with them, and saying, "do this here" and "do that there", he taught them so much in one day that they were able to continue the works during many weeks. The masons seeing themselves thus disgraced as well as deprived of their employment, and knowing that they would find no work equally profitable, sent messengers to Filippo, declaring that they would willingly return, and recommending themselves to his consideration. Filippo kept them for several days in suspense, and seemed not inclined to admit them again; they were afterwards re-

[16] Ghiberti's friends had earlier obtained his appointment as co-architect, but the unhappy Brunelleschi had managed to have Lorenzo's incompetence as an architect displayed and himself restored as sole architect.
[17] A carpenter who in 1423 received a florin in payment for a device for raising stone.
[18] The construction of the huge dome was intricate and ingenious. Two concentric, interjoined octagonal domes, 140 to 150 ft. in diameter, spring 130 ft. above their base, an octagonal drum, at a height of 175 ft. above the ground, for a total height of 305 ft. Iron clamps join huge oaken girders and an invisible chain circles the base, which lacks any heavy piers as supports. The dome is comparable to that of St. Peter's, but higher, lighter, and stronger.

instated, but with lower wages than they had received at first: thus where they had thought to make gain they suffered loss, and by seek- to revenge themselves on Filippo, they brought injury and shame on their own heads.[19]

When the building was seen to proceed so happily, the genius of Filippo obtained its due consideration; and, by all who judged dispassionately, he was already held to have shown a boldness which has, perhaps, never before been displayed in their works, by any architect ancient or modern. This opinion was confirmed by the fact that Filippo now brought out his model, in which all might see the extraordinary amount of thought bestowed on every detail of the building. The varied invention displayed in the staircases, in the provision of lights, both within and without, so that none might strike or injure themselves in the darkness, were all made manifest, with the careful consideration evinced by the different supports of iron which were placed to assist the footsteps wherever the ascent was steep. In addition to all this, Filippo had even thought of the irons for fixing scaffolds within the cupola, if ever they should be required for the execution of mosiacs or pictures; he had selected the least dangerous positions for the places of the conduits, to be afterwards constructed for carrying off the rain water, had shown where these were to be covered and where uncovered; and had moreover contrived different outlets and appertures, whereby the force of the winds should be diminished, to the end that neither vapours nor the vibrations of the earth should have power to do injury to the building: all which proved the extent to which he had profited by his studies, during the many years of his residence in Rome. When in addition to these things, the superintendents considered how much he had accomplished in the shaping, fixing, uniting, and securing the stones of this immense pile, they were almost awe-struck on perceiving that the mind of one man had been capable of all that Filippo had now proved himself able to perform. His powers and facilities continually increased, and that to such an extent, that there was no operation, however difficult and complex, which he did not render easy and simple; of this he gave proof in one instance among others, by the employment of wheels and counterpoises to raise heavy weights, so that one ox could draw more than six pairs could have moved by the ordinary methods. The building had now reached such a height, that when a man had once arrived at the summit, it was a very great labour to descend to the ground, and the workmen lost much time in going to their meals, and to drink; they also suffered great inconvenience in the heat of the day from the same cause; arrangements were therefore made by Filippo, for opening wine-shops and eating-houses in the Cupola; where the required food being sold, none were compelled to leave their labour until the evening, which was a relief

[19] Note 15th-century labor relations and trials of an architect-contractor.

and convenience to the men, as well as a very important advantage to the work. Perceiving the building to proceed rapidly, and finding all his undertakings happily successful, the zeal and confidence of Filippo increased, and he laboured perpetually; he went himself to the ovens where the bricks were made, examined the clay, proved the quality of the working, and when they were baked he would select and set them apart, with his own hands. In like manner, while the stones were under the hands of the stone-cutters, he would look narrowly to see that they were hard and free from clefts; he supplied the stone-cutters with models in wood or wax, or hastily cut on the spot from turnips, to direct them in the shaping and junction of the different masses; he did the same thing for the men who prepared the iron-work; Filippo likewise invented hooked hinges, with the mode of fixing them to the door-posts, and greatly facilitated the practice of architecture, which was certainly brought by his labours to a perfection that it would else perhaps never have attained among the Tuscans. ...

... Filippo was now at an age which rendered it impossible that he should live to see the lanthorn completed; he therefore left directions, by his will, that it should be built after the model here described, and according to the rules which he had laid down in writing, affirming that the fabric would otherwise be in danger of falling, since, being constructed with the pointed arch, it required to be rendered secure by means of the pressure of the weight to be thus added. But, though Filippo could not complete the edifice before his death, he raised the lanthorn to the height of several braccia,[1] causing almost all the marbles required for the completion of the building to be carefully prepared and brought to the place. At the sight of these huge masses as they arrived, the people stood amazed, marvelling that it should be possible for Filippo to propose the laying of such a weight on the Cupola. It was, indeed, the opinion of many intelligent men that it could not possibly support that weight. It appeared to them to be a piece of good fortune that he had conducted it so far, and they considered the loading it so heavily to be a tempting of Providence. Filippo constantly laughed at these fears. ...

How beautiful this building is, it will itself bear testimony. With respect to the height, from the level ground to the commencement of the lanthorn, there are one hundred and fifty-four braccia;[2] the body of the lanthorn is thirty-six braccia high; the copper ball four braccia; the cross eight braccia; in all two hunderd and two braccia.[3] And it

---

[1] The first stone of the lanthorn was laid in 1443, the last in 1461. The lanthorn, or lantern, is a small tower placed atop the dome and admitting light.

[2] A braccio (*pl.* braccia) was nearly two feet. The top of the dome is actually said to be about 305 ft. above ground.

[3] This would bring the tip of the cross to about 400 ft. above ground.

may be confidently affirmed that the ancients never carried their buildings to so vast a height, nor committed themselves to so great a risk as to dare a competition with the heavens, which this structure verily appears to do, seeing that it rears itself to such an elevation that the hills around Florence do not appear to equal it.[4] And of a truth it might seem that the heavens did feel envious of its height, since their lightnings perpetually strike it.[5] While this work was in progress, Filippo constructed many other fabrics.[6] ...

In a place called Ruciano, outside the gate of San Niccolò at Florence, Filippo constructed a rich and magnificent palace for Messer Luca Pitti, but this was not by any means equal to that which he commenced for the same person within the city of Florence;[7] and which he completed to the second range of windows, with so much grandeur and magnificence, that no more splendid or more beautiful edifice in the Tuscan manner has yet been seen. ...

The Marquis of Mantua,[8] among others, desiring to secure the services of Filippo, wrote with very earnest instances respecting him to the Signoria of Florence, by whom the master was accordingly sent to the Marquis in that city, where, in the year 1445, he prepared designs for the construction of dams on the Po, with other works, according to the wish of that prince, who caressed him infinitely, being wont to say that Florence was as worthy to number Filippo among her citizens as he to have so noble and beautiful a city for his birthplace. ... .[9]

In the church of Santo Spirito, the sermons during Lent were one year preached by Maestro Franceso Zoppo, then very popular with the Florentines. In these sermons the preacher had earnestly recommended the claims of the convent and schools for youth, but more particularly those of the church which had been burnt about that time, to the consideration of his hearers. Thereupon the chief persons of that quarter, Lorenzo Ridolfi, Bartholommeo Corbinelli, Neri di Gino Capponi, and Goro di Stagio Dati, with many other citizens, obtained an order from the Signoria for the rebuilding of the church of Santo Spirito, of which they made Stoldo Frescobaldi *proveditor*. ... When the matter had been fully resolved on, Filippo was sent

---

4 Although it is said slightly to exceed the dome of St. Peter's, both in height and circumference, by a couple of braccia, Brunelleschi's dome is lighter and stronger.
5 This is hardly an exaggeration. Thus the ball with the cross was thrown down by lightning in 1601, being later replaced by one somewhat larger.
6 Fabrics: structures. Famous among these are the Pazzi Chapel, Pitti Palace, Foundling Hospital of the Silk Guild, and Churches of San Lorenzo and Spiritu Sancto, all in Florence.
7 The famous Pitti Palace, Florence. Important alterations were made after Brunelleschi's time.
8 Probably Luigi III, Gonzaga, Marquis of Mantua 1444–78.
9 Brunelleschi's versatility is here exemplified.

for, and he made a model, comprising all the requisites demanded for the due completion of a Christian temple, whether as regards utility or beauty.[10] . . .

Filippo was truly facetious in conversation, and acute in repartee, as was shown on a certain occasion, when he desired to vex Lorenzo Ghiberti, who had bought a farm at Monte Morello, called Lepriano, on which he spent double the income that he derived from it. This caused Lorenzo great vexation, insomuch that he sold the farm. Filippo was asked about that time, what was the best thing that Lorenzo had done — being expected perhaps to answer in terms of depreciation respecting the works of Lorenzo on account of the enmity between them — when he replied, "To sell Lepriano." . . .

The Florentine Sculptor Donato[1]

The sculptor Donato, called by his contemporaries Donatello, and who subscribes himself thus on some of his works, was born in Florence in the year 1386. He devoted himself to the arts of design and was not only an excellent sculptor and admirable statuary, but was beside very skilful in works of stucco, well versed in the study of perspective, and highly esteemed as an architect. The productions of Donatello displayed so much grace and excellence, with such correctness of design, that they were considered to resemble the admirable works of the ancient Greeks and Romans more closely than those of any other master had ever done. Nor is it without good reason that he is acknowledged to be the first who conducted the practice of historical composition, in basso-rilievo,[2] into the right path; his works of that kind giving proof of so much thought, power, and facility, that he is at once perceived to have had the true intelligence and mastery of that branch of art, which he exercised with extraordinary success, insomuch that he has not only remained unsurpassed in that style, but has never been equalled by any artist, even down to our own days. . . .

In the church of San Giovanni in the same city, Donato executed the sepulchral monument of the pope, Giovanni Coscia,[3] who had been deposed from the pontificate by the Council of Constance. The monument to Coscia was erected at the cost of Cosimo de' Medici, who was the intimate friend of the deposed pontiff. For this tomb, Donato

---

[10] The noted Church of Santo Spiritu or Spiritu Sancto (the Holy Ghost), Florence, done in the Renaissance style.

[1] Donato di Niccolo, or Donatello (c. 1386–1466).

[2] Low relief.

[3] The "Pisan Pope," John XXIII, now considered an Antipope. Baldassare Cossa, of Neapolitan birth, was a corsair before entering the service of the Church. He became a cardinal, largely through his administrative abilities, and Pisan Pope 1410–1415, when he was constrained by the Council of Constance to resign.

executed the figure of the departed pope in gilded bronze, with those of Hope and Charity, in marble, all with his own hand; but the figure of Faith was done by his pupil Michelozzo. . . .

The same master, while still very young, executed a figure of the prophet Daniel, in marble, for the facade of Santa Maria del Fiore;[4] and at a later period he produced one of San Giovanni Evangelista[5] seated; this figure is four braccia high, it is clothed in very simple vestments, and is much celebrated. . . . Donato likewise executed for the same church the decorations of the organ, which stands over the door of the old sacristy, where are those figures, so boldly sketched as we have before said, that in looking at them one almost believes them really to live and move.[6] . . .

. . . It may indeed be truly said of this master, that he effected as much by the superiority of his judgment as by the skill of his hand; seeing that many works are produced which appear very beautiful in the work-rooms where they are executed, but which, when taken thence and placed in another situation, in a different light or higher position, present a much changed aspect, and turn out to be the reverse of what they appeared. Donato, on the contrary, treated his figures in such a manner, that while in the rooms where they were executed they did not produce one-half the effect, which he had in fact secured to them, and which they exhibited when placed in the positions for which they had been calculated.

For the new sacristy of Santa Maria del Fiore, Donatello gave the design of those boys who support the festoons, which decorate the frieze; as also that of the figures executed in the circular window beneath the cupola. Donato also produced the statue of St. Peter, still to be seen in San Michele, in Orto, in the same city, (Florence); an admirable figure, full of spirit, which he executed for the Guild of Butchers; with the figure of San Marco,[7] undertaken in the first instance in concert with Filippo Brunelleschi, for the Guild of Joiners, but which Donatello afterwards finished by himself, an arrangement to which Filippo had consented. This figure was executed by Donato with so much judgment, that while standing on the ground its excellence was not obvious to those who were but imperfectly acquainted with matters of art, insomuch that the syndics of the Guild were not disposed to have it placed in the situation intended for it; whereupon Donato bade them suffer him to raise it to its due position, when he would so work at it that they should see a different figure from that they then beheld. Having placed the statue accordingly, he shut it

---

[4] The Florentine Cathedral.

[5] St. John the Baptist, one of Donatello's masterpieces, found its way to the tribune of the Cathedral.

[6] The dancing cupids and other parts of this famous organ loft, since dismantled, are now to be found in the Bargello and the Cathedral Museum, Florence.

[7] Both of these statues remain.

up for a fortnight, and then, without having touched it, uncovered his work to the admiration of all.

For the Guild of Armourers, Donatello executed a most animated figure of St. George, in his armour. The brightness of youthful beauty, generosity, and bravery shine forth in his face; his attitude gives evidence of a proud and terrible impetuosity; the character of the saint is indeed expressed most wonderfully, and life seems to move within that stone. It is certain that in no modern figure has there yet been seen so much animation, nor so life-like a spirit in marble, as nature and art have combined to produce by the hand of Donato in this statue.[8] On the pedestal which supports the tabernacle enclosing the figure, the story of St. George killing the dragon is executed in basso-rilievo, and also in marble: in this work there is a horse, which has been highly celebrated and much admired: in the pediment is a half-length figure of God the Father, also in basso-rilievo. . . . In that façade of Santa Maria del Fiore, which faces the Campanile, Donato executed four[9] figures, each five braccia high, two of which are portraits from the life, one of Francesco Soderini when a youth, the other of Giovanni di Barduccio Cherichini, now called the Zuccone.[10] The latter is considered the most extraordinary and most beautiful work ever produced by Donatello, who, when he intended to affirm a thing in a manner that should preclude all doubt, would say, "By the faith that I place in my Zuccone." And while he was working on this statue he would frequently exclaim, while looking at it, "Speak then! why wilt thou not speak?"

For the Signoria of Florence, Donatello cast, in bronze, a statue of Judith cutting off the head of Holofernes. This was placed on the piazza, in an arch of their loggia. It is a work of great excellence, and proves the mastery of the author over his art. There is much grandeur and simplicity in the aspect and vestments of Judith; her greatness of mind, and the power she derives from the aid of God, are made clearly manifest, while the effects of wine and sleep are equally visible in the countenance of Holofernes, as is the result of death in his limbs, which have lost all power, and hang down cold and flaccid. This work was so carefully executed by Donato, that the casting turned out most successfully, and was delicately beautiful: he then finished it so diligently, that it is indeed most wonderful to behold. The basement, also, which is a balustrade, in granite, of simple arrangement, is very graceful in its effect, and the appearance is extremely pleasing to the eye. Donatello himself was so well satisfied with the whole of this

---

[8] Story has it that Michelangelo, on beholding this noted statue, said to it: "March!" For greater safety the St. George was moved to the Bargello in Florence.

[9] Three. These three statues represent St. John, the prophet Jeremiah or Solomon, and evidently King David in later life (the "Zuccone").

[10] "Pumpkin-head" (because of its utter baldness).

work, that he determined to place his name on it (which he had not done on the others), as is seen in the words *Donatelli Opus*.[11]

In the court of the before-mentioned Palazzo de' Signoria is a David, in bronze, by this master, naked, and of the size of life.[12] He has cut off the head of Goliath, and, raising his foot, he places it on the head; in his right hand is the sword. The animation, truth to nature, and softness manifest in this figure, make it almost impossible to artists to believe that it has not been moulded on the living form. . . .

Now it chanced that at this time the Signoria of Venice, having heard of his fame, sent for Donato, to the end that he might erect the monument of Gattamelata,[13] in the city of Padua, whither he repaired very willingly, and where he erected the bronze horse, still on the Piazza di Sant' Antonio, in which the chaffing and neighing of the horse are made clearly obvious, while the pride and spirit of the rider are also expressed with infinite force and truth by the art of the master.[14] Notwithstanding the great size of this casting, Donatello preserved an admirable justice in all the proportions; and the excellence of the work is such that it may be compared with those of any ancient master for design, animation, art, harmony, and care in execution. . . . The Paduans, moved by the merit of this work, did their utmost to obtain the artist for their fellow-citizen, and sought, by all sorts of caresses, to prevail on him to stay with them. In the hope of retaining him, they gave him the commission to execute stories from the life of Sant' Antonio of Padua on the predella of the high altar, in the church of the Friars Minor. These stories are in basso-rilievo, and are executed with so much ability, that the most excellent masters in this art stand amazed and confounded before them, when they consider the beautiful and varied composition they display, with the vast amount of extraordinary figures they contain, and the careful consideration of the perspective manifest in all their parts.[15] . . . A vast number of works by this master exist in all parts of that city. They caused him to be considered a wonder among the Paduans, and won him the commendations of all good judges. . . .

But fully to narrate the life and enumerate the works executed by this master, would necessitate a longer story than we have proposed

---

11 "Work of Donatello." It found its way to the Loggia di Lanzi. The gestures are restricted to the point of stiffness for purposes of safety, according to some.

12 This is the "young David," as opposed to the "old David." This was, according to one authority, "the earliest attempt of the Renaissance to restore the nude to honor." It was later removed to the Bargello.

13 This colossal statue of Erasmo da Nardi, general of the Venetians, known as "Gattamelata," was erected 1444–53 at the expense of his son.

14 The Gattemalata was the first full-length bronze equestrian statue attempted since antiquity, and a vast success.

15 The bronze reliefs, together with a large relief in stone, were dispersed when a new altar was provided in the later 16th century, but they were reassembled and replaced at the close of the 19th century.

to ourselves in writing the lives of our artists, seeing that he occupied himself with so many things; giving his attention not only to works of importance, of which we have spoken sufficiently, but also to the smallest matters connected with art. . . .

As the friend and servant of the house of Medici, Donato lived in cheerfulness and free from cares all the rest of his days. When he had attained his eighty-third year, he became paralytic, and could no longer labour in any manner, whereupon he took to his bed, where he lay constantly, in a poor little house which he had in the Via del Cocomero, close to the nuns of San Niccolo. Here, becoming worse from day to day, and declining by degrees, he died on the 13th of December, 1466.

12

The New Politique

MACHIAVELLI

Machiavelli and his Prince have become synonymous with the doctrine of political expedience: that the end justifies the means, and that governments and their ministers are exempt from the moral laws that bind private individuals, and hence are at liberty to employ falsehood and perfidy, dishonesty and duplicity, cruelty and injustice, in the name of the public welfare. This revolutionary new doctrine, openly advocated by a Florentine statesman and political theorist, both summarizes the concepts and practices which had developed in Italian politics during the Later Middle Ages and reflects the climate which gave rise to them: the diminished respect for the Church and its teachings, the augmented scope of secular governments, the impotence of republican forms, the political instability and unrestrained competition between internal factions and among rival states.

The author of The Prince was born in Medicean Florence in 1469. His father was a lawyer of modest circumstances, and the family owned a little landed property, enough to support Machiavelli in some of his later lean years. He apparently received a good humanist education, strong in literature and history, both classical and Italian, but weak in Scholastic philosophy, religion, and rhetoric. In his twenty-fifth year (1494) Machiavelli entered the service of the recently restored Republic of Florence, in which he soon became, in today's terms, a bureaucrat and a braintruster. Starting as a clerk in the second Chancery, he became its head (Second Chancellor) within four years, and soon thereafter one of the government's chief advisers. He served on numerous important embassies to such powerful personages as Cesare Borgia, Louis XII, Pope Julius II, and Emperor Maximilian. Placed in charge of the Florentine War Department, he had an opportunity to put into operation his favorite idea that Italian states should rely on citizen-troops rather than on foreign mercenaries.

Machiavelli's efforts in these various capacities did not prevent the overthrow of the Republic and the restoration of the Medici by a Spanish army in 1512. Although thrown out of office, Machiavelli — like Talleyrand three centuries later — did not despair of regaining governmental employment. He soon discovered, however, that his services were no longer desired and that he was suspect. In consequence of an abortive republican plot, he was even temporarily jailed and racked in 1513, after which he was exiled to his modest country villa.

For some time he had been working on a political treatise concerned with republican governments, later published under the title Discourses on the First Ten Books of Titus Livy. Now he undertook a guidebook for monarchical governments, intended for the recently restored Medici. Completed in 1513, this brief but influential work was entitled The Prince. It was originally addressed to Giuliano de' Medici, who ruled Florence from 1513 to 1515; but after Giuliano's early death, Machiavelli readdressed it to Lorenzo II de' Medici (not "The Magnificent"), who succeeded Guiliano and ruled until 1519. Meanwhile Cardinal Giovanni de' Medici had become Pope Leo X, and reportedly schemed to invest first Giuliano and then Lorenzo II with the princedoms of Urbino or Parma and Modena. It was apparently to advise on the assumption and retention of such states and on possible steps toward new acquisitions that The Prince was written. Since 1494, foreign powers — France, Spain, the Swiss, and the Germans — had been intervening in Italian affairs, and Machiavelli envisioned their eviction by the Medici. The Prince thus stemmed from two consuming interests: Machiavelli's personal ambition to regain political employment, and his patriotic dream of a unified Italy liberated from foreign control.

Medieval guidebooks for rulers had been idealistic and even pietistic, stressing the monarch's responsibilities to God and the moral law, and often picturing the desired ruler as a crowned saint. The Prince was written in the guidebook tradition, but in outlook and content it was a radical departure. What Machiavelli did was to compile a body of practical, down-to-earth advice, based on his own experience and observations, as well as on classical and recent history, and divorced from ethical considerations. It is a short work, most of which is given in the following pages, and it is easy reading. After dealing with the acquisition and retention of various types of principalities (Chapters 1-11), Machiavelli discusses the military means by which they are to be defended and controlled (12-14). He lays down principles to guide the conduct of princes, in which expediency, rather than morality, is the norm (15-19); this is the core of the work. After miscellaneous practical advice on such subjects as the use of fortresses, the choice of ministers (or secretaries), and the role of luck (20-25), Machiavelli concludes with an exhortation to the addressee to liberate Italy from the "stinking tyranny" of the "barbarian" invaders from beyond the Alps.

The Prince did not regain early important official employment for Machiavelli in the Florentine government, nor did it stir the quiescent Medici to liberate Italy. Still, after some years he was restored to a measure of Medicean favor. In 1520 he was commissioned by Pope Leo X to write a history of Florence; and he became an occasional adviser to the later Medicean Pope Clement VII, for whom he accomplished some minor missions. When a sudden revolution overthrew the Medicean government in Florence in 1527, Machiavelli hastened back in his usual quest of employment with the successful regime; but his Prince and his recent associations made him again unwanted and suspect. Mercifully, he died in 1527 before he could learn of his rejection.

Machiavelli was a versatile and prolific author. In addition to The Prince and his Discourses on republican government, he wrote an Art of War, a History of Florence, and a historical romance, The Life of Castruccio Castricane. Although he was a first-rate writer of Italian prose, his poetry was indifferent; but his plays, such as his Mandragola and his Clizia, are praised. He also left a voluminous correspondence.

The Prince tells us a great deal about Italian history at the watershed between medieval and modern times, about the unscrupulous political practices and views which had come to prevail in Renaissance Italy, about the general state of contemporary ideas and ideals, and about Machiavelli himself. Here are mirrored the ascendant despots, the widespread failure of republican government, the political involvements of the Papacy, clerical worldliness and nepotism, the far-reaching power of the Medici, and the chronic instability of the Florentine government, wherein, as Dante says, "pride, envy, and avarice were the sparks that set hearts on fire." Since the Italian despots had typically come to power by illegitimate and violent methods, they were compelled to maintain themselves and their governments by the same means. This bred a disregard for human law and a growing insensibility to natural morality, as well as admiration for political success regardless of how it was attained.

Machiavelli's view of human nature is a pessimistic and cynical one, stemming from classical rather than Christian sources: a pagan human nature, unenlightened by divine revelation, unsaved by divine grace. Also evident are the newly-resurrected classical ideals of virtu and fama (manliness and reputation) and the concept of fortuna (capricious Lady Luck). But though Machiavelli's thinking was colored by the classical revival, his ideas of human nature and of effective statesmanship were essentially formed from his own observations and experience in contemporary Italian politics. Brilliant, shrewd, and unquenchably ambitious, chameleon-like in his ability to change his colors, yet "patriotic" in his dreams of a unified Italy, he reflects and formulates rather than creates the "new politique" — the sacrifice of morality to political considerations. "Machiavellian" tactics were to become standard operating procedure for many modern dictators, including Napoleon I, Bismarck, Cavour, Mussolini, Hitler, and Stalin; nor have they been yet abandoned in our own day.

NICCOLÒ MACHIAVELLI

The Prince *

CHAPTER I
Of the Various Kinds of Princedom, and of the Ways In Which They Are Acquired

All the States and Governments by which men are or ever have been ruled, have been and are either Republics[1] or Princedoms. Princedoms are either hereditary, in which the sovereignty is derived through an ancient line of ancestors, or they are new. New Princedoms are either wholly new, as that of Milan to Francesco Sforza;[2] or they are like limbs joined on to the hereditary possessions of the Prince who acquires them, as the Kingdom of Naples to the dominions of the King of Spain.[3] The States thus acquired have either been used to live under a Prince or have been free; and he who acquires them does so either by his own arms or by the arms of others, and either by good fortune or by merit.

CHAPTER II
Of Hereditary Princedoms

Of Republics I shall not now speak, having elsewhere spoken of them at length. Here I shall treat exclusively of Princedoms,[4] and,

* Translated by J. H. Thompson (Oxford: University Press, 1897).

[1] The government of republics is the subject of Machiavelli's *Discourses*, which, it appears, he had already begun, but did not finish until some time later.

[2] Francesco Sforza, a former *condottiere*, had overthrown the short-lived Ambrosian Republic and mounted to supreme power in Milan in 1450.

[3] King Ferdinand of Aragon and Castile added the Kingdom of Naples to his dominions in 1502.

[4] Princedom: a state ruled by one person, as in the case of a monarchy or a dictatorship.

filling in the outline above traced out, shall proceed to examine how such States are to be governed and maintained.

I say, then, that hereditary States, accustomed to the family of their Prince,[5] are maintained with far less difficulty than new States, since all that is required is that the Prince shall not depart from the usages of his ancestors, trusting for the rest to deal with events as they arise. So that if an hereditary Prince be of average address, he will always maintain himself in his Princedom, unless deprived of it by some extraordinary and irresistible force; and even if so deprived will recover it, should any, even the least, mishap overtake the usurper. We have in Italy an example of this in the Duke of Ferrara, who never could have withstood the attacks of the Venetians in 1484, nor those of Pope Julius in 1510, had not his authority in that State been consolidated by time.[6] For since a Prince by birth has fewer occasions and less need to give offence, he ought to be better loved, and will naturally be popular with his subjects unless outrageous vices make him odious. Moreover, the very antiquity and continuance of his rule will efface the memories and causes which lead to innovation. For one change always leaves a dovetail into which another will fit.

CHAPTER III

Of Mixed Princedoms

But in new Princedoms difficulties abound. And, first, if the Princedom be not wholly new, but joined on to the ancient dominions of the Prince, so as to form with them what may be termed a mixed Princedom, changes will come from a cause common to all new States, namely, that men, thinking to better their condition, are always ready to change masters, and in this expectation will take up arms against any ruler; wherein they deceive themselves, and find afterwards by experience that they are worse off than before. This again results naturally and necessarily from the circumstance that the Prince cannot avoid giving offence to his new subjects, either in respect of the troops he quarters on them, or of some other of the numberless vexations attendant on a new acquisition. And in this way you may find that you have enemies in all those whom you have injured in seizing the Princedom, yet cannot keep the friendship of those who helped you to gain it; since you can neither reward them as they expect, nor yet, being under obligations to them, use violent remedies against them. For however strong you may be in respect of your army it is essential that in entering a new Province you should have the good will of its inhabitants.

Hence it happened that Louis XII of France, speedily gaining pos-

---

5 Such as the hereditary monarchs then ruling France and Aragon.
6 The d'Este family had ruled Ferrara since the 12th century.

session of Milan, as speedily lost it; and that on the occasion of its first capture, Lodovico Sforza was able with his own forces only to take it from him.[7] For the very people who had opened the gates to the French King, when they found themselves deceived in their expectations and hopes of future benefits, could not put up with the insolence of their new ruler. True it is that when a State rebels and is again got under, it will not afterwards be lost so easily. For the Prince, using the rebellion as a pretext, will not scruple to secure himself by punishing the guilty, bringing the suspected to trial, and otherwise strengthening his position in the points where it was weak. So that if to recover Milan from the French it was enough on the first occasion that a Duke Lodovico should raise alarms on the frontiers, to wrest it from them a second time the whole world had to be ranged against them, and their armies destroyed and driven out of Italy.[8] And this for the reasons above assigned. And yet, for a second time, Milan was lost to the King. The general causes of its first loss have been shown. It remains to note the causes of the second, and to point out the remedies which the French King had, or which might have been used by another in like circumstances to maintain his conquest more successfully than he did.

I say, then, that those States which upon their acquisition are joined on to the ancient dominions of the Prince who acquires them, are either of the same Province and tongue as the people of these dominions, or they are not. When they are, there is great ease in retaining them, especially when they have not been accustomed to live in freedom. To hold them securely it is enough to have rooted out the line of the reigning Prince; because if in other respects the old condition of things be continued, and there be no discordance in their customs, men live peaceably with one another, as we see to have been the case in Brittany, Burgundy, Gascony, and Normandy, which have so long been united to France. For although there be some slight difference in their languages,[9] their customs are similar, and they can easily get on together. He, therefore, who acquires such a State, if he mean to keep it, must see to two things; first, that the blood of the ancient line of Princes be destroyed; second, that no change be made in respect of laws or taxes; for in this way the newly acquired States speedily becomes incorporated with the hereditary.

But when States are acquired in a country differing in language, usages, and laws, difficulties multiply, and great good fortune, as well as address, is needed to overcome them. One of the best and most efficacious methods for dealing with such a State, is for the Prince who

[7] Louis XII took Milan in 1499, but Ludovico il Moro Sforza regained it quickly with Swiss aid.

[8] After the Swiss turned Ludovico over to Louis in 1500, Louis held Milan for 12 years, and it took the powerful "Holy League" with Swiss assistance to oust the French this time.

[9] Different dialects.

acquires it to go and dwell there in person, since this will tend to make his tenure more secure and lasting. This course has been followed by the Turk with regard to Greece, who, had he not, in addition to all his other precautions for securing that Province, himself come to live in it, could never have kept his hold of it.[10] For when you are on the spot, disorders are detected in their beginnings and remedies can be readily applied; but when you are at a distance, they are not heard of until they have gathered strength and the case is past cure. Moreover, the Province in which you take up your abode is not pillaged by your officers; the people are pleased to have a ready recourse to their Prince; and have all the more reason, if they are well disposed, to love, if disaffected, to fear him. A foreign enemy desiring to attack that State would be cautious how he did so. In short, where the Prince resides in person, it will be extremely difficult to oust him.

Another excellent expedient is to send colonies into one or two places, so that these may become, as it were, the keys of the Province; for you must either do this, or else keep up a numerous force of men-at-arms and foot soldiers. A Prince need not spend much on colonies. He can send them out and support them at little or no charge to himself, and the only persons to whom he gives offence are those whom he deprives of their fields and houses to bestow them on the new inhabitants. Those who are thus injured form but a small part of the community, and remaining scattered and poor can never become dangerous. All others being left unmolested are in consequence easily quieted, and at the same time are afraid to make a false move, lest they share the fate of those who have been deprived of their possessions. In few words, these colonies cost less than soldiers, are more faithful, and give less offence, while those who are offended, being, as I have said, poor and dispersed, cannot hurt. And let it here be noted that men are either to be kindly treated, or utterly crushed, since they can revenge lighter injuries, but not graver. Wherefore the injury we do to a man should be of a sort to leave no fear of reprisals.

But if instead of colonies you send troops, the cost is vastly greater, and the whole revenues of the country are spent in guarding it; so that the gain becomes a loss, and much deeper offence is given; since in shifting the quarters of your soldiers from place to place the whole country suffers hardship, which, as all feel, all are made enemies; and enemies who, remaining, although vanquished, in their own homes, have power to hurt. In every way, therefore, his mode of defence is as disadvantageous as that by colonizing is useful.

The Prince who establishes himself in a Province whose laws and language differ from those of his own people, ought also to make himself the head and protector of his feebler neighbours, and endeavour

---

[10] The Ottoman Turks took what remained of the Byzantine or "Greek" Empire, including Greece proper, in the 15th century and moved their capital to Constantinople.

to weaken the stronger, and must see that by no accident shall any other stranger as powerful as himself find an entrance there. For it will always happen that some such person will be called in by those of the Province who are discontented either through ambition or fear; as we see of old the Romans brought into Greece by the Aetolians,[11] and in every other country that they entered, invited there by its inhabitants. And the usual course of things is that so soon as a formidable stranger enters a Province, all the weaker powers side with him, moved thereto by the ill-will they bear towards him who has hitherto kept them in subjection. So that in respect of these lesser powers, no trouble is needed to gain them over, for at once, together, and of their own accord, they throw in their lot with the government of the stranger. The new Prince, therefore, has only to see that they do not increase too much in strength, and with his own forces, aided by their good will, can easily subdue any who are powerful, so as to remain supreme in the Province. He who does not manage this matter well, will soon lose whatever he has gained, and while he retains it will find in it endless troubles and annoyances.

In dealing with the countries of which they took possession the Romans diligently followed the methods I have described. They planted colonies, conciliated weaker powers without adding to their strength, humbled the great, and never suffered a formidable stranger to acquire influence. A single example will suffice to show this. In Greece the Romans took the Achaians and Aetolians into their pay; the Macedonian monarchy was humbled; Antiochus[12] was driven out. But the services of the Achaians and Aetolians[13] never obtained for them any addition to their power; no persuasions on the part of Philip[14] could induce the Romans to be his friends on the condition of sparing him humiliation; nor could all the power of Antiochus bring them to consent to his exercising any authority within that Province. And in thus acting the Romans did as all wise rulers should, who have to consider not only present difficulties but also future, against which they must use all diligence to provide; for these, if they be foreseen while yet remote, admit of easy remedy, but if their approach be awaited, are already past cure, the disorder having become hopeless; realizing what the physicians tell us of hectic fever,[15] that in its beginning it is easy to cure, but hard to recognize; whereas, after a time, not having been detected and treated at the first, it becomes easy to recognize but impossible to cure.

And so it is with State affairs. For the distempers of a State being

[11] To intervene in Greek quarrels in the so-called "Macedonian Wars," 215 B.C. and after.
[12] Antiochus III (d. 187 B.C.), ruler of the large Seleucid Empire in southwest Asia, who attempted to intervene in the Balkans.
[13] The Greek Achaean League, and the rival Greek Aetolian League.
[14] Philip V of Macedon (d. 179 B.C.).
[15] Consumption.

discovered while yet inchoate, which can only be done by a sagacious ruler, may easily be dealt with; but when, from not being observed, they are suffered to grow until they are obvious to every one, there is no longer any remedy. The Romans, therefore, foreseeing evils while they were yet far off, always provided against them, and never suffered them to take their course for the sake of avoiding war; since they knew that war is not so to be avoided, but is only postponed to the advantage of the other side....

CHAPTER V
How Cities or Provinces Which Before Their Acquisition Have Lived Under Their Own Laws Are to Be Governed

When a newly acquired State has been accustomed, as I have said, to live under its own laws and in freedom, there are three methods whereby it may be held. The first is to destroy it; the second, to go and reside there in person; the third, to suffer it to live on under its own laws, subjecting it to a tribute, and entrusting its government to a few of the inhabitants who will keep the rest your friends. Such a Government, since it is the creature of the new Prince, will see that it cannot stand without his protection and support, and must therefore do all it can to maintain him; and a city accustomed to live in freedom, if it is to be preserved at all, is more easily controlled through its own citizens than in any other way.

We have examples of all these methods in the histories of the Spartans and the Romans. The Spartans held Athens and Thebes by creating oligarchies in these cities, yet lost them in the end.[16] The Romans, to retain Capua, Carthage, and Numantia, destroyed them and never lost them. On the other hand, when they thought to hold Greece as the Spartans had held it, leaving it its freedom and allowing it to be governed by its own laws, they failed, and had to destroy many cities of that Province before they could secure it.[17] For, in truth, there is no sure way of holding other than by destroying, and whoever becomes master of a City accustomed to live in freedom and does not destroy it, may reckon on being destroyed by it. For if it should rebel, it can always screen itself under the name of liberty and its ancient laws, which no length of time, nor any benefits conferred will ever cause it to forget; and do what you will, and take what care you may, unless the inhabitants be scattered and dispersed, this name, and the

---

[16] After the Peloponnesian War (431–404 B.C.), Sparta was temporarily ascendant in Greece, and ruled Athens through the "Thirty Tyrants" from 404 to 403 B.C. and Thebes from 382 to 379 B.C.; but its hegemony was broken by Thebes at Leuctra in 371 B.C.

[17] At first the Romans tried to allow the Greeks to retain their independence, but were finally obliged to take it away for the sake of peace.

old order of things, will never cease to be remembered, but will at once be turned against you whenever misfortune overtakes you, as when Pisa rose against the Florentines after a hundred years of servitude.[18]

If, however, the newly acquired City or Province has been accustomed to live under a Prince, and his line is extinguished, it will be impossible for the citizens, used, on the one hand, to obey, and deprived, on the other, of their old ruler, to agree to choose a leader from among themselves; and as they know not how to live as freemen, and are therefore slow to take up arms, a stranger may readily gain them over and attach them to his cause. But in Republics there is a stronger vitality, a fiercer hatred, a keener thirst for revenge. The memory of their former freedom will not let them rest; so that the safest course is either to destroy them, or to go and live in them.

CHAPTER VII

Of New Princedoms Acquired By the Aid of Others and By Good Fortune

They who from a private station become Princes by mere good fortune, do so with little trouble, but have much trouble to maintain themselves. They meet with no hindrance on their way, being carried as it were on wings to their destination, but all their difficulties overtake them when they alight. Of this class are those on whom states are conferred either in return for money, or through the favour of him who confers them; as it happened to many in the Greek cities of Ionia and the Hellespont to be made Princes by Darius, that they might hold these cities for his security and glory;[19] and as happened in the case of those Emperors who, from privacy, attained the Imperial dignity by corrupting the army.[1] Such Princes are wholly dependent on the favour and fortunes of those who have made them great, than which supports none could be less stable or secure; and they lack both the knowledge and the power that would enable them to maintain their position. They lack the knowledge, because, unless they have great parts and force of character, it is not to be expected that having always lived in a private station they should have learned how to command. They lack the power, since they cannot look for support from attached and faithful troops. Moreover, States suddenly acquired, like all else that is produced and that grows up rapidly, can never have such root or hold as that the first storm which strikes them shall

---

[18] Pisa, subjected in 1406, revolted in 1494.

[19] Darius I, great Persian ruler (522–486 B.C.) governed the Greek city-states of western Asia Minor and the eastern Aegean area by means of cooperative Greek dictators or "tyrants."

[1] Some Romans obtained the imperial office by bribing the praetorian guard, as did Claudius, Didius Julianus, etc.

not overthrow them; unless, indeed, as I have said already, they who thus suddenly become Princes have a capacity for learning quickly how to defend what Fortune has placed in their lap, and can lay those foundations after they rise which by others are laid before.

Of each of these methods of becoming a Prince, namely, by merit and by good fortune, I shall select an instance from times within my own recollection, and shall take the cases of Francesco Sforza and Cesare Borgia. By suitable measures and singular ability, Francesco Sforza rose from privacy to be Duke of Milan, preserving with little trouble what it cost him infinite efforts to gain.[2] On the other hand, Cesare Borgia, vulgarly spoken of as Duke Valentino, obtained his Princedom through the favourable fortunes of his father, and with these lost it,[3] although, so far as in him lay, he used every effort and practised every expedient that a prudent and able man should, who desires to strike root in a State given him by the arms and fortune of another. For, as I have already said, he who does not lay his foundations at first, may, if he be of great parts, succeed in laying them afterwards, though with inconvenience to the builder and risk to the building. And if we consider the various measures taken by Duke Valentino, we shall perceive how broad were the foundations he had laid whereon to rest his future power.

These I think it not superfluous to examine, since I know not what lessons I could teach a new Prince, more useful than the example of his actions.[4] And if the measures taken by him did not profit him in the end, it was through no fault of his, but from the extraordinary and extreme malignity of Fortune.

In his efforts to aggrandize the Duke his son, Alexander VI had to face many difficulties, both immediate and remote. In the first place, he saw no way to make him Lord of any State which was not a State of the Church, while, if he sought to take for him a State belonging to the Church, he knew that the Duke of Milan and the Venetians would withhold their consent; Faenza and Rimini being already under the protection of the latter. Further, he saw that the arms of Italy, and those more especially of which he might have availed himself, were in the hands of men who had reason to fear his aggrandizement, that is, of the Orsini, the Colonnesi, and their followers. These therefore he could not trust. It was consequently necessary that the existing order of things should be changed, and the States of Italy thrown into confusion, in order that he might safely make himself master of some part of them; and this became easy for him when he found that the Venetians, moved by other causes, were

[2] Francesco Sforza won Milan by marriage, intrigue, and force in 1450. He and his descendants ruled Milan 1450–1500 and 1512–35.

[3] Cesare Borgia (1476–1507) was the natural son of Rodrigo Borgia, who became Pope Alexander VI in 1492 and died in 1503.

[4] Cesare Borgia and his methods were greatly admired by Machiavelli. In fact, Cesare is considered the "Prince" incarnate.

plotting to bring the French once more into Italy. This design he accordingly did not oppose, but furthered by annulling the first marriage of the French King.[5]

King Louis therefore came into Italy at the instance of the Venetians, and with the consent of Pope Alexander, and no sooner was he in Milan than the Pope got troops from him to aid him in his enterprise against Romagna, which Province, moved by the reputation of the French arms, at once submitted.[6] After thus obtaining possession of Romagna, and after quelling the Colonnesi, Duke Valentino was desirous to follow up and extend his conquests. Two causes, however, held him back, namely, the doubtful fidelity of his own forces, and the waywardness of France. For he feared that the Orsini, of whose arms he had made use, might fail him, and not merely prove a hindrance to further acquisitions, but take from him what he had gained, and that the King might serve him the same turn. How little he could count on the Orsini was made plain when, after the capture of Faenza, he turned his arms against Bologna, and saw how reluctantly they took part in that enterprise. The King's mind he understood, when, after seizing on the Dukedom of Urbino, he was about to attack Tuscany; from which design Louis compelled him to desist. Whereupon the Duke resolved to depend no longer on the arms or fortune of others. His first step, therefore, was to weaken the factions of the Orsini and Colonnesi in Rome. Those of their following who were of good birth, he gained over by making them his own gentlemen, assigning them a liberal provision, and conferring upon them commands and appointments suited to their rank; so that in a few months their old partisan attachments died out, and the hopes of all rested on the Duke alone.

He then awaited an occasion to crush the chiefs of the Orsini, for those of the house of Colonna[7] he had already scattered, and a good opportunity presenting itself, he turned it to the best account. For when the Orsini came at last to see that the greatness of the Duke and the Church involved their ruin, they assembled a council at Magione in the Perugian territory, whence resulted the revolt of Urbino, commotions in Romagna, and an infinity of dangers to the Duke, all of which he overcame with the help of France.[8] His credit thus restored, the Duke trusting no longer either to the French or to any other foreign aid, that he might not have to confront them openly, resorted to strategem, and was so well able to dissemble his designs, that the

---

[5] Alexander VI annulled the marriage of Louis XII to Jeanne of France in 1498 so that Louis could marry Anne of Brittany in 1499. At the time, Louis made Cesare Duke of Valentinois, and Cesare married Charlotte, sister of the King of Navarre.

[6] Cesare's conquest of the Romagna in northeast central Italy began in 1500.

[7] The Orsini and Colonna were old-time Roman families — wealthy, powerful, aristocratic rivals of the Borgias for control of the Papal States.

[8] After initial successes, the so-called "Conspiracy of La Magione" collapsed when the French king promised to aid Cesare Borgia.

Orsini, through the mediation of Signor Paolo (whom he failed not to secure by every friendly attention, furnishing him with clothes, money, and horses), were so won over as to be drawn in their simplicity into his hands at Sinigaglia.[9] When the leaders were thus disposed of, and their followers made his friends, the Duke had laid sufficiently good foundations for his future power, since he held all Romagna together with the Dukedom of Urbino, and had ingratiated himself with the entire population of these States, who now began to see that they were well off.

And since this part of his conduct merits both attention and imitation, I shall not pass it over in silence. After the Duke had taken Romagna, finding that it had been ruled by feeble Lords, who thought more of plundering than correcting their subjects, and gave them more cause for division than for union, so that the country was overrun with robbery, tumult, and every kind of outrage, he judged it necessary, with a view to render it peaceful and obedient to his authority, to provide it with a good government. Accordingly he set over it Messer Remiro d'Orco, a stern and prompt ruler, who being entrusted with the fullest powers, in a very short time, and with much credit to himself, restored it to tranquillity and order. But afterwards apprehending that such unlimited authority might become odious, the Duke decided that it was no longer needed, and established in the centre of the Province a civil Tribunal, with an excellent President, in which every town was represented by its advocate. And knowing that past severities had generated ill-feeling against himself, in order to purge the minds of the people and gain their good-will, he sought to show them that any cruelty which had been done had not originated with him, but in the harsh disposition of his minister. Availing himself of the pretext which this afforded, he one morning caused Remiro to be beheaded, and exposed in the market place of Cesena with a block and bloody axe by his side. The barbarity of which spectacle at once astounded and satisfied the populace.

But, returning to the point whence we diverged, I say that the Duke, finding himself fairly strong and in a measure secured against present dangers, being furnished with arms of his own choosing and having to a great extent got rid of those which, if left near him, might have caused him trouble, had to consider, if he desired to follow up his conquests, how he was to deal with France, since he saw he could expect no further support from King Louis, whose eyes were at last opened to his mistake. He therefore began to look about for new alliances, and to waver in his adherence to the French, then occupied with their expedition into the kingdom of Naples against the Spaniards,

---

[9] On the pretext of a conference and reconciliation at Sinigaglia, Cesare ensnared and arrested surprised leaders of the revolt and executed some of them on the spot (1502).

at that time laying siege to Gaeta;[10] his object being to secure himself against France; and in this he would soon have succeeded had Alexander lived.

Such was the line he took to meet present exigencies. As regards the future, he had to apprehend that a new Head of the Church might not be his friend, and might even seek to deprive him of what Alexander had given. This he thought to provide against in four ways. First, by exterminating all who were of kin to those Lords whom he had despoiled of their possessions, that they might not become instruments in the hands of a new Pope. Second, by gaining over all the Roman nobles, so as to be able with their help to put a bridle, as the saying is, in the Pope's mouth. Third, by bringing the College of Cardinals, so far as he could, under his control. And fourth, by establishing his authority so firmly before his father's death, as to be able by himself to withstand the shock of a first onset.

Of these measures, at the time when Alexander died,[11] he had already effected three, and had almost carried out the fourth. For of the Lords whose possessions he had usurped, he had put to death all whom he could reach, and very few had escaped. He had gained over the Roman nobility, and had the majority in the College of Cardinals on his side.

As to further acquisitions, his design was to make himself master of Tuscany.[12] He was already in possession of Perugia and Piombino, and had assumed the protectorship of Pisa, on which city he was about to spring; taking no heed of France, as indeed he no longer had occasion, since the French had been deprived of the kingdom of Naples by the Spaniards under circumstances which made it necessary for both nations to buy his friendship. Pisa taken, Lucca and Siena would soon have yielded, partly through jealousy of Florence, partly through fear, and the position of the Florentines must then have been desperate.

Had he therefore succeeded in these designs, as he was succeeding in that very year in which Alexander died, he would have won such power and reputation that he might afterwards have stood alone, relying on his own strength and resources, without being beholden to the power and fortune of others. But Alexander died five years from the time he first unsheathed the sword, leaving his son with the State of Romagna alone consolidated, with all the rest unsettled, between two powerful hostile armies, and sick almost to death. And yet such were the fire and courage of the Duke, he knew so well how men must either be conciliated or crushed, and so solid were the foundations he had laid in that brief period, that had these armies not been

[10] In 1502. After agreeing to split the Kingdom of Naples with Louis XII, Ferdinand I seized the whole on the pretext of a quarrel over the spoils.
[11] In 1503 both Alexander VI and Cesare took ill with fever. Alexander died, and Cesare was seriously ill for some time.
[12] In west central Italy.

upon his back, or had he been in sound health, he must have surmounted every difficulty.

How strong his foundations were may be seen from this, that Romagna waited for him for more than a month; and that although half dead, he remained in safety in Rome, where though the Baglioni, the Vitelli, and the Orsini came to attack him, they met with no success. Moreover, since he was able, if not to make whom he liked Pope, at least to prevent the election of any whom he disliked, had he been in health at the time when Alexander died, all would have been easy for him. But he told me himself on the day on which Julius II[13] was created, that he had foreseen and provided for everything else that could happen on his father's death, but had never anticipated that when his father died he too should be at death's-door.

Taking all these actions of the Duke together, I can find no fault with him; nay, it seems to me reasonable to put him forward, as I have done, as a pattern for all such as rise to power by good fortune and the help of others. For with his great spirit and high aims he could not act otherwise than he did, and nothing but the shortness of his father's life and his own illness prevented the success of his designs. Whoever, therefore, on entering a new Princedom, judges it necessary to rid himself of enemies, to conciliate friends, to prevail by force or fraud, to make himself feared yet not hated by his subjects, respected and obeyed by his soldiers, to crush those who can or ought to injure him, to introduce changes in the old order of things, to be at once severe and affable, magnanimous and liberal, to do away with a mutinous army and create a new one, to maintain relations with Kings and Princes on such a footing that they must see it for their interest to aid him, and dangerous to offend, can find no brighter example than in the actions of this Prince.

The one thing for which he may be blamed was the creation of Pope Julius II, in respect of whom he chose badly.[14] Because, as I have said already, though he could not secure the election he desired, he could have prevented any other; and he ought never to have consented to the creation of any one of those Cardinals whom he had injured, or who on becoming Pope would have reason to fear him; for fear is as dangerous an enemy as resentment. Those whom he had offended were, among others, San Pietro ad Vincula,[15] Colonna,[16] San Giorgio,[17] and Ascanio;[18] all the rest, expecting d'Amboise and the Spanish Cardinals (the latter from their connexion and obligations, the former from the power he derived through his relations with the French Court), would on assuming the Pontificate have had reason

[13] Nov. 1, 1503, after the brief rule of the elderly Pius III.
[14] In 1504 Julius II forced Cesare out of the Romagna and the Papal States.
[15] Cardinal Giuliano Della Rovere, who became Julius II.
[16] Cardinal Giovanni Colonna.
[17] Cardinal Raphael Riorio, Papal Grand Chamberlain.
[18] Cardinal Ascanio Sforza, son of the Duke of Milan.

to fear him. The Duke, therefore, ought, in the first place, to have laboured for the creation of a Spanish Pope; failing in which, he should have agreed to the election of d'Amboise, but never to that of San Pietro ad Vincula. And he deceives himself who believes that with the great, recent benefits cause old wrongs to be forgotten.

The Duke, therefore, erred in the part he took in this election; and his error was the cause of his ultimate downfall.

CHAPTER VIII

Of Those Who By Their Crimes Come to Be Princes

But since from privacy a man may also rise to be a Prince in one or other of two ways, neither of which can be referred wholly either to merit or to fortune, it is fit that I notice them here, though one of them may happen to be discussed more fully in treating of Republics.

The ways I speak of are, first, when the ascent to power is made by paths of wickedness and crime; and second, when a private person becomes ruler of this country by the favour of his fellow-citizens. The former method I shall make clear by two examples, one ancient, the other modern, without entering further into the merits of the matter, for these, I think, should be enough for any one who is driven to follow them.

Agathocles the Sicilian came, not merely from a private station, but from the very dregs of the people, to be King of Syracuse.[19] Son of a potter, through all the stages of his fortunes he led a foul life. His vices, however, were conjoined with so great vigour both of mind and body, that becoming a soldier, he rose through the various grades of the service to be Praetor[1] of Syracuse. Once established in that post, he resolved to make himself Prince, and to hold by violence and without obligation to others the authority which had been spontaneously entrusted to him. Accordingly, after imparting his design to Hamilcar,[2] who with the Carthaginian armies was at that time waging war in Sicily, he one morning assembled the people and senate of Syracuse as though to consult with them on matters of public moment, and on a preconcerted signal caused his soldiers to put to death all the senators, and the wealthiest of the commons. These being thus got rid of, he assumed and retained possession of the sovereignty without opposition on the part of the people; and although twice defeated by the Carthaginians, and afterwards besieged, he was able

---

[19] Agathocles, son of a potter, rose to wealth, became a leader of mercenaries, and, with cruelty and bloodshed, seized control of Sicily about 317 B.C., remaining its tyrant until his death in 289 B.C.

[1] Highest magistrate.

[2] Hamilcar Barca (c. 276–228 B.C.), father of Hannibal, distinguished himself in Sicily in the First Punic War.

not only to defend his city, but leaving a part of his forces for its protection, to invade Africa with the remainder, and so in a short time to raise the siege of Syracuse, reducing the Carthaginians to the utmost extremities, and compelling them to make terms whereby they abandoned Sicily to him and confined themselves to Africa....

In our own times, during the papacy of Alexander VI, Oliverotto of Fermo,[3] who some years before had been left an orphan, and had been brought up by his maternal uncle Giovanni Fogliani, was sent while still a lad to serve under Paolo Vitelli,[4] in the expectation that a thorough training under that commander might qualify him for high rank as a soldier. After the death of Paolo, he served under his brother Vitellozzo,[5] and in a very short time, being of a quick wit, hardy and resolute, he became one of the first soldiers of his company. But thinking it beneath him to serve under others, with the countenance of the Vitelleschi[6] and the connivance of certain citizens of Fermo who preferred the slavery to the freedom of their country, he formed the design to seize on that town.

He accordingly wrote to Giovanni Fogliani that after many years of absence from home, he desired to see him and his native city once more, and to look a little into the condition of his patrimony; and as his one endeavour had been to make himself a name, in order that his fellow-citizens might see that his time had not been mis-spent, he proposed to return honourably attended by a hundred horsemen from among his own friends and followers; and he begged Giovanni graciously to arrange for his reception by the citizens of Fermo with corresponding marks of distinction, as this would be creditable not only to himself, but also to the uncle who had brought him up.

Giovanni accordingly, did not fail in any proper attention to his nephew, but caused him to be splendidly received by his fellow-citizens, and lodged him in his house; where Oliverotto having passed some days, and made the necessary arrangements for carrying out his wickedness, gave a formal banquet, to which he invited his uncle and all the first men of Fermo. When the repast and the other entertainments proper to such an occasion had come to an end, Oliverotto artfully turned the conversation to matters of grave interest, by speaking of the greatness of Pope Alexander and Cesare his son, and of their enterprises; and when Giovanni and the others were replying to what he said, he suddenly rose up, observing that these were matters to be discussed in a more private place, and so withdrew to another

---

[3] Oliverotto was a successful Italian *condottiere*, who, after becoming a party to the conspiracy of La Magione, was decoyed and strangled by Cesare Borgia at Sinigaglia in 1502.

[4] An Italian *condottiere* in the service of Florence, suspected of treachery and put to death by Cesare Borgia's orders in 1499.

[5] Vitellozo Vitelli, Italian *condottiere*, brother of Paolo, and in the service of Cesare Borgia since 1500, was also strangled at Sinigaglia in 1502, as a party to the conspiracy of La Magione.

[6] The Vitelli clan.

chamber; whither his uncle and all the other citizens followed him, and where they had no sooner seated themselves, than soldiers rushing out from places of concealment put Giovanni and all the rest to death.

After this butchery, Oliverotto mounted his horse, rode through the streets, and besieged the chief magistrate in the palace, so that all were constrained by fear to yield obedience and accept a government of which he made himself the head. And all who from being disaffected were likely to stand in his way, he put to death, while he strengthened himself with new ordinances, civil and military, to such purpose, that for the space of a year during which he retained the Princedom, he not merely kept a firm hold of the city, but grew formidable to all his neighbours. And it would have been as impossible to unseat him as it was to unseat Agathocles, had he not let himself be overreached by Cesare Borgia on the occasion when, as has already been told, the Orsini and Vitelli were entrapped at Sinigaglia; where he too being taken, one year after the commission of his parricidal crime, was strangled along with Vitellozzo, whom he had assumed for his master in villany as in valour.

It may be asked how Agathocles and some like him, after numberless acts of treachery and cruelty, have been able to live long in their own country in safety, and to defend themselves from foreign enemies, without being plotted against by their fellow-citizens, whereas, many others, by reason of their cruelty, have failed to maintain their position even in peaceful times, not to speak of the perilous times of war. I believe that this results from cruelty being well or ill employed. Those cruelties we may say are well employed, if it be permitted to speak well of things evil, which are done once for all under the necessity of self-preservation, and are not afterwards persisted in, but so far as possible modified to the advantage of the governed. Ill-employed cruelties, on the other hand, are those which from small beginnings increase rather than diminish with time. They who follow the first of these methods, may, by the grace of God and man, find, as did Agathocles, that their condition is not desperate; but by no possibility can the others maintain themselves.

Hence we may learn the lesson that on seizing a state, the usurper should make haste to inflict what injuries he must, at a stroke, that he may not have to renew them daily, but be enabled by their discontinuance to reassure men's minds, and afterwards win them over by benefits. Whosoever, either through timidity or from following bad counsels, adopts a contrary course, must keep the sword always drawn, and can put no trust in his subjects, who, suffering from continued and constantly renewed severities, will never yield him their confidence. Injuries, therefore, should be inflicted all at once, that their ill savour being less lasting may the less offend; whereas, benefits should be conferred little by little, that so they may be more fully relished.

But, before all things, a Prince should so live with his subjects that no vicissitude of good or evil fortune shall oblige him to alter his behaviour; because, if a need to change come through adversity, it is then too late to resort to severity; while any leniency you may use will be thrown away, for it will be seen to be compulsory and gain you no thanks.

CHAPTER IX
Of the Civil Princedom

I come now to the second case, namely, of the leading citizen who, not by crimes or violence, but by the favour of his fellow-citizens is made Prince of his country. This may be called a Civil Princedom,[7] and its attainment depends not wholly on merit, nor wholly on good fortune, but rather on what may be termed a *fortunate astuteness*. I say then that the road to this Princedom lies either through the favour of the people or of the nobles.[8] For in every city are to be found these two opposed humours having their origin in this, that the people desire not to be domineered over or oppressed by the nobles, while the nobles desire to oppress and domineer over the people. And from these two contrary appetites there arises in cities one of three results, a Princedom, or Liberty, or Licence. A Princedom is created either by the people or by the nobles, according as one or other of these factions has occasion for it. For when the nobles perceive that they cannot withstand the people, they set to work to magnify the reputation of one of their number, and make him their Prince, to the end that under his shadow they may be enabled to indulge their desires. The people, on the other hand, when they see that they cannot make head against the nobles, invest a single citizen with all their influence and make him Prince, that they may have the shelter of his authority.

He who is made Prince by the favour of the nobles, has greater difficulty to maintain himself than he who comes to the Princedom by aid of the people, since he finds many about him who think themselves as good as he, and whom, on that account, he cannot guide or govern as he would. But he who reaches the Princedom by the popular support, finds himself alone, with none, or but a very few about him who are not ready to obey. Moreover, the demands of the nobles cannot be satisfied with credit to the Prince, nor without injury to others, while those of the people well may, the aim of the people being more honourable than that of the nobles, the latter seeking to oppress, the former not to be oppressed. Add to this, that a Prince can never secure himself against a disaffected people, their number being too great, while he may against a disaffected nobility, since their

---

[7] As opposed to a Princedom or dictatorship set up by crime or violence.

[8] Many Princedoms or dictatorships in ancient, medieval, and modern times, including those of the Caesars, and of Fascism, Communism, and Nazism, have thus arisen.

number is small. The worst that a Prince need fear from a disaffected people is, that they may desert him, whereas when the nobles are his enemies he has to fear not only that they may desert him, but also that they may turn against him; because, as they have greater craft and foresight, they always choose their time to suit their safety, and seek favour with the side they think will win. Again, a Prince must always live with the same people, but need not always live with the same nobles, being able to make and unmake these from day to day, and give and take away their authority at his pleasure. . . .

CHAPTER X

How the Strength of All Princedoms Should Be Measured

In examining the character of these Princedoms, another circumstance has to be considered, namely, whether the Prince is strong enough, if occasion demands, to stand alone, or whether he needs continual help from others. To make the matter clearer, I pronounce those to be able to stand alone who, with the men and money at their disposal, can get together an army fit to take the field against any assailant; and, conversely, I judge those to be in constant need of help who cannot take the field against their enemies, but are obliged to retire behind their walls, and to defend themselves there. Of the former I have already spoken and shall speak again as occasion may require. As to the latter there is nothing to be said, except to exhort such Princes to strengthen and fortify the towns in which they dwell, and take no heed of the country outside. For whoever has thoroughly fortified his town, and put himself on such a footing with his subjects as I have already indicated and shall hereafter speak of, will always be attacked with much circumspection; for men are always averse to enterprises that are attended with difficulty, and it is impossible not to forsee difficulties in attacking a Prince whose town is strongly fortified and who is not hated by his subjects.

The towns of Germany enjoy great freedom.[9] Having little territory, they render obedience to the Emperor only when so disposed, fearing neither him nor any other neighbouring power. For they are so fortified that it is plain to every one that it would be a tedious and difficult task to reduce them, since all of them are protected by moats and suitable ramparts, are well supplied with artillery, and keep their public magazines constantly stored with victual, drink and fuel, enough to last them for a year. Besides which, in order to support the poorer class of citizens without public loss, they lay in a common stock of materials for these to work on for a year, in the handicrafts which

[9] Germany at this time was divided into between two and three hundred practically independent states, many of them city-states, such as Lübeck and Hamburg.

are the life and sinews of such cities, and by which the common people live. Moreover, they esteem military exercises and have many regulations for their maintenance.

A Prince, therefore, who has a strong city, and who does not make himself hated, cannot be attacked, or should he be so, his assailant will come badly off; since human affairs are so variable that it is almost impossible for any one to keep an army posted in leaguer for a whole year without interruption of some sort. Should it be objected that if the citizens have possessions outside the town, and see them burned, they will lose patience, and that self-interest, together with the hardships of a protracted siege, will cause them to forget their loyalty; I answer that a capable and courageous Prince will always overcome these difficulties, now, by holding out hopes to his subjects that the evil will not be of long continuance; now, by exciting their fears of the enemy's cruelty; and, again, by dexterously silencing those who seem to him too forward in their complaints. Moreover, it is to be expected that the enemy will burn and lay waste the country immediately on their arrival, at a time when men's minds are still heated and resolute for defence. And for this very reason the Prince ought the less to fear, because after a few days, when the first ardour has abated, the injury is already done and suffered, and cannot be undone; and the people will now, all the more readily, make common cause with their Prince from his seeming to be under obligations to them, their houses having been burned and their lands wasted in his defence. For it is the nature of men to incur obligation as much by the benefits they render as by those they receive.

Wherefore, if the whole matter be well considered, it ought not to be difficult for a prudent Prince, both at the outset and afterwards, to maintain the spirits of his subjects during a siege; provided always that victuals and the other means of defence do not run short.

CHAPTER XI

Of Ecclesiastical Princedoms[10]

It now only remains for me to treat of Ecclesiastical Princedoms, all the difficulties in respect of which precede their acquisition. For they are acquired by merit or good fortune, but are maintained without either; being upheld by the venerable ordinances of Religion, which are all of such a nature and efficacy that they secure the authority of their Princes in whatever way they may act or live. These Princes alone have territories which they do not defend, and subjects whom they do not govern; yet their territories are not taken from them through not being defended, nor are their subjects concerned at not being governed, or led to think of throwing off their allegiance; nor

[10] Such as the Prince Bishoprics of Germany and the Papal States in Italy.

is it in their power to do so. Accordingly these Princedoms alone are secure and happy. But inasmuch as they are sustained by agencies of a higher nature than the mind of man can reach, I forbear to speak of them: for since they are set up and supported by God himself, he would be a rash and presumptuous man who should venture to discuss them.

Nevertheless, should any one ask me how it comes about that the temporal power of the Church, which before the time of Alexander was looked on with contempt by all the Potentates of Italy, and not only by those so styling themselves, but by every Baron and Lordling however insignificant, has now reached such a pitch of greatness that the King of France trembles before it, and that it has been able to drive him out of Italy and to crush the Venetians,[11] though the causes be known, it seem to me not superfluous to call them in some measure to recollection.

Before Charles of France passed into Italy,[12] that country was under the control of the Pope, the Venetians, the King of Naples, the Duke of Milan, and the Florentines.[13] Two chief objects had to be kept in view by all these powers; first, that no armed foreigner should be allowed to invade Italy; second, that no one of their own number should be suffered to extend his territory. Those whom it was especially needed to guard against, were the Pope and the Venetians.[14] To hold back the Venetians it was necessary that all the other States should combine, as was done for the defence of Ferrara; while to restrain the Pope, use was made of the Roman Barons, who being divided into two factions, the Orsini and Colonnesi, had constant cause for feud with one another, and standing with arms in their hands under the very eyes of the Pontiff, kept the Popedom feeble and insecure.

And although there arose from time to time a courageous Pope like Sixtus, neither his prudence nor his good fortune could free him from these embarrassments. The cause whereof was the shortness of the lives of the Popes. For in the ten years, which was the average duration of a Pope's life, he could barely succeed in humbling one of these factions; so that if, for instance, one Pope had almost exterminated the Colonnesi, he was followed by another, who being the enemy of the Orsini had no time to rid himself of them, but so far from completing the destruction of the Colonnesi, restored them to life. This led to the temporal authority of the Popes being little esteemed in Italy.

[11] Pope Julius II defeated Venice by means of papal armies and the powerful League of Cambrai (1508 ff.), and France by means of the formidable Holy League (1512 ff.).

[12] Charles VIII of France invaded Italy in 1494, thus bringing about a renewed period of foreign intervention.

[13] Since the balance-of-power system was established in Italy by Cosimo de' Medici in 1454.

[14] From a Florentine point of view.

Then came Alexander VI, who more than any of his predecessors showed what a Pope could effect with money and arms, achieving by the instrumentality of Duke Valentino, and by taking advantage of the coming of the French into Italy, all those successes which I have already noticed in speaking of the actions of the Duke. And although his object was to aggrandize, not the Church but the Duke, what he did turned to the advantage of the Church, which after his death, and after the Duke had been put out of the way, became the heir of his labours.

After him came Pope Julius, who found the Church strengthened by the possession of the whole of Romagna, and the Roman Barons exhausted and their factions shattered under the blows of Pope Alexander. He found also a way opened for the accumulation of wealth, which before the time of Alexander no one had followed. These advantages Julius not only used but added to. He undertook the conquest of Bologna, the overthrow of the Venetians, and the expulsion of the French from Italy; in all which enterprises he succeeded, and with the greater glory to himself in that whatever he did, was done to strengthen the Church and not to aggrandize any private person. He succeeded, moreover, in keeping the factions of the Orsini and Colonnesi within the same limits as he found them; and, though some seeds of insubordination may still have been left among them, two causes operated to hold them in check; first, the great power of the Church, which overawed them, and second, their being without Cardinals, who had been the cause of all their disorders. For these factions while they have Cardinals among them can never be at rest, since it is they who foment dissension both in Rome and out of it, in which the Barons are forced to take part, the ambition of the Prelates thus giving rise to tumult and discord among the Barons.

His Holiness, Pope Leo,[15] has consequently found the Papacy most powerful; and from him we may hope, that as his predecessors made it great with arms, he will render it still greater and more venerable by his benignity and other countless virtues.

CHAPTER XII

How Many Different Kinds of Soldiers There Are, and of Mercenaries

Having spoken particularly of all the various kinds of Princedom whereof at the outset I proposed to treat, considered in some measure what are the causes of their strength and weakness, and pointed out the methods by which men commonly seek to acquire them, it now remains that I should discourse generally concerning the means for

---

[15] Pope Leo X, formerly Cardinal Giovanni de' Medici, had just become Pope in 1513. It is to be remembered that Machiavelli was courting the favor of the Medici.

attack and defence of which each of these different kinds of Princedom may make use.

I have already said that a Prince must lay solid foundations, since otherwise he will inevitably be destroyed. Now the main foundations of all States, whether new, old or mixed, are good laws and good arms.[16] But since you cannot have the former without the latter, and where you have the latter, are likely to have the former, I shall here omit all discussion on the subject of laws, and speak only of arms.

I say then that the arms wherewith a Prince defends his State are either his own subjects, or they are mercenaries, or they are auxiliaries, or they are partly one and partly another. Mercenaries and auxiliaries are at once useless and dangerous, and he who holds his State by means of mercenary troops can never be solidly or securely seated. For such troops are disunited, ambitious, insubordinate, treacherous, insolent among friends, cowardly before foes, and without fear of God or faith with man. Whenever they are attacked, defeat follows; so that in peace you are plundered by them, in war by your enemies. And this because they have no tie or motive to keep them in the field beyond their paltry pay, in return for which it would be too much to expect them to give their lives. They are ready enough, therefore, to be your soldiers while you are at peace, but when war is declared they make off and disappear. I ought to have little difficulty in getting this believed, for the present ruin of Italy is due to no other cause than her having for many years trusted to mercenaries,[17] who though heretofore they may have helped the fortunes of some one man, and made a show of strength when matched with one another, have always revealed themselves in their true colours so soon as foreign enemies appeared. Hence it was that Charles of France was suffered to conquer Italy *with chalk;*[18] and he who said our sins were the cause, said truly, though it was not the sins he meant, but those which I have noticed. And as these were the sins of Princes, they it is who have paid the penalty.

But I desire to demonstrate still more clearly the untoward character of these forces. Captains of mercenaries are either able men, or they are not. If they are, you cannot trust them, since they will always seek their own aggrandizement, either by overthrowing you who are their master, or by the overthrow of others contrary to your desire. On the other hand, if your captain be not an able man the chances are you will be ruined. And if it be said that whoever has arms in his hands will act in the same way whether he be a mercenary or no, I answer that when arms have to be employed by a Prince or a Republic,

---

[16] Cf. Justinian, in the Preface to the *Institutes*, in his *Corpus Juris Civilis*.
[17] For some time, and especially from the 14th century on, partly as a by-product of lapses in the Hundred Years War, bands of foreign mercenaries, led by *condottieri*, had been the chief protection of Italian states. Of late there had been an increasing trend to Italian mercenaries, but from other states.
[18] I.e., without any trouble, by merely designing to do so.

the Prince ought to go in person to take command as captain, the Republic should send one of her citizens, and if he prove incapable should change him, but if he prove capable should by the force of the laws confine him within proper bounds. And we see from experience that both Princes and Republics when they depend on their own arms have the greatest success, whereas from employing mercenaries nothing but loss results. Moreover, a Republic trusting to her own forces, is with less danger than one which relies on foreign arms brought to yield obedience to a single citizen. Rome and Sparta remained for ages armed and free. The Swiss are at once the best armed and the freest people in the world.

Of mercenary arms in ancient times we have an example in the Carthaginians, who at the close of their first war with Rome, were well-nigh ruined by their hired troops, although these were commanded by Carthaginian citizens.[19] So too, when, on the death of Epaminondas, the Thebans made Philip of Macedon captain of their army, after gaining a victory for them, he deprived them of their liberty.[1] The Milanese, in like manner, when Duke Filippo died, took Francesco Sforza into their pay to conduct the war against the Venetians. But he, after defeating the enemy at Caravaggio, combined with them to overthrow the Milanese, his masters. His father[2] too while in the pay of Giovanna, Queen of Naples, suddenly left her without troops, obliging her, in order to save her kingdom, to throw herself into the arms of the King of Aragon.

And if it be said that in times past the Venetians and the Florentines have extended their dominions by means of these arms, and that their captains have served them faithfully, without seeking to make themselves their masters, I answer that in this respect the Florentines have been fortunate, because among those valiant captains who might have given them cause for fear, some have not been victorious, some have had rivals, and some have turned their ambition in other directions.

Among those not victorious, was Giovanni Acuto,[3] whose fidelity, since he was unsuccessful, was not put to the proof: but any one may see, that had he been victorious the Florentines must have been entirely in his hands. The Sforzas, again, had constant rivals in the Braccheschi, so that the one following was a check upon the other;

---

[19] Plutocratic Carthage was notorious for the use of mercenaries. After the First Punic War, Carthaginian mercenaries, clamoring unsuccessfully for arrears of pay, revolted and besieged Carthage, which was relieved by Hamilcar Barca (241 B.C.).

[1] After the death of Epaminondas (362 B.C.), Thebes called in Philip II of Macedon to help them in a war against the Phocians. Philip thereby occupied territory next to Thebes, which thus became a Macedonian satellite.

[2] Giacomo or Muzio Sforza, father of Francesco, served Joanna II of Naples and later Pope Martin V. He was drowned in 1424.

[3] Sir John Hawkwood, English soldier of fortune, who served as *condottiere* for various Italian states in the wars of the 14th century, and died in 1394.

moreover, the ambition of Francesco was directed against Milan, while that of Braccio was directed against the Church and the kingdom of Naples. Let us turn, however, to what took place lately. The Florentines chose for their captain Paolo Vitelli, a most prudent commander, who had raised himself from privacy to the highest renown in arms. Had he been successful in reducing Pisa, none can deny that the Florentines would have been completely in his power, for they would have been ruined had he gone over to their enemies, while if they retained him they must have submitted to his will.[4]

Again, as to the Venetians, if we consider the growth of their power, it will be seen that they conducted their affairs with glory and safety so long as their subjects of all ranks, gentle and simple alike, valiantly bore arms in their wars; as they did before they directed their enterprises landwards. But when they took to making war by land, they forsook those methods in which they excelled and were content to follow the customs of Italy.

At first, indeed, in extending their possessions on the mainland, having as yet but little territory and being held in high repute, they had not much to fear from their captains; but when their territories increased, which they did under Carmagnola, they were taught their mistake. For as they found him a most valiant and skilful leader when, under his command, they defeated the Duke of Milan, and, on the other hand, saw him slack in carrying on the war, they made up their minds that no further victories were to be had under him; and because, through fear of losing what they had gained, they could not discharge him, to secure themselves against him they were forced to put him to death.[5] After him they have had for captains, Bartolommeo of Bergamo, Roberto of San Severino, the Count of Pitigliano, and the like, under whom their danger has not been from victories, but from defeats; as, for instance, at Vaïla,[6] where they lost in a single day what it had taken the efforts of eight hundred years to acquire. For the gains resulting from mercenary arms are slow, and late, and inconsiderable, but the losses sudden and astounding.

And since these examples have led me back to Italy, which for many years past has been defended by mercenary arms, I desire to go somewhat deeper into the matter, in order that the causes which led to the adoption of these arms being seen, they may the more readily be corrected. You are to understand, then, that when in these

---

[4] Paolo Vitelli was eventually executed by the Florentines for treachery (see above).

[5] Carmagnola was an Italian *condottiere*, who first served the Dukes of Milan and then the Doges of Venice. But in his dilatory war on behalf of the Venetians he was eventually suspected of infidelity and beheaded for treachery by the Venetian government (1432).

[6] At Agnadello, in 1510, the Venetians suffered so severe a defeat at the hands of the League of Cambrai that they stood likely to lose most of their peninsular holdings.

later times the Imperial control began to be rejected by Italy, and the temporal power of the Pope to be more thought of, Italy suddenly split up into a number of separate States. For many of the larger cities took up arms against their nobles, who, with the favour of the Emperor, had before kept them in subjection, and were supported by the Church with a view to add to her temporal authority; while in many others of these cities, private citizens became rulers. Hence Italy, having passed almost entirely into the hands of the Church and of certain Republics, the former made up of priests, the latter of citizens unfamiliar with arms, began to take foreigners into her pay.

The first who gave reputation to this service was Alberigo of Conio[7] in Romagna, from whose school of warlike training descended, among others, Braccio and Sforza, who in their time were the arbiters of Italy; after whom came all those others who down to the present hour have held similar commands, and to whose merits we owe it that our country has been overrun by Charles, plundered by Louis, wasted by Ferdinand,[8] and insulted by the Swiss.

The first object of these mercenaries was to bring foot soldiers into disrepute, in order to enhance the merit of their own followers; and this they did, because lacking territory of their own and depending on their profession for their support, a few foot soldiers gave them no importance, while for a large number they were unable to provide. For these reasons they had recourse to horsemen, a less retinue of whom was thought to confer distinction, and could be more easily maintained. And the matter went to such a length that in an army of twenty thousand men, not two thousand foot soldiers were to be found. Moreover, they spared no endeavour to relieve themselves and their men from fatigue and danger, not killing one another in battle, but making prisoners who were afterwards released without ransom. They would attack no town by night; those in towns would make no sortie by night against a besieging army. Their camps were without rampart or trench. They had no winter campaigns. All which arrangements were sanctioned by their military rules, contrived by them, as I have said already, to escape fatigue and danger; but the result of which has been to bring Italy into servitude and contempt.

CHAPTER XIII

Of Auxilliary, Mixed, and National Arms

The second sort of unprofitable arms are auxiliaries, by whom I mean troops brought to help and protect you by a potentate whom you summon to your aid; as when in recent times, Pope Julius II, ob-

---

[7] Machiavelli calls him Ludovico da Conio towards the end of the first book of his *History of Florence*.

[8] Charles VIII of France, Louis XII of France and Ferdinand V of Spain.

serving the pitiful behaviour of his mercenaries at the enterprise of Ferrara,[9] betook himself to auxiliaries, and arranged with Ferdinand of Spain to be supplied with horse and foot soldiers.[10]

Auxiliaries may be excellent and useful soldiers for themselves, but are always hurtful to him who calls them in; for if they are defeated, he is undone, if victorious, he becomes their prisoner. Ancient histories abound with instances of this, but I shall not pass from the example of Pope Julius, which is still fresh in men's minds. It was the height of rashness for him, in his eagerness to gain Ferrara, to throw himself without reserve into the arms of a stranger. Nevertheless, his good fortune came to his rescue, and he had not to reap the fruits of his ill-considered conduct. For after his auxiliaries were defeated at Ravenna, the Swiss suddenly descended and, to their own surprise and that of every one else, swept the victors out of the country, so that, he neither remained a prisoner with his enemies, they being put to flight, nor with his auxiliaries, because victory was won by other arms than theirs.[11] The Florentines, being wholly without soldiers of their own, brought ten thousand French men-at-arms to the siege of Pisa, thereby incurring greater peril than at any previous time of trouble.[12] To protect himself from his neighbours, the Emperor of Constantinople summoned ten thousand Turkish soldiers into Greece, who, when the war was over, refused to leave, and this was the beginning of the servitude of Greece to the Infidel.[13]

Let him, therefore, who would deprive himself of every chance of success, have recourse to auxiliaries, these being far more dangerous than mercenary arms, bringing ruin with them ready made. For they are united, and wholly under the control of their own officers; whereas, before mercenaries, even after gaining a victory, can do you hurt, longer time and better opportunities are needed; because, as they are made up of separate companies, raised and paid by you, he whom you place in command cannot at once acquire such authority over them as will be injurious to you. In short, with mercenaries your greatest danger is from their inertness and cowardice, with auxiliaries from their valour. Wise Princes, therefore, have always eschewed these arms, and trusted rather to their own, and have preferred defeat with the latter to victory with the former, counting that as no true victory which is gained by foreign aid.

I shall never hesiate to cite the example of Cesare Borgia and his actions.[14] He entered Romagna with a force of auxiliaries, all of them French men-at-arms, with whom he took Imola and Forli. But it

---

[9] In 1510.   [10] In 1511.   [11] In 1512.
[12] The Florentine siege of Pisa took place 1507–1509.
[13] In the mid-14th century, usurping Emperor John V, Cantecuzene brought the Ottoman Turks into the Gallipoli peninsula to help him against John VI, and when the latter won the civil war the Ottoman Turks stayed on in the peninsula.
[14] In the period 1500–1503, as above.

appearing to him afterwards that these troops were not to be trusted, he had recourse to mercenaries from whom he thought there would be less danger, and took the Orsini and Vitelli into his pay. But finding these likewise while under his command to be fickle, false, and treacherous, he got rid of them, and fell back on troops of his own raising. And we may readily discern the difference between these various kinds of arms, by observing the different degrees of reputation in which the Duke stood while he depended upon the French alone, when he took the Orsini and Vitelli into his pay, and when he fell back on his own troops and his own resources; for we find his reputation always increasing, and that he was never so well thought of as when every one perceived him to be sole master of his own forces. . . .

Charles VII,[15] the father of Louis XI, who by his good fortune and valour freed France from the English, saw this necessity of strengthening himself with a national army, and drew up ordinances regulating the service both of men-at-arms and of foot soldiers throughout his kingdom. But afterwards his son, King Louis,[16] did away with the national infantry, and began to hire Swiss mercenaries. Which blunder having been followed by subsequent Princes, has been the cause, as the result shows, of the dangers into which the kingdom of France has fallen; for, by enhancing the reputation of the Swiss, the whole of the national troops of Frances have been deteriorated. For from their infantry being done away with, their men-at-arms are made wholly dependent on foreign assistance, and being accustomed to co-operate with the Swiss, have grown to think they can do nothing without them. Hence the French are no match for the Swiss, and without them cannot succeed against others.

The armies of France, then, are mixed, being partly national and partly mercenary. Armies thus composed are far superior to mere mercenaries or mere auxiliaries, but far inferior to forces purely national. And this example is in itself conclusive, for the realm of France would be invincible if the military ordinances of Charles VII had been retained and extended. But from want of foresight men make changes which relishing well at first do not betray their hidden venom, as I have already observed respecting hectic fever. Nevertheless, the ruler is not truly wise who cannot discern evils before they develop themselves, and this is a faculty given to few. . . .

CHAPTER XIV

Of the Duty of a Prince In Respect of Military Affairs

A Prince, therefore, should have no care or thought but for war, and for the regulations and training it requires, and should apply

[15] Charles VII of France (1422/29–61).   [16] Louis XI (1461–83).

himself exclusively to this as his peculiar province; for war is the sole art looked for in one who rules, and is of such efficacy that it not merely maintains those who are born Princes, but often enables men to rise to that eminence from a private station; while, on the other hand, we often see that when Princes devote themselves rather to pleasure than to arms, they lose their dominions. And as neglect of this art is the prime cause of such calamities, so to be a proficient in it is the surest way to acquire power. Francesco Sforza, from his renown in arms, rose from privacy to be Duke of Milan, while his descendants, seeking to avoid the hardships and fatigues of military life, from being Princes fell back into privacy. For among other causes of misfortune which your not being armed brings upon you, it makes you despised, and this is one of those reproaches against which, as shall presently be explained, a Prince ought most carefully to guard.

Between an armed and an unarmed man no proportion holds, and it is contrary to reason to expect that the armed man should voluntarily submit to him who is unarmed, or that the unarmed man should stand secure among armed retainers. For with contempt on one side, and distrust on the other, it is impossible that men should work well together. Wherefore, as has already been said, a Prince who is ignorant of military affairs, besides other disadvantages, can neither be respected by his soldiers, nor can he trust them. A Prince, therefore, ought never to allow his attention to be diverted from warlike pursuits, and should occupy himself with them even more in peace than in war. This he can do in two ways, by practice or by study.

As to practice, he ought, besides keeping his soldiers well trained and disciplined, to be constantly engaged in the chase, that he may inure his body to hardships and fatigue, and gain at the same time a knowledge of places, by observing how the mountains slope, the valleys open, and the plains spread; acquainting himself with the characters of rivers and marshes, and giving the greatest attention to this subject. Such knowledge is useful to him in two ways; for first, he learns thereby to know his own country, and to understand better how it may be defended; and next, from his familiar acquaintance with its localities, he readily comprehends the character of other districts, when obliged to observe them for the first time. For the hills, valleys, plains, rivers, and marshes of Tuscany, for example, have a certain resemblance to those elsewhere; so that from a knowledge of the natural features of that province, similar knowledge in respect of other provinces may readily be gained. The Prince who is wanting in this kind of knowledge, is wanting in the first qualification of a good captain, for by it he is taught how to surprise an enemy, how to choose an encampment, how to lead his army on a march, how to array it for battle, and how to post it to the best advantage for a siege. . . .

As to the mental training of which we have spoken, a Prince

should read histories,[17] and in these should note the actions of great men, observe how they conducted themselves in their wars, and examine the causes of their victories and defeats, so as to avoid the latter and imitate them in the former. And above all, he should, as many great men of past ages have done, assume for his models those persons who before his time have been renowned and celebrated, whose deeds and achievements he should constantly keep in mind, as it is related that Alexander the Great sought to resemble Achilles, Caesar Alexander, and Scipio Cyrus. And any one who reads the life of this last-named hero, written by Xenophon, recognizes afterwards in the life of Scipio, how much this imitation was the source of his glory, and how nearly in his chastity, affability, kindliness, and generosity, he conformed to the character of Cyrus as Xenophon describes it.[18]

CHAPTER XV

Of the Qualities In Respect of Which Men, and Most of All Princes, Are Praised or Blamed

It now remains for us to consider what ought to be the conduct and bearing of a Prince in relation to his subjects and friends. And since I know that many have written on this subject, I fear it may be thought presumptuous in me to write of it also; the more so, because in my treatment of it I depart from the views that others have taken.

But since it is my object to write what shall be useful to whosoever understands it, it seems to me better to follow the real truth of things than an imaginary view of them. For many Republics and Princedoms have been imagined that were never seen or known to exist in reality. And the manner in which we live, and that in which we ought to live, are things so wide asunder, that he who quits the one to betake himself to the other is more likely to destroy than to save himself; since any one who would act up to a perfect standard of goodness in everything, must be ruined among so many who are not good. It is essential, therefore, for a Prince who desires to maintain his position, to have learned how to be other than good, and to use or not to use his goodness as necessity requires.[19]

Laying aside, therefore, all fanciful notions concerning a Prince, and considering those only that are true, I say that all men when they are spoken of, and Princes more than others from their being set so high, are characterized by some one of those qualities which attach

[17] Machiavelli, like most political scientists, is a great booster and user of history. He is also a noted history-writer.
[18] Xenophon's *Cyropaedia*, purporting to describe the training and character of Cyrus the Great, was actually an idealized presentation of many of the author's own philosophical and pedagogical ideas.
[19] This paragraph summarizes the political theory of Machiavelli presented in this work, and the reasoning behind it.

either praise or blame. Thus one is accounted liberal, another miserly (which word I use, rather than *avaricious*, to denote the man who is too sparing of what is his own, *avarice* being the disposition to take wrongfully what is another's); one is generous, another greedy; one cruel, another tender-hearted; one is faithless, another true to his word; one effeminate and cowardly, another high-spirited and courageous; one is courteous, another haughty; one impure, another chaste; one simple, another crafty; one firm, another facile; one grave, another frivolous; one devoted, another unbelieving; and the like. Every one, I know, will admit that it would be most laudable for a Prince to be endowed with all of the above qualities that are reckoned good; but since it is impossible for him to possess or constantly practise them all, the conditions of human nature not allowing it, he must be discreet enough to know how to avoid the infamy of those vices that would deprive him of his government, and, if possible, be on his guard also against those which might not deprive him of it; though if he cannot wholly restrain himself, he may with less scruple indulge in the latter. He need never hesitate, however, to incur the reproach of those vices without which his authority can hardly be preserved; for if he well consider the whole matter, he will find that there may be a line of conduct having the appearance of virtue, to follow which would be his ruin, and that there may be another course having the appearance of vice, by following which his safety and well-being are secured.

CHAPTER XVI
Of Liberality and Miserliness

Beginning, then, with the first of the qualities above noticed, I say that it may be a good thing to be reputed liberal, but, nevertheless, that liberality without the reputation of it is hurtful; because, though it be worthily and rightly used, still if it be not known, you escape not the reproach of its opposite vice. . . .

A Prince, therefore, since he cannot without injury to himself practise the virtue of liberality so that it may be known, will not, if he be wise, greatly concern himself though he be called miserly. Because in time he will come to be regarded as more and more liberal, when it is seen that through his parsimony his revenues are sufficient; that he is able to defend himself against any who make war on him; that he can engage in enterprises against others without burdening his subjects; and thus exercise liberality towards all from whom he does not take, whose number is infinite, while he is miserly in respect of those only to whom he does not give, whose number is few.

In our own days we have seen no Princes accomplish great results save those who have been accounted miserly. All others have been ruined. Pope Julius II, after availing himself of his reputation for liberality to arrive at the Papacy, made no effort to preserve that reputation when making war on the King of France, but carried on all his numerous campaigns without levying from his subjects a single extraordinary tax, providing for the increased expenditure out of his long-continued savings. Had the present King of Spain[1] been accounted liberal, he never could have engaged or succeeded in so many enterprises.

A Prince, therefore, if he is enabled thereby to forbear from plundering his subjects, to defend himself, to escape poverty and contempt, and the necessity of becoming rapacious, ought to care little though he incur the reproach of miserliness, for this is one of those vices which enable him to reign. . . .

And if it be further urged that many Princes reputed to have been most liberal have achieved great things with their armies, I answer that a Prince spends either what belongs to himself and his subjects, or what belongs to others; and that in the former case he ought to be sparing, but in the latter ought not to refrain from any kind of liberality. Because for a Prince who leads his armies in person and maintains them by plunder, pillage, and forced contributions, dealing as he does with the property of others, this liberality is necessary, since otherwise he would not be followed by his soldiers. Of what does not belong to you or to your subjects you should, therefore, be a lavish giver, as were Cyrus, Caesar, and Alexander; for to be liberal with the property of others does not take from your reputation, but adds to it. What injures you is to give away what is your own. And there is no quality so self-destructive as liberality; for while you practise it you lose the means whereby it can be practised, and become poor and despised, or else, to avoid poverty, you become rapacious and hated. For liberality leads to one or other of these two results, against which, beyond all others, a Prince should guard.

Wherefore it is wiser to put up with the name of being miserly, which breeds ignominy, but without hate, than to be obliged, from the desire to be reckoned liberal, to incur the reproach of rapacity, which breeds hate as well as ignominy.

CHAPTER XVII

Of Cruelty and Clemency, and Whether It Is Better To Be Loved or Feared

Passing to the other qualities above referred to, I say that every Prince should desire to be accounted merciful and not cruel. Nevertheless, he should be on his guard against the abuse of this quality of mercy. Cesare Borgia was reputed cruel, yet his cruelty restored Romagna, united it, and brought it to order and obedience;

---

[1] Ferdinand V, the Catholic (d. 1516), husband of Isabella of Castile.

so that if we look at things in their true light, it will be seen that he was in reality far more merciful than the people of Florence, who, to avoid the imputation of cruelty, suffered Pistoja to be torn to pieces by factions.[2]

A Prince should therefore disregard the reproach of being thought cruel where it enables him to keep his subjects united and obedient. For he who quells disorder by a very few signal examples will in the end be more merciful than he who from too great leniency permits things to take their course and so to result in rapine and bloodshed; for these hurt the whole State, whereas the severities of the Prince injure individuals only.

And for a new Prince, of all others, it is impossible to escape a name for cruelty, since new States are full of dangers. Wherefore Virgil, by the mouth of Dido, excuses the harshness of her reign on the plea that it was new, saying: —

> 'A fate unkind, and newness in my reign
> Compel me thus to guard a wide domain.'[3]

Nevertheless, the new Prince should not be too ready of belief, nor too easily set in motion; nor should he himself be the first to raise alarms; but should so temper prudence with kindliness that too great confidence in others shall not throw him off guard, nor groundless distrust render him insupportable.

And here comes in the question whether it is better to be loved rather than feared, or feared rather than loved. It might perhaps be answered that we should wish to be both; but since love and fear can hardly exist together, if we must choose between them, it is far safer to be feared than loved. For of men it may generally be affirmed that they are thankless, fickle, false, studious to avoid danger, greedy of gain, devoted to you while you are able to confer benefits upon them, and ready, as I said before, while danger is distant, to shed their blood, and sacrifice their property, their lives, and their children for you; but in the hour of need they turn against you.[4] The Prince, therefore, who without otherwise securing himself builds wholly on their professions is undone. For the friendships which we buy with a price, and do not gain by greatness and nobility of character, though they be fairly earned are not made good, but fail us when we have occasion to use them.

Moreover, men are less careful how they offend him who makes himself loved than him who makes himself feared. For love is held by the tie of obligation, which, because men are a sorry breed, is broken on every whisper of private interest; but fear is bound by the apprehension of punishment which never relaxes its grasp.

---

[2] By not forcibly suppressing two rival families that kept the city in turmoil.
[3] Virgil, *Aeneid*, I, 563–4.
[4] Note Machiavelli's pessimistic view of human nature.

Nevertheless a Prince should inspire fear in such a fashion that if he do not win love he may escape hate. For a man may very well be feared and yet not hated, and this will be the case so long as he does not meddle with the property or with the women of his citizens and subjects. And if constrained to put any to death, he should do so only when there is manifest cause or reasonable justification. But, above all, he must abstain from the property of others. For men will sooner forget the death of their father than the loss of their patrimony. Moreover, pretexts for confiscation are never to seek, and he who has once begun to live by rapine always finds reasons for taking what is not his; whereas reasons for shedding blood are fewer, and sooner exhausted.

But when a Prince is with his army, and has many soldiers under his command, he must needs disregard the reproach of cruelty, for without such a reputation in its Captain, no army can be held together or kept under any kind of control. Among other things remarkable in Hannibal[5] this has been noted, that having a very great army, made up of men of many different nations and brought to fight in a foreign country, no dissension ever rose among the soldiers themselves, nor any mutiny against their leader, either in his good or in his evil fortunes. This we can only ascribe to the transcendent cruelty, which, joined with numberless great qualities, rendered him at once venerable and terrible in the eyes of his soldiers; for without this reputation for cruelty these other virtues would not have produced the like results. . . .

CHAPTER XVIII
How Princes Should Keep Faith

Every one understands how praiseworthy it is in a Prince to keep faith, and to live uprightly and not craftily. Nevertheless, we see from what has taken place in our own days that Princes who have set little store by their word, but have known how to overreach men by their cunning, have accomplished great things, and in the end got the better of those who trusted to honest dealing.

Be it known, then, that there are two ways of contending, one in accordance with the laws, the other by force; the first of which is proper to men, the second to beasts. But since the first method is often ineffectual, it becomes necessary to resort to the second. A Prince should, therefore, understand how to use well both the man and the beast. And this lesson has been covertly taught by the ancient writers, who relate how Achilles and many others of these old Princes were given over to be brought up and trained by Chiron the Centaur;[6]

---

[5] Hannibal, great Carthaginian general, so successful in Spain and especially in Italy during the Second Punic War (218–201 B.C.).

[6] Chiron the Centaur, son of Cronus and a sea-nymph, was famous for his wisdom and was supposed to have instructed many celebrated heroes, according to Greek mythology.

since the only meaning of their having for instructor one who was half man and half beast is, that it is necessary for a Prince to know how to use both natures, and that the one without the other has no stability.

But since a Prince should know how to use the beast's nature wisely, he ought of beasts to choose both the lion and the fox; for the lion cannot guard himself from the toils, nor the fox from wolves. He must therefore be a fox to discern toils,[7] and a lion to drive off wolves.

To rely wholly on the lion is unwise; and for this reason a prudent Prince neither can nor ought to keep his word when to keep it is hurtful to him and the causes which led him to pledge it are removed. If all men were good, this would not be good advice, but since they are dishonest and do not keep faith with you, you, in return, need not keep faith with them; and no prince was ever at a loss for plausible reasons to cloak a breach of faith. Of this, numberless recent instances could be given, and it might be shown how many solemn treaties and engagements have been rendered inoperative and idle through want of faith in Princes, and that he who was best known to play the fox has had the best success.

It is necessary, indeed, to put a good colour[8] on this nature, and to be skilful in simulating and dissembling. But men are so simple, and governed so absolutely by their present needs, that he who wishes to deceive will never fail in finding willing dupes. One recent example I will not omit. Pope Alexander VI had no care or thought but how to deceive, and always found material to work on. No man ever had a more effective manner of asseverating, or made promises with more solemn protestations, or observed them less. And yet, because he understood this side of human nature, his frauds always succeeded.

It is not essential, then, that a Prince should have all the good qualities which I have enumerated above, but it is most essential that he should seem to have them; I will even venture to affirm that if he has and invariably practises them all, they are hurtful, whereas the appearance of having them is useful. Thus, it is well to seem merciful, faithful, humane, religious, and upright, and also to be so; but the mind should remain so balanced that were it needful not to be so, you should be able and know how to change to the contrary.

And you are to understand that a Prince, and most of all a new Prince, cannot observe all those rules of conduct in respect whereof men are accounted good, being often forced, in order to preserve his Princedom, to act in opposition to good faith, charity, humanity, and religion. He must therefore keep his mind ready to shift as the winds and tides of Fortune turn, and, as I have already said, he ought not to quit good courses if he can help it, but should know how to follow evil courses if he must.[9]

[7] Snares. [8] Appearance.
[9] There can be no doubt that Machiavelli argued for suspension of the moral law in the case of princes, and supported the doctrine that the end justifies the means, as we see here and elsewhere in *The Prince*.

A Prince should therefore be very careful that nothing ever escapes his lips which is not replete with the five qualities above named, so that to see and hear him, one would think him the embodiment of mercy, good faith, integrity, humanity, and religion. And there is no virtue which it is more necessary for him to seem to possess than this last; because men in general judge rather by the eye than by the hand, for every one can see but few can touch. Every one sees what you seem, but few know what you are, and these few dare not oppose themselves to the opinion of the many who have the majesty of the State to back them up.

Moreover, in the actions of all men, and most of all of Princes, where there is no tribunal to which we can appeal, we look to results. Wherefore if a Prince succeeds in establishing and maintaining his authority, the means will always be judged honourable and be approved by every one. For the vulgar are always taken by appearances and by results, and the world is made up of the vulgar, the few only finding room when the many have no longer ground to stand on.

A certain Prince of our own days, whose name it is as well not to mention,[10] is always preaching peace and good faith, although the mortal enemy of both; and either of them, had he practised them as he preaches them, would oftener than once, have lost him his kingdom and authority.

CHAPTER XIX

That a Prince Should Seek To Escape Contempt and Hatred

Having now spoken of the chief of the qualities above referred to, the rest I shall dispose of briefly with these general remarks, that a Prince, as has already in part been said, should consider how he may avoid such courses as would make him hated or despised; and that whenever he succeeds in keeping clear of these, he has performed his part, and runs no risk though he incur other infamies.

A Prince, as I have said before, sooner becomes hated by being rapacious and by interfering with the property and with the women of his subjects, than in any other way. From these, therefore, he should abstain. For so long as neither their property nor their honour is touched, the mass of mankind live contentedly, and the Prince has only to cope with the ambition of a few, which can in many ways and easily be kept within bounds.

A Prince is despised when he is seen to be fickle, frivolous, effeminate, pusillanimous, or irresolute, against which defects he ought therefore most carefully to guard, striving so to bear himself that

[10] This is apparently a reference to Ferdinand V of Aragon and Spain, who had recently acquired the Kingdom of Naples by duplicity, and was ruling Castile on questionable grounds after the death of his wife Isabella.

greatness, courage, wisdom, and strength may appear in all his actions. In his private dealings with his subjects his decisions should be irrevocable, and his reputation such that no one would dream of overreaching or cajoling him.

The Prince who inspires such an opinion of himself is greatly esteemed, and against one who is greatly esteemed, conspiracy is difficult; nor, when he is known to be an excellent Prince and held in reverence by his subjects, will it be easy to attack him. For a Prince is exposed to two dangers, from within in respect of his subjects, from without in respect of foreign powers. Against the latter he will defend himself with good arms and good allies, and if he have good arms he will always have good allies; and when things are settled abroad, they will always be settled at home, unless disturbed by conspiracies; and even should there be hostility from without, if he has taken those measures, and has lived in the way I have recommended, and if he never abandons hope, he will withstand every attack. . . .

CHAPTER XX

Whether Fortresses, and Certain Other Expedients to Which Princes Often Have Recourse, are Profitable or Hurtful

To govern more securely some Princes have disarmed their subjects, others have kept the towns subject to them divided by factions; some have fostered hostility against themselves, others have sought to gain over those who at the beginning of their reign were looked on with suspicion; some have built fortresses, others have dismantled and destroyed them. . . .

It has been customary for Princes, with a view to hold their dominions more securely, to build fortresses which might serve as a curb and restraint on such as have designs against them, and as a safe refuge against a first onset. I approve this custom, because it has been followed from the earliest times. Nevertheless, in our own days, Messer Niccolò Vitelli[11] thought it prudent to dismantle two fortresses in Città di Castello in order to secure that town: and Guido Ubaldo, Duke of Urbino,[12] on returning to his dominions, whence he had been driven by Cesare Borgia, razed to their foundations the fortresses throughout the Dukedom, judging that if these were removed, it would not again be so easily lost. A like course was followed by the Bentivogli[13] on their return to Bologna.

[11] Niccolò Vitelli, father of Vitellozo and Paolo Vitelli (see above) was a soldier of fortune who became tyrant of Città di Castello (15th century).
[12] Guido Ubaldo, son of Frederigo, was Duke of Urbino 1482–1508. Expelled by Cesare Borgia in 1497, Guido returned to Urbino in 1503.
[13] The Bentivoglio family ruled Bologna from 1438 to 1506, when they were driven out by Pope Julius II, who was reclaiming former territories of the Papal States.

Fortresses, therefore, are useful or no, according to circumstances, and if in one way they benefit, in another they injure you. We may state the case thus: the Prince who is more afraid of his subjects than of strangers ought to build fortresses, while he who is more afraid of strangers than of his subjects, should leave them alone. The citadel built by Francesco Sforza in Milan, has been, and will hereafter prove to be more dangerous to the House of Sforza than any other disorder of that State. So that, on the whole, the best fortress you can have, is in not being hated by your subjects. If they hate you no fortress will save you; for when once the people take up arms, foreigners are never wanting to assist them.

Within our own time it does not appear that fortresses have been of service to any Prince, unless to the Countess of Forli[14] after her husband Count Girolamo was murdered; for by this means she was able to escape the first onset of the insurgents, and awaiting succour from Milan, to recover her State; the circumstances of the times not allowing any foreigner to lend assistance to the people. But afterwards, when she was attacked by Cesare Borgia, and the people, out of hostility to her, took part with the invader, her fortresses were of little avail. So that, both on this and on the former occasion, it would have been safer for her to have had no fortresses, than to have had her subjects for enemies.

All which considerations taken into account, I shall applaud him who builds fortresses, and him who does not; but I shall blame him who, trusting in them, reckons it a light thing to be held in hatred by his people.

CHAPTER XXI

How a Prince Should Bear Himself So As to Acquire Reputation

Nothing makes a Prince so well thought of as to undertake great enterprises and give striking proofs of his capacity.

Among the Princes of our time Ferdinand of Aragon, the present King of Spain,[15] may almost be accounted a new Prince, since from one of the weakest he has become, for fame and glory, the foremost King in Christendom. And if you consider his achievements you will find them all great and some extraordinary.

In the beginning of his reign he made war on Granada, which enterprise was the foundation of his power.[16] At first he carried on the war leisurely, without fear of interruption, and kept the attention and thoughts of the Barons of Castile so completely occupied with it, that

[14] Caterina Sforza, strenuous and unpopular Countess of Forli and Imola, was forcibly deposed by Cesare Borgia in 1500. She never regained power.
[15] Like Cesare Borgia, a hero of Machiavelli's.
[16] Ferdinand and Isabella first attacked Granada in 1481, but did not complete its conquest until 1492.

they had no time to think of changes at home. Meanwhile he insensibly acquired reputation among them and authority over them. With the money of the Church[17] and of his subjects he was able to maintain his armies, and during the prolonged contest to lay the foundations of that military discipline which afterwards made him so famous. Moreover, to enable him to engage in still greater undertakings, always covering himself with the cloak of religion, he had recourse to what may be called *pious cruelty,* in driving out and clearing his Kingdom of the Moors; than which exploit none could be more wonderful or uncommon.[18] Using the same pretext he made war on Africa, invaded Italy, and finally attacked France;[19] and being thus constantly busied in planning and executing vast designs, he kept the minds of his subjects in suspense and admiration, and occupied with the results of his actions, which arose one out of another in such close succession as left neither time nor opportunity to oppose them. . . .

And here let it be noted that a Prince should be careful never to join with one stronger than himself in attacking others, unless, as already said, he be driven to it by necessity. For if he whom you join prevails, you are at his mercy; and Princes, so far as in them lies, should avoid placing themselves at the mercy of others. The Venetians, although they might have declined the alliance, joined with France against the Duke of Milan, which brought about their ruin.[1] But when an alliance cannot be avoided, as was the case with the Florentines when the Pope and Spain together led their armies to attack Lombardy,[2] a Prince, for the reasons given, must take a side. Nor let it be supposed that any State can choose for itself a perfectly safe line of policy. On the contrary, it must reckon on every course which it may take being doubtful; for it happens in all human affairs that we never seek to escape one mischief without falling into another. Prudence therefore consists in knowing how to distinguish degrees of disadvantage, and in accepting a less evil as a good.

Again, a Prince should show himself a patron of merit, and should honour those who excel in every art. He ought accordingly to encourage his subjects by enabling them to pursue their callings, whether mercantile, agricultural, or any other, in security, so that this

---

[17] Over the Church, Ferdinand and Isabella enjoyed the *Real Patronato,* or royal right of patronage, which enabled them to participate in its revenues.

[18] Ferdinand and Isabella, by laws of 1492 and 1502, ordered that all Jews and Moors in their dominions who refused to be converted should be driven out, and they used the Inquisition to track down false converts.

[19] Ferdinand engaged in war in Africa in 1497 and invaded Italy in 1495. Besides fighting France in Italy, he invaded Navarre in 1512 and held it against French forces.

[1] Venice joined Louis XII of France against Milan in 1499; but the Venetians were themselves defeated in 1509 by the French and the League of Cambrai.

[2] The Florentines were aided by France against Pope Alexander VI and Spain, and against Pope Julius II and Spain. Florence was allied with France 1494–1512.

man shall not be deterred from beautifying his possessions from the apprehension that they may be taken from him, or that another refrain from opening a trade through fear of taxes; and he should provide rewards for those who desire so to employ themselves, and for all who are disposed in any way to add to the greatness of his City or State.

He ought, moreover, at suitable seasons of the year to entertain the people with festivals and shows. And because all cities are divided into guilds and companies, he should show attention to these societies, and sometimes take part in their meetings; offering an example of courtesy and munificence, but always maintaining the dignity of his station, which must under no circumstances be compromised.

CHAPTER XXII

Of the Secretaries of Princes

The choice of Ministers is a matter of no small moment to a Prince. Whether they shall be good or no depends on his prudence, so that the readiest conjecture we can form of the character and sagacity of a Prince, is from seeing what sort of men he has about him. When they are at once capable and faithful, we may always account him wise, since he has known to recognize their merit and to retain their fidelity. But if they be otherwise, we must pronounce unfavourably of him, since he has committed a first fault in making this selection. . . .

CHAPTER XXIV

Why the Princes of Italy Have Lost Their States

The lessons above taught, if prudently followed, will make a new Prince seem like an old one, and will soon seat him in his place more firmly and securely than if his authority had the sanction of time. For the actions of a new Prince are watched much more closely than those of an hereditary Prince; and when seen to be good are far more effectual than antiquity of blood in gaining men over and attaching them to his cause. For men are more nearly touched by things present than by things past, and when they find themselves well off as they are, enjoy their felicity and seek no further; nay, are ready to do their utmost in defence of the new Prince, provided he be not wanting to himself in other respects. In this way there accrues to him a twofold glory, in having laid the foundations of the new Princedom, and in having strengthened and adorned it with good laws and good arms, with faithful friends and great deeds; as, on the other hand, there is a double disgrace in one who has been born to a Princedom losing it by his own want of wisdom.

And if we contemplate those Lords who in our own times have lost their dominions in Italy, such as the King of Naples,[3] the Duke of Milan,[4] and others, in the first place we shall see, that in respect of arms they have, for reasons already dwelt on, been all alike defective; and next, that some of them have either had the people against them, or if they have had the people with them, have not known how to secure themselves against their nobles. For without such defects as these, States powerful enough to keep an army in the field are never overthrown.

Philip of Macedon,[5] not the father of Alexander the Great, but he who was vanquished by Titus Quintius, had no great State as compared with the strength of the Romans and Greeks who attacked him. Nevertheless, being a Prince of a warlike spirit, and skilful in gaining the good will of the people and in securing the fidelity of the nobles, he maintained himself for many years against his assailants, and in the end, though he lost some towns, succeeded in saving his Kingdom.

Let those Princes of ours, therefore, who, after holding them for a length of years, have lost their dominions, blame not Fortune but their own inertness. For never having reflected in tranquil times that there might come a change (and it is human nature when the sea is calm not to think of storms), when adversity overtook them, they thought not of defence but only of escape, hoping that their people, disgusted with the arrogance of the conqueror, would some day recall them.

This course may be a good one to follow when all others fail, but it were the height of folly, trusting to it, to abandon every other; since none would wish to fall on the chance of some one else being found to lift him up. It may not happen that you are recalled by your people, or if it happen, it gives you no security. It is an ignoble resource, since it does not depend on you for its success; and those modes of defence are alone good, certain, and lasting, which depend upon yourself and your own worth.

CHAPTER XXV

What Fortune Can Effect in Human Affairs, and How She May Be Withstood

I am not ignorant that many have been and are of the opinion that human affairs are so governed by Fortune and by God, that

[3] King Frederigo of Naples lost his kingdom to France and Spain, who were leagued against him, 1501–2. Although Louis XII and Ferdinand had agreed to partition the kingdom, they fell out over the spoils and Ferdinand seized the whole.

[4] Duke Ludovico il Moro of Milan lost his duchy to Louis XII of France 1499–1500. Although the French were later expelled by the Holy League (1513), they returned in 1516 and regained control of Milan.

[5] Philip V of Macedone (220–179 B.C.) was utterly defeated by the Romans at Cynoscephalae in 197 B.C., but remained King of Macedon until his death.

men cannot alter them by any prudence of theirs, and indeed have no remedy against them; and for this reason have come to think that it is not worth while to labour much about anything, but that they must leave everything to be determined by chance.

Often when I turn the matter over, I am in part inclined to agree with this opinion, which has had the readier acceptance in our own times from the great changes in things which we have seen, and every day see happen contrary to all human expectation. Nevertheless, that our free will be not wholly set aside, I think it may be the case that Fortune[6] is the mistress of one half our actions, and yet leaves the control of the other half, or a little less, to ourselves. And I would liken her to one of those wild torrents which, when angry, overflow the plains, sweep away trees and houses, and carry off soil from one bank to throw it down upon the other. Every one flees before them, and yields to their fury without the least power to resist. And yet, though this be their nature, it does not follow that in seasons of fair weather, men cannot, by constructing weirs and moles, take such precautions as will cause them when again in flood to pass off by some artificial channel, or at least prevent their course from being so uncontrolled and destructive. And so it is with Fortune, who displays her might where there is no organized strength to resist her, and directs her onset where she knows that there is neither barrier nor embankment to confine her. . . .

To be brief, I say that since Fortune changes and men stand fixed in their old ways, they are prosperous so long as there is congruity between them, and the reverse when there is not. Of this, however, I am well persuaded, that it is better to be impetuous than cautious. For Fortune is a woman who to be kept under must be beaten and roughly handled; and we see that she suffers herself to be more readily mastered by those who so treat her than by those who are more timid in their approaches. And always, like a woman, she favours the young, because they are less scrupulous and fiercer, and command her with greater audacity.[7]

CHAPTER XXVI

An Exhortation to Liberate Italy from the Barbarians

Turning over in my mind all the matters which have above been considered, and debating with myself whether in Italy at the present hour the times are such as might serve to confer honour on a new

[6] *Fortuna*, like *fama*, and *virtù*, was a Renaissance concept stemming from classical antiquity.
[7] Machiavelli himself is said to have had an eye for and a way with women.

Prince, and whether a fit opportunity now offers for a prudent and valiant leader to bring about changes glorious for himself and beneficial to the whole Italian people, it seems to me that so many conditions combine to further such an enterprise, that I know of no time so favourable to it as the present.[8] And if, as I have said, it was necessary in order to display the valour of Moses that the children of Israel should be slaves in Egypt,[9] and to know the greatness and courage of Cyrus that the Persians should be oppressed by the Medes,[10] and to illustrate the excellence of Theseus that the Athenians should be scattered and divided,[11] so at this hour, to prove the worth of some Italian hero, it was required that Italy should be brought to her present abject condition, to be more a slave than the Hebrew, more oppressed than the Persian, more disunited than the Athenian, without a head, without order, beaten, spoiled, torn in pieces, over-run and abandoned to destruction in every shape.

But though, heretofore, glimmerings may have been discerned in this man or that, whence it might be conjectured that he was ordained by God for her redemption, nevertheless it has afterwards been seen in the further course of his actions that Fortune has disowned him; so that our country, left almost without life, still waits to know who it is that is to heal her bruises, to put an end to the devastation and plunder of Lombardy, to the exactions and imposts of Naples and Tuscany, and to staunch those wounds of hers which long neglect has changed into running sores. . . .

Nor is it to be marvelled at if none of those Italians I have named[12] has been able to effect what we hope to see effected by your illustrious House; or that amid so many revolutions and so many warlike movements it should always appear as though the military virtues of Italy were spent; for this comes from her old system being defective, and from no one being found among us capable to strike out a new. Nothing confers such honour on the reformer of a State, as do the new laws and institutions which he devises; for these when they stand on a solid basis and have a greatness in their scope, make him admired and venerated. And in Italy material is not wanting for improvement in every form. If the head be weak the limbs are strong, and we see daily in single combats, or where few are engaged, how superior

---

[8] In *The Prince* Machiavelli is trying to persuade the Medici, recently restored in Florence (1512), to undertake the liberation and unification of Italy. This advice was originally meant for Giuliano; but since he died in 1514, before it was delivered, it was then addressed to Lorenzo de' Medici, his successor.
[9] Exodus 1–12.
[10] The Medes ruled over the related Persians until the latter revolted, about 550 B.C. under the leadership of Cyrus, and turned the tables.
[11] Theseus, Greek legendary hero, was credited, among his many exploits, with having unified Attica and Athens into one strong state.
[12] Such as Cesare Borgia.

are the strength, dexterity, and intelligence of Italians.[13] But when it comes to armies, they are nowhere, and this from no other reason than the defects of their leaders. For those who are skilful in arms will not obey, and every one thinks himself skilful, since hitherto we have had none among us so raised by merit or by fortune above his fellows that they should yield him the palm. And hence it happens that for the long period of twenty years, during which so many wars have taken place, whenever there has been an army purely Italian it has always been beaten. To this testify, first Taro, then Alessandria, Capua, Genoa, Vaila, Bologna, Mestri.[14]

If then your illustrious House should seek to follow the example of those great men who have delivered their country in past ages, it is before all things necessary, as the true foundation of every such attempt, to be provided with national troops, since you have no braver, truer, or more faithful soldiers; and although every single man of them be good, collectively they will be better, seeing themselves commanded by their own Prince, and honoured and esteemed by him. That you may be able, therefore, to defend yourself against the foreigner with Italian valour, the first step is to provide yourself with an army such as this. . . .

This opportunity then, for Italy at last to look on her deliverer, ought not to be allowed to pass away. With what love he would be received in all those Provinces which have suffered from the foreign inundation, with what thirst for vengeance, with what fixed fidelity, with what devotion, and what tears, no words of mine can declare. What gates would be closed against him? What people would refuse him obedience? What jealousy would stand in his way? What Italian but would yield him homage? This barbarian tyranny stinks in all nostrils.[15]

Let your illustrious House therefore take upon itself this enterprise with all the courage and all the hopes with which a just cause is undertaken; so that under your standard this our country may be ennobled, and under your auspices be fulfilled the words of Petrarch: —

> Brief will be the strife
> When valour arms against barbaric rage;
> For the bold spirit of the bygone age
> Still warms Italian hearts with life.[16]

---

[13] This Italian patriotism, manifested by Machiavelli, was characteristic of the humanists and the Renaissance, and was especially stimulated by foreign invasions and hegemony in Italy.

[14] Famous battles resulting in Italian defeats at the hands of foreigners.

[15] Machiavelli refers to foreign invasions, French, Spanish, Swiss, and German, into Italy, 1494–1513.

[16] Petrarch, in a poem lamenting the decline of Rome. Note the continuing influence of Petrarch and his humanistic patriotism.

SECTION V

The Reformation:
The Rending of Religious Unity

❧

EVERY AGE has its share of crises, and in the Age of the Reformation the initial crisis arose over theological matters. The religious controversies which followed Luther's action in posting his theses on the church door at Wittenberg in 1517 resulted in the division of the Christian world into hostile camps. The Reformation also had a profound effect upon many other aspects of man's life, for the theologians of the sixteenth century contributed to that alteration of outlook which the ferment of the Renaissance, the overseas expansion, and the acceleration of European economic activity were already bringing about. The invention of printing was a great stimulus to the widespread dissemination of the polemical literature of the period. Hitherto, laboriously handwritten manuscripts had taken a long time to produce and had circulated among a limited reading audience. The success of Protestantism in the sixteenth century was in no small measure due to the printing press which placed pamphlets and books, speedily and in quantity, in the hands of the literate.

In an age of controversy the individual leaders of particular movements play a significant role. This is especially true of Luther, Loyola, and the Tudors. Luther was the first to challenge successfully the authority of the Papacy and the Roman communion. Loyola created a force which effectively countered and checked the non-Roman religious movements, and his religious order spearheaded the Catholic Reformation. The Tudors created a *via media* in theological matters between the extremes of religious conservatism and religious radicalism. The documents in this section thus not only provide clues to the personalities, minds, and religious experiences of leading figures, but give insights into the movements to which they gave impetus and the times in which they lived.

13

The Protest Begins

Martin Luther

One of the most significant works produced in the Age of the Reformation was Martin Luther's Address to the Christian Nobility of the German Nation. It was written by its author under extremely trying circumstances. Friar Martin had recently concluded a heated debate at Leipzig (July, 1519) with the papal champion, John Eck. He was aware that his ideas had been transmitted to Rome for consideration, and he further knew that his excommunication from the Catholic Church could be expected momentarily. Excommunication could mean for him arrest, trial, imprisonment, and even death. It was in this atmosphere that he decided to explain more fully the position at which he had arrived on matters of doctrine and reform.

Luther was born of peasant stock in 1483 in the town of Eisleben, Saxony. His parents determined that he should have a university education in order to become a member of the legal profession. However, after receiving his master's degree from the University of Erfurt in 1505, he entered an Augustinian monastery. Ordained as a priest in 1507, Luther was sent to the University of Wittenberg to complete his doctoral studies. In 1510 he journeyed to Rome for his superior, Johann von Staupitz, and some historians argue that this trip affected his attitude towards Catholicism. Two years later he was granted a doctorate in biblical exegesis, and he soon won fame as a brilliant teacher. On October 31, 1517, to protest against what he considered abuses in the preaching of indulgences, he posted ninety-five theses on the church door at Wittenberg — the customary academic way of advertising one's views and one's willingness to defend them in debate. The theses attracted more than ordinary attention, and copies were printed and distributed throughout Germany. His views and actions aroused the ire of the Papacy, and after numerous debates and hearings his excommunication was imminent. In these circumstances he penned his Address to the Christian Nobility.

The Address is actually a pamphlet which runs over ninety pages in English translation. It was dedicated to Luther's political superior, the Emperor Charles V, and was printed by Melchio

Lotther and distributed in August, 1520. The extracts printed here are from the second German edition, which Luther revised at the suggestion of his lifelong friend, George Spalatin, who was also the confessor to Luther's immediate secular lord, Frederick of Saxony.

The Address has been called "the prophecy and pioneer of the Protestant Reformation." It includes an opening "Salutation"; "The Appeal," which is a call to the German nobility to aid in the reformation of the Church; "The Three Walls," which is an attack upon the asserted prerogatives of the Catholic Church, and especially those of the Pope; a list of "Subjects to be Discussed by the Councils"; and finally "Twenty-Seven Proposals for Improving the State of Christendom."

In reading this selection the student should note Luther's frequent reference to the Bible to support his position, and also his appeal to German nationalism and particularism. The author is very strong in his criticism of the Roman clergy, their lives, and what he considers their exploitation of the German people. The work also contains the seeds of Luther's mature theological ideas, such as his advocacy of individual interpretation of the Scriptures, his doctrine of the priesthood of all believers, and his central spiritual theme — justification by faith alone. In addition, he proposes a long list of disciplinary reforms, such as the abolition of monasticism, of clerical vows, of pilgrimages, and of masses for the dead. His suggestions stemmed in part from his personal beliefs and in part from his personal experiences.

Luther wrote the Address with a hurried and frenzied determination, as was his wont in any crisis which arose to challenge him. The work is somewhat verbose and at times repetitious, but it is interesting reading. Luther here directly appeals to German secular princes to take an active role in effecting his proposed reformation of the Christian Church. Historians' judgments of Luther depend, to a great extent, upon their own religious predilections; but, whatever pronouncement is made upon him, his role in the Reformation deserves the careful attention of student and historian alike.

MARTIN LUTHER

from *An Address to the Christian Nobility of the German Nation on the Reformation of the Christian Church* *

Jesus

Dedicated by Dr. Martin Luther to his dear friend, the honourable and worthy gentleman, Nicholas Von Amsdorft,[1] Licentiate in Holy Scripture, and Canon in Wittenberg.

The Salutation

May the grace and peace of God be yours, my honourable, worthy, and dear friend.

The time for silence is over, and the time for speech has come, as Ecclesiastes says. In accordance with our project, I have put together a few paragraphs on the amelioration of the condition of Christendom. I intend the writing for the consideration of Christians belonging to the ruling classes in Germany. I hope that God will grant help to His church through the laity, since the clergy, who should be the more appropriate persons, have grown quite indifferent. I am sending to your worthy self all I have written. Please examine, and, where desirable, modify it. I know that I shall not escape the criticism that I presume too much, in that I, an unimportant and inferior person, dare to address such a high and responsible class of society on very special and important subjects. I am acting, I confess, as if there were no other in the world than Doctor Luther to play the part of a Christian, and give advice to people of culture and education. But I shall not apologize, no matter who demands it. Perhaps I owe God and the world another act of folly. For what it is worth, this pamphlet is an attempt to pay that debt as well as I can, even if I become for once a Court-fool. No one needs to buy me a fool's cap nor shave

---

* From Bertram Lee Woolf, ed., *The Reformation Writings of Martin Luther*, Vol. 1, *The Basis of the Protestant Reformation* (New York: The Philosophical Library, 1953); reprinted by permission. The title of this Address, or Appeal, is variously translated.

[1] Amsdorf or Amsdorft had been a fellow student of Luther's at Erfurt and later became a convert to his cause.

me my poll. The question is, Which of us is to put the bells on the other? I must act according to the proverb, "A Monk must be in it whatever the world is doing, even if he has to be painted in." A fool often says wise things and frequently sages speak very foolishly. St. Paul said: "If any wishes to be wise, he must become a fool." Moreover, since I am not only a fool, but also sworn in as a Doctor of Holy Scripture, I am glad that I have the opportunity to fulfil my oath even in the guise of a fool. I beg you to make my apologies to those of average understanding, for I make no pretence of attempting to win the favour and goodwill of the super-intelligent. I have often tried hard to do it, but never again will I attempt it, nor worry about it. God help us not to seek our own glory but His alone. Amen

Wittenberg, The Augustinian Monastery, on the eve of John the Baptist's day,[2] A.D. 1520.

The Appeal

Doctor Martin Luther to His Most Illustrious, Most Mighty and Imperial Majesty,[3] and to the Christians of the German Ruling Class.

Grace and power from God to his Illustrious Majesty, and to you, most gracious and honourable Gentlemen.

It is not due to sheer impertinence or wantonness that I, a lone and simple man, have taken it upon myself to address your worships. All classes in Christendom, particularly in Germany, are now oppressed by distress and affliction, and this has stirred not only me but everyman to cry out anxiously for help. It has compelled me to beg and pray that God will endow someone with His Spirit to bring aid to this unhappy nation. Proposals have often been made at councils, but have been cunningly deferred by the guile of certain men, and matters have gone from bad to worse. Their artifices and wickedness I intend with God's help to lay bare in order that, once shown up, they may never again present such hindrances or be so harmful. God has given us a young man of noble ancestry to be our head and so has raised high hopes in many hearts. In these circumstances, it is fitting for us to do all we can to make good use of the present time and of God's gracious gift to us.

The first and most urgent thing just now is that we should each prepare our own selves in all seriousness. We must not begin by assuming we possess much strength or wisdom, even if we had all the authority in the world. For God cannot and will not suffer a goodly enterprise to be begun if we trust in our own strength and wisdom. God will surely abase such pride, as is said in Psalm 33, "No king stands by the multitude of his host, and no lord by the greatness of

[2] June 24.
[3] The Emperor Charles V, a Hapsburg (Charles I of Spain and the Spanish Empire overseas).

his strength." For this reason, I fear, it came to pass in former times that the good princes, emperors Frederick I and II,[4] and many other German emperors, were shamelessly trodden under foot and oppressed by the popes whom all the world feared. Perhaps they relied more on their own strength than on God, and therefore had to fall. And what else, in our day, has raised the bloodthirsty Julius II[5] so high, if it were not, as I fear, that France, Germany, and Venice depended on themselves? The children of Benjamin slew 42,000 Israelites because they relied on their own strength (Judges 19).

Lest we have the same experience under our noble emperor, Charles, we must be clear that we are not dealing permanently with men in this matter, but with the princes of hell who would fill the world with war and bloodshed, and yet avoid letting themselves be caught by the flood. We must go to work now, not depending on physical power, but in humble trust in God, seeking help from Him in earnest prayer, with nothing else in mind than the misery and distress of all Christendom suffering over and above what sinful men have deserved. Otherwise our efforts may well begin with good prospects, but, when we get deeply involved, the evil spirit will cause such confusion as to make the whole world swim in blood, and then nothing will be accomplished. Therefore, in this matter let us act wisely, and as those who fear God. The greater the power we employ, the greater the disaster we suffer, unless we act humbly and in the fear of God. If hitherto the popes and Romanists have been able, with the devil's help, to bring kings into conflict with each other,[6] they will be able to do it again now, if we set forth without God's help, and armed only with our strength and shrewdness.

I. The Three Walls

The Romanists have very cleverly surrounded themselves with three walls, which have protected them till now in such a way that no one could reform them. As a result, the whole of Christendom has suffered woeful corruption. In the first place, when under the threat of secular force, they have stood firm and declared that secular force had no jurisdiction over them;[7] rather the opposite was the case, and

---

[4] Striking a patriotic note in this sentence, Luther reminds Germans that he regards the medieval conflict between the Empire and the Papacy as "the graveyard of the German Empire."

[5] Julius II (1503–13), "the warrior pope," was criticized by contemporaries for his militant policies aimed at preserving the independence of the Papal States. He was absent from Rome when Luther sought an audience in 1511.

[6] A pointed reminder of the internal and external disorders caused by papal excommunication and deposition of European sovereigns during the Middle Ages.

[7] Study, for example, the conflict between Boniface VIII and Philip IV of France.

the spiritual was superior to the secular. In the second place, when the Holy Scriptures have been used to reprove them, they have responded that no one except the pope was competent to expound Scripture. In the third place, when threatened with a council, they have pretended that no one but the pope could summon a council.[8] In this way, they have adroitly nullified these three means of correction, and avoided punishment. Thus they still remain in secure possession of these three walls, and practise all the villainy and wickedness we see to-day. When they have been compelled to hold a council, they have made it nugatory by compelling the princes to swear in advance that the present position shall remain undisturbed. In addition they have given the pope full authority over all the decisions of a council, till it is a matter of indifference whether there be many councils or none, for they only deceive us with make-believes and sham-fights. So terribly fearful are they for their skins, if a truly free council were held. Further, the Romanists have overawed kings and princes till the latter believe it would be impious not to obey them in spite of all the deceitful and cunning dodges of theirs.

May God now help us, and give us one of those trumpets with which the walls of Jericho were overthrown; that we may blow away these walls of paper and straw, and set free the Christian, corrective measures to punish sin, and to bring the devil's deceits and wiles to the light of day. In this way, may we be reformed through suffering and again receive God's blessing.

1. Let us begin by attacking the first wall.[9]

To call popes, bishops, priests, monks, and nuns, the religious class, but princes, lords, artizans, and farm-workers the secular class, is a specious device invented by certain time-servers; but no one ought to be frightened by it, and for good reason. For all Christians whatsoever really and truly belong to the religious class, and there is no difference among them except in so far as they do different work. That is St. Paul's meaning, in I Corinthians 12, when he says: "We are all one body, yet each member hath his own work for serving others." This applies to us all, because we have one baptism, one gospel, one faith, and are all equally Christian. For baptism, gospel, and faith alone make men religious, and create a Christian people. When a pope or bishop anoints, grants tonsures, ordains, consecrates, dresses differently from laymen, he may make a hypocrite of a man, or an anointed image, but never a Christian or a spiritually-minded man. The fact is that our baptism consecrates us all without exception, and makes us all priests. As St. Peter says, "You are a royal priesthood

---

[8] Appeal to a church council was forbidden by Pius II in his bull *Execabilis* (1460).
[9] The following passages are the nucleus of Luther's opinions about the "priesthood of all believers."

and a realm of priests," and Revelation, "Thou hast made us priests and kings by Thy blood." If we ourselves as Christians did not receive a higher consecration than that given by pope or bishop, then no one would be made priest even by consecration at the hands of pope or bishop; nor would anyone be authorized to celebrate Eucharist, or preach, or pronounce absolution.

When a bishop consecrates, he simply acts on behalf of the entire congregation, all of whom have the same authority. They may select one of their number and command him to exercise this authority on behalf of the others. It would be similar if ten brothers, king's sons and equal heirs, were to choose one of themselves to rule the kingdom for them. All would be kings and of equal authority, although one was appointed to rule. To put it more plainly, suppose a small group of earnest Christian laymen were taken prisoner and settled in the middle of a desert without any episcopally ordained priest among them; and they then agreed to choose one of themselves, whether married or not, and endow him with the office of baptizing, administering the sacrament, pronouncing absolution, and preaching; that man would be as truly a priest as if he had been ordained by all the bishops and the popes. It follows that, if needs be, anyone may baptize or pronounce absolution, an impossible situation if we were not all priests. The fact that baptism, and the Christian status which it confers, possess such great grace and authority, is what the Romanists have overridden by their canon law, and kept us in ignorance thereof. But, in former days, Christians used to choose their bishops and priests from their own members, and these were afterwards confirmed by other bishops without any of the pomp of present custom. St. Augustine, Ambrose, and Cyprian each became bishops in this way.[10]

Those who exercise secular authority have been baptized like the rest of us, and have the same faith and the same gospel; therefore we must admit that they are priests and bishops. They discharge their office as an office of the Christian community, and for the benefit of that community. Every one who has been baptized may claim that he has already been consecrated priest, bishop, or pope, even though it is not seemly for any particular person arbitrarily to exercise the office. Just because we are all priests of equal standing, no one must push himself forward and, without the consent and choice of the rest, presume to do that for which we all have equal authority. Only by the consent and command of the community should any individual person claim for himself what belongs equally to all. If it should happen that anyone abuses an office for which he has been chosen, and is dismissed for that reason, he would resume his former status. It follows that the status of a priest among Christians is merely that of an office-bearer; while he holds the office he

[10] This statement involves the matter of "personal" interpretation of the circumstances of their consecration.

exercises it; if he be deposed he resumes his status in the community and becomes like the rest. Certainly a priest is no longer a priest after being unfrocked. Yet the Romanists have devised the claim to *characteres indelebiles*,[11] and assert that a priest, even if deposed, is different from a mere layman. They even hold the illusion that a priest can never be anything else than a priest, and therefore never a layman again. All these are human inventions and regulations.

Hence we deduce that there is, at bottom, really no other difference between laymen, priests, princes, bishops, or in Romanist terminology, between religious and secular, than that of office or occupation, and not that of Christian status. All have spiritual status, and all are truly priests, bishops, and popes. But Christians do not all follow the same occupation. . . .

Therefore those now called "the religious," i.e., priests, bishops, and popes, possess no further or greater dignity than other Christians, except that their duty is to expound the word of God and administer the sacraments — that being their office. In the same way, the secular authorities "hold the sword and the rod", their function being to punish evil-doers and protect the law-abiding. A shoemaker, a smith, a farmer, each has his manual occupation and work; and yet, at the same time, all are eligible to act as priests and bishops. Every one of them in his occupation or handicraft ought to be useful to his fellows, and serve them in such a way that the various trades are all directed to the best advantage of the community, and promote the well-being of body and soul, just as all the organs of the body serve each other.

Now let us consider whether it is Christian to affirm and declare that secular authorities do not exercise jurisdiction over religious office-bearers, and should not inflict penalties on them.[12] That is as much as to say that the hand ought to do nothing to help when the eye suffers severely. Would it not be unnatural, or indeed unchristian, for one organ not to help another and not ward off what is destroying it? Rather, the more precious an organ is, the more ought the other to help. Therefore, I maintain, that since the secular authorities are ordained by God to punish evil-doers and to protect the law-abiding, so we ought to leave them free to do their work without let or hindrance everywhere in Christian countries, and without partiality, whether for pope, bishops, pastors, monks, nuns, or anyone else. If, to prevent the exercise of secular authority, it were enough to say that the civil administration was, from the Christian standpoint, a lower function than that of preacher or confessor or the religious status, then surely

---

[11] Literally, "indelible character." The Catholic Church teaches that ordination is a sacrament which, when conferred, stamps the recipient with a mark which is forever with him and sets him, as a priest, apart from all other people.

[12] Luther reopens the age-old problem: "Render to Caesar the things that are Caesar's and to God the things that are God's."

tailors, shoemakers, stonemasons, carpenters, cooks, manservants, farmers, and all secular craftsmen, being lower still, should be forbidden to make shoes, clothes, houses, things to eat and drink, or pay rents and tributes to the pope, bishops, priests, and monks. But if these laymen are to be allowed to do their work undisturbed, what is the purpose of Romanist writers who make laws by which they exempt themselves from the secular Christian authorities? It is simply that they may do evil unpunished, and fulfil what St. Peter said, "There shall arise false teachers among you, moving among you with false and imaginary sayings, selling you a bad bargain."

Hence secular Christian authorities should exercise their office freely and unhindered and without fear, whether it be pope, bishop, or priest with whom they are dealing; if a man is guilty let him pay the penalty. What canon law says to the contrary is Romish presumptuousness and pure invention. . . .

That in my view overturns the first wall — of paper. The reason is that the social corpus of Christendom includes secular government as one of its component functions. This government is spiritual in status, although it discharges a secular duty. It should operate, freely and unhindered, upon all members of the entire corpus, should punish and compel where guilt deserves or necessity requires, in spite of pope, bishops, and priests; and whether they denounce or excommunicate to their hearts' desire. That is why guilty priests, before being handed over to the secular arm, are previously deprived of the dignities of their office.[13] This would not be right unless the secular "sword"[14] already possessed authority over them by divine ordinance. Moreover, it is intolerable that in canon law, the freedom, person, and goods of the clergy should be given this exemption, as if laymen were not exactly as spiritual, and as good Christians, as they, or did not equally belong to the church. Why should your person, life, possessions, and honour be exempt, whereas mine are not, although we are equally Christian, with the same baptism, guilt, and spirit and all else? If a priest is killed, a country is placed under interdict; why not also if a farmer is killed? Whence comes such a great difference between two men equally Christian? Simply from human law and fabrications.

It cannot have been a man of goodwill who devised such distinctions, and made some sins exempt and immune. For it is our duty to strive as much as we can against the Evil One and his works and to drive him away, for so Christ and His apostles bade us. How comes it then that we are told to hold our peace and be silent when the pope or his supporters design impious words or deeds? Are we, on

---

[13] In the Middle Ages the juridical conflict over "clerics" accused of crimes produced many disputes. One of the most famous was that between King Henry II of England and Thomas à Becket, Archbishop of Canterbury, in the 12th century.

[14] The "two swords" theory of the Middle Ages was still a bitterly contested issue.

account of certain men, to neglect divine commands and God's truth which we swore at our baptism to defend with life and limb? Of a truth we shall be held responsible for the souls of all who are abandoned and led astray thereby. Surely, it must be the archdevil himself who propounded that canon law which declares, "Even if the pope were so wicked that he led men in multitudes to the devil, nevertheless he could not be deposed." This is the accursed and impious foundation on which they build at Rome, maintaining that we should sooner let all the world go to the devil than oppose their villainy. . . .[15]

II. The second wall is more loosely built and less indefensible. The Romanists profess to be the only interpreters of Scripture, even though they never learn anything contained in it their lives long. They claim authority for themselves alone, juggle with words shamelessly before our eyes, saying that the pope cannot err as to the faith, whether he be bad or good; although they cannot quote a single letter of Scripture to support their claim.[16] Thus it comes about that so many heretical, unchristian, and even unnatural laws are contained in the canon law — matters of which there is no need for discussion at the present juncture. Just because the Romanists profess to believe that the Holy Spirit has not abandoned them, no matter if they are as ignorant and bad as they could be, they presume to assert whatever they please. In such a case, what is the need or the value of Holy Scripture? Let it be burned, and let us be content with the ignorant gentlemen at Rome who "possess the Holy Spirit within", who, however, in fact, dwells in pious souls only. Had I not read it, I should have thought it incredible that the devil should have produced such ineptitudes at Rome, and have gained adherents to them. But lest we fight them with mere words, let us adduce Scripture. St. Paul says, I Corinthians 14, "If something superior be revealed to any one sitting there and listening to another speaking God's word, the first speaker must be silent and give place." . . .

Therefore it is a wicked, base invention, for which they cannot adduce a tittle of evidence in support, to aver that it is the function of the pope alone to interpret Scripture, or to confirm any particular interpretation. And if they claim that St. Peter received authority when he was given the keys — well, it is plain enough that the keys were not given to St. Peter only, but to the whole Christian community. Moreover the keys have no reference to doctrine or policy, but only to refusing or being willing to forgive sin. Whatever else the Romanists claim in virtue of the keys is an idle invention. . . .

Think it over for yourself.[17] You must acknowledge that there are

[15] A pope may resign but he may not be deposed if canonically elected.
[16] Papal infallibility, though not to be expressly stated until Vatican Council I in 1870, was implicit in Catholic doctrine. Luther was not the first to challenge this claim.
[17] A characteristic and effective technique of Luther's is the appeal to individual religious judgments.

good Christians among us who have the true faith, spirit, understanding, word, and mind of Christ. Why ever should one reject their opinion and judgment, and accept those of the pope, who has neither that faith nor that spirit? That would be to repudiate the whole faith and the Christian church itself. . . .

In addition, as I have already said, each and all of us are priests because we all have the one faith, the one gospel, one and the same sacrament; why then should we not be entitled to taste or test, and to judge what is right or wrong in the faith? . . . We ought to march boldly forward, and test everything the Romanists do or leave undone. We ought to apply that understanding of the Scriptures which we possess as believers, and constrain the Romanists to follow, not their own interpretation, but that which is in fact the better. In former days, Abraham had to listen to Sarah, who was more completely subject to him than we are to anyone in the world. Similarly, Balaam's ass was more perspicacious than the prophet himself. Since God once spoke through an ass, why should He not come in our day and speak through a man of faith and even contradict the pope? . . . Hence it is the duty of every Christian to accept the implications of the faith, understand and defend it, and denounce everything false.

III. The third wall falls without more ado when the first two are demolished; for, even if the pope acts contrary to Scripture, we ourselves are bound to abide by Scripture. We must punish and constrain him, according to the passage, "If thy brother sin against thee, go and tell it him between thee and him alone; but if he hear thee not, take with thee one or two more; and if he hear them not, tell it to the church; and if he hear not the church, let him be unto thee as a Gentile." This passage commands each member to exercise concern for his fellow; much more is it our duty when the wrongdoer is one who rules over us all alike, and who causes much harm and offence to the rest by his conduct. And if I am to lay a charge against him before the Church, then I must call it together.

Romanists have no Scriptural basis for their contention that the pope alone has the right to summon or sanction a council. This is their own ruling, and only valid as long as it is not harmful to Christian well-being or contrary to God's laws. If, however, the pope is in the wrong, this ruling becomes invalid, because it is harmful to Christian well-being not to punish him through a council.

Accordingly, we read in Acts 15 that it was not St. Peter, but all the apostles and elders, who called the Apostolic Council. If that had been the sole right of St. Peter, it would not have been a Christian council, but an heretical *conciliabulum*. Further, the bishop of Rome neither called nor sanctioned the council of Nicea, the most celebrated of all, but the emperor, Constantine.[18] After him, many

[18] Luther's opinions are at variance with Catholic interpretation of these same events. In the case of Nicaea, Pope Sylvester I was too advanced in years to attend, but he sent representatives.

other emperors did the same, and these councils were the most Christian of all. But if the pope had really had the sole authority, then they would necessarily all have been heretical. Moreover, when I examine decisions of those councils which the pope himself called, I find they did nothing of special importance.[19]

Therefore, when need requires it, and the pope is acting harmfully to Christian well-being, let anyone who is a true member of the Christian community as a whole take steps as early as possible to bring about a genuinely free council.[1] No one is so able to do this as the secular authorities, especially since they are also fellow Christians, fellow priests, similarly religious, and of similar authority in all respects. They should exercise their office and do their work without let or hindrance where it is necessary or advantageous to do so, for God has given them authority over every one. Surely it would be an unnatural proceeding, if fire were to break out in a town, if everyone should stand still and let it burn on and on, simply because no one had the mayor's authority, or perhaps because it began at the mayor's residence. In such a case, is it not the duty of each citizen to stir up the rest, and call upon them for help? Much more ought it to be the case in the spiritual city of Christ, were a fire of offence to break out, whether in the pope's régime or anywhere else. . . .

. . . The church has no authority except to promote the greater good. Hence, if the pope should exercise his authority to prevent a free council, and so hinder the reform of the church, we ought to pay no regard to him and his authority. If he should excommunicate and fulminate, that ought to be despised as the proceedings of a foolish man. Trusting in God's protection, we ought to excommunicate him in return, and manage as best we can; for this authority of his would be presumptuous and empty. . . .

And now, I hope that I have laid these false and deceptive terrors, though the Romanists have long used them to make us diffident and of a fearful conscience. It is obvious to all that they, like us, are subject to the authority of the state, that they have no warrant to expound Scripture arbitrarily and without special knowledge. They are not empowered to prohibit a council or, according to their pleasure, to determine its decisions in advance, to bind it and to rob it of freedom. But if they do so, I hope I have shown that of a truth they belong to the community of Antichrist and the devil, and have nothing in common with Christ except the name. . . .

II. *Subjects to be Discussed by the Councils*

Now let us consider the subjects which might properly be discussed in the councils, or with which popes, cardinals, bishops, and all

---

[19] The accomplishments of various councils are a matter of record, and Luther's statement may be disputed.
[1] From the Catholic viewpoint, no council would be valid unless summoned by a legitimately elected pope.

scholars might well busy themselves day and night if they held Christ or His church dear. Otherwise, Christians at large, and those who exercise authority in the state, ought to do so despite the Romanists' excommunications or fulminations. For one undeserved excommunication is better than ten justifiable absolutions; and one undeserved absolution is worse than ten justifiable excommunications. Therefore let us wake up, my dear fellow countrymen, and fear God rather than men, lest we suffer like all those poor folk who have gone astray so pitiably through the shameless and impious régime of Rome. Under this régime, the devil prospers more and more every day; and, if such a thing were possible, this impious régime must become worse as a consequence, although I still cannot conceive nor believe how.[2]

1. In the first place, it is painful and shocking to see that the head of Christendom, proclaiming himself the Vicar of Christ and the successor of St. Peter, lives in such a worldly and ostentatious style that no king or emperor can reach and rival him.[3] He claims the titles of "Most Holy" and "Most Spiritual," but there is more worldliness in him than in the world itself. He wears a triple crown, whereas the mightiest kings wear only one. If that is like the lowly Christ or St. Peter, it is to me a new sort of likeness. The Romanists bleat that it would be heretical to speak against it; they refuse to consider how unchristian and ungodly such conduct is. In my view, however, if the pope were to pray before God with fear, he would have to lay aside his triple crown, for our God tolerates no haughtiness. . . .

2. What Christian purpose is served by the ecclesiastics called cardinals? I will tell you. In Italy and Germany there are many wealthy monasteries, institutions, benefices, and parishes. No better way has been devised of bringing them into Rome's possession than by creating cardinals and giving them bishoprics, monasteries, and prelacies as their property, thus destroying the service of God. The consequence is that Italy is now almost devastated; monasteries are in disorder, bishoprics despoiled, the revenues of prelacies and all the churches drawn to Rome, cities devastated, land and people ruined, because no longer are services held or sermons preached. Why so? Because the cardinals must have their revenues. The Turk himself could not have ruined Italy in like manner nor put an end to divine worship to such an extent.

Now that Italy is drained dry, they are coming into the German countries, and beginning with calculated restraint. But let us watch, for the German countries will soon become like Italy. Already we have a few cardinals. They think the drunken Germans will not understand what the game is, till there is not a single bishopric, monastery, parish or benefice, not a cent or farthing, left for them. . . .

[2] In the revised editions of this tract, Luther's language becomes more violent.
[3] The reigning pope was Leo X.

3. If ninety-nine per cent. of the papal court were abolished and only one per cent. were left, it would still be large enough to deal with questions of Christian faith. At present there is a crawling mass of reptiles, all claiming to pay allegiance to the pope, but Babylon never saw the like of these miscreants. The pope has more than 3,000 secretaries alone,[4] and no one can count the others he employs, as the posts are so numerous. It is hardly possible to number all those that lie in wait for the institutions and benefices of Germany, like wolves for the sheep. I fear that Germany to-day is giving far more to the pope in Rome than she used to give formerly to the emperors. Some have estimated that more than 300,000 guilders go annually from Germany to Rome, quite uselessly and to no purpose, while we get nothing in return except contempt and scorn. It is not at all astonishing if princes, aristocracy, towns, institutions, country, and people grow poor. We ought to marvel that we still have anything left to eat. . . .

The German nation, including their bishops and princes, should remember that they too are Christian. They should protect the populace whom it is their duty to rule; they should defend them by means of their temporal and spiritual possessions against these ravening wolves who come dressed in sheep's clothing as shepherds and rulers. Further, since the annates[5] are so shamefully misused, and agreements are not kept, the German bishops and princes ought not to allow their country and people to be so pitiably harassed and impoverished without any regard for justice. Rather, by an imperial decree, or a national law, they ought to suspend payment of the annates, or abolish them entirely. . . .

Finally, the pope has built a market-house for the convenience of all this refined traffic, viz.: the house of the *datarius* in Rome. This is where all those resort who deal in this way in benefices and livings. From him they must buy these "glosses" and transactions, and get power to practise their arch-villainy. . . .

But, if you bring money to this ecclesiastical market, you can buy any of the goods I have described. Here any one can pay and then legally charge interest[6] on loans of any sort. You can get a legal right to goods you have stolen or seized. Here vows are annulled; here monks receive liberty to leave their orders; here marriage is for sale to the clergy; here bastards can become legitimate, and any form of dishonour and shame can achieve dignity; all kinds of iniquity and evil are knighted and ennobled. Here a marriage is permitted which is within the forbidden degrees, or which is otherwise objectionable. O what a jugglery and extortion go on here! until it would seem that

[4] This figure is an exaggeration — or else Luther is referring to *all* employees of the Vatican in Rome.
[5] Portion of the first year's income from a benefice, paid to Rome.
[6] The receipt of money from the loaning of money, usury, not interest, was prohibited by the Catholic Church.

all the laws of the canon were only given to produce gilded nooses, from which a man must free himself if he would become a Christian. Indeed, here the devil becomes a saint and a god: what cannot be done anywhere else in heaven or earth, can be done in this house. . . .[7]

This wicked régime is not only barefaced robbery, trickery, and tyranny appropriate to the nether regions, but also a destruction of the body and soul of Christendom. Therefore we ought to make every effort to protect Christendom from this hurt and damage. If we are willing to make war on the Turks, let us begin here where they are most iniquitous. If we are right in hanging thieves and beheading robbers, why should we leave Avarice of Rome unpunished? Here is the greatest thief and robber that has ever come or is likely to come on earth, and the scandal is perpetrated in the holy names of Christ and St. Peter. Who can go on tolerating it or keeping silence? . . .

III. Twenty-seven Proposals for Improving the State of Christendom

Although I am really of too little consequence to make proposals for the improvement of such a terrible state of affairs, I will go on, although foolishly, to the end, and declare, as far as I understand the case, what might well be done and should be done, either by the secular arm or an ecumenical council.

1. Firstly, I suggest that every prince, peer, and city should strictly forbid their subjects to pay the annates to Rome, and should do away with them entirely. For the pope has broken the agreement about the annates, and so stolen them, to the hurt and shame of the whole German people. He bestows them on his friends, sells them for large sums, and endows certain offices with them. Hence he has lost the right to them, and deserves to be punished. The secular arm is now under obligation to protect the innocent and prevent injustice. . . .

2. With his Romish practices, viz., commends, coadjutors, reservations, *gratiae expectativae*, "papal months," incorporations, unions, pensions, palliums, rules in chancery, and similar villainies, the pope is engulfing all foundations of German origin, without authority or justice, and bestowing and selling them in Rome to strangers who do nothing for Germany in return. . . . This is sufficient reason for the Christian ruling classes to set their faces against the pope as a common foe, who is wreaking destruction in Christendom; and to do so for the sake of saving the poor, who cannot avoid perishing under this tyranny. They should decree, command, and ordain that not another benefice shall in future be transferred to Rome, and that by no device whatever shall a single further appointment be obtained there.

[7] Similar charges had been made by many others. See, for example, Petrarch's comments on the Avignon Papacy.

Rather, the benefices shall be rescued and kept from this tyrannical power; the proper incumbents should have their rights and offices restored, so that those benefices, which belong to Germany, may be brought into the best possible order. . . .[8] They would then take note in Rome that Germans are not silly and besotted all the time, but that they are really converted Christians, and such that they will no longer tolerate the holy name of Christ to be scoffed at and scorned, thus permitting rogues to live and souls to perish. Rather they reverence God's honour more than man's power.

3. An imperial law should be decreed, whereby no bishop should go to Rome for his pallium, or for the confirmation of any other dignity, from now onwards. Instead of this, the ordinance of Nicea, the holiest and most celebrated of all the councils, should be re-established. This regulation declares that a bishop shall be confirmed by the two nearest bishops, or by the archbishop. If the pope intends to abolish the statute of this and all other councils, what is the value of having councils? Moreover, who has given him authority to despise and nullify councils? All the more reason for us to depose all bishops, archbishops, and primates, and make plain pastors of them, with the pope as their sole superior, as in fact he is. For he leaves no regular authority or office to the bishops, archbishops, and primates. He appropriates everything for himself, and allows them to retain only the name and the empty title. . . .

4. It should be decreed that no secular matter is to be referred to Rome. All such issues should be left to the secular arm,[9] as the Romanists themselves affirm in their canon laws, which, however, they do not observe. It should be the pope's part, as the man most learned of all in the Scriptures, and as actually and not merely nominally the holiest of all, to regulate whatever concerns the faith and holy life of Christians. . . .

Besides the above, the gross malpractices of the judges in the ecclesiastical courts ought to be forbidden.[10] They ought to be concerned only with matters of faith and good morals; whereas money, property, life, and honour should be left for the secular judges to deal with. . . .

5. Not another reservation[11] should hold good, and not another living should be taken possession of by Rome, even if the incumbent die, or a dispute arise about it, or the incumbent is a cardinal, or

[8] Luther voices current criticisms about the appointment of foreigners to benefices.
[9] This was a constant source of annoyance to many Germans who felt that the Papacy had too frequently interfered in purely secular affairs in the Empire.
[10] Catholic canon law held that a cleric who had received minor orders could not be tried by a secular court for purely secular crimes. It was often difficult to determine what was a purely secular crime.
[11] A practice whereby certain benefices were "reserved" and would go to the person holding the reservation when the incumbent died. It was subject to considerable abuse at the time.

one of the pope's staff. A court follower must be strictly forbidden, and prevented from beginning, litigation against the holder of any benefice, or citing and disturbing any dutiful priests, or driving them to some compromise. If, as a consequence, Rome pronounces excommunication or exercises spiritual pressure, it should be ignored just as it would be if a thief excommunicated someone who would not let him steal. Indeed, the Romanists ought to be severely punished for blasphemous misuse of excommunication and of God's name in support of their robberies. . . .

6. The reserved cases (*casus reservati*),[12] which the pope alone can absolve, should be abolished. Not only are the people cheated of much money by them, but the ravenous tyrants ensnare and confuse tender consciences with intolerable harm to their faith in God. . . .

Really every priest ought to know, and a public decree should declare, that no private and undenounced trespass constitutes a reserved case; and that every priest is empowered to pronounce absolution, no matter what the sin, or whatever it may be called. . . .

7. The Holy See of Rome should abolish the *officia*[13] and lessen the creeping and crawling swarms of hirelings in the city. The object of this abolition is that the papal staff should be supported out of the pope's own income, and his court not outvie in magnificence and extravagance that of any king. Regard should be paid to the fact that such a state of affairs has never been of any service to the Christian faith, but has been a very great hindrance to study and prayer, until the court officials now know scarcely anything about Christian faith. This was proved plainly at the last council which was held recently at Rome. . . .

8. The far-reaching and fearful oaths, which bishops are wrongfully compelled to swear to the pope, should be abolished.[14] They keep the bishops bound like domestic servants. . . . Is it not enough that their numerous foolish laws should burden us in body, soul, and property, to the weakening of faith and the ruin of Christian estate? But now they make a prisoner of the bishop with his office and duties, including his very investiture. Formerly, this last was performed by the German emperor, and still is carried out by the king in France and other countries. On this point, the Romanists struggled and disputed hotly with the emperors, until at last they had the barefaced effrontery to seize the right and retain it to the present day. They must think the German Christians are, to a greater extent than any others, the household fools of the pope and the papacy, for doing and suffering what no one elsewhere will suffer or do. . . .

[12] These were certain offenses in which only the Pope or his authorized delegate could give absolution to the sinner.
[13] The Papacy controlled certain offices which only the Pope could confer. It was a common practice to make an offering to the Pope after the position had been confirmed.
[14] Bishops pledged their loyalty to the Pope and to his commands.

9. The pope should exercise no authority over the emperor, except the right to anoint and crown him at the altar as a bishop crowns a king. Never again should his iniquitous Arrogance be permitted to make the emperor kiss the pope's feet, or sit at them, or, as it is said, hold the stirrup and bridle of his mule when he mounts to go riding.[15] Still less should he do homage to the pope, and swear faithfulness to him as his liege lord, as the popes shamelessly presume to demand as if by right. The chapter entitled *Solite*,[16] which raises the power of the pope above that of the emperor, is not worth a farthing. . . .

. . . The pope seems almost the Counter-Christ, called in Scripture the Antichrist, for the whole of his system, his efforts, and his pretensions are contrary to Christ, and directed solely to blotting out and destroying whatever Christ has informed with His spirit, and whatever work He has done. . . .

10. The pope should withdraw from temporal affairs, take his finger out of the pie, and lay no claim to the throne of the kingdom of Naples and Sicily.[17] He has no more right to it than I have, and yet wants to be its overlord. It is robbery by violence, like almost every other of his possessions. Therefore, the emperor ought not to confirm him in such tenures, and, in cases where he has already done so, withdraw his support. . . . The pope should let temporal lords rule land and people, while he himself preaches and prays.

The same principle should also apply to Bologna, Imola, Vincenza, Ravenna, and everywhere else in the provinces of Ancona, Romagna, and other parts of Italy, which the pope has seized by force and keeps without justification, meddling in these matters contrary to all the commandments of Christ and St. Paul. . . .

11. No one should ever again kiss the pope's feet. It is unchristian, indeed antichristian, that a pitiable and sinful man should let his feet be kissed by another who may be a hundred times better than himself. If it is intended to pay tribute to his authority, why does the pope not do it to others as a tribute to their sanctity? Compare them with one another, Christ and the pope; Christ washed and dried His disciples' feet, but the disciples never washed His. The pope, presuming to be higher than Christ, reverses the relation, and with much condescension allows his feet to be kissed. But it would be proper for him, if any one were to ask permission, to refuse at all costs to allow it. . . .

---

[15] Ancient traditions observed when Emperor met Pope, to symbolize the supremacy of spiritual power over secular power. These traditions produced conflicts such as that occasioned by the meeting of Frederick Barbarossa and Hadrian IV in 1155, outside of Rome.

[16] Luther here refers to the Decretals of Pope Gregory VII. Their authenticity is sometimes questioned because of the extreme statements contained in the document.

[17] The imperialistic policy of the Emperors, which dates back to Charlemagne, was partially concerned with the control of all Italy. The Papacy violently resisted this throughout the Middle Ages for fear that if they lived in imperial land their freedom would be lost.

12. Pilgrimages to Rome should be disallowed. No person actuated merely by curiosity or his own religious feelings should be permitted to make a pilgrimage. Rather, he must be previously recognized by his minister, city council, or liege lord as having sufficient good reasons for making the pilgrimage. I do not say this because pilgrimages are wrong, but because they are ill-advised just now; for what one sees in Rome is not exemplary, but scandalous. The Romanists themselves have coined the saying, "The nearer Rome, the worse the Christians,,' and they bring about contempt of God and God's commandments. Another saying runs, "The first time one goes to Rome, one has to look for a rogue; the second time, one finds him; the third time, one brings him back." But they have become so slick by now that the three journeys are made at the same time, and indeed, in Rome they have coined us the catch-phrase, "It would be better not to have seen or known Rome."

Even if this were not true, there is a more cogent reason, namely, these pilgrimages seduce untrained minds into a false idea and a misapprehension of the divine commandments; simple folk hold that pilgrimages are works of rare merit, which is untrue. They are works of little merit, and, if frequently repeated, they are evil and seductive; God never gave such a commandment. . . .

13. We now come to the great multitudes who swear many vows, but keep few. Do not be angry, my dear readers; I mean nothing wrong. For it is the truth, at once sweet and bitter, that no more mendicant houses[18] should be built. God knows, there are already far too many of them. Would to God they were all dissolved, or all combined into two or three Orders. There is no merit, and there never will be any merit, in simply walking about over the face of the earth. I would therefore counsel that ten, or as many as may be necessary, should be joined together into one house and made into a single institution. Let this be endowed sufficiently so as to require no mendicancy. . . .

The pope must be forbidden to institute, or set his seal on, any more of these Orders. Indeed, he must be ordered to dissolve some, or force them to reduce their numbers. . . .

14. We know also how the priesthood has declined. Many a poor priest is responsible for wife and child, and has a troubled conscience; yet no one lends a hand, although it would be a very kindly act to help them. The pope and the bishop may let these abuses go on untouched, even though ruin ensue, if ruin it must be. So I will obey my conscience, and speak my mind freely, in spite of hurting the pope, the bishops, or anyone else. . . . The Scriptures know nothing of the present-day kind of bishops who, by ordinances of the Christian church, have authority over several pastors.

Thus the Apostle teaches us plainly that the method to be followed

[18] The monasteries of the mendicant orders which took an oath to live only on what they could beg.

among Christians is that each separate town should choose from its church a scholarly and devout citizen, and lay upon him the duties of a pastor; his maintenance being cared for by the church. He should be quite free to marry, or not. At his side, he should have several priests or deacons, either married or not, as he prefers, to help him in ministering to the church and the people at large with sermons and the sacraments. . . .

. . . My advice is, Break the bonds, let each follow his own preference whether to marry or not to marry. But then there will have to be quite a different arrangement and order of things in regard to salaries; also the whole of the canon law must be razed to the ground; nor must many benefices become Rome's. . . .[19]

I do not wish either to encourage or discourage those, who have as yet no wife, on the question whether they should marry or remain single. I leave that to be pronounced by an ecumenical, Christian council, and also by the conscience of the man's better self. But I will not conceal my own real view from the many who are distressed, nor will I withhold from them words of comfort. I mean those who have fallen into disgrace with a woman, and have a child, and who suffer grievously in conscience because she is called a priest's prostitute and the children scorned as "priest-brats". . . .

Let him who has faith enough to make the venture, boldly follow my word; I shall not lead him astray. I have not the power of a pope, but I have the power of a Christian to help and advise my neighbour to escape from his sins and temptations; and that not without rhyme or reason. . . .

15. Nor would I forget the sad condition of the monasteries. The evil spirit, who to-day confuses all classes by man-made laws and makes life intolerable, has taken possession of certain abbots, abbesses, and prelates. The result is that they so govern the brothers and sisters that they consign them the more speedily to hell; meanwhile, the poor things lead a lamentable existence here on earth, as do all martyrs to the devil. To go into detail, the papists reserve to their own dispensation all, or at least some, of the deadly sins which are committed in private, and from which no friar is allowed to absolve his fellow under his vow of obedience and on penalty of excommunication. . . .

. . . Hence I give this counsel to those same poor creatures, whether friars or nuns. If your Superior will not allow you to confess your secret sins to someone of your own choice, nevertheless take them and bewail them to the brother or sister whom you prefer. Receive your absolution and comfort; go away, follow your bent, and do your duty. Only remain firm in the faith that you have been absolved, and that nothing further is necessary. Do not let yourself be troubled or led

[19] These passages prefigure Luther's later tracts urging clerics to leave the monasteries and to forgo the vow of chastity.

astray by threats of excommunication, or of being *"irregulares"*, or anything of this kind. . . .

16. Further, masses on anniversaries, or at celebrations, and for the dead, ought to be either entirely abolished, or at least reduced in number. It is plain to see that they become merely subjects for contempt, things with which God will be greatly angered, seeing that they will be celebrated only for money, and as an excuse for eating and drinking to excess. . . .

17. Certain of the penances or penalties of canon law ought to be abolished, especially the *interdict* which is undoubtedly a device of the Evil One. Is it not a trick of Satan to wipe away one sin by causing many sins of a worse character? . . .

Excommunication must never be employed as a penalty except where the Scriptures prescribe its use, i.e., against those who believe amiss, or who live in open sin; but it should not be used for the sake of temporal advantages. But, to-day, the opposite is the case; everyone lives and believes as he will, most of all those who harass and plunder other people with interdicts; and every one of the bans is pronounced purely for the sake of temporal property. . . .

18. All festival days should be abolished, and Sundays alone retained. But, if it is preferred to keep the festivals of Our Lady and of the greater saints, they should all be transferred to Sundays, or observed only at morning Mass, after which the whole day should be a working day. The reason for the proposed change is the present misuse of festival days in drinking, gaming, idleness, and all sorts of sins. In this way, we incur the wrath of God more on holy days than on the rest. . . .[1]

19. The grades or degrees within which marriage is forbidden should be altered, such as those affecting godparents, or third and fourth degrees of kinship. Here the pope, in his scandalous traffic, grants a dispensation for a fee, where every individual pastor should be able to grant dispensations without fee, and for the eternal good of the people concerned. Would God that every pastor might do or permit gratis everything that Rome must be paid for. . . .

In this connection, it should be said that the question of fasting ought to be a matter of free choice, and the foods which may be eaten left unrestricted, as the gospel has ordained. . . .

20. The extra-parochial chapels and churches, away from inhabited parts, should be pulled down. I mean those which have recently become the goal of pilgrimages, e.g., Wilsnack, Sternberg, Trèves, the Grimmenthal, and now Regensburg and many others. Oh, what a heavy and pitiful reckoning inevitably awaits the bishops who agree to these tricks of the devil's own, and get profit out of them! . . .

---

[1] In a society where most people enjoyed little respite from toil, church festivals and holy-days provided about the only opportunity for relaxation and recreation.

It is relevant here to say that we should abolish, ignore, or else make common to all churches, the licences, the bulls, and whatever else the pope may have for sale in Rome at the place where he fleeces people. For if he sells or gives rights to livings, if he grants privileges, indulgences, graces, advantages, faculties, to Wittenberg, Halle, Venice, and especially to his own city of Rome, why does he not give them to the churches in general? . . .

21. Probably one of our greatest needs is to abolish all mendicancy everywhere in Christendom. No one living among Christians ought to go begging. It would be an easy law to make, if only we dared, and were in earnest that every town should support its own poor. No outside beggars should be allowed in, whatever they called themselves, whether pilgrims, friars, or mendicant orders. Every town could provide for its own poor, or, if it were too small, the surrounding villages could be urged to contribute. . . .

But certain people think that, if my proposals were adopted, the poor would fare properly, and that fewer great stone houses and cloisters would be built, and fewer so well adorned. All this I can well believe. Nor is any of it necessary. He who has chosen poverty, ought not to be rich; but if a man chooses wealth, let him put his hand to the plough and get his wealth for himself out of the earth. It is sufficient if the poor are decently provided for, in such a way that they do not die of hunger or cold. . . .

22. I am also concerned to think that the numerous masses, which have been endowed in benefices and cloisters, are both of very little use, and greatly incur the wrath of God. For that reason, it would be wise to endow no more of them, but to abolish many of those that are already endowed. For it is obvious that they are only held to be sacrifices and good works in spite of the fact that, like baptism and penance, they are sacraments which are of value, not to others, but only to him who receives them. . . . Therefore, my advice to a man in future would be to become a shepherd, or else learn a handicraft, rather than become a priest or a monk, unless he were well aware in advance what it means to celebrate mass.

What I have said here does not apply to the ancient monasteries and cathedral chapters, which were undoubtedly founded for the sake of noblemen's children. According to German custom, only some of a nobleman's issue can become landowners or rulers, and it was intended that the rest should enter these monasteries, and there be free to serve God, to study, to become scholarly people, and to help others to do so. . . .

23. The "fraternities,"[2] indulgences, letters of indulgence, butterbriefs,[3] mass briefs,[4] dispensations and the like, ought all to be

[2] Congregations of laymen gathered together to perform spiritual activities.
[3] Dispensations to eat butter at certain times.
[4] Special benefits to be gained from masses said for special intentions.

drowned and destroyed as containing nothing good. If the pope can grant you a dispensation to eat butter, or from hearing mass, he should allow a pastor the power to grant it; indeed he has no right to deprive him of the power. . . .

The first thing is to chase out of Germany the papal legates[5] with the "faculties" which they sell to us at a high figure, although the traffic is nought but trickery. As things are, they take the money, and make unrighteousness righteous, dissolve vows, oaths, and agreements, thereby destroying and teaching us to destroy faithfulness and faith, which men have promised one another; and they plead that the pope has authority to do all these things. This means that the Evil One speaks through them; also, that they are selling impious doctrine, and taking our money to teach us to sin and lead us to hell. . . .

24. It is high time that we took up the Hussite question and dealt with it seriously. We ought to make an earnest effort to get the Hussites[6] to join us, and for us to unite ourselves with them. It would put an end to defamation, hatred, and envy on both sides. In accord with my present boldness, I will be the first to propound an opinion, but I will defer to any one with a better grasp of the situation. . . .

I have no desire to justify at this stage John Huss's propositions or defend his error, although to my way of thinking he wrote nothing erroneous. . . . I am not to be understood as meaning that John Huss was a saint or a martyr, as certain of his fellow-countrymen maintain. But I do declare my belief that he suffered a wrong, and that his books and his teaching were wrongly condemned. . . .[7]

Nor is it my view that the Hussites be compelled to abandon taking the sacrament in both kinds,[8] for that practice is neither unchristian nor heretical. Let them be free to follow that custom if they prefer it. . . .

25. The universities need a sound and thorough reformation. I must say so no matter who takes offence. Everything that the papacy has instituted or ordered is directed solely towards the multiplication of sin and error. Unless they are completely altered from what they have been hitherto, the universities will fit exactly what is said in the Book of Maccabees: "Places for the exercise for youth, and for the Greekish fashion." Loose living is practised there; little is taught of the Holy Scripture or the Christian faith; the blind pagan teacher, Aristotle, is of more consequence than Christ. In my view, Aristotle's

---

[5] Luther's initial conflict with Rome was precipitated by his attack upon the Dominican, John Tetzel, who was a special legate of Pope Leo X and a much-hated preacher of indulgences.

[6] A popular religious movement in Bohemia, and composed of the followers of John Huss who was burned as a heretic in Constance in 1415.

[7] Luther had defended Huss in a debate with John Eck at Leipzig in 1519.

[8] The receiving of communion in the dual form of the chalice of wine as well as the wafer.

writings on *Physics, Metaphysics, On the Soul,* and *Ethics,* hitherto regarded as the most important, should be set aside along with all others that boast they treat of natural objects, for in fact they have nothing to teach about things natural or spiritual. Remember too that no one, up to now, has understood his teaching, but much precious time and mental energy have been uselessly devoted to wasteful work, study, and effort. I venture to say that a potter has more understanding of the things of nature than is written down in those books. It pains me to the heart that this damnable, arrogant, pagan rascal has seduced and fooled so many of the best Christians with his misleading writings. God has made him a plague to us on account of our sins. . . .

I leave the medical men to reform their own faculties, but I claim to speak for the jurists and theologians. In regard to the former, I aver that it would be well if the canon law, in particular the Decretals,[9] were completely blotted out, from the first letter to the last. There is a superabundance of material at our disposal in the Biblical writings, telling what our conduct should be in all circumstances. . . . To-day, the canon law does not consist of what is written in books, but in the arbitrary choices preferred by the pope and his lickspittles. Even if your case is most firmly established according to the written canon law, the pope still retains his *"scrinium pectoris"*[10] superior to it, and by which he will settle what is legal, and rule the world. Often a villain, or even the devil himself, controls that chamber, although the popes proudly claim that the Holy Spirit rules it. . . .

Moreover, even if the universities diligently studied the Holy Scriptures, we should not, as now, send everyone there for the mere sake of having many students, or because everyone wants a doctor in the family. Only the cleverest should be sent, and after having received a good education in the lower schools. The prince and the local town council ought to see to this, and send only those who are well qualified. But I would not advise anyone to send his son to a place where the Holy Scriptures do not come first. . . .

[26.[11] I am well aware that the crew in Rome will object and cry aloud that the pope took the Holy Roman empire from the Greek emperor, and transferred it to the German people.[12] In exchange for

---

9 Ecclesiastical pronouncements included in canon law. Luther burned the book of canon law on December 10, 1520, at Wittenberg, along with the bull of his excommunication.

10 This is an excerpt from a phrase widely used by canon lawyers in the Middle Ages. This phrase read *"omnia jura sunt in scrinio pectoris Romae pontificis,"* which freely translated meant that the Pope was supreme over all ecclesiastical rights.

11 This section does not occur in Luther's first edition.

12 A reference to the fact that all Western Emperors since Charlemagne in 800 had received their imperial crown, in a ceremony, from the Pope. Some Germans felt that this subordinated the position of the Emperor to that of the Pope. Charles V, in 1530, was the last Emperor to be so crowned. "Greek" here means Byzantine.

this honour and favour, he deserves, and should have received, our willing submission, and thanks, and every other expression of gratitude. For this reason, they will perhaps attempt to scatter to the winds every effort to reform them, and let nothing happen except things like making a present of the Roman empire. From this starting-point, they have till now persecuted and oppressed many an excellent emperor so arbitrarily and arrogantly that it is distressing to talk of. And they have used the same adroitness in making themselves the overlords of every secular authority and government, contrary to the holy gospel. I must therefore say a word on that subject.

It is unquestionable that the real Roman empire perished and ended long ago. . . .

When the pope could no longer force the Greeks and the emperor to suit his arbitrary preferences, he invented the device of robbing him of his empire and title, and transferring them to the Germans, who, at that time, were warlike and of good repute. In so doing, the Romanists wished to make the power of the Roman empire subject to themselves, and then give it away in the form of feudal states. All happened according to plan. It was taken from the emperor at Constantinople, and its name and title ascribed to us Germans. Thereby we became the pope's feudatories, and there is now a second Roman empire, one built by the popes, but on German foundations. . . .

. . . Nevertheless, we have unhappily paid far too dearly for this empire, through pontifical cunning and unscrupulousness, at the cost of immeasurable bloodshed, with the suppressions of our freedom, the loss and theft of our property, especially of our churches and canonries, and the suffering of unspeakable fraud and contempt. We have the title of empire, but the pope has our goods, our honour, our bodies, lives, souls, and all we possess. That is the way to cheat the Germans, and, because they are Germans, to go on cheating them. The popes had this in mind when they wanted to become emperors; when they could not accomplish this, they set themselves above the emperors. . . .

For these reasons, the pope and his entourage have no room to boast that they have conferred great benefit on the German people by giving this Roman empire to them. Firstly, because they did not grant it to us for our benefit. Rather, they took advantage of our simplicity when they did so, in order to give support for their arrogance towards the true Roman emperor in Constantinople. The pope took it from him contrary to God and the right, and without authority. Secondly, because the pope's objective was not to give the empire to us, but to keep it for himself, to claim all our power, freedom, property, our bodies and souls; and with us, if God had not prevented it, all the world besides. He has said so himself plainly in the Decretals and tried to carry it out, with many a trick on several German emperors. How beautifully have we Germans been taught our German! While we supposed we were to become masters, we have become serfs of the most cunning tyrant. We have come into possession of the name, the titles, and the coat of arms of empire; but the treasures, the powers, the rights, and liberties of it remain the pope's. So the pope eats the nut while we play with the empty shell. . . .

. . . Let the pope give us the Roman empire and all it means, but let our country be free from his intolerable taxes and frauds. Give us back our freedom, our power, our honour, our bodies and souls; and let us be an empire as an empire ought to be, and let there be an end of his word and claims! . . .]

27. And now I have spoken at sufficient length about the transgressions of the clergy, though you may and will find more of them if you look in the right place. We shall now devote a section to the consideration of temporal failings.

In the first place, there is urgent need of a general order and decree on behalf of the German people against the overflowing abundance and the great expensiveness of the clothing worn by so many nobles and rich folk. To us, as to other people, God has given enough wool, fur, flax, and everything that would provide proper, suitable, and worthy garments for each class. . . . I believe that, even if the pope did not rob us Germans with his intolerable, fraudulent practices, we should still have had too many of these native robbers, the silk and velvet merchants. . . .

In the same way, the spice traffic ought to be reduced, for it is another of the great channels by which money is conveyed out of Germany. By the grace of God, more things to eat and drink are indigenous to our own country than to any other, and are just as precious and wholesome. Perhaps I am now bringing forward foolish and impossible suggestions which would endanger the principal trade of the merchants. But I am expressing my own views. . . .

The next thing is the abuse of eating and drinking, a matter which gains us no good repute abroad, but is thought a special failing of ours. Preaching never makes any impression on it, so firmly is it rooted and so well has it gained the upper hand. The waste of money would be its least evil; but it often entails the vices of murder, adultery, robbery, blasphemy, and every form of immorality. Here is something for the secular government to prevent. . . .

Finally, is it not a lamentable thing that we Christians should openly tolerate in our midst common houses of ill-fame, though we all took the oath of chastity at our baptism? I am well aware of the frequent reply, that it is a custom not confined to any one people, that it would be difficult to stop, and that it is better to have such houses than that married women, or maidens, or others held in greater respect, should be dishonoured. Nevertheless, ought not the secular but Christian government to consider that that is not the way to get rid of a heathen custom? ...

But on account of avoiding the many sins which gnaw their way within us so disgustingly, I will give the faithful advice that neither youths nor maidens should take the vows of continence or the "spiritual" life before they are thirty. ... Further: I say that if you trust God so little that you doubt whether you could support yourself and a wife, and if that doubt is your only reason for entering the clerical status, then I beg you for the good of your soul not to become a cleric, but rather a farmer; or else make some other choice. ...

... I am aware that I have spoken strongly, and suggested much that will be felt impossible, and attacked many subjects too severely. But what am I to do? I cannot but speak. If I were able, I would also act. I would rather that the world were wroth with me than that God were. No man can do more than take away my life. Many times heretofore I have proposed peace with my enemies. But as it seems to me, God has used them to compel me to raise my voice even more insistently; and because they are not satisfied, I must speak, shout, shriek, and write till they have had enough. Oh well! I have still a little song[13] about Rome and about them. Their ears are itching for me to sing it to them, and pitch the notes in the treble clef. Do you grasp my meaning, oh worthy Rome?

I have offered to stand and be cross-examined for what I have written, but without avail.[14] Nevertheless, I know that if my cause is just, though of necessity condemned on earth, it must be justified in heaven. For the whole Bible shows that the cause of Christians and Christianity shall be judged by God alone; it has never yet been judged on earth by men, but has always been too great and strong for my enemies. My great concern and primary fear are that my case may remain uncondemned; that would show me it was not yet pleasing to God. Therefore, let them but come boldly forward, whether pope, bishop, priest, monk, or scholar; they are the right people to pursue the truth. They should have done so all the time. God grant to us a Christian mind, and, in particular, God grant a truly religious courage to the ruling class of the German people, to do the best they can for the church that is so much to be pitied.

Amen.

Wittenberg. A.D. 1520.

[13] A reference to Luther's equally famous Latin tract, *On the Pagan Servitude*, which was his attack upon the Catholic sacramental system. It appeared shortly after the original edition of this pamphlet.
[14] By 1520 Luther had been given "hearings" at Heidelberg, Augsburg, and Leipzig.

14

A Soldier Forges a Militant Spiritual Army

Ignatius of Loyola

The sixteenth century, a time of religious turmoil and upheaval, abounded in theological treatises dealing with the spiritual struggles of the writers. Leaders as diverse as Martin Luther, John Calvin, and Ignatius of Loyola, despite their obvious differences, had several things in common: personal doubts about their early lives, intense psychological struggles, a repudiation of old ways of living and an embarkation upon new ways, concerning which they wrote for their followers and for posterity. The testament or autobiography of Ignatius of Loyola is such a document.

Iñigo de Oñez y Loyola (1491–1556), Spanish nobleman, soldier, and founder of the Company (or Society) of Jesus, was one of the most influential figures of his time. He served as a page in the court of King Ferdinand V and later was wounded at the siege of Pamplona (1521) while serving the Duke of Najera. Loyola's period of convalescence wrought a profound change in his life, and he determined to enter the service of the Roman Church as a missionary to convert the infidels of the Holy Land. However, a journey to Jerusalem (1523–24) convinced him of the need to extend his education, which had been quite limited. After a time as a hermit he entered the University of Salamanca, but difficulties with ecclesiastical authorities prompted him to migrate to the University of Paris in 1528. It was at this university that he founded the religious order which came to be known as the Jesuits and which soon won renown for its discipline and military character, features which were the result of his earlier experiences. In 1541, having received papal approval of his order, Loyola became its superior or general; and he continued to direct its destinies until his death in 1556.

The Autobiography of Ignatius of Loyola occupies a unique place in the literature of the Reformation era. It was rather casually dictated to a young Spanish Jesuit, Luis González de Cámera, recently arrived in Rome, where Loyola spent his last years. Father González had been sent to Rome to place before

Loyola the problems of the Portuguese province of the Jesuits. Loyola was favorably impressed by the young priest; and at González' urging, he began to recount some of the details of his life. For many years the Jesuits had attempted to persuade their founder to give such an account, but he had refused on the grounds that to do so would seem vain. Where others had failed, González now prevailed; Loyola began his dictation in September, 1553, and continued intermittently until March, 1555. González would take Loyola's account down in a kind of shorthand; then in the evening would expand his notes. The final draft was completed by González in December, 1555, in Genoa, where he had been sent. The manuscript was then corrected and expanded by Father Jerome Nadal, a longtime confidant of Loyola.

The Autobiography, written in the third person, is one of the few sources of information about the early life of Loyola. It is therefore a valuable historical document and key source on one of the major figures of a pivotal era. The work itself is at times vague as to details and dates of events in the author's life, but it provides the essential framework. For example, at one point Loyola speaks of visiting the sick and dying in Paris in a time of plague, but gives no date. However, since it is known that Paris suffered a severe plague in 1531, the historian can estimate the date of this incident as probably 1531.

The Autobiography should be read carefully and perhaps slowly. It is a moving account of Loyola's struggle to find his place in the world and to live a constructive and helpful life. The difficulties he encountered with religious authorities are indicative of the suspicion with which the Church viewed religious innovators. This was true throughout Catholic Europe, which had been shaken by the rise of many groups that questioned the ancient authority of Rome; but in Spain the feeling was intensified, partly because of the seven-centuries struggle of the Spaniards against the Moors and the Jews, and partly too because of the presence of the Alumbrados, whose practices had brought them under ecclesiastical censure. Protestantism, also, had begun in Loyola's time to make some limited progress in the universities, and it is not surprising that Loyola's conduct, as he himself describes it, should have aroused suspicion and hostility. His trials and tribulations served, however, to strengthen his determination to continue his work; and his efforts produced, in the Society of Jesus, probably the most effective force of the Catholic Reformation.

Ignatius of Loyola

Autobiography *

CHAPTER I

His Military Life — He Is Wounded at the Siege of Pampeluna — His Cure — Spiritual Reading — The Apparition — The Gift of Chastity — His Longing for a Holier Life

Up to his twenty-sixth year the heart of Ignatius was enthralled by the vanities of the world. His special delight was in the military life, and he seemed led by a strong and empty desire of gaining for himself a great name. The citadel of Pampeluna[1] was held in siege by the French. All the other soldiers were unanimous in wishing to surrender on condition of freedom to leave, since it was impossible to hold out any longer; but Ignatius so persuaded the commander, that against the views of all the other nobles, he decided to hold the citadel against the enemy.

When the day of assault came, Ignatius made his confession to one of the nobles, his companion in arms. The soldier also made his to Ignatius. After the walls were destroyed, Ignatius stood fighting bravely until a cannon ball of the enemy broke one of his legs and seriously injured the other.

When he fell, the citadel was surrendered. When the French took possession of the town they showed great admiration for Ignatius. After twelve or fifteen days at Pampeluna, where he received the best care from the physicians of the French army, he was borne on a litter to Loyola.[2] His recovery was slow, and doctors and surgeons were summoned from all parts for a consultation. They decided that

---

* Reprinted from *The Autobiography of St. Ignatius: The Account of His Life Dictated to Father González by St. Ignatius*, edited by J. F. X. O'Connor, S.J. (New York: Benziger Brothers, 1900).

[1] Pampeluna (Pamplona), a key fortress in the province of Navarre, was besieged by Henri d'Albert whose family claimed the province as their heritage. The king of France, Francis I, had urged the campaign and supplied troops for d'Albert, as part of his program to weaken the Hapsburgs and thus assure the ascendancy of the Valois dynasty and France. The date is 1521, when Loyola was about 30 years old. A few authorities suggest that Loyola was born in 1495.

[2] Loyola was the family home of Ignatius, situated in the Basque province of Guipuzcoa. The Loyolas could trace their lineage back to the thirteenth century when Inés of Loyola married Lope Garcia de Oñez, a member of a neighboring family. The Loyolas rose to prominence through military service to the kings of Castile. The provincial term, Guipuzcoa, means "to terrify the enemy."

the leg should be broken again, that the bones, which had knit badly, might be properly reset; for they had not been properly set in the beginning, or else had been so jostled on the journey that a cure was impossible. He submitted to have his flesh cut again. During the operation, as in all he suffered before and after, he uttered no word and gave no sign of suffering save that of tightly clenching his fists.

In the meantime his strength was failing. He could take no food, and showed other symptoms of approaching death. On the feast of St. John the doctors gave up hope of his recovery, and he was advised to make his confession. Having received the sacraments on the eve of the feasts of Sts. Peter and Paul, toward evening the doctors said that if by the middle of the night there were no change for the better, he would surely die. He had great devotion to St. Peter, and it so happened by the goodness of God that in the middle of the night he began to grow better.

His recovery was so rapid that in a few days he was out of danger. As the bones of his leg settled and pressed upon each other, one bone protruded below the knee. The result was that one leg was shorter than the other, and the bone causing a lump there, made the leg seem quite deformed. As he could not bear this, since he intended to live a life at court, he asked the doctors whether the bone could be cut away. They replied that it could, but it would cause him more suffering than all that had preceded, as everything was healed, and they would need space in order to cut it. He determined, however, to undergo this torture.

His elder brother[3] looked on with astonishment and admiration. He said he could never have had the fortitude to suffer the pain which the sick man bore with his usual patience. When the flesh and the bone that protruded were cut away, means were taken to prevent the leg from becoming shorter than the other. For this purpose, in spite of sharp and constant pain, the leg was kept stretched for many days. Finally the Lord gave him health. He came out of the danger safe and strong with the exception that he could not easily stand on his leg, but was forced to lie in bed.

As Ignatius had a love for fiction, when he found himself out of danger he asked for some romances to pass away the time. In that house there was no book of the kind. They gave him instead, "The Life of Christ," by Rudolph, the Carthusian, and another book called the "Flowers of the Saints," both in Spanish. By frequent reading of these books he began to get some love for spiritual things. This reading led his mind to meditate on holy things, yet sometimes it wandered to thoughts which he had been accustomed to dwell upon before.

---

[3] Presumably this was Ignatius's oldest surviving brother, Martin Garcia. It is estimated that there were thirteen children in the Loyola family, although definite records prove the existence of only ten, seven sons and three daughters.

Among these there was one thought which, above the others, so filled his heart that he became, as it were, immersed and absorbed in it. Unconsciously, it engaged his attention for three and four hours at a time. He pictured to himself what he should do in honor of an illustrious lady, how he should journey to the city where she was, in what words he would address her and what bright and pleasant sayings he would make use of, what manner of warlike exploits he should perform to please her. He was so carried away by this thought that he did not even perceive how far beyond his power it was to do what he proposed, for she was a lady exceedingly illustrious and of the highest nobility.

In the meantime the divine mercy was at work substituting for these thoughts others suggested by his recent readings. While perusing the life of Our Lord and the saints, he began to reflect, saying to himself: "What if I should do what St. Francis did?" "What if I should act like St. Dominic?" He pondered over these things in his mind, and kept continually proposing to himself serious and difficult things. He seemed to feel a certain readiness for doing them, with no other reason except this thought: "St. Dominic did this; I, too, will do it." "St. Francis did this; therefore I will do it." These heroic resolutions remained for a time, and then other vain and worldly thoughts followed. This succession of thoughts occupied him for a long while, those about God alternating with those about the world. But in these thoughts there was this difference. When he thought of worldly things it gave him great pleasure, but afterward he found himself dry and sad. But when he thought of journeying to Jerusalem,[4] and of living only on herbs, and practising austerities, he found pleasure not only while thinking of them, but also when he had ceased.

This difference he did not notice or value, until one day the eyes of his soul were opened and he began to inquire the reason of the difference. He learned by experience that one train of thought left him sad, the other joyful. This was his first reasoning on spiritual matters. Afterward, when he began the Spiritual Exercises,[5] he was enlightened, and understood what he afterward taught his children about the discernment of spirits. When gradually he recognized the different spirits by which he was moved, one, the spirit of God, the other, the devil, and when he had gained no little spiritual light from the reading of pious books, he began to think more seriously of his past life, and how much penance he should do to expiate his past sins.

---

[4] The Holy Land was ruled by the Mohammedans and had been since the fall of Jerusalem in the thirteenth century. The Papacy had constantly, and unavailingly, sought to launch new crusades to free the birthplace of Christ from the infidels.

[5] See note 10, page 422.

Amid these thoughts the holy wish to imitate saintly men came to his mind; his resolve was not more definite than to promise with the help of divine grace that what they had done he also would do. After his recovery his one wish was to make a pilgrimage to Jerusalem. He fasted frequently and scourged himself to satisfy the desire of penance that ruled in a soul filled with the spirit of God.

The vain thoughts were gradually lessened by means of these desires — desires that were not a little strengthened by the following vision. While watching one night he plainly saw the image of the Blessed Mother of God with the Infant Jesus, at the sight of which, for a considerable time, he received abundant consolation, and felt such contrition for his past life that he thought of nothing else. From that time until August, 1555, when this was written, he never felt the least motion of concupiscence. This privilege we may suppose from the fact to have been a divine gift, although we dare not state it, nor say anything except confirm what has been already said. His brother and all in the house recognized from what appeared externally how great a change had taken place in his soul.

He continued his reading meanwhile, and kept the holy resolution he had made. At home his conversation was wholly devoted to divine things, and helped much to the spiritual advancement of others.

CHAPTER II

Ignatius Leaves His Native Land — What He Did at Montserrat and at Manresa

Ignatius, starting from his father's house, set out upon his journey on horseback. About this time he began his habit of taking the discipline every night. His brother desired to accompany him as far as Ogna, and during the journey was persuaded by the Saint to pass one night of watching at the shrine of Our Blessed Lady at Aruncuz.[6] Having prayed some time at the shrine for new strength for his journey, leaving his brother at Ogna at the house of their sister, to whom he paid a short visit, he journeyed on to Navarre. Remembering that an official in the Duke's palace owed him some money, he collected it by sending in a written account to the treasurer, and distributed it among persons to whom he felt indebted. A portion of the money he devoted to the restoration of a picture of the Blessed Virgin. Then dismissing his two remaining servants, he rode forth

---

[6] This shrine was of recent origin and had developed when a shepherd found a statue of Mary in a shrub. Visitors to the area attested to the performance of miracles and a church was subsequently built on the site. Loyola maintained a lifelong and deep devotion to Mary. Aruncuz (Aranzazu) means, "You are in the shrub."

alone from Navarre in the direction of Montserrat,[7] a mountain town of Catalonia in the northern part of Spain.

It will not be amiss to recall an event that occurred during this journey, to show the manner in which God directed him. Although filled with an ardent desire of serving God, yet his knowledge of spiritual things was still very obscure. He had undertaken to perform extraordinary penances, not so much with a view to satisfy for his sins as with the intention of doing something pleasing to his Lord. He declared indeed that though filled with the liveliest abhorrence of his past sins, he could not assure himself that they were forgiven; yet in his austerities so intense was his desire to do great things for Christ that he did not think of his sins. When he recalled the penances practised by holy persons, his whole mind was bent on doing something to equal and even surpass them. In this holy ambition he found his consolation, for he had no interior motive for his penances, knowing as yet very little about humility or charity or patience, for to obtain these many holy men have led austere lives. He knew still less the value of discretion, which regulates the practice of these virtues. To do something great for the glory of his God, to emulate saintly men in all that they had done before him — this was the only object of Ignatius in his practices of external mortification.

While he journeyed on, a Saracen mounted on a horse came up with him. In the course of the conversation mention was made of the Blessed Virgin. The stranger remarked that though he admitted that the Mother of Christ had conceived without detriment to her virginal purity, yet he could not believe that after the conception of her divine Son she was still a virgin. He was so obstinate in holding this opinion, that no amount of reasoning on the part of Ignatius could force him to abandon it. Shortly afterward the Saracen rode on, leaving the pilgrim to his own reflections. These were not of the most peaceful nature. He was sorely troubled as he thought over the conduct of his recent fellow-traveler, and felt that he had but poorly acquitted himself of his duty of honoring the Mother of God. The longer his mind thought upon the matter, the more his soul was filled with indignation against himself for having allowed the Saracen to speak as he had done of the Blessed Virgin, and for the lack of courage he fancied he had shown in not at once resenting the insult. He consequently felt impelled by a strong impulse to hasten after him and slay the miscreant for the insulting language he had used. After much internal conflict with these thoughts, he still remained in doubt, nor could he decide what course to follow. The Saracen, who had ridden

---

[7] Ignatius arrived in Montserrat on March 21, 1522. He was attracted by the spiritual history of the town. A Benedictine monastery was founded there in the middle of the sixth century, and during the Moorish wars a special devotion had developed for Mary. At Montserrat, Loyola came under the influence of a French Benedictine, Jean Chanones, who is considered to be his first "spiritual father."

on, had mentioned to him that it was his intention to proceed to a town not far distant from the highroad. At length, Ignatius, wearied by his inward struggle and not arriving at any determination, decided to settle all his doubts in the following novel way: he would give free rein to his horse, and if, on coming to the cross-road, his horse should turn into the path that led to the destination of the Moor, he would pursue him and kill him; but if his horse kept to the highroad he would allow the wretch to escape. Having done as he had decided, it happened through the Providence of God that his horse kept to the highroad, though the place was distant only about thirty or forty yards, and the way leading to it was very wide and easy.

Arriving at a large village situated a short distance from Montserrat, he determined to procure a garment to wear on his journey to Jerusalem. He therefore bought a piece of sackcloth, poorly woven, and filled with prickly wooden fibres. Of this he made a garment that reached to his feet. He bought, also, a pair of shoes of coarse stuff that is often used in making brooms. He never wore but one shoe, and that not for the sake of the comfort to be derived from it, but because as he was in the habit of wearing a cord tied below the knee by way of mortification, this leg would be very much swollen at night, though he rode all day on horseback. For this reason, he felt he ought to wear a shoe on that foot. He provided himself also with a pilgrim's staff and a gourd to drink from. All these he tied to his saddle.

Thus equipped, he continued on his way to Montserrat, pondering in his mind, as was his wont, on the great things he would do for the love of God. And as he had formerly read the stories of Amadeus of Gaul[8] and other such writers, who told how the Christian knights of the past were accustomed to spend the entire night, preceding the day on which they were to receive knighthood, on guard before an altar of the Blessed Virgin, he was filled with these chivalric fancies, and resolved to prepare himself for a noble knighthood by passing a night in vigil before an altar of Our Lady at Montserrat. He would observe all the formalities of this ceremony, neither sitting nor lying down, but alternately standing and kneeling, and there he would lay aside his worldly dignities to assume the arms of Christ.

When he arrived at Montserrat, he passed a long time in prayer, and with the consent of his confessor he made in writing a general confession of his sins. Three whole days were employed in this undertaking. He begged and obtained leave of his confessor to give up his horse, and to hang up his sword and his dagger in the church, near the altar of the Blessed Virgin. This confessor was the first to whom he unfolded his interior, and disclosed his resolution of devoting him-

[8] The *Amadis de Gaula* was a romantic novel about chivalry in Wales and England. It appeared in book form in Saragossa in 1508 and was widely read by Spaniards who felt that its ideals were closely suited to the Spanish character. Ignatius, commenting on the novel, and speaking in the third person, said, "His whole mind was full of those things, *Amadis de Gaula* and similar books."

self to a spiritual life. Never before had he manifested his purpose to anybody.

The eve of the Annunciation of Our Blessed Lady in the year 1522 was the time he chose to carry out the project he had formed. At nightfall, unobserved by any one, he approached a beggar, and taking off his own costly garments gave them to the beggar. He then put on the pilgrim's dress he had previously bought, and hastened to the church, where he threw himself on his knees before the altar of the Blessed Mother of God, and there, now kneeling, now standing, with staff in hand, he passed the entire night.

After receiving the Blessed Sacrament, to avoid recognition he left the town at daybreak.[9] He did not go by the direct route that leads to Barcelona, as he might have met those who knew him and would honor him, but he took a byway that led him to a town called Manresa.[10] Here he determined to remain a few days in the hospital and write out some notes in his little book, which for his own consolation he carefully carried about with him. At about a league's distance from Montserrat, he was overtaken by a man who had ridden after him at a rapid pace. This man accosted him and inquired if he had given certain garments to a poor man, as the latter had declared. Ignatius answered that it was true that he had given them to a beggar. On learning that the latter had been ill-treated because he was suspected of having stolen the clothes, the eyes of Ignatius filled with tears, in pity for the poor man.

Although he had fled so anxiously from the praise of men, he did not remain long at Manresa before many marvellous things were narrated of him. This fame arose from what had occurred at Montserrat. His reputation increased day by day. Men vied with each other in adding some particulars about his sanctity, declaring that he had abandoned immense revenues, and other wonderful things without much regard to real facts.

At Manresa he lived on the alms that he daily begged. He never ate meat nor partook of wine, though they were offered him. On Sundays, however, he never fasted, and if wine were offered him, he drank of it sparingly. In former days he had been very careful of his hair, which he had worn, and, indeed, not unbecomingly, in the fashionable manner of the young men of his age; but now he determined to cease to care for it, neither to comb it nor to cut it, and to dispense with all covering for his head both day and night. To punish himself for the too great nicety which he had formerly had in the care of his hands and feet, he now resolved to neglect them.

---

[9] Loyola's conduct had brought ridicule and criticism from his former friends and suspicion from the ecclesiastical authorities.

[10] The date of his arrival was March 25, 1522. Manresa was originally an episcopal see but in 888 the bishopric was transferred to the town of Vich. The cathedral of Manresa, dedicated to Mary, remained, as did a score of lesser churches and monasteries. It was at Manresa that Loyola began his famous work of devotional readings, *The Spiritual Exercises.*

It was while he was living at the hospital at Manresa that the following strange event took place. Very frequently on a clear moonlight night there appeared in the courtyard before him an indistinct shape which he could not see clearly enough to tell what it was. Yet it appeared so symmetrical and beautiful that his soul was filled with pleasure and joy as he gazed at it. It had something of the form of a serpent with glittering eyes, and yet they were not eyes. He felt an indescribable joy steal over him at the sight of this object. The oftener he saw it, the greater was the consolation he derived from it, and when the vision left him, his soul was filled with sorrow and sadness.

Up to this period he had remained in a constant state of tranquillity and consolation, without any interior knowledge of the trials that beset the spiritual life. But during the time that the vision lasted, sometimes for days, or a little previous to that time, his soul was violently agitated by a thought that brought him no little uneasiness. There flashed upon his mind the idea of the difficulty that attended the kind of life he had begun, and he felt as if he heard some one whispering to him, "How can you keep up for seventy years of your life these practices which you have begun?" Knowing that this thought was a temptation of the evil one, he expelled it by this anwser: "Can you, wretched one, promise me one hour of life?" In this manner he overcame the temptation, and his soul was restored to peace. This was his first trial besides what has already been narrated, and it came upon him suddenly one day as he was entering the church. He was accustomed to hear Mass daily, and to assist at Vespers and Compline — devotions from which he derived much consolation. During Mass, he always read over the history of the Passion, and his soul was filled with a joyful feeling of uninterrupted calm.

Shortly after the temptation just spoken of, he began to experience great changes in his soul. At one time he was deprived of all consolation, so that he found no pleasure in vocal prayer, in hearing Mass, or in any spiritual exercise. At another, on the contrary, he suddenly felt as if all sorrow and desolation were taken from him, experiencing the relief of one from whose shoulders a heavy cloak had suddenly been lifted. On noticing all this, he was surprised, wondering what could be the import of these changes which he had never before experienced, and he said to himself, "What new kind of life is this upon which I am entering?"

At this time he became acquainted with some holy persons who manifested great confidence in him, and gladly conversed with him; for though he had, as yet, little knowledge of spiritual things, still he spoke with great fervor on religious subjects, and incited his hearers to make greater progress in the way of God's service. Among those holy persons who dwelt at Manresa, there was one lady well advanced in years who had long been given to the service of God, and who was so well known in many places in Spain that his Catholic

Majesty,[11] the King of Spain, had desired her presence on one occasion in order to take counsel with her about certain projects that he had in his mind. This lady, speaking one day to our new soldier of Christ, said to him, "Would that the Lord Jesus might appear to you some day!" Ignatius, wondering at her words, understood in a literal sense, and asked her, "What would He look like if He were to show Himself to me?"

He always persevered in his custom of approaching the Sacraments of Confession and Holy Communion every week. But herein he found a great source of anxiety on account of the scruples with which he was annoyed. For though he had written out his general confession at Montserrat, and with great diligence and care had tried to make it complete, yet he always felt that he had forgotten something in his confession, and this caused him much anxiety. Even though he should now confess it again, he received no consolation. He tried then to find a spiritual person, who could give him relief in his trouble, but he found no one. Finally, a certain doctor who had experience in spiritual things, and who was a preacher in the church, advised him to write down anything he remembered and feared that he had not confessed. He obeyed, and even after he had confessed these sins, his scruples still continued to fill his soul, and he was constantly recalling minor details that he had not confessed. In this way he was cruelly tormented. He knew well that these scruples caused no little harm to the spiritual life, and that it was most expedient to get rid of them, yet they continued to torture him. At times it occurred to him that it would be well if he could have his confessor command him in the name of the Lord Jesus not again to confess anything of his past sins; and he inwardly prayed that his confessor would give him some such command, but he could not bring himself to ask him to do so.

CHAPTER III

Scruples — Heavenly Favors — Journey to Barcelona

At last his confessor, without any suggestion on the part of the penitent, commanded him to confess nothing of his past life, except what was very clear and evident. But as he regarded everything of the past as evident, the confessor's order did not help him at all. He was in constant anxiety. At that time he lived in the Dominican monastery, in a little cell which the Fathers had allotted to him. He kept up his usual custom of praying on bended knees for seven hours a day, and scourged himself three times a day and during the night. But all this did not remove his scruples, which had been torment-

[11] Charles I.

ing him for months. One day, when terribly tormented, he began to pray. During his prayer, he cried out to God in a loud voice: "O Lord, help me, for I find no remedy among men, nor in any creature! If I thought I could find one, no labor would seem too great to me. Show me some one! O Lord! where may I find one? I am willing to do anything to find relief."

While tortured by these thoughts, several times he was violently tempted to cast himself out of the large window of his cell. This window was quite near the place where he was praying. But since he knew that it would be a sin to take his own life, he began to pray, "O Lord, I will not do anything to offend Thee." He repeated these words frequently with his former prayer, when there came to his mind the story of a certain holy man, who, to obtain of God some favor which he ardently desired, spent many days without food, until he obtained the favor he asked. He determined to do the same. He resolved in his heart neither to eat nor drink until God should look upon him in mercy, or until he should find himself at the point of death; then only should he eat.

This resolution was taken on a Sunday after communion, and for a whole week he neither ate nor drank anything; in the meantime he practised his usual penances, recited the Divine Office, prayed on bended knees at the appointed times, and rose at midnight. On the following Sunday, when about to make his usual confession, as he had been in the habit of making known to his confessor everything he had done, even the smallest detail, he told him that he had not eaten anything during the past week. Hereupon his confessor bade him break his fast. Although he felt that he still had sufficient strength to continue without food, nevertheless he obeyed his confessor, and on that day and the next he was free from scruples. On the third day, however, which was Tuesday, while standing in prayer, the remembrance of his sins came back to him. One suggested another, until he passed in review, one after another, all his past sins. He then thought he ought to repeat his general confession. After these thoughts a sort of disgust seized him, so that he felt an inclination to give up the life he was leading. While in this state, God was pleased to arouse him as it were from sleep, and to relieve him of his trouble. As he had acquired some experience in the discernment of spirits, he profited by the lessons he had learned of God, and began to examine how that spirit had entered into possession of his soul; then he resolved never again to speak of his past sins in confession. From that day he was free from scruples, and felt certain that it was the will of our merciful Lord to deliver him from his trouble of soul.

Besides the seven hours devoted to prayer, he spent a portion of his time in assisting souls who came to him for advice. During the rest of the day he gave his thoughts to God, pondering on what he had read or meditated that day. When he retired, it often happened that wonderful illuminations and great spiritual consolations came to him, so that he abridged the short time he had already allotted to sleep. Once while thinking over this matter he concluded that he had given sufficient time for conversation with God, and that moreover the whole way was also given to Him. Then he began to doubt whether these illuminations were from the Good Spirit. Finally he came to the conclusion that it would be better to give up a portion and to give sufficient time to sleep. This he did.

While he persevered in his resolution to abstain from meat, it happened on a certain morning after rising, that a dish of cooked meat seemed to be set before him. He appeared to see it with his eyes, although he had felt no previous craving for it. At the same time he afterward experienced within himself a certain movement of the will, urging him to eat meat. Although the remembrance of his former resolution came to mind he had no doubt about determining to eat meat. When he made this known to his confessor, the latter advised him to consider whether it was a temptation or not. Pondering over it, he felt certain that he was right. At that period God dealt with him as a teacher instructing a pupil. Was this on account of his ignorance or dulness, or because he had no one else to teach him? Or on account of the fixed resolve he had of serving God, with which God Himself had inspired him, for the light given him could not possibly be greater? He was firmly convinced, both then and afterward, that God had treated him thus because it was the better spiritual training for him. The five following points will prove what he says: —

In the first place, he had a great devotion to the Blessed Trinity. Every day he prayed to each of the three Persons and to the whole Trinity. While thus praying to the Blessed Trinity, the thought came of how to offer fourfold prayers to the Divinity. This thought, however, caused him little or no trouble. Once, while reciting on the steps of the monastery the little hours in honor of the Blessed Virgin, his vision carried him beyond the earth. He seemed to behold the Blessed Trinity in the form of a lyre or harp; this vision affected him so much that he could not refrain from tears and sighs. On the same day he accompanied the procession from the church, but even up to the time of dinner he could not withhold his tears, and after dinner his joy and consolation were so great that he could speak of no subject except the Blessed Trinity. In these conversations he made use of many different comparisons to illustrate his thoughts. Such an impression was made on him on that occasion that during his after life, whenever he prayed to the Blessed Trinity, he experienced great devotion.

At another time, to his great joy, God permitted him to understand how He had created this world. This vision presented to him a white object, with rays emanating from it. From this object God sent forth light. However, he could not clearly explain this vision, nor could he recall the illuminations given to him by God on that occasion. During his stay of about a year at Manresa, after he had begun to receive from God consolations, and fruitful lights for the direction of others, he gave up his former rigorous penances. At that time he trimmed his nails and hair. During the time of his residence at Manresa, while assisting at Mass, he had another vision in the church of the monastery. At the elevation of the body of Christ Our Lord he beheld, with the eyes of his soul, white rays descending from above. Although he cannot, after so long an interval, explain the details of this vision, still the manner in which Our Lord Jesus Christ is present in the Blessed Sacrament was clearly and vividly stamped upon his mind. Often in prayer, and even during a long space of time, did he see the humanity of Christ with the eyes of the soul. The form under which this vision appeared was that of a white body, neither large nor small; besides, there seemed to be no distinction of members in His body. This vision appeared to him often at Manresa, perhaps twenty or even forty times, once at Jerusalem, and once when he was at Padua. He saw the Blessed Virgin under the same form, without any distinction of members. These visions gave him such strength that he often thought within himself, that even though Scripture did not bear witness to these mysteries of faith, still, from what he had seen, it would be his duty to lay down his life for them.

One day he went to the Church of St. Paul, situated about a mile from Manresa. Near the road is a stream, on the bank of which he sat, and gazed at the deep waters flowing by. While seated there, the eyes of his soul were opened. He did not have any special vision, but his mind was enlightened on many subjects, spiritual and intellectual. So clear was this knowledge that from that day everything appeared to him in a new light. Such was the abundance of this light in his mind that all the divine helps received, and all the knowledge acquired up to his sixty-second year, were not equal to it.

From that day he seemed to be quite another man, and possessed of a new intellect. This illumination lasted a long time. While kneeling in thanksgiving for this grace, there appeared to him that object which he had often seen before, but had never understood. It seemed to be something most beautiful, and, as it were, gleaming with many eyes. This is how it always appeared. There was a cross near which he was praying, and he noticed that near the cross the vision had lost some of its former beautiful color. He understood from this that the apparition was the work of the devil, and whenever the vision appeared to him after that, as it did several times, he dispelled it with his staff.

During a violent fever at Manresa, he thought he was near his death. The thought then came to his mind that he was already justified before God. Calling to mind his sins, he tried to combat the thought, but could not overcome it, and this struggle to overcome the temptation caused him much more suffering than the fever itself. After the fever had somewhat abated, and he was out of danger, he cried out to some noble ladies who had come to visit him, and asked them for the love of God, to cry out aloud the next time they should find him near death, "O sinner!" and "Remember the sins by which you have offended God."

On another occasion, while sailing from Valencia to Italy, in the midst of a violent storm, the rudder was broken, and he and every one on board were convinced that the ship must founder unless help came from above. Then, as he examined his conscience and prepared for death, he had no dread on account of past sins, nor fear of eternal punishment, but he experienced intense shame and sorrow at the thought of not having made a good use of the favors and graces which God had bestowed upon him. Again, in the year 1550, he was dangerously ill, and in his own judgment and that of others he was about to die. This time, however, whenever he thought of death, such consolation poured into his soul that he wept tears of joy. He continued in this state so long that he often had to divert his mind from the thought of death, lest he should find in the thought too much consolation.

In the beginning of another winter he became very ill, and was placed under the care of the father of a man named Ferrera, who afterward entered the service of Balthasar Faria.[12] Here he was very carefully attended. Several ladies of the highest rank were very devoted to him, and came every night to watch beside him. When he began to recover, he was still extremely weak, and suffered from severe pains in the stomach. These two causes, together with the intense cold and the entreaties of his attendants, induced him to wear shoes, warmer clothing, and a cap. He was obliged to accept two small coats of coarse grayish stuff, and a small cap of the same color. During that illness his constant wish was to speak of spiritual things, and to find some one who could talk upon such subjects. Meanwhile the time which he had determined upon for his journey to Jerusalem was approaching.

In the beginning of the year 1523, therefore, he set out for Barcelona. Many offered to accompany him, but he refused, as he wished to go alone. He expected to derive great advantage from placing his whole trust in God alone. Several were very earnest, and insisted that as he knew neither Latin nor Italian, he should not go alone, but should take with him a certain companion whom they praised very much. Ignatius replied that even were he the son or brother of the Duke of Cordova,[13] he would not take him as a companion, as he wished only

---

[12] Faria later became the Portuguese ambassador of King John III at the papal court, a position which permitted him to continue his association with Loyola.

[13] This is a reference to the Cardona (Cardova) family whose head, Duke Ferdinand, became a close friend of Loyola in the 1540's.

three virtues, — Faith, Hope, and Charity. If he took a companion, when hungry he would look to his companion for food; if exhausted, he would call on his companion for help; and so he would confide in his companion, and have some affection for him: whereas he wished to place all this confidence, hope, and affection in God alone. These words were not a mere expression of the lips, but they were the true sentiments of his heart. For these reasons he wished to embark not only alone, but even without any provision for the voyage. When he arranged about his passage, the captain agreed to take him free, as he had no money; but on condition that he should take with him as much sailors' bread as would suffice for his sustenance. Were it not for this condition imposed by the captain, Ignatius would have refused to take with him any provision at all.

When he thought of procuring bread, he was much troubled with scruples. "Is this your hope and faith in God, who, you were sure, would not fail you?" The force and violence of the temptation were such that he was greatly distressed. Good reasons on both sides presented themselves. Finally, in his perplexity, he determined to leave the matter to his confessor. He told him first of his great desire to go go to Jerusalem, and to do everything for the greater glory of God. Then he gave the reasons for not taking provisions for the voyage. His confessor decided that he ought to beg what was necessary and take it with him. He went to a lady of rank to ask for what he needed. When she asked where he was going, he hesitated, and replied that he was going to Italy and Rome. She was somewhat astonished at this, and replied: "To Rome? Why, as to those who go there — well, I do not like to say what they are when they return." She meant by this that as most of those who went to Rome did not go through motives of piety and devotion, when they returned they were not much better. The reason of his not openly declaring that he intended to go to the holy city of Jerusalem was his dread of yielding to vain glory. In fact, he was so much troubled by this fear that he was afraid to make known even the place of his birth or the name of his family. When he had secured the bread, before going on board he took care to leave behind him, on a bench on the wharf, five or six Spanish coins, which had been given to him as alms.

He was obliged to remain at Barcelona more than twenty days before the ship was ready to sail. During that time, in accordance with his custom, in order to speak with spiritual men about his soul, he sought them out even though dwelling in hermitages at a long distance from the city. But neither then, nor during the whole time of his stay at Manresa, could he find any one who could help him to advance as he wished. He met one woman, however, who seemed to be thoroughly acquainted with the spiritual life. She promised to pray to Jesus Christ and to ask Him to appear to Ignatius in person. In consequence of this promise, after leaving Barcelona, he gave up all anxiety about finding souls advanced in the spiritual life.

CHAPTER IV

His Journey to Rome, Venice, Jerusalem, and the Holy Land

After a voyage of five days and nights the vessel in which they set out from Barcelona reached Gaeta,[14] and the pilgrim disembarked and started for Rome, although there was danger there on account of the plague. After reaching the city, he found the gates closed. He spent the night in a damp church, and in the morning sought to enter the city, but could not obtain permission. As no alms could be obtained outside of the city, he wished to go on to a neighboring village, but for sheer weakness, the pilgrim could go no farther. On that day it happened that a great procession came out of the city. On inquiry the pilgrim learned that the Duchess was in the throng. He approached her, told her that his malady was simply the effect of weakness, and asked permission to enter the city to get relief. She readily consented. He was successful and his strength returned, and two days later he resumed his journey, reaching Rome on Palm Sunday.

Those whom he met at Rome knew he had no money for his journey to Jerusalem. They tried to dissuade him from his undertaking, alleging that such a journey was impossible without money. He felt assured, however, that everything needed for his voyage would be at hand when required. Accordingly, on the octave of Easter, he received the blessing of Adrian VI[15] and left Rome for Venice. He had in his possession six or seven pieces of gold which they had given him to pay his passage from Venice as far as Jerusalem. He had taken this money with him from Venice only because they had convinced him that without it he could not reach Jerusalem. On the third day from the time he set out from Rome, he realized that this fear had come from a want of confidence, and was sorry he had accepted the money, and was deliberating about giving it away. Finally, however, he determined to spend it on those he met, who were chiefly beggars. The result was that when he came to Venice he had only four coins left, and these were necessary for his lodging that night.

On this journey to Venice, on account of sentinels placed around the cities, he was obliged to sleep outside the walls. The dread of the pestilence was so great that one morning on rising he saw a man

---

[14] A fortified seaport in central Italy.

[15] Adrian was elected Pope in January, 1522, and received news of his elevation while in Spain. Adrian was a Dutchman from Utrecht in the Spanish Netherlands. He owed his election to the influence of King Charles of Spain, whose tutor he had been. Loyola did not have a private audience with the Pope; he merely received the papal blessing, along with other pilgrims, on some public occasion. He left Rome in April 1523.

fleeing from him in terror. Pursuing his journey, he reached Chizoa[16] with several others who had joined him on the road. There he learned that he would not be allowed to enter the city. He then proceeded with his companions to Padua, to get the testimony of a notary that the party was not stricken with the plague. Ignatius could not, on account of his weakness, keep pace with the others, and was left alone in an open field. Then Christ appeared to him, as He had appeared on former occasions. By this vision he was greatly strengthened and consoled. The next morning, filled with new courage, he came to the gate of the city, and although provided with no certificate, entered unquestioned by the guard. In the same way he left the city unquestioned. His companions were surprised at this, for they had to present a certificate, which he had taken no pains to procure. At Venice they begged their food, and slept in St. Mark's Square. Ignatius refused to go to the house of the Ambassador, and although he made no effort to get money for his voyage to Jerusalem, he felt sure nevertheless that God would provide him with means.

One day he met a rich Spaniard, who asked him whether he was going, and having learned his intention, brought him to dine at his house. Here he remained for several days. From the time he left Manresa, Ignatius, while seated at table with others, had made it a practice never to speak except to give a brief answer to questions. However, he heard all that was said, and took occasion after dinner to give the conversation a spiritual turn. His host and all his family were so filled with admiration for him that they tried to induce him to remain with them, and introduced him to the Doge of Venice.[17] The latter offered him accommodations on the government ship about to sail for Cyprus. Many pilgrims had assembled at Venice to go to Jerusalem, but the greater part hesitated through fear, as the Island of Rhodes had fallen into the hands of the Turks. Thirteen sailed in the pilgrims' ship, which was the first to weigh anchor. The government ship carried eight or nine. About the time of departure Ignatius was taken ill with a fever, which lasted several days. On the day of sailing he took the prescribed medicine, and asked the doctor if he could go. The doctor replied he could if he wished the vessel to be his tomb. Nevertheless he went on board, and after a fit of illness soon recovered.

The licentious conduct of those on board Ignatius severely censured. The Spaniards advised him not to do this, as the rest thought of abandoning him on an island. But the wind quickly conveyed them to Cyprus. From Cyprus they went to another port called Salinae,[18] ten leagues distant. Here he went on board the ship of the pilgrims, with no other provision than his hope in Providence. During all that voy-

---

[16] Chius, in the central Italian province of Sienna.
[17] Andrea Gritti.
[18] Salamis, a port on the eastern coast of Cyprus.

age, the Lord often appeared to him, and gave him great consolation. The visions seemed to take the form of something large, round, and golden. The travelers reached Joppa,[19] and seated on asses after the custom of that region, they journeyed to Jerusalem. A noble Spanish gentleman, named Didacus Minez,[1] as the pilgrims came in sight of the city, recommended silence and recollection.

All followed his suggestion, and when they saw a monk approaching with a crucifix, dismounted. On beholding the city, Ignatius was deeply affected, and the rest affirmed that they experienced a sort of heavenly joy. He always felt this same devotion whenever he visited the holy places. He decided to remain in Jerusalem, in order to visit the holy places often. For this purpose he had taken with him letters of recommendation to the Father Guardian.[2] On presenting them, he said that he intended to remain there to satisfy his own devotion, but said nothing of his purpose of helping others. The Father Guardian told him he did not see how this could be possible, as his house was not even capable of providing for his own Religious, and he intended to send some away from the Holy Land. Ignatius said he wished him merely to hear his confession, since he had come to make it. The Father Guardian said this could be done, but he should wait for the arrival of the Provincial, who was then at Bethlehem. Relying on this promise, Ignatius began to write letters to spiritual persons at Barcelona. He had written some on the day before he was to depart when he was summoned in the name of the Father Guardian and the Provincial. Then the Provincial, addressing him kindly, said he had heard of his pious determination to remain in the holy places, and had given it serious thought. Many others had the same desire, some had died, others had been taken prisoners, and to his Order was left the work of ransoming captives, wherefore he should prepare himself to resume his journey with the pilgrims on the following day. To this Ignatius answered that his resolution was very fixed, and he did not think that anything would keep him from executing it. If the precept did not bind him under pain of sin, he would not allow any fear to keep him from carrying out his desire. The Provincial said he had authority from the Holy See to detain those he thought fit, and to even excommunicate those who would not obey when stopped by him, and he thought in this case it was better for him not to remain. When he wished to show the pontifical papers giving him power to excommunicate, Ignatius said there was no need, as he believed his word. If they had the authority, he would obey.

After this, returning to where he was before, he was seized with a great longing to visit Mount Olivet[3] again before he departed, since

---

[19] Jaffa.
[1] Diego Manes.
[2] The superior of the Franciscan monastery.
[3] Mount of Olives.

the Divine Will would not suffer him to remain in those holy places. On that mountain is a rock from which Our Lord ascended to heaven, on which even now His footprints are visible. And this is what he wished to see again. Therefore, without telling any one, and without a guide, although it was a dangerous thing to go without a Turkish guard, secretly withdrawing he went to Mount Olivet alone. As the guards would not allow him to enter, he gave them his knife. After great consolation in prayer he desired to go to Bethphage.[4] When he reached that place, he thought that on Mount Olivet he had not noticed the position of the right foot of Our Lord and that of the left. He came a second time, and gave his scissors to the guards to allow him to enter. Afterward when at the monastery it was discovered he had gone without a guide, a great search was made for him. Coming down from Mount Olivet he met a girdled Christian, those who are bound to wear a girdle to distinguish them from the Mussulmans;[5] this man, pretending to be very angry, threatened him with a large stick, and approaching, firmly grasped him by the arm. He allowed himself to be led, but the good man once he had hold of him did not let him go. In the meantime, as he was thus led along a captive, he was visited with great consolation, as he seemed to see Christ walking above him. And this continued until he reached the monastery.

CHAPTER V

His Arrival in Apulia, Venice, Ferrara, and Genoa — He Is Apprehended as a Spy — He Is Despised as a Fool — His Studies at Barcelona and Alcala

On the following day the pilgrims took their departure, and arriving at Cyprus, were assigned to different vessels. In the harbor of that place were three or four ships bound for Venice. Of these one belonged to some Turks; another was too small; but the third, the property of a wealthy Venetian, was very large and strong.

Some of the band asked the captain of this last to take the pilgrim aboard; but, finding that no pay was to be offered, he refused, in spite of the fact that many begged him and were loud in their praises of the pilgrim. His reply was, that if the pilgrim were indeed a holy man, he might cross the sea as St. James did.

The favor they asked was easily obtained of the captain of the smaller ship.

On a certain day they set sail with a favorable wind, but toward evening a storm arose, which tossed the vessels about in different

---

[4] A village east of Jerusalem which, by tradition, was said to be situated on the Mount of Olives. The name means "House of Unripe Figs."
[5] Another term for Moslem.

directions. The large ship, whose captain had refused to take Ignatius, was driven by the tempest against the Island of Cyprus, and dashed to pieces. A like fate overtook the Turkish vessel. The small ship, however, though for a long time severely tried by wind and waves, finally reached the shores of Apulia in safety.

Although the winter had set in with intense cold and a heavy fall of snow, Ignatius had no garments save a pair of knee-breeches of a very rough texture, leaving the legs naked, a black waistcoat open and quite ragged about his shoulders, a light cloak made of coarse hair, and a pair of shoes. He arrived at Venice about the middle of January,[6] having spent a good part of the preceding month and all of November aboard the ship which carried him from Cyprus.

At Venice, he met a friend who had been kind to him on his way to Jerusalem. From him he received alms and some cloth, which he wrapped about his body as a protection against the intense cold.

When Ignatius understood that God did not wish him to remain at Jerusalem, he began to consider what he should do. The plan he approved and adopted was to enter upon a course of study in order to be better fitted to save souls. For this purpose he determined to go to Barcelona, and setting out from Venice he traveled toward Genoa.

While praying at the principal church of Ferrara, he gave five or six coins to a beggar who asked an alms. To a second beggar he was equally generous. As soon as the beggars saw him so prodigal of his alms, they flocked around him, until he had spent all the money that he had; so when others approached to ask for assistance, he excused himself on the plea that he had nothing left.

While proceeding from Ferrara to Genoa, he met some Spanish soldiers, who treated him kindly, and who were not a little surprised at his choosing such a route, since by so doing he was compelled to pass through the very midst of the armies of France and Spain. They entreated him therefore to take a safer road, which they would point out to him, and to withdraw from the highway.

Not following their counsel, however, he kept straight on until he came to a town fortified by strong walls. Seized as a spy, the guards cast him into a small house not far from the gate, and, as is customary in such suspicious times, closely questioned him. On all points, however, he professed the greatest ignorance. Finally they searched his clothes and shoes to see if he bore any messages, and finding nothing, they led him into the presence of the captain. They deprived him of his cloak, leaving him only his waistcoat and knee-breeches.

As he was compelled to go about in this condition, he recalled to mind the thought of Christ led about as a captive. Although he was forced to walk through the three principal streets of the town, he did so, not with sadness, but feeling great joy and consolation.

In addressing others he was in the habit of saying "*you*," employ-

[6] 1524.

ing no other word either of reverence or dignity, believing that such was the simplicity as well of the Apostles as of Christ Himself.

While being conducted through the different streets, it occurred to him that it would be well to depart somewhat from his ordinary custom, and to show greater respect to the commander of the place. Such a thought was by no means the outcome of the fear of any punishment which they might inflict. He felt, however, that this was a temptation; he said, "In that case I'll neither address him as a person of dignity, nor bend the knee as a mark of respect, nor even remove my hat in his presence."

Having reached the residence of the commander, he was made to wait sometime in the courtyard before being summoned into his presence. Then, without manifesting the slightest degree of civility, he so paused after each word he spoke as to be taken for a fool by the commander, who said to his captors, "This man is an idiot; restore what belongs to him and send him away."

A certain Spaniard met Ignatius coming from the house of the commander, led him home, just as he was, and gave him food and whatever was necessary for that night.

The next morning he resumed his journey until toward evening, when, espied by the soldiers of a fort, he was seized and brought to the commander of the French forces. The latter, among other things, asked where he came from. When Ignatius answered, "Guipuscoa,"[7] the officer said, "I also come from near that place;" and immediately he ordered Ignatius to be conducted within to supper and to be treated with great kindness.

At Genoa, he was recognized by a Cantabrian, who had spoken with him elsewhere, when in the army of his Catholic Majesty.[8] Through his influence, he was taken on a ship bound for Barcelona. He came very near being taken captive by Andrea Dorea,[9] who was at that time in the service of the French, and gave chase to the vessel.

At Barcelona,[10] he was enabled to study through the assistance of a noble and very pious lady, Isabel Roser,[11] and a teacher, named Ardebal.[12] Both highly approved his plan, Ardebal promising to give him instruction free, while Isabel generously offered to provide him with everything necessary.

At Manresa, there was a very holy monk, of the Order of St. Bernard, with whom Ignatius wished to remain, as well for his own personal guidance as to prepare himself to direct others. He accord-

---

[7] Cf. n. 2, page 436.   [8] Charles I.
[9] The Doge of Genoa, and one of the most illustrious of Italian Renaissance soldiers.
[10] Lent, 1524. Loyola remained there until 1526.
[11] Isabel Roser was from the noble family of Ferrers. She became one of Loyola's benefactresses and maintained a lifelong friendship with him.
[12] Jerome Ardevoll was a Master of Arts and a regent of the University of Barcelona. He tutored Loyola in grammar.

ingly accepted the offer of his two generous friends on condition that what he sought could not be obtained at Manresa. Finding, however, that the monk had died, he returned to Barcelona and applied himself to study. In this, however, he was destined to meet with some difficulties. In his studies, the principles of grammar caused new spiritual thoughts and tastes to arise so abundantly, as to render him incapable of committing anything to memory, and though he strove hard, he could not dispel these thoughts.

Noticing, however, that while praying at Mass he did not experience similar thoughts, he considered this a temptation. Accordingly, after praying for some time, he asked his teacher to come to the Church of Blessed Mary of the Sea, not far from the professor's house, and there to listen to what he would tell him. Ignatius faithfully made known the whole state of his mind, and why he had as yet learned so little. "But," he said, "I promise not to be wanting in attention in school during these two years, provided that at Barcelona I may be able to find bread and water."

Such an acknowledgement was of the greatest efficacy, and he never after experienced that temptation. The pains of the stomach, which afflicted him at Manresa, ceased, and, in fact, they did not trouble him from the time he set out for Jerusalem.

While studying at Barcelona, he wished to practise his former penances. Accordingly, making a hole in the soles of his shoes, he tore them, little by little, until nothing but the upper portion was left.

His two years of study being completed, in which, they say, he greatly advanced, he was advised by his master to go to Alcala[13] to study philosophy, as he was deemed ready for it.

Before setting out, however, he wished to be examined by a certain theologian. As he also gave him the same advice, Ignatius, unaccompanied, started for Alcala. Here he began to beg and live upon alms. After ten or twelve days, this kind of life drew upon him the contempt of a priest and of some others. They began to insult him as one who preferred to live on alms, although quite able to support himself.

The superior of a new hospital, seeing him thus rudely treated, took him home, placed him in a room, and liberally provided for his needs.

The time of his arrival at Barcelona was about Lent of the year 1524; and as he remained there upwards of two years, we do not find

---

[13] Ignatius arrived at the University of Alcalá in June, 1526. The university was founded by Cardinal Ximenes de Cisneros, the leading Spanish prelate of the fifteenth and early sixteenth centuries, in 1500. Alcala was officially authorized in 1509 and opened its first classes in 1513. It soon became renowned; Francis I said of it in 1526, "The University of Paris, the pride of my kingdom, is the work of centuries. Ximenes has created its equal singlehanded." Loyola spent sixteen months at Alcalá, where he mastered the elements of Latin, logic, physics, and theology.

him at Alcala until the year 1526. At the latter place he spent his time in studying the works of Scotus, Albertus, Alcuin, and the Master of the Sentences.[14] He was diligent also in giving the Spiritual Exercises[15] and explaining the Christian doctrine, by which he gave great glory to God, as very many were thereby led to a knowledge and taste of spiritual things. Many, however, fell victims to various temptations, an example of which is to be seen in one who was unable to scourge himself, because, as he fancied, his hand was held by some invisible agent. Because of such affairs, and especially by reason of the great crowd of men coming to him when he explained the Christian doctrine, various rumors began to spread among the people.

When he first came to Alcala a friendship sprang up between him and one Didacus Guya, who lived with his brother, a painter.[16] Through that friendship, Ignatius was abundantly supplied with all that was necessary; hence he would bestow upon the poor the alms that he himself obtained, and besides three other pilgrims stayed with him.

One day Ignatius went to Didacus to ask for alms in order to assist some poor people. He replied that he had no money. Opening, however, a chest which belonged to him, he took from it trappings of various colors, candlesticks, and other objects, which he gave to Ignatius, who distributed them to the poor.

Many rumors, as was stated above, became widespread in Alcala, and reached the ears even of the Inquisitors[17] who were at Toledo, and who, as their host testified, styled Ignatius and his associates, Legati or Illuminati,[18] and threatened him with capital punishment.

The Inquisitors who had come to Alcala to investigate their actions left the entire affair in the hands of the Vicar Figueroa,[19] who was then negotiating with the Emperor,[1] and returned to Toledo without having even once summoned them. Figueroa granted them the right to continue the work in which they were engaged, and the Inquisitors,

---

14 Peter Abelard.

15 The *Exercises*, though begun at Manresa, were given additions and changes during Loyola's lifetime. Their purpose is perhaps best explained by the subtitle, which reads, "Spiritual exercises for the conquest of oneself and the ordering of one's life so that one's decisions are uninfluenced by any inordinate affections." And again, they are "A method in which the soul may prepare and dispose itself to free itself of its disordered affections and, this achieved, set itself to seek and find the will of God concerning the ordering of its life, for that soul's salvation."

16 This is a reference to Dedacus Guia or Diego de Eguia, who entered the Society some years later at Venice. His brother Estevan was a publisher, not a painter.

17 Many pious Spaniards such as John of the Cross and Teresa of Avila were also denounced to the Inquisition, but, like Loyola, were exonerated.

18 Spanish religious factions sympathetic to Protestantism. Legati: "bewitched."

19 Juan Rodrígues de Figueroa was the vicar general of Alcalá for the Archbishop of Toledo. Among his duties was the investigation of suspected heretics.

1 Charles V of the Empire and Charles I of Spain.

after mature deliberation, discovered error neither in their doctrines nor in their manner of life.

They did not, however, favor their custom of dressing alike, as they were not Religious. Ignatius replied that the wish of the Vicar would be obeyed, but he added: "I do not see the fruit of these examinations, since but a few days ago a certain priest refused holy communion to one, on the plea that he had communicated but eight days before; and to me, indeed he gave it very reluctantly. We would like to know whether or not we have been guilty of any heresy?" "None," replied Figueroa, "else you would have been led to the stake." "And they would likewise have led you to the stake," responded Ignatius, "had you been convicted of heresy."

The dress was changed according to the wish of Figueroa, who also desired that the pilgrim should not go around barefooted for at least fifteen or twenty days. This command was also obeyed.

Four months after, Figueroa, a second time, brought the Inquisition to bear upon them, influenced, as I think, by the fact that a certain married woman of rank, who chanced to be singularly devoted to the pilgrim, went in disguise at daybreak to visit Ignatius at the hospital where he was staying. But even on this occasion Ignatius was not summoned to appear before the Inquisition; nor was any sentence pronounced against him.

CHAPTER VI

The Prisons at Alcala and Salamanca

After the space of four months, Ignatius, who did not remain at the hospital, was taken from his lodging by a public officer, who cast him into prison, with the command not to depart until otherwise ordered.

This took place during the summer months, and as the discipline of the prison was not very strict, an opportunity of visiting him was afforded many persons, to whom he explained the principles of Christian faith and the Exercises, as was his wont when enjoying perfect freedom.

Many persons of rank were anxious to help him, but he did not wish to avail himself of their offers. One person especially, Lady Teresa de Cardena[2] sent frequently, offering to deliver him from prison. He replied in these words, "He, for whose love I am imprisoned, will free me when it may be His good pleasure."

He passed seventeen days in prison, — yet was totally ignorant of the cause, — when Figueroa came to question him. Among other things, he asked whether he commanded the observance of the Sabbath.

[2] Doña Teresa de Cardenas was the mother of the Duke of Maqueda and a prominent figure in Alcalá.

Among those who had frequently come to see Ignatius were two persons, a mother and daughter, the latter of whom was young and beautiful. These, especially the daughter, had made great progress in the spiritual life, and although ladies of rank, had determined to make a pilgrimage alone and on foot, and beg their way to the shrine of Veronica, in the city of Jaen.[3]

This occasioned so great a sensation throughout the city of Alcala that Dr. Giruellus,[4] who was the guardian of the two women, thinking that Ignatius was the cause of their action, ordered him to be cast into prison.

As the Vicar[5] was willing to be fully informed, Ignatius said: "These women made known to me their desire of going about from place to place to assist the poor they found in the different hospitals. I, however, disapproved of their design, on account of the daughter, who was quite young and beautiful, representing to them at the same time that if they felt strongly urged to assist the poor, Alcala presented a broad enough field for their labors, and they could satisfy their devotion by accompanying the Blessed Sacrament as it was being carried to the sick." When Ignatius had finished his account, Figueroa and the notary[6] departed, after writing down what had taken place.

Calisto,[7] a companion of Ignatius, and who on recovering from a severe illness had heard of the imprisonment of Ignatius, hastened from Segovia, where he was staying, and came to Alcala, that he, too, might be cast into prison.

Ignatius advised him to go to the Vicar, who received him kindly, and promised to send him to prison. It was necessary, he said, for him to be detained until the return of the women. It could then be seen whether or not their account agreed with what he and Ignatius had stated.

As the confinement was undermining Calisto's health, Ignatius, through the intervention of a professor who was a friend of his, obtained his liberation.

When Ignatius had been in prison forty-two days,[8] the women returned. He was once more visited by the notary, who made known to

---

[3] A city in Andalusia which purported to contain the handkerchief which Veronica used to wipe the face of Christ. The women were Maria del Vado and her daughter Luisa.

[4] Dr. Pedro Ciruelo. The investigation was conducted by Dr. Miguel Carrasco, Canon of San Justo, and the licentiate, Alonzo Mejía of Toledo. The Protestant movement had caused Catholic authorities to increase their investigations of "unfamiliar" preachers.

[5] Figueroa.

[6] Francisco Ximénes.

[7] Calixto or Calisto de Saa, a man of Portuguese extraction from Seville, was a student with Loyola at the university and one of his first disciples. He made a pilgrimage to Jerusalem at Ignatius' suggestion but did not become a member of the Society.

[8] Loyola also mentions this imprisonment in a letter to King John III of Portugal, but at a later date.

him the condition on which he was to regain his freedom. It was this: He and his companions should wear the same style of clothing as the other students, and refrain from preaching the truths of faith until they had finished four more years of study. Ignatius, indeed, had made more progress in his studies than the rest, yet he confessed that he had not been solidly grounded. And this he was always wont to say whenever he was questioned.

When Ignatius heard the judgment passed upon himself and his companions, he was at a loss what to do, for he saw very little chance of advancing the salvation of souls, hindered as he was for no other reason than that of not having completed a full course of study.

He finally resolved to trust the entire affair to the good sense and judgment of Fonseca,[9] Archbishop of Toledo, whom, after leaving Alcala, he found at Valladolid.

To the Archbishop, then, he made known everything with the utmost fidelity, and said that, although it was not a matter pertaining either to his court or judgment, he determined to act as the Archbishop should advise.

The Archbishop received him cordially, approving his intention of going to Salamanca, and assuring him that he would find friends there. Supplying him with everything necessary for his journey, he dismissed him.

When sentence had been pronounced against them at Alcala, Ignatius promised obedience, but at the same time observed that they were too poor to provide themselves with new clothing. Hearing this, the Vicar himself supplied what they needed, and they set out for Alcala.

Four of his companions had already taken up their abode at Salamanca. When he reached the city Ignatius went to church to pray, and was recognized by a pious lady, who, asking his name, conducted him to his companions. About ten or twelve days after their arrival at Salamanca, a Dominican monk, to whom Ignatius had made his confession, pressed him to visit the convent, as some of the Religious wished to see him.

Ignatius accepting the invitation "in the name of the Lord," his confessor thought it well for him to come to dine the Sunday following, at the same time adding that many questions would be put to him. On Sunday, therefore, as was appointed, the pilgrim came in company with Calisto.

When dinner was over, the Superior, together with the confessor and others, conducted Ignatius to a chapel, and after expressing his pleasure at the good account received of him and his apostolic zeal, manifested a desire of hearing a more full and exact account of his teaching.

---

[9] The approximate date of this meeting is June, 1527. Alfonso de Fonseca was Primate of Spain. Loyola arrived in Salamanca in October, 1527.

He was first questioned in reference to his studies. Ignatius answered that he had spent more time in studying than his companions, yet he confessed that his knowledge was not very extensive, as he had never laid a solid foundation.

"Why, then, do you preach?" broke in the monk. "We do not preach," replied Ignatius; "we are wont to talk familiarly about divine things with some, in much the same as after dinner we converse with our host."

"About what divine things?" continued the monk; "this is the very point upon which we wish information."

"About different virtues and vices," rejoined Ignatius, "endeavoring to inculcate a love of virtue and a detestation of vice."

"How comes it," said the monk, "that you who are not learned should presume to converse upon virtue and vice? No one is wont to engage in such a task unless he has acquired knowledge or has been taught by the Holy Ghost. You confess ignorance of letters; it follows then that He has been your director. We wish to learn, therefore, what He has been pleased to make known to you."

Ignatius at first made no reply, as he felt such reasoning was without value. Soon, however, breaking the silence, he remarked that there seemed no reason why he should say more upon the subject. As the monk still pressed him, giving as a reason the fact that many were once more thrusting forward the erroneous doctrine of Erasmus and others, Ignatius answered, "I will add no more to what has already been said, unless questioned by those who have a right to expect an account from me."

Previous to the present proceedings the monk wished to know why Calisto was so strangely clothed, for, although of tall stature, he went about almost barelegged, holding a staff in his hand, and wearing a cloak much too short, and a hat of enormous size. The whole costume formed a rather ludicrous picture.

Ignatius replied that although at Alcala they were ordered to dress as the other students, Calisto had charitably given his clothes to a poor priest.

The monk showed himself displeased at this, remarking, "Charity begins at home."

But to return to our former narrative. When the monk saw Ignatius fixed in his resolution, "You shall remain here," he said, "and we shall easily find a way of compelling you to make everything known." Immediately all the monks withdrew, the subprior signifying his wish that Ignatius should remain in the chapel. The matter was then laid before the judges. Both Ignatius and Calisto remained three days in the monastery, taking their meals with the community, before any decision of the judges was made known to them. During this time the Religious frequently visited their cells, and Ignatius never failed to speak with them in his accustomed manner. This caused the monks to be divided in their opinion of him, and many, indeed, showed themselves very kindly disposed.

On the third day a notary came to conduct them to prison. They were not put with the common criminals, but their place of confinement was nevertheless very repulsive. In the centre of the cell there was a pillar to which was attached a chain but a few feet in length, and so riveted to the prisoners that when either moved the other was obliged to follow him. They passed that night without any sleep. On the following day, however, the report spread that they were prisoners. The people then hastened to supply them with all they needed.

Ignatius, as may readily be supposed, lost no opportunity of speaking upon spiritual things with those who came to see them.

They were each separately examined by a friar, to whom Ignatius delivered all his writings. Among these were his Spiritual Exercises, that it might be seen whether or not they contained any false doctrine. When asked about his other companions, he told who and where they were. They were arrested also, and confined in separate apartments from that in which Ignatius was placed.

Although help was offered on this occasion, he declined to accept it.

After a few days he was called into the presence of the judges and professors, who made him answer many questions, not only on his Spiritual Exercises, but even on articles of faith, as, for example, the Trinity and the Blessed Sacrament, requiring him to explain these mysteries.

So clear and exact was his explanation that his examiners could not find the least flaw in his doctrine. He was equally correct in the answer to the friar who proposed a difficulty in Canon Law.

In every case he said that he did not know the decision of the professors.

When ordered to speak on the first commandment, he gave so full and exhaustive an explanation as to leave to his hearers no further chance of questioning him.

Although he had not completed his studies, he frequently showed the difference between a mortal and a venial sin of thought. While speaking about his Exercises, he was closely questioned. To their questions, however, he replied, "What I say is either false or true; if false, condemn it." The doctrine remained uncondemned.

Francis de Mendoza,[10] afterward Cardinal of Valencia, was one of those who came to the prison to visit Ignatius. One day, while accompanied with the friar, he asked him whether the prison and chains were not insupportable. "I shall give," said Ignatius, "the reply made

[10] Don Francisco de Mendoza, though only nineteen at the time of this visit, was professor of Greek at the University of Salamanca. He was to be created a cardinal in 1545, and became Archbishop of Burgos in 1550. They were to meet once again in Rome, towards the end of Loyola's life.

to-day to a woman who bewailed my lot. For the love of Jesus Christ, I gladly would wear all the handcuffs and chains that could be found in Salamanca. And if you consider this an evil, you show that as yet you are not desirous of suffering imprisonment for the love of Our Lord."

About this time it happened that all the inmates of the prison managed to escape, leaving only Ignatius and his companions. When this became known it caused a reaction in their favor, and they were placed for the time in a large building adjoining the prison.

On the twenty-second day of their imprisonment they were summoned to hear their sentence.

Although they were declared to be free from reproach both in their lives and their doctrines, and were allowed to continue their work of teaching the Christian doctrine and of speaking on spiritual subjects, yet they were forbidden to draw any distinction between mortal and venial sin, until they should have spent four more years in study.

Although Ignatius was unwilling to accept the sentence, because, though condemned in no respect, he was nevertheless prevented from assisting his neighbor, he declared that he would submit as long as he remained in Salamanca.

Recommending the affair to God, Ignatius began to deliberate on his future plan of action. He considered it a waste of time to remain at Salamanca, as the restriction laid upon him prevented him from assisting those for whose salvation he wished to labor.

He resolved, accordingly, to set out for Paris for the purpose of there continuing his studies.

While studying at Barcelona, Ignatius was in doubt whether, after completing his studies, he should enter some Religious Order, or go from place to place, according to his custom.

He decided to enter upon the religious life. His next step was to find some Order where the primitive fervor had not relaxed, as he felt that there he would be more sure of satisfying his desire of suffering and assisting others spiritually by bearing, for the love of God, any injury or insult to which he might be subjected.

Even while at Salamanca these desires were ever present to him. To this end he directed all his studies, endeavoring at the same time to persuade others to adopt a like course, and to strengthen in their good resolutions those who had already embraced it.

When he had resolved to go to Paris, he communicated his design to his companions, telling them to remain where they were, until he could find a means of helping them in their studies.

Many persons of rank endeavored to dissuade him from departing, but all to no purpose.

Placing the few books he possessed upon a little ass, he took leave of his companions about fifteen or twenty days after they came out of prison.

Those who met him at Barcelona sought to deter him from going to

France, as at that time the war between the two countries was raging with great fierceness. Notwithstanding the many acts of cruelty inflicted by the French upon the Spaniards, many of whom had been impaled, he persevered in his intention.

CHAPTER VII

His Studies in Paris, and Other Incidents of His Life

He left for Paris on foot and alone, and, according to his own reckoning, arrived there toward the beginning of February, 1528. While in prison, the Prince of Spain[11] was born, and from this event we can determine the date of what preceded and followed. At Paris he lived with some Spaniards, and attended the lectures given at the College of Montaigu.[12] As he had been advanced too rapidly to the higher studies, he returned to those of a lower grade, because he felt that in great part he lacked the proper groundwork. He therefore studied in a class with children. When he first came to Paris, he received from a merchant twenty-five gold crowns on an order sent from Barcelona.[13] These he put for safekeeping in the hands of one of the Spaniards with whom he lived. This latter very soon appropriated them for his own use, and when called upon, could not restore them. The result was that when Lent was over Ignatius found himself unprovided for, partly on account of the loss mentioned, and partly on account of other expenses. In consequence, he was forced to seek his livelihood by begging, and to leave the house where he lived.

Afterward he was received into the Hospital of St. James, near the Church of the Holy Innocents. This residence proved no slight hindrance to his studies. The hospital was at a great distance from the college, and while he could not gain admission at night unless he returned before the sound of the Angelus, in the morning he was not allowed to depart before daylight. He could not, in consequence, be present at, nor give his time to, the lectures with profit. He found another hindrance, also, in loss of the time needed in getting alms wherewith to purchase food.

As he had not experienced interior spiritual suffering for almost five years, he mortified himself by austere fasts and penances. After he had spent some time in this way, living in the hospital and begging

---

[11] The future Philip II.

[12] Loyola enrolled at the College de Montaigu to acquire a firmer grounding in Latin as preparation for his actual university work at Paris. The college had a predominance of Spanish and Portuguese students. Due to a lack of funds, Loyola was classified as a "martinet," one who shifted for himself in finding food and lodging and who was a resident of the college only during lectures and other class hours.

[13] The money was sent by Isabel Roser.

his food, he noticed that his progress in letters was not rapid. He then considered what course to follow. He had observed that many who lived as servants of the lecturers in the colleges had abundant time for study. He resolved to seek some one whom he might serve in the same way. He weighed the matter well, and not without consolation thought of it as follows: "I shall imagine that my master is Christ, and I shall call one of the students Peter, another John, and to the rest I shall give the names of the remaining Apostles. Then, when my master gives me a command, I shall think that Christ commands me. When any one else gives orders, I shall think that the order comes from St. Peter or some other Apostle." He was very diligent in seeking a master, and spoke of the matter to a bachelor and to a Carthusian monk, who knew many masters, and to others, but he was never able to find one.

Deprived of every resource, he was told by a Spanish monk that it would be a wise step for him to go every year to Flanders, and there in two months he could procure enough for the whole year. He approved of the plan, after recommending the matter to God. On adopting this plan, he brought back yearly from Flanders whatever he needed for his maintenance. Once even he passed over into England,[14] and from there brought greater alms than he had gathered in the previous years.

When he first returned from Flanders he began to devote himself earnestly to spiritual work. About the same time he gave the Exercises to three persons, — to Peralta,[15] to Castro,[16] a friend who dwelt at Sorbonne, and to a Cantabrian who lived in the College of St. Barbara, by name Amator.[17] A great change was made in the lives of these men. At once they gave to the poor whatever they had, even their books, while they themselves began to live on the alms they begged, and to dwell in the Hospital of St. James, where Ignatius had previously dwelt, and which he left as stated above. This incident aroused a great outcry in the University of Paris, because the two first were very famous men. The other Spaniards at once undertook to oppose them, but unable to persuade them by any argument to return to the university, a great crowd went armed to the hospital and led, or rather dragged, them away.

On coming to the university they agreed with their captors to complete their course of studies, and afterward to follow out their determination. Castro went afterward to Spain, and after preaching for a while at Burgos, joined the Order of the Carthusians at Valencia. Peralta undertook a journey to Jerusalem on foot and after the fashion of a pilgrim. In this garb he was seized in Italy by a military leader, his relative, who found a pretext for bringing him before the Sovereign

---

[14] This was in September, 1531.
[15] Pedro de Peralta. [16] Dr. Juan Castro.
[17] Amador (Amator) was a fellow Basque countryman of Loyola.

Pontiff,[18] from whom he obtained a command for Peralta to return to Spain. All these events did not occur then, but years afterward. Exaggerated reports arose against Ignatius at Paris, especially among the Spaniards. De Govea[19] was wont to say that Amator, who remained in his college, had been brought by Ignatius to the verge of insanity. He therefore made up his mind that as soon as Ignatius came to the College of St. Barbara, he would give him a public whipping as a seducer of the pupils.

Now the Spaniard who had spent the money of Ignatius and had not paid him, had set out to journey to Spain and fallen sick. As soon as Ignatius learned of this, he was seized with a longing to visit and help him, hoping by this to lead him to abandon the world and give himself wholly to God. And indeed to accomplish this he wished to make the journey barefooted, without food or drink. While praying for this purpose, he felt himself seized with great fear until, entering the Church of St. Dominic, he resolved to make the journey in this manner. The fear that it might be tempting God then left him; on the morning of the following day, upon arising, so great a fear seized him that it seemed to him that he could not even put on his clothes. In this interior strife he left the house and went out of the city, and the fear did not leave him till he was nine miles from Paris. At this distance there is a village which the inhabitants call Argenteuil, where the Holy Coat of Our Lord is said to be preserved. As he left this place in great trouble of spirit, a feeling of great consolation and strength filled his soul with such joy that he began to shout aloud and to talk with God as he walked through the fields. That night, having completed forty-five miles, he went to rest with a beggar in a hospital. On the next day toward nightfall he lodged in a straw-thatched cabin. On the third day he arrived on foot. According to his resolve, he took neither foor nor drink. Upon his arrival he consoled the sick man, helped him on board a vessel which was about to sail for Spain, and gave him letters to his companions, Calisto, Caceres, and Artiaga,[1] who were in Salamanca. Here we may dwell for a moment on the fate of these companions. While Ignatius was at Paris he often sent them letters, telling them of the little hope left of calling them to Paris for their studies. Still he urged by letter Donna Leonora de Mascarenas[2] to use her influence with the King of Portugal[3] for Calisto, that he might receive one of the burses which the King had established. A certain yearly aid is called a burse. Donna Leonora gave Calisto a mule and money to take him to the court of the King of Portugal. He

[18] Clement VII (1523–34).

[19] Diego De Gouvea (Govea) was the principal of the Collège de Ste. Barbe (St. Barbara).

[1] Diego Caceres and Juan de Arteaga were attracted to Loyola but did not join the Society.

[2] Doña Leonor de Mascarenas, a former lady-in-waiting to Queen Isabella, governess for Prince Philip of Spain, had met Ignatius at Alcalá.

[3] John III (1521–77), called "the pious," was later to invite the Jesuits into Portugal.

set out, but never reached that place. He came back afterward to Spain and went to India. He returned rich, to the great surprise of all at Salamanca, who had known him in former days. Caceres, after returning to Segovia, his native city, began to grow unmindful of his former purpose and life. Artiaga was first made a magistrate. Afterward, when the Society was established at Rome, a bishopric was given to him. He wrote to Ignatius, "I wish this bishopric to be given to one of the Society." But as soon as the answer came that this was not to be done, he went to India, was made bishop, and died there a strange death. While sick it chanced that two phials of liquid were placed in water to cool, one containing a medicine ordered for him by the doctor, the other a diluted poison called Sollimanus. His attendant gave him by mistake the poisoned draught, which he drank, and thus ended his life.

Returning to Paris Ignatius heard many rumors connecting his name with that of Caceres and Peralta, and learned that he had been summoned before the judge. As he did not wish to remain in doubt, he went of his own accord to the Inquisitor, a Domican friar. "I heard that I had been sought for, and I now present myself." During the conversation he asked the Inquisitor to terminate the matter speedily. He had determined to begin his course in arts on the approaching feast of St. Remigius, and therefore wished all other business completed in order to apply himself to his studies with greater profit. The Inquisitor on his part told him that certain charges had been made against him, but he allowed him to depart, and did not summon him again.

Toward the first of October, the feast of St. Remigius, he began his course under the preceptor Master John Pegna,[4] with the intention of fostering the vocations of those who wished to serve God. He intended to add others in order the more freely to give his mind to his studies. He followed the lectures in philosophy, and experienced the same temptations with which he had been assailed when studying grammar at Barcelona. During the lectures he was troubled by so many spiritual thoughts that he could not listen attentively. Accordingly, as he saw he was making but little progress in his studies, he spoke to his preceptor and promised to attend the lectures, as long as he could find bread and water enough to keep him alive. After making this promise, all these untimely devotions ceased to disturb him, and he quietly pursued his studies. He was at this period a friend of Peter Faber[5] and Francis Xavier,[6] whom he afterward led to the

[4] Juan de la Pena (John Pegna) was a Valencian who instructed Loyola, Francis Xavier and Pierre Favre in philosophy.
[5] Pierre Favre (Peter Faber) was a poor student from Savoy who became the first steadfast disciple of Ignatius and who was later to become significant in the activities of the Jesuits in the Empire.
[6] Francis Xavier (Francisco de Javier) was from a Basque noble family that had fought with the French against the Loyolas in 1521. Francis Xavier was to become famous as the "Apostle of the Indies."

service of God by giving them the Exercises. During the last years he was not persecuted as at first. Speaking of this to him one day, Doctor Fragus[7] remarked that he was surprised that no one molested him. Ignatius replied: "This is owing to the fact that I do not speak on religious topics. But when the course is completed, we shall act as formerly."

During the course of this conversation a monk approached Doctor Fragus and begged his aid in visiting a house, in which there were many corpses of those whom he thought died of the plague. At that time the plague was beginning to spread in Paris. Doctor Fragus and Ignatius wished to visit the house, and procured the aid of a woman who was very skilful in detecting the disease. After she had entered the house she answered that the plague was certainly there. Ignatius, also, entered and consoled and revived a sick man he found lying there. When he had touched the wounds with his hand, Ignatius departed alone. His hand began to cause him great pain, and it seemed as if he had caught the disease. The fear that came upon him was so great that he was unable to vanquish and drive it away, until with a great effort he placed his fingers in his mouth, and for a long time kept them there, saying, "If you have the plague in your hand, you will also have it in your mouth." As soon as this was done, the illusion left him and the pain he had felt in his hand ceased.

He was not allowed to enter the College of St. Barbara where he was then living, for all fled from him when they learned that he had entered a house infected with the plague. He was obliged to remain several days outside of the college.

At Paris it is customary for those who follow the philosophical studies to receive in their third year the Petra, as it is called, in order to obtain the bachelor's degree. Now those who are very poor are unable to comply with this custom, as it costs a gold crown. While Ignatius was in great hesitation, he submitted the matter to the judgment of his preceptor. The latter advised him to receive it. He did so, but not without a complaint on the part of some, especially of a certain Spaniard who had taken note of the fact.

While in Paris he suffered great pains of the stomach for several days. On the twenty-fifth day, for the space of an hour, a very severe pain seized him, bringing with it a fever. One day the pains lasted for sixteen or seventeen hours. At that time he had already concluded his course, had spent some years in the study of theology, and had collected his companions.

As the disease grew worse day by day, and the many remedies employed brought no relief, the doctors said that the only one left for him was to revisit his native land, as nothing but his native air

---

[7] Dr. Jeronimo Frago (Fragus) of the Sorbonne, later Bishop of Pamplona. The date of the visitation is probably 1531.

could cure him. His companions gave him the same advice. By this time all had determined on their future conduct, namely, to go first to Venice, and then to Jerusalem, where they would pass their whole life in helping souls. If, however, they should not be allowed to remain in Jerusalem, they were to return to Rome and offer themselves to the Sovereign Pontiff,[8] Christ's Vicar, that he might use their aid as he thought would be for God's glory and the salvation of souls. They also agreed to wait one year at Venice for ships to carry them to the Holy Land; but if during the year no ship were at hand, they should be absolved from the vow, and go to the Sovereign Pontiff. Finally Ignatius yielded to the advice of his companions, in order to attend to their business in Spain. It was agreed among them, that after the recovery of his health he should settle their affairs and they should go to Venice, and there await him.

He left Paris in the year 1535, but according to the agreement his companions were to leave two years afterward on the feast of the conversion of St. Paul. However, owing to the wars, they were obliged to anticipate that time, and to set out from Paris in the month of November in the year 1536. On the very eve of his departure, as Ignatius had heard that an accusation had been made against him before the Inquisitor,[9] while no summons had as yet been served, he went to that official and stated what he had heard. At the same time he told him that he had several companions, and that he himself was about to travel to Spain, and requested that sentence should be passed upon him. The Inquisitor admitted that the accusation had been made, but that he did not think it worthy of consideration. He said that he wished merely to see the writings of Ignatius, meaning the Exercises. Having seen these he approved of them very highly, and begged Ignatius to give him a copy. Ignatius complied with his request, but insisted that his trial be brought to an end, and that judgment be passed. As his request met with a refusal, he brought a notary and witnesses to the Inquisitor's house, and received their testimony in writing concerning his innocence of the charges.

CHAPTER VIII

His Arrival in His Native Land — His Journey into Spain and Italy — The Famous Apparition and His Life in the Same Place

After the event related in the last chapter, Ignatius mounted the little horse which his companions had purchased for him, and began his journey toward his native land. Even on the way he found his

---

[8] Clement VII (1523–34).
[9] The Inquisition was not formally established in France, but delegated Inquisitors were sent there from time to time.

health improving. As soon as he arrived in the province of Guipuscoa, his native country, abandoning the common highway he followed a road through the mountains because it was less frequented. He had advanced a short distance by this path when he saw two armed men approaching. The place was famous as the haunt of murderers. The men passed him a little and then turning, hurried after him. He was not a little frightened, but still, addressing them, he learned that they were his brother's servants sent to meet him. For he had reason to believe that a warning of his coming was sent to his brother from Bayonne in France, where he had been recognized by several persons. Still Ignatius kept on in the direction he had taken, and shortly before he arrived in the town he met some priests coming to meet him. They wished to bring him to his brother's home; but their efforts were unavailing. He went to a public hospital, and afterward, at a suitable time, begged for alms through the town.

Many came to see him in the hospital. He spoke to them, and through God's grace gathered no little fruit. Upon his arrival, he resolved to teach the Christian doctrine to children every day. His brother objected to this, and assured him that no one would come. In answer Ignatius said, "One is enough for me." However, as soon he began to teach many came regularly, his brother among the number. In addition to this, on Sundays and feast days, he also preached to the people with great fruit, and thousands came many miles to hear him. He labored also for the removal of many abuses, and through God's grace good results were obtained in many cases. To give an example: By his representations to the governor he obtained an order forbidding gambling and other disorders, under great penalties. He took means that the poor should be provided for publicly and regularly, and that thrice a day, morning, noon, and evening, according to the Roman custom, a signal should be given by ringing a bell for the recital of the Angelus by the people.

Although at first he enjoyed good health, he afterward fell seriously ill. For this reason, after his recovery, he determined to depart in order to accomplish the business which he had undertaken for his companions. He resolved to set out on foot and without money. His brother was grieved at this, and looked on it as a disgrace to himself. Ignatius concluded to yield this point, and at last, toward evening, he consented to be carried to the boundary of the province in company with his brother and relatives.

But as soon as he had left the province, he dismounted and without receiving any sustenance for the journey he set out for Pampeluna and thence to Almazonus, the birthplace of Father Laynez.[10] Then he traveled on to Siguensa and to Toledo, and afterward from Toledo to Valencia. In all these cities, the birthplaces of his companions, he

---

[10] Diego Laynez came to the University of Paris from Alcala, where he had received a Master of Arts degree. He was to become one of the outstanding papal champions at the Council of Trent.

would receive nothing from their parents and relations, although they offered him a great many things, and begged him to accept them. At Valencia he had a conversation with Castro. When ready to embark at Valencia to sail to Genoa, several of his well-wishers dissuaded him, because, as they asserted, the Barbary pirates were on the sea with many large ships. However, though they said a great deal to inspire fear, still he did not hesitate. Having gone aboard a vessel, a great storm arose during the voyage. This was mentioned before, where Ignatius describes the three occasions on which he was in danger of death. On this journey he suffered a great deal, as I shall now relate. One day after landing he wandered from his path and followed a road which ran along the bank of a river. The road was high, while far below was the river deep and sluggish. The farther he advanced, the narrower grew the road. At last he came to a spot where he could go neither forward nor backward. He then began to advance on hands and feet and continued thus for a long time, full of fear. For as often as he moved it seemed to him that he would fall into the river. This was the greatest of all the bodily labors that he ever experienced. At last he escaped, but just as he was entering Bologna he fell from a little bridge and was so wet and dirty from the mud and water as to afford much laughter to a great crowd who observed the accident. From his entrance into Bologna until his departure he begged for alms, and though he went through the whole city, he did not receive so much as a farthing. As he was ill, he rested for a while at Bologna. Thence he directed his steps toward Venice, traveling always in the same way. At Venice he spent his time in giving the Exercises and in other spiritual works. Those to whom he gave the Exercises were Peter Contarenus,[11] Gaspar a Doctis,[12] and another Spaniard named Hozes,[13] who, like the pilgrim, was a great friend of the bishop. Hozes at first would not make the Exercises, although he felt drawn to do so. At last he resolved to undertake the work, and on the third or fourth day he opened his mind to Ignatius. He said that he had feared that by the Exercises his mind might be imbued with false doctrines. Indeed, he had been persuaded by a man to be on his guard, and for this reason he had brought along with him a book to use in case he were imposed on. He made great progress in the Exercises, and finally embraced that manner of life which Ignatius had established. He was the first of the companions of the Saint to die.

At Venice another persecution was stirred up against Ignatius.

---

[11] Peter Contarenus (Pietro Contarini), from a famous Venetian family, subsequently became Bishop of Cyprus.
[12] Gaspare de Doctis was a powerful Venetian figure who became governor of Loreto, at which time he wanted to resign his position and enter the Jesuit order but was refused permission by Loyola.
[13] Diego Hoces (Hozes), from Malaga, in later life was torn between entering the Jesuits and entering the Theatine order of Gian Pietro Carafa. Eventually he followed Loyola and became a member of the Society.

Some asserted that he had been burned in effigy both in Spain and in Paris. The matter went so far that he was brought to trial, but obtained a favorable sentence. At the beginning of the year 1538 the nine companions[14] came to Venice and were scattered about the city in various hospitals to minister to the sick. After two or three months all journeyed to Rome to receive the Pope's blessing before going to Jerusalem. Ignatius, however, did not go to Rome on account of Doctor Ortiz[15] and the Theatine Cardinal[16] recently raised to that dignity. The companions on their return brought the value of two or three hundred gold crowns which had been given to them as alms for their projected journey to Jerusalem.[17] They would accept it only in the forms of bills, and when they were unable to make the voyage to Jerusalem they returned it to those who had made the gift. They returned to Venice in the same manner that they had set out for Rome. They traveled on foot and begging, divided into three parties, as they were of different nationalities. Those who were not priests were ordained at Venice, having received faculties from the Nuncio, who was then in that city and who was afterward called Cardinal Verallus.[18] They were promoted to the priesthood[19] *sub titulo paupertatis*,[1] having made vows of poverty and chastity. That year no ships left for the East, on account of the breach of the treaty between the Venetians and Turks. When, therefore, they saw their hopes deferred, they dispersed into various parts of the Venetian territory, with the understanding that they should wait one year, as they had previously resolved; when that time had elapsed, they were to return to Rome if it was not possible to make the voyage. Vicenza[2] fell to the lot of Ignatius. His companions were Faber and Laynez. Outside of the city they found a house that had neither door nor windows. Here they lived, sleeping on a little straw which they had brought with them. Two of the three entered the city twice daily, in the morning and evening, to ask for alms. They returned with so little that it hardly sufficed for their nourishment. Their usual food was bread, when they could get it. The one who chanced to remain at home did the baking. In this way they spent forty days, intent upon nothing but prayer.

[14] The original group, in addition to Loyola, included Pierre Favre, Diego Laynez, Alfonso Salmerón, Nicholas Bobadilla, Simón Rodrigues, and Francis Xavier. This group took their vows at Montmartre on August 15, 1534. They were later joined by Gabriel-François Le Jay, Pachase Broet, and John Codure in 1537.

[15] Pedro Ortiz, doctor of the Sorbonne, who subsequently gave Ignatius' name to Matthieu Ory, prior of the Dominican convent in Paris, on suspicion of heresy. Ortiz was the guardian of one of Loyola's early followers, Peralta. Loyola was later cleared of any charge.

[16] Gian Pietro Carafa (cf. n. 13, above). Afterwards Paul III (1534-49).

[17] A portion of the money came from Paul III.

[18] Monsignor Veralli received their vows of poverty and chastity.

[19] By Bishop Vincenzio Negusanti of Arbe, who ordained them on June 24, 1537.

[1] "Under the title of poverty."   [2] Venezia.

After the forty days were over, Master John Cordurus[3] arrived, and the four determined to begin preaching. On the same day and at the same hour, in different squares, all began to preach, having first uttered a great cry, and having waved their hats with their hands to call the people. These sermons caused great talk in the city, and led many citizens to a devout life. Now the needed nourishment was supplied to them more abundantly. While the pilgrim was at Vicenza, he had many spiritual visions. Consolations were sent to him in great number. This was especially so at Venice, while he was preparing for the priesthood and for celebrating Mass.[4] On all his journeys, he received great supernatural visitations, like those which he had been wont to receive at Manresa.

While still at Venice he learned that one of his companions was sick unto death at Bassanum.[5] He was himself ill with fever, still he undertook the journey, and walked so rapidly that Faber, his companion, was unable to keep up with him. On the way he received an assurance from God that his companion would not die of this illness. As soon as they arrived at Bassanum, the sick man was very much consoled, and not long after grew better. After this, all returned to Vicenza, and there the ten tarried for a whole, some going about the neighboring towns to beg for alms.

In the year that passed, as no means could be had of journeying to Jerusalem, they set out on their way to Rome, divided into three or four parties. On the journey Ignatius experienced singular visitations from God. After his reception of the priesthood, he had resolved to put off the offering of his first Mass for one year, in order to prepare himself better, and to ask the Most Blessed Virgin to place him near her Son. One day, when he was a few miles from Rome, he entered a church to pray, and there felt his soul so moved and changed, and saw so clearly that God the Father placed him with Christ His Son, that he did not dare to doubt it. When Ignatius was told that several other details were related by Laynez, he replied: "Whatever Laynez said about the matter is true. For my part, I do not remember the particulars; but," he added, "I know for certain that when I related what happened I told nothing but the truth." These were his words about the vision.[6] He referred me to Laynez to verify what he narrated.

Once Ignatius left Rome for Monte Cassino,[7] to give the Exercises to Doctor Ortiz,[8] and spent forty days there. One day, at a certain hour, in a vision, he saw Hozes entering heaven. In this vision he

---

[3] John Codure, who entered the Society.
[4] Loyola was ordained on June 24, 1537, but did not celebrate his first Mass for eighteen months. This was performed at the church of Mary Major in Rome.
[5] Presumably Rodrigues, who had been sent by Loyola to Bassano.
[6] Laynez tells us that this was the occasion which decided Loyola to call his group "The Company of Jesus." The term "Jesuit" was originally used in 1544 by critics of Loyola.
[7] In 1538.   [8] Cf. n. 15, page 472.

shed abundant tears of consolation. He saw this so clearly that if he were to say the contrary, it would seem to him as if he were telling a lie. He brought with him from Monte Cassino Francis Strada[9] After his return to Rome, he labored for the help of souls, and gave the Exercises to two different persons, one of whom dwelt near the Sixtine Bridge, the other near the Church of St. Mary Major. Soon the people began to persecute Ignatius and his companions. Michael[10] was the first of all to be troublesome and to speak wickedly of Ignatius, and had him summoned before the governor for trial. Ignatius showed the governor a letter written by the same Michael, in which he commended Ignatius very highly. The governor examined Michael, and the result was that he was exiled from Rome. After him followed Mindarra and Berrera,[11] who said that Ignatius and his companions were fugitives from Spain, Paris, and Venice. Finally, however, in the presence of the governor and ambassador then at Rome, both acknowledged that they had nothing which they could say against them with regard to their doctrines or their lives. The ambassador ordered this lawsuit to be abandoned. Ignatius objected, saying that he wished the sentence to be made clear and public. This did not please the ambassador and the governor, nor even those who had previously taken sides with Ignatius. A few months afterward the Roman Pontiff[12] returned. While he was at Tusculum[13] Ignatius was admitted to an audience with the Holy Father, and having given some of his reasons, he obtained what he wished. The Pope ordered sentence to be passed, and it was given in favor of Ignatius and his companions.

Through the labors of Ignatius and his companions, certain pious works were established at Rome.[14]

[9] Francis Strada (Estrada), who entered the Society.
[10] Miguel Landivar from Navarre, who had known the companions of Loyola in Paris. He resented Francis Xavier's devotion to Loyola, and sought revenge on Loyola, who had refused him admission to the Society.
[11] Jealous of the Loyola group, they unsuccessfully sought to have the companions denounced to the Inquisitions.
[12] Pope Paul III, who confirmed the Society of Jesus in the papal bull *Regimini ecclesiae militantis,* on September 27, 1540, and who referred to the group as "Societas Jesu."
[13] An ancient town about 12 miles southeast of Rome.
[14] The manuscript ends abruptly at this point. Loyola was canonized by Pope Gregory XV on May 22, 1622. At the time of his death, in 1556, the Society had over a thousand members and members-in-training.

15

Political and Religious Unrest in Reformation Europe

Venetian Diplomatic Reports

The art of diplomacy, developed in the Middle Ages by the representatives of the Papacy, was perfected by the Venetians, whose controlling position in the lucrative commerce between East and West made them peculiarly sensitive to currents of political unrest and encouraged a talent for shrewd observation of foreign affairs. To the Venetian, diplomacy was a game, an intriguing one with high stakes. Venice employed countless agents, many of them secret, to assemble the multitudinous details which made up the present and to fit these together with the materials of the past in a way that would predict the shape of the future. The periodical reports, often in code, which accredited envoys and other agents sent home, provided the Venetian authorities with a barometer by which to gauge the shifting political climate in Europe, and were invaluable aids in the making of foreign policy.

In an age which was not noted for its objectivity or moderation, these Venetian papers are, on the whole, surprisingly accurate and restrained. Astute representatives of a state that had long been schooled in the realities of commerce and in the subtleties of Italian politics, the Venetian diplomats developed a technique of reporting that by the standards of any age would rate high in factual accuracy, completeness, and freedom from personal bias. There are, to be sure, the built-in predilections of an era which the historian must take into account in assessing any source; nonetheless the Venetian diplomatic reports remain today an invaluable archive of reliable facts and shrewd deductions on European politics in the Age of the Reformation.

In the excerpts which follow, the state of affairs in England provides a unifying theme, as we see the impact of the Reformation upon the domestic and foreign policies of four nations: England, France, Spain, and Scotland. Each of these states, in its own way, was forced to alter its policies in the light of religious developments both at home and abroad. These alterations the Venetian ambassadors sought to identify for the present and to prophesy for the future. To read these dispatches from the front line of sixteenth-century European politics is indeed to read history in the making.

FROM

Venetian Papers Relating to English Affairs *

REPORT of ENGLAND made to the SENATE by GIACOMO SORANZO, late Ambassador to Edward VI. and Queen Mary. Aug. 18, 1554.

The business of the Signory's ambassadors consists chiefly in three things: in the diligent execution of the commissions received by them, in sending detailed and speedy advices of what occurs in the courts where they reside, and in acquainting the Senate on their return with whatever may be worth knowing; so having been ambassador to King Edward VI., and after his death to Queen Mary, for the term in all of 41 months, and having to the best of his ability done what was required touching the two first points, will allude to them no further, save inasmuch as shall be necessary, and coming to the third, will divide it into three principal parts. In the first, will tell of the Queen's qualities, and with what difficulty she obtained the crown, and will also speak of her nearest kindred. In the second, will tell of her realms, and military and naval forces, and of her revenues and expenditure. In the last, will speak of the mode of government, both with regard to church, realm, and state, and conclude with a few remarks about her Majesty's understanding with such neighbouring foreign powers as trade with England.

The most Serene Madame Mary is entitled Queen of England and of France, and Defendress of the Faith. She was born on the 18th February 1515,[1] so she yesterday completed her 38th year and six months. She is of low stature, with a red and white complexion, and very thin; her eyes are white and large, and her hair reddish; her face is round, with a nose rather low and wide; and were not her age

---

* From the *Calendar of State Papers and Manuscripts Relating to English Affairs Existing in the Archives and Collections of Venice and in Other Libraries of Northern Italy*, edited by Rawdon Brown and others, 38 vols. (London: Longmans, Green, Reader and Dyer, 1864ff). The excerpts given here are taken from Volume 5, pp. 532–544; Vol. 7, pp. 322–332 and 414–418.

[1] The correct date is 1516.

on the decline she might be called handsome rather than the contrary. She is not of a strong constitution, and of late she suffers from headache and serious affection of the heart [query, physical palpitation of the heart, or mental anxiety], so that she is often obliged to take medicine, and also to be blooded. She is of very spare diet, and never eats until 1 or 2 p.m., although she rises at daybreak, when, after saying her prayers and hearing mass in private, she transacts business incessantly, until after midnight, when she retires to rest; for she chooses to give audience not only to all the members of her Privy Council, and to hear from them every detail of public business, but also to all other persons who ask it of her. Her Majesty's countenance indicates great benignity and clemency, which are not belied by her conduct, for although she has had many enemies, and though so many of them were by law condemned to death, yet had the execuions depended solely on her Majesty's will, not one of them perhaps would have been enforced;[2] but deferring to her Council in everything, she in this matter likewise complied with the wishes of others rather than with her own. She is endowed with excellent ability, and more than moderately read in Latin literature, especially with regard to Holy Writ; and besides her native tongue she speaks Latin, French, and Spanish, and understands Italian perfectly, but does not speak it. She is also very generous, but not to the extent of letting it appear that she rests her chief claim to commendation on this quality.

She is so confirmed in the Catholic religion that although the King her brother[3] and his Council prohibited her from having the mass celebrated according to the Roman Catholic ritual, she nevertheless had it performed in secret, nor did she ever choose by any act to assent to any other form of religion, her belief in that in which she was born being so strong that had the opportunity offered she would have displayed it at the stake, her hopes being placed in God alone. Her Majesty takes pleasure in playing on the lute and spinet, and is a very good performer on both instruments; and indeed before her accession she taught many of her maids of honour. But she seems to delight above all in arraying herself elegantly and magnificently, and her garments are of two sorts; the one, a gown such as men wear, but fitting very close, with an under-petticoat which has a very long train; and this is her ordinary costume, being also that of the gentlewomen of England. The other garment is a gown and boddice, with wide hanging sleeves in the French fashion, which she wears on state occasions; and she also wears much embroidery, and gowns and mantles of cloth of gold and cloth of silver, of great value, and changes every day. She also makes great use of jewels, wearing them both on her chaperon and round her neck, and trimming for her

[2] Historians disagree on Mary's role in the persecution of her Protestant subjects, but the majority place the responsibility on her.
[3] Edward VI (1547–53).

gowns; in which jewels she delights greatly, and although she has a great plenty of them left her by her predecessors, yet were she better supplied with money than she is, she would doubtless buy many more.

Her Majesty's father was the most serene King Henry VIII., and her mother the most serene Katharine, daughter of King Ferdinand, the Catholic, of Spain, and sister of the Emperor's mother;[4] and therefore on her Majesty's birth, the King her father proclaimed her heiress of the realm, although shortly after, she was bastardized, the cause being, that after the King her father had cohabited during 20 consecutive years with the Queen her mother in the most complete love and concord, he became enamoured of a damsel in the Queen's service, an English girl, by name Anne Boleyn, and wishing to enjoy her, not merely as his mistress, but if possible as his wife, his flatterers, and principally the Cardinal of York,[5] at that time the King's chief favourite, and who was unfriendly towards the Queen, had it represented to him by his Confessor that his marriage with Queen Katharine was invalid, she having previously been the wife of his brother Prince Arthur.[6] The King, therefore, although he had had a dispensation from Pope Julius,[7] empowering him to contract this marriage, did nevertheless not scruple to send ambassadors to Pope Clement,[8] to hear his opinion, whether this marriage was valid or not; hoping that as the Pope was then at enmity with the Emperor, he would favour his wishes; and his Holiness gave such ear to this matter, that, according to the English, he encouraged almost certain hope that the divorce would take place; but a little later, the Pope having come to a better understanding with the Emperor, by reason of the assistance rendered for the enterprise against Florence by his Imperial Majesty, who made great suit in favour of Queen Katharine, the Pope sent Cardinal Campeggio to London,[9] in order that, together with the Cardinal of York, he might settle the difficulty; but the King and Queen not agreeing to [abide by] the sentence Cardinal Campeggio went back without any decision, although, had they agreed to accept the award, the Queen would have consented to the divorce, provided the King took oath, that the first time he consummated marriage with her, he had not found her a virgin; offering moreover to prove that long before the death of Prince Arthur, he was known to be consumptive, and of so bad a constitution, that although they lived five months together, he had been unable to consummate marriage with her.[10]

[4] Joanna, mother of Charles V.   [5] Thomas Wolsey.
[6] It is not certain who first suggested the idea of a divorce to Henry VIII, or if it was his own idea. Presumably it developed between 1525 and 1527.
[7] Julius II (1503–13).   [8] Clement VII (1523–34).   [9] In 1529.
[10] This is incorrect. Catherine never agreed to a divorce, and the secret addendum to the original bull of dispensation stated that the question of sexual intercourse was not relevant to the dispensation.

On the return to Rome, therefore, of Cardinal Campeggio, the Pope had the King summoned to restore the Queen — from whom he was already separated — to her matrimonial rights, but the King not only refused obedience, but repudiated the Queen entirely; and celebrated his marriage with Anne,[11] and had her crowned, causing his daughter, The Lady Mary, to be declared a bastard,[12] and therefore deprived of the succession to the Crown; on which account, the Pope having excommunicated him,[13] he withdrew his obedience from his Holiness and the Church; and Parliament declared him Supreme Head of the Church of England and Ireland,[14] which title he subsequently held until his death, as did his son Edward likewise. Her present Majesty resigned the title, but when she wished Parliament to pass an Act rescinding it from the Crown, the bill was rejected, it being merely carried that she was at liberty to assume the title or not, in order not utterly to deprive her successors of it, as written by me to your Serenity after the first coronation.

Not long after the marriage of Ann Boleyn, the Lady Elizabeth was born, and immediately declared heir to the Crown, in which grade she remained a very short time, because her mother being beheaded on suspicion of adultery, she in like manner was deposed from the succession, and proclaimed a bastard.

Subsequently in 1547, the late King Edward being 10 years old, his father, by reason of his great corpulence, having little hope of life, and wishing to make his last testament, assembled Parliament, and made it pass an Act, whereby he was given liberty, notwithstanding a law to the contrary, to institute his daughters heirs to the Crown in case his son should be childless; and this he had done, as by the statutes of the realm bastards cannot succeed to the Crown; so he made his will, leaving the kingdom to Edward, on condition that, should he die without children, the Lady Mary was to succeed him, provided she had not married, save with the consent of his Council; and in case she also should leave no legitimate heirs, she was to be succeeded by the Lady Elizabeth, who, if she also died childless, was to be succeeded by the Lady Jane, eldest daughter of the Duchess of Suffolk, late Queen widow of France, King Henry's sister; and after the Lady Jane, she not having children, her two other sisters, one after the other, were to succeed, and in the event of their leaving no chlidren, the Crown was to pass to the Lady Margaret, daughter of the Lady Eleanor Countess of Cumberland, second daughter of the Lady Mary, late Queen widow of France aforesaid.

On the death of King Henry he was succeeded by King Edward,

---

[11] Secretly, about January 25, 1533. Anne was pregnant. The marriage was publicly "validated" on June 1.

[12] Act of Succession, 1534.

[13] September, 1533.

[14] Act of Supremacy, 1534.

a youth of very handsome presence, with which his mental endowments corresponded. Whilst under the guardianship of his uncle, the Duke of Somerset,[15] he attended to his studies with marvellous success, learning not only Latin but Greek likewise, though when the government was changed and Somerset replaced by the Duke of Northumberland,[16] who was a soldier at heart and by profession, he changed the King's studies accordingly, and had him taught to ride and handle his weapons, and to go through other similar exercises, so that his Majesty soon commenced arming and tilting, managing horses, and delighting in every sort of exercise, drawing the bow, playing rackets, hunting, and so forth, indefatigably, though he never neglected his studies.

By these means the Duke obtained great favour with him, and to gain him more completely not only caused entertainments to be made for his diversion, but supplied him freely with money, appointing a Lord Privy Purse, recommending him to make presents, and show that he was King; but what mattered more, he made him acquainted with all public business, and chose to have his opinion, in such wise that his commands might then be executed without delay. But although his Majesty seemed much satisfied with this proceeding on the part of the Duke, yet such was the excellence of his natural disposition that he would never do any act, either of grace or justice, without the approval of his Council, by which means he became so popular with his councillors and the whole country that there is perhaps no instance on record of any other King of that age being more beloved, or who gave greater promise, his Majesty's obstinate adherence to the heresy, alone detracting from so many merits, though for this also he may be excused as he was educated according to its precepts.

Last year, however, precisely at the moment when it was hoped he would commence ruling in person, he was seized with a malady, which the physicians soon knew to be consumption, and in a few days his life was despaired of.

Thereupon, the Duke of Northumberland, whose mode of proceeding had rendered him all powerful with the King, devised a plan, whereby, in the event of the well nigh certain death of his Majesty, the kingdom was to pass into Northumberland's own hands; and his first act was to obtain from the King that the Duke of Suffolk should give his eldest daughter, Lady Jane Grey, in marriage to Northumberland's fourth son, Guilford Dudley, the only one of his five sons then unmarried. Thus was it done, and after performance of the marriage ceremony, with a display truly regal, his Majesty becoming daily worse, they persuaded him to make a will, represent-

---

[15] Edward Seymour, Earl of Hertford, executed in 1551 by Northumberland.
[16] Thomas Dudley, Earl of Warwick, executed for treason by Queen Mary in 1553.

ing to him that the King, his father, had acted illegally by making the will he did, as bastards may not succeed to the Crown; and if the King obtained this from Parliament it was an unlawful act, as, without legitimate cause, Parliament could not deprive the legitimate line of the succession, so that the Act, to the prejudice of the Lady Jane, was null, she being the next legitimate heir after King Edward; in addition to which, the Lady Mary having chosen to persist in her old opinion about the religion, and having thus disobeyed the decrees of Parliament and of his Majesty himself, she deserved on this account likewise to forfeit the succession; and, moreover, as neither Mary nor Elizabeth had a husband, it might easily come to pass that they would marry an alien, and place the country under foreign jurisdiction, she [Mary] having clearly demonstrated how little love she bore the English nation. The King being moved by these arguments, but yet more by his wish to oblige Northumberland in everything, made his testament, instituting Lady Jane Grey his heir, and having summoned all his councillors, announced his will to them, making them read his testament, which he then signed with his own hand, and had it sealed with the great seal of the realm, ordering all the councillors to sign it in like manner, as they did, immediately; and a few days afterwards, namely on the 6th July 1553, he died at the age of 14 years, eight months, and 28 days, having reigned about six years.

In the mean while, Northumberland did not fail doing his utmost to ensure the success of this great scheme, endeavouring, above all, that his negotiations should be kept very secret, and especially from the Lady Mary (notwithstanding which they were known to him, Soranzo,[17] who gave a detailed account of them to the Signory); and having by divers means contrived to enjoy no less credit with the Lady Mary than with the King, he[18] imagined that by continuing to perform similar offices he should convince her of his good will, and retain his influence. Amongst other things he gave her to understand that, without any doubt, she would be Queen, although but few of the members of the Council wished it, but he, on the contrary, would risk his life and whatever else he had for her service. He thus convinced her so completely, and so secured her favour, that, although those who really wished her to be Queen knew of the Duke's deceit, having discovered his intrigues, yet did they not dare divulge anything to the Lady Mary from fear, lest, instead of providing for her own safety, she might reveal everything to him, and thus ruin them completely; but, by secret means, having let her know how the plot was proceeding, they suggested that she could do nothing more advantageous for herself than to simulate with the Duke, and evince greater trust in him than ever, as he would

---

[17] The previous Venetian ambassador.
[18] Northumberland.

thus feel sure, whereas any fear of detection might make him seek to guard himself against her by some worse means.

Her Majesty — as it pleased God — gave ear to the warning of her friends, and followed their advice to the letter; so Northumberland, thinking he could get possession of her whenever he pleased, did not change his conduct towards the Lady Mary, whose friends however, considering all that might occur, contrived when the King was at the point of death to let her know it; whereupon, although it was night, she took flight with six attendants, including two of her maids of honour, and went to Norwich, where having been refused admittance, she stopped a short way off; and although without money or other aid, she nevertheless in a few days mustered an army of 30,000 men, and formed a council from amongst the most faithful of those adherents who joined her.

On the other hand, shortly after the King's death, Northumberland sent to arrest her, but she was gone, and at the very moment when he took Lady Jane to the Tower, as is usually done to those who are to be crowned, news reached him that the Lady Mary had commenced mustering an army, and in many places had been proclaimed Queen, and hearing that her forces increased he determined to march against them in person, but could not raise more than 2,000 horse and foot;[19] so the Lords in the Tower with Lady Jane became alarmed, especially on perceiving how dissatisfied the city of London was; and when they heard that eight of the largest ships had gone over from the Duke to the Lady Mary, giving her all their guns and ammunition, they quitted the Tower, leaving the Lady Jane a prisoner there, issuing also an order for the Duke's arrest; and having assembled in the house of the Earl of Pembroke,[1] they immediately proclaimed the Lady Mary Queen. This took place on the 19th July 1553, when her Majesty's proclamation took place to the great joy of the people, which was evinced to the utmost by bell-ringing, bonfires and shouts of applause; so that in those few days she settled the business, and on the 3rd of August following, made her entry into London with 1,000 horse, being met by all the ambassadors including him (Soranzo), who went towards her a distance of 10 miles from London, with 150 mounted attendants. On the 22nd of August she had Northumberland beheaded on the scaffold as usual at Tower Hill, and on the 1st of October she was crowned by the Bishop of Winchester.

Immediately after this ceremony she assembled Parliament, and forthwith repealed the Acts passed at the instigation of her father, concerning the divorce from Queen Katharine, so that the marriage being declared valid, Her Majesty remained legitimate daughter, the Lady Elizabeth being consequently bastardized, because born in the life-time of the Catholic Queen. From that time forth a great change

[19] This estimate is probably too high.
[1] William Herbert, 1st Earl of Pembroke.

took place in Queen Mary's treatment of her, for whereas until then she had shown her every mark of honour, especially by always placing her beside her when she appeared in public, so did she now by all her actions show that she held her in small account. This disquieting her Excellency, she asked leave to go to her country house [Ashridge], and although some persons were of opinion that the Queen should have refused it, Her Majesty, not loving her (as she had demonstrated by very clear signs, even in the lifetime of King Edward), granted the permission. After Wyatt's[2] insurrection, she was accused of being his accomplice; so both on this account, and also by reason of some suspicion of a matrimonial alliance between her and Courtenay, Earl of Devon, she was sent for to London, although indisposed, and after remaining under custody for a few days in the Queen's palace [at Whitehall], she was at length taken to the Tower. But what perhaps gave more cause for suspicion than anything else, was, that at the time of these insurrections the French ambassador being strongly suspected of having an understanding with the rebels, the Council seized a packet of letters which he was sending to France, and in it they found the copy of a letter sent a few days previously to the Queen by the Lady Elizabeth, in reply to a certain communication made to her by her Majesty about the marriage with the Prince of Spain;[3] and as it contained certain words to which a suspicious meaning was attributed, they inferred that she herself had given the copy to the ambassador for the King, by reason of her secret understanding with him. But although her Excellency confuted all these charges, yet was she not set quite at liberty, for on being released from the Tower, they took her to a palace [Woodstock], where she is in the custody of certain gentlewomen sent by the Queen to keep her company.[4]

She was the daughter of Henry VIII. and Queen Anne Boleyn, and was born on the 7th September 1533, so she is now about twenty-one years old; her figure and face are very handsome, and such an air of dignified majesty pervades all her actions that no one can fail to suppose she is a queen. She is a good Greek and Latin scholar, and besides her native tongue she speaks Latin, French, Spanish, and Italian most perfectly; and her manners are very modest and affable. During the life-time of King Edward she held his opinion about the religion, but since the Queen's accession she has adapted herself to the will of her Majesty.

According to the will of King Henry, the next in succession after the Lady Elizabeth were the daughters of the Duchess of Suffolk, the eldest of whom, Lady Jane Grey, having been beheaded, two remain,[5]

[2] Sir Thomas Wyatt, who led a rebellion in Devonshire, perhaps to dethrone Mary.
[3] Philip.   [4] Elizabeth remained in the Tower until May 19. 1554.
[5] Catherine, who married Edward, Earl of Hertford; and Mary, who married Thomas Keys.

the eldest of them having been promised to the eldest son of the Earl of Pembroke, a most powerful and popular nobleman; but as he knows that this alliance could but cause him great embarrassment, by reason of the marriage of Philip and Mary, he was on the point of breaking it off when he (Soranzo) left England. According to this same will, the next in succession to the crown after the ladies Grey, would be the Countess of Cumberland,[6] who is not yet married, but holds place in the Queen's privy chamber.

The next in blood to the crown is Courtenay, Earl of Devon, descended from a younger daughter of Edward IV.; he is twenty-nine years old, and when his father, the Marquis of Exeter, was beheaded[7] on the charge of having had an understanding with Cardinal Pole, this son of his was also put in the Tower, where he remained fifteen years, but the present Queen released him and restored the earldom, with 15,000 ducats[8] revenue, supposing that he was to marry her; but after the stipulation of the marriage with the Prince of Spain, being suspected of complicity with the Kentish insurgents, Courtenay was again sent to the Tower, but as there were no proofs against him they took him out and placed him in a palace under custody of some gentlemen sent by the Queen.[9] He is of well proportioned frame, has had a very good literary education, and speaks several languages, but having been so long in prison he has neither that spirit nor experience which his position would require.

The kingdom of Scotland is held by Queen Mary, of the Stuart family, sole heir of her father King James,[10] son of Queen Margaret, the eldest sister of Henry VIII.; so that had Lady Jane Grey remained Queen, the Queen of Soctland being descended from the elder sister, and Lady Jane from the younger, she would have had a strong claim, although not mentioned in King Henry's will.

Queen Mary of Scotland, being now twelve years old, is out of her minority, during which she was under the guardianship of the Earl of Arran, who is also styled Duke of Chatelherault, in right of a duchy given him by the King of France. On the death of the King of Scotland,[11] Arran assumed the government as next of kin to the

---

[6] Lady Margaret Clifford, daughter of Henry Clifford, Earl of Cumberland, by his first wife Eleanor Brandon, youngest daughter of the Duke of Suffolk by Mary Tudor, Queen Dowager of France. This Mary Tudor was the sister of Henry VIII.

[7] In 1538 on a charge of treason for corresponding with Reginald (later Cardinal) Pole, who was abroad working with Charles V and Francis I to restore Catholicism in England. Most of Pole's family, including his mother and brother, were executed at the same time.

[8] Ducat: a gold coin in use in several European countries.

[9] On May 25, 1554, Courtenay was brought from the Tower and conveyed to Fordingham Castle in Northamptonshire under the care of Sir Thomas Tresham.

[10] James V (1513–42).

[11] James V.

crown, according to the national law, the post being tenable during the Queen's minority, with power to dispose of all the revenues of the country, and of everything else, without rendering any account; and although it was supposed that he would make a difficulty about resigning his trust, he nevertheless retired a few months ago, as Soranzo wrote to the Senate; and the young Queen appointed as Regent her mother, the Queen Dowager Mary, sister of the Duke de Guise, and she is now in Scotland and rules it, the Queen Regnant being in France, the affianced wife of the Dauphin,[12] she having been taken thither chiefly by the will and exertion of her mother, who well knew that many of the Scots were inclined to marry her to King Edward of England, as had been already promised him. The fortresses are all in the hands of the French or of the Queen Dowager, who being a Frenchwoman, it may be said that everything is in the power of his most Christian Majesty, who keeps some thousand infantry there as garrison, that force being sufficient, as in two days they can send over as many troops as they please.

The kingdom is almost all mountainous and marshy, and the climate very cold, so the soil produces but little grain or fruit, and no grapes, but abounds in fish and animals for the use of man, especially in sheep, which yield very fine wool, though but little of it is manufactured at home, it being exported for the most part to France and Denmark, from which countries they import such commodities as they stand most in need of. The kingdom is divided into twelve bishoprics, the chief of which is St. Andrews, and twelve counties, which are well peopled, as the Kings of Scotland have often brought armies of 30,000 men into the field, for the most part against their natural enemies, the English, because Scotland being very poor, and England plentifully supplied, the Scots have always invaded the country, carrying off great booty, this discord being fomented by France; and by donatives and privileges they have induced the French always to prefer the Scottish alliance to that of England. Part of these Scots are savages, and those who are the most civilized either reside at the court or are on the borders of England. The Scots are rigid Catholics, nor is there public heresy of any sort amongst them.[13] Such is the poverty of the county that royal revenues do not amount to 100,000 ducats.

The other three parts of the island are held by the most serene Queen of England, as they were by her predecessors, commencing with William the Conqueror; that is to say, from 1067[14] down to the present time, the Crown having always been in that descent, although

[12] The future Francis II. These Franco-Spanish marriages joined the two countries against their common enemy, England. The last portions of this selection deal with Scotland.
[13] This was an incorrect observation, for the Scottish Lords were already making preparations to introduce Protestantism.
[14] 1066.

there have been many wars, and especially those which originated with the sons of Edward III., the one, Duke of York,[15] from whom the House of York sprang; and the other, Duke of Lancaster,[16] who founded the Lancastrian family; the first bearing on their shield the white rose, the second the red. Finally, after much bloodshed, the Crown passing from one side to the other, and the male line of the then reigning King Edward IV. of the white rose, becoming extinct, there remaining only daughters, the eldest[17] of them was given in marriage to Henry Earl of Richmond, the sole remaining heir of the red rose, who afterwards became Henry VII., grandfather of the present Queen; so these two families were again united, and her Majesty is thus the legitimate heir of both.

The air of England is thick, so it often generates clouds, wind, and rain, but in calm weather the climate is so temperate that the extremes of heat and cold are rarely felt, and never last long, so that persons clad in fur may be seen all the year round. They have some little plague in England well nigh every year, for which they are not accustomed to make sanitary provisions, as it does not usually make great progress; the cases for the most part occur amongst the lower classes, as if their dissolute mode of life impaired their constitutions; but in 1551, the first year of Soranzo's residence in England, there was an atmospheric putrescence which produced the disease called "the Sweat,"[18] which, according to general report, was never known in other countries, and only twice before in England, at intervals of upwards of 20 years; it commenced in Wales, and then traversed the whole kingdom, the mortality being immense amongst persons of every condition, save that children under 10 years of age did not seem subject to this epidemic The malady was a most profuse sweat, which without any other indisposition seized patients by the way and the remedies at first administered taking no effect they died in a few hours, so that during the three first days of its appearance there died in London alone upwards of 5,000 persons, but some remedy having been devised subsequently, it ceased in 20 days.[19] The alarm, however was great and universal, especially at the courts, some of the King's chamber attendants having died, so that his Majesty and all who could made their escape, all business being suspended, the shops closed, and nothing attended to, but the preservation of life.

The soil, especially in England proper, produces wheat, oats, and barley, in such plenty that they have usually enough for their own consumption, but were they to work more diligently, and with greater skill, and bring the soil into higher cultivation, England might supply grain for exportation, but they do not attend much to this, so that

[15] Edmund.
[16] John of Gaunt.
[17] Margaret.
[18] Apparently a form of influenza, rampant in 1485, 1529, 1543, and 1551.
[19] Incorrect; the epidemic continued active in London in 1528–29.

they sometimes need assistance both from Flanders and Denmark, and occasionally from France likewise. They grow no other sort of grain, and their only lentils[1] are beans and peas. Although they have vines they do not make wine of any sort, the plant serving as an ornament for their gardens rather than anything else, as the grapes do not ripen save in very small quantity, partly because the sun has not much power, and partly because precisely at the ripening season cold winds generally prevail, so that the grapes wither, but in lieu of wine they make beer, with wheat, barley, and hops, which [last?] they import from Flanders, boiling all the ingredients together in water, and making it stronger or weaker by adding more wheat and less barley, and producing a contrary result by reversing the process. This potion is most palatable to them, and all persons drink it, even their sovereigns, although they also consume a great quantity of wine, which is brought from Candia,[2] Spain, the Rhine, and from France, this last being prized more than the rest, but it is sold at a very high price, so that it is usually worth from 36 to 40 ducats per butt, and in his (Soranzo's) time it cost as much as 50. As there are no olive trees in England they import oil from Spain and the Venetian possessions, but the consumption is small, as for food they mostly use butter, and for the cloth manufactures rape oil, which is imported from Flanders and Spain. They have great plenty of white salt at home, and the black is brought from Normandy, nor is there any salt duty. They have abundance of fish, both from the ocean and the Thames, of the same sort as is common in Venice, but they have also salmon, a fish not found in Italy. They have an immense quantity of oysters, so that occasionally as many as 20 smacks are seen filled with them, but during four months in the summer it is forbidden either to take or sell them.

The country is almost all level, with few rivers and springs, and such hills as they have are not very high, and one advantage of the climate is that the grass remains green at all seasons, affording excellent pasturage for animals, especially for sheep, of which there is an incredible number, supplying that wool which is in such universal repute under the name of "Frankish," the French having been the first to bring it into Italy. Great part of this wool is manufactured in England, where cloths and kerseys of various sorts are wrought, which amount annually to 150,000 pieces of cloths of all sorts, and 150,000 pieces of kersey,[3] the rest of the wool being exported, and taken usually to Calais on account of the staplers, who then sell it on the spot, and have the monopoly of the wool exports from England, though occasionally export-permits are conceded by favour to other persons, though the staplers do their utmost to prevent it. The quantity of

[1] The seed of a podbearing plant related to the bean and the pea.
[2] Crete.
[3] A coarse, ribbed woollen cloth, named after the town of Kersey in Suffolk.

unwrought wool exported is said to amount to about 2,000 tons [annually]; they also export hides to the values of 500,000 ducats. In Cornwall they have lead and tin mines, from which they extract metal in great quantity, and of such good quality that the like is not to be found elsewhere. For some time they have not exported much lead because permits are refused, but they export annually from five to six thousand weight of unwrought tin, and to the value of 100,000 ducats in the wrought metal, the greater part to Spain.

In Derbyshire there are some iron mines, but in small quantity, but none of gold nor of silver.

In the north towards Scotland they find a certain sort of earth well nigh mineral,[4] and which burns like charcoal, and is extremely used, especially by blacksmiths, and but for a certain bad odour which it leaves it would be yet more employed, as it gives great heat and costs little.

The principal cities of the kingdom are London and York, but London is the most noble, both on account of its being the royal residence, and because the river Thames runs through it, very much to the convenience and profit of the inhabitants, as it ebbs and flows every six hours like the sea, scarcely ever causing inundation or any extraordinary floods; and up to London Bridge it is navigable for ships of 400 butts[5] burden, of which a great plenty arrive with every sort of merchandise. This bridge connects the city with the borough, and is built of stone with twenty arches; and shops on both sides. On the banks of the river there are many large palaces, making a very fine show, but the city is much disfigured by the ruins of a multitude of churches and monasteries belonging heretofore to friars and nuns. It has a dense population, said to number 180,000 souls; and is beyond measure commercial, the merchants of the entire kingdom flocking thither, as, by a privilege conceded to the citizens of London, from them alone can they purchase merchandise, so they soon become very wealthy; and the same privileges placed in their hands the government of the city of London, which is divided into 24 trades or crafts, each of which elects a certain individual, styled alderman, the election being made solely in the persons of those who are considered the most wealthy, and the office is for life; the which aldermen, after assembling these trades, create annually a person as their head for the current year entitled Mayor, and they call him Lord, which signifies *signor;* and he assumes the magistracy on the day of Saints Simon and Jude,[6] on which day he goes to the court and swears allegiance to the King, and then gives a banquet to the ambassadors and lords, and to the judges of the city and others, in such number, that in one and the same hall upwards of a thousand persons sit down to table, all

---

[4] Peat.
[5] Butt: a large cask containing, by modern measuring standards, 129.7 gallons.
[6] October 28.

being served at the same time with the most perfect order. The Lord Mayor is always preceded by the sword in virtue of the privilege conceded to the city for its deserts in 1190 by King Richard the First. This mayor usually keeps a most excellent table with open doors, and in one year spends at least 4000 ducats out of his own purse; and on the expiration of his office he is for the most part knighted. His chief charge is to superintend the victualling department, to legislate for the populace in minor suits, and to have care for the custody of the city day and night, the keys of its gates being in his posession.

The English for the most part are of handsome stature and sound constitution, with red or white complexions, their eyes also being white. According to their station they are all as well clad as any other nation whatever. The dress of the men resembles the Italian fashion, and that of the women the French.

The nobility are by nature very courteous, especially to foreigners, who however are treated with very great arrogance and enmity by the people, it seeming to them that the profit derived by the merchants from their country is so much taken from them, and they imagine that they could live without foreign intercourse. They are also by nature of little faith both towards their sovereigns and with each other, and are therefore very suspicious. The nobility, save such as are employed at Court, do not habitually reside in the cities, but in their own country mansions, where they keep up very grand establishments, both with regard to the great abundance of eatables consumed by them, as also by reason of their numerous attendants, in which they exceed all other nations, so that the Earl of Pembroke has upwards of 1,000 clad in his own livery. In these their country residences they occupy themselves with hunting of every description, and with whatever else can amuse or divert them; so that they seem wholly intent on leading a joyous existence, the women also being no less sociable than the men, it being customary for them and allowable to go without any regard either alone or accompanied by their husbands to the taverns, and to dine and sup where they please.

The English do not delight much either in military pursuits or literature, which last, most especially by the nobility, is not held in much account, and they have scarcely any opportunity for occupying themselves with the former, save in time of war, and when that is ended they think no more about them, but in battle they show great courage and great presence of mind in danger, but they require to be largely supplied with victuals; so it is evident that they cannot endure much fatigue.

REPORT of FRANCE by Signor GIOVANNI MICHIEL, Venetian Ambassador there, 1561.

Unless it otherwise pleases the Almighty, religious affairs will soon be in an evil case in France, because there is not one single province uncontaminated.[7] Indeed in some provinces, such as Normandy, almost the whole of Britany, Touraine, Poitou, Gascony, and a great part of Languedoc, of Dauphiny, and of Provence, comprising three-fourths of the kingdom, congregations and meetings, which they call assemblies, are held; and in these assemblies they read and preach, according to the rites and uses of Geneva, without any respect either for the ministers of the King or the commandments of the King himself. This contagion has penetrated so deeply that it affects every class of persons, and, what appears more strange, even the ecclesiastical body itself. I do not mean only priests, friars, and nuns, for there are but few monasteries that are not corrupted, but even bishops and many of the principal prelates, who hitherto had not shown any such disposition; and it is only on account of the rigorous execution of the law that other persons besides the populace have not disclosed themselves, because they have restrained themselves for the time being from fear of the loss of their property and lives.[8] But your Serenity[9] must learn that while the people and the populace show fervent devotion by frequenting the churches and observing the Catholic rites, all other classes are supposed to be disaffected, and the nobility perhaps more than any other class, and, particularly, persons of forty years of age and under. If these disaffected individuals continue to attend mass and the Divine offices, and externally to practise Catholic rites, they do so for show and from fear; because when they either are, or believe themselves to be, unobserved, they avoid and even fly from the mass above all things, and also from the churches as far as they are able, and more so since it became known that by imprisonment, chastisement, and burnings, no remedy was found. It has now been determined not to proceed against any disaffected persons unless they venture to preach, persuade, and to take part publicly in congregations and assemblies. All other such persons are allowed to live, and some have been set at liberty, and released from the prisons of Paris and of other parts of the kingdom. A great number of these last have still remained in the kingdom, preaching and speaking publicly, and boasting that they have gained their cause against the Papists, as they delight to style their adversaries; so that, now, every one of them is assured against the fear of being questioned; and there exists thus a silent truce, because whilst formerly all suspected persons had to quit the kingdom, and to retire some to Geneva, some to Germany, and some to England, now they not only do not leave the country, but a large number of those who had already emigrated have returned. It was told me, whilst passing through Geneva on my way

[7] A reference to the French Calvinists, called Huguenots, who numbered perhaps 400,000 at this time.

[8] This seems to be an exaggerated account of the influence and numbers of the Huguenots. Since France was in a constant state of turmoil, most dissident persons were indiscriminately labeled Huguenots.

[9] The Doge of Venice, Girolamo Pruili.

to Italy, that, after the death of the King,[10] a great number of gentlemen who had fled thither after the conspiracy of Amboise,[11] had come back to France, and, in particular, Monsieur de Mombrun, who was the author of the late disturbances in Provence and in Dauphiny, and who had been burnt in effigy; besides these, more than fifty others, who are called ministers, were summoned from various parts of France to travel, and teach and preach the "Word," for thus they term the Gospels, and their own doctrine. Your Serenity will hardly believe the influence and the great power which the principal minister of Geneva, by name Calvin, a Frenchman, and a native of Picardy, possesses in this kingdom; he is a man of extraordinary authority, who by his mode of life, his doctrines, and his writings, rises superior to all the rest; and it is almost impossible to believe the enormous sums of money which are secretly sent to him from France to maintain his power. It is sufficient to add that if God does not interfere, there is great and imminent danger that one of two things will happen in this kingdom: either that the truce, which is desired and sought publicly, will end by the heretics having churches wherein they can preach, read, and perform their rites, according to their doctrine, without hindrance, and in like manner as they obtained churches by command of the late King, given at Fontainebleau, at the end of August, in compliance with a petition presented to him by the Admiral;[12] or, else, that we shall see an obedience to the Pope and to the Catholic rites enforced, and shall have resort to violence and imbrue our hands in noble blood. For these reasons I foresee a manifest and certain division in the kingdom, and civil war as a consequence; and this will be the cause of the ruin both of the kingdom and of religion, because upon a change in religion a change in the State necessarily follows.

Orleans is called Edward, having received this name after Edward, King of England. He is 8 years old, one year less than the King;[13] he is a very fine child, but of a more grave and subdued nature than the King, and enjoys better health than his Majesty.

The King of Navarre,[14] before he became King, took his title from the House of Vendôme, as successor to the states and inheritance of his mother, who belonged to that house, and who married under a contract that her heir should take that title. This house became extinct this very year, on the death of the Vidame of Chartres. The King is 44 or 45 years of age, but his beard has already begun to turn grey. He is a man of good presence, and far more prepossessing in appearance than his brothers, who are undersized and ill made, while the

[10] Francis II.
[11] A Huguenot conspiracy to capture the duke and cardinal of Guise.
[12] Coligny, the leader of the Huguenots.
[13] Charles IX (1560–74).
[14] Anthony Bourbon.

King's stature is above the ordinary height. He is of a jovial and friendly disposition, and has a reputation for courage and ardour, which he has shown in the war, but he is thought to be a better soldier than a captain or general. But still he is ranked amongst the principal commanders of the kingdom, and will not give precedence either to the Constable[15] or M. de Guise. He is a prince of great affability towards everybody indifferently, without any pretence or emptiness about him, and with a free and open manner of proceeding, according to the French custom; and he is so liberal that he is always in debt, and never has money to spend. By these two qualities of liberality and affability he has obtained great popularity with all classes, and especially with the nobles, by whom he is much loved. He has a reputation for a good intellect and power of speech, but as to actions he is reputed vain, inconsiderate, and inconstant, with little ability to undertake great enterprises, or to carry them out with spirit. He has hitherto been under suspicion of being unfriendly to the religion, as one who had been persuaded to abandon the mass and to accept all the rites of Geneva. Still everybody agrees that he has done this more for the purpose of creating a division in the kingdom and for becoming the head of a party, than for any respect or zeal in religious matters; for the very Protestants themselves believe him to be a great hypocrite and deceiver, and that he will fall in with whatever may turn most to his advantage, because he has allowed himself to be persuaded to live according to the Catholic religion, and to send to Rome to render public obedience to the Pope, simply in order to do less in this way than the Kings of France and of Spain.

The brothers of the King (of Navarre) are the Cardinal of Bourbon and the Prince of Condé, who are opposed to one another in religious opinion. The Cardinal is considered one of the best Catholics in the whole kingdom, while the Prince of Condé, on the other hand, is believed to be most disaffected, and to be agitating as much as he can with all those who are not corrupted, with the intent to form a party in order to defeat the Lords de Guise, against whom he professes open enmity on account of his being excluded from the Government at their instance. He was the author of the insurrections and conspiracies which lately took place under pretext of religion, but which were formed with the object of assassinating the Lords de Guise; and there is no doubt that if the late King had not died, the Prince would have worked much greater evil against many others, and particularly against the house of the Constable, and with danger even to the Constable himself, notwithstanding that the Constable had never done nor even imagined any of the acts that were to be laid to his charge; but the death of the King, as if by a miracle, put an end to all these contemplated proceedings.

[15] Duc Anne de Montmorency, French soldier, created Constable of France in 1537; the leader of the Catholics against the Huguenots.

The peace concluded with England[16] by the intervention of the ministers of the King of Spain continues outwardly to be observed, but whoever considers the real dispositions of these two nations, who are natural enemies, cannot believe that any good understanding can ever exist between them; and, to say the truth, there is no such understanding, nor will there ever be any, because the English have greatly at heart the recovery of Calais, which they lost in the last war, and the French desire to revenge the injuries which they have received at the hands of the English in the kingdom of Scotland, and which resulted in little less than the complete loss of that kingdom by an agreement which was so disgraceful to the crown of France that the late King refused to ratify it. But as neither the French nor the English are in a position to go to war openly, they, from the necessity of the case, take advantage of the present time of peace, and especially the English, who, from the condition of affairs in Scotland since the death of the late King, have less reason to fear than formerly an open invasion by the French, and await with greater tranquillity the expiration of the seven years for which they have signed peace, when Calais is to be restored, with the alternative of the payment of 100,000 crowns; and according to the position in which these nations will then be, they will either break or maintain the treaty.

COMMENTARY and OBSERVATIONS on the Kingdom of FRANCE by MICHIEL SURIANO, Venetian Ambassador at the Court of France, 1561.

The kingdom of France has always possessed adequate means for self-defence. It has never been conquered except by the English, who, after a long and protracted war waged within the very bowels of the land, occupied a great portion of the country; but their victory endured only a short time, for they were deprived not only of those portions of the kingdom which they had held by force, but also of Normandy and Guienne, the ancient patrimony of the Kings of England; and this is the origin of the mortal hatred which exists between the two nations, and which will never end.

The country itself is delightful and pleasing, full of navigable rivers; it has no rugged mountains except at one extremity and on the frontiers, and the centre consists of fertile and cultivated plains and hills, which produce a quantity of wheat, wine, flax, hemp, and other things, which are not only sufficient for the use of the kingdom, but which are exported to Spain, Portugal, Flanders, England, Denmark, and to other countries even more distant. Although there are no mines of gold and silver, as in Germany and Spain, yet in France there is no lack of money received from the various countries which

[16] Treaty of Cateau-Cambresis, concluded on April 3, 1559.

consume its produce; Portugal alone sends to France gold and silver in large quantities; Spain sends the like, notwithstanding that the prohibitions are most strict, because the profit that is derived amounts to 15 or 20 per cent. at the least; and I remember that during the war with the Catholic King,[17] the trade with the Flemings did not cease, from the necessity which compelled the latter to obtain provisions and merchandise from France. It is therefore not surprising that in time of war the French soldiers not only in Italy, but within the kingdom itself, were paid in Spanish crowns and silver reals.

If any authority in France can control the absolute power of the King it is the Assembly of the Three Estates, who represent the whole kingdom, like the Parliament in England and in Scotland and the Diet in Germany. A meeting is held nearly every year, when matters of importance are considered.

With regard to matters of religion, every one knows that the first person [Luther] who revived the old heresies, and who is the origin of the new sects of our time, was a man of humble origin and fortune; nevertheless he has infected so large a part of the world in a few years that he has not only caused religion to be changed in Germany, which was his native country, but also in Denmark, Sweden, Prussia, Poland, and all the northern countries. He has also ruined England and Scotland, corrupted France and Flanders, thrown Italy and Spain into confusion, and his influence extends even to the Indies, so that there is now no part of Christendom which is free from this pestilence; and although from the three branches which this evil root has produced, namely, one of Lutherans, one of Sacramentarians, and one of Anabaptists, thirty and more sects all different one from another have sprung, they nevertheless derive their origin from him alone. The main principles which the authors of the new doctrines profess are, to teach the purity of the Gospel, and to preach Christian liberty.

The Pope[18] is interested in these matters, because these new sects greatly prejudice his authority, and the treaties which he has with this kingdom. The Emperor[19] is also interested on account of Metz, the Queen of England for Calais, and the Duke of Savoy[1] for the fortresses of Piedmont.

The Pope is not considered to have much power in France, because the weakness of the Church was proved during the last war, and because at one time the French thought to occupy Italy if a Frenchman were made Pope. The authority of his Holiness has also greatly declined on account of these new sects, which, although of contrary

---

[17] Charles I of Spain.
[18] Pius IV (Gian-Antonio de' Medici).
[19] Ferdinand I.
[1] Emanuel Philibert.

opinions and various kinds, are united in their endeavor to destroy the Papal authority.

His Holiness, moreover, is not a Prince by blood, and many Catholics consider that the name of the House of Medici is fatal to Christianity, because during the time of Pope Leo[2] Germany was lost, in the time of Clement,[3] England, and now in the time of this Pius, France is threatened with a danger which every one perceives.

The authority of his Holiness having thus declined so greatly, proposals have been discussed to satisfy the heretics, to suspend the payments of annates, and to annul the Pragmatic agreed to many years since.

REPORT concerning KING PHILIP OF SPAIN, presented by MICHIEL SORIANO (Surian), late Ambassador with his Majesty, to the MOST SERENE SIGNORY. 1561.

Describes the respective geographical positions of Burgundy and the Low Countries, which latter, he states, are defended by twenty-four so called fortresses, which, however, according to his opinion, do not merit that name.

The Low Countries, by reason of the extent of their frontiers, the multitude of their population, their riches, their proximity to the sea and to rivers, and the beauty and the grandeur of their land, are not inferior to any kingdom in Europe, and there is no other country in the world which is at the same time more sterile and more wealthy. Their sterility is due partly to the climate, which is cold and damp, and partly to want of care on the part of the inhabitants, who busy themselves more with commerce and the arts of manufacture than with agriculture, and the land is allowed to run to pasture and to woods after the manner in which the English deal with their lands.

Their wealth is derived from the large trade which is carried on with England, Flanders, Spain, Germany, Italy, and the whole world, because much merchandise is exported to those countries, and much merchandise imported from them, and these importations are partly consumed at home and partly forwarded elsewhere. The goods which are exported to all parts of the world are tapestries, cloth, and linen.

In these States two causes for apprehension constantly exist; the first is the disposition of the people, who are discontented on account of continual burdens, and because the whole government which was formerly in their hands is now entirely carried on by the Spaniards. The second cause is the power and proximity of the French, who neither in time of war nor in time of peace allow any opportunity to pass which may be useful to them and damaging to their adver-

---

[2] Leo X (1513–21).
[3] Clement VII (1523–34).

...aries. Therefore the Emperor,[4] to protect himself against the people, decided to maintain a large force of Spanish soldiers in these provinces, besides the fortress which he made in Ghent, and others which he proposed to make in other places also. And in order to secure himself against the French, he thought it expedient to avail himself of the arms of England, which have always been fatal to the kingdom of France; so he entered into a league with King Henry the Eighth, which bound each party to furnish certain forces for the common defence of their States.

But after the death of Henry and of Edward, and upon the accession of Queen Mary, the Emperor, who always entertained large designs, thought that he might acquire the kingdom of England by contracting a marriage between the Queen and his son; but his expectations were disappointed, because the King (Philip) met with so many obstacles and difficulties that I remember having heard a great personage say that his Majesty daily repented more and more having applied himself to this undertaking, because in that kingdom he had neither authority, obedience, nor peace, but only a title which was empty rather than real. And now, as I am on the subject of England, it seems to me desirable to write some brief details concerning that kingdom.

England is the most wealthy and powerful of all the kingdoms of the north, and although the Crown levies small import duties (usually about 100,000 ducats), it has nevertheless sufficient supplies under ordinary circumstances for the public service both in time of peace and also in time of war, because in time of war subsidies, great and small, are levied upon owners of property according to the assessment of individuals appointed for that purpose; and the sums fixed are paid within two months without any complaint or the slightest tumult, notwithstanding, as has happened frequently, that the amount has reached one million and a half of gold.

The power of the country consists in its number of warlike men, and in the strength of its fleet, in which respect this kingdom is superior to all its neighbours, and also in the advantage of its natural position, which is easy to defend and difficult to attack. But from the disposition of the people, and from the incapacity of the Council, the kingdom has lately suffered more detriment than advantage from the above forces, for Calais has been lost because no steps were taken in time to provide against the danger, and the country itself is weakened by many intestine discords.

The English are universally partial to novelty, hostile to foreigners, and not very friendly amongst themselves; they attempt to do everything that comes into their heads, just as if all that the imagination suggests could be easily executed; hence a greater number of insurrections have broken out in this country than in all the rest of

[4] Charles V.

the world, the most recent of these being that raised by Thomas Stafford[5] nephew of the Cardinal [Pole], who endeavoured to obtain the kingdom with only sixty men brought by him from France, and he paid the penalty of his temerity.

From the same cause has arisen the change of faith, which is the greatest alteration that could possibly arise in a nation, because besides the offence which is thus committed against our Lord God, a revolution in customs, laws, obedience, and, lastly, in the very State itself, necessarily follows, as has happened in Asia, Africa, Germany, and in a great part of Europe.

Hence also have resulted many depositions of great men and promotions of the unworthy, many imprisonments, exiles, and deaths. It is also a fact, incredible though true, namely, that during the last twenty years three Princes of the blood, four Dukes, forty Earls, and more than three thousand other persons have died by violent death. It may therefore be easily imagined that no foreigner could rule this kind of people, when even their own countrymen are not safe, yet nevertheless the King [Philip] used every endeavour and every means suggested by his father and his friends to acquire authority over them. To obtain their favour he showed himself most gracious towards all; he trusted his own life in their hands; he professed openly to require nothing from them; he spent money freely amongst all classes; he reduced the Council of the Queen from the old number of twenty-five to six confidential persons only; and he did everything he possibly could without resorting to force.

But seeing the suspicion against him continually on the increase, and being aware that if he had no son he would be excluded from the throne, and foreseeing that the people would then incline to the Lady Elizabeth, who is now Queen, the King, in order not to lose with shame that which he could not retain, determined to marry her to the Duke of Savoy, who was a friend and dependent of his Majesty, and thus to preserve the friendship of that kingdom, which he could not otherwise subdue.

This scheme involved two difficulties: the first was to gain the consent of that Queen (Elizabeth), who seemed unwilling to marry without the consent of Parliament, which the King her father had ordained as necessary; and Parliament appeared indisposed to consent to her marrying a foreigner. The other difficulty was to induce the Queen (Mary), her sister, to consent that she (Elizabeth) should marry with the hope of [succeeding to] the kingdom. This difficulty appeared greater than the other, because the Queen was very illdisposed towards her (Elizabeth), and would not acknowledge her as a sister; and as she (Mary) was of a terrible and obstinate nature,

---

[5] On April 24, 1557, Sir Thomas Stafford landed on English soil from Dieppe, France, promising to overthrow the "foreigner" Philip II and the hated Mary. His invasion failed and he was executed at Tyburn on May 28.

neither the King nor any other person dared to reason with her against
her will. Therefore a mission was given to the King's Confessor, who
was a man of great ability and very acceptable to the Queen, to
undertake the business, and he performed this duty with such assidu-
ity and dexterity that he induced her to alter her mind, so that she
expressed her satisfaction, and promised to speak to the King on the
subject the following evening; but as the Queen then said nothing
about it, the Confessor returned to her on the following day, when he
found her mind altogether changed, and the blame was laid on
Cardinal Pole, who was supposed, because he had not been first
consulted, to have persuaded the Queen in a contrary sense.

This Cardinal was a man of singular goodness, who spent his life
in the practice and teaching of religion, and his sole object was to
confirm that kingdom in the Catholic religion, and to maintain it
in tranquillity. Knowing therefore that the Lady Elizabeth must
succeed to the throne, and that in order that she might not relapse
into the heresy in which she was born and educated, it was imperative to give her a husband who was a Catholic, or who might have
authority over her, he, the Cardinal, would not have thought of
hindering the proposal above mentioned, as he would have been
opposing his own chief design.

But this imputation was put upon him because he had always
been under suspicion at the court of the Emperor and of the King,
for while he held the principal dignity in the kingdom, he had
never been willing to use his power to make the King absolute, as
the Spaniards desired. Indeed, one day the Bishop of Arras, speaking
of the Cardinal, said that the Cardinal neither understood nor knew
anything about affairs of State or of the Court, and added that he
was good for nothing in that kingdom, either for counsel or for government. This was said because it is the habit of the Spaniards,
when they cannot or do not know how to carry their point, always
to suspect that they have been thwarted by some one from whom
they ought to have had assistance; and therefore they came to the
conclusion that this most holy and innocent man could have served
their ends if he had wished to do so.

But before they were able to execute their plan, the Queen's state
of health became seriously worse, and then, taking advantage of
the opportunity, the Count de Feria[6] was sent to England with
orders, with or without the consent of the Queen, to acquaint Lady
Elizabeth that the King was the author of the project for her ag-
grandisement; and both the Count and the Confessor intimated that
in the matter of such importance no regard was to be paid to the
mere displeasure of a woman. But the King lost one point and failed

---

[6] The Count de Feria was sent by Mary's husband, Philip II, to congratulate
her on her supposed pregnancy. Feria had married Jane Dormer, one of Mary's
maids of honor. As Philip's agent he constantly intrigued in English affairs.

to gain the other, because Queen Mary, partly from rage, which was natural to her, and partly from being compelled to consent against her will, fell into such a state of passion that she departed this life.

Queen Elizabeth, who has succeeded to the throne, owing to her courage and to her great power of mind, being similar to that of the King her father, declines to rely upon anyone save herself, although she is most gracious to all. And while she has not as yet changed the religion for reasons of her own it is nevertheless believed that she favours the sect in which she was born and educated, and, having regard to the individuals whom she has appointed to govern the kingdom, that she will return to the manner in which she lived in the time of King Edward.

With regard to the Queen's marriage, the English are of opinion that she will not marry a foreigner, and if there be a report that she is treating with the Catholic King, his Majesty has no inclination to any such negotiation, partly because he is indisposed to resume his responsibilities in England, and partly for other reasons which are secret.

The only hope his Majesty has of remaining friendly with the Queen is her distrust of the French, who have pretensions to her kingdom through the Queen of Scotland, as a descendant from a sister of King Henry, and the nearest to him in legitimate succession, should the Queen (Elizabeth) be adjudged ineligible by reason of having been born while the legitimate wife of her father was still alive.

I will conclude with the brief observation that the Catholic King, for the preservation of his estates in Flanders, and to keep the sea open between Flanders and Spain, will do his utmost to remain ever at peace with that kingdom, and prevent it falling into the hands of any Prince from whom he might at any time apprehend war.

* * * * * *

The Catholic King was born in Spain in the month of May 1527. He passed his early days and the greater part of his youth in that kingdom, where either from the custom of the country or by the will of his mother, who was a Portuguese, he was educated with all the care and respect which could become the son of the greatest Emperor who ever reigned in Christendom and the heir of possessions of such vast magnitude.

Having been brought up after this manner, his Majesty, when he first quitted Spain, passed through Italy and Germany to Flanders, and conveyed a universal impression that he was of a severe and intractable disposition, and therefore he was not much liked by the Italians, thoroughly disliked by the Flemings, and hated by the Germans. Consequently he was first warned by the Cardinal of Trent,[7] then by Queen Mary, and even more effectually by his father,[8]

---

[7] Reginald Pole.   [8] Charles I of Spain; the Emperor Charles V.

that a character for severity did not become the ruler of various nations and people of various habits and customs. He thenceforward changed so completely that since he left Spain to proceed to England, he has shown continually such great sweetness of temper, and such affability, as not to be surpassed by any Prince in these respects; and although he preserves his reputation and royal dignity, which are natural to him, in all his actions, the urbanity which his Majesty shows towards all persons is not the less acceptable to them.

His personal appearance, his manly presence, and his manner of speaking sweetly, add to his graciousness of demeanour; and although he is small in stature he is so well made, and his limbs so well proportioned and symmetrical, and he dresses with so much cleanliness and taste, that it is not possible to behold anything more perfect than himself.

His Majesty is of a very delicate constitution, and for this reason he lives invariably according to rule; his habit is to partake only of highly nutritious food, and he abstains from fish, fruit, and similar aliments, which have a tendency to produce ill humours.

He sleeps a great deal, takes little exercise, and his habits of life are of a tranquil character; and although in the field he has shown more readiness and vivacity, it is apparent that he has overcome his nature, which inclined to tranquillity rather than activity, and to repose rather than to fatigue. Hence it follows that although his time of life is apt to engender generous aspirations, and an insatiable desire to govern, his efforts are directed not to increase his possessions by war, but to preserve them by peace; for at the commencement of his reign he made a truce with the King of France,[9] notwithstanding that the Emperor refused his consent, and that the Bishop of Arras publicly condemned it. He regulated the disorders of the ministers of his realms; he restored the courts of law; he expedited the grants of favours and the decrees of justice, which the Emperor was accustomed to delay; he showed liberality towards all persons, and never permitted anyone to leave his presence dissatisfied. But when the Emperor, who had by his great reputation for prudence and experience maintained the authority of his son, departed for Spain, his Majesty was too weak to support so great a burden, and soon found himself involved in serious difficulties, which might have overthrown him had he not been aided by fortune, and the imprudence of his enemies. Then, if he had desired to imitate the Emperor, he might have done so by the strength of his power and the prosperity of his fortune, which are most formidable to the world; but although he resembles his father in his features, in his mode of speech, in his observance of religion, and in his kindness and good faith, he is dissimilar in many other respects which constitute the crowning point of the greatness of Princes. The Emperor delighted in all that pertained to war, but his Majesty has neither knowledge

[9] Henry II (1547–59).

of warlike matters, nor delight in them. The Emperor undertook great expeditions, but these the King avoids. The Emperor planned great designs, and conducted them with dexterity, and to his great benefit; but the King thinks less of increasing his own power, than of obstructing the power of others. The Emperor never yielded to threats or to fear, but the King under very small apprehensions has given away states.

The Emperor governed entirely according to his own views, but the King governs according to the views of others, and he has no esteem for any nation except the Spanish; he consorts only with Spaniards, and with these only he takes counsel and governs. Moreover, contrary to the custom of the Emperor, he takes no notice of Italians and Flemings, and least of all Germans, and although he retains the chief men of each nation in his kingdom, still it is observed that he declines to admit any one of them to his secret councils, but keeps them only for affairs of war; and he probably acts thus, not so much because he has a good opinion of them, as to prevent their services being employed by his enemies. For this reason he has never summoned either the Duke of Savoy or the Duke Ottavio to the council of state, but only to the council of war, into which all the chief officers, and even the colonels, are admitted. The Duke Ottavio has nicknamed this council "the council of the populace."

* * * * * *

According to my opinion the kingdom of England will always be in alliance with his Majesty, from fear of being harassed by France, which already possesses Calais and Boulogne this side of England, and the kingdom of Scotland on the other.

Reports concerning Mary, Queen of Scotland

Giovanni Correr, Venetian Ambassador in France, to the Signory.

A gentleman came from Scotland with confirmation of the Queen's flight, which took place thus.

The Queen of Scotland was advised by Lord Seton her most confidential Catholic friend, and a very brave gentleman, by means of a lad of the house who never returned, that he on an appointed day would be with about fifty horsemen at the lake of Lochleven, where the Queen was held a prisoner. Seton remained with forty horsemen in the mountains at a short distance, so as not to be discovered by the occupants of the castle in the lake, and the other ten, approaching nearer, entered a village, pretending to be travellers; and one of these men went to the edge of the lake itself, and prostrating himself on the ground, so as not to be seen, waited, according to the order given, until the Queen should come forth, as arranged.

Guard was continually kept at the castle day and night, except during supper, at which time the gate was locked with a key, every one going to supper, and the key was always placed on the table where the Governor took his meals, and before him. The Governor is the uterine brother of the Earl of Murray, Regent of Scotland, the Queen's illegitimate brother and her mortal enemy. The Queen, having attempted to descend from a window unsuccessfully, contrived that a page of the Governor's, whom she had persuaded to this effect, when carrying a dish, in the evening of the 2nd of May, to the table of his master with a napkin before him, should place the napkin on the key, and in removing the napkin take up the key with it, and carry it away unperceived by anyone. Having done so, the page then went directly to the Queen, and told her all was ready; and she, having in the meanwhile been attired by the elder of the two maids who waited upon her, took her by the hand the younger maid, a girl ten years old, and with the page went quietly to the door, and he having opened it, the Queen went out with him and the younger girl and locked the gate outside with the same key, without which it could not be opened from within. They then got into a little boat which was kept for the service of the castle, and displaying a white veil of the Queen's with a red tassel, she made the concerted signal to those who awaited her, that she was approaching. On seeing this, the person stretched on the ground on the bank of the lake arose, and by another signal summoned the horsemen from the village, amongst whom a principal person was he [John Beaton] who is now come to give account of these facts to these Majesties, and who is the brother of the Scottish Ambassador here [James Beaton, Bishop of Glasgow]. The horsemen from the mountains being also informed came immediately to the lake, and received the Queen with infinite joy, and having placed her on horseback with the page and the girl, they conveyed her to the sea coast, at a distance of five miles from thence, because to proceed by land to the place which had been designated appeared manifestly too dangerous. All having embarked, the Queen was conducted to Niddry, a place belonging to Lord Seton, and from thence to Hamilton, a castle of the Duke of Châtellerault, where his brother, the Archbishop of St. Andrew's, with other principal personages of those parts, acknowledged her as Queen.

Hamilton is a favourable basis for military operations, and four leagues distant from Dumbarton, which is a seaport and a very strong fortress, but the Queen will not proceed thither because she feels quite safe in Hamilton, for the Archbishop of St. Andrew's has command over all the adjacent country, and she can thus more easily receive at Hamilton the friends who may come to her assistance than in the fortress of Dumbarton, whither, however, she might proceed at any time in case of necessity.

All Scotland is in motion, some declaring for the Queen, and some against her and for the Earl of Murray.

She sends this gentleman to ask the King of France,[10] for her present need, for a thousand harquebusiers,[11] but should she wish to recover Edinburgh and other fortresses occupied by the rebels, she would require to be assisted by a greater number. She has also written a letter to the Cardinal of Lorraine which should move every hard heart to have compassion upon her; the first lines express that she begs pardon of God, and of the world, for the past errors of her youth, which she promises to amend for the future; then she acknowledges her release solely from His Divine Majesty, and returns Him most humble thanks for having given her so much strength in these her afflictions; and she declares that she has never swerved in the least from her firm purpose to live and die a Catholic, as she now intends to do more than ever.

With regard to her flight it is judged here, by those who know the site, and how strictly she was guarded, that her escape was most miraculous, most especially having been contrived by two lads, under ten years of age, who could not be presupposed to have the requisite judgment and secrecy.

To the greater satisfaction with the result may be added, that the inmates of Lochleven castle perceived the flight; but being shut up within it, and thus made prisoners, they had to take patience, and to witness the Queen's escape, while they remained at the windows of the castle.

But now, if the current report be true, the Queen of Scotland, following the course of her fickle fortune, gives news of her troops having been routed near Glasgow; all her chief adherents being killed, or made prisoners, and the Captain of Domberdran having fled to England by sea. We are now awaiting information, as the Scotch here support themselves with the hope that all may not be true, assigning reasons for their doubts.

The English Ambassador [Sir Henry Norris], before he knew this last fact, went to his most Christian Majesty, and told him he had heard that there was a project to succour the Queen of Scotland, which in his opinion would be superfluous, because his Queen would not fail to favour and assist her with what was needed. These words were instantly repeated to the Queen [of France], who told the Ambassador that this was precisely the time to have compassion on the Queen of Scotland and to favour her, after having taken refuge in England.

The Ambassador seemed not to know the last news, but affirmed that his Queen would certainly do as anticipated.

10 Charles IX.
11 A soldier armed with a wheel or flint firing gun, which had been invented in the previous century.

Her Majesty [of France] has despatched a gentlemen to know in what condition the Queen of Scotland is, and whether she is in Scotland or in England.

Paris, 26th May 1568.

GIOVANNI CORRER, Venetian Ambassador in France, to the SIGNORY.

The news of the defeat of the troops of the Queen of Scotland was true. She had assembled about eight thousand men, who had flocked to her from divers parts, and for greater security she wished to shut herself up in Dumbarton, which is a very strong castle, but she could not get there without crossing the Clyde, over which there is but one bridge near Glasgow, and that was already occupied by the enemy. It was therefore determined to cross the river where it flows into the sea, a number of boats being sent to the spot for that purpose. The Regent, aware of this, went in pursuit with four thousand men; whereupon the Queen appointed as her Lieutenant-General the Earl of Argyle, who had just joined her, and who is her brother-in-law through his wife, Queen Mary's natural sister, and he with six thousand men gave Murray battle.

The contest last for three-quarters of an hour, when the Queen's troops were worsted, but only one hundred and fifty of her followers were killed, for the Regent exerted himself extremely to prevent his troops shedding blood. The prisoners exceeded three hundred, including many noblemen, amongst whom, moreover, is that Lord Seton who was the chief instrument and leader in effecting the Queen's escape. Finding herself defeated, the Queen set out for England, accompanied by a son of the Duke of Châtellarault, by Lord Fleming, by the Earl of Maxwell, and some twenty-five other attendants, and she travelled a distance of one hundred and twenty-five miles without any rest. She stopped at a place called Workington, which is four miles within the English border. She did not discover herself, but was recognised by a Scotchman, who informed the warden of the castle, and the latter went immediately to receive her, with great marks of respect, and posted guards on all sides to prevent pursuit by the enemy.

When the Queen of England heard this news she appeared much pleased, and immediately despatched to Carlisle, where the Queen of Scotland now is, her Lord Chamberlain and the Governor of the place [Lord Scroop, Warden of the Marches], with clothes of silk and jewels for her wear, and in London a palace is being prepared for her with great pomp. Queen Elizabeth promises to give her all aid for the recovery of her kingdom, and has written to this effect to their Majesties here, who have besought her warmly thus to do; but it is said that she will not allow Queen Mary to come to France, as was believed to be her intention, but will detain her in England until she sees the result, it appearing that there is already some talk of an adjustment.

The same Scottish gentleman, John Beaton, who brought the news of Queen Mary's escape, in which he indeed took part, has come to me in her name, to say that all her valuables, and especially her jewels, are in the hands of the enemy, who got possession of them when they imprisoned her. She is now apprehensive of their being sent for sale abroad, and possibly to Venice, which is one of the chief and wealthiest marts in the world; and he therefore requested me to co-operate with him in assisting her by writing to your Serenity, in order that should any jewels reach our city and be recognised, from their extreme beauty and quality, or through any other circumstance, the Signory may be pleased to have them detained until the Queen can send the necessary proofs. This I readily promised him to do, assuring him at the same time, that out of the love ever borne by your Serenity towards his Queen, you would willingly comply with the present request or any other that could possibly be of service to her.

Paris, 6th June 1568.

GIOVANNI CORRER, Venetian Ambassador in France, to the SIGNORY.

The Queen of Scotland is approaching London, and has sent Lord Fleming to Queen Elizabeth, who has given him leave to go to the French Court, where Queen Catherine de' Medici and the Guises are expecting the return of Montmorin, whom they had sent to England for news of the real situation of their daughter-in-law and niece, for it was already rumoured that instead of aiding the Queen of Scotland, Queen Elizabeth intended to detain her; and the ground of this suspicion rested on the fact of Middlemore's mission to the Regent Murray, demanding his rejoinder to the charges brought against him by his half-sister, and requesting leniency in favour of her adherents.

Paris, 24th June 1568.

GIOVANNI CORRER, Venetian Ambassador in France, to the SIGNORY.

The Scottish royalists intercepted a packet of letters on their way from England to the Regent Murray; one of them was addressed to him by his own secretary then resident with Queen Elizabeth; and five of the other letters were from members of her Privy Council, including Secretary Cecil.

The writers unanimously urged Murray to be of good cheer, as Queen Elizabeth would most assuredly not aid Queen Mary in the least against him; adding that he was not to credit whatever he might hear to the contrary.

The packet also contained some letters from certain Scotch archers of the guard of Charles IX., who in like manner assured the Regent that he had nothing to fear from France.

This intercepted correspondence was immediately consigned to Queen Mary, who forwarded the letters of the archers to her mother-in-law at Paris, and the rest to Queen Elizabeth, requesting her, if she disapproved of their contents, to give some manifest proof of resentment. Some little stir was therefore made to save appearances; all the Privy Councillors stoutly denied their own handwriting; Murray's secretary alone confessing that he had written thus in order to "comfort" his master; and so it becomes daily more and more evident that Queen Mary has nothing to hope from England.

It was also said in Paris that the Earl of Leicester ranked amongst the bitterest of Queen Mary's enemies; and that when told of her demand for leave to go to France, Queen Elizabeth exclaimed, "My prudence would weigh but lightly were I to permit the departure of her who lays claim to be mistress of this realm, and who of yore assumed its arms and title."

Paris, 28th July 1568.[12]

GIOVANNI CORRER, Venetian Ambassador in France, to the SIGNORY.

News has been received in Paris of Queen Mary's removal from Carlisle to Bolton Castle.

It was expected that an interview would take place there between the two Queens, and that as Queen Elizabeth had commenced her usual progress, she would hold it on the way.

Queen Mary was also reported to have denied ever having consented to the murder of Darnley, adding that if permitted to confer with Queen Elizabeth, she promised to give a detailed account of all the circumstances, and to prove her innocence.

Paris, 28th July 1568.[12]

---

[12] Mary was to remain Elizabeth's prisoner for two decades, until 1587, when she was executed for allegedly plotting Elizabeth's overthrow.